How to Use Maps in This Textbook

Here are some basic map concepts and simple tips to help you get the most from the maps in this textbook.

- There are many different types of maps intended to illustrate different types of information. A few of the kinds most frequently used in history books are political, demographic, topographic, and military maps.

  - **Political maps** traditionally show territorial boundaries (such as state and country borders).
  - **Demographic maps** use shading or cross-hatching to show trends relating to population density and distribution.
  - **Topographic maps** illustrate both natural and man-made surface features, such as mountain ranges, rivers, and dams.
  - **Military maps** zoom in on a specific battlefield or show a broad theater of war, and illustrate troop movements over a period of time.

  Many maps, such as the one in this foldout, combine multiple features into one document, illustrating more than one kind of information.

- Always look at the scale, which allows you to determine the distance, in miles or kilometers, between locations on the map.

- Examine the legend carefully (it's usually contained in a boxed inset). It explains the colors, shading, and symbols used on the map.

- If the map is accompanied by a caption, read it thoroughly. Captions usually provide clues to what the author thinks is important about the geography, and offer additional interesting details that may not be covered in the surrounding text.

- Note the mountains, rivers, oceans and other topographic features and consider how these features would affect human activities such as agriculture, trade, communication, travel, and warfare during the period being discussed.

- Refer often to the maps as you read surrounding text, and go back to study them after you have finished reading. Maps can enhance your understanding of events and places discussed.

0-495-12925-9

World History

COMPACT FOURTH EDITION
VOLUME II
SINCE 1500: THE AGE OF GLOBAL INTEGRATION

Jiu-Hwa L. Upshur
EASTERN MICHIGAN UNIVERSITY

Janice J. Terry
EASTERN MICHIGAN UNIVERSITY

James P. Holoka
EASTERN MICHIGAN UNIVERSITY

Richard D. Goff
EASTERN MICHIGAN UNIVERSITY

George H. Cassar
EASTERN MICHIGAN UNIVERSITY

THOMSON
™
WADSWORTH

Australia • Canada • Mexico • Singapore • Spain
United Kingdom • United States

THOMSON

★ ™

WADSWORTH

Executive Editor: Clark Baxter
Assistant Editor: Paul Massicotte
Editorial Assistant: Richard Yoder
Technology Project Manager: Melinda Newfarmer
Marketing Manager: Lori Grebe-Cook
Marketing Assistant: Mary Ho
Advertising Project Manager: Stacey Purviance
Project Manager, Editorial Production: Matt Ballantyne
Art Director: Maria Epes
Print/Media Buyer: Rebecca Cross

Permissions Editor: Chelsea Junget
Production Service: Lachina Publishing Services
Photo Researcher: Connie Hathaway, Penmarin Books
Illustrator: Graphic World, Inc.
Cover Designer: Janet Bollow Design
Cover Images: Art Today, Corel Corporation,
   Instructional Resources Corporation
Cover Printer: Coral Graphic Services
Compositor: Lachina Publishing Services
Printer: Courier–Westford

For more information about our products,
contact us at:
Thomson Learning Academic Resource Center
1-800-423-0563

For permission to use material from this text
or product, submit a request online at
http://www.thomsonrights.com.
Any additional questions about permissions
can be submitted by email to
thomsonrights@thomson.com.

Library of Congress Control Number: 200408492

ISBN-13: 978-0-495-12925-7
ISBN-10: 0-495-12925-9

Thomson Wadsworth
10 Davis Drive
Belmont, CA 94002-3098
USA

Asia
Thomson Learning
5 Shenton Way #01-01
UIC Building
Singapore 068808

Australia/New Zealand
Thomson Learning
102 Dodds Street
Southbank, Victoria 3006
Australia

Canada
Nelson
1120 Birchmount Road
Toronto, Ontario M1K 5G4
Canada

Europe/Middle East/Africa
Thomson Learning
High Holborn House
50/51 Bedford Row
London WC1R 4LR
United Kingdom

About the Authors

JIU-HWA L. UPSHUR received her B.A. at the University of Sydney in Australia and Ph.D. in history at the University of Michigan. She is the author of two catalogs on Chinese art and many articles on Chinese history and has lived and traveled extensively in China, Taiwan, and other parts of Asia. She is co-author of *The Twentieth Century: A Brief Global History* (6th edition, 2001) and co-editor of *Lives and Times: Readings in World History* (1994). She served on the world history committee of the College Board between 1993 and 1999. She is currently a member of the review board of Teaching World History for the Twentieth Century, funded by the National Endowment for the Humanities and the National Advisory Committee for Social Studies of the Educational Testing Service.

JANICE J. TERRY is a graduate of the School of Oriental and African Studies, University of London. She is author of *The Wafd, 1919–1952: Cornerstone of Egyptian Political Power, Mistaken Identity: Arab Stereotypes in Popular Writing,* and numerous articles on contemporary events in western Asia. Dr. Terry has lived and traveled extensively throughout western Asia and Africa. She is co-author of *The Twentieth Century: A Brief Global History* (6th edition, 2001). In 1990, she received an award for excellence in teaching from the state of Michigan.

JAMES P. HOLOKA received his B.A. from the University of Rochester, his M.A. from SUNY, Binghamton, and his Ph.D. from the University of Michigan, where he was a Rackham Prize Fellow. He has taught Greek and Latin, classical humanities, and ancient history since 1974; he received a teaching excellence award in 1980 and a scholarly recognition award in 1991. He is a published translator and the author of three textbooks and over eighty scholarly articles and reviews in such journals as *American Historical Review; Classical World; Greek, Roman, and Byzantine Studies;* and *Transactions of the American Philological Association.*

RICHARD D. GOFF received his B.A. and Ph.D. from Duke University and his M.A. from Cornell University. He has taught courses in Western civilization and specializes in teaching twentieth-century world history. He is the author of *Confederate Supply* and encyclopedia articles on southern U.S. history and culture. In 1983 he received a distinguished faculty service award. He is co-author of *The Twentieth Century: A Brief Global History* (6th edition, 2001), and lead author of R. Goff et al., *A Survey of Western Civilization* (2nd edition, 1997).

GEORGE H. CASSAR received his B.A and M.A. from the University of New Brunswick and his Ph.D. from McGill University. He is currently Professor of History at Eastern Michigan University, where he has taught European and military history since 1968. His output is extensive and includes half a dozen books on various aspects of the First World War as well as co-authorship of *A Survey of Western Civilization* (2nd edition, 1997). In 1985 he received the prestigious Faculty Award for Research and Publication from Eastern Michigan University. He is currently working on a book about Kitchener and British strategy during the Great War.

Brief Contents

Contents

Maps

Preface

Modern communications and transportation have linked the world's continents closer together and made them more integrated politically, economically, and culturally than ever before. Our technological society is predicated on a world economy and depends on a precarious ecological balance that makes events in the forests of Brazil or the deserts of Africa and Asia vitally important to people all around the globe.

Many institutions of higher learning have come to realize that students need insights into the historical backgrounds of other cultures in order to respond effectively to the currents that make us all citizens of a global village. As a result, many are now emphasizing world history as an essential part of the basic undergraduate curriculum, rather than traditional courses in Western civilization.

The five of us have aimed to produce a truly global and well-balanced world history text, since we have expertise in different regions, periods, and topics of history: the classics and Greco-Roman history, modern Europe, military history, the Western Hemisphere, the Islamic world, the United States, and South and East Asia. We are conversant in more than a half-dozen ancient and modern languages. Each has more than thirty years' experience teaching college survey courses of Western and world history and advanced courses in special subjects. All have extensive experience in writing successful textbooks and editing primary source materials in world history and Western civilization. The result is a smooth integration of diverse materials.

Our first edition, widely adopted across the United States and Canada, was a success. Our second and third editions were even more successful. Thus encouraged, we have now updated the current edition.

While other world history textbooks have stressed specific themes, human civilizations, in our view, have produced too rich a tapestry of experience to limit our examination of them to any single theme. Our consistent goal has been not only to show students the diversity and distinctive qualities of the various civilizations, but to trace their social, cultural, and economic influences and interactions. Furthermore, we point out the many dimensions of the lives of individual men and women across cultures, religions, social classes, and times.

Several distinctive features of our book bear enumeration.

First, we have divided world history into seventeen chapters, each highlighting a major trend (emergence of civilization, early empires, invasion and disruption, and so on) during a distinct chronological era. The subsections of each chapter are devoted to the areas of the world affected by this trend. This effective organization has been continued from previous editions, with revisions based on the latest discoveries and advances in scholarship. Chapter 17 has been carefully reworked and updated to incorporate recent events up to 2004.

Second, we have placed twelve comparative essays at strategic points in the book. These lay the groundwork for the historical concepts examined in detail in subsequent chapter sections. For example, the essay "The Defining Characteristics of Great Empires," which discusses the dynamics of large states, precedes Chapter 4, which covers the roughly contemporary Hellenistic, Roman, Mauryan, and Han Empires. For this edition, we have added quotations from original sources at the opening of each essay to demonstrate the pertinence of such material and to heighten the essays' interest and relevance.

Third, we have included many charts and maps; each chapter features helpful maps to accentuate the geographical contexts of historical events. In each chapter the "Summary and Comparisons" section is accompanied by a timeline of important events that occurred during the period covered by that chapter, an important learning aid for students.

Fourth, we have added new boxes to each chapter; most of these consist of quotations from primary sources. Students, reviewers, and professors have praised this engaging and useful enhancement of the text.

Fifth, expanding on a successful feature, we have added more short essays entitled "Lives and Times Across Cultures." These informative, often unusual, and entertaining pieces present facts and details of life not found in traditional textbooks.

Sixth, the chapter summaries, titled "Summary and Comparisons," stress the comparative aspect of historical study. Since each chapter contains much information about diverse regions of the world, this emphasis on comparison ensures a better integration of the various materials of a given chapter and a clearer overall view of world events.

Seventh, at the end of each chapter we have compiled an updated list of sources to guide interested students to well-written monographs, fiction, dramas, films, and television programs that provide historical perspective.

Eighth, the publisher has put together an invaluable package of ancillary materials. These include aids for instructors:

- **Instructor's Manual and Testbank.** Includes a multimedia guide, chapter outlines, recommended readings, paper topics, identification questions, multiple-choice questions, short-essay questions, and new to this edition, Internet resources. One comprehensive volume.
- **ExamView for Windows and Macintosh.** Create, deliver, and customize tests and study guides (both print and online) in minutes with this easy-to-use assessment and tutorial system. ExamView offers both a Quick Test Wizard and an Online Test Wizard that guide you step by step through the process of creating tests, while its unique "WYSIWYG" capability allows you to see the test you are creating on the screen

exactly as it will print or display online. You can build tests of up to 250 questions using up to 12 question types. Using ExamView's complete word-processing capabilities, you can enter an unlimited number of new questions or edit existing questions.

- **Map Acetates and Commentary for World History.** Contains maps from the text and from other sources as well as commentary on each map. The commentary, by James Harrison of Siena College, includes not only the text caption but also additional points of interest about the map, such as what it shows and its relevance to the study of world history. Possible discussion questions for student involvement are included.

- **Wadsworth Video Library: History.** Recommended Films for the Humanities & Sciences videos are available free upon adoption, subject to terms of the Wadsworth video policy.

- **CNN Today Video: *World History, Volumes I and II.*** Launch lectures with riveting footage from CNN, the world's leading twenty-four-hour global news television network. CNN Today: *World History, Volumes I and II,* allows you to integrate the news-gathering and programming power of CNN into the classroom to show students the relevance of course topics to their everyday lives. Organized by topics covered in a typical course, these videos are divided into short segments—perfect for introducing key concepts. A Wadsworth/Thomson exclusive.

- **Sights and Sounds of History Videodisk/Video.** Short, focused video clips, photos, artwork, animations, music, and dramatic readings are used to bring life to historical topics and events that are most difficult for students to appreciate from a textbook alone. For example, students will experience the grandeur of Versailles and the defeat felt by a German soldier at Stalingrad. The video segments (average length, four minutes) are available on VHS and make excellent lecture launchers.

The following ancillaries are also available for students:

- **Study Guide for World History, Volumes I and II.** The study guide contains identifications, true-or-false questions, essay study questions for further reading, and map exercises.

- **Migrations in History CD-ROM.** An interactive multimedia curriculum on CD-ROM by Patrick Manning and the World History Center. Includes over 400 primary source documents; analytical questions to help the student develop his/her own interpretations of history; timelines; and additional suggested resources, including books, films, and websites.

- **Journey of Civilization CD-ROM.** This CD-ROM takes the student on eighteen interactive journeys through history. Enhanced with QuickTime movies, animations, sound clips, maps, and more, the journeys allow students to engage in history as active participants rather than as readers of past events.

- **Magellan World History Atlas.**

- **Lives and Times: A World History Reader.** Assembled by two of the text authors, James Holoka and Jiu-Hwa Upshur, the reader includes 150 short and lively selections, most of them biographical.

■ **Web page.** Both instructors and students will enjoy our web page. Visit Historic Times, the Wadsworth History Resource Center at http://history.wadsworth.com. From this full-service site, instructors and students can access many selections, such as a career center, lessons on surfing the web, and links to great history-related websites.

In sum, we have striven to make this book not only accurate and informative but also exciting for students and other readers. Our textbook combines key characteristics to work effectively in various learning situations. It offers a clear narrative focusing on major historical forces and concepts, uncluttered by minute detail. This edition gives greater attention to social, economic, cultural, and gender history in order to provide a more balanced and comprehensive account of human experience.

We have nevertheless kept our book relatively short—short enough to be suitable for courses at most colleges, so that instructors may assign supplementary readings without overwhelming their students.

To provide a true world perspective, we have adopted several special conventions. First, because the text will be used mostly in North American colleges, we have based our general chronology on the traditional Christian/Western calendar; however, we have designated year dates as B.C.E. (Before the Common Era) instead of B.C. (Before Christ) and C.E. (Common Era) instead of A.D. (Anno Domini). Next, wherever possible we have eliminated Eurocentric geographical terms such as *Far East, Levant, New World,* and the like. Finally, we have generally transliterated (rather than Latinized or Anglicized) names and terms from their original language; thus, *Qur'an* instead of *Koran, Tanakh* instead of *Old Testament,* and (post–1949) *Mao Zedong* instead of *Mao Tse-tung* and *Beijing* instead of *Peking* (see also "Romanizing Chinese Words" at the end of this volume). However, we have made exceptions of such familiar Westernized spellings as *Confucius, Averroës, Christopher Columbus,* and *Aztec.*

An enterprise of this magnitude and complexity succeeds only through the dedicated efforts of many people. Wadsworth Publishing secured the services of reviewers whose insights and information materially strengthened this and the previous three editions. The list follows this preface.

We wish to thank our colleagues at Eastern Michigan University—in particular, Ronald Delph and Joseph Engwenyu for their assistance at several stages in the writing—and Gersham Nelson, head of the History Department, for his constant support and encouragement. Nancy Snyder and her assistants were stalwart helpers in handling innumerable practical and technological chores. Raymond Craib at Yale University supplied information and text on women's history and Mexican history. From the outset of this project, Sally Marks, in Providence, Rhode Island, has been exceptionally helpful in suggesting improvements. We also wish to thank Margot Duley of Eastern Michigan University and Richard Edwards of the University of Michigan for making available to us photographs of historical interest from their personal collections. We are grateful to John Nystuen of the University of Michigan for photographing some of the artifacts illustrated in this edition. The authors' spouses furnished copious practical and moral support and showed a high tolerance for hectic writing and production schedules. Thanks also go to Pat Manning at the World History Center at Northeastern University and his graduate assistants, Stacy Tweedy, Tiffany Olson, and Bin Yang. A final word of thanks goes to Clark Baxter, Sharon Adams Poore, Nancy Crochiere, and other members of the Wadsworth Publishing team for their patient attention to all manner of details. Their collective skills have once again transformed our project into a most attractive textbook.

THE AUTHORS

Reviewers

Charles F. Ames, Jr.
Salem State College

Jay Pascal Anglin
University of Southern Mississippi

Gary Dean Best
University of Hawaii at Hilo

Charmarie Blaisdell
Northeastern University

Edward L. Bond
Alabama Agricultural and Mechanical University

Patricia Bradley
Auburn University at Montgomery

Cynthia Brokaw
University of Oregon

Antoinette Burton
Indiana State University

Antonio Calabria
University of Texas

Daniel P. Connerton
North Adams State College

Lane Earns
University of Wisconsin at Oshkosh

John Anthony Eisterhold
University of Tennessee

Angela Hudson Elms
University of Louisiana

Edward L. Farmer
University of Minnesota

William Wayne Farris
University of Tennessee

Gary R. Freeze
Erskine College

Ronald Fritze
Lamar University

Ray C. Gerhardt
Texas Lutheran College

Marc Jason Gilbert
North Georgia College

Steven A. Glazer
Graceland College

Joseph M. Gowaskie
Rider College

Zoltan Kramar
Central Washington University

Susie Ling
Pasadena City College

Lawrence S. Little
Villanova University

Craig A. Lockard
University of Wisconsin at Green Bay

Raymond M. Lorantas
Drexel University

Delores Nason McBroome
Humboldt State University

Susan Maneck
Murray State University

C. P. Mao
Texas Lutheran University

Robroy Meyers
El Camino College

Timothy E. Morgan
Christopher Newport University

Terry Morris
Shorter College

Henry Myers
James Madison University

Cecil C. Orchard
Eastern Kentucky University

James L. Owens
Lynchburg College

Oliver B. Pollak
University of Nebraska at Omaha

Dennis Reinhartz
University of Texas at Arlington

Cynthia Schwenk
Georgia State University

Wendy Singer
Kenyon College

Paul D. Steeves
Stetson University

Cheryl Thurber
Shippensburg University

Hubert van Tuyll
Augusta State University

Pingchao Zhu
University of Idaho

9

Emerging Global Interrelations

•

• The Rival Ottoman and Safavid Empires •

• The Culture of the Renaissance in Europe •

• European Nation-States and the Reformation •

• African Kingdoms, European Contacts, and the Slave Trade •

• European Colonial Empires in the Western Hemisphere •

• Summary and Comparisons •

Wednesday, November 28, 1520, we debouched from [the Strait of Magellan, at the tip of South America], engulfing ourselves in the Pacific Sea. We were three months and twenty days without getting any kind of fresh food. We ate bisquit, which was no longer bisquit, but powder of bisquit swarming with worms. . . . It stank strongly of the urine of rats. We drank yellow water that had been putrid for many days. We also ate oxhides . . . and sawdust from boards. Rats were sold for one-half ducados apiece, and even [then] we could not get them. [But the worst was that] the gums . . . of some of our men swelled [from scurvy], so that they could not eat under any circumstances and therefore died. . . . Had not God and His blessed mother given us . . . good weather we would have all died of hunger in that exceeding vast sea. Of a verity I believe no such voyage will ever be made again. . . .

On Monday, September eight [1522] we cast anchor near the quay of [Seville, Spain] . . . with only [twenty-one] men and the majority of them sick. . . . Some died of hunger; some deserted . . . and some were put to death for crimes. . . . We had sailed fourteen thousand, four hundred and sixty leguas [about 40,000 miles] and furthermore completed the circumnavigation of the world from east to west. . . . Tuesday we all went in shirts and barefoot, each holding a candle, to visit [shrines]. . . .*

*Antonio Pigafetta, in Charles E. Nowell, ed., Magellan's Voyage around the World (Evanston, IL: Northwestern University Press, 1962), pp. 122–124, 259.

The (appropriately named) Portuguese ship *Victoria*, which limped into the harbor near Seville on September 6, 1522, with its sick and ragged surviving crew, had made history by circumnavigating the globe. Although the expedition's commander, Ferdinand Magellan, did not live to savor the triumph, his crew had done what no humans had done before.

Magellan's expedition was the culmination of a century of European voyages of discovery that had begun with Prince Henry the Navigator of Portugal. The European appetite for adventure and taste for the luxuries of Asia dated back to the First Crusade (1096–1099); Marco Polo's accounts of his travels in the thirteenth century had also created great interest in Asian lands far removed from Europe. But not until the fifteenth century did advances in shipbuilding and navigational knowledge permit oceangoing vessels to sail around the Cape of Good Hope and across the Indian Ocean to Asia. At the end of the century, Christopher Columbus sailed across the Atlantic and stumbled onto a "New World" in the Western Hemisphere while seeking an alternative route to Asia. Magellan proved the existence of such a route by sailing around South America, past Cape Horn, and across the Pacific to Asia.

Whereas major civilizations had developed in relative isolation from each other in the preceding 5,000 years, the voyages of discovery of the fifteenth and sixteenth centuries began to meld the world into an interrelated whole. The earth today is truly an interdependent "global village."

This chapter begins with a discussion of the highly centralized and powerful Ottoman and Safavid Empires, based in western Asia, and their interactions and confrontations with one another and with Europe. Commercial interactions between Asian empires and Europe had fueled Europeans' appetites for Asian luxury goods and also helped to foster the new intellectual and artistic climate of the Renaissance, which began in Italy and spread through the rest of Europe. Following a description of the Renaissance, this chapter will trace the development of centralized monarchies in Europe and the religious and political changes brought about by the Reformation.

The chapter will then examine how European horizons in the fifteenth century expanded to include—for Europeans—the newly discovered continents of Africa south of the Sahara and North and South America. The impacts of the slave trade on African societies and the Western Hemisphere will be described. The chapter closes with a discussion of the creation of colonial empires by Europeans in the Western Hemisphere.

The Rival Ottoman and Safavid Empires

The Sultan was seated on a rather low sofa, not more than a foot from the ground and spread with many costly coverlets and cushions embroidered with exquisite work. Near him were his bow and arrows. His expression . . . is anything but smiling, and has a sternness which, though sad, is full of majesty.

The Sultan's head-quarters were crowded by numerous attendants, including many high officials. All the cavalry of the guard were there . . . and a large number of Janissaries. . . . The Sultan himself assigns to all their duties and offices, and in doing so pays no attention to wealth or the empty claims of rank. . . . He only considers merit and scrutinizes the character, natural ability, and disposition of each.

The Turks were quite as much astonished at our manner of dress as we at theirs. They wear long robes which reach almost to their ankles, and are not only more imposing but seem to add to the stature; our dress, on the other hand, is so short and tight that it disclosed the forms of the body, which would be better hidden.

What struck me as particularly praiseworthy in that great multitude was the silence and good discipline. . . . Each man kept his appointed place. . . . The officers . . . were seated; the common soldiers *stood up. The most remarkable body of men were several thousand Janissaries, who stood in a long line apart and so motionless that . . . I was for a while doubtful whether they were living men or statues.**

*The Turkish Letters of Ogier Ghiselin De Busbecq, trans. Edward S. Forster (Oxford: Clarendon Press, 1927), pp. 58–62. Another brief excerpt of the letters can be found in Peter N. Stearns, ed., *Documents in World History,* vol. 2 (Oxford: Clarendon Press, 1988), pp. 73–77.

In these words, the imperial ambassador for the Holy Roman Empire described the court of Suleiman the Magnificent, the ruler of the Ottoman Empire. While Christian Europe was entering a period of religious turmoil (discussed later in the chapter), Suleiman's empire and its powerful rival, the Safavid state in Persia, were both in the ascendant. Indeed, the Ottoman Empire profited from Christian turmoil and dynastic rivalries, extending its rule into central Europe and advancing to the gates of Vienna. Religious differences also existed in the Islamic world, however; the Ottoman and Safavid states were sectarian as well as political rivals. Although Ottoman taxation of international trade helped to stimulate European interest in developing new trade routes to Asia, the two Muslim empires were far too strong in this period to feel adverse effects from European expansion.

Ottoman Territorial Expansion and Government

Immediately following the conquest of Constantinople in 1453, the Ottoman Sultans moved to extend their control over the Balkans. Aided by the rugged terrain in the region, the predominantly Christian but politically divided Balkan peoples repelled Ottoman advances until late in the sixteenth century. Papal calls for crusades against the Ottomans were ignored as Europeans, more interested in economic gains than religious confrontations with the Muslim Ottoman government, sought to establish commercial and political relations.

Sultan Selim I (reigned 1512–1520) sought territorial gains in the east and south. After successfully thwarting the threat of expansion by the Safavid emperors in Persia, in 1517 Selim routed the Mamluks in Egypt and gained control of Palestine and Syria. The defeat of the Mamluks gave the Ottomans control over most of the Arab world, including the key Muslim cities of Mecca, Medina, and Jerusalem. The Ottoman rulers moved the caliphate to Istanbul and assumed leadership over the Sunni Islamic world. They now viewed themselves as the guardians of Islam and the military might of their empire as the Sword of Islam. Later, the sultans also took the title of caliph.

Ottoman expansion continued during the reign of Suleiman the Magnificent (reigned 1520–1566), when the empire reached the apex of its power. Suleiman brilliantly led his armies against rulers in central Europe and in 1521 seized the Serbian capital of Belgrade. In an age of mighty kings, Suleiman was probably the most powerful and dynamic. He was a successful military commander and a clever diplomat; competing European powers, such as France, sought and secured his protection. By exploiting the rivalry between the Austrian Habsburg emperors and the French kings, Suleiman's forces conquered most of Hungary. His political alliance with the French soon expanded into mutually beneficial economic relations.

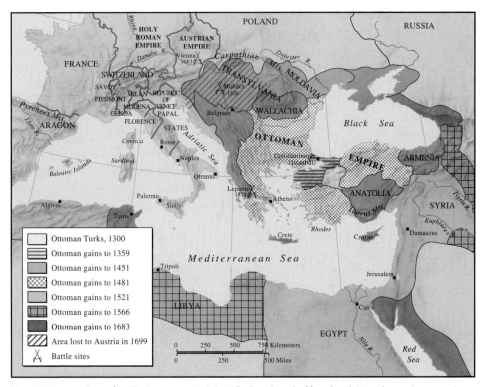

Map 9.1 Ottoman Expansion. The Ottomans expanded rapidly throughout the fifteenth and sixteenth centuries, conquering vast territories around the Black Sea, in the Balkans, and in the Arab provinces along the eastern Mediterranean and North Africa.

In 1529 Suleiman laid siege to Vienna, but because of overextended communication lines and heavy rainfall that made transporting heavy cannon difficult, the Ottoman forces failed to take the city before the onset of winter. Because the Janissaries (the elite, professional soldiers of the Ottoman army) and the cavalry refused to campaign during the winter months, Suleiman was forced to retreat without taking the Habsburg capital. Reportedly, the Ottoman army left behind sacks of coffee, a new product that soon gained popularity among the Europeans.

At its height in 1566, Suleiman's empire incorporated Hungary and the Balkan Peninsula; extensive territory around the Black Sea; the entire Anatolian Peninsula; Arab territories bordering the eastern Mediterranean and the Red Sea; Egypt and the northern Sudan; most islands in the eastern Mediterranean, including the strategic islands of Rhodes and Crete; and the coastal areas of North Africa east of Morocco.

Like many emperors in other powerful empires before him, Suleiman failed to leave a worthy successor to his throne. Influenced by his most beloved wife, Hurrem Haseki ("the Joyous One"), to make her son the successor, Suleiman had his favorite and more able son killed, just as rulers in China and the Roman Empire had killed members of their own families in order to ensure their own power or the succession of particular favorites. Following Suleiman's death in 1566, Hurrem Haseki's son succeeded to the throne as Selim II, but this alcoholic, nicknamed The Sot, proved unworthy of his capable and abstemious father. Ottoman military and naval supremacy waned under his rule, and at the Battle of Lepanto in 1571, the navies of the Habsburgs and the Italian city-states crushed the Ottoman fleet. This defeat marked the beginning of a military decline that lasted more than 200 years.

The administration of the Ottoman Empire, like the Safavid in Persia and the earlier T'ang in China, was highly centralized. The Sultan acted as the supreme political, religious, and military ruler, subject only to divine law. Below him, the grand vizier and the divan (imperial council) were responsible for political and economic administration. Ottoman administration was highly complex and required a multitude of bureaucrats, drawn from an elite whose prestige was based on ownership of land and booty acquired in military campaigns. They were responsible for matters as diverse as the translation of documents to the supervision of the vast royal palace complex of Topkapi in Istanbul, where the Sultan maintained his harem, with separate chambers for his mother, wives, children, and servants.

Without a firm tradition of primogeniture (succession of the eldest son), all the half-brothers in the harem were potential candidates for the throne. Consequently, wives, mothers, sisters, and sons often intrigued to gain the sultan's favor. As the example of Hurrem Haseki demonstrates, the mothers and favorite wives of sultans could exercise considerable political power. When the sultans were strong rulers, the harem did not pose a threat to effective government. For example, the first ten sultans, from 1299 to 1566, all led their military forces directly into battle and were personally in charge of military strategy and governmental policy. Indeed, the personal dynamism and strength of the first Ottoman sultans were major factors in Ottoman expansion. However, the less able sultans who succeeded Suleiman frequently became virtual prisoners of the royal court, the harem, and the Janissaries.

Like the Safavids in Persia, Ottoman rulers placed the major provinces under appointed governors who ruled for about two years. As authorities in Istanbul correctly feared, provincial governors often tried to establish their own bases of authority. Generally, the central Ottoman government retained tight controls over its Anatolian territories, which lay close to Istanbul. The more distant European and Arab territories tended to enjoy more autonomy.

© Bettmann/Corbis

Suleiman the Magnificent. Here Suleiman, who wrote poetry under the pen name *muhibbi,* or beloved, wearing a white turban, stands before an archway inscribed with the name of Allah. Through the arch may be seen the mosque of Suleiman.

Elegy for Suleiman the Magnificent

That master-rider of the realm of bliss
For whose careering steed the field of the world was
*   narrow.*

The infidels of Hungary bowed their heads to the
*   temper of his blade,*
The Frank admired the grain of his sword.

He laid his face to the ground, graciously, like a fresh
*   rose petal,*
The treasurer of time put him in the coffer, like a jewel.

May the sun burn and blaze with fire of your parting;
In grief for you, let him dress in black weeds of cloud.

Weeping tears of blood as it recalls your skill,
May your sword plunge into the ground from its
*   scabbard.*

May the pen tear its collar in grief for you,
The standard rend its shirt in affliction.*

This elegy was written by Muhammad Baki (1527–1600), one of the greatest Ottoman poets. It is a lyrical idealization of the imperial ruler, much in the vein of the celebrations of great rulers as mighty heroes in ancient Greek and Latin poetry.

*Wayne S. Vucinich, The Ottoman Empire: Its Record and Legacy, trans. Bernard Lewis (Princeton: Van Nostrand, 1965), pp. 146–147.

The administration was financed through new wealth acquired from the expansion of the empire and from taxes. The collection of taxes was assigned to "tax farmers," who collected as much as possible from a given territory in return for a percentage of the total amount collected. As in Rome and China, tax farming became a source of abuse and corruption within the empire.

Founded by the military, the Ottoman Empire remained dependent upon the army, which, like the government, was rigidly structured. The Janissaries, along with the cavalry, were the backbone of the military. They quickly adapted to the use of European military technology, especially siege and field artillery, and became a major military force of the age.

In this Islamic empire, the Sheik al-Islam was responsible for religious life, and since there was no separation of civil and religious law, he served as supreme judge, handing down *fatwas,* or legal opinions. In the provinces, *qadis* (judges) appointed by Istanbul joined with local experts in religious law to settle legal disputes. They also served as overseers of such charitable religious endowments as orphanages, soup kitchens, and hospitals.

Social and Economic Life in the Ottoman Empire

During the golden age of the empire under Suleiman, Ottoman society was remarkably open. The Ottomans did not see fit to settle Turkish tribes throughout their empire; most Turks remained peasants scattered in remote and poor agricultural villages throughout the Anatolian Peninsula. Ottoman rulers initially made no attempt to impose the Turkish language or customs on their subjects or to force non-Muslims to convert to Islam. On the contrary, Ottoman society allowed diversity, and considerable "upward mobility" occurred. Under the *millet* system, religious and ethnic minorities retained their own educational, religious, and judicial institutions, and enjoyed considerable economic autonomy in return for the payment of an additional tax. Arabs, Armenians, Christians, and Jews were able to reach the highest levels of society, and some served as advisors and doctors to the sultan himself. Only the sultanate was denied them, for it was solely reserved for the heirs of the Osman rulers. This open society, remarkable for the age, was one of the sources of Ottoman strength.

The Ottoman Empire was at the center of a lively international trade from East to West and West to East that persisted despite rivalries among Western and Eastern monarchs. Istanbul and Cairo became major centers on the route between India and Europe. Slaves, gold, and ivory were transported from sub-Saharan Africa through Cairo to European markets. New foodstuffs like potatoes, tomatoes, and tobacco came from the Western Hemisphere into the Ottoman Empire and into Asia. Coffee from Ethiopia and Yemen was traded to Europe. Coffeehouses became major gathering spots for the elite in Ottoman, Safavid, and European cities. The use of tobacco quickly spread from Europe to the Ottoman Empire, where pipe smoking became a common practice among both men and women.

Despite the rich trade that passed through the empire, the Ottoman elite, reflecting the values of a still predominantly agrarian society, held commerce, banking, and most manufacturing businesses in low esteem. As a result, they permitted and encouraged subject peoples (such as Armenians) and foreigners to organize and maintain these economic activities. Under the system of capitulations, which had also been used by the Mamluks and the Safavids, foreign Christians living in the empire were given freedom of activity and were exempted from Ottoman taxes and laws. When the empire flourished, these special privileges fostered international trade and increased revenues, but as the empire declined and European nations grew stronger, the capitulations enabled Europeans and minorities to dominate economic life.

Ottoman authorities encouraged international trade across their domains in part, of course, to benefit the imperial treasury. Taxes on trade had often gone uncollected in the Arab provinces in the period of political instability before the Ottomans conquered them. The Ottoman government began to collect these taxes with more efficiency, and in some cases raised them. Traders in turn raised prices, which angered European consumers, especially those at the end of the line. Consequently, the newly centralized and energetic nations became increasingly eager to find new trade routes to Asia.

Cultural and Artistic Achievements

The noteworthy cultural achievements of the Ottoman Empire began at the top. According to custom, Ottoman Sultans were all trained in a craft, and some achieved considerable artistic and literary skill. Suleiman, for example, was an accomplished goldsmith. Ottoman Sultans were great patrons of the arts; and as in most Islamic societies, literary skills, especially the ability to write poetry, were much admired. An accomplished poet in his own right, Suleiman strongly supported the cultural life of Istanbul in an effort to make his court the most splendid of the age. The Turkish language continued to develop, borrowing many words from both Arabic and Persian. Some poets wrote in Turkish and Arabic. Turkish historians chronicled the development of the empire and the exploits of the military, and although most literature was highly derivative of Persian or Arab forms, a lively folk literature continued to flourish.

Like many imperial rulers, Suleiman was also a great builder. He financed the construction of monumental buildings, many designed by Sinan, one of the most prolific architects of all time. Originally a slave from the conquered Greek provinces, Sinan was recruited as a Janissary and became a military engineer. His skills attracted the attention of the sultan, who enlisted him as the royal architect. Living to the (at the time) incredible advanced age of ninety-nine, Sinan designed buildings to commemorate Ottoman imperial power. His massive, interconnecting buildings surmounted by domes became the hallmark of Ottoman architecture throughout the empire. Although the Suleimaniye complex of mosque, schools, hospital, bath, shops, and cemetery in Istanbul is the largest of Sinan's creations, the Selimiye Mosque in Edirne, outside Istanbul, finished in 1575, is generally considered his masterpiece.

In the fine arts, Ottoman artisans synthesized earlier Islamic/Arab designs and techniques with Chinese and European motifs and crafts. They decorated Sinan's structures with Isnik (named after a Turkish city) tiles whose glazed surfaces contained painted floral designs. Clearly an imitation of Chinese porcelains, these tiles still retain their crystal-clear coloring. Such glazing techniques and designs were copied in much of Europe. Ottoman artisans also produced textiles, silver work, bookbindings, and calligraphy of remarkable beauty and luxury. The Ottomans were known for their woven textiles and carpets. "Oriental" carpets from Turkey and Persia became popular decorative items among wealthy classes around the world. Although Ottoman culture, like Roman culture, has been criticized for its lack of originality, the synthesis of disparate cultural ideas and motifs from West and East enabled Ottoman artisans to fashion unique objects of remarkable beauty.

The Imperial Safavids

During the sixteenth and seventeenth centuries the Ottoman Empire's chief rival in the Muslim world was the neighboring Safavid Empire centered in Persia (present-day Iran). The Safavid realm differed from that of the Ottomans in two major respects. First, it was based upon Shi'i Islam rather than on Orthodox Sunni Islam. Second, the Safavids maintained and reinforced the separate identity of Persian society and language. In contrast, the Ottoman Empire sought to assimilate many new cultural styles while retaining cultural pluralism. The Ottomans made no attempt to impose their language or values over the diverse peoples they ruled. In particular, the Arabs, the single largest linguistic and ethnic group within the empire, were allowed to retain their linguistic and cultural identity.

Founded by Shah Isma'il, who ruled from 1500 to 1524, the Safavid Empire reached its zenith under Shah Abbas the Great (reigned 1587–1629), an autocrat who ruled with an iron hand. He killed or blinded three of his five sons and, like Suleiman the Magnificent, left no able successor. In the Safavid Empire, as in most other empires, whenever the central authority was strong, the local chieftains remained submissive, paid taxes, and rendered homage to the shah. Whenever the shah or central authority was weak, the local rulers assumed more power. One of Shah Abbas's first moves in consolidating his power was to curb the influence of the local chieftains.

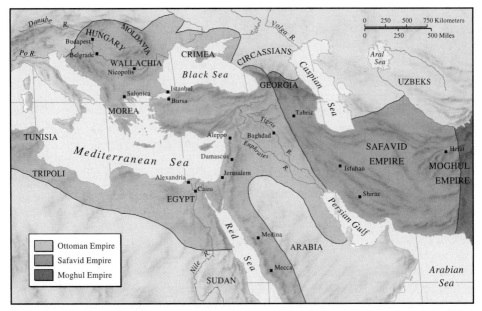

Map 9.2 The Ottoman and Safavid Empires. By 1689 the Ottoman Empire had reached its zenith and included most of the Arab provinces of the eastern Mediterranean, the holy cities of Mecca and Medina, and most of North Africa. However, the Safavid Empire, with its glorious capital at Isfahan in Persia, competed for control in the region; despite many wars, neither empire could conquer its rival.

The populace of Safavid Iran consisted largely of peasants who lived in small rural villages. There were a few nomadic pastoralists as well as a small urban middle class that engaged in cottage industries and trade. In this predominantly rural setting, the Safavid government was organized along feudal lines, and officials acquired fiefs from the shah in return for services to the central government. The Safavids divided their territories into provinces, placed under the administration of appointed governors. The shahs also depended upon the *ghulams,* or slave elite. Obtained mainly from central Asia, these slaves were converts to Islam and gradually achieved prominent positions in the royal court, thereby following a tradition in other Muslim empires.

The mullahs, or Shi'i clergy, also exercised considerable power within the empire; like the feudal landowners, the mullahs tended to be more powerful whenever the shah was ineffective. Their authority was particularly strong in rural areas, where the peasants looked to them for both religious and political guidance.

Taxes, land, and commerce were the major sources of wealth in the Persian economy. Crown lands were owned directly by the royal court to use as it wished; as in the Ottoman Empire, state lands were given as payment or rewards to officials or army officers, generally for a specific time, after which they reverted to the crown to be parceled out again at the pleasure of the court. Some land was owned directly by religious authorities; the revenues from these lands provided the mullahs with an independent source of income and also helped to finance mosques, religious schools, and welfare projects for the poor.

The Safavid Shah Writes to His Ottoman Rival

Shah Isma'il of Persia to the Ottoman Sultan Selim [c. 1514]:

Now to begin: Your honored letters have arrived one after another.... Their contents, although indicative of hostility, are stated with boldness and vigor. The latter gives us much enjoyment and pleasure, but we are ignorant of the reason for the former.... In the time of your late blessed father . . . when our royal troops passed through the lands of [eastern Anatolia] . . . complete concord and friendship was shown on both sides. . . . Thus now, the cause of your resentment and displeasure yet remains unknown. If political necessity has compelled you on this course, then may your problems soon be solved.

Dispute may fire words to such a heat

That ancient houses be consumed in flames. The intention of our inaction in this regard is twofold:

(1.) Most of the inhabitants of the land of Rum are followers of our forefathers....

(2.) We have always loved the ... Ottoman house.... Nevertheless, there is no cause for improper words: ... At this writing we were engaged upon the hunt near

Isfahan, we now prepare provisions and our troops for the coming campaign. In all friendship we say do what you will.

Bitter experience has taught that in this world of trial

He who falls upon the house of Ali always falls. Kindly give our ambassador leave to travel unmolested. ...When war becomes inevitable, hesitation and delay must be set aside, and one must think on that which is to come. Farewell.*

In this letter Shah Isma'il of Persia very diplomatically, but firmly, expressed his views on the conflict between the Safavid (Persian) and the Ottoman Empires. Between them, these two great Muslim empires dominated much of the eastern Mediterranean and West Asia from the fifteenth to the nineteenth centuries and were almost continually in a state of war with one another. Although neither succeeded in destroying the other, the perpetual conflicts drained the economic and military strength of both, thereby contributing to their downfalls.

*William H. McNeill and Marilyn Robinson Waldman, eds., The Islamic World (New York: Oxford University Press, 1973; reprint, Chicago: University of Chicago Press, 1983), pp. 342–344.

The manufacture and sale of textiles, particularly silk fabrics and carpets, was a major source of Safavid income. Soon after coming to power, Shah Abbas added the silk-producing areas in the north to his empire. Although Abbas did not directly confiscate the land, the sale of silk became a royal monopoly. Anxious to expand the silk industry, Abbas encouraged foreign traders and Christian communities, particularly the Armenians, who formerly had been silk producers, to settle in his domain. Although earlier Safavid rulers had persecuted religious minorities and forced religious conversion to Shi'i Islam by sword, Abbas was known for his relative tolerance. To some extent, his more liberal policies regarding the Armenians and other Christian minorities, who dominated the silk manufacturing and commercial trade with the West, were motivated by economic considerations.

To strengthen the Persian economy, Shah Abbas established a new Safavid capital in Isfahan, situated at an intersection of key trade routes. He moved a number of Armenians into a new community on the outskirts of the city and provided interest-free loans for them to rebuild their houses and businesses. As a result of Shah Abbas's tolerance and patronage, Isfahan quickly became a world center for trade in luxury textiles.

In search of new markets, Shah Abbas sent emissaries with samples of luxurious silks to Venice, Spain, Portugal, Holland, Russia, and Poland. Foreign traders were encouraged to establish businesses in Persia by special financial inducements, including tax breaks. These privileges contributed to an economic boom from which the royal court benefited. As early as 1617, agents from the English East Indian Company arrived along the Persian Gulf and petitioned the shah for permission to trade. By the middle of the seventeenth century, Bandar Abbas on the Persian Gulf had become a major seaport for trade with Europe. The Safavids also enjoyed a lively trade through northern routes with Russia. Trade through the northern provinces often continued even during periods of open warfare with the Ottoman Empire.

Control of the silk trade provided the Safavid rulers with the economic means to extend their control over all of Persia. As was true for the sultans in the Ottoman Empire, when the central authority of the Shahs was strong, the special privileges for foreign communities were not a threat. However, as subsequent Safavid leaders became weaker, and the European nations strengthened and augmented their global power, these privileges enabled foreign governments, acting in support of their subjects, to undermine the central government and to dominate Persia.

Architecture, the Fine Arts, and Literature in Persia

Literature, painting, music, and architecture flourished under the Safavids. Like imperial rulers in China, Egypt, Rome, and elsewhere, the Safavids encouraged and patronized the arts. The new capital of Isfahan became a glittering cultural center; as the Persians said, "Isfahan is half the world."

Shah Abbas ordered numerous mosques, inns, schools, and baths built in Isfahan and along the important trading routes. His Shah Mosque in Isfahan with its ornate tile work, large entrance facades, and bulbous dome epitomizes Safavid architecture at its best. Safavid artists also continued to excel in painting complex miniatures on paper and ivory. Many such miniatures adorned and illustrated Persian manuscripts.

The Safavids and the aristocrats were conspicuous in their love of luxury items. They lived lavishly and wore ornate silk and gold-brocaded attire. Persian artisans were noted for their skills in weaving gold brocade and large, extremely fine carpets. Many weavers of carpets were women and children. European traders often

The Textile Museum, Washington, D.C., 1985.5.1, Ruth Lincoln Fisher Fund

Persian Silk Robe. This elaborate brocaded taffeta robe in rich blues, oranges, and gold shows the floral designs favored by high-ranking Safavid courtiers.

commented on the conspicuous consumption of Safavid lifestyles. Nonetheless, the Safavids were early believers in recycling. Every seven years the used clothes from the royal court were burned and the gold and silver threads collected for use in new garments. For relaxation, the upper class enjoyed games such as chess (a Persian invention) and polo. The entire population participated in religious festivals marking the Shi'i calendar, particularly services commemorating the death of Ali (the Shi'i believe that the ruling authority of the Muslim community should have passed through Ali's descendants) and the martyrdom of his son, Husayn. Husayn's death was reenacted in protracted and moving passion plays.

Indeed, much Safavid literature was devoted to religious themes, and the Safavids financed numerous religious schools that reinterpreted and reinforced Shi'i theological tenets. Religious differences between the Shi'i Safavids and Sunni Ottomans were one of the sources of conflict between the two empires. In contrast to the religious written works, romantic love poetry continued to be highly popular, and Persian poets and poetry dominated and influenced literary life in both the Ottoman and Moghul Empires. Like the Ottoman sultans, Safavid rulers also encouraged writers to immortalize their military and political achievements in long histories and biographies.

Wars between the Rival Empires

Throughout their long histories, the Ottomans and Safavids were rivals for control over the territories around the Tigris-Euphrates Valley (present-day Iraq). As Sunni Muslims, the Ottomans also clashed with the Shi'i Safavids over domination of Islamic territories and interpretations of basic Islamic doctrines. The long struggle drained both of needed military power and resources. Neither delivered a fatal military blow to the other, but debilitating intermittent warfare made both increasingly vulnerable to other outside enemies.

The conflicts began when Suleiman's father, Selim I, initiated a "holy war" against the Shi'i and the Safavid dynasty. In 1514 Ottoman forces equipped with cannon decisively defeated the Safavids in the northern provinces of present-day Iran, but Selim failed to follow through on his victory. Suleiman continued the struggle by launching several campaigns against the Safavid ruler, Shah Tahmasp, who employed a policy of "scorched earth" as a defensive measure, thereby forcing the Ottomans to bring all their supplies with them. Suleiman successfully conquered the major northern city of Tabriz, but found it costly to maintain its control. In 1555 his difficulties holding the northern territories forced him to arrange a treaty with the Safavids. Suleiman retained Iraq, with the major trading center of Baghdad and a port on the Persian Gulf, but had to withdraw from the northern Persian provinces.

The Safavids countered Ottoman power by allying with the Habsburgs, the major Ottoman enemy in eastern Europe. Taking advantage of the power vacuum following Suleiman's death, Shah Abbas occupied present-day Iraq and parts of the Anatolia Peninsula. By 1623 the Ottomans, now strengthened by internal reforms, took advantage of Safavid weakness after Shah Abbas's death to oust the Safavids from these territories. A peace treaty between these two mighty empires in 1639 established boundaries that approximate those of present-day western Iran.

In spite of several attempts to implement internal reforms, the Safavid Empire never regained the power wielded by Shah Abbas. As a consequence, it was ill prepared to meet the challenges of expansionist neighbors. By the eighteenth century, tribes from Afghanistan began to expand into Safavid territories and by 1722, Afghan forces took Isfahan. Safavid weakness allowed Ottoman forces then to move into northern Persian provinces. Under Shah Tahmasp II, the Safavids unsuccessfully counterattacked the Afghan forces. The assassination of Nader Shah in 1747 ended the Safavid dynasty. With the collapse of effective centralized government, numerous rival local rulers vied for political and military control until the Qajar dynasty emerged as the dominant power in 1794.

The Culture of the Renaissance in Europe

If then we are to call any age golden, it is beyond doubt that age which brings forth golden talents in different places. That such is true of our age, he who wishes to consider the illustrious discoveries of this century will hardly doubt. For this century, like a golden age, has restored to light the liberal arts, which were almost extinct: grammar, poetry, rhetoric, painting, sculpture, architecture, music . . . and all this in Florence. Achieving what had been honored among the ancients, but almost forgotten since, the age has joined wisdom with eloquence, and produce with the military art . . . and in Florence it has recalled the Platonic teaching from darkness into light.*

**Letter of Marsilio Ficino to Paul of Middleburg, trans. M. M. McLaughlin, in *The Portable Renaissance Reader* (New York: Viking, 1953), p. 79.

In this excerpt, the Florentine philosopher Marsilio Ficino (1433–1499) expresses his joy at living in a time of intellectual revolution, sparked by a reawakened interest in the values and culture of ancient Greece and Rome. Ficino and his contemporaries scorned what they perceived as the ignorance and barbarism of the "dark ages," the thousand years between the collapse of the Roman Empire and their own era, to which they applied the term *Renaissance,* meaning "rebirth" in French. They believed that they were living in a "golden age" that had broken abruptly with the immediate past.

Although Renaissance thinkers were aware of the contrast between their own and the medieval period, they failed to appreciate the full dimensions of their age. To them, the revival of cultural antiquity was the outstanding characteristic of their progressive era. Yet artistic creativity was only one aspect of the Renaissance. In fact, changes affected every element of European society—political, social, and religious as well as cultural. Nor did the Renaissance develop in complete isolation from the era that preceded it. Indeed, the Renaissance continued many trends of medieval civilization. The difference lay in the faster pace of change, not in the creation of something entirely new.

This is not to say that there were no differences in attitude between the Middle Ages and the Renaissance. The medieval cultural perspective had centered on theology, with emphasis on God's will, human sinfulness, and heavenly existence after earthly life. That outlook permeated all intellectual life: education, philosophy, theology, art, and architecture. Medieval religion had firmly rejected life in this world as evil, useless, and perilous to the salvation of the soul. Abandoning secular culture in favor of a monastic life seemed to many the surest way to gain salvation and please God. During the Renaissance, however, thinkers, writers, and artists made man, not God, the chief center of interest. They glorified the human body as beautiful and the human intellect as capable of unlocking the deepest mysteries of nature by rational processes. Renaissance thinkers known as humanists argued that God in fact wanted men to engage in political and civic life, to create and discover, and to marry and have families. In short, fulfillment within the secular sphere was in accord with God's will. Thus a major innovation of the humanists was to reconcile the new urban culture and life with Christianity and the possibility of salvation.

The Origins of the Renaissance: Italian Literature and Humanism

The Renaissance was an age of rapid transition, linking medieval to early modern ways of life. The chronology of the Renaissance raises some problems for historians in deciding when it began and how long it continued. Most accept early fourteenth century as the start and mid-sixteenth century as the end. The Renaissance began and took shape in Italy before spreading across the Alps.

There are many reasons why Italy was the birthplace of the Renaissance. For one thing, the survival of Roman artistic and architectural heritage and the continued use of Latin had kept memories of classical civilization alive. Italy also had profited from both Islamic and Byzantine cultural influences. Trade remained important in Italy, which gave rise to early modern capitalism, and furnished the material resources for cultural development. Less feudal than northern Europe, Italy enjoyed renewed vigor in its urban centers in the wake of the Crusades. Political developments fostered the growth of independent city-states, and prominent commercial cities like Genoa, Venice, and Milan competed with one another in cultural as well as commercial affairs. These cities gave rise to an affluent, middle/upper class with the leisure for education and a sense of political responsibility. Such individuals sought models of civic duty, social responsibility, and governmental values. The urbanized, sophisticated world of ancient Greece and Rome provided just such models in an extensive body of literature and art. Thus, the humanists returned to classical literature and found inspiration there for an active life of political involvement and reasoned analysis of morals and beliefs.

The early Renaissance in Italy during the fourteenth century centered on a few eloquent writers from Tuscany (the area around Florence) who stimulated interest and delight in the physical world. Francesco Petrarca, or Petrarch (1304–1374), sometimes called the father of humanism, idolized the ancient Roman authors and emulated their literary compositions and writing styles; he also adopted the ancient writers' secular outlook on life in his own works. Petrarch as a man of letters gained enduring fame from his poetry, written in the Tuscan vernacular. A keen observer of nature, he wrote tender sonnets and exquisite odes in celebration of his burning love for Laura, a married woman whom he adored at a distance. Although Petrarch expresses real love for a living woman and rhapsodizes over her physical features, his devotion to her is essentially spiritual, so that a conflict between body and mind underlies his poems. Being ambitious and desiring fame and fortune, he struggled against the medieval notion that God

LIVES AND TIMES ACROSS CULTURES

Racy Tales

Renaissance writers, with their interest in describing society as they observed it, tended to be tolerant of human behavior. The following racy passages illustrate how far Renaissance society had departed from Christian moral restraint.

The first excerpt centers on an adulterous relationship. A young wife, Petronella, tells her lover, Gianello, to get into a tub when her husband returns home unexpectedly. Petronella explains that she has sold the old tub to a man who is inspecting it from the inside. Gianello leaps out of the tub and expresses satisfaction with it, except for an area that is coated with a hard substance. The wife tells her husband to climb into the tub to scrape it off.

While she was busy instructing and directing her husband in this fashion, Gianello, who had not fully gratified his desires that morning before the husband arrived, seeing that he couldn't do it in the way he wished, contributed to bring it off as best he could. So he went up to Petronella, who was completely blocking up the mouth of the tub, and in the manner of a wild and hot-blooded stallion mounting a Parthian mare in the open fields, he satisfied his young man's passion, which no sooner reached fulfillment than the scraping of the tub was completed, whereupon he stood back,

*Petronella withdrew her head from the tub and the husband clambered out.** *

The second excerpt contains a wife's justification for taking on a lover.

*As you can see, Lusca [her maid], I am young and vigorous, and I am well supplied with all the things a woman could desire. In short, with one exception I have nothing to complain about, and the exception is this: that my husband is much older than myself, and consequently I am ill provided with the one thing that gives young women their great pleasure.*** *

The third excerpt describes a young man's clumsy and crude efforts to seduce a noble Parisian lady.

"Would you like a bolt of bright crimson velvet, striped with green, or some embroidered satin, or maybe crimson? What would you like—necklaces, gold things, things for your hair, rings? All you have to do is say yes. Even fifty thousand gold pieces doesn't bother me...."

"No. Thank you, but I want nothing from you."

*"By God," said he, "I damned well want something from you, and it's something that won't cost you a cent, and once you've given it you'll still have it, every bit of it. Here"—and he showed her his long codpiece—"here is my John Thomas, who wants a place to jump into."**** *

* Giovanni Boccaccio, The Decameron, trans. G. H. McWilliam (London: Penguin, 1995), p. 494.

** Ibid., p. 534.

*** François Rabelais, Gargantua and Pantagruel, trans. Burton Raffel (New York: Norton, 1990), p. 201.

wished men to renounce the material things of this world. Petrarch's work thus exemplifies the typical Renaissance propensity to elevate the secular.

The new interest in worldly life that marks Petrarch's thought is evident also in the work of his friend, Giovanni Boccaccio (1313–1375), the first great Italian prose writer. His *Decameron* is concerned with everyday life, portraying people from all social classes, often with a strong satirical flavor. With Boccaccio, the lustfulness and earthy wit of the lower classes enter serious literature during the Renaissance. In contrast to Dante's *Divine Comedy*, the *Decameron* is sometimes termed the "Human Comedy."

Although many humanist literary works were written in Italian, most writers maintained that the Latin of Cicero was the supreme literary language. Shunning "corrupt" medieval Latin, they found in classical literature a purity of style, form, and eloquence absent from most medieval literature, and they argued that to speak and write correctly one should imitate the ancients. Petrarch, for example, developed the finest Latin style of his age. Succeeding Renaissance writers and scholars, stimulated by the migration of Byzantine scholars who had begun to flee Constantinople before its fall in 1453, promoted the study of Greek.

An important aspect of humanist activity was the recovery of manuscripts of classical literary, scientific, and historical works. Searchers discovered many Latin manuscripts in European monasteries and churches. Increasingly, during the fifteenth century, Greek history and literature became available in the West as humanists obtained copies of Greek manuscripts through contacts with Byzantine scholars. Manuel Chrysoloras, a Byzantine diplomat, began a regular course of lectures on Greek in Florence in 1397; his grammar textbook gained wide circulation (it was used by Erasmus, discussed later in this section) and in 1471 became the first Greek grammar to be printed.

The recovery of so many texts gave rise to modern textual criticism, including the disciplines of paleography (the analysis of manuscripts and the handwriting in which they are transcribed) and philology (the critical study of language and literature). Dictionaries, grammars, indices, and commentaries were produced, and the texts of ancient authors were put on a sound footing by scholars who collected and compared manuscripts. From their careful textual studies, the humanists learned how to assess authenticity, showing, for example, that "The Donation of Constantine," used by popes to support their territorial sovereignty over Rome and its environs, was in fact a forgery written 400 years after the Roman emperor's death.

The Genius of Petrarch

[Petrarch] dwarfs his precursors in every respect: he was an immeasurably greater poet and greater man than any of them; his horizons were wider and his influence, never cramped within the limits of town or province, extended over most of Western Europe; he had the vision and the ability to unite the two existing strands of humanism, the literary and the scholarly, and to combine aims which reached for the moon with the capacity for painstaking research; he went further than anyone else in trying to revive within the framework of a Christian society the ideals of ancient Rome, and his attempts to get close to the great figures of the past, and indeed to rival their achievement, though flirting with the vainglorious, unleashed passions and ambitions which were to reanimate the whole cultural legacy of the ancient world and bring it to bear upon contemporary modes of thought and literature.*

Petrarch is the archetypal figure of the humanist as scholar poet. While he assembled a personal library of thousands of manuscripts, with special emphasis on his beloved Cicero, he was no mere antiquarian book collector. He read with intensity and absorbed the thought of the classical authors to his very marrow.

*L. D. Reynolds and N. G. Wilson, Scribes and Scholars: A Guide to the Transmission of Greek and Latin Literature, 2nd ed. (Oxford: Clarendon Press, 1974), pp. 113–114.

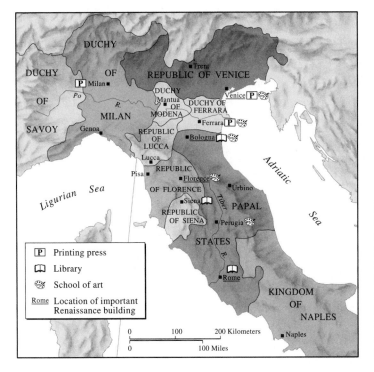

Map 9.3 Renaissance Italy. The commercial vitality and political disunity of northern Italy stimulated cultural creativity. Prosperous towns patronized and promoted artists and scholars. A remarkable number of Italian cities contributed significantly to Renaissance thought, literature, and art.

The spread of classical learning was accelerated by print. The use of movable type to print books, a momentous innovation for Europe, though known earlier in China and Korea, is attributed to Johannes Gutenberg of Mainz about 1450. The mass production of texts that printing facilitated soon made the cultural heritage of the classical world and, with it, the Renaissance widely available in Europe.

Classical texts were the basis of humanistic elementary and secondary education; the curricula included literature, mathematics, music, science, and athletics. In contrast to medieval scholars, teachers and students achieved a direct familiarity with classical Greek authorities in most subject areas. Students who received such classical training excelled in law and theology, or became secretaries for princes, prelates, and town councils.

Renaissance historians modeled their work on the classical authors, producing histories of their city or state, rather than the universal histories or annalistic accounts favored by medieval scholars. They departed from medieval precedents in emphasizing politics and stressing the role of human motives over divine intervention. Renaissance historians were also more critical in their evaluation of source materials.

The philosophers of the Renaissance were proponents of the new humanist outlook. Unlike the Scholastics of the late Middle Ages, they tended to prefer Plato to Aristotle because of the former's superior literary style and the more mystical nature of his thought. Marsilio Ficino translated into Latin all the works of Plato as well as many commentaries on his philosophy. Renaissance Platonists drew on Plato's fascination with numbers and harmonies to promote interest in geometry and mathematics. Ficino and the brilliant young scholar Giovanni Pico della Mirandola (1463–1494) also held that humans were free, perfectible individuals, with social responsibilities and a dignity derived from their position midway between the material world and the spiritual God. Pico's "Oration on the Dignity of Man," delivered in Rome in 1486, was a manifesto of humanism:

> O unsurpassed generosity of God the Father, O wondrous and unsurpassed felicity of man, to whom it is granted to have what he chooses, to be what he wills to be! The brutes, from the moment of their birth, bring with them . . . from their mother's womb all that they will ever possess. The highest spiritual beings [angels] were, from the very moment of creation, or soon thereafter, fixed in the mode of being which would be theirs through measureless eternities. But upon man, at the moment of his creation, God bestowed seeds pregnant with all possibilities, the germs of every form of life. Whichever of these a man shall cultivate, the same will mature and bear fruit in him. If vegetative, he will become a plant; if sensual, he will become brutish; if rational, he will reveal himself a heavenly being; if intellectual, he will be an angel and the son of God. . . . Who then will not look with awe upon this our chameleon, or who, at least, will look with greater admiration on any other being? (A. R. Caponigri, trans., Giovanni Pico della Mirandola: Oration on the Dignity of Man [Chicago: Regnery, 1956], pp. 8–9).

Renaissance Art in Italy

During the fourteenth century, Renaissance painters and sculptors, like Italian writers, drew inspiration from classical models. They could do so partly because Roman antiquities (monuments and ruins) were unusually numerous and near at hand and partly because Gothic art, popular elsewhere in Europe, had penetrated only slightly into Italy.

Art in the Middle Ages tended to be subservient to the church and its purposes. The object was to emphasize spiritual aspiration at the expense of physical beauty. Italian painting, usually religious figures against solid backgrounds, had been stiff and flat, with the human form covered almost entirely with clothing. In short, the art of the Middle Ages had tended to ignore nature and the physical features of the human figure, because these were thought to be sources of evil and corruption that distracted from the contemplation of God. Renaissance artists, by contrast, following the lead of the humanists, depicted a world in which nature, human beauty, the family, and even fame were pleasing to God. Because human beings were to fulfill themselves as Christians in this world, the things of this world were now, in wonderful detail, suitable subjects for artists.

A serious difficulty in the imitation of nature in painting was the simulation of movement and depth on a flat surface. A late medieval painter, the Florentine Giotto di Bondone (1266–1337), overcame this obstacle by discarding the flat forms, aloof figures, and formal compositions of the Byzantine style that had dominated Italian painting. Allegedly able to draw a fly so realistically that viewers attempted to brush it away, he skillfully contrasted light and shadow to create an illusion of depth that made his human figures look solid and round. Among the artists influenced by Giotto was Tomasso Guidi (1401–1428), better known as Masaccio. He employed the laws of atmospheric perspective to show objects receding into a background and to make figures appear round and truly three-dimensional. Although only twenty-seven when he died, Masaccio's innova-

The School of Athens. In this painting, Renaissance master Raphael presented his version of the humanist ideal of classical antiquity. Many Greek and Roman cultural heroes are depicted in the dress of sixteenth-century Italians in a setting of Renaissance architecture and sculpture. At the center of the composition, framed by the arch, Plato and Aristotle are deep in discussion.

tions inspired succeeding generations of painters, including Michelangelo and the other giants of the High Renaissance.

The first of these was Leonardo da Vinci (1452–1519), who more than any other person of his age personified the Renaissance ideal of versatility. As an artist, he was keenly interested in the natural world and was a masterly portrayer of human psychology and personality. *The Last Supper* is a careful study of the emotions that each of Jesus' disciples was likely to have expressed on that occasion. In the *Mona Lisa,* he skillfully employed light and shadow and perspective to make the figure fully human, enigmatic and mysterious, and forever fascinating.

The most popular of the Renaissance painters, Raphael Sanzio (1483–1520), excelled in composition and use of soft colors. His *School of Athens* is a symbolic and allegorical portrayal of the classical philosophers Plato and Aristotle with their students. Raphael was best known for his many Madonnas, which are warm, pious, and graceful.

Michelangelo Buonarroti (1475–1564) considered himself a sculptor first of all, but as painter he was unsurpassed in technical excellence and grandeur of conception. He painted with a sculptor's eye and made the muscular male figure his ideal of beauty. His most ambitious project, perhaps the greatest single achievement in Renaissance art, was the painting of the frescoes covering the ceiling of the Sistine Chapel in the Vatican. This masterpiece, which required four years to complete, often with the artist lying flat on his back on a scaffold, depicts nine scenes from the Old Testament, from the creation to the flood.

Sculpture followed a parallel course to painting in its development. The first major artist in this medium was Donato di Niccolì di Betto Bardi, known as Donatello (c. 1386–1466). He drew on models of classical antiquity for inspiration, traveling to Rome to study ancient art remains. His studies included anatomy and the human body, and he employed models. Donatello's *David*, the first nude statue of the Renaissance, is graceful, well proportioned, and superbly balanced.

Michelangelo brought to sculpture the same scientific accuracy, endowment of life, and deep emotion that distinguished his paintings. His statues, whether standing like *David* or seated like *Moses,* show dramatic and emotional postures and expressions. His absolute mastery of sculptural technique powerfully served the Renaissance glorification of man. Especially moving is his exquisite *Pietà,* which depicts a grief-stricken Mary looking at the dead body of Jesus lying across her lap.

Michelangelo's later works exemplify an important change that took place in the art of the sixteenth century. His later sculptures show an exaggeration, elongation, and distortion that heightens their emotional and religious qualities. For example, his crowded *Last Judgment* painting on the Sistine Chapel's end wall is full of violence, tragedy, and horror, in contrast to the classical harmony and restraint of the ceiling figures.

Architects, though slower in exploring new directions, were still more strongly influenced by classical models. In his church designs, Filippo Brunelleschi (1377–1446) combined the Romanesque cruciform floor plan with such classical features as columns, rounded windows, and arches. His greatest triumph was the cupola (dome) atop the Florence cathedral, which echoes both Rome's Pantheon and Constantinople's Hagia Sophia.

The Renaissance Outside Italy

A great watershed in western European literature and thought was the spread of the Renaissance outside of Italy between 1490 and 1530. Italian humanists accepted positions as secretaries and diplomats with northern kings and princes. Scholars from the north studied in Italy and returned home to write and teach humanism. Northern universities incorporated humanist studies into their curricula, and humanist historians used their critical skills in writing the histories of northern lands.

Italian humanism, fostered in the republics and communes of Italy, had a strong civic strain that was believed to be acceptable to God and quite consistent with Christian life. In northern Europe, humanists wrote less about civic and political duty and more about personal morality, though they still drew heavily upon both Christian and pagan (that is, non-Christian Greek and Roman) authors. Although they stressed the Bible and the words of the church fathers over classical writings, northern humanists believed that by absorbing the wisdom of both, they could improve individual morality and revitalize and purify contemporary social and religious life. Nevertheless, like their Italian predecessors, northern humanists also believed, as Thomas More (1478–1535) said, that education in Latin and Greek "doth train the soul in virtue." More, who was a lawyer and diplomat (even becoming lord chancellor of England) as well as a humanist, is best known for his *Utopia*. The *Utopia* contrasted the evil conditions of sixteenth-century Europe with an idealized, peaceful, and prosperous society living communally in accord with reason and Christian values.

The foremost northern humanist was Desiderius Erasmus (c.1466–1536), a native of Rotterdam. His wit, marvelous writing style, and extensive travels earned him international renown and ensured that his works would be "best sellers." Erasmus formulated a humanist religion of simple piety and noble conduct based on a belief in human dignity and free will. He embraced the naturalism, tolerance, and humanitarianism he found in classical writings and used his formidable satiric power to oppose war, violence, ignorance, and irrationality. His *Adages* collected apt sayings from classical Latin writers and the *Praise of Folly* attacked the pedantic dogmatism of scholars and the ignorance of the masses. Erasmus's fresh edition of the Greek New Testament became the basis of various translations into the vernacular languages.

In areas of Europe outside Italy, vernacular literatures, already developing in the thirteenth century, now registered remarkable achievements. In England, Geoffrey Chaucer (1340–1400) made the East Midland dialect the ancestor of modern English. His highly entertaining *Canterbury Tales* are filled with realistic and humorous portrayals of men and women from various social classes and occupations.

By the fifteenth century, humanist stimulation had fostered a quickening of literary achievement in western Europe. In France, François Rabelais (1490–1553) produced a prose masterpiece, *Gargantua and Pantagruel,* that glorified the human and the natural, rejected Christian doctrine and morality, and satirized scholasticism, bigotry, and church practices with bawdy humor. At the abbey where many of the book's episodes occur, the only rule is "do what you will." A little later Michel de Montaigne (1533–1592) introduced the essay as an important literary form. His great collection of *Essays* is a kind of extended intellectual autobiography, ranging over a wide variety of topics in an engaging conversational tone. Characteristic of Montaigne's essays is a healthy skepticism regarding human opinions, doctrines, institutions, and customs, as in the following passage from "On Cannibals":

> *I am not so anxious that we should note the horrible savagery of these [cannibalistic] acts as concerned that, whilst judging their faults so correctly, we should be so blind to our own. I consider it more barbarous to eat a man alive than to eat him dead; to tear by rack and torture a body still full of feeling, to roast it by degrees, and then to give it to be trampled and eaten by dogs and swine—a practice which we have not only read about but seen within recent memory, not between ancient enemies, but between neighbors and fellow-citizens and, what is worse, under the cloak of piety and religion—than to roast and eat a man after he is dead. (J. M. Cohen, trans., Michel de Montaigne: Essays [Harmondsworth: Penguin, 1958], p. 113.)*

For the most part, the golden age of Spanish literature came somewhat later than that of France. Miguel de Cervantes's (1547–1616) *Don Quixote,* sometimes regarded as the greatest novel ever written, is a rich depiction of human nobility and folly. Cervantes ridicules the nobles' pretensions to be champions of honor by recounting the adventures of a Spanish gentleman who, after reading too many chivalric romances, becomes a wandering knight. Imagining windmills to be giants and inns to be castles, the hero (mis)behaves in accord with those (mis)perceptions. His squire, Sancho Panza, is, by contrast, a practical man untroubled by romantic dreams and content with the simple creature comforts of eating, drinking, and sleeping.

England's literary developments were contemporary with those of Spain and were most impressive in drama. William Shakespeare (1564–1616) drew themes and story lines from Greek and Roman literature and from English history. Extremely adept in the use of language and the analysis of character, he showed a deep understanding of human potential, both for good and for evil. The following is an example:

> What a piece of work is a man! How noble in reason! How infinite in faculty! In form and moving how express and admirable! In action how like an angel! In apprehension how like a god! The beauty of the world! The paragon of animals! (Hamlet 2.2.315–319.)

In an ironic vein reminiscent of Greek tragedy, Shakespeare's heroes are responsible for their own dilemmas and suffer by their own sins and mistakes. His strongest plays express bitterness and overwhelming pathos, as the characters conduct a troubled search into life's mysteries. Of these plays, the later ones present an overall view of the universe as benevolent and just, despite individual tragedy and grief.

Northern Renaissance art represented physical and emotional reality by use of detail, careful observation of nature, and skill in the technique of foreshortening. Jan van Eyck (1370–1440) capitalized on the advantages of oil paints, excelling in the painting of portraits in which the subjects seem to live and breathe; each detail, from a blade of grass to the hair of a dog, is meticulously rendered. Albrecht Dürer (1471–1528) studied the human form carefully and gave attention to both detail and harmonious composition in woodcuts, engravings, and paintings. He admired Martin Luther (see the next section) and often chose biblical themes for his work. Many of his pieces have a pervasive somber and often gloomy quality. The great Spanish painter, Doménikos Theotokópoulos (1541–1614), known as El Greco from his birth on the island of Crete, was an avid admirer of Michelangelo. He used severe colors and elongated features to express Spanish religious zeal in his powerful and emotional paintings. His greatest work, *The Burial of Count Orgaz,* conveys the Catholic spirit of communion among God, saints, and humans.

Architects outside Italy continued to use Gothic techniques in building both churches and secular structures, but as they reached the structural and decorative limits of the Gothic, they began to employ the classical Greco-Roman style revived by fifteenth-century Italians. Those Italian influences are especially evident in central France's Loire Valley chateaux, country houses for French kings, nobles, and wealthy townspeople.

Women and the Renaissance

In the Renaissance, as in earlier periods of European history, education and intellectual professions were accessible almost exclusively to males. Laws were designed to keep women in a subservient role. As a rule they could not hold public office, testify in a court of law, make their own wills, or buy and sell property. Most women from the nobility and wealthy merchant class had few career options: they either entered into arranged marriages or became nuns. A few women, however, did receive schooling based on the revival of classical learning during the Renaissance; they were typically daughters of aristocrats or royalty instructed by fathers or husbands or by private tutors.

Despite the restrictions imposed by male-oriented societies, some females achieved personal and intellectual fulfillment. Christine de Pizan (1365–c. 1430), for example, was the first woman known to have made her living as a professional writer. In 1390, the death of her husband, a secretary at the court of the French king (Charles V), left her with three children, her mother, and two brothers to support. To do so, she developed her skills in a variety of genres: love poetry, literary criticism, histories of eminent women, political theory, religious meditations, a biography of King Charles V, and poetry written for aristocratic patrons; her last work was a poem celebrating the victory of Joan of Arc at the siege of Orléans during the Hundred Years' War (see the next section). She also penned a fascinating autobiography entitled *Christine's Vision*.

Even for learned women, a life of scholarship did not combine easily with wifely duties and maternal obligations of child bearing and rearing. Ginerva Nogarola (c. 1417–1468) and Cataruzza Caldiera (d. 1463), both of whom showed exceptional promise as young women, abandoned their studies and writings altogether after they

Melancholia I. The melancholy figure by Albrecht Dürer sits amid symbols of the new learning of the sixteenth century, suggesting that greater knowledge does not necessarily produce happiness. If meant as a self-portrait, it is a very early example of the "tormented artist" theme so familiar in modern times. The work shows the exquisite detail that a master engraver could achieve.

married and bore children. Described by some humanists as a prodigy, Cassandra Fedele (1465–1558) married reluctantly at age thirty-three and continued her scholarly work only haphazardly, failing to complete any of the three major works she had planned.

There were a few exceptions, however, when privileged women were able to study, write, marry, and have children. Marguerite of Navarre (1492–1549) was one of the greatest women literary writers of the sixteenth century. Although a poet of unusual sensitivity, her fame rests on her principal prose work, the *Heptameron,* a collection of short stories modeled on Boccaccio's *Decameron.*

Some women found themselves in conflict with their family and society as they followed a literary career outside of marriage. Constanza Barbaro (born c. 1419), daughter of a Venetian humanist, became a nun so that she could devote all her time to study. Isotta Nogarola (1418–1466) was probably the best known among women writers who created their own cloistered world. She was trained by a private tutor and at age eighteen started a correspondence with male humanists in Verona. Though her letters show great promise and were praised by some, others advised her that she would have to "become a man" if she wished to continue her career as a writer. Isotta decided against both the alternatives of married life and the nunnery and lived as a recluse in her mother's home, producing some fine Latin verse and an important theological tract.

Women who aspired to paint had to overcome the same disadvantages as those drawn to the intellectual movement. Still, many succeeded in earning a living by selling their works to, or accepting commissions for portraits from, wealthy patrons. Levina Bening Teerline (c. 1520–1576) was invited by Henry VIII to come from Flanders to paint miniature portraits. The English monarch was so delighted with her paintings that he paid her a life annuity of £40, then a generous sum. The portraitist Sofonisba Anguissola (c. 1535–1625), the daughter of an Italian noble family, drew a similar commission from Philip II of Spain, who rewarded her lavishly with a pension, a dowry on her marriage, and appointment as lady-in-waiting to the court.

During the Baroque phase of the Italian Renaissance, Artemisia Gentileschi (1593–c. 1652), trained by her father and other artists, achieved a reputation on a par with that of Leonardo Da Vinci and Michelangelo. She often chose women for her subjects: for example, the biblical heroines Susannah and Judith beheading Holofernes. In another medium Properzia de' Rossi (c.1500–1530) was singled out by the biographer Vasari for the excellence of her relief sculptures in the Church of St. Peter in Bologna and for her great versatility: "[she was] skilled not only in household matters . . . but in infinite fields of knowledge. . . . She was beautiful and played and sang better than any woman in the city." Few women of the Renaissance were able (or allowed) to be so multitalented.

European Nation-States and the Reformation

[At the Diet of Worms in 1521, the spokesman said:] "Martin, how can you assume that you are the only one to understand the sense of Scripture? Would you put your judgment above that of so many famous men and claim that you know more than they all? You have no right to call into question the most holy orthodox faith, instituted by Christ the perfect lawgiver, proclaimed throughout the world by

the apostles, sealed by the red blood of the martyrs, confirmed by the sacred councils, defined by the Church in which all our fathers believed until death and gave to us as an inheritance, and which now we are forbidden by the pope and the emperor to discuss lest there be no end of debate. I ask you, Martin—answer candidly and without horns—do you or do you not repudiate your books and the errors which they contain?"

Luther replied, "Since then Your Majesty and your lordships desire a simple reply, I will answer without horns and without teeth. Unless I am convicted by Scripture and plain reason—I do not accept the authority of popes and councils, for they have contradicted each other—my conscience is captive to the Word of God. I cannot and I will not recant anything, for to go against conscience is neither right nor safe. God help me. Amen." [In the earliest printed version the words "Here I stand. I cannot do otherwise," were added.]*

*Roland H. Bainton, Here I Stand: A Life of Martin Luther (New York: Mentor, 1958), p. 144.

This exchange was the culmination of a sequence of events that produced the Protestant Reformation, a broad revolt against the medieval church. Although religious dissent was the root of the problem, the Reformation was also intimately bound up with political, social, economic, and intellectual matters. Within a generation of Luther's defiant act, many Europeans had set up separate religious organizations outside the Catholic church, ending the centuries-long religious unity of western Europe. Although the various Protestant denominations disagreed among themselves on minor theological points, they were firmly united in their opposition to Catholicism. The confrontation inspired a long period of bloody strife that would profoundly affect Western civilization.

The Reformation was closely associated with the formation of powerful national states in western Europe, a process that had begun some two centuries earlier. The pride, power, and resources of these states found expression in various forms of political and commercial rivalry, including developing trade overseas (see the following sections). The emergence of these nation-states of western Europe will open this section.

The Centralization of Western European Monarchies

The High Middle Ages had witnessed the resurgent power of the monarchy in Europe as the prelude to the development of the modern state. However, the troubles of four-teenth- and fifteenth-century Europe—civil and foreign wars, economic depression, and the plague—undid much of the earlier work of consolidation. The powers of government came to be divided between the king and his semiautonomous vassals, the great nobles of the realm. Royal vassals maintained private armies, dispensed justice in the courts, and served as advisors and royal officials. The nobles were monarchs in minia-ture, often having the power of life and death over the people in their territories. As a result, a country like France was not a single nation under one king; rather, it was a mosaic of principalities, each with its own ruler. At times of a major threat, vassals would sometimes temporarily join forces under their king.

For the peasants or serfs, it made little difference whether they were exploited by king or duke, because life close to the soil was harsh in either case. For dwellers in manufacturing and trading towns, the situation was less clear. The city fathers longed to win self-rule and, to that end, liked to play one great lord off against another or against the king. At the same time, however, those who aspired to trade over larger areas found the political fragmentation of their country a hindrance.

The trend towards decentralization was dramatically reversed during the second half of the fifteenth century with the emergence of strong, ambitious kings in France, England, and Spain. They ended internal disorders in their lands, reduced the power of the nobility, and extended greater control over their subjects. The achievements of these "New Monarchs" served as examples for lesser kings to follow.

Several factors led to the recovery of the monarchy in western Europe. As already noted, in the centralized states around the world, the European kings needed to generate an assured source of income sufficient to create an army and a bureaucracy under their control. The new towns provided a potential source of new money. In a mutually beneficial arrangement, the kings granted the towns privileges and rights in return for money payments to the royal treasury. In this way, towns and monarchs became allies against the great lords, who often sought to encroach on the independence of both. These arrangements not only reduced the kings' dependence on the great nobles but resulted in the growth of semi-independent towns in early modern Europe.

With the new revenue, the kings moved to abandon feudal levies and create a powerful army. In the traditional feudal levy, vassals supplied forces for temporary service, but so long as the great nobles controlled the military, the king's power was limited. Accordingly, the monarchs began to build up armies of paid soldiers commanded by loyal officers who were willing to follow orders and even make war on the nobles, if necessary.

The kings further strengthened their position through marriages calculated either to neutralize powerful antagonists or to add territory to their own realm. No less important was the development of bureaucracies. Civil servants attached to districts collected taxes and administered in the king's name. Kings selected their officials from outside the nobility and paid them in money and in small, scattered estates instead of huge blocks of territory. In this way, the kings ensured that the officials would be dependent on them and thus loyal to the crown.

In France, the first of the New Monarchs, Louis XI (reigned 1461–1483), inherited a realm devastated by the Black Death and the Hundred Years' War (1337–1453). The latter was a debilitating struggle fought between the English and the French, and among the French, over a maze of feudal claims and commercial competition. At a dark moment for France, a young woman, later known as Joan of Arc (1412–1431) changed the course of the war. Believing herself to be acting at God's urging, she persuaded Charles VII (reigned 1422–1461) to appoint her to a military command. Her prestige reached its height in 1429 when she succeeded in relieving the besieged city of Orléans and cutting a path for Charles to Rheims, where he was properly crowned in the place and manner of his ancestors. Joan, who was later captured and executed, came to symbolize the French national spirit.

Louis XI was nicknamed the "Spider," in part because his misshapen body appeared spiderlike, but more because he devised political traps and plots reminiscent of a spiderweb. He attracted the loyalty of the lesser nobility and employed many of them as royal officials. Louis used the army to expand royal power within France, and in a series of adroit, if underhanded, moves, he suppressed the great nobles, already weakened by losses during the Hundred Years' War. At the same time, he curbed town autonomy and asserted administrative control over the provinces. He seldom convened the Estates General, France's rudimentary representative assembly. By his death in 1483 Louis had united France, strengthened its economy, and laid the foundations for royal absolutism.

Like France, fifteenth-century England was wracked by factionalism, which culminated in a civil war (the War of the Roses, 1455–1485) between the great feudal families of Lancaster and York. The civil war ended in 1485 when Henry Tudor, the foremost surviving Lancastrian, seized the crown as Henry VII (reigned 1485–1509) and married Elizabeth of York, the leading Yorkist claimant, thereby uniting the two feuding groups. With peace temporarily assured, Henry set out to centralize his power. He drew his officials from the ranks of the lesser gentry and townsmen and seated many of his councilors in Parliament, where they could manipulate matters to the king's liking. Henry received such ample revenues from customs duties on increased international trade and from fines derived from active law enforcement that he needed to summon Parliament only once in the last twelve years of his reign. He supplemented traditional English law with Roman law for many purposes. Roman law, formulated to govern a far-flung empire, favored central authority over the rights of aristocrats and common people alike and helped Henry legally justify seizing the lands and revenues of "overmighty subjects." At his death in 1509, Henry left a powerful monarchy to his son, Henry VIII.

Events in the Iberian Peninsula paralleled those in France and England. Beginning in the eleventh century, the salient feature of Iberian history was the Christian *Reconquista* (Reconquest) against the Muslims, who controlled most of the peninsula. By the mid-fifteenth century, the three kingdoms of Aragon, Castile, and Portugal dominated the peninsula. Portugal was the first national state to emerge in Europe. There the House of Avis centralized royal administration by suppressing revolts of nobles and executing many of their leaders. Partly as a result of this centralization, Portugal was the first European nation to use its resources to expand overseas (discussed later in this chapter).

The marriage of Ferdinand, King of Aragon (reigned 1479–1516), to Isabella, Queen of Castile (reigned 1474–1504), in 1469 united their two realms into the Kingdom of Spain. Ferdinand and Isabella moved against the nobles, who objected to any increase in the crown's power and opposed the introduction of Roman law, which the royal couple supported. They forged alliances with the towns, ostensibly to combat bandits but actually to counter the power of feudal levies. The Cortes, the representative assembly dominated by the nobility, steadily lost power.

The desire to consolidate their strength led the Spanish rulers to establish the Inquisition, a tribunal for the detection and punishment of heresy. It operated as an agency of the state, free from papal or church control. Ferdinand, who was not religious, did not hesitate to use it as well as an instrument to enforce civil despotism; in particular, to suppress rebellious churchmen and nobles. Most of the inquisition's fury, however, was aimed at achieving religious uniformity. Its officials energetically and carefully examined the religious purity of all, searching for blasphemers and heretics. The officials conducted trials and passed sentence, often gathering information and confessions through torture. The state then executed those found guilty. When Ferdinand and Isabella conquered Granada (1492), the last Muslim outpost on the peninsula, they ordered all unconverted Muslims and Jews to leave the country with only what they could carry. The confiscated property of the religious exiles, coupled with the profits from discoveries overseas, greatly enriched the crown.

The Background of the Protestant Reformation

The Reformation, the religious upheaval that splintered the Roman Catholic church, took place during the sixteenth and seventeenth centuries, at the same time that centralized monarchy was on the rise in western Europe. Earlier, in 1054, Christianity had split into two main branches, the Eastern or Orthodox church, which prevailed in the Byzantine Empire, and the Western or Roman Catholic church, which was dominant in central and western Europe. In the High Middle Ages, the popes had succeeded in centralizing the administration of the church under their control, permitting them to impose religious uniformity and to exercise a potent influence on European political life. The Catholic church reached the height of its power under Pope Innocent III (reigned 1198–1216). Laxity and worldliness characterized Innocent III's successors, weakening the papacy's moral authority and opening the way for increasing defiance and contempt. Papal power eroded at the same time that the prestige of the new national states was on the rise.

The turning point in papal history occurred when the strong and consolidated monarchy of France challenged the secular pretensions of the papacy. The result was the humiliation of the pope, Boniface VIII (reigned 1294–1303), in 1303 and the removal of the papacy to Avignon, in southern France, two years later. From 1305 to 1378 the popes resided at Avignon, where, to all appearances, they became tools of French interests and, consequently, objects of suspicion and hostility to France's enemies. The long period of papal exile at Avignon, known as the Babylonian Captivity, was a minor scandal compared to what followed during the next half century.

Pope Gregory XI (reigned 1370–1378) ended the Babylonian Captivity when he moved back to Rome, where he died in 1378. The cardinals met and, amid scenes of mob violence, first elected an Italian pope, Urban VI (reigned 1378–1389), who publicly scolded them for their worldliness and attempted to reduce their revenues. Most of the cardinals thereupon withdrew from Rome, declared Urban's election invalid because it had been held under threat of violence, chose a Frenchman as Pope Clement VII (reigned 1378–1394), and settled with him at Avignon. To the bewilderment of conscientious Christians, there were now two popes, one at Rome and the other at Avignon, each with competing systems of church administrations, courts, and taxation. Corruption and financial abuses worsened as each pope, seeking to oust the other, became more involved than ever in politics. At the urging of bishops and powerful laymen, a church council was summoned with the object of ending the schism.

The second church council, held at Constance (1414–1417), reunited the Catholic church. The delegates deposed the rival popes and elected a new pope, Martin V (reigned 1417–1431). Radical elements wanted to go further and strip away papal powers and have councils govern the church, but the efforts of these conciliarists were thwarted by papal intransigence and by their own inability to agree. In the meantime Martin and his successors tried to win over the temporal rulers in western and central Europe who had initially supported the conciliarists. The popes achieved their objective, but only after permitting the monarchs to assume more control over the church in their respective countries. Before the end of the fifteenth century, the papacy had once again asserted its dominance over the church, although it was unable to recapture the spiritual and moral leadership it had formerly enjoyed. The price for the papacy's triumph was high. Preoccupied for many years in combating the conciliarist movement and practicing power politics, the popes showed little interest in undertaking the reforms that sincere Christians were demanding.

A number of abuses had arisen in the church in the fourteenth and fifteenth centuries. Simony, the sale of church offices, was one such problem. Some 2,000 church offices were for sale, and the resulting revenues formed a significant part of papal income. A case in point was the Archbishop of Mainz, who paid the astronomical sum of 30,000 ducats for his office—equivalent to fifteen years' salary for a mid-level functionary in the papal bureaucracy. Another serious problem was pluralism, where one individual held several church offices at the same time. Priests and bishops often hired stand-ins to fulfill their duties. In Germany in 1500, more than 90 percent of the parishes were served by part-time priests. The practice of nepotism, giving lucrative church offices to relatives of the higher clergy, was widespread. Churchmen, from the highest rank to the lowest, were frequently affected by the secular spirit of the Renaissance and showed more interest in worldly pleasures and pursuits than in attending to their spiritual responsibilities. Popes led a life of luxury rivaling that of the secular rulers of their time. The church's ever-growing fiscal demands, together with the immorality and secular interests of the clergy, aggravated the resentment and sense of alienation felt by many Christians.

When church leaders did not initiate reform, some priests and laity on the local level tried to make changes, while in other areas, secular princes led popular reform movements. Appealing to scriptural precedents, the life of Jesus, and the activities of the early church described in the Book of Acts, most reformers demanded back-to-basics change. Such was the general situation on All Saints' Eve, 1517, when Martin Luther made his famous demand for reform of church practices and doctrines.

Martin Luther Breaks with the Church

Martin Luther was born in 1483 at Eisleben in Saxony (central Germany), the second son of a moderately prosperous miner. To please his father he went to the University of Erfurt in 1505 to study law. That same year, according to his account, he was caught in a fearsome thunderstorm and thrown to the ground by a flash of lightning. Following his miraculous survival, which affected him emotionally, he entered an Augustinian monastery at Erfurt, where he was ordained a priest in 1507. He returned to the university and became a doctor of theology. From 1511 until his death thirty-five years later, he served as professor of theology at the newly founded University of Wittenberg.

Luther before the Diet of Worms, 1521. Luther was resolute in his defense, partly because of the support he received from Germans of all classes. His journey to Worms was made triumphant by the acclamation of cheering crowds who lined the road.

Luther's growing reputation as a biblical scholar masked his torment about gaining God's grace and his own salvation. Beyond scrupulous monastic observance, he had been diligent in confessing his sins, praying, and fasting. Yet performing good works, as commanded by the church, did not give him the comfort and spiritual peace he was seeking. Through the study of the Bible he found the answer to his dilemma in one of St. Paul's letters to the Romans, especially in the phrase "the just shall live by faith." It dawned on him that people could be saved only by repenting their sins and throwing themselves on God's mercy and accepting His grace. Salvation was a gift from God as a reward for faith in His mercy and could not be earned by doing good works. This doctrine struck at the heart of orthodox Catholic belief, which held that only through the sacraments of the church could sinners be redeemed and made worthy of salvation. Luther was at first unaware of the conflict. He thought he was simply giving more emphasis to the Bible in Christian education. Only after he was drawn into the indulgence controversy did he realize the revolutionary implications of his religious views.

According to Catholic teaching, an indulgence was supposed to remit punishment in purgatory for sins for which insufficient penance had been done while on earth. It was granted on condition that the sinner was repentant and was willing to perform some pious deed such as going on a crusade or a pilgrimage. By the sixteenth century, however, the practice had become perverted. Church agents made extravagant claims, implying that indulgences secured total remission of sins, on earth and in purgatory, without bothering to mention the acts of contrition and confession demanded of every sinner as

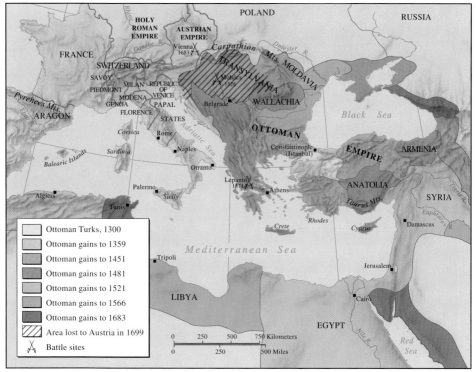

Ottoman Expansion
The Ottoman's expanded rapidly throughout the fifteenth and sixteenth centuries, conquering vast territories around the Black Sea, in the Balkans, and in the Arab provinces along the eastern Mediterranean and North Africa.

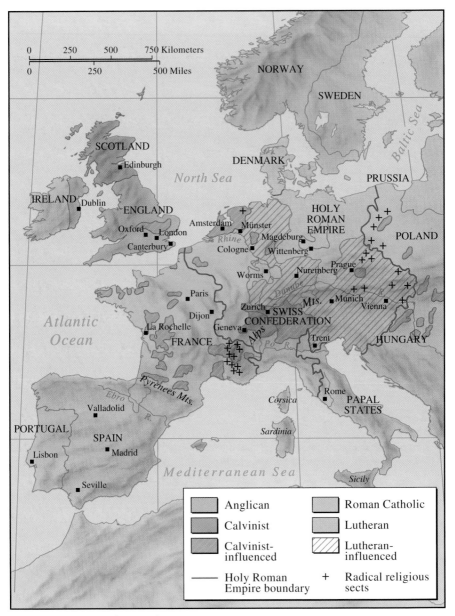

Catholics and Protestants in Europe by 1560

Reformation religious upheavals affected most of Europe, with Protestant faiths predominant in the north. Protestantism also made substantial headway in France, the Habsburg dominions, southern Germany, and Poland, but these areas eventually reverted to Roman Catholicism.

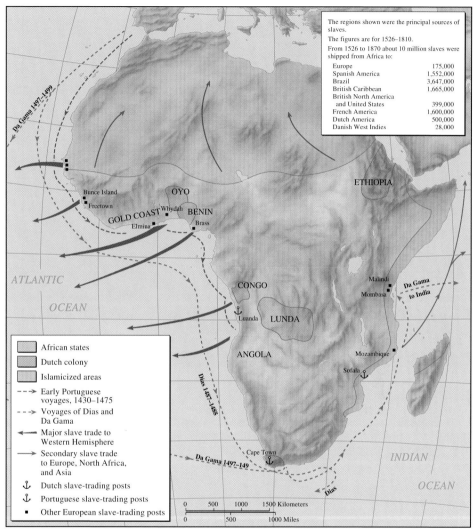

The regions shown were the principal sources of slaves.

The figures are for 1526–1810.

From 1526 to 1870 about 10 million slaves were shipped from Africa to:

Europe	175,000
Spanish America	1,552,000
Brazil	3,647,000
British Caribbean	1,665,000
British North America and United States	399,000
French America	1,600,000
Dutch America	500,000
Danish West Indies	28,000

Da Gama 1497–1499

ETHIOPIA

Bunce Island
Freetown
GOLD COAST Whydah BENIN
Elmina Brass
OYO

ATLANTIC

OCEAN

CONGO

Luanda LUNDA

ANGOLA

Malindi
Mombasa
Da Gama to India

Mozambique
Sofala

African states

Dutch colony

Islamicized areas

- - - ► Early Portuguese voyages, 1430–1475
- - - ► Voyages of Dias and Da Gama
◄━━ Major slave trade to Western Hemisphere
───► Secondary slave trade to Europe, North Africa, and Asia
⚓ Dutch slave-trading posts
⚓ Portuguese slave-trading posts
■ Other European slave-trading posts

Dias 1497–1488

Cape Town

Da Gama 1497–149

Dias

INDIAN

OCEAN

| 0 | 500 | 1000 | 1500 Kilometers |
| 0 | 500 | 1000 Miles |

Africa, 1500–c. 1750, and the Slave Trade

By the sixteenth century, Islam had spread throughout much of North and East Africa, while many independent kingdoms and city-states continued to prosper. Along the African coasts, European explorers also founded small trading posts, where the slave trade flourished as growing numbers of Africans were transported as slave labor for plantations in the Western Hemisphere.

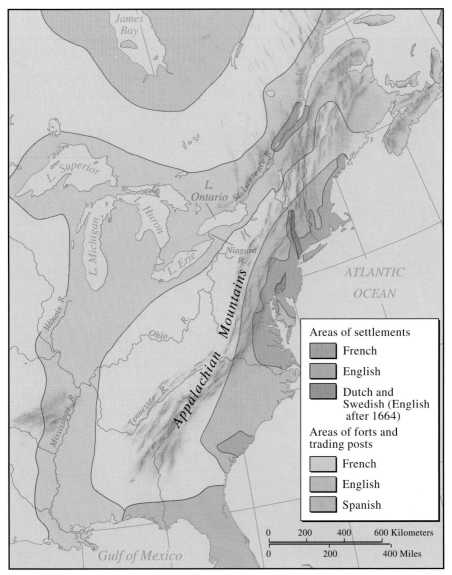

European Holdings in North America, c. 1685
After nearly a century of activity in North America, the French and the English had secured very disparate colonial holdings. The French presence centered on fur and deerskin trading posts radiating from a small settlement in Quebec. The English controlled an area smaller in extent, but greater in population, dominated by family farms.

a prerequisite for forgiveness. An indulgence, so it was advertised, guaranteed swift entry in heaven for the purchaser himself or for a loved one in purgatory. As one hawker put it: "As soon as the coin in the coffer rings, the soul from purgatory springs." Many flocked to buy indulgences; the huge sums collected went either into the pockets of leading political and church officials or to Rome to pay for such papal projects as Saint Peter's basilica.

Luther was outraged to see poor people being deprived of their hard-earned money under false pretenses. He objected to the sale of indulgences on the grounds that the pope had no control over purgatory and, most important of all, that it did not mandate repentance as a condition for forgiveness of sins. On October 31, 1517, Luther posted a list of ninety-five theses (statements of error) on the church door at Wittenberg. His purpose in doing so was to challenge the defenders of indulgences to a debate. Luther had expected reaction to be confined to the university community, but to his surprise printed copies of his theses circulated throughout Germany, arousing widespread public interest. To the consternation of church authorities, the sale of indulgences fell off sharply.

As Luther was forced by critics to define his theological position, it became increasingly apparent that his beliefs were sharply at odds with those of the Catholic church. In 1520 Pope Leo X (reigned 1513–1521) condemned Luther's teachings and ordered him to recant within two months or face excommunication. Luther responded by publicly burning the document. The pope then formally excommunicated Luther and called upon the Holy Roman Emperor, Charles V, to punish him as a heretic. But Luther had become a national figure, and the German princes did not feel he could be condemned without a hearing.

In the spring of 1521 Luther, under the protection of an imperial safe conduct, appeared before Charles V at a diet (meeting) at Worms. There he refused to recant unless it could be proved that his writings were contrary to Scripture. Branded an outlaw with a price on his head, he traveled home with the assistance of agents of Frederick, elector of Saxony, under whose protection he would remain for the rest of his life. In 1522 Luther returned to Wittenberg where he gathered his supporters and established the first Protestant church.

The rapid spread of Lutheranism was in marked contrast to other reform movements, which had failed to divide the church. Luther was a brilliant theologian and possessed nearly every quality essential to a revolutionary leader. He also enjoyed advantages that had been denied to his predecessors. First, his revolt against Rome occurred when the church was in a state of decline and was being strongly criticized from within. The abuses resulting from the Great Schism and a series of worldly Renaissance popes had lowered public support for the church. Meanwhile, the writings of Erasmus and other humanists generated a critical spirit that challenged many accepted beliefs. Erasmus's scholarly edition of the New Testament (1516) and the publication of the writings of the church fathers, including all of Jerome's letters, in the vernacular, coupled with other humanist texts, revealed that some church doctrines had shaky foundations. Second, the invention of the printing press allowed for the mass production of books, including the Bible, at relatively low cost. Published materials thereafter became available to larger numbers of people, permitting the rapid spread of new ideas. Third, an unusual political situation existed in Germany. Charles V, the Holy Roman Emperor, was committed to maintaining an alliance with the papacy and also wanted to extend his authority over Germany. About half of the 300-odd German rulers supported Lutheranism as a way to resist Charles V. Some among them may have been moved as much by material considerations as by religious concerns. By adopting Lutheranism, the princes could confiscate the rich and extensive Catholic holdings in their domains. Finally, the rising capitalistic classes, finding Catholicism incompatible with the practices of trade and banking, were willing to push for a system that suited them better.

Many of Luther's early followers broke away from his guidance. The largest group to do so was the Anabaptists, a radical religious sect whose social ideas included a refusal to bear arms and the abolition of private property. Luther disavowed them because, apart from sharp religious differences, his views on the social order were extremely conservative. The humanists, who had scorned and ridiculed church practices, hailed Luther for his efforts to restore the purity of Christianity. But the humanists, placing unity ahead of doctrine, wanted to reform the church from within, not start a new religion. When Luther refused to patch up his differences with Rome, most of them, including Erasmus, decided to remain within the Catholic fold. In 1524–1525 the Peasants' Revolt had far more serious consequences. Thousands of downtrodden peasants in southwest Germany, seeking relief from economic and manorial burdens, revolted against their landlords. At first, Luther had shown considerable sympathy for the commoners' cause but, when they resorted to violence, endangering the fabric of society and the structure of the state, he called for their suppression. The princes did so with unspeakable cruelty, causing Lutheranism to lose much of its appeal among the poor of southern Germany.

Luther saw himself not as a social and economic reformer but as a restorer of true doctrine and practices of the early Christian church. In final form, Luther's religion differed from the Catholic church in a number of important ways. Luther believed that salvation came through faith in God rather than through good works, sacraments, and rituals. The true church, he contended, consisted of all believers and not just an organization of ecclesiastics; thus he eliminated the hierarchy of pope, cardinals, and bishops and reduced the importance of the clergy. For Luther, ultimate authority rested with the Scriptures, not with church traditions and papal pronouncements. Of the seven Catholic sacraments, he retained only baptism and communion, the two found in the Bible. He abolished monasteries and the celibacy of the clergy. Luther himself married a former nun, by whom he had six children. He replaced the Latin liturgy with a German service that included Bible reading and the singing of hymns. So that the Bible would be available in German, Luther translated both the New and Old Testaments. Finally, unlike Catholicism, Luther gave the state supreme authority over his church except in matters of doctrine.

The spectacular progress of Lutheranism troubled Charles V, who sought to find an accommodation that would prevent Germany from being divided by religion. His political skirmishing with the Lutheran princes only intensified matters, however, and led to open war in 1546, the same year that Luther died. Although Charles was determined to crush the Lutheran states, he was unable to intervene forcefully because of his preoccupation with wars against the French and the Turks. With neither side able to gain a clear advantage, the Peace of Augsburg in 1555 ended the nine-year conflict. By this compromise sovereign princes and cities were given the right to decide between Catholicism and Lutheranism; subjects who objected to their ruler's choice would be permitted to emigrate. The peace of Augsburg left Lutheranism firmly entrenched in the northern half of Germany. From there it spread to Scandinavia and to the Baltic lands under the control of Sweden. Lutheranism would also have a great influence on all subsequent Protestant movements.

Protestant Reformers after Luther

Luther may have been the first to revolt against the established church, but others soon followed. Ulrich Zwingli (1484–1531) led a reform movement in Zurich, Switzerland, that incorporated many of Luther's teachings. Zwingli believed in the supreme authority of Scripture and simplified church services, taught justification by faith instead of good works, and opposed clerical celibacy. But he went beyond Luther in considering baptism and communion to be merely symbolic ceremonies. These doctrinal differences proved irreconcilable and marked the first in a long series of Protestant schisms. Zwingli also maintained that the church needed to take the lead in imposing Christian discipline on civil life. The Swiss confederation of cantons could not agree on which church to follow, so it allowed each canton to make its own decision.

The reform tradition that Zwingli started in Zurich was carried on by John Calvin (1509–1564) in Geneva a generation later. Calvin, who next to Martin Luther was the most celebrated Protestant leader of the sixteenth century, was born in the French town of Noyon, the son of a prosperous lawyer. His heart was set on becoming a priest, but at his father's insistence, he abandoned theology for law. Early in life he associated with followers of Luther and about 1534 converted to Protestantism. Forced into hiding to avoid persecution, Calvin fled to Switzerland and settled in Geneva where, as a dynamic agent of change, he rose to become virtual dictator of the city.

Calvin outlined his religious views in *The Institutes of the Christian Religion,* published in 1536 when he was only twenty-six. The book was a clear, logical, and superb synthesis of Protestant theology. On the surface Calvin's beliefs resembled those of Luther. He accepted the sinfulness of humans and their impotence to save themselves, denied the value of good works as a means of salvation, regarded the Bible as the sole authority in matters of faith, and rejected all the Catholic sacraments except baptism and communion. But Calvin's differences with Luther were significant enough to rule out collaboration between the two. Calvin favored suppressing anything that was not clearly sanctioned in the Bible, which he regarded as the supreme authority in every aspect of life. Luther, regarding the Bible as a vehicle for Christ's teachings, permitted anything that it did not specifically forbid. Far more than Luther, Calvin stressed the omnipotence of God. Calvin accepted Luther's concept of salvation through God's grace, but believed more strongly than the latter that this priceless gift was granted only to some men. According to Calvin, people were condemned to live in perpetual sin as punishment for

Adam and Eve's fall from grace. But God through his infinite mercy had chosen some human beings to be saved and had damned all the rest to suffer in hell. Men and women could do nothing to change their fate, which was predestined before they were born. The doctrine of predestination was at the core of Calvin's theology. The doctrine itself was not new, but Calvin's emphasis on it was. Luther's belief in justification by faith implied divine predetermination, but he was too consumed with other matters to follow through. Calvin, with his rigorous logic, was driven to carry the doctrine to its ultimate conclusion.

Logically, one might think that if individuals could have no effect on their destiny, they would be indifferent about their personal conduct. Calvin took another position on that point, however: although people had no sure way of knowing who would be saved and who would be damned, those living in accordance with God's will could take it as a hopeful sign. Even if a pious life did not ensure salvation, an immoral life proved that one was not among the chosen. Calvin's doctrine had an enormous appeal. It gave believers a powerful motive to do God's work in order to convince themselves that they would be saved.

Calvinism was not confined to Switzerland. Geneva became a training center for Calvinist preachers who came from many parts of Europe. Impelled by a sense of militancy and dedication, they returned to promote Calvin's teachings in their homeland. Calvinism triumphed in Scotland under the leadership of John Knox (c. 1510–1572), in the German Palatinate, and in the Dutch Netherlands, where it played a major role in overthrowing Spanish tyranny. It gained many converts in England (Puritans) and a vigorous following in France (Huguenots), Bohemia, and Hungary. From Europe Calvinism made its way to America, where it contributed significantly to the growth of constitutional government.

The act that sparked the English Reformation had little to do with Calvinism or church doctrine, however. The king, Henry VIII, wanted to annul his marriage to his wife, Catherine of Aragon, by whom he had only a daughter, Mary. Although England had no law that barred a woman from the throne, Henry and his advisors felt that the country should be ruled by a male. While divorce was contrary to church law, ecclesiastical authorities sometimes allowed marriages to be annulled, especially when monarchs were involved. The problem in this case was that Catherine was the aunt of the powerful Holy Roman Emperor, Charles V, whose troops not only controlled Rome but held the pope captive. Henry was not a patient man; when the pope delayed acting on his request he turned to the compliant Archbishop of Canterbury, Thomas Cramner, who granted the annulment in 1533. The following year Parliament passed the Act of Supremacy, which repudiated papal primacy and declared the king head of an independent Anglican church. In this capacity, Henry subsequently dissolved the monasteries and enriched his treasury with their great wealth.

Despite his break with Rome, Henry continued to think of himself as a devout Catholic. The official theology of the Church of England made few departures from Catholicism. When Henry died in 1547, his nine-year-old son, Edward VI, ascended the throne. During the regency government of the youth, Protestants gradually moved Anglican doctrine closer to mainstream Protestant tenets through the Book of Common

LIVES AND TIMES ACROSS CULTURES

Life in Geneva and Venice in the Sixteenth Century

Under a constitution Calvin helped write, Geneva became a theocratic republic in which the administration of church and state were closely interwoven. Calvin's objective was to transform the city into his version of the ideal Christian community. Ruling with the assistance of a council known as the Consistory, he considered it his duty to supervise every aspect of the city's life and to enforce God's will. Guided by the Bible, laws were passed forbidding such things as idleness, dancing, frivolous pastimes, card playing, profanity, adultery, and marriage to Catholics. There were instructions for the way people dressed, on how women were to arrange their hair, even for the selection of names for infants. Calvin demanded sobriety, regular church attendance, hard work, frugality, and pursuit of a trade. Secret agents were on the lookout for wrongdoing.

Calvin had no tolerance for human weaknesses, and even common sins were punished with unprecedented rigor. The most notorious example of Calvin's harshness was the execution of Michael Servetus, a Spanish refugee, for publicly denying the doctrine of the Trinity. Gradually, as the more liberal-minded people left the city and were replaced by zealots from all over Europe, the character of the city changed. In 1546 John Knox reported that Geneva was the most perfect community of Christ seen anywhere on earth since the days of the apostles.

In many ways unique among Italian cities, Venice stood in sharp contrast to Geneva. Built almost exclusively on trade and shipping, Venice was a rich, highly cultural and cosmopolitan city. It was governed by a hereditary oligarchy of wealthy merchants comprising only about 2 percent of the population. Although members of this aristocracy, as they styled themselves, tolerated no opposition, they ruled wisely and did much to improve the economic welfare of the disenfranchised masses.

Venice was untroubled by internal disorder, social tensions, or party factionalism. Travelers were struck by the paradoxical nature of the city. On the one hand, they saw a city that projected a sober image of republican restraint and judicious modesty, founded on the principles of equality, magnanimity, domestic harmony, and justice for all of its citizens. On the other hand, they reported that Venice was a pleasure-seeking community—full of festive people, indulgent of gambling, of roisterous parties, of the theatre, and of lax sexual mores. As early as the fourteenth century Petrarch noted with disapproval his impression of the city: "Much freedom reigns there in every respect, and what I should call the only evil prevailing—but also the worst—far too much freedom." Freedom was possible because there was no opposition to the government; and there were few grounds for criticism because the government had adopted progressive social policies and secured boundless wealth.

Laws in Venice were enacted without reference to God's will. In fact the government was anticlerical and as a rule ignored interdicts issued by the papacy. During the Counter-Reformation the papacy rejuvenated the Inquisition as a means to maintain orthodoxy and effectively extend the church's power in the Catholic world. Most Catholic countries rallied behind this institution without reservation. However, Venice, long impervious to papal influence, adopted a middle position, designed to contain heresy without compromising the authority of its secular government or severely restricting rights traditionally enjoyed by its citizens.

Prayer. When Edward died without an heir in 1553, the crown passed to Mary, a devout Catholic, who dedicated herself to restoring the Roman Catholic church in England. Persecution of Protestants during Mary's rule earned her the nickname "Bloody Mary." In 1558 the childless Mary died unexpectedly, and the crown went to her Protestant half-sister,

Elizabeth, who quickly restored the Anglican church and declared herself its governor. During her long reign (1558–1603), Elizabeth successfully steered a middle course between Roman Catholicism and Calvinism. The Anglican church's beliefs were spelled out in a modified Book of Common Prayer and in the Thirty-nine Articles, published in 1563.

A great upheaval, such as the Protestant revolt, was bound to produce extremist groups. The most radical among the reformers were the Anabaptists, the ancestors of the modern Mennonites and Amish. They generally came from the lower classes and stressed a literal interpretation of the Scripture, seeking a return to the simplicity of primitive Christianity. The name *Anabaptist* meant "baptize again," and came from their rejection of infant baptism and their belief that only adults capable of free choice should be baptized. Adults who had been baptized as children had to be rebaptized. Generally the Anabaptists rejected any association between church and state, refused to recognize civil authority when it conflicted with their religious ideals, and favored the creation of egalitarian communities like those of the early Christians. Because they posed a religious and political threat to established society, they were intensively and cruelly persecuted by both Catholics and Protestants.

The aim of early Protestant movements was to modify rather than reject the medieval church. All, to varying degrees, retained features of the old Roman church, but their sharp differences could not be harmonized. By the middle of the sixteenth century, Protestantism had triumphed in nearly half of Europe and the existence of the Catholic church itself seemed threatened.

Women and the Reformation

Women showed as much interest in the Reformation as did men. For most women, exposure to Protestant doctrines came through their husbands or fathers. Some, inspired by what they heard and anxious to promote their new faith, did so in ways open to them. Anabaptist women were allowed to preach and administer baptism, and, occasionally, zealous wives of evangelizers were active alongside their husbands from the pulpits. However, larger Protestant groups, as with Catholics, closed the ministry to women. As John Calvin put it: "The custom of the church . . . may be elicited first of all from Tertullian [church father, c. 160–230], who held that no woman in church is allowed to speak, teach, baptize or make offerings; this in order that she may not usurp the functions of men." Apart from the lack of theological training, women serving conspicuously in nontraditional roles would have been objectionable to most men.

The most common venue in which women conveyed their views and feelings was the home. Here they discussed doctrinal matters and instructed occasional visitors and friends on the virtues of their new faith. Some educated women composed hymns or wrote devotional works. Married women taught their children the catechism, pronounced prayers, and sang hymns. There were even instances of noblewomen pressuring their husbands into converting to their faith.

The Reformation affected women not only through new religious ideas but also through institutional and political changes. Protestant reformers stressed the value and sanctity of marriage, challenging the medieval tendency to denigrate women and encourage celibacy. Luther considered marriage a divinely ordained union and a natural vocation for women. Although he and other Protestant reformers exalted the state of marriage and urged that husbands treat their wives in a kindly manner and share authority with them within the household, they nevertheless insisted that women remain subject to men in that union. Convinced that women's primary duty was to obey their husbands and bear children, the reformers did not want them to serve as ministers or hold too many public responsibilities. A strong patriarchal family seemed indispensable to the social stability of the state.

Laws regulating marriage were quite equitable: if a marriage failed, women had the same right as men to divorce and remarry. Unlike Catholics, who permitted only separation from bed and board, Protestant reformers allowed divorce under circumstances such as abuse, abandonment, or adultery. Still, the various Protestant denominations discouraged the breakup of families, permitting divorce only after all efforts to reconcile had failed. Even "liberated" women rarely sought divorce, which was apt to leave them without financial support.

The closing of convents in Protestant territories imposed a cruel hardship on many nuns. Some married or returned to their paternal homes, but most were left alone to face the hazards of life. They took whatever employment was available; some found no work, while others, in desperation, even turned to prostitution.

Protestant leaders, eager to increase biblical literacy and make individuals better Christians, encouraged education for women and men alike. They established schools for both sexes at the primary and secondary levels, as well as academies and colleges to train pastors and male lay church workers. Education gave women an opportunity to find employment as teachers or become authors. Although illiteracy remained pervasive in Europe, a base for expanding educational opportunity had been laid: it proved to be one of the most enduring legacies of the Reformation.

The Roman Catholic or Counter-Reformation

Rome responded hesitantly and slowly to the Protestant challenge and to calls for changes from within. But as hopes for reconciliation dimmed and Protestantism continued to make gains, the Catholic church launched a vigorous counterattack on a number of fronts, a response termed variously the Catholic Reformation or Counter-Reformation. First and foremost, success in halting the spread of Protestantism and reclaiming lost lands depended heavily on reform within the Roman Catholic church. Long before Luther acted at Wittenberg, many sincere and devout Catholics, disturbed at the deterioration of the church, had urged that a general council be held to carry through needed reforms. The popes had resisted summoning a church council, in part because they were mindful of the efforts of the conciliar movement in the fifteenth century to strip them of their authority. Ultimately, however, the pressure for reform became too great, and Pope Paul III (reigned 1534–1549) called for a church council.

The most important work of the council, which met at Trent, in northern Italy, between 1545 and 1563, dealt with doctrinal matters. All doctrines, especially those under Protestant attack, were reaffirmed. They were set out in clear and precise terms and their differences with Protestantism were specified. The council also outlined a comprehensive

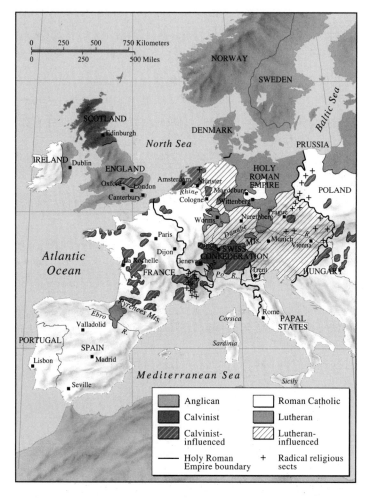

Map 9.4 Catholics and Protestants in Europe by 1560. Reformation religious upheavals affected most of Europe, with Protestant faiths predominant in the north. Protestantism also made substantial headway in France, the Habsburg dominions, southern Germany, and Poland, but these areas eventually reverted to Roman Catholicism.

program of reform. It condemned such corrupt practices as simony, pluralism, and nepotism and made provisions for better discipline and higher educational standards among the clergy.

Besides reforming itself, the Catholic church took measures to halt the spread of Protestant beliefs. The council instituted the Index of Forbidden Books—a list of books, periodically revised, that Catholics were forbidden to read. The council also revived and extended the Inquisition to combat heresy and the practice of witchcraft. The work of the Council of Trent created a foundation on which a new, more vibrant Catholic church could be built.

The most effective single weapon of the Catholic church in battling the Protestants was the Society of Jesus, popularly called the Jesuit order. Founded by Ignatius Loyola (1491–1556), a Basque noble and former soldier, the order was modeled on military lines, highly disciplined, and devoted to actively promoting and defending the teachings of the church. Applicants for membership were carefully screened, and those selected had to pass rigorous training and a long apprenticeship. When found ready, they were sent to whatever field seemed most in need of their services.

The Jesuits were effective missionaries, carrying the gospel to nations as far away as China, Japan, and South America. Some became priests and from the pulpits preached simple sermons that stressed morality. As confessors and advisers to kings and princes, they were able to influence state policy to the benefit of Catholicism. They won their greatest fame, however, in the field of education. In Europe the Jesuits built schools or took over existing ones and in many areas were the dominant force in education. Their results were impressive. Through their dedication and zeal, they played a key role in holding southern Germany and France and in bringing Poland and much of Hungary back to Catholicism.

The zealous efforts of the Catholic church to stamp out Protestantism led to bitter religious wars in the late sixteenth century and first half of the seventeenth. England experienced an attempted invasion by Catholic Spain in 1588, and heavy sectarian fighting occurred in the Netherlands, France, and elsewhere in Europe (see Chapter 11). In Germany the Peace of Augsburg proved to be only an uneasy truce. The growing tensions finally erupted into a destructive conflict, known as the Thirty Years' War, which began in 1618 and continued until 1648. Over time, every major power became involved in the struggle, and the character of the war changed from religious to political. Protestant and Catholic armies, mostly composed of mercenaries, crisscrossed the German landscape, wreaking havoc.

The stalemated Thirty Years' War ended in 1648 with the Treaty of Westphalia. Most of the contending major powers demanded and received grants of territory as compensation for their efforts. Politically the settlement practically dissolved the Holy Roman Empire, though it continued to exist as a formal entity. Each German prince was recognized as a sovereign ruler, free to govern his state without interference by the emperor. The key religious clause accorded Calvinist rulers the same right to determine the religion practiced in their territories that Catholic and Lutheran princes had enjoyed since 1555. All in all, Germany was the big loser. Perhaps 300,000 soldiers and civilians were killed during campaigns, and several times that number died from malnutrition and disease. The damage wrecked the economy of the German states and caused many Germans to migrate to North America.

The Treaty of Westphalia, like the Peace of Augsburg, did not quell religious enmities. Religious strife continued to plague Europe, but on a far smaller scale than in the previous century. By regenerating itself and taking the offensive, the Catholic church had staged a strong comeback, stemming the Protestant tide and even winning back some lands that seemed irretrievably lost. But it could not regain domination over all of Western Christendom. After 1648 the religious map of Europe would not change appreciably.

European Expansion

Beginning in the fifteenth century the new European monarchies, which, as discussed earlier in this chapter, had achieved a high degree of national unification, embarked on five centuries of expansion that brought European power to every continent on the globe. Most of the indigenous societies around the world felt the impact of this movement in one way or another. Some were relatively untouched; many were profoundly altered; a number were destroyed. In the process Western society would itself feel the impact of other cultures.

European overseas expansion occurred for numerous reasons. The new national states of western Europe were now sufficiently centralized to support and finance exploration and expansion. Technological advances in navigational systems and ship design enabled sailors to undertake longer voyages. Moreover, Europeans had visions of wealth; gold, pepper, ivory, and slaves from Africa were all valued commodities on world markets. European governments and merchants were also eager to find alternative ocean routes so they could avoid the high import taxes imposed by the Ottoman Empire on goods coming overland from Asia by caravans. For Spain and Portugal, religion also played a role. After the long struggle (*Reconquista*) that ended Muslim supremacy of the Iberian Peninsula, the devoutly Christian rulers of Spain and Portugal were eager to dominate the Islamic states in North Africa and to convert non-Christians. Some Europeans even dreamed of forging links with the legendary African kingdom of the Christian leader Prester John.

Portugal was the first to move. With a long maritime tradition and an advantageous geographic position on the Atlantic, Portugal was the first European nation to look for a seaborne route to tap the wealth of the Atlantic Islands, Africa, and (hopefully) Asia. Beginning in the 1430s, Prince Henry (later called the "Navigator" by the English), the brother of the king of Portugal, used the royal treasury to finance voyages of discovery down the African coast; by 1498 the Portuguese were in Asia. In 1492, with the voyage of Columbus, Spain moved westward to the Americas. A century later, England, France, and the Netherlands joined in. The text will take up European expansion in the context of the cultures of each geographic area the Europeans entered; this chapter will discuss Africa and the Western Hemisphere, and Chapter 10 will deal with Asia.

African Kingdoms, European Contacts, and the Slave Trade

Your people . . . seize many of our people, freed and exempt men; and very often it happens that they kidnap even noblemen and the sons of noblemen, and our relatives, and take them to be sold to the white men. . . .

And as soon as they are taken by the white men they are immediately ironed and branded with fire, and when they are carried to be embarked, if they are caught by our guards' men the whites allege that they have bought them but they cannot say from whom. . . .

And so to avoid such a great evil we passed a law so that any white man living in our Kingdoms and wanting to purchase goods in any way should first inform three of our noblemen and officials of our court . . . who should investigate if the mentioned goods are captives or free men. . . . But if the white men do not comply with it they will lose the aforementioned goods. *

*A letter by King Afonso of the Kongo to the King of Portugal, October 18, 1526, in *Horizon History of Africa* (New York: American Heritage, 1971), p. 334.

In this letter in 1526, King Afonso, a convert to Christianity, complains of the excesses of European slave traders in his Kongo Kingdom. The slave trade became an important aspect of a dynamic and complex situation in Africa during the period from the fifteenth to the seventeenth century. The Portuguese moved down the West African coast and eventually to southern and eastern Africa, beginning the trade for the riches of those regions. In the fourteenth century, when Europeans first began to make extensive contact, many societies in West Africa had been, in economic terms, nearly as prosperous as those in most of Europe. The slave trade substantially altered that balance. As it turned out, the greatest wealth for European traders was to be found in the labor of human beings. The slave trade devastated many regions of Africa; it also profoundly changed the Western Hemisphere (see the following section). The ensuing discussion will focus on a number of African societies beginning about the fifteenth century, when European explorers and traders began to have extensive contact with local African rulers and peoples.

European Entry into Africa

In the early fifteenth century, the Portuguese began to move into Africa. Portugal's first target was Morocco, where it conquered small coastal areas. During the next half-century the Portuguese worked down the West African coast to Angola. The voyages of Bartholomeu Dias in 1487–1488 and Vasco da Gama in 1497–1499 opened up the Cape of Good Hope and East Africa to Portuguese traders and explorers; in 1498 da Gama arrived in India (see Chapter 10). At the East African city-state of Malindi, a king seated on a bronze chair and wearing an ornate robe trimmed in green satin greeted da Gama. The leaders of Malindi welcomed an alliance with the Portuguese as an aid in their commercial rivalry against traders in Mombasa.

Traders and adventurers, the Portuguese were not initially interested in founding colonies in Africa. However, they did establish fortified trading posts at strategic ports along the western and eastern coasts. Fort Sao Jorge was established at Elmina on the west coast in 1482. In 1576 it was followed by Luanda, which became a major center for the transport of slaves from Angola. Along the East African coast the Portuguese extracted tribute from the local rulers of Kilwa and later extended their domination over the older commercial city-states of Malindi and Mombasa.

African forces from the interior frequently attacked the Portuguese enclaves, limiting Portuguese domination to the coastal regions. Mombasa resisted for so many decades that the Portuguese nicknamed it the Island of War. In 1592 the Portuguese finally seized Mombasa and largely destroyed local opposition. Afterward they built a new outpost, called Fort Jesus, which still stands as evidence of Portuguese presence in Africa.

Although the Portuguese struggled to monopolize the African trade routes and the access they provided for the Asian trade, they were quickly challenged by the Spanish, Dutch, English, and other European powers. By 1630 English traders were operating along West Africa; the French and Dutch soon followed them. The Swedes and Danes also competed for territorial footholds in Ghana, or the Gold Coast. The Dutch proved a particularly formidable rival, and by 1610 they had effectively ended Portuguese dominance in the Indian Ocean. These rival European powers build many forts and military installations along the West African coast; these installations were intended primarily to defend the nation's trading interests against competing Europeans, not as protection against the African states.

As Portuguese naval power waned in the seventeenth century, first Mombasa and then other East African city-states revolted. Mombasa requested aid from fellow Muslims, most notably from the *imam* (leader) of Oman, on the Arabian coast. The Omanis, who had a long naval tradition, quickly responded and after several failures succeeded in ousting the Portuguese from Mombasa in 1698 and subsequently from neighboring East African city-states. The Omanis then established a Muslim empire in coastal East Africa that lasted into the nineteenth century.

Dutch Settlements in South Africa

In 1652, at Table Bay in South Africa, the Dutch founded Africa's first European settlement. Originally, the settlement was intended as a reprovisioning station for ships of the Dutch East India Company undertaking the long voyage between Europe and Asia; it was not meant to be an outpost for further Dutch settlement or colonial expansion. However, the persistent need for fresh food supplies led the Dutch East India Company to bring in colonists to establish farms in South Africa in 1657. Slaves were then brought in as forced laborers.

As the colony expanded, the Dutch attacked the indigenous Khoi, who were forcibly dispersed. The colonists recruited single Dutch women so that the predominantly male population of the colony could marry Europeans. French Huguenots who fled the persecution of Louis XIV reinforced the Dutch settlers. These frontier farmers, who called themselves both Boers (farmers) and Afrikaners, were strict Calvinists. Their descendants continued to dominate South Africa well into the twentieth century.

The Boers viewed black Africans as inferior human beings and used their strict Calvinist tenets to justify their attitude of racial superiority. They established a system of strict social and racial stratification in which the Dutch Boers were placed at the top, followed by later Asian immigrants and coloreds (people of mixed race), with blacks at the bottom. This racial hierarchy based on white European domination continued into the 1990s. Racism, the belief in the superiority and inferiority of differing peoples based on race, was not, however, confined to the Dutch in South Africa. It was common in European and American societies and was frequently used to justify the enslavement of African peoples.

The Slave Trade in Africa

The slave trade was a key factor of European expansion and had disastrous results for African peoples. As in many other societies and cultures, slavery had very deep roots in Africa and was known in antiquity. Africans had enslaved other Africans, and, although there were Qur'anic injunctions against such practices, Islamic societies in Africa had perpetuated the system. It persisted throughout Africa and especially in the Sudan in the ninth century, and it was practiced in other parts of the continent as well. African slaves could be found throughout the Islamic world, in India, and perhaps also in China prior to European expansion into these areas. Slavery in Africa and the Islamic world was not based on race or religion, however. Animists, Christians, and Muslims in Africa and elsewhere had historically enslaved members of their own and other religions. As in most civilizations up to this time, Africans acquired slaves from raids or victories in wars. In African and Islamic cultures, slaves were generally treated as part of the family and were integrated into the larger society. Most such slaves in the Islamic world served as domestic servants, concubines, or slave-soldiers.

The extensive trade in African slaves by the Western nations between the late fifteenth and the nineteenth centuries severely affected the social, cultural, economic, and even political life of the African societies. Although experts disagree on how adversely this

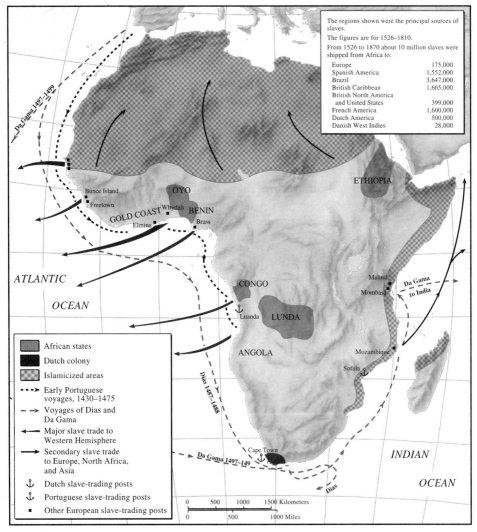

Map 9.5 Africa, 1500–c. 1750, and the Slave Trade. By the sixteenth century, Islam had spread throughout much of North and East Africa, while many independent kingdoms and city-states continued to prosper. Along the African coasts, European explorers also founded small trading posts, where the slave trade flourished as growing numbers of Africans were transported as slave labor for plantations in the Western Hemisphere.

Memoirs of a Slave

The first object which saluted my eyes when I arrived on the coast was the sea, and a slave ship which was then riding at anchor and waiting for its cargo. These filled me with astonishment, which was soon converted into terror when I was carried on board. I was immediately handled and tossed up to see if I were sound ... and I was now persuaded that I had gotten into a world of bad spirits and that they were going to kill me. Their complexions too differing so much from ours, their long hair and the language they spoke (which was very different from any I had ever heard) united to confirm me in this belief. ...

I now saw myself deprived of all chance of returning to my native country. ... I became so sick and low that I was not able to eat. ... In a little time after, amongst the poor chained men I found some of my own nation. ... I inquired of these what was to be done with us; they gave me to understand we were to be carried to these white people's country to work for them.*

The slave trade persisted for centuries. In the above excerpt, Olaudah Equiano, from present-day Nigeria, described his reactions to being captured and taken into slavery. Equiano was taken to the West Indies, Canada, England, and the United States; he was freed in 1766 and became a spokesperson for the antislavery movement (see Chapter 11). His memoirs offer a moving testimony to the human cost of slavery and its disruption of African society.*

*Olaudah Equiano, in Modern Asia and Africa, *ed. William H. McNeill and Mitsuko Iriye (New York: Oxford University Press, 1971), pp. 82–84.*

trade affected African development, none deny its social and economic consequences. Although Muslims and Europeans took some African slaves for sale in Europe, the Canary and Madeira Islands, Muslim North Africa, the Ottoman Empire, and Asia, the vast majority of those taken by the Europeans and their African allies were sent to the Western Hemisphere for sale.

In contrast to the work of slaves in other societies, the overwhelming majority of slaves in the Western Hemisphere were used as agricultural workers on vast cotton, tobacco, or sugar plantations or as laborers in copper and silver mines. As only able-bodied men and women were suitable for such hard labor, most slaves taken from Africa were young males from fifteen to thirty years of age. Although experts disagree on the exact numbers, it appears that between 10 and 15 million Africans were forcibly removed from their homelands to become slaves in the Americas; in addition, possibly several million more were killed or died during armed raids to secure the slaves, and the forced marches and brutal conditions to which the captives were subjected.

The first African slaves were shipped from Spain to Latin America in 1501. By 1518 Spanish slave traders had established direct trade routes between Africa and the Americas. Recognizing the enormous profits to be made in this human traffic, the Portuguese, English, French, and Dutch also engaged in the slave trade. For the most part, European slave traffickers did not capture the slaves, but paid professional African slave traders, or local political leaders, to secure slaves from the interior and to bring them to ports or marshaling yards on the coast. They were then herded into ships for the long voyage to the Western Hemisphere.

Although their African owners or rulers sold some slaves as punishment, most were captured through wars and raids. Slave hunting was a violent activity. Able-bodied men and women were torn from their villages, shackled in chains, and fastened together in long lines by strips of rawhide. These long human chains were then forcibly marched to either the East or West African coast, where European traders purchased them. Many slaves died of abuse or committed suicide before they ever reached the coasts. Others (at least 15 percent) died of inadequate food or diseases in the overcrowded, vermin-infested ships that transported the slaves to the Americas. Slave revolts were not uncommon, particularly among Muslim Africans, especially after they reached the Western Hemisphere.

African leaders who cooperated with European slave traders became rich from the slave trade. They coveted European armaments with which to extend their authority. The Songhai leaders in northwest Africa, for example, sold slaves for horses and guns. On Goree Island off the coast of present-day Senegal, one of the major trading depots for the traffic in human beings, West African women, who often engaged in commerce, controlled the sale of slaves brought from the interior regions. Likewise, some Muslim African traders became wealthy from the slave trade in East Africa and the Sudan. On the other hand, some African leaders sought to stop or to contain the trade. The obas in Benin banned the export of males from their territories until the end of the seventeenth century. King Afonso I in the Kongo also protested the trade and made numerous attempts to control and to curtail it.

In Angola, where the Portuguese were particularly active, Africans fiercely opposed the slave trade and foreign intervention. The Portuguese had made considerable inroads into Angola during the reign of weak monarchs, but in 1623–1624 Nzinga Mbandi ascended to the throne. As strong a ruler as Cleopatra of Egypt or Catherine the Great of Russia, Nzinga was an astute diplomat and politician. Forbidding her subjects to call her queen, Nzinga took the title king and promptly launched a lifelong struggle against the Portuguese. She joined forces with the Dutch against the Portuguese and lured Portuguese slave-soldiers to desert by promising them freedom and land. In spite of several uneasy treaties with the Portuguese, she continued fighting them until her death in

© Bethmann/Corbis

Slave Ship. This diagram shows how slaves were "packed" into ships for the long and often fatal journey to the Americas. Crowded on and below decks, slaves frequently died of asphyxiation, thirst, and disease during the long Atlantic crossing.

1663. No strong ruler followed Nzinga. As a result, the Portuguese were able to prevail, and slave raids increasingly decimated Angolan villages.

While coastal areas of Africa frequently prospered because of the slave trade, many villages, farms, and political institutions in the interior were weakened or destroyed. Damage to the cultural and economic life of African societies varied greatly from region to region. The forced removal of vital segments of their populations had lasting impact on some African societies. Many major states, however, particularly West African states like Benin, survived the attacks. Most African states remained independent of outside rule until the nineteenth century (see Chapter 13).

One of the most abusive and inhumane enterprises shared between Africa and the West, slavery spread throughout much of the Western Hemisphere in the following century. Slavery profoundly altered traditional social, economic, and political patterns in both Africa and the Western Hemisphere.

European Colonial Empires in the Western Hemisphere

Strange people have come to the shores of the great sea [the Caribbean]. . . . Their trappings and arms are all made of iron; they dress in iron and wear iron casques on their heads. Their swords are made of iron; their shields are iron; their spears are iron. Their deer carry them on their backs wherever they wish to go. Those deer, our lord, are as tall as the roof of a house. . . . The strangers' bodies are completely covered, so that only their faces can be seen. Their skin is white, as if it were made of lime. They have yellow hair, though some of them are black[-haired]. Their dogs are enormous, with flat ears and long dangling tongues. . . . Their eyes flash fire. [Referring to a gun:] a thing like a ball of stone comes out of its entrails; it comes out shooting sparks and raining fire. The smoke that comes out has a pestilent odor, like rotten mud. . . . If the cannon is aimed against a mountain, the mountain splits and cracks open.*

*Miguel Leon-Portilla, ed., The Broken Spears: The Aztec Account of the Conquest of Mexico, trans. A. M. Garibay and L. Kemp (Boston: Beacon Press, 1969), pp. 30–31.

This vivid description of the Spanish arrival in Mexico was in a report given to Moctezuma, the Aztec ruler, by his spies who observed the landing and advance of the Spaniards in 1519. The presence of the Spanish in the heartland of Mesoamerican civilization was but one aspect of a remarkable phenomenon, the expansion of European power around the globe during the sixteenth century. As has been seen in the previous section, Europeans were already constructing fortified trading posts along the African coast and building up the slave trade. Europeans were also appearing on the shores of Asia (see Chapter 10).

Early European Exploration of the Western Hemisphere

Spanish and Portuguese explorers and settlers were the first Europeans to make a lasting impact on the Western Hemisphere. Christopher Columbus, an Italian financed by Queen Isabella of Castile, led the way. By sailing west, Columbus hoped to find a shorter route to Asia than the one the Portuguese were pursuing around the African coast. He calculated Japan to be about 2,400 miles west of the Canary Islands (off the northwestern coast of Africa), putting Asia within range of the sailing ships of that day. On

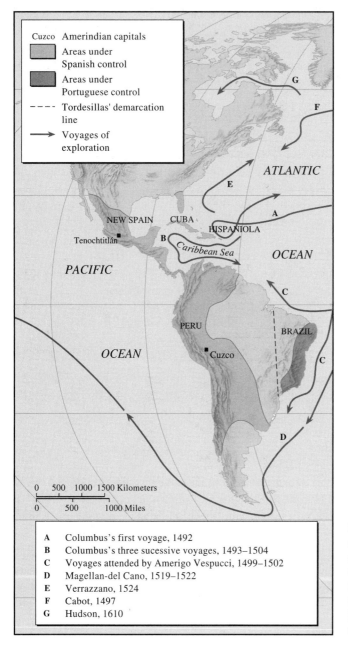

Map 9.6 The Western Hemisphere, c. 1600.

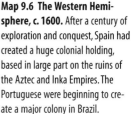

A	Columbus's first voyage, 1492
B	Columbus's three sucessive voyages, 1493–1504
C	Voyages attended by Amerigo Vespucci, 1499–1502
D	Magellan-del Cano, 1519–1522
E	Verrazzano, 1524
F	Cabot, 1497
G	Hudson, 1610

Map 9.6 The Western Hemisphere, c. 1600. After a century of exploration and conquest, Spain had created a huge colonial holding, based in large part on the ruins of the Aztec and Inka Empires. The Portuguese were beginning to create a major colony in Brazil.

October 12, 1492, Columbus made landfall in the Bahamas, approximately where he had calculated Asia to be. Assuming that he was off the coast of Asia, he called the islands the "Indies" and their inhabitants "Indians" (in this text, Amerindians). In 1493 Columbus triumphantly returned to Spain.

In January 1492, just a few months before Columbus's first voyage, the Spanish had conquered Granada, the last Muslim enclave on the Iberian Peninsula. The victory marked the completion of seven centuries of the *Reconquista* (Reconquest) of the Iberian Peninsula from the Muslims, a crusade that left a profound impact on Spanish institutions and practices. The struggle against the Muslims had forged a powerful partnership between church and state in Spanish society. The end of the *Reconquista* left a large number of men who were looking for new and profitable adventures and for new areas for Christianity to conquer.

During the quarter-century after Columbus's landing in the Bahamas, the Spanish occupied the major Caribbean islands. They found that European crops and domestic animals could thrive in the Western Hemisphere. Eventually it became clear that the islands could produce valuable crops of sugar and tobacco. These products, however, required constant attention and thus a large labor force.

To get this labor, the Spanish instituted the *encomienda* system, in which the Spanish king gave individuals control over Amerindian lands and villages. The *encomiendero* had the right to force the Amerindians under his control to work in his mines and fields. This brutal labor system and the ravages of new diseases from Europe, plus secondary factors, killed nearly all of the Amerindians in the Caribbean. Deprived of a native work force, the Spanish imported large numbers of black slaves from Africa.

To avoid confrontation, the Spanish and Portuguese negotiated a treaty to divide the Western Hemisphere between them. Under the Treaty of Tordesillas in 1494, the pope selected a line of longitude in which Spain received everything west of the line and Portugal everything east of it. The treaty technically gave Asia, the East Indies, and Brazil to Portugal, while everything else in the Western Hemisphere went to Spain. In 1500 Pedro Cabral landed in Brazil and formally claimed the area for Portugal. Brazil eventually became a major sugar-producing area.

Meanwhile, Europeans were readjusting their thinking about the nature of the lands that Columbus had found. After two voyages to the Western Hemisphere in which he visited much of the eastern coast of South America, Amerigo Vespucci claimed in 1501 that he had seen a "new land . . . a continent." In 1507 cartographers putting out a new map labeled the area representing present-day Brazil "America" in his honor.

By the early sixteenth century it was becoming clear that Asia was far away from Europe, with the new "America" in between. In 1513 Vasco Núñez de Balboa crossed the Panamanian isthmus and saw what he called the South Sea (the present-day Pacific Ocean), a sea that ships might sail on to Asia if a way could be found to get through or around America to enter it. Various European expeditions searched for a "Passage to India," a water route around or through America that led to Asia. They all failed, confirming the dismaying proposition that America was an unbroken barrier that extended northward and southward from the Caribbean to the stormy and icy waters of the Arctic and Antarctic seas.

In 1519 the Spanish government dispatched an expedition under Ferdinand Magellan to find a passage to Asia that would justify a Spanish claim to some of the southeast Asian Spice Islands held by the Portuguese. Magellan fought his way for thirty-eight days through a stormy water passage (later called the Straits of Magellan) at the tip of South America. Afterwards, Magellan pushed across the enormous stretches of Balboa's South Sea, which Magellan termed the Pacific (from Latin for "calm") Ocean. His men died from lack of water and ate rats to survive. In 1521 he reached the Philippines, where he was killed in a skirmish. His navigator, Juan Sebastián del Cano, and one surviving ship pushed on across the Indian Ocean, reaching Spain in September 1522, three years after their departure. This first circumnavigation of the globe was one of the great epics of human bravery and was the high mark of the age of European exploration. The discoveries of Magellan and del Cano demonstrated that Asia was too far away, and the trip too dangerous, for a successful trade route westward to Asia. Although holding on to the Philippine Islands, Spain would have to derive its main colonial wealth from the Western Hemisphere, not the Eastern.

Spanish Conquests in Mexico and South America

Great wealth was not long in coming to the Spanish. For years Spaniards had heard tales of Amerindian empires of gold and silver on the mainland of present-day Mexico. In 1519 Hernán Cortés organized an expedition of 11 vessels, 550 men, 16 horses, and 10 cannon, and sailed from Cuba to the Mexican coast. Marching inland, Cortés swiftly reached the outer fringes of the Aztec Empire.

Aided by large forces of Amerindian allies disaffected by the parasitic rule of the Aztecs, Cortés and his tiny band of Spaniards defeated the Aztecs and conquered Mexico. The key reasons were clear. Cortés himself gave much credit to his Amerindian allies, both as warriors and porters. The Tlaxcalans, armed with razor-sharp obsidian weapons, were especially effective. The Spanish firearms and cannon, as well as metal armor and weapons, totally outclassed the Aztec's stone-age weapons and cotton armor. In battle the Spanish horses and huge mastiffs, which were unknown to the Amerindians, often unnerved them. Cortés also capitalized on prophecies in Mexican folklore that seemed to foretell his coming.

Disease was perhaps the greatest ally of Cortés. An epidemic of smallpox saved Cortés from an Amerindian revolt in 1520. Since Amerindians did not have natural immunities to the many diseases the Europeans carried, including smallpox, measles, and influenza, the ravages of these diseases continued unabated. When Cortés landed, there were about 28 million persons in the Mexican heartland. Fifty years later the population had plummeted to 3 million. By 1620 only 1 million Amerindians lived in the area. As a result of the massive depopulation, Amerindian culture in the Western Hemisphere was substantially demolished.

In 1532 the Mexican story was repeated in Peru when Francisco Pizarro led a force of 170 men into the Andes, looking for the gold and silver of the Inka Empire. Inka rule centered in the mountains of present-day Peru, Ecuador, Bolivia, and northern Chile. Like the Aztecs, the Inkas had only lately come to power (see Chapter 7). By the time the Spanish arrived, the Inkas ruled about 8 million persons living in an area about half the size of the Roman Empire at its height. The Inka state was a rigid autocracy in which all power focused in the person of the ruler, the Inka; this proved to be a fatal weakness.

Finding this highly structured civilization divided by civil war and racked by an epidemic, Pizarro captured, imprisoned, and murdered the Inka ruler Atahualpa and destroyed every element of the Inka leadership; by 1533 he had gained control over the empire.

The *conquistadores* in Mexico and Peru were well rewarded for their ruthless daring. They robbed the Amerindians of their gold and silver objects and then searched for deposits to mine. In both Mexico and the Andes they found substantial supplies of gold and huge amounts of silver. Their search for precious metals and other opportunities for wealth took them into the southern third of the present-day United States, throughout Central America and across much of South America outside Brazil. A very rich lode was discovered at Cerro Potosí in Bolivia in 1545, which supplied enormous quantities of silver to the Spaniards. Potosí had a population of 160,000 persons in 1650, when the silver mine was at its most productive. It shrank to a minor town of 8,000 persons by 1825, when the mine had been largely depleted.

To exploit the wealth of the Inka Empire, the Spanish instituted a forced labor regime that was, if anything, more brutal than those in Mexico or the Caribbean. Inka rulers had demanded *mit'a* (forced labor) from their subjects. The Spanish claimed that their own demand for forced labor was an extension of the mit'a; under the Inkas, however, mit'a demands were harsh, but could be met without starvation and other ills that became prevalent under the Spanish. The dangerous and arduous labor in the mines killed many Amerindians. Coupled with recurrent epidemics, the Andean population declined in the same proportion as in Mexico, with the same devastating cultural results.

It is likely that the Amerindians gave their conquerors syphilis in exchange for the terrible plagues that had been let loose among them. Syphilis raged for decades as an epidemic, mortal disease in Europe. Eventually it became a slow-acting but still immensely dangerous disease.

In the middle of the sixteenth century, the Amerindians were proclaimed subjects under the protection of the crown. As such they could no longer be legally enslaved, but many were still worked to death in the mines, businesses, and fields of their Spanish overlords. Over time, racial interrelationships created many individuals of mixed ancestry called *mestizos,* who eventually formed a major element in the Latin American population.

Based on the toil of this Amerindian and *mestizo* work force, fleets carried enormous wealth in silver, hides, gold, dyes, cacao, and quinine from the mainland of the Western Hemisphere to Spain. The Spanish monarchy, from its share of the precious metals and from taxes, received 40 percent of the value of these shipments. Two fleets from Spain carrying food, clothing, wine, tools, household items, and a few settlers sailed to the Western Hemisphere annually, but the goods sent over were inadequate for the colonial population.

The Spanish and Portuguese, in name at least, made their colonies Roman Catholic. In many areas church teachings mixed with indigenous Amerindian and African religious practices. Some of the Spanish religious leaders went to great lengths to destroy all remnants of the Amerindian heritage on the grounds that their pre-Conquest culture was based on devil worship, sodomy, and cannibalism. A Spanish bishop destroyed all the pre-Conquest Maya books that he could locate because they contained aspects of the old religion. Of the hundreds of Maya books that once existed, only four survived to modern times. In many areas Catholic churchmen were responsible for exploration and settlement. Some priests also led the fight for more humane treatment for the Amerindians.

Several aspects of the Western Hemisphere were transmitted to Europe. Foods such as potatoes, maize, several varieties of peppers, tomatoes, chocolate, and many others became a part of the European diet; maize became a staple in China.

Rival Empires in the Western Hemisphere

By the middle of the sixteenth century, the Spanish and Portuguese had used the Western Hemisphere as an arena to create enormous colonial empires. Unlike the collection of fortified coastal towns and trading depots set up by the Portuguese in Africa and Asia, the Spanish colonies constituted a territory many times larger than Spain itself. Portugal created an equivalently huge colony in Brazil.

During most of the sixteenth century, while the Spanish and Portuguese exploited the riches of Latin America, the English, French, and Dutch, preoccupied with religious wars and other domestic problems, stayed home. Late in the century, however, these nations were ready to compete with the Spanish and Portuguese; in particular, they had devised effective economic incentives to foster their own colonialism. The Spanish and Portuguese had allowed a small percentage of their business community to monopolize opportunities abroad, thus limiting available investment resources. In contrast, the English, French, and Dutch governments encouraged merchants and bankers to invest in overseas commerce by granting charters to new "joint stock" companies specializing in trading and colonization. Participants in joint stock companies had their risks limited to the proportion of their investment; this restricted liability encouraged smaller investors to put their money in new overseas companies. Investment was further encouraged by

Forced Labor in Peru, 1652

According to His Majesty's warrant, the mine owners on this massive range have a right . . . to 13,300 Indians in working and exploitation of the mines. It is the duty of the Corregidor of Potosi [governor] to have them rounded up and to see that they come in from all the provinces. . . . These Indians are sent out every year under a captain. . . . This works very badly, with great losses and gaps in the quotas of Indians, the villages being depopulated. . . . After each has eaten his ration, they climb up the hill, each to his mine, and go in, staying there from that hour until Saturday evening without coming out of the mine; their wives bring them food, but they stay constantly underground, excavating and carrying out the ore from which they get the silver. They all have tallow candles, lighted day and night; that is
the light they work with, for as they are underground, they have need of it all the time. The mere cost of these candles used in the mines . . . will amount every year to more than 300,000 pesos, even though tallow is cheap in that country, being abundant; but this is a very great expense, and it is almost incredible, how much is spent for candles in the operation of breaking down and getting out the ore.*

The above description of forced Amerindian labor in silver mines provided insight both into the working conditions for the miners and attitudes of Spanish observers. This report revealed rather more concern over the cost of candles than for the health or well-being of the Amerindian workers.

*"The Potosi Mine and Indian Forced Labor in Peru," in Antonio Vasques de Espinosa, Compendium and Description of the West Indies, trans. C. U. Clark (Washington: Smithsonian Institution, 1942), pp. 623–625, in Peter N. Stearns, ed., Documents in World History, vol. 2 (New York: Harper & Row, 1988), pp. 83–84.

LIVES AND TIMES ACROSS CULTURES

New Stuff on Your Plate

We have already seen two important results of European conquests in the Western Hemisphere: one was the migration of millions of Europeans and Africans to the Americas, and the second was the spread of diseases, especially smallpox, which decimated the Amerindian populations. A third effect was the reciprocal introduction of new foods. Europeans brought with them both field crops and livestock. Wheat now supplemented the indigenous maize, and citrus fruits and grapes also enjoyed local success in the Americas. On the other hand, cash crops like sugar, rice, bananas, and tobacco (indigenous) enriched the landowning elite in the Americas.

Before Columbus, the Amerindians had domesticated only dogs, turkeys, ducks, alpacas, and llamas—none of which provided much food or hauling power. Worst of all, the Amerindians had few animals that could turn grass into meat. The European introduction of sheep, goats, swine, cattle, and horses varied the diet of many and furnished powerful draft animals. Later, horses, cattle, and sheep became the basis of full-scale Amerindian herding and riding cultures among, for example, the Navaho and the Apache.

At the same time, Amerindian field and tuber crops had a tremendous impact in Europe after 1500.

Maize and potatoes spread through the Eastern Hemisphere, superseding indigenous staples because they supplied more nutrients per hectare.

The potato, native to the cool valleys of the Andes, adapted very readily to temperate northern Europe, providing the dietary mainstay from Ireland to Russia. The Dutch peasant family portrayed in Van Gogh's *The Potato Eaters* could just as well have been Peruvian. Maize, native to warm Mesoamerica, was adopted in much of southern Europe; its cultivation in Africa increased steadily till, by the 1990s, it had become the leading consumer crop on that continent. Maize and sweet potatoes became major crops in Asia, surpassed only by rice and wheat. Other Amerindian foods that proliferated around the world were tomatoes, squash, certain beans, and peanuts. Manioc (cassava) was an important food crop, first in Brazil and later in Africa.

Enormous economic consequences flowed from the improvement of diet ensured by maize and potato farming. In the British Isles, for example, the new crops spurred population growth, thereby furnishing both the labor and the consumer basis for the Industrial Revolution.

---

easier access to marine insurance. The wealth brought into Europe from the Western Hemisphere later helped to fuel further European expansion into Asia (see Chapter 10).

At first the northern nations concentrated on finding a share of the Asia trade. During the sixteenth century, despite the discouraging news of earlier explorers, many northern Europeans hoped that a water route to Asia might yet be found somewhere in the northern latitudes. Beginning in 1497 English, French, and Dutch expeditions hunted for a "Northwest Passage" around North America, but to their dismay found the northern seas clogged with impenetrable ice. However, the explorers did learn that the northern parts of North America contained valuable timber and furs and that the North Atlantic teemed with fish.

As hopes of finding a northern route to Asia faded, the northern European nations turned their attention to the Western Hemisphere. Since Spain and Portugal monopolized the wealth of the most valuable parts of the Americas, England, France, and the Netherlands had to fight their way in. In the beginning this meant smuggling goods and slaves into the Spanish colonies; the Dutch were particularly active in this. Soon the interlopers were attacking Spanish and Portuguese ships laden with wealth bound for Europe. Pirates, both freelance "buccaneers" and marauders secretly outfitted by European governments, pillaged the "Spanish Main," raiding Spanish silver fleets and attacking Caribbean ports.

By the mid-seventeenth century, the English, French, and Dutch were strong enough to attempt the conquest of the Spanish and Portuguese colonies in the Western Hemisphere, as well as in Africa and Asia. The Spanish and Portuguese held on to their main possessions in the Americas, but the newcomers did capture a number of small islands in the West Indies, turning them into agricultural plantations for growing sugar and tobacco. To work the crops, the English, French, and Dutch shipped in slaves from their trading posts in West Africa. The constant importation of slaves into the European plantation colonies quickly transformed the racial composition of the eastern fringe of the Western Hemisphere, replacing the original Amerindian population with a few Europeans and masses of black slaves.

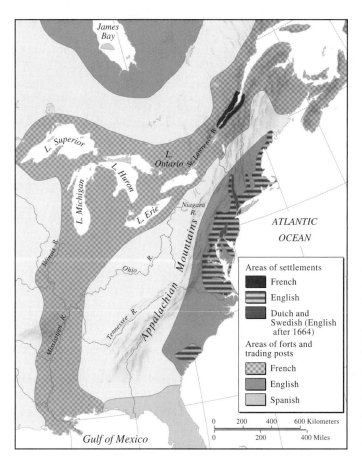

Map 9.7 European Holdings in North America, c. 1685. After nearly a century of activity in North America, the French and the English had secured very disparate colonial holdings. The French presence centered on fur and deerskin trading posts radiating from a small settlement in Quebec. The English controlled an area smaller in extent but greater in population, dominated by family farms.

Slavery in Virginia. In 1619, at Jamestown, England's Virginia colony, a Dutch ship has landed with the first blacks offered for sale. The Virginians stare at the strangers, trying to gauge the economic and social consequences of purchasing them. Their decision to buy slaves radically transformed the racial composition of the Western Hemisphere.

© Bethmann/Corbis

During the seventeenth century the northern European states established new colonies on the east coast of North America. The Dutch, Swedes, and French were primarily interested in developing a lucrative fur trade with the Amerindians, but their colonies proved to be only modestly profitable, considering the cost of maintenance and defense. To cut down on costs, they brought over a few farmers to provide food.

In 1607 the English established a new kind of colony on the east coast of North America. In such colonies, often termed "New Europes," large numbers of European settlers landed, killing off or driving out the Amerindian inhabitants and setting up replicas of European society. The English authorities had originally hoped to trade with the Amerindians for skins and furs, as the French and Dutch were doing. Failing that, they wanted to find or grow the products that had made the Spanish and Portuguese rich: gold, silver, silk, spices, and tea. They had other motives as well: outflanking the Spanish; converting Amerindians to Christianity; and removing from England some of its criminals, paupers, unemployed, religious dissenters, and political unreliables. English leaders believed that the work of these people would be profitable to the merchant trading companies. Encouraged by such "boosters" as Richard Hakluyt and with varying degrees of pressure by the government and the trading companies, more than 100,000 settlers came to English North America by the middle of the seventeenth century.

To the disappointment of the English investors, many of the colonies produced little in the way of Asian and Latin American wealth. North of Chesapeake Bay, the natural products were timber, fish, grain, and meat; only the first was wanted in England. The foodstuffs, however, could be sent to the Caribbean, allowing the planters there to keep their slaves at work exclusively growing sugar and tobacco. From the Chesapeake southward, the English had more luck: Here settlers could grow tobacco and (later) rice, indigo, and cotton—all valuable products. Slave traders brought in slaves from the Caribbean and from Africa to raise these products; as a result some areas from the Chesapeake southward rapidly took on the brutal economic and social characteristics of the plantation culture of the Caribbean and Brazil.

By the mid-seventeenth century, the center of economic power in Europe had shifted from the Iberian to the North European nations. Having sufficient power and economic stability, these nations created, enlarged, and protected their colonial empires. Increasingly efficient in mercantile and banking affairs, they augmented the profits obtained from their colonies and avoided dissipating their wealth in European wars. Many English and Dutch families became wealthy from overseas trade, and company investors plowed profits from their colonial enterprises into new manufacturing and trading projects in Europe (see Chapter 11).

Summary and Comparisons

The fifteenth, sixteenth, and seventeenth centuries were marked by the rise and fall of absolutist states. The Ottoman and Safavid Empires were flourishing; several of the Atlantic-facing nations of Europe were building up centralized monarchies; and the papacy was beleaguered. The Renaissance reissue of classical histories and biographies gave some new perspective to this process. Largely as a result of European exploration and expansion, the Aztec and Inka Empires in the Western Hemisphere were overthrown.

Authoritarian government was well established in the Ottoman and Safavid Empires. Although old enemies, these empires were remarkably similar. Each was highly centralized politically and economically, and their cultural and social life shared a common Islamic heritage. Differences did exist, however, because the Ottoman Empire adhered to Sunni Islam while the Safavids were ardent believers in Shi'i Islam.

As a leading military power in the eastern Mediterranean, the Ottomans successfully absorbed the Balkans, Hungary, and the Arab lands of the eastern Mediterranean and North Africa. Ottoman attempts to take Vienna and to destroy Safavid power failed. The Ottoman Empire reached its zenith under Suleiman the Magnificent, a great patron of the arts, but steadily declined in world status afterwards.

The Safavid Empire entered its golden age under Shah Abbas, who created a new, glorious capital at Isfahan and made Persia a cultural center. Control of the silk industry provided the Safavids with economic wealth and enabled them to become patrons of the arts. Like the Ottoman Empire, the Safavids encouraged trade with European nations

CHRONOLOGY

1300

Petrarch and the Italian Renaissance

The Black Death

Renaissance in northern Europe

1450

Johannes Gutenberg's printing press

Benin kingdom in West Africa

End of Muslim rule in Spain

Voyage of Christopher Columbus

1500 Centralization of western European monarchies

Leonardo da Vinci

Michelangelo Buonarroti

Desiderius Erasmus

Beginnings of the Safavid Empire

Voyages of Balboa and Magellan

Martin Luther's ninety-five theses

Spain conquers Aztecs and Inkas

Ottoman Turks conquer Arab territories

Suleiman the Magnificent

Suleimaniye complex in Istanbul

John Calvin

Afonso I, king of the Kongo

Henry VIII

Roman Catholic Reformation

Slave trade in Africa

Queen Elizabeth I

Shah Abbas the Great

1600 William Shakespeare

British and French establish colonies in North America

Miguel de Cervantes, *Don Quixote*

The Thirty Years' War

"King" Nzinga in Angola

Ashanti kingdom

Louis XIV, the Sun King

Dutch make settlement in South Africa

1700

and granted special privileges to European traders. Both the Safavids and the Ottomans also maintained economic links with Asia, where other centralized empires flourished during the sixteenth and seventeenth centuries.

During these centuries European societies also underwent profound changes. In Europe, the otherworldly orientation of the Catholic church gave way to a secular outlook in thought and in art. Spurred on by refugee scholars who fled Ottoman advances in the eastern Mediterranean, Italy became the center of a remarkable intellectual, literary, and artistic reawakening called the Renaissance. Deriving inspiration from recently recovered manuscripts by classical authors of Greece and Rome, and from contacts with Islamic scholars, humanists produced superb works in history, philosophy, and philology. Drawing from nature, painters and sculptors now concentrated on capturing and interpreting the world about them. By the sixteenth and seventeenth centuries, the practices and perspectives of the Italian Renaissance also spread into western Europe. Vernacular literature flourished, and humanism became a strong force. France, England, and Spain enjoyed golden ages of literary productivity, particularly in drama.

During the fifteenth and sixteenth centuries national monarchies also developed in western Europe. These national monarchies established territorial unity and centralized governmental functions, and their monarchs overcame the opposition of the nobles by allying with towns and relying on advisers and bureaucrats from outside the aristocracy. Expanding centralized monarchies also had impacts on the relationships of European governments with the Catholic church.

The Protestant Reformation of the sixteenth century had several causes. A weakened papacy lowered popular support and abuses of simony, indulgences, and pluralism stirred reformers to action. Luther and Calvin led the movement to break with the Catholic church and to establish Protestant Christianity. Within the Roman Catholic church, humanists and clergy led reforming activities, and Pope Paul III made reform a churchwide activity. The Council of Trent reaffirmed traditional Roman Catholic doctrines and sought to eliminate abuses. Religious wars disrupted European societies until 1648, when the Treaty of Westphalia recognized both Protestant and Catholic states in Europe.

The newly unified European states along the Atlantic Ocean had also amassed the economic resources and technology necessary to explore new trade routes. Spurred on by Ottoman taxes on goods from Asia, and to some degree by a desire to make converts to Christianity, they began to search for routes to Asia that they could control. In the process they explored much of the globe and brought European power not only to Asia but to Africa and the Western Hemisphere as well.

The Portuguese, Dutch, French, and English all established trading routes along the coasts of Africa. The Portuguese were initially strongly entrenched in both West and East Africa, but they gradually lost their favored positions to the Dutch and English.

In East Africa, indigenous African and Arab opposition drove out the Portuguese, who had been weakened by Dutch naval victories in the Indian Ocean. In South Africa, the Dutch established a permanent colony based on the racial supremacy of the white

Boers. This initially small colony would have many long-term ramifications for the history of South Africa.

Finally, the slave trade, which lasted some 400 years, affected all of Africa. Millions of Africans were shipped by force to the Americas. Although some Africans cooperated and benefited from this trade, many, like "King" Nzinga of Angola, fought against it. The slave trade had many disastrous results on individual African societies, particularly in the interior of the continent. In spite of the negative impacts of the slave trade, most of Africa remained independent and continued to develop under its own political and cultural institutions until the nineteenth century.

During this era, Spain led the European expansion across the Atlantic and established a vast empire, exceedingly rich in silver, in Mexico and South America. In the course of this conquest, the great majority of Amerindians died from European diseases. Europeans also transformed the Caribbean into sugar and tobacco plantations worked by black slaves who lived and died under brutal conditions. Portugal established a similar plantation-based economy in Brazil. Three key characteristics of Iberia—paternalistic government, aristocratic privilege, and mercantilist economics—were essentially replicated in Latin America, but in this case imposed on populations who were predominantly Amerindian and black. Amerindian and black culture—especially food, clothing, textiles, music, and speech—modified the lifestyles of Europeans, both in Latin America and elsewhere.

In the seventeenth century, the French, Dutch, and English also became active overseas. Although they failed to find passages to Asia through the Arctic ice, the northern European states did establish colonies on the Atlantic seaboard of North America and used the wealth from these colonies for financial and industrial developments in Europe. Thousands of Europeans settled in North America, displacing and often massacring the Amerindians. These colonies began to exhibit more liberal social, political, and religious values and practices than Europe.

These major upheavals mark the beginning of a remarkable five-century period in which some European nations extended their power into four other continents. In the process they destroyed or profoundly altered many indigenous cultures in the Western Hemisphere and also in Africa and Asia. As a result of these developments, the center of political and economic power shifted from Mediterranean to Atlantic societies.

Selected Sources

Items indicated with an asterisk (*) are available in paperback.

Adas, Michael, ed. *Technology and European Overseas Enterprise: Diffusion, Adaptation, and Adoption.* 1996.

*Atil, Esin. *The Age of Sultan Suleyman the Magnificent.* 1987. Lavishly illustrated discussion of art, crafts, and culture during the zenith of Ottoman power.

Augustijn, Cornelius. *Erasmus: His Life, Works and Influence.* Trans. J. C. Grayson. 1991. Presents a balanced account of Erasmus's life and works.

*Bailyn, Bernard. *Origins of American Politics.* 1970. Examines colonial roots of American political theory and practice.

*Balewa, Abubakar Tafawa. *Shathu Umar.* 1967. A novel about the life of a slave by a former prime minister of Nigeria.

Barber, Noel. *The Sultans.* 1973. Readable account of the Ottoman Empire, based on the lives of the Sultans.

Benesch, Otto. *The Art of the Renaissance in Northern Europe.* 1965. Well-illustrated presentation relating northern European art to contemporary trends in thought and religion.

Bethell, Leslie, ed. *Colonial Spanish America.* 1987. *Colonial Brazil.* 1988. Both books contain essays concerning Latin America from the conquest to independence. Noted authorities write about rural society and the hacienda, urbanization, and Amerindian cultures matters.

*Bouwsma, William J. *John Calvin: A Sixteenth-Century Portrait.* 1988. An essential biography of Calvin.

Boxers, Charles R. *Four Centuries of Portuguese Expansion, 1415–1825.* 1969. Overview of Brazil within the context of the Portuguese Empire.

Braudel, Fernand. *The Mediterranean and the Mediterranean World in the Age of Philip II.* Abridged 1992. Excellent background for understanding Spain and Spanish transplantations in the Americas.

Brown, Judith C., and Davis, Robert C., eds. *Gender and Society in Renaissance Italy.* 1998. A useful collection of essays on the interplay between gender and society.

*Costain, Thomas B. *The Moneyman.* 1947. Historical novel on the life of a French merchant.

Cutter, Donald C. *Quest for Empire: Spanish Settlement in the Southwest.* 1996. An overview of Spanish policies.

Ferro, Marc. *Colonization: A Global History.* 1997. A good general account.

Fuentes, Carlos. *The Buried Mirror: Reflections on Spain and the New World.* 1992. Excellent introduction to Spain and the Americas; beautifully crafted with prints, maps, and artwork.

*Goodwin, Godfrey. *A History of Ottoman Architecture.* 1971; reprinted 1992. Includes hundreds of illustrations and dozens of floor plans for mosques, government complexes, and homes; also a particularly informative chapter on Sinan, the noted Ottoman architect.

"Gorée: Door of No Return." Films for the Humanities. A moving historical description of Gorée, a slave-trading center in West Africa.

Green, Guy, dir. *Luther.* 1974. Stirring film interpretation of Luther's reforming activities.

Grimm, Harold J. *The Reformation Era: 1500–1650.* 2d ed. 1973. Focuses on the religious issues and personalities of the Reformation era.

*Haring, Clarence H. *The Spanish Empire in America.* 1975. An authoritative study that is sympathetic to the Spanish.

*Hodgson, Marshall G. S. *The Venture of Islam: The Gunpowder Empires and Modern Times.* Vol. 3. 1974. Scholarly analysis and truly global approach to the confrontation of Islamic states, including the Ottoman and Persian Empires and Muslim India, with the West.

*Innes, Hammond. *The Conquistadors.* 1969. A lively, beautifully illustrated account.

The Isfahan of Shah Abbas. 1987. This 28-minute film is a stunning visual presentation of Safavid culture with narration by art expert Oleg Grabar.

Jensen, De Lamar. *Reformation Europe.* 1992. The best one-volume account.

Joffe, Roland, dir. *The Mission.* 1986. A visually spectacular film about a Jesuit mission in the jungles of Brazil and its destruction by the greed of merchants and factionalism within the church.

*Kinross, Patrick Balfour. *The Ottoman Centuries: the Rise and Fall of the Turkish Empire.* 1977. Well-written account of Ottoman history, with good analysis of strengths and weaknesses of the empire.

Labalm, Patricia, ed. *Beyond Their Sex: Learned Women of the European Past.* 1980. Contains a number of useful articles analyzing educational and scholarly roles open to females in Renaissance society.

*Leonard, Irving A. *Baroque Times in Old Mexico: Seventeenth-Century Persons, Places, and Practices.* 1959. A colorful insight into the society and culture of Latin America.

Leon-Portilla, Miguel. *The Broken Spears: Aztec Accounts of the Conquest.* 1962. An enduring classic, employing Amerindian accounts of the fall of the Aztecs.

——. *Pre-Colombian Literatures of Mexico.* 1992. An anthology of poetry and prose, including indigenous accounts of the Conquest.

*Maalouf, Amin. *Leo Africanus.* 1986; reprinted 1992. A novel based on the celebrated traveler's life, with vivid, historically accurate descriptions of Moorish Spain, Timbuktu, and Italy during the Renaissance.

Marks, Richard L. *Cortés: The Great Adventurer and the Fate of Aztec Mexico.* 1993. A biography of the Spanish conqueror against the backdrop of a clash between the Aztec and European civilizations.

Marshall, Sherrin, ed. *Women in Reformation and Counter-Reformation Europe.* 1989. Explores the role and status of women in the Reformation era, and their contribution to spiritual renewal and reform.

*Morison, Samuel E. *Christopher Columbus, Mariner.* 1983. A lively, if traditional, introduction to Columbus.

Oberman, Heiko O. *Luther: Man between God and Devil.* Trans. E. Walliser-Schwarzbart. 1989. Examines Luther and his theology against the intellectual currents of the later medieval world.

*Pernoud, Regine. *Joan of Arc, by Herself and Her Witnesses.* Trans. Edward Hyams. 1969. Powerful biography; also the film *Joan of Arc,* dir. Victor Fleming, 1948, starring Ingrid Bergman.

*Perroy, Edouard. *The Hundred Years' War.* 1965. Combines social and political history with military events.

*Perry, Glenn E. *The Middle East: Fourteen Islamic Centuries.* 3d ed. 1997. Concise overview of the region from early times to the present day.

Ptak, Roderich, ed. *Portuguese Asia: Aspects in History and Economic History, Sixteenth and Seventeenth Centuries.* 1987.

Rubin, Nancy. *Isabella of Castile: The First Renaissance Queen.* 1991. A lively biography of the strong-willed queen.

Sale, Kirkpatrick. *The Conquest of Paradise: Christopher Columbus and the Columbian Legacy.* 1990. A fervent exposition of the concept that a sickly, dispirited post–Black Death Europe essentially destroyed the environment, native population, and indigenous culture of the Americas.

Shaffer, Peter. *The Royal Hunt of the Sun.* 1981. A moving play depicting the story of the capture, imprisonment, and execution of the Inka emperor by Pizarro.

Sobel, Dava. *Galileo's Daughter.* 1999. Based on the surviving letters of his illegitimate daughter, a cloistered nun in Florence, this study reveals much about Galileo the man, accenting his struggle to reconcile his scientific discoveries with his beliefs as a good Catholic.

*Stone, Irving. *The Agony and the Ecstasy.* 1961. An historical novel based on Michelangelo's life; also the basis for a movie of the same title.

Suleiman the Magnificent. 1987. This one-hour film, produced by the National Gallery of Art, is a colorful, historically accurate account of the Ottoman empire at its zenith.

*Thompson, Vincent Bakpetu. *The Making of the African Diaspora in the Americas 1441–1900.* 1988. Full account of the slave trade and its cultural impacts.

Williams, Selma. *Demeter's Daughters.* 1976. A survey of the various roles of women in British North America, stressing the stories of individuals.

Wölfflin, Heinrich. *Classic Art: An Introduction to the Italian Renaissance.* 3d ed. 1968. Brief, comprehensive, well-illustrated introduction to this large topic.

Wood, Betty. *The Origins of American Slavery: Freedom and Bondage in the English Colonies.* 1997.

Zili, Madeline C. *Women in the Ottoman Empire.* 1997. A scholarly study of the lives of women over the many centuries of Ottoman rule.

Zophy, Jonathan W. *A Short History of Reformation Europe.* 1997. A concise, readable overview of the period. Tailored for students who have not had much exposure to the subject.

——. *A Short History of Renaissance Europe.* 1997. Like its above companion, a useful introduction for the beginning student.

 Additional resources, exercises, and Internet links related to this chapter are available at the Book Companion Web site: http://history.wadsworth.com/upshurcompact4/

10

Asia in the Early Modern Era

•

• Early European Colonization of Southeast Asia •

• The Moghul Dynasty •

• The Ming Dynasty •

• The Ch'ing (Manchu) Dynasty at Its Height •

• A Centralized Feudal State in Japan •

• Summary and Comparisons •

All the face of the earth, so far as we could see, was covered with people, troops of horses, elephants, etc., with innumerable flags small and great, which made a most gallant show; for it is the custom of every great man to go with a great many of these flags carried before him.

Then thousands of horsemen going breadthwise; then came about 19 or 20 elephants of state with coverings and furniture; most of them of cloth of gold, the rest rich stuff, velvets, etc.; some of them carrying a flag with the king's arms, which is a tiger crouching with the sun rising over his back. . . . Then came the king himself mounted on a dark gray horse, and with him Mahabat Khan. A little distance behind rode his eldest son Dara-Shikot all alone, all the rest of the lords on foot, before and behind, and on each side of him. All this moving in one, on so many huge elephants [that it] seemed like a fleet of ships with flags and streamers. So that all this together made a most majestical, warlike and delightsome sight.*

*Peter Mundy, The Travels of Peter Mundy in Europe and Asia, 1608–1667, vol. 2 (Cambridge: Hakluyt Society, 1907–1936), p. 188.

This awestruck description was written in 1632 by Englishman Peter Mundy after the Moghul Emperor Jahangir's entry into Ahmadabad. The great splendor of the Moghul court reflected the wealth of India and led Europeans to call the Moghul emperors Great Moghuls. Rulers have always tried to impress the world with pomp and circumstance; in seventeenth-century India with horses, elephants, and many retainers; in the modern West with jet planes, helicopters, and fleets of limousines. Such showmanship is designed to inspire awe and obedience.

Similar accounts by Westerners record the court splendors of Ming and Ch'ing China and Tokugawa Japan, whose leaders ruled more people and wealthier territories than their European counterparts. This is why European adventurers and traders fought to control new trading routes to Asia.

This chapter describes the last great imperial age in Asia, when India, China, and Japan experienced political success and cultural flowering. Southeast Asia continued to be influenced culturally by China, India, and West Asia and remained politically divided. During this period, European voyages to find a direct sea route to Asia culminated in Vasco da Gama's arrival in India in 1498 via the southern tip of Africa and the Indian Ocean. Europeans were happy to be granted permission to trade in India, China, and Japan by those countries' powerful governments. The Portuguese mercantile empire in Southeast Asia, where no strong governments existed, eventually failed for lack of manpower. In time the Netherlands dominated trade in Southeast Asia, while Spain colonized the Philippines and England focused on India.

This chapter continues to examine the Moghul Empire that unified India for the first time in almost 1,000 years. By securing almost 200 years of peace, it allowed Indians to evolve an Indo-Islamic style of art and to attain great heights in other cultural areas. The chapter also looks at the Ming and Ch'ing dynasties, under which China enjoyed great economic prosperity and a final flourishing of traditional culture and arts. It concludes with Japan, which emerged from civil war to achieve unity under feudal warlords called shoguns.

Early European Colonization of Southeast Asia

From ancient times the country of Siam was known as Shahru'n-nuwi, and all princes of these regions below the wind were subject to Siam. . . . And when the news reached Siam that Malaka was a great city but was not subject to Siam, the [king] sent an envoy to Malaka to demand a letter of 'obedience': but Sultan Muzaffar Shah [reigned 1446–1459] refused to own allegiance to Siam. The Raja of Siam was very angry and ordered an expedition to be made ready for the invasion of Malaka. . . . [Later] the men of Siam arrived, and they fought with the men of Malaka. After a long battle, in which many of the soldiers of the Raja of Siam were killed, Malaka still held out and the Siamese withdrew. . . .*

*From the Sejarah Melayu (Malay Annals), in Asia on the Eve of Europe's Expansion, eds. Donald F. Lach and Carol Flaumenhaft (Englewood Cliffs, N.J.: Prentice-Hall, 1965), pp. 86–87.

The *Malay Annals* tell this story of how the city of Malacca came to be founded (near the tip of the Malay Peninsula opposite Sumatra) in the early fifteenth century. The *Annals* are a mixture of myths and oral history and provide a rare indigenous account of the early greatness of the city. Malacca was a center of trade for China, the East Indies, India, and West Asia, and, after the coming of Europeans, for Europe as well.

A Kaleidoscope of States and Cultures

Southeast Asia is a rich mosaic of many peoples and cultures. Blessed with varied natural resources, it was since early times the destination of traders and immigrants from India and China, and later also from West Asia. Each group brought along its culture, language, technology, and religion, contributing to a melting pot.

Few indigenous writings describe conditions in Southeast Asia, especially the islands, prior to the coming of Europeans. Thus scholars must reconstruct the history of the region from a combination of external written sources, mainly Chinese, incidental local inscriptions, traditional accounts, and oral history and corroborate them with archaeological evidence.

Mongol invasions launched from China during the late thirteenth century are a good point of demarcation. As elsewhere in continental Asia, Mongols established overlordship over the mainland states. They destroyed the Burmese kingdom and its capital city Pagan. After the Mongol era, several petty Burmese states fought one another and fought periodically with neighboring Siam. Mongol invasions into southwestern China had accelerated the southward migration of the Buddhist (mainly Theravada) Shan or Thai people into Thailand. The Thais defeated the Khmers and in 1350 established a state, Siam, whose capital city was Ayuthia (named after Ayodhia in India, the legendary capital of King Rama of the *Ramayana* epic). Though culturally influenced by India and Khmer, the Thai gradually developed a national art style no longer dependent on Gupta Indian and Khmer models. Many monuments and great quantities of elegant religious sculptures survive from post-fourteenth-century Siam, but few written records remain because a Burmese invasion destroyed Ayuthia and its perishable contents in 1767. In 1782 King Rama I founded a new Siamese dynasty with its capital city at Bangkok. His descendants escaped European colonization and rule the country to the present.

The Mongols were unable to dominate island Southeast Asia, as their expensive failed attempt to conquer Java in the 1290s proved. Afterward a new Javanese commercial empire was established over Borneo, Sumatra, the Malay Peninsula, and parts of the Philippines and lasted for about 100 years. In the early fifteenth century many Malay and island East Indian states accepted Chinese suzerainty in the wake of the massive naval expeditions commanded by Ming admiral Cheng Ho (discussed later in this chapter). Rising Arab commercial power centered in Malacca in Sumatra led many states in the region to accept Islam, with rulers adopting the new religion to facilitate trade with Muslim Indians and Arabs. When the Portuguese under Alfonso d'Albuquerque first came to Southeast Asia, they found no powerful empires in the region but a mosaic of many faiths and numerous petty states.

Southeast Asia: Magnet for Europeans

When the first Europeans, Portuguese explorers, sailed around the coast of Africa in the fifteenth century in search of a direct route to Asia, they found strong governments in parts of India, China, and Japan. Too weak to attempt establishing territorial bases on mainland Asia, the Portuguese were grateful to be allowed to trade. However, island Southeast Asia's political fragmentation and desirable products made the region easy prey for European domination.

Once established in Asia, the Portuguese carefully guarded charts of the navigation routes and defended their trading posts against other European nations, forcing them to seek other routes. Thus England's King Henry VII commissioned John Cabot (or Giovanni Caboto) to find a northwest passage to Asia by following the American coast northward along the Atlantic Ocean in 1497. Cabot failed, but in 1519 Spain's Ferdinand Magellan rounded the tip of South America and in 1521 reached a chain of islands that the Spanish later named the Philippines, after King Philip II of Spain. Spain later colonized the Philippines not because the islands possessed many valuable products but because Chinese sailing junks had been trading there for centuries. Control over the islands gave Spain access to goods made in China and Japan. Spain ruled the Philippines until it was ousted by the United States at the end of the nineteenth century.

In the seventeenth century, for economic, religious, and nationalistic reasons, England and the Netherlands challenged Portuguese and Spanish dominance of the Asian trade. A small nation that lacked the population to sustain its Asian enterprise, Portugal encouraged its men stationed overseas to marry local women. Their sons, raised as Catholics, supplied some of the needed manpower. Portugal also recruited displaced samurai from Japan to serve in its garrisons. Despite these measures, Portugal could not successfully defend its empire after the sixteenth century and lost its holdings in Ceylon, Taiwan, and the East Indies to the Dutch. The Dutch prevented England from establishing a firm foothold in Southeast Asia until the nineteenth century, forcing the English to concentrate their energies on commercial and later territorial expansion on the Indian subcontinent.

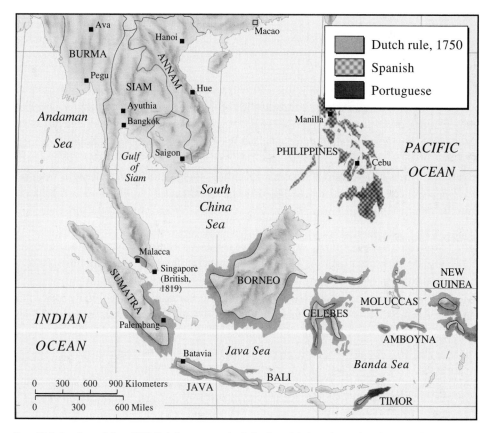

Map 10.1 Southeast Asia, c. 1750. Early European empires in Southeast Asia focused on trade and were mainly interested in the spices that had made the islands famous. By the mid-seventeenth century, the Portuguese had been largely expelled from their trading outposts in the region, replaced by the Dutch in the East Indies. Spain ruled the Philippine Islands. Indigenous states, many of them vassals to China, ruled mainland Southeast Asia.

Portuguese and Spanish Empires

The rise of the Ottoman Empire and political changes in Persia during the fifteenth century disrupted established overland trade routes to the east (see Chapter 9), forcing Europeans to seek alternative sea routes to India and East Asia. Technological improvements in shipbuilding and the adoption of the compass in navigation during the fifteenth century made the long sea voyages possible. With its advantageous location along the Atlantic Ocean, Portugal under Prince Henry the Navigator took the lead in sponsoring voyages of exploration. At the same time that the Portuguese were developing a slave trade in Africa, they were also heading east across the Indian Ocean in search of spices and other exotic goods. In 1497 four Portuguese ships led by Vasco da Gama (1469–1525) left Lisbon and sailed down the west coast of Africa, around the Cape of Good Hope, and across the Indian Ocean, arriving at Calicut on the west coast of India in 1498. In 1508 another Portuguese squadron under Alfonso d'Albuquerque (1453–1515) sailed for Southeast Asia. He built permanent fortified stations at Aden near the mouth of the Red Sea, Ormuz near the mouth of the Persian Gulf in East Africa, Goa on the west coast of India, and in 1511 at Malacca, on the Malay Peninsula. Strategically located to control trade between East and South Asia, Malacca was also a center of trade within Southeast Asia.

The voyage of da Gama and others began a century of Portuguese domination of Southeast Asia. Albuquerque became the first governor-general of a string of fortified trading ports of Portugal's newly established trading empire, administered from Goa. Later Portuguese commanders established additional outposts on the coast of India, on Ceylon (Sri Lanka), and the Sunda Isles and Malacca in Southeast Asia. They fought some local rulers and formed alliances with others for control of the lucrative trade in spices and other exotic and precious goods either produced in Southeast Asia or obtainable there. Other intrepid Portuguese sailors ventured to China and Japan, briefly establishing and manning an outpost on the Chinese island of Taiwan (which Portuguese explorers named Ilha Formosa, or beautiful island). In the mid-sixteenth century, the Chinese government granted Macao, a small peninsula in southern China near Canton, to Portugal for a trading base, but excluded them from other Chinese ports.

Zealous Catholics and fanatically anti-Muslim, the Portuguese carried their hatred for Muslims (who had ruled their homeland for several centuries) to Asia, where to their horror they found many Muslim communities. Catholic missionaries followed in the wake of the explorers and introduced Christianity to the region.

Portugal reaped immense wealth from its Asian trade. Malacca, the linchpin to its trading empire, was guarded by 200 intrepid Portuguese soldiers and 300 adventurous civilians. For much of the sixteenth century, the Portuguese government derived immense wealth from this domination. To ensure a steady supply of the spices, they made some of the weak local rulers vassals and compelled them to pay tribute in the desired items. Annually, a fleet of up to twenty *carracks,* or sailing ships, plied the ocean lanes between Portugal and Asia. On the outward voyage, they carried silver, glass, linens, woolen textiles, and metal manufactures for sale in Asia, and returned to Lisbon laden with pepper, spices, nutmeg (highly prized and expensive in Europe because it was believed to enhance male sexual powers), other spices, precious stones, porcelains, and silks. Portugal also controlled interisland trade throughout the region and collected tolls. Portuguese ships engaged in piracy in areas not under their control. By the late sixteenth century, however, the Portuguese commercial empire was declining because of inadequate manpower and shipping technology that lagged behind new advances made by the Dutch.

Spain also sought to engage in the Asian trade, but because Portugal closely guarded its trade lanes across the Indian Ocean, the Spanish had to discover a different route to the East. This quest culminated in Ferdinand Magellan's voyage in 1519 through the straits at the tip of South America (thereafter named after the explorer) into the Pacific Ocean (see Chapter 9). He reached an archipelago in 1521 and named one of the islands St. Lazarus (the chain of islands was renamed the Philippines in 1542). Although Magellan was killed, one of his ships returned to Spain in 1522 via the Indian Ocean and Africa, the first to circumnavigate the globe.

Spain easily established control over the numerous petty states of the Philippines. Most of its people were preliterate and were followers of animistic religions. Spanish missionaries eventually Christianized most Filipinos, except for the inhabitants of Mindanao and the Sulu islands who retained their Muslim faith. Spain also introduced distinctively European clothing styles and Christian names to the Filipinos, making them closer culturally to Spaniards and Latin Americans than to other Asians.

Spanish rule of the Philippines followed precedents and patterns set in Spanish America. From the capital at Manila, a governor supervised many provinces. Land was granted to a privileged class of Spaniards and local chiefs, who ruled over the peasants in

Catholic Cathedral. This Baroque cathedral in Cebu City was one of many built by the Spanish when they ruled the Philippines.

a feudal fashion. The Catholic church dominated religious life. It also provided education, from village schools for boys and girls, convent schools to daughters of the elite, and the College of St. Thomas in Manila for select young men. Founded in 1619, the latter was the first university in Southeast Asia; as St. Thomas University, it remains one of the most prestigious universities in the Philippines.

Although plantations were developed for commercial crops such as tobacco and hemp, Spain did not undertake major economic development of the islands. The port of Manila served an important function as the hub and entrepôt of trade between China, Spanish America, and Spain. Chinese sailing junks, which had been coming to the Philippines since the first millennium to trade with local peoples, now brought silks, tea, porcelain, and other Chinese and Japanese goods to Manila for the Spanish and Spanish-American market as well. From Manila they were shipped across the Pacific to Acapulco in Mexico. There they were carried by porters across the isthmus to Vera Cruz and other ports on the Atlantic coast, where they were loaded onto ships that sailed across the Atlantic to Spain. Thus Spain was able to obtain East Asian goods despite the Portuguese stranglehold on the Pacific-African route.

Spain paid for its imports from China and Japan mainly with silver mined in Mexico and Peru, minted as coins or in bars. The high-quality Spanish coins were widely accepted throughout Southeast Asia, Japan, and China. Many Chinese middlemen settled in Manila to participate in this trade. From Spanish America new crops such as maize, tobacco, sweet potatoes, potatoes, and peanuts were brought to the Philippines, whence they were introduced to China and Japan, with important and lasting impact. So secondary were the products of the Philippines that only one "Manila galleon" carrying local products sailed annually from the islands to Spain.

In 1580 Spain annexed Portugal. This event motivated the Dutch, who were in revolt against Spain, to expand their anti-Spanish activities to include attacks on Portuguese outposts and commercial interests. When the Spanish Armada that set out to conquer England was destroyed by a storm in 1588, the era of Portuguese and Spanish naval supremacy ended. By the time Portugal recovered its independence in 1640, its Asian commercial empire had all but collapsed and could never be revived.

Dutch and English Empires

During the seventeenth century the Portuguese were supplanted in much of Asia by the Dutch and English. The Dutch first appeared in Southeast Asia in the late sixteenth century. Needing money to support their war of independence from Spain, they attacked the Spanish-Portuguese trading posts whenever possible and traded with Asians wherever they could. An early example of commercial espionage occurred in 1595, when a Dutchman who had spent some years in service of the Portuguese in Goa and other parts of Asia published a manual on sailing to the eastern seas. Armed with this "inside" information, a Dutch expedition immediately set sail for Southeast Asia. It was welcomed by some local rulers who wanted assistance in ousting the unpopular Portuguese. Some Muslim rulers were happy to conclude treaties with the Dutch for the additional reason that unlike the Portuguese, the Dutch had no interest in converting local peoples to Christianity.

How the Dutch Eliminated the English from the East Indies

[Through three treaties, concluded in] 1613, 1615, and 1619 . . . it was agreed, that in regard of the great blood-shed and cost, pretended to be bestowed by the Hollanders, in winning of the trade of the Iles of the Molluccos, Banda, and Amboyna, from the Spaniards and Portugals, and in building of Forts for the continual securing of the same, the said Hollanders therefore should enjoy two thirds parts of that trade, and the English the other third; and the charges of the Forts to be maintained by taxes and impositions, to be levied upon the merchandise. Wherefore, in consequence of this agreement, the English East India Company planted certain factories for their share of this trade, some at Molluccos, some at Banda, and some at Amboyna. . . .

Upon these islands of Amboyna, and the point of Seran, the Hollanders have four Forts; the chief . . . at Amboyna [with] . . . four bulwarks . . . upon each of which six great pieces of ordnance mounted, most of them of brass. The one side of this castle is washed by the sea, and the other is divided from the land with a ditch of four or five fathoms broad, very deep, and ever filled with the sea. The garrison of this Castle consists of about two hundred Dutch soldiers, and a company of free burgers. . . . The English lived, not in the Castle, but under the protection thereof, in a house of their own in the town; holding themselves safe, as well in respect of the ancient bonds of amity between both nations. . . . They continued here for some two years, conversing and trading together with the Hollanders, by virtue of the said treaties. . . .

[On the] fifteenth of February, 1622 . . . they [the Dutch] sent for Captain Towerson, and the rest of the English that were in the town, to come to speak with the governor of the Castle: they all went. . . . Being come to the governor, he told Captain Towerson, that he himself and others of his nation were accused of a conspiracy to surprise the Castle, and therefore, until further trial, were to remain prisoners. Instantly they . . . took the merchandise of the English Company . . . and seized all the chests, boxes, books, writings, and other things in the English house. . . . The same day also the Governor sent to the two other Factories in the same island, to apprehend the rest of the English there. . . .

[All prisoners were tortured and condemned to death] all protesting their innocence. . . . [Despite] the manifold testimonies of their innocence by their own writings before their death, devout and deep protestations at their death. . . . At the instant of the execution, there arose a great darkness, with a sudden and violent gust of wind and tempest; whereby two of the Dutch ships, riding in the harbour, were driven from their anchors, and with great labour and difficulty saved from the rocks. . . . Forthwith also fell a new sickness at Amboyna, which swept away about a thousand people, Dutch and Amboyners: in the space wherein, there usually died not above thirty at other seasons. . . . These signs were by the Amboyners interpreted as a token of the wrath of God for this barbarous tyranny of the Hollanders.*

This is a survivor's account of the Dutch massacre of English traders at Amboyna in 1622. It shows the cut-throat nature of Anglo-Dutch trade rivalry in the East Indies. Unable to retaliate, the English withdrew from trading in the East Indies, conceding a monopoly to the Dutch.

*Samuel Purchas, Hakluytus Posthumus or Purchas His Pilgrimes, vol. 10 (Glasgow: MacLehose and Sons, 1905), pp. 508, 510, 516–517.

These developments brought a lucrative trade to Dutch merchants. Between 1595 and 1601, sixty-five Dutch ships sailed for the East Indies under various commercial companies. In 1602, the newly formed Dutch government granted a charter to the United Dutch East India Company and gave it monopoly rights to trade, make treaties, and establish forts in lands bordering the Indian and Pacific Oceans. With capital of 6.5 million guilders, this company was the largest commercial enterprise to date in the world.

Stocks sold to private shareholders soon soared in price as enormous profits poured in. Dividends averaged 37 percent annually, and in some years went as high as 75 percent.

To monopolize the spice trade, the Dutch launched a systematic war of attrition against the Portuguese, which culminated in the siege and fall of the Portuguese stronghold of Malacca in 1640. Portuguese commerce in Asia, long since in decline, would be miniscule from now on. A similar fate had earlier befallen the English in Southeast Asia. Beginning in 1600, the English East India Company had also sought a share in the lucrative spice trade of the East Indies. Initially, when they were both interlopers, the English and Dutch had cooperated against the Portuguese, but as Portuguese power waned, the two newly emerging commercial powers became bitter rivals. The massacre of the entire staff of an English trading post by the Dutch in 1623 ended English trade in the East Indies. In 1658 the Dutch expelled the Portuguese from Ceylon, a valuable way station and the sole producer of cinnamon. With the capture of Ceylon, the Netherlands gained control of the entire lucrative spice trade from Asia to Europe—a control they would maintain for the next century and a half.

The Dutch Asian administrative and governing headquarters were located at Batavia (present-day Jakarta), a port on the northwestern coast of the island of Java. Batavia was an entrepôt of intra-Asian trade from Japan to Persia and the clearinghouse of Asian goods shipped by the Dutch to Europe. The port was guarded by a great fortress, manned by 1,200 Dutch soldiers and Japanese mercenaries. The governor-general and an advisory council, appointed by the East India Company and only indirectly responsible to the Dutch government, supervised trade, defense, and administration.

Like the Portuguese before them, the Dutch in the seventeenth century were mainly interested in trade and not colonization or direct territorial control. Dutch ships, now the best in the world, patrolled the sea lanes and controlled strategically important ports. They eliminated rivals, exacted a tariff on all traffic, and maintained the Dutch monopoly on the spices that all Europeans sought. They intervened in local wars to ensure that friendly rulers stayed in power and acquired territory only when trade demanded territorial control.

Interestingly, the Dutch in Batavia and other ports in Asia tried to maintain their accustomed northern European mode of life even in the tropical climate: they wore heavy woolen clothes, seldom bathed, lived in Dutch-style houses with windows tightly closed, ate heavy European meals, and drank large quantities of gin, beer, and wine. Many died prematurely. Few bothered to learn the native languages and instead learned a form of debased Portuguese that remained the international trading language of Southeast Asia for a long time. Because few women came from the Netherlands to the East Indies, many Dutch men formed unions with local women. In fact, a shortage of Dutch immigrants of either sex led the company to encourage Chinese and Japanese immigrants; the business acumen of Chinese merchants and the fighting qualities of Japanese samurai were especially appreciated. New Japanese laws cut off fresh supplies of Japanese immigrants in the early seventeenth century, but a large influx of southern Chinese refugees fleeing the Manchu conquest of China in the late seventeenth century spurred the economic development of Java. The Netherlands also established an outpost on Tai-

An Oppressive Agricultural Policy

The coffee-plant, which is only known on Java by its European appellation, and its intimate connexion with European despotism, was first introduced by the Dutch early in the eighteenth century, and has since formed one of the articles of their exclusive monopoly. The labor by which it is planted, and its produce collected, is included among the oppressions of forced services of the natives, and the delivery of it into the government stores, among the forced deliveries at inadequate rates ... [after 1809] this shrub usurped the soil destined for yielding the subsistence of the people, every other kind of cultivation was made subservient to it, and the withering effects of a government monopoly extended their influence indiscriminately throughout every province of the island.

In the Sunda districts, each family was obliged to take care of one thousand coffee plants; and in the eastern districts, where new and extensive plantations were now to be formed, on soils and in situations in many instances by no means favourable to the cultivation, five hundred plants was the prescribed allotment. No negligence could be practised in the execution of this duty: the whole operations of planting, cleaning, and collecting, continued to be conducted under the immediate superintendance of European officers, who selected the spot on which new gardens were to be laid out, took care that they were preserved from weeds and rank grass, and received the produce into store when gathered. ...

A government of colonial monopolists, eager only for profit, and heedless of the sources from which it was derived, sometimes subjected its native subjects to distresses and privations, the recital of which would shock the ear of humanity. Suffice it to say, that the coffee culture in the Sunda districts has sometimes been so severely exacted, that together with the other constant and heavy demands made by the European authority on the labour of the country, they deprived the unfortunate peasants of the time necessary to rear food for their support. Many have thus perished by famine, while others have fled to the crags of the mountains, where raising a scanty subsistence in patches of gaga, or oftener dependent for it upon the roots of the forest, they congratulated themselves on their escape from the reach of their oppressors. Many of these people, with their descendants, remain in these haunts to the present time: in their annual migrations from hill to hill, they frequently pass over the richest lands, which still remain uncultivated and invite their return; but they prefer their wild independence and precarious subsistence, to the horrors of being again subjected to forced services and forced deliveries at inadequate rates.*

This account of the forced delivery of coffee to the Dutch East India Company on Java is a scathing indictment of the cruelty of a colonial administration that was motivated purely by profit. During his short tenure as Lieutenant Governor of Java under a British administration, Sir Stamford Raffles, the author of this account, reformed some of the abuses of Dutch rule.

*Thomas S. Raffles, The History of Java, vol. 1 (1817); reprint ed. by John Bastin (Kuala Lumpur: Oxford University Press, 1965), pp. 125, 129–130.

wan, ousting the Portuguese garrison, and held it until they were expelled in the midseventeenth century by China. Local peoples on southern Taiwan respect the geckos (a tropical lizard), because, as the story goes, they alerted Chinese forces of a Dutch night attack by squawking loudly.

By the late seventeenth century, British power had overtaken the Dutch. Nevertheless, Dutch control continued in Java, where they established plantations to grow exportoriented commercial crops; the most important were coffee (introduced from Arabia), sugarcane (from China), indigo (for dye making), and, later, tea (also from China). The Netherlands either established direct rule or began to exert strong political supervision over local rulers to ensure the success of the plantations. Many local rulers saw mutual benefits to be derived from plantations and willingly joined forces with the Dutch authorities to exploit the peasants, sometimes requiring them to grow cash crops rather than the food they needed, as shown by Raffles's account quoted in the preceding box.

Anglo-Dutch colonial rivalry continued throughout the eighteenth century. Together with France, the Netherlands fought against Great Britain during the American War of Independence. Although Britain lost its North American colonies, it emerged from the war as the dominant naval power, with overseas interests that shifted from North America to Asia. In 1793, war broke out between revolutionary France and its subordinate ally, the Netherlands, against Britain and several other European powers. To deprive France of the benefits of the Dutch Empire, Britain seized Dutch outposts and colonies throughout the world: the Cape of Good Hope and Malacca in 1795, Ceylon in 1796, and finally Java in 1811. Sir Stamford Raffles, a rising young administrator of the British East India Company, ruled Java and other Dutch possessions in the East Indies between 1811 and 1816 and instituted many liberal reforms, including the ending of forced delivery of cash crops. A keen amateur antiquarian, Raffles commissioned the first archaeological survey of Borobodur.

To Raffles's intense chagrin, the valuable former Dutch possessions in the East Indies were returned to the Netherlands in 1816 in the territorial settlement that ended the Napoleonic Wars. To compensate, Raffles purchased Singapore for Britain from a Malay prince in 1819. Situated at the southern extremity of the Malay Peninsula, Singapore, then a fishing village, possessed a wonderful deep-water port and was strategically located to control trade between the Indian and Pacific Oceans. Under British rule, it attracted many Chinese settlers, and as a free port it became a thriving entrepôt of international trade, supplanting Malacca. It also became a major British naval base.

From Singapore, Britain developed control over Malaya, but except for a part of the island of Borneo it stayed clear of island Southeast Asia. With its huge naval base in Singapore, Britain controlled the eastern approaches to the Indian Ocean and thus maintained its preeminent trading position in East Asia.

Life in Southeast Asia

Life varied so much in the diverse region that few generalizations are possible. Most people were subsistence farmers; fishing produced food that supplemented the diet. A benign tropical climate made living relatively easy and clothing uncomplicated. Most people wore a blouse and, below the waist, a sarong or a wrap, made of locally woven or traded cotton or silk cloths. Locally made tie dyed and intricately woven cloths, called *ikat,* were also made into the simply tailored blouses and sarongs. Housing was also simple; most houses had open sides to allow ventilation, and were raised on stilts to avoid insects and flooding.

Many island Southeast Asians were unwilling to work under the onerous conditions imposed by European commercial farming. Some ran away from the exactions of European and local rulers, causing labor shortages. To rectify the problem, the British encouraged Chinese and Indians to immigrate to their colonies. Accustomed to a more rigorous and competitive life, Chinese and Indian immigrants were willing to endure the discipline of plantation farming or mining. Many also had good business acumen, and thus rose to dominate commerce throughout the region.

While most Filipinos became Roman Catholics, other Southeast Asians remained Buddhists and Muslims, with a small pocket of Hindus on Bali in the East Indies. Chinese immigrants remained Buddhists and Confucians, while most Indian immigrants were Hindus. The different religious groups tended to live in separate communities, the life of each dictated by its religious and social practices.

The Moghul Dynasty

The emperor [Akbar] came to Fatehpur. There he used to spend much time in the Hall of Worship in the company of [Muslim] learned men and shaikhs . . . continually occupied in discussing questions of religion. . . . The learned men used to draw the sword of the tongue on the battlefield of mutual contradiction and opposition, and the antagonism of the sects reached such a pitch that they would call one another fools and heretics. . . .

[Then he had] Samanas [Hindu or Buddhist ascetics] and Brahmans . . . [bring] forward proofs, based on reason and additional testimony, for the truth of their own, and the fallacy of our religion, and inculcated their doctrine with such firmness and assurance that they affirmed mere imaginations as though they were self-evident facts. . . . [They also] instructed His Majesty in the secrets and legends of Hinduism, in the manner of worshipping idols, the fire, the sun and stars, and of revering the chief gods of these unbelievers, such as Brahma. . . .

Sometimes . . . His Majesty listened the whole night to Shaikh Taj ud-din's Sufic obscenities and follies. The shaikh, since he did not in any great degree feel himself bound by the injunctions of the law, introduced arguments concerning the unity of existence, such as idle Sufis discuss, and which eventually led to license and open heresy. . . .

Learned monks also from Europe, who are called Padre *. . . brought the Gospel, and advanced proof of the Trinity. His Majesty firmly believed in the truth of the Christian religion. . . .*

Fire worshippers also came from Nousari in Gujarat, proclaimed the religion of Zarathustra as the true one, and declared reverence to fire to be superior to every other kind of worship. They also attracted the emperor's regard, and taught him the peculiar terms, the ordinances, the rites and ceremonies of [Zoroastrianism].*

*William T. de Bary, ed., *Sources of Indian Tradition,* vol. 1 (New York: Columbia University Press, 1958), pp. 432–434.

Emperor Akbar, third ruler of the Moghul dynasty, was raised as a Sunni Muslim. Open-minded on religious matters, he summoned teachers of other religions, including Hindus, Buddhists, Jains, Christians, and Zoroastrians, to the Hall of Worship in his new capital city, Fatehpur Sikri, to discuss and debate their religious teachings. Akbar eventually proclaimed a Divine Faith, based on what he considered the best of Islam and Hinduism, but did not enforce it among his subjects. Akbar's radical religious ideas scandalized orthodox Muslims like Bada'muni, the author of the passage quoted above.

The Moghul dynasty (1524–1857) ruled most of India efficiently in the sixteenth and seventeenth centuries and nominally until 1857. It is called the Moghul, or Mughal, a corruption of Mongol, because the Moghuls came from central Asia and were descended from Timurlane, and more remotely from Genghis Khan. Like the Mongols, they were expert horsemen and professional raiders, adventurers, and conquerors. Babur, founder of the Moghul dynasty, had reputedly been inspired to conquer India from stories he had heard about Timurlane's exploits in that land.

Many surviving documents show that the Moghul dynasty is important for several reasons. It unified India for the first time since Harsha nearly 1,000 years earlier, and its administrative framework became the basis of government for the British and later for independent India. The dynasty provided several capable rulers who were lavish patrons of art, sponsoring major monuments and works of art. Akbar, the greatest Moghul emperor, achieved a degree of religious reconciliation between Hindus and Muslims; in contrast, earlier Muslim conquerors had typically opposed Hinduism and pursued a divisive religious policy.

Rise and Fall of Moghul Rule

India was divided and turbulent in the early sixteenth century. North India and the Deccan were ruled by Muslim dynasties, mostly of Afghan origin. In Rajasthan in the west, Rajput nobles (Hindus and professional warriors) battled one another and the Muslims. Hindu dynasties controlled South India. Central Asia, too, had been in chaos since Timurlane's death in 1404, and had been the battleground between his numerous descendants.

The founder of the Moghul dynasty was born in 1483, the son of the ruler of a small central Asian state called Ferghana, north of the Hindu Kush Mountains. He was named Babur, which means panther in Turkish. A great deal is known about him because of details he provides in his *Memoirs,* a book of considerable literary merit. Only eleven when he inherited a very shaky throne following his father's death, Babur struggled for the next twelve years against many dangers.

In 1504 Babur was driven out of central Asia. He then seized the throne at Kabul in Afghanistan, where he planned to build his fortune in India. In 1524 he set out for India with 12,000 soldiers and camp followers. Two years later he met the Afghan king of Delhi at the Battle of Panipat, the historic battleground in the gap between the mountains and desert fifty miles north of Delhi, where the fate of India had already been decided more than once. Although outnumbered ten to one, Babur had cannons and guns (acquired from the Ottomans) that his adversaries did not have. The battle ended with the enemy in rout and the Afghan king dead. Babur entered Delhi and Agra and was proclaimed emperor of Hindustan. A prize of the battle was the Koh-i-nor (mountain of light) diamond, one of the world's largest and now part of the British crown jewel collection.

Babur had a hard time persuading some of his followers to remain in India through the torrid North Indian summer instead of returning to Kabul with the loot. To alleviate the effects of the fierce heat, he immediately laid out gardens and fountains and planted trees in Delhi and Agra. His successors continued to do so and have left a legacy of beautiful Moghul gardens in many North Indian cities. Seeking to enlarge his domains,

Babur subdued some of the Rajputs and was beginning to create administrative offices when he died suddenly in 1530.

Humayun (reigned 1530–1556) succeeded his father, but possessed none of Babur's abilities; he drank to excess and was addicted to opium. As a result Humayun lost most of his patrimony to the Afghans, and ten years after inheriting the throne, had been reduced to a fugitive. It was up to his son Akbar (reigned 1556–1605), who had many of the great qualities of his grandfather, to turn the family's fortunes around.

Partly because his youth was spent in wandering and adversity, Akbar never learned to read. But he had a keen intellect and inquiring mind; he collected an extensive library of books in several languages and during his spare moments had others read books to him. Fatherless at thirteen, he took up the immense responsibility of recovering his family's fortunes. In 1557 he met the Afghan king at the Second Battle of Panipat. The Afghans had a huge army with 1,500 war elephants, but their forces dissolved in confusion when their leader became injured. After this victory Akbar was able to regain Delhi, Agra, and the rest of Hindustan and then reconquer Afghanistan. He devoted the remaining years of his reign until his death in 1605 to building a stable administration.

Europeans, who began arriving in India during the early Moghul dynasty, called its rulers the Great Moghuls. This title is an apt description, because until the end of the seventeenth century most Moghul rulers were talented men. Akbar was succeeded by his son Jahangir (reigned 1605–1627), also a good ruler. Jahangir's son, Shah Jahan (reigned 1627–1657), is best remembered for building the Taj Mahal, a mausoleum for his favorite wife, Mumtaz Mahal, which remains an architectural wonder of the world. But Shah Jahan lived too long for some of his many sons' ambitions. One of them, Aurengzeb, revolted in 1657, seized the throne, and proclaimed himself emperor. In action reminiscent of the Ottoman sultans, Aurengzeb (reigned 1659–1707) then killed his brothers. He imprisoned his father in a suite of rooms in the palace with a view of the Taj Mahal and later buried him beside his mother. Shah Jahan had planned to build another mausoleum for himself beside that for his wife. The civil war and fratricide that brought Aurengzeb to power were but one instance of the bloody politics of the Moghul royal family, where sons often revolted against fathers and family members murdered each other for possession of the throne.

Although Aurengzeb was a capable ruler, his strictly pro-Muslim and anti-Hindu religious policy put the clock back on the development of better relations between the two religious groups. He surrounded himself with religious bigots, and harshly persecuted Hindus. He restored discriminatory and humiliating taxes on Hindus and razed many of their temples, thus re-igniting bad relations between members of the two faiths. The Hindus were provoked to revolt, and the ensuing wars permanently weakened the empire. Wars of succession plagued his heirs. In 1739 the Persians invaded and took Afghanistan, and even captured and looted Delhi, taking with them the fabled jewel-encrusted peacock throne of the Moghuls.

The Moghul Empire lost all effective power after 1760. North India was invaded by Afghans, and over much of the subcontinent Hindus, Muslims, and Sikhs (a new religious group begun in India in the sixteenth century) contended for control. Indians call the century after 1760 the Great Anarchy or Time of Troubles. Order was only restored with the consolidation of British power. Some Indians who opposed British rule during the Indian Mutiny in 1857 used the figurehead Moghul then reigning in Delhi as a symbol for their rebellion. When Great Britain suppressed the mutiny, it deposed the Moghul emperor, ending the dynastic era of Indian history.

Moghul Absolutism

Akbar created an absolute government that endured for two centuries, an accomplishment that made him one of the great rulers of Indian history. In theory the Moghul emperor's power was unlimited; his word was law and he commanded the military directly. As caliph (secular ruler of a Muslim state), his only restraints were to obey the Qur'an and Islamic tradition. The early Moghul emperors exercised their power wisely and were dedicated to improving the lives of their subjects.

Because of the foreign origins of the dynasty, a large portion of the bureaucracy and military that maintained the Moghul government was foreign also, as had been true of the earlier Yuan Mongol Empire of China and the il-khanate that ruled Persia. Maintaining military power was essential, so every official had to be enrolled in the military. The state maintained a large army, partly commanded by the emperor himself. Vassal chiefs, such as the Rajputs, provided supplemental levies. Aside from ships to keep coastal areas free of pirates, the Moghuls had no navy. Even after Akbar's reforms opened public service careers to Hindus, the Moghul bureaucracy remained tilted against indigenous Indians. Seventy percent of the high imperial officers were Persians and central Asians, the remainder equally divided between Indian Muslims and Hindus. However, these foreigners were expected to remain in India and could not take their wealth out of the country. In later times the proportion of Indians increased.

The keystone of Akbar's statesmanship was his conciliation of his Hindu subjects. Like many other successful rulers, Akbar was a good listener, chose his advisors based on ability, took advice on its merit, and paid attention to detail. He often put on disguises and mixed with the people to learn their points of view. Akbar married Hindu Rajput princesses, one of whom was the mother of his successor, raised many Hindus to positions of power, and abolished the special taxes levied on them. He also encouraged members of his court and other high-ranking Muslims to marry Hindus. However, these intermarriages did not produce genuine cultural fusion because Hindu women were merely transferred to Muslim households, whereas Muslim women seldom married Hindu men. As before, leaders of the various religious communities administered civil laws according to the tenets of their respective religions—Islam, Hinduism, or one of the other religions. The *ulema*, or Muslim theologians, interpreted Islamic civil and criminal law.

The principal functions of the Moghul government were the collection of taxes, maintenance of order, enforcement of the law, building and maintenance of roads and bridges, and encouragement of cultural life by court patronage. It did not concern itself with irrigation works and water conservancy or with relief for those in distress. Nor did the government remit taxes even during famines, which caused enormous hardships.

During the widespread famines of 1594–1598 and 1630–1632, desperate people even resorted to cannibalism.

Since the Moghul emperor was the sole source of power, the whole government moved with him wherever he traveled. According to custom, the emperor presented himself before the public at least once daily, usually at sunrise. He spent most of the morning holding public audience, receiving petitions, and giving orders. Other business was conducted in a more confidential manner with his ministers and advisors.

The emperor supervised a centralized administration with ministers who controlled the secretariat and other government bureaus. Much of the imperial service was borrowed from Persia, including the ranking system of thirty-two grades. The official language was Persian. Because good communications were vital to effective government, the early Moghuls built and maintained a system of roads that linked parts of the empire to the two capitals, Delhi and Agra. Rest houses along the roads provided for the needs of people on government business and the postal service.

As in the Ottoman, Manchu, and Russian Empires, land under direct imperial rule was divided into provinces, districts, and subdistricts down to the village. The efficient revenue system devised by the early Moghuls persisted to British times. For most Indians the payment of land taxes was their main contact with the government; custom duties, import and transit dues, and tolls on domestic trade provided minor sources of revenue. A detailed land register, including the type of crops grown, was compiled under Akbar and became the basis of taxation, which was usually set at a third of the gross product. In addition to land taxes imposed on the centrally governed parts of the empire, a tribute was levied on the territories ruled by local princes, such as the lands under the Rajputs. The bulk of tax revenues went to the imperial treasury. After paying for the military and bureaucracy, the remaining funds were spent on erecting imposing buildings, entertainment, and luxurious living by the rulers.

Akbar insisted on paying official salaries in cash, so that all revenue went to the central treasury, which then disbursed all payments. As administrative efficiency deteriorated under later rulers, officials came to be assigned the revenues from various lands in lieu of salaries. Here again, the Moghuls and the Ottomans followed similar patterns.

Whereas the divided state of India prior to Moghul rule produced chaotic coinage systems, Akbar centralized the mint and struck gold, silver, and copper coins. In purity of metal, constancy of weight, and artistic merit, they were in general superior to coins struck by European rulers of the same era. Most of the gold and silver used for coinage came from the Americas and Africa to pay for Indian goods desired by Europeans.

Society and Economy under the Moghuls

Much is known about the lives of Moghul emperors and aristocrats from their own memoirs and from accounts by European ambassadors, merchants, and missionaries. The emperors lived and entertained lavishly, supported by over a hundred offices and workshops that looked after their boats, horses, elephants, dogs, and other animals, and made many luxury items for their households. The imperial harem reputedly had as many as 5,000 women, each with a separate apartment and an allowance. The women

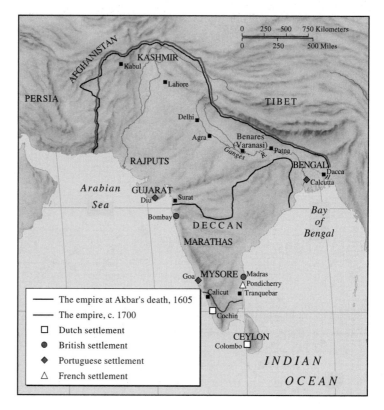

Map 10.2 The Moghul Empire. The seventeenth century was the great age of the Moghul Empire. Under talented rulers and able generals, the empire expanded until it included all of the Indian subcontinent except for Cape Comorin in the extreme south, as well as part of present-day Afghanistan. Moghul power and wealth became legendary in Europe.

were looked after by eunuchs and protected by female guards. A number of the ladies of the imperial family—consorts, mothers, sisters, and daughters—managed their own estates, painted, wrote poetry, and patronized the arts. After Akbar's reign a unique problem confronted the sisters and daughters of the emperors. Because civil wars and revolts killed many of the males of the imperial clan, and men outside the imperial clan were considered beneath the princesses for marriage, few suitable husbands could be found and many of the princesses did not marry.

Several Moghul queens and princesses influenced state affairs; the most powerful was Persian-born Nur Jahan, the daughter of a courtier. She married a Persian nobleman at seventeen and had a daughter by him. Later her husband rebelled against Emperor Jahangir and was killed. She was brought to court, where the emperor became infatuated with her and made her his principal wife. Nur Jahan was noted for her beauty, intellect, and patronage of the arts. She achieved great influence over her husband, and successfully schemed to influence the succession, marrying her daughter to one of her husband's sons and a niece (Mumtaz Mahal) to another (his successor Shah Jahan).

Moghuls traveled in great style and liked to hunt along the way, as the following description of Shah Jahan's trip in 1633 illustrates:

A city of canvas, 100,000 horsemen, 50,000 men on foot, as many functionaries, slaves, and eunuchs, the whole retinue of the Queens, Princesses, and favourites escorting them. The elephants sniffed the snow of the passes. At night, in front of the master's pavilion, a giant beacon signalled the sovereign will that moved this tumultuous mass, the soul of the horde. They traveled by short stages. There were two camps, so that one was always pitched on the arrival of the train. On the road they hunted the wild boar, the tiger, the lion even . . . by means of nets, of armies of beaters, or of a donkey drunk with opium that served as a bait.

Such expeditions resembled military campaigns, and are similar to the arena "hunts" staged by the Roman emperor Commodus. Beaters enclosed a huge tract of land and drove the animals into ever-smaller areas for the slaughter. Once, in the seventh year of his reign, Jahangir hunted for eighty consecutive days. At age forty-seven he had a scribe list all the animals he had personally killed; the number totaled 17,167. The roundups also captured primitive jungle-dwelling people, who were sold as slaves. Other favored sports were polo, pigeon flying, and wrestling. Like the Romans, the Moghuls also loved to watch animal combat, the favorite being elephant fighting. Popular indoor games included cards and chess. Akbar had a large chess board of marble squares laid out on a palace floor and used dancing girls as chess pieces.

Like the ancient Macedonian rulers and their Mongol ancestors, many Moghul rulers and noblemen drank strong alcoholic spirits, sometimes mixed with hemp and opium. Babur's *Memoirs* reveal how he loved to lie in the shade of trees in a state of intoxication with his boon companions. Several Moghul princes died young of alcohol-related diseases. Aurengzeb differed from most of his relatives by strictly observing the Islamic prohibition against alcohol.

Although nobles imitated the ruling house in lavish living and entertaining, ordinary people, Hindus and Muslims alike, rarely engaged in heavy drinking. Their lives were enlivened by special events such as weddings, fairs, and religious celebrations. Hindus enjoyed pilgrimages to sacred shrines, which, since Akbar's reign, did not require payment of a special tax. He abolished the levy on the ground that no one should be taxed for worshiping God, although some of his officials lamented the loss of revenue from its abolition. Muslims made the *hajj*, or pilgrimage, to Mecca, by sea in large sailing vessels, and the needy often received imperial financial assistance for their trip. For fear of revolts during his absence, no emperor undertook the pilgrimage. Rulers sometimes got rid of troublesome ministers by sending them to Mecca.

A small middle class of merchants worked hard and lived frugally. Most commerce was in Hindu hands. Muslims who came to India with the Moghuls considered themselves the ruling class and disdained commerce. The Islamic rule against charging interest for loans also discouraged Muslims from trading.

Tradition prevailed in the villages, and agriculture followed its age-old pattern, relying on the monsoon rains. Most farmers engaged in subsistence agriculture and crafts, but commercial crops such as cotton, mulberry trees (for silkworms), sugarcane, spices, and indigo (for dyeing textiles) increased in importance due to domestic and foreign demand. Although most farmers were free, some became serfs when they could not repay their debts. Most artisans were poor, working under contract. The economic condition of most Indians deteriorated during the late Moghul period.

Slavery was permitted under both Hindu and Muslim law. Some crimes were punished by enslavement of the perpetrator. Debtors could be enslaved until they worked off their debt, and thus resembled indentured servants. Some poor parents sold their children into slavery. Other slaves were captured tribal people, who were looked upon as being beyond the pale of civilization. A regular slave trade brought additional slaves from East Africa. Most slaves performed domestic duties.

Specialized artisans were dependent upon the patronage of the emperor and the nobles. Foreigners with special skills were welcomed and came from many Asian and European lands; Persians were most especially skilled in rug making, which became an important industry in India and remains so to the present. India was best known for cotton textiles, and the Western names of many types of cotton cloth, such as calico, dungaree, muslin, madras, and cambric were of Indian origin. European travelers in Moghul India marveled that every part of India excelled in some kind of textile making, including an extensive silk industry; one traveler estimated that the province of Bengal alone produced 2.5 million pounds of silk, mostly for local consumption, but also for export. Markets for Indian cotton cloths ranged from Southeast Asia to Arabia, east Africa and Egypt, and Europe. In addition, India exported pepper, indigo, opium and other drugs, saltpeter for gunpowder, and various luxury handicrafts. Indians imported horses from central Asia, porcelain from China, bullion and costly knickknacks from Europe, and other luxuries such as coral, amber, and gems. After about 1620, Indians began to cultivate tobacco and took up smoking, both the crop and the habit introduced by Europeans. Many great cities thrived on trade. Unlike the Safavids in Persia, the Moghuls did not play an active role in developing commerce and did not rely on its taxation as a key source of revenue.

Rulers and nobles took pride in patronizing learning and establishing or endowing schools, usually associated with mosques, where boys and sometimes girls received an elementary education. Sons of Hindu farmers and craftsmen received a rough primary education given by local brahmans in vernacular languages. Learned men called *pandits* (compare the English word *pundit*) taught the sons of the upper castes in Sanskrit such subjects as logic, law, and grammar. Daughters of the imperial and noble families were privately educated; some, like men, were patrons of the arts, while others wrote poetry and prose, though mostly anonymously.

The condition of women varied, depending on religion and class, but generally it deteriorated during this era. The Islamic *purdah* kept Muslim women secluded or heavily veiled in public. While Hinduism did not require the veiling of women, the practice became common among high-caste Hindu women in North India. Muslim law allowed daughters to inherit property, but Hindu law generally forbade daughters from inheriting landed property to prevent the transferring of the joint family's land to another family. In both communities a daughter joined her husband's family upon marriage. Early arranged marriages were common, especially for girls who were expected to be virgins at marriage and chaste afterward. Hindu parents also had to provide dowries for daughters. Except for aristocrats, most Hindus were monogamous; in contrast, Muslim men could have several wives and concubines. Divorces were almost unknown among Hindus but were allowed among Muslims. Muslim widows were allowed to remarry, but Hindu widows were discouraged from remarrying, and the practice of *suttee* (or *sati,* the suicide of a widow on her husband's funeral pyre) was encouraged among high castes in certain communities, for example, the Rajputs. Members of both faiths relied on astrology for guidance before making important decisions such as marriage.

Diverse and Divisive Religions

The religious situation in Moghul India was complex. More than three-fourths of Moghul subjects were Hindus. Hindus lived by caste rules and tended to look at Muslims and followers of other religions as members of castes. The ranks of the minority Muslims were continually swelled by immigrants from Persia and central Asia and by Hindu converts, mostly from lower castes; these converts tended to retain their former ways of living. In time Hindus and Muslims shared many tastes and habits.

Most Indian Muslims were Sunnis and were concentrated in the northwest and along the western coast of the Indian subcontinent, where Arab traders had settled and intermarried with Hindus. However, most immigrants from Persia were Shi'i Muslims. There were also Muslims in northeastern India and scattered throughout the subcontinent. Many Moghul rulers were eclectic in their religious practices. Akbar was religiously tolerant. He allowed his Hindu wives their own places of worship in the palace, and he also forbade the destruction and desecration of Hindu temples and allowed new ones to be built. For his personal and political needs, Akbar synthesized what he thought were the best elements of Hinduism and Islam and proclaimed a state religion called Divine Faith, with himself as its chief interpreter and head.

Divine Faith taught people to pursue virtue. From Islam, it borrowed the idea of one god and no priesthood, but it rejected the Muslim belief in a last judgment in favor of the Hindu idea of the transmigration of souls. It also borrowed many Hindu ceremonies. This syncretic religion failed to gain the support of the people, but many Hindus honored Akbar for the generosity of his intentions. Conversely, many orthodox Muslims bitterly resented his religious ideas and regarded his Divine Faith as a heresy. Like Akhenaton's religious innovations in ancient Egypt, Divine Faith did not survive its founder. Aurengzeb ended Moghul religious tolerance and persecuted Hindus.

Sikhism, another religion that began during the early sixteenth century, also stemmed from the desire to find common ground between Hinduism and Islam. Guru Nanak (1469–1538), founder of Sikhism, taught about the one loving god, whom he called the True Name, did not care about one's caste or creed, but demanded goodness and charity. He rejected asceticism, an established clergy, and vegetarianism, commanding Sikhs (disciples) to live healthy, clean lives. Nanak wrote poems and hymns that were later collected in the Granth, the sacred book of Sikhism, which is honored in the Golden Temple, a holy shrine in the city of Amritsar.

Nanak was followed by ten gurus. The first gurus won the respect of the Moghul emperors by their saintly lives. The fifth guru, Arjan (1581–1606), backed the losing

A Moghul Pleasure Garden

One of the great defects of Hindustan being its lack of running-waters, it kept coming to my mind that waters should be made to flow by means of wheels erected wherever I might settle down, also that grounds should be laid out in an orderly and symmetrical way. With this object in view, we crossed the Jun-water to look at garden-grounds a few days after entering Agra. These grounds were so bad and unattractive that we traversed them with a hundred disgusts and repulsions. So ugly and displeasing were they, that the idea of making a char-bagh in them passed from my mind, but needs must! as there was no other land near Agra that same ground was taken in hand a few days later.

The beginning was made with the large well from which water comes from the hot-bath, and also with the piece of ground where the tamarind-trees and the octagonal tank now are.... Then in that charmless and disorderly Hind, plots of garden were seen laid out with order and symmetry, with suitable borders and parterres in every corner, and in every border rose and narcissus in perfect arrangement.*

Not much remains of Babur's Persian gardens in Agra. When he died, his remains were taken to Kabul, via a road he had ordered built and planted with shade trees (sections of which remain). Humayun's troubles gave him no opportunity to build, but he did plan a noble mausoleum for himself at Delhi that his son completed. It was the model on which the plan of the Taj Mahal was based.

*Memoirs of Babur, trans. A. S. Beveridge (New Delhi: Oriental Book Reprint Corporation, 1979), pp. 531–532.

side in a Moghul war of succession, refused to pay a fine exacted by the winner, Emperor Jahangir, and was tortured and executed. Before his death, Arjan told his followers to arm themselves and organize into a disciplined movement. After this episode relations between the Sikhs and the Moghul government continued to deteriorate, and Sikhs became implacably opposed to Islam. Arjan's successors instilled in Sikhs a belief that they were an elect group and organized them into a fighting brotherhood with an initiation and a distinctive dress. Most early Sikhs were from Punjab in northern India and some were converts from the Hindu kshatriya (warrior) caste, which made their transition into warriors an easy one. Thus Sikhism failed to reconcile Hinduism and Islam and has continued as a separate religion. Sikhs and Hindus were on amicable terms and often intermarried.

Artistic Fusion in Architecture and Painting

Early Moghul rulers were patrons and connoisseurs of the arts and lavish builders. They attracted artists and artisans from many lands, who worked alongside their Indian counterparts. The interactions of these artists produced a sophisticated common culture and a new style called Indo-Islamic that is a fusion of many elements and traditions.

Akbar and Shah Jahan were the great builders among Moghuls. They left their monuments in the magnificent forts, palaces, and mosques of red sandstone and white marble in the cities of Agra, Delhi, and Fatehpur Sikri. Agra was Akbar's capital city during most of his reign. Starting in 1558, he built a fort and palaces and surrounded them with a massive wall, all made from local red sandstone. Eleven years after the start of his building activities in Agra, Akbar began a new capital at Sikri. As his son Jahangir said in his memoirs:

My revered father, regarding the village of Sikri, my birthplace, as fortunate to himself, made it his capital, and in the course of fourteen or fifteen years the hills and desert, which abounded in beasts of prey, became converted into a magnificent city, comprising numerous gardens, elegant edifices and pavilions, and other places of great attraction and beauty. After the conquest of Gujrat, the village was named Fatehpur (the town of victory).

The fifteen years that Akbar ruled from this "rose-red city" marked the zenith of his reign. Then he resumed his residence in Agra. Except for occasional visits by later emperors, Fatehpur Sikri has remained deserted but intact, protected by the dry climate and the absence of portable treasures.

Moghul rulers built many mausoleums; the most famous was the Taj Mahal, built by Shah Jahan for his favorite wife at Agra. It took 20,000 men seventeen years to complete. Since Akbar's reign artists, architects, and craftsmen from central Asia, Persia, Arabia, and elsewhere had been working in India. With their Indian colleagues, they gradually synthesized their various traditions into an eclectic Moghul style, epitomized in the Taj Mahal. It commemorated the emperor's devotion to his wife and the zenith of Moghul power.

In addition to architecture, the Moghuls left a rich legacy in the visual arts. Moghul painting had its origin in Persia, whose painters had earlier learned their skills from China via the Mongols and the Timurids. Babur encouraged Persian painters to settle in India and commissioned them to paint portraits, documents of state occasions, and landscapes. Indian painters soon assimilated Persian techniques and by Akbar's reign the

© Brian A. Vikander/Corbis

Mausoleum for an Empress. The Taj Mahal, built of white marble and a masterpiece of Indo-Islamic art, was the mausoleum of the beautiful empress Mumtaz Mahal, wife of Shah Jahan. Surrounding the reflecting pool is a Persian formal garden with cypresses, flowering trees, and flower beds.

majority of court painters were Hindus. They fused Sino-Persian and Muslim artistic traditions with the Hindu-Buddhist tradition of India and created two distinctive schools, the Moghul and Rajput.

The Moghul school concentrated on court life and the illuminating of manuscripts, while the Rajput school emphasized scenes from the Indian classics and domestic subjects. Both schools excelled in painting miniatures. The Moghul school reached maturity under Jahangir, a great connoisseur and accomplished critic of painting. He invited Jesuit artists to his court to teach the painting techniques of Italian Renaissance masters. Jahangir said in his *Memoirs*:

> As regards myself, my liking for painting and my practice in judging it have arrived at such a point that when any work is brought before me, either of deceased artists or of the present day, without the names being told me, I say on the spur of the moment that it is the work of such and such a man. And if there be a picture containing many portraits, and each face be the work of a different master, I can discover which face is the work of each.

Calligraphy, or the art of penmanship, which was highly esteemed in China, Persia, the Arab world, and India, was closely associated with Moghul painting. Painters and calligraphers often worked side by side, and, as in Chinese paintings, many pictures had space reserved for calligraphic inscriptions. The art of illuminating manuscripts (similar to the tradition established in medieval European monasteries) also flourished.

Numerous minor arts thrived. Artisans created decorative relief carving on stone or marble and latticework screens to shield ladies from public view and to filter strong light. Those that survive in Agra and Fatehpur Sikri continue to filter the bright light of the hot Indian summer and still give cooling relief. Indian craftsmen who did mosaic work and inlay decoration acquired familiarity with an Italian form of inlay called *pietra dura:* semiprecious and precious stones were cut into thin slivers and imbedded into sockets prepared in the marble to form patterns and pictures. Lapidaries (those who cut and polish gemstones) and jewelers benefited from the Moghul love of pomp and display, for both men and women wore extravagantly rich jewels and clothes. The rich clothes, sumptuous jewels, and lavish furnishings of the Moghul court dazzled early European visitors, and their descriptions gave Europeans visions of India's fabulous wealth. Europeans referred to the emperor as the Great Moghul; the word *mogul* (Anglicized form) entered English as an epithet for a powerful man, though a business entrepreneur rather than a ruler.

The Ming Dynasty

> From time immemorial whenever emperors and kings have ruled over the universe, the Middle Kingdom has always been considered the center of government, from which the emperors and kings rule over the barbarians.
>
> The barbarians are left outside but they are subject to the Middle Kingdom. It is unheard of that barbarian tribes have ever come to rule the universe.*

*Albert Chan, *The Glory and Fall of the Ming Dynasty* (Norman, Okla.: University of Oklahoma Press, 1982), p. 378.

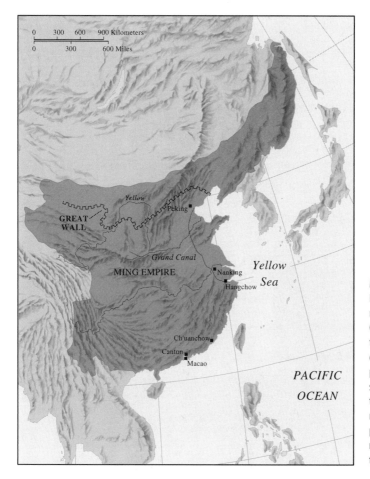

Map 10.3 The Ming Empire. The Ming dynasty ruled over all lands inhabited by Chinese people. Early Ming military campaigns and naval expeditions reestablished Chinese prestige and ensured Chinese suzerainty throughout most of the region. The northern nomads, however, continued to pose a threat, which prompted major reconstructions of sections of the Great Wall.

This ringing statement was the rallying cry of Chu Yuan-chang, founder of the Ming dynasty (1368–1644), who welded together many of the disparate groups that had risen against the tyrannical rule of the Mongols. When the last Mongol emperor fled his capital, Tatu, to his ancestral homeland beyond the Great Wall in 1368, all China was once again ruled by Chinese. The Ming government emulated many Han and T'ang institutions and policies and invoked their memory.

Ming History

The last three decades of Mongol rule (1330s–1360s) were marked by murderous palace intrigues and by civil and military collapse. Merciless taxation, neglect of water conservation for agriculture, and natural disasters drove desperate peasants to revolt. One rebel was Chu Yuan-chang, who at age sixteen had lost both his parents and most of his relatives to drought-induced famine. To survive, he abandoned his small family farm and joined a Buddhist monastery, but the monastery, too, ran out of food, and he was reduced to beggary. Chu then joined a secret society dedicated to driving out the Mongols and

Emperor Hung-wu, Founder of the Ming Dynasty. Chu Yuan-chang (who reigned under the name Hung-wu) was the second commoner to found a dynasty in China. His humble origin and physical ugliness (not evident in this formal portrait) contributed to his paranoia as a ruler.

National Palace Museum, Taipei, Taiwan, Republic of China

distinguished himself in military action. In 1356 his forces captured Nanking, a city of great wealth and historic importance on the southern bank of the lower Yangtze River, and there he set up a rudimentary government.

In 1368 Chu proclaimed himself the Hung-wu ("Bounteous Warrior," reigned 1368–1398) Emperor and founded a dynasty called the Ming or "brilliant." He thus became the second commoner (after the founder of the Han) to rise to the Chinese throne. In that same year the last Mongol emperor fled to Mongolia, ending the Yuan dynasty. During the next fourteen years, Ming armies brought all China under control. Further, they campaigned deep into Mongolia, burnt Karakorum (Genghis Khan's capital), nearly reached the shores of Lake Baikal in present-day Russia, and ventured westward to central Asia. Not since the T'ang had Chinese armies reached so far and been so successful. Korea and states in central and Southeast Asia once again acknowledged Chinese suzerainty. Hung-wu built a wall twenty miles long and sixty feet tall around his capital at Nanking, making it the largest enclosed city in the world.

Although he had little formal education, Hung-wu was an intelligent man who clearly understood the needs of his subjects. He not only restored the pride of the Chinese but also labored to rebuild their prosperity. His character also had a dark side: he was suspicious, despotic, cruel, and increasingly paranoid in his later years, especially after the deaths of his wife and eldest son. When it was revealed after his death in 1398 that he had passed over his capable fourth son, the Prince of Yen, the experienced commander of a large army stationed near the former Yuan capital, Tatu, in favor of his eldest grandson, a youth of sixteen, China was plunged into a three-year civil war. When the Prince of Yen captured Nanking, the young emperor disappeared in the ensuing confusion (he escaped disguised as a monk; several decades later he was identified by an aged eunuch and was allowed to live out his life in obscurity).

The Prince of Yen became Emperor Yung-lo (reigned 1402–1424). A powerful general and forceful ruler, he personally led five expeditions into Mongolia and humbled the Mongols. Using a political crisis in Vietnam as pretext, his army conquered and annexed that country. His most spectacular exploits were seven huge naval expeditions led by a eunuch admiral, Cheng Ho; the expeditions were made possible by advances in shipping

China's Brief Maritime Supremacy

The largest ocean vessel was about 500 feet in length and 211.5 feet broad. The first expedition consisted of 27,000 men and 62 large vessels, each of which carried about four or five hundred people, valuable gifts of silk, embroideries, and curiosities, as well as all the necessary provisions....

The fleet set sail from Liuchia Ho on the Yangtze estuary [on a southward course. After passing] . . . the Malacca Straits it entered the Indian Ocean. Its object was to reach the country of Kuli, the present Calicut on the Malabar coast of India, which was then the focal point of all sea routes in the Indian Ocean, and held the key position between many states in Southern Asia and the Near East.... For some years Kuli had maintained very amicable relations with China. On account of its frequent delivery of tribute to the Ming court, Cheng Ho was authorized to entitle the chief, Sami, king of Kuli. Cheng Ho handed Sami the imperial gifts and Sami in return gave a great celebration for their visit....

Two years later, the expedition sailed homeward. As the fleet passed by Chiu Kang . . . present Palembang [on Sumatra in Indonesia], it encountered the fleet of a powerful Chinese pirate named Ch'en Tsu-i who had for years been a threat to the voyagers passing the Malacca Straits. . . . After a major sea battle, Ch'en's fleet was badly defeated. More than five thousand of his crew were killed, ten of his vessels were burned, seven others damaged and Ch'en . . . was captured alive. The victory undoubtedly gave great prestige to the . . . Ming dynasty in Southern Asia.

On their way back the whole expedition visited Java [where a civil war was raging. Cheng intervened on behalf of the rightful ruler and] . . . raised the heir of the East King to regain his kingdom. In the summer of 1407, Cheng Ho returned to Peking and reported to the Emperor.*

Cheng Ho's fleets roamed Southeast Asia and the Indian Ocean as far as East Africa, attesting to China's advanced maritime technology and its dominance of the seas. The Ming government did not establish naval bases or plant colonies, however. Later it discontinued the expeditions for political reasons; China never recaptured world naval supremacy. Portugal and Spain became the leading naval powers later in the fifteenth century.

*Kuei-sheng Chang, "Chinese Great Explorers: Their Effect upon Chinese Geographic Knowledge prior to 1600" (Diss., University of Michigan, 1955), in James P. Holoka and Jiu-Hwa L. Upshur, eds., Lives and Times: A World History Reader, vol. 1 (Minneapolis/St. Paul: West Publishing, 1995), p. 358.

since the Sung dynasty, including the development of compartmentalized, water-tight ships and the magnetic compass. They proclaimed the resurgence of Chinese power under the Ming, enrolled vassal states, and promoted trade. In their wake the Ryukyu Islands, Champa, Cambodia, Siam, and states in Borneo, Java, Sumatra, Malacca, Sri Lanka, South India, and others sent tribute. Cheng also had a secret mission: to find out whether the missing young emperor had fled abroad. Never before or since has the Chinese navy attained such power.

Chinese naval dominance of the Indian Ocean lasted only from 1405 to 1433, ending as suddenly as it had begun. The expeditions sent by Emperor Yung-lo were sharply different in motive and nature from European ventures that began later in the century. Being largely self-sufficient economically, the Chinese did not seek to expand their empire or to establish colonies, naval bases, or even new trading partners. The primary purpose of these expeditions was to show the flag and display the power and prestige of the Ming empire. When it proved necessary to use force to obtain submission to the Ming emperor's claim of suzerainty, Cheng Ho landed troops and intervened in the affairs of numerous minor states.

The expeditions also collected strange and exotic products to flatter the emperor and entertain the court. For example, a giraffe was brought back from Africa and presented to Yung-lo with the suggestion that it was the *chi-lin* of Chinese mythology, a fabulous beast said to come down to earth when a sage ruled. The emperor welcomed the strange gift but dismissed the suggestion. The civil service opposed such extravagant and largely futile expeditions because they produced few tangible results and were commanded by

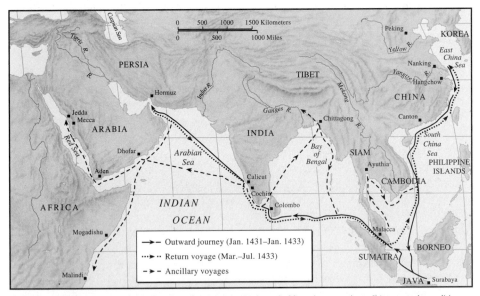

Map 10.4 Chinese Sea Voyages during the Ming Dynasty. In the early fifteenth century, large Chinese naval expeditions reached the Red Sea and East Africa. But China planted no colonies and established no naval bases in this area. After the return of the last expedition in 1433, China lost interest in overseas explorations.

eunuchs who were personal servants of the emperor and not members of the bureaucracy. After Cheng Ho's death, the officials conveniently "lost" the navigation charts. Thus China left exploration to European nations.

Yung-lo's reign was also notable for great public works projects. The silted-up Grand Canal was dredged, facilitating north-south trade and improving drainage, transport, and food distribution. The eastern section of the Great Wall was rebuilt to guard against nomad incursions. Yung-lo was anxious to leave Nanking, where unpleasant memory of his usurpation lingered, and to return to the north, where his power base lay. He therefore built Peking, near the site of the Yuan capital, which had been flattened to obliterate the hated Mongol rule from memory. Most of the great palaces and temples in Peking that survive today date from his reign. He also chose a valley near the city to build his mausoleum. Peking was a bad choice for a capital for two principal reasons. First, situated only 40 miles south of the Great Wall, it was vulnerable to attacks by nomads. Second, the capital was located on a dry, infertile plain, and the nearby region was not productive enough to support the city's population. Thus resources of the prosperous south had to be diverted to Peking.

Yung-lo's successors were mostly undistinguished and often grossly incompetent. For example the Emperor Wan-li (reigned 1572–1620) ascended the throne at age eight, led a debauched life surrounded by eunuchs and palace ladies, and indulged in drinking and opium smoking. For years he avoided meeting with officials and conducted the business of government through eunuch intermediaries. By the end of his unfortunately long reign, thousands of official posts were vacant because he refused to appoint replacements. The dynasty nonetheless survived because of the strength of the bureaucracy and the durability of tested institutions. In time, however, the toll of misgovernment mounted. By the early seventeenth century, decline was all too apparent, and a natural disaster drove the disaffected peasants to revolt. Most Chinese interpreted these disasters as symptomatic of the dynasty's loss of the mandate of heaven, or authority to rule. In 1644 Peking fell to a rebel army; to avoid capture, the last Ming emperor killed his wife and daughters and committed suicide.

An Autocratic Government and a Conservative Military

Ming government was consciously patterned after that of the T'ang but was more autocratic, for several reasons. One is the disappearance of the great families of the Han and T'ang dynasties. Another is the dominance of a nonhereditary civil service, recruited through the rigorous examination system, but consisting of men with no independent power base. A third was the legacy of absolutist Mongol rule. After discovering a planned attempt by the prime minister on his life, Emperor Hung-wu abolished the office and concentrated all power in his own hands, assisted by a Grand Secretariat and various ministries in the central government. The empire was divided into fifteen provinces and subdivided into counties, which have largely survived to the present. All officials belonged to a strictly ordered bureaucracy.

Emperor Hung-wu sternly ruled over his officials and ruthlessly punished disloyalty or disobedience. Although his successors continued his autocratic practices, they discarded

Ming Dynasty Great Wall.
The continuing need to defend its territory against Mongol raids led the Ming government to rebuild parts of the Great Wall. This section protected the capital city, Peking.

Courtesy of Jiu-Hwa Upshur

his unequivocal admonition that "eunuchs should not be allowed to interfere with affairs of state; death to the offender," because the rise of eunuchs to power had been traditionally associated with dynastic decline. In contrast, the usurper emperor Yung-lo executed many officials who had been loyal to his nephew. He also distrusted his relatives, who might do to his descendants what he had done to his nephew. Accordingly, he gave his relatives and in-laws honors and lavish stipends, but no political positions or power. He turned to eunuchs—for example, appointing the eunuch Cheng Ho admiral of his fleet. Most eunuchs came from poor families and were despised by officials and the people alike for their profession. In revenge, many eunuchs ruthlessly enriched themselves and when possible humiliated the officials.

Yung-lo's eunuchs served him loyally, but the self-indulgent later Ming emperors who feared criticism by the bureaucracy undercut it by entrusting authority to eunuchs and tolerating their abuses of power. A prominent eunuch who fell from power in 1510 owned coins and bullion totaling 251 million ounces of silver, twenty-four pounds of unmounted precious gems, over 7,000 pieces of precious-stone jewelry mounted in gold, 500 gold plates, two suits of armor in solid gold, and several mansions. He had amassed all this wealth in one lifetime. The power of eunuchs demoralized the civil service and contributed to the fall of the dynasty.

Despite the corruptions that eventually weakened the dynasty at the top, China was relatively well governed during this period. The greatness of the Ming dynasty was largely due to its able and dedicated bureaucracy recruited through impartial examinations, which drew the most talented men to public service.

The military constituted the largest component of the Ming government and consumed most of its revenue. In practices similar to their Ottoman contemporaries, Emperor Hung-wu allotted state land as farms to his million-plus soldiers. After the initial expense of setting up the farms, the emperor boasted that it cost the treasury nothing to maintain the army. In fact, the treasury had to allocate ever-increasing sums to subsidize an army that increased to 4 million men.

Military service became hereditary and was not esteemed. Officers' sons became officers once they passed a relatively easy examination on military techniques and rudimentary book learning. There was little innovation in military technology, particularly in firearms, during this dynasty, and China began to fall behind the West militarily. By the seventeenth century, the army was unable either to put down peasant revolts or to ward off nomadic incursions.

The Economy, Society, and Educational System

Much of China, especially the north, was ravaged and depopulated when the Ming dynasty was first established. Although early figures are only estimates, the population of China was probably around 150 million in the early thirteenth century, on the eve of the Mongol invasion of North China. By 1368 the population was reduced to about 60 million, down to the T'ang level. It recovered to approximately 100 million by 1500, and then rose steadily to around 200 million by 1600. Even more telling was the distribution of the population. Whereas numbers were about evenly divided between the north and south in the early Sung, the brutal Mongol conquest of the north and the bubonic plague (which was at least as terrible in China as in western Europe) reduced the population of the north during the Yuan dynasty to less than a quarter (some say as little as a tenth) of the land.

Emperor Hung-wu, the son of a poor farmer, was particularly solicitous of farmers. He took his heir on visits to farms to show him the farmers' hard life, once lecturing him in the following words:

> Now, you see the hard life of these people. They hardly ever leave their fields, and their hands are always on the plow. They work hard throughout the year, and hardly ever take any rest. They live in crude straw huts, their clothes are made of rough cloth, and their food consists of unrefined rice and vegetables. Nevertheless the government depends chiefly on them for revenue. I wish therefore that in your daily life you shall remember the hardships of the farmers. When you exact anything from them, be reasonable and use what you receive from them with great care, so that they may not have to suffer from hunger and cold.

Early Ming rulers took vigorous and effective measures to repopulate the north by emancipating slaves and encouraging refugees to settle on confiscated Mongol estates as freehold farmers. They remitted taxes and provided land grants, free seeds, tools, and animals. These measures led to the reinvigoration of the economy during the first century of the dynasty. Later rulers forgot the founder's admonitions and led ever more extravagant lives that caused general economic misery.

To stimulate agricultural production, the government also undertook major projects in hydraulic engineering. It built a sea wall that protected the coast between Shanghai and Hangchow (south of the Yangtze River) to prevent floods by storm tides. Improvements in printing allowed the government to offer farmers agricultural and technical manuals that further contributed to greater productivity.

Farmers took up the cultivation of mulberries and the raising of silkworms even more than before. Silk production became widespread in all provinces, especially those south of the Yangtze River, and techniques improved greatly; Nanking and Soochow were the best-known silk manufacturing centers. Women and girls were trained for raising silkworms; men, women, and children were employed in silk manufacturing. As before, Chinese silks were sought after in many lands. After the opening of direct sea trade with Europe, southern coastal cities prospered because they became the principal ports of export. Just as several different types of cotton cloth were named after Indian towns, many varieties of silk were named after their places of production in China; for example, shantung, honan, and satin. Cotton cultivation and manufacture also became widespread, but unlike India, China produced cotton textiles mainly for affordable domestic consumption.

New food crops stimulated population growth. Maize, sweet potatoes, peanuts, and (despite official discouragement) tobacco were introduced from the Americas by the

The Temple of Heaven. The Chinese emperor performed many ritual duties, the most important being the worship of heaven at the Temple of Heaven in Peking.

Spaniards via the Philippines. However, the potato, the least nutritious staple food, which became important in Europe in the eighteenth century, never became popular in China. As a result of the new foods, the late Ming Chinese were among the best-fed people in the world, consuming on average more than 2,000 calories a day in a wide variety of grains, vegetables, fish, and meats. Beneficial dietary practices, such as a preference for hot cooked foods and an insistence on drinking tea and boiled water, promoted public health and productivity.

While the population was predominantly rural, the number of town dwellers grew steadily. Peking had over 700,000 registered citizens, while Nanking and Hangchow had over a million people each. Soochow, China's most populous city, had over 2 million. Soochow and Hangchow were manufacturing and cultural centers as well as resort cities for the rich. The popular saying "Above are the Halls of Heaven; here below, Soochow and Hangchow" suggests the pleasures afforded by each of these cities. Slavery existed, but the Ming code was more humane to slaves and gave them greater protection than had the Han and T'ang codes. Prisoners of war were the major sources of slaves early in the dynasty; certain political prisoners were enslaved, and poor parents could sell their children into slavery. On numerous occasions, however, the government intervened to free children sold into slavery by poor parents or during famines.

Another indicator of prosperity was the stable currency. During the Southern Sung and Yuan dynasties inflation had undermined paper currency. Although paper money still continued to circulate and was even required for payment of certain taxes, silver became the preferred medium of exchange. Trade with Europe generated a favorable balance for China, as the Europeans paid for the goods in silver, the basis of China's currency.

Intermediate-sized manufacturing and market towns proliferated, many with over 100,000 people. Ching-te-chen was a prime example of a market town and surrounding district devoted to a single product—porcelain manufacturing. By the mid-Ming era it had a population of almost a million people and nearly 3,000 factories making porcelains that were sought after worldwide. A fifteenth-century poet described the scene created by all the burning kilns:

Like a glowing cloud arising from a crimson city,
it is transformed into a piece of beautiful silk; or
like the sun arising from a violet sea, its brilliant
rays spread all over.

Or, as a Jesuit missionary said more prosaically:

The finest specimens of porcelain are made from clay found in the province of Kiam [Kiangsi, where Ching-te-chen is located] and these are shipped not only to every part of China but even to the remotest corners of Europe, where they are highly prized by those who appreciate elegance at their banquets rather than pompous display.

Porcelain production was highly specialized and technically advanced. Division of labor and assembly-line techniques expedited and accelerated production. For a moment China seemed on the verge of an industrial revolution, but then Chinese technology stagnated, while that of less advanced Europe caught up and forged ahead. Why China failed to make the transition to industrialism is not clear, but the explanation must lie partly in the nature of Chinese government and society, which esteemed book learning that emphasized such subjects as philosophy, literature, and history and denigrated the sciences. An abundant labor force and a moral code that disdained the profit motive and the merchant class channeled creative minds away from scientific and technological fields. The conditions that prepared western Europe for the industrial revolution will be explored in Chapter 11.

Next to textile and porcelain in importance were the metal, lacquer, and paper industries, the last supplying the needs of the growing reading public. Up to the end of the Ming, more books had been published in China than in the rest of the world combined.

In many cities and towns, many types of artisans plied their trade; some were itinerant artisans who moved from place to place. Not only did some cities specialize in certain products, but within cities shops engaged in the same business or craft grouped together. As in medieval European towns, many street names identified the trade conducted there; for example, Scissors Lane, Lane of Oil Manufacturers, and Handkerchief Lane. Nanking had forty streets and lanes named after trades and crafts.

Although officially merchants as a class ranked low in the Chinese social system, they nevertheless became very important. The growth of cities, commerce, and industry led to the development of an urban middle class of shopkeepers, wholesalers, manufacturers, and artisans with a sophisticated lifestyle. They demanded paintings and decorations for their homes and required places of pleasure and entertainment for their leisure hours. Beginning in the sixteenth century, coastal cities prospered from growing trade with Europe; from Europeans the Chinese learned to enjoy luxury items such as clocks and other mechanical devices, enameled decorative articles, and woolen textiles.

Whereas the tone of society under the Han and T'ang dynasties was aristocratic, that of the Ming was decidedly bourgeois. The growing egalitarianism or leveling of society owed in part to government policy, which deliberately favored ordinary citizens and broke up large estates. The spread of education, made possible by growing prosperity and advances in printing, favored the middle class.

Education had suffered sadly under Mongol rule. To remedy this situation, and to provide the state with a pool of well-educated talent, Hung-wu founded the most extensive public education system in premodern China. He encouraged village elementary schools, and ordered each county to maintain at least one school where the state provided financial support for some students. After matriculating, the best graduates from these schools then attended the state university in the capital city as honor students. Educational reforms particularly benefited those who lived in the prosperous south. Millions of families were able to educate their sons, who in turn could advance up the social ladder by passing the examinations.

Two years after the founding of the dynasty, Hung-wu restored and improved the examination system, which remained essentially unchanged to the end of the nineteenth century. Those who passed the county examination were called Cultivated Talents, a degree comparable to the modern B.A. Recipients of this degree were exempted from corvée labor and entitled to wear distinctive robes. Those who passed the provincial examination were called Elevated Men, a degree equivalent to the M.A., and were entitled to take the metropolitan examination. Held triennially in Peking, this examination, like all exams, required mastery of the Confucian classics. About 300 men passed the metropolitan examination each time it was administered; those who passed were further tested in the palace and ranked.

Men who passed these additional tests received a degree similar to the modern Ph.D. and were called Presented Scholars. Those with first, second, and third places acquired the status of national heroes, and their families and communities shared in their reflected glory. High scorers received appointments to the Hanlin Academy, where they perfected their scholarship and acquired familiarity with government functions and business. They were then selected to fill vacancies in important posts. Men without degrees could hold only minor administrative and clerical jobs; no civil service position in the ladder of promotion was given to anyone without a degree. While individual family fortunes rose and fell with the success of its sons, the scholar-gentry class as a group dominated society. There were no schools for girls. With society esteeming education, girls from educated families received an education at home from their mothers and teachers. Many biographies of famous men cite their mothers as their first teachers. Ming histories and biographies list many famous women painters and writers.

The examination system had both strengths and weaknesses. When Jesuit missionaries came to China in the late sixteenth century, they reported on the Chinese method of selecting officials with wonder and unconcealed admiration. After Yung-lo forbade imperial clansmen to hold positions of power, examinations served as the only recognized road to high government service, status, and social esteem; this system constantly added new blood to the corps of the elite. More than half of all doctoral degree holders throughout the dynasty came from families that had not produced any degree holders for three generations. A geographical quota system of degree holders ensured that government positions would be distributed nationally.

A major disadvantage of the system was the restrictive nature of its curriculum. It was confined to the mastery of Confucian classics, along with approved commentaries by scholars from the Sung neo-Confucian school. This narrow focus curbed individual creativity and discouraged the investigation of science and technology.

Vibrant Culture and Arts

Scholarship thrived during the peaceful centuries of Ming rule. The state officially sponsored some scholarly endeavors, especially those in historiography, the most esteemed field of study. Scholars wrote local histories and gazettes (over 1,000 have been preserved), poetry, and prose. They also produced substantial numbers of collected writings; the 1,500 that survive possess considerable literary distinction. The Ming craze for anthologies proved fortuitous, for thousands of books that otherwise might have perished were thereby preserved.

The Ming era was noted for drama. During the preceding Yuan dynasty, Chinese scholars had been forced out of government and could hold only subordinate positions.

Some took to writing for the stage as a new form of expression. Drawing on history and contemporary life, they made drama a popular form of entertainment. This interest in drama persisted into the Ming.

Chinese theaters resembled those of Elizabethan England; both used a three-sided stage with no scenery, and regardless of the time the play was set, actors were gorgeously attired in contemporary costumes. For reasons of propriety casts were either entirely male or entirely female. Even today, all stage costumes used in modern theatrical production are those of the Ming period. As in many other cultures, actors were designated "mean" people and held the lowest social status. Because of actors' poor moral reputation, their sons were forbidden to sit for the examinations.

The novel was another important literary development of the Ming. Written in the mode of popular speech, it was enjoyed by both poorly educated people and scholars. The first great Ming novel was Lo Kuan-chung's *The Romance of the Three Kingdoms*. Set in the waning years of the Han dynasty in the third century, it was the story of politics, war, and intrigue and is considered seven parts history and three parts fiction; it gave readers the color that formal histories lacked. Lo reputedly also wrote another novel, *All Men Are Brothers*. Its heroes are a band of men and women, who, like England's folk hero Robin Hood, were driven to banditry by corrupt government officials. Although set in the Northern Sung era, the novel undoubtedly was intended as a criticism of the corrupt government of the late Ming. Both novels have supplied plots for countless later Chinese plays and operas and remain immensely popular to the present.

The Golden Lotus, of unknown authorship, is Ming China's third great novel. Focusing on domestic life in an upper-middle-class provincial household, it is the first novel to give female characters, who are depicted with skill and sympathy, equal importance with males. *The Golden Lotus* paints an exceedingly frank picture of human relationships and offers explicit descriptions of the sexual lives of the characters.

Early Contacts with Europeans

In 1515 the Portuguese arrived at the southern Chinese port of Canton. The Ming government greeted them with the same hospitality and tolerance that earlier Chinese governments had shown to peaceful Persian, Arab, and Malay merchants. However, the violent and bigoted conduct of Portuguese sailors soon convinced Ming officials that the Portuguese were little better than pirates and should be dealt with as such. Their appearance and conduct led ordinary Chinese to call the Portuguese "devils," an epithet that was soon applied to all Europeans.

Despite their repugnance for Portuguese merchants, the Ming nevertheless desired to engage in profitable trade and formulated a plan to deal with them. In rules promulgated in 1557, the government allowed Portugal to establish a trading station at Macao, situated at the tip of the Pearl River estuary, not far from Canton but sufficiently remote from China's other major cities to make aggression difficult. As a further protection, the Chinese built a wall across the peninsula, separating Macao from the rest of China, and guarded the wall with a strong garrison.

A mutually profitable trading pattern evolved at Macao. The Portuguese eagerly purchased tea, porcelain, silks, spices, lacquerware, and other luxury items from China and shipped them to Europe. Each round trip from Lisbon required two years, a voyage so rigorous that half the crew did not live to return. Some ships were lost, but both merchants and rulers profited enormously. One Portuguese writer declared in 1541 that a piece of Chinese porcelain was worth several slaves. European royalty and aristocrats eagerly snapped up the porcelain and other luxury goods, and in time began to order specially decorated chinaware, silk embroideries, and other items from Chinese workshops.

After 1571 between thirty and forty Chinese sailing junks annually brought porcelain, silks, and other products to Spanish-controlled Manila, where they were shipped to Mexico and transferred to other ships bound for Spain. Dutch sailors, who first arrived at Macao in 1602, behaved as abominably as had the Portuguese, and the Ming government reacted by closing the entire Chinese coast to them. However, the Dutch established a base in northern Taiwan, an island outpost of Ming China. Between 1604 and 1656 more than 3 million pieces of Chinese porcelain were imported to the Netherlands by the Dutch East India Company. Neither the English nor the French played an important role in trade with Ming China.

When Catholic missionaries arrived in China, they found that the traders had given Europeans a bad reputation among the Chinese. Thus when the Jesuit Francis Xavier, who spent many years proselytizing in India, the East Indies, and Japan, arrived in China, he was denied permission to land and died on an island off Macao while waiting for a favorable ruling. In 1583 another Jesuit missionary, Matteo Ricci, received permission to build a church near Canton. Twenty years elapsed before Ricci obtained permission to proceed to Peking. Meanwhile he established a high reputation among Chinese scholar-officials as a mathematician, astronomer, cartographer, and clockmaker. Until his death in 1610, Ricci wrote treatises explaining the Christian religion in Chinese and also translated Chinese classics into Latin. He converted a number of respected officials to Catholicism.

Ricci was followed by other learned missionaries of the Jesuit order, who introduced aspects of the culture of Renaissance Europe to China. Some Jesuits served the Ming government in various nonreligious capacities in order to gain protection for their brethren who worked as missionaries in the field. In 1611 the Ming government appointed Jesuits learned in astronomy to reform China's calendar. After successfully making these reforms, one of them was named director of the prestigious Bureau of Astronomy. A late Ming observatory built in Peking by the Jesuits remains standing. Confronted by rebels, the government even prevailed on one Jesuit to cast 200 cannons for the Ming army. Having little choice, he eased his conscience by naming each piece after a saint. On the whole, the Jesuits did much to change the unfavorable view of Europeans that the sailors and merchants had created. Significantly, Chinese records refer to the missionaries as men from the western oceans and not as devils. Grateful for their services, the Ming government granted the Jesuits a piece of land outside Peking for a mission home, church, and cemetery.

The Ch'ing (Manchu) Dynasty at Its Height

On hunting expeditions, as on campaigns, one must look after the officials and men in the retinue. In hot weather, when possible [there should be] cold drinks ready by the roadside to refresh the marchers—iced water, or herbal wines, or plum cider. When it was snowing, I used to send guards officers over to the camel drovers' tents with food and charcoal, so that hot meals could be prepared for the carters who had not yet arrived, and they could rest up. . . . So planning and attention to details are essential, and the advice of the veteran commanders should always be considered. . . . For my part, I reviewed the campaign instructions of my ancestors' victories and combined them with the demands of this new campaign. . . .

Giving life to people and killing people—those are the power that the emperor has. He knows that administrative errors in government bureaus can be rectified, but that a criminal who has been executed cannot be brought back to life any more than a chopped string can be joined together again. He knows, too, that sometimes people have to be persuaded into morality by the example of an execution.

On tours I learned about the common people's grievances by talking with them, or by accepting their petitions. In northern China I asked peasants about their officials, looked at their houses, and discussed their crops. In the South I heard pleas from a woman whose husband had been wrongfully enslaved, from a monk whose temple was falling down, and from a man who was robbed on his way to town of 200 taels of someone else's money that he had promised to invest—a complex predicament, and I had him given 40 taels in partial compensation. But if someone was attacked in an anonymous message, then I refused to take action, for we should always confront a witness directly; and if someone exaggerated too stupidly, then too I would not listen.*

*Jonathan D. Spence, Emperor of China: Self-Portrait of K'ang-hsi (New York: Vintage, 1975), pp. 16–18, 31, 43.

Emperor K'ang-hsi (reigned 1661–1722), the longest-ruling emperor in Chinese history and one of the greatest, wrote the above passages about war, justice, and administration. Like Louis XIV of France and Akbar of Moghul India, he inherited a shaky government, which he consolidated into a powerful, autocratic state. He bequeathed to his son the largest, most prosperous dominion of the time. A man of keen intellect, a capable general, and an indefatigable administrator, K'ang-hsi, in his personal qualities and rule, exemplified autocracy at its best. This was in sharp contrast with the capricious and self-indulgent rulers of the late Ming dynasty that the Ch'ing replaced.

The Consolidation of Ch'ing Rule

The Ming was overthrown and replaced by the Ch'ing dynasty in 1644. As Ming authority tottered, rebellions swept the countryside. A combination of accidental circumstances, superior organization, and effective leadership brought to power the Manchus, a nomadic people from northeastern China called Manchuria. Originally forest dwelling vassals of the Ming, the Manchus claimed descent from an earlier nomadic group, the Jurchens of the Chin dynasty that ruled North China in the twelfth century. Living in frontier communities intermixed with the Chinese, they learned agriculture and Chinese ways. Just as the Mongols had relied on the organizing and military genius of Genghis Khan, the Manchus owed their rise to the skills of Nurhachi (1559–1626), a petty chief who defeated rival nomads and proclaimed himself Khan in 1616, establishing his capital at Shenyang (later also called Mukden, which later became the secondary capital of the Manchu dynasty). His work was continued by his son, Abahai (1592–1643), who subdued Korea and conquered all Ming territories northeast of the Great Wall and all eastern Mongol tribes. In 1635 Abahai adopted the dynastic name of Ch'ing (pure) to signal his ambition to rule all China.

Although they patterned their state after the Chinese model, Nurhachi and Abahai organized the Manchus into an efficient fighting machine through the banner system, which enrolled all men for compulsory military service in one of eight banners. As non-Manchus were conquered and incorporated into the Manchu state, Manchu males were freed from the pursuit of agriculture and trade and restricted to fighting and administration in the same manner as the ancient Spartans; the conquered peoples worked their lands, as the helots had worked for the Spartans. As the Manchus expanded their power, eight Mongol and eight Chinese (Han) banners were added.

Nurhachi and Abahai adopted the traditional Chinese bureaucracy to rule their expanding state, and recruited Chinese to fill many posts. Because many Chinese admired the good discipline of the Manchu troops and recognized the Manchu leaders' keen appreciation of Chinese civilization, increasing numbers of Ming officials and officers defected to the Manchus. Thus the rise of Manchu power was clearly different from that of the Mongols.

However, the Manchus became a national dynasty by accident. In 1664 rebel forces captured Peking and subjected it to a reign of terror. With the last Ming emperor dead, a loyal Ming general asked the Manchus for help in expelling the rebels, and opened the gates of the Great Wall to let their army in. Their combined armies defeated the rebels, captured Peking, and installed the son of Abahai on the throne. Manchus thus claimed to be the avengers of the last Ming emperor, whom they buried with honor, and liberators of the people. Most northern Chinese preferred the Sinicized Manchus to the rapacious and destructive rebels and accepted their rule with little resistance. However, Ming supporters in South China resisted the conquerors for several decades.

In 1661 the first Manchu ruler on the Chinese throne died while still a young man; he was succeeded by his seven-year-old son, K'ang-hsi, in part because the boy had survived smallpox, a dreaded childhood disease. One of the great sovereigns in all Chinese history, K'ang-hsi was raised by his devoted grandmother. However, until the mid-nineteenth century, no woman was permitted to act as regent, and she made no attempt to influence the government. K'ang-hsi's uncle acted as his regent and wisely retained most of the Ming administration intact, weeding out the corruption.

K'ang-hsi had awesome physical and intellectual abilities. Accomplished in Chinese and Manchu, he also learned Latin, music, the sciences, and higher mathematics from his Jesuit tutors. He was a careful and decisive general and took personal charge of the campaigns to subjugate South China. In 1683 a naval expedition to Taiwan defeated the last Ming loyalist general and brought that island under Ch'ing rule. All China was now under firm Manchu grip, but two bitter campaigns in South China left southern Chinese–Manchu relations embittered throughout the dynasty.

The father of fifty-six children born to his empress and twenty-nine consorts of varying ranks, K'ang-hsi was plagued in his later years by intrigues among some twenty sons who vied for the succession. Chinese emperors had one empress at any time but could have many consorts of varying ranks. The empress was generally chosen by the parents of the reigning emperor, often in consultation with high officials. She had many ceremonial duties. Han Chinese dynasties practiced primogeniture, preferring the eldest son of the empress. Manchu custom also preferred sons borne by the empress, but not necessarily the eldest one. Unlike the Ottoman and Moghul dynasties, no wars or succession plagued the Ch'ing dynasty. K'ang-hsi's final choice was his fourth son, whom he said most resembled him, who ruled as the Emperor Yung-cheng (reigned 1723–1735). Vigorous and capable, Yung-cheng worked as hard as his father. He personally led campaigns, maintained government discipline, and sternly punished corruption. Already forty-five when he ascended the throne, he had a relatively short reign.

Yung-cheng's son, the Emperor Ch'ien-lung (reigned 1735–1796), ruled for sixty years and abdicated in 1796 out of filial piety, so as not to exceed his revered grandfather's reign. Like his father and grandfather, Ch'ien-lung was an accomplished man of letters, patron of the arts, and dynamic military commander. He personally led military expeditions to the north and west, where he crushed Mongol power and brought Tibet and part of central Asia under Chinese control. In 1792 a Ch'ing army marched into Nepal, inflicting an unprecedented defeat on the Gurkhas (later renowned as warriors for the British Empire) and ensuring the submission of Nepal as a Ch'ing tributary state.

The Education of a Prince

[His] training began at home, under the personal direction of his father. It consisted largely of private tutorials—a confrontation between father and son. . . . Later Ch'ien-lung paid tribute to [his father] Yung-cheng's untiring and detailed direction of his studies. . . . From nine sui *[eight years] on Ch'ien-lung was a school boy. He began classes in the classics and history and later, from the age of fourteen* sui *[thirteen years] in composition. The classes were first held at home [under a] highly respected tutor. . . . With Yung-cheng's assumption of power, Ch'ien-lung's education became more intensive, more highly structured, and less isolated . . . in a Palace School for Princes [that his father had established]. . . .*

Class hours were long, from 5:00 A.M. to 4:00 P.M., and the school operated throughout the year. Only five official holidays were recognized: New Year's Day, the Dragon Boat Festival, Mid-Autumn Festival, the emperor's birthday, and the prince's own birthday. . . .

Classroom procedures appear to have differed according to the needs of individual students and both individual instruction and small group study sessions were employed. The princes learned to read by rote. . . .

None of the princes enrolled was exempted from attendance, and if the emperor learned of any inexcusable truancy he would have the culprit punished regardless of his age, marital status, or accumulated official honors. Even on days when a prince was in attendance at court he was expected to proceed to the school directly upon being relieved. *

This account of the future Emperor Ch'ien-lung's schooling (his father had not been designated crown prince when it began) shows the rigorous attention early Ch'ing rulers paid to the education of their sons. The strict training produced conscientious rulers that served the dynasty well for almost two centuries.

*Harold L. Kahn, Monarchy in the Emperor's Eyes: Images and Reality in the Ch'ien-lung Reign (Cambridge: Harvard University Press, 1971), pp. 116, 118–119.

The three great early Ch'ing monarchs ruled for almost a century and a half. Under them traditional Chinese civilization achieved a last great flowering, and Chinese power and prosperity overawed neighboring peoples. Prolonged peace, increased food production (including government-sponsored introduction of early-ripening strains of rice from southern Indochina), and improved public health (including widespread smallpox inoculations for children with serum from infected cows) resulted in steady population growth. By the end of the eighteenth century, China's population had reached the saturation point for a preindustrial economy. Jesuit missionary reports on the luxury and elegance of Chinese court life and the justice of their governmental system made China the model for the European Enlightenment intellectuals and made Confucius their patron saint. By the time Ch'ien-lung's reign drew to a close, however, the dynasty had passed its zenith. During the next century the Ch'ing dynasty rapidly declined, and China was almost destroyed by the growing power of the West.

The Manchu Government: Traditions Continued

The Ch'ing maintained the government and bureaucracy they had inherited from the Ming with a minimum of changes. They retained the three-tier examination system for recruiting scholar-bureaucrats, with its geographical quotas and educational requirements, but liberalized it to admit previously ineligible groups. Bannermen, however, were allowed to take special, less rigorous exams. The Manchus represented only about 2 percent of the population, but preferential treatment allowed them to hold 10 percent of all official appointments. Although Han Chinese officials held most provincial and county government positions, they shared positions equally with Manchus at the top levels of the central government. Statutes required that the emperor's top advisors include equal numbers of bannermen and Han Chinese, and each government ministry had dual Manchu and Han Chinese ministers and vice-ministers. This system, called dyarchy, produced a collegial form of government; it also maintained a system of checks and balances.

The Manchus enacted laws aimed at preventing their total assimilation by the Han Chinese. One law prohibited intermarriage between bannermen and Han Chinese, another stipulated that all official documents be bilingual (a written script, derived from the Mongol alphabet, was invented for writing Manchu in the early seventeenth century). Although the ban on intermarriages persisted until the last years of the dynasty, bilingualism ended once the Manchus learned Chinese. All instruction in the palace school was in Chinese by the early eighteenth century, with the result that most Manchus quickly lost facility in their own language.

The three great early Ch'ing emperors exercised power more forcefully and decisively than their weak and self-indulgent Ming predecessors. As a secretary of the Grand Council (the highest advisory body to the emperor) wrote: "Ten or more of my comrades would take turns every five or six days on early morning duty and even so would feel fatigued. How did the emperor do it day after day?" Such a government worked well so long as the ruler was capable and hardworking. Unfortunately, Ch'ing monarchs of the nineteenth century, like the Spanish Habsburgs, French Bourbons, and Moghuls ruling during the same period, lacked the ability that distinguished their forebears.

Because they embraced Chinese culture and values, conciliated all classes among the Chinese, and created an essentially humane and fair government, the Manchus were successful where the Mongols had failed. In contrast to the Mongols, who only cared about their luxuries for themselves, the Manchus built granaries to control famine, subsidized local schools and academies to propagate classical learning, sacrificed to local deities and heroes, bestowed honors on the aged and virtuous, and commissioned top scholars to compile the official history of the Ming dynasty. Thus early Ch'ing was one of the best periods in Chinese history.

The dynasty was ultimately sustained by its military might. The 169,000 banner forces that wrested control of China in 1644 were concentrated in the capital and its environs, in strategic spots in the northwest to prevent nomad invasions, and in key metropolitan centers. Commanding officers were drawn from the Banner aristocracy. As Manchu power grew, additional Chinese levies (around 500,000 men), called the Green Standard Army, were put on garrison duty across the land. Early Ch'ing monarchs labored to keep up the fighting spirit and readiness of the banner armies. Like their Ming predecessors, they purchased artillery from the Portuguese and put Jesuit missionaries to work casting cannons. Artillery played an important role in campaigns against the Mongols and ensured the final destruction of their nomadic power. While cannons were incorporated into Ch'ing military strategy, Manchu troops continued to rely on archery and swords and did not adopt muskets. No advances were made in military technology in the seventeenth and eighteenth centuries, while Europeans were rapidly forging ahead, with disastrous consequences for China in the nineteenth century.

National Palace Museum, Taipei, Taiwan, Republic of China

Royal Favorite. Each emperor had one empress and also consorts of various ranks. Above is an oil painting of Hsiang Fei, a Turkic Muslim consort of Emperor Ch'ien-lung, dressed in European armor; this painting is attributed to the Italian Jesuit Giuseppe Castiglione.

The Final Flowering of the Traditional Economy and Society

The transition from Ming to Ch'ing was the least disruptive major dynastic change in Chinese history. However, as conquering rulers, they ordered Han Chinese men to adopt

Manchu hair fashion—shaving the front part of the head and wearing a long queue in the back—and to wear a tight-fitting Manchu-style robe with side slits designed originally to facilitate mounting horses (in contrast, Chinese men in Ming times had worn their long hair knotted on the crown, and had worn loose-fitting long robes). Han women, however, continued to wear their long skirts with jackets and vests, and upper-class women bound their feet, as their standard of beauty dictated (despite early Ch'ing government efforts to stop the custom), which distinguished them from Manchu women who had unbound feet and wore one-piece long dresses with side slits originally designed for riding on horseback.

Sweet potatoes, maize, and peanuts, introduced during the Ming dynasty, became basic crops by the mid-Ch'ing. Rice dropped from about 70 percent of the total national staple output in the late Ming to about 36 percent in the nineteenth century. It became the staple diet of the wealthy, as sweet potatoes and maize became staples for the poor. These new crops transformed agricultural life and resulted in a population explosion, from around 150–200 million in early Ch'ing to about 450 million in the mid-nineteenth century.

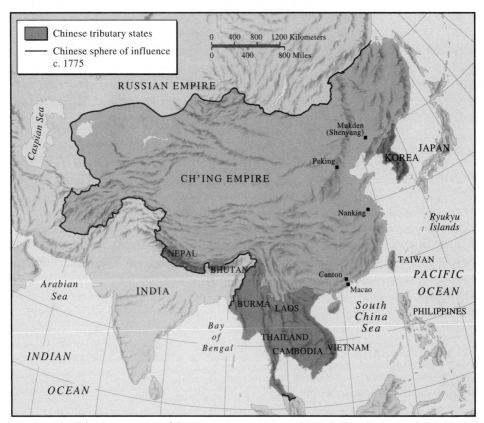

Map 10.5 The Ch'ing Dynasty at Its Height. At its maximum extent, around 1775, the Ch'ing Empire controlled more lands than any other empire in Chinese history and was surrounded by vassal states from Korea to Siam (present-day Thailand).

Food for an Emperor's Table

Main course dishes:
  A dish of fat chicken, pot boiled duck, and bean curd
  A dish of swallows' nests and julienned smoked duck
  A bowl of clear soup
  A dish of julienned pot-boiled chicken
  A dish of smoked fat chicken and Chinese cabbage
  A dish of salted duck and pork
  A dish of court-style fried chicken
Pastries:
  A dish of bamboo-stuffed steamed dumplings
  A dish of rice cakes
  A dish of rice cake with honey
Pickles:
  Chinese cabbage pickled in brine
  Cucumber preserved in soy
  Pickled eggplant
Rice:
  Boiled rice*

This menu for Emperor Ch'ien-lung's dinner in 1754 shows the emperor ate well but not extravagantly. It was a typical good Chinese meal and demonstrates the Sinicization of the Manchus in contrast with the earlier Yuan rulers' preservation of Mongol eating habits.

Good cuisine was considered one of life's pleasures. Many cookbooks from the Ch'ing period survive, and many famous chefs left their names to their special dishes. Several regional cuisines rose to prominence, and famous restaurants and eating clubs in major cities catered to the eating fancies of the rich; some also had take-out and delivery services and rented out chefs for special occasions to clients. Small eateries and mobile snack stands were everywhere in cities and villages.

*K. C. Chang, ed. Food in Chinese Culture (New Haven: Yale University Press, 1977), p. 282.

Ch'ing policy prohibiting the migration of Han Chinese into Manchuria kept the region sparsely settled and much of the land virgin. Elsewhere in China, the expanding population stripped forests, plowed marginal lands, and colonized areas that had hitherto been the homes of aboriginal tribal peoples. The government failed to adjust to population growth. Whereas the county magistrate in the year 1000 governed an average of 80,000 people, he was responsible for over 250,000 in mid-Ch'ing. Inevitably, the government became more remote for the ordinary person. Similarly, the number of doctoral degrees awarded after each triennial examination did not increase between the eleventh and the nineteenth centuries; thus in late imperial China many brilliant and ambitious young men were doomed to frustration, a dangerous situation for any regime.

Missionaries, Foreign Relations, and Trade

Jesuit missionary activities, begun during the Ming dynasty, increased under the Ch'ing. Jesuits continued to head the Board of Astronomy, which forecast eclipses and issued calendars. One tutored young Emperor K'ang-hsi in Western sciences and learning. Others worked as cartographers, interpreters, court painters, and architects; several Jesuits even designed and supervised the building of a villa outside Peking for the emperor that resembled a scaled-down Versailles. Such activities won favor for their brothers who proselytized in the field. The number of Chinese converts to Christianity grew to an estimated 150,000 in the mid-seventeenth century. Jesuit successes were due in part to their acceptance of so-called Chinese rites. They allowed Chinese converts to honor Confucius and to practice ancestor worship, reasoning that they were secular rites and did not contradict monotheistic Christian beliefs. Thus Chinese converts could continue to behave as good, moral Chinese.

Christian influence in China began to decline when Franciscan and Dominican missionaries arrived and challenged Jesuit concessions allowing Chinese converts to maintain their customs. They even proclaimed that Confucius had gone to hell since he was not a Christian. The bitter dispute between the different missionary groups was called the Rites Controversy; it generated 262 books. The pope was finally called on for a ruling. Two cardinals were sent to China to investigate. One was received by Emperor K'ang-hsi, who was outraged that a European leader would presume to rule on what his subjects should believe.

In 1715 the pope decided against the Jesuits and decreed that Chinese practices of honoring Confucius and ancestor worship were incompatible with Catholicism. Henceforth, all Catholic missionaries embarking for China were required to vow not to permit Chinese rites (this ban was not lifted by the Vatican until the 1930s). K'ang-hsi retaliated by drastically restricting all missionary activities and severely limiting all missionaries from entering China in the future. When the pope dissolved the Society of Jesus in 1773, two centuries of Catholic missionary activity came to an end. Of the 500 Jesuits sent to China during that time, 80 substantially contributed to cultural exchange. The Jesuits not only aided the Chinese in astronomy and calendar making but also conducted geographical explorations and compiled a detailed atlas of China, the first showing longitudes and latitudes, though they diplomatically placed China at the center of the world. Jesuit translators also provided the Chinese with European works on geometry, trigonometry, physiology, geography, and other subjects.

The Jesuits also successfully introduced Europeans to the riches of Chinese culture. In 1688 they presented the pope with translations of more than 400 Chinese works in Latin and other European languages, exposing Europeans to the riches of Chinese philosophy and literature for the first time. Great scholars and thinkers such as Spinoza, Leibnitz, Goethe, Adam Smith, Voltaire, and Diderot became admirers of Chinese culture. They were particularly impressed with the Chinese rational approach to government and of the separation of church and state. In art, the Rococo movement reflected Chinese influence: Chinese gardens became a rage (for example, Kew Garden, outside London, was built in the Chinese style) as did Chinese porcelains and artworks.

In the long run, the Jesuits were more successful in presenting Chinese civilization to the West than vice versa, for several reasons. First, as men of religion rather than the sciences, they influenced China only in those facets of European civilization to which the Chinese were receptive, such as astronomy and cartography. Second, most Chinese scholars were ethnocentric, which impeded their reception of alien cultures. Few scholar-bureaucrats could be convinced that they could learn from a culture they deemed inferior. Opportunities for those Chinese who did see profit in Western study ended with the dissolution of the Jesuit missions in the eighteenth century.

In dealing with European states, the early Ch'ing emperors shared the world view of their Ming predecessors and relied on Ming precedents in their foreign relations. They assumed Chinese cultural and diplomatic superiority, a position totally intolerable to

European monarchs. The Ming dynasty had created a Reception Department in charge of its extensive network of tributaries (many had been enrolled by Cheng Ho during his naval expeditions). The Ch'ing modified the Reception Department, giving it charge of the tributaries from southern and eastern Asia, plus the Western countries, and added a Court of Colonial Affairs to deal with the peoples of Inner Asia. The latter defined the tribal territories of Mongols and other nomads, regulated their relations with the court, arranged marriage alliances between tribal chieftains and members of the imperial clan with such success that after the mid-eighteenth century, the nomads ceased to be a source of trouble.

In its trade policy, the Ch'ing government continued the Ming's quarantine that restricted the Portuguese to Macao. Canton was later opened to trade with all Western countries. Here, the government licensed a number of Chinese merchant houses and granted them a monopoly in foreign trade. Correspondingly, Western commercial companies from thirteen countries established "factories," or trading agencies, subject to Chinese regulations. Factory offices were located along the riverfront outside of Canton.

Trade steadily increased, and until the closing years of the eighteenth century, the balance remained in China's favor. Exports consisted of porcelains, tea, silks, and various handicrafts, all in great demand in the West. China's self-sufficiency and small demand for European manufactured goods limited imports to such luxuries as furs from Siberia and North America and clocks, mechanical items, and art objects from Europe. The balance was made up in silver, the basis of Chinese currency.

Anxious to gain the privilege of trade, the Portuguese and Dutch did not object to being enrolled as Chinese tributaries. Between 1655 and 1793, seventeen European missions traveled to Peking bearing tributes, and the leaders of sixteen of them performed the ritual of three kneelings and nine *kowtows* (touching the ground with one's head) before the emperor. Only the British refused to kowtow. An embassy sent by the government of King George III and led by Lord Macartney, arrived in China in 1793. Great Britain, now the major world sea power and China's main trading partner, sought to establish formal diplomatic relations and to negotiate a new and less restrictive trading agreement.

China refused to change the established mode of international relations, continued to treat the British diplomats as tribute bearers from a vassal state, and after entertaining them lavishly, sent them home empty-handed. Although sorely disappointed, the British were too involved in European wars to press the Chinese. Macartney, however, noted that China was behind Europe technologically and predicted that it would be easy to defeat.

China's relations with Russia were an exception to this pattern in that the two nations treated each other as equals. Russian ambassadors performed the kowtows before the Chinese emperor, while Chinese ambassadors saluted the tsars according to Russian court protocol. Since the sixteenth century, Cossacks had spearheaded the Russian advance eastward across Siberia in pursuit of furs, especially sable. They arrived at the Amur River in northern Manchuria at the same time as the Manchus rose to power. Preoccupied with consolidating their power in China, the Ch'ing government endured Cossack raids without retaliating. After quelling a revolt in South China, K'ang-hsi turned his attention to Russia. He was anxious to come to terms with the Russians so that the yet unsubdued western Mongol tribes would not ally themselves with Russia. Two Jesuit priests acted as interpreters for the Ch'ing delegation and also as mediators between the two camps. The Treaty of Nerchinsk in 1689 and another treaty concluded in 1714 defined the boundaries between the two empires and regulated trade and other relations. These treaties were written in five languages—Chinese, Russian, Manchu, Mongol, and Latin; the Latin version served as the official text.

The Last Great Era of Traditional Culture and the Arts

Since the Ch'ing rulers admired Chinese civilization, cultural life experienced little disruption with the transfer of power from Ming to Ch'ing. Early Ch'ing emperors patronized artists and artisans, as did wealthy scholars and merchants, most notably the flamboyant millionaire salt merchants of Yangchow on the lower Yangtze River, a city noted for its eccentric artist colony and beautiful gardens.

Painting, considered the most important form of artistic expression, continued along the styles established since the Sung dynasty with some modifications on perspective introduced by Jesuit court painters. Just as the Moghul emperor Jahangir patronized European artists to teach Renaissance art forms to Indians, Emperor Ch'ien-lung employed Jesuit artists to introduce new techniques to the Chinese. The most notable Jesuit painter was the eighteenth-century Italian Giuseppe Castiglione (better known as an artist by his Chinese name Lang Shih-ning). Dozens of Castiglione's paintings, many documenting Emperor Ch'ien-lung's military campaigns and hunting expeditions, others portraying the monarch's favorite ladies, horses, and dogs, survive in Chinese and Western museums and private collections.

Scholarly pursuits also continued along traditional lines. Historians wrote many local histories. Scholars also made significant contributions in historiography and philology and compiled and published major dictionaries and encyclopedias. In the 1770s a government board published a monumental work called the *Complete Writings of the Four Treasuries* (classics, histories, philosophies, and belles lettres). It consisted of all major works published to date and came to 36,000 volumes. They were so expensive to print that only seven complete sets were made; fortunately, several have survived. The benefits of this monumental effort are obvious, but the Emperor Ch'ien-lung also had a dark motive for sponsoring the project—to expurgate from the collected writings derogatory mentions of the Manchus and other dynasties with nomadic origins. About 3,000 works were tampered with and some works by Ming authors were suppressed altogether.

Poets, essayists, and novelists continued to work in the Ming tradition. *The Dream of the Red Chamber* is the most noted novel of the Ch'ing. It focused on women, as did many other popular novels. The admired women in these novels are described as "literary and talented," because they studied the classics, wrote poetry, painted, and played musical instruments. Although precise figures are not available, more women received an education than in previous eras. An anthology of Ch'ing women poets made in 1831 had 933 names, while a supplement made in 1835 listed an additional 513 names. A collection of songwriters had 783 female composers who wrote 22,045 songs.

LIVES AND TIMES ACROSS CULTURES

Marriage Customs in India and China

In India since medieval times, arranged marriages between children became common in well-to-do families. The bride's parents had to provide her with a dowry and to pay for the festivities, often incurring heavy debts to do so. The marriage was solemnized by a brahman priest according to the Vedas. The first part was held in the bride's parents' home when her father formally gave her to the groom, who promised not to be false to her in respect to the three goals of life—piety, wealth, or pleasure. The newly wed couple then returned to the groom's home to perform further rites. The proceedings lasted for about a week before the marriage was consummated. The solemnity of the ceremony indicated the importance, sanctity, and binding nature of marriage to Hindus. Divorces were virtually forbidden among the upper castes but were permitted by custom among the lower castes. The ideal marriage was monogamous; though rulers and some rich men took secondary wives, the senior wife was held in the highest respect.

Likewise, in China marriages were arranged by family elders, often with the help of go-betweens, and involved contracts specifying the number and value of presents from the groom's family and the bride's dowry; the husband generally managed his wife's property, but to her benefit and that of her children. The prospective bride and groom did not see each other until the wedding, generally when the couple were in their late teens. The marriage ceremony was secular in nature, and no priests officiated. On the wedding day the groom's party traveled to the bride's home to escort her to his home, where the wedding ceremony consisted of obeisance by the two before the groom's ancestral shrine and his parents, followed by feasting. The pair subsequently returned to the bride's home to pay honor to her ancestors' shrine and her parents, followed by festivities hosted by her family. As in India, the bride lived with her husband's family. Divorces were permitted, under more lenient terms when initiated by the husband, but family and societal pressure made them rare. A man could have only one legal wife at a time, but was allowed to have concubines if his financial position permitted, especially if the wife was childless.

The theater remained popular. Both the Peking opera and regional style operas presented historical stories and stories taken from popular novels, through a combination of singing, dancing, and acrobatics. Storytellers in teahouses in villages and towns also retold these stories. Operas were patronized by everyone from emperors to common people. Other popular modes of recreation were religious and folk festivals, many of which featured distinctive foods and drinks.

The Chinese and other East Asians followed the lunar calendar and did not have a seven-day week. Thus there was no regular day of rest on Sundays. Holidays followed cycles of the moon or some other form of rotation. The most important holidays were the lunar New Year, which was celebrated for fifteen days until the first full moon of the first month and climaxed with the lantern festival. Other popular festivals were holidays to visit ancestral graves in the spring, the Dragon Boat festival on the fifth day of the fifth month, a lovers' festival on the seventh day of the seventh month, and a mid-autumn full moon festival to celebrate the harvest. Gift giving, visiting friends and families, and special foods were associated with each holiday. Some holidays were specific to a profession; for example, Confucius's birth was celebrated in schools and fishermen honored the goddess Ma-tsu of the sea. Others were local in nature. Tobacco smoking through long pipes, introduced by Westerners during the Ming dynasty, and taking snuff, a powdered tobacco, had become very prevalent among both men and women.

Families celebrated betrothals, weddings, births of children, and birthdays, especially those of old people. Social etiquette segregated upper-class men and women in most entertainments and parties. When the emperors K'ang-hsi and Ch'ien-lung celebrated their birthdays in old age, they sometimes invited old men from throughout the empire to attend an elaborate banquet at the palace where they were served by the emperors' sons and grandsons. In cities men had added opportunities of visiting pleasure quarters and being entertained by singing girls and prostitutes. Dominos, playing cards, and *mah jong* were popular gambling games. People also wagered on various contests, the most popular being cricket fights and kite flying contests.

Imperial patronage and general prosperity also led to a flowering of many minor arts, most importantly ceramics. Porcelains produced from the K'ang-hsi reign to the latter part of the eighteenth century provided a dazzling grand finale to the cavalcade of several thousand years of the Chinese potters' art. An extremely wide variety of porcelains produced in imperial and private kilns catered to the tastes of Chinese, other Asians, and Europeans. On the one hand, the craze for porcelains led to the establishment of pottery works in Europe based on information provided by the Jesuits. On the other hand, Chinese fondness for European novelties resulted in the adoption of European methods of decoration and designs in Chinese ceramics. For example, the Jesuits introduced a rose pink color in Chinese porcelain decoration. Pieces so decorated became popular from the Yung-cheng reign onward and are called "famille rose" in the West but "foreign colors" in China. Ch'ing ceramics are prized in public and private collections the world over.

Although most artisans were men, women and girls continued to be important in the textile industries. Even girls in rich households were taught to sew and embroider, which were considered feminine accomplishments. Women also helped their husbands and sons run family businesses, farm women labored alongside the men, and poor women worked as maids, nurses, and governesses and in such "women's professions" as midwifery.

A Centralized Feudal State in Japan

[In 1534] there appeared off our western shore a big ship. No one knew whence it had come. It carried a crew of over a hundred whose physical features differed from ours, and whose language was unintelligible. . . . In their hands they carried something two or three feet long . . . made of a heavy substance. . . . To use it, fill it with powder and small lead pellets. . . . Grip the object in your hand, compose your body, and close one eye, apply fire to the aperture. Then the pellet hits the target squarely. The explosion is like lightning and the report like thunder. . . . This thing with one blow can smash a mountain of silver and a wall of iron. If one sought to do mischief in another man's domain and he was touched by it, he would lose his life instantly.

> *Lord Tokitaka saw it and thought it was the wonder of wonders. . . . Thus, one day, Tokitaka spoke to the two alien leaders through an interpreter: "Incapable though I am, I should like to learn about it." Whereupon, the chiefs answered, also through an interpreter: "If you wish to learn about it, we shall teach you its mysteries."*
>
> *Tokitaka procured two pieces of the weapon and studied them, and with one volley of the weapon startled sixty provinces of our country. Moreover, it was he who made the iron-workers learn the method of their manufacture and made it possible for the knowledge to spread over the entire length and breadth of the country.**

*As described by Nampo Bunshi, "Teppo-ki," in *Sources of Japanese Tradition*, ed. William T. de Bary (New York: Columbia University Press, 1958), vol. 1, pp. 308–312.

This account of the introduction of firearms by Portuguese traders to Japan was recounted sixty years after the event by a descendant of the southern Japanese lord in whose domain the first Portuguese ships had landed. Japanese lords immediately appreciated the significance of firearms and widely adopted them for use against their local enemies. As a result, Japanese battle tactics and castle construction were revolutionized. Firearms also were important in the wars that unified Japan in the late sixteenth century.

Although Europeans did not attempt to conquer Japan, their success in establishing control over strategic points in Southeast Asia and the proselytizing success of Catholic missionaries in Japan inspired alarm in Japanese leaders. They feared Europeans lest they might be tempted to conquer Japan, and lest Japanese Catholic converts declare allegiance first to the pope. These fears and domestic political reasons propelled early-seventeenth-century leaders of the newly unified Japan to expel most foreigners, ban Christianity, and severely restrict the outside contacts of Japanese.

The Building of a Centralized Feudal State

The Kamakura shogunate ended in 1336. It had controlled Japan since the twelfth century, but had been fatally weakened by costly military expenditures to halt the invading Mongols. General Ashikaga Takauji established his family as hereditary shoguns in 1338. Although the Ashikaga shogunate lasted until 1573, it exerted effective central control only for a brief initial period. Then civil wars broke out between the *daimyo* (literally meaning "great name," but referring to the feudal lords; in feudal Europe and Japan only the lords and knights had surnames). The imperial court at Kyoto remained impotent.

Although the Ashikaga period was marked by a long succession of civil wars, it was also a time of rapid cultural and economic development. Increasing yields in the rice crop fueled an expanding economy. In the growing towns, specialized artisans organized in guilds similar to their counterparts in Europe, specializing in paper, textiles, metal wares, and art objects. Trade flourished, especially with China. Japan imported copper coins, books, and artworks from China and exported copper, painted folding fans, screens, and, most importantly, swords. The shogunal government, daimyo, and Buddhist monasteries all participated in a lucrative trade with China. To facilitate trade the Ashikaga shoguns acknowledged the Ming emperors as overlords and were in turn invested as "kings of Japan." Other Japanese turned to piracy, which the ineffectual shoguns were powerless to control. Cultural contact with China ensured the growing

Courtesy of the Freer Gallery of Art, Smithsonian Institution, Washington, D.C.
F1965.23

Screens Showing Europeans. Richly painted screens decorated the interiors of wealthy Japanese households; during the seventeenth century, European subjects were popular. This one shows curious Japanese watching Portuguese sailors and priests as they walk along a street.

importance of Zen Buddhism, tea drinking, the tea ceremony, flower arranging, and landscape gardening.

In the midst of these civil wars, the first Europeans, with their novel firearms, arrived in Japan. The warring daimyo immediately appreciated their importance and began first to purchase and then to manufacture their own. The winning side in a battle fought in 1575 had 38,000 soldiers and 10,000 matchlocks.

The advent of firearms hastened the process of unification, led by three successive leaders. Oda Nobunaga (1534–1582), a daimyo from near Kyoto, quickly grasped the importance of learning about new weaponry from the Europeans. He treated Christian missionaries cordially, because he and others had noticed that Portuguese traders tended to land in the domain of those daimyo who were friendly toward missionaries. He also adopted firearms and other Western battle tactics, built himself a virtually impregnable fortress, destroyed his monastic and secular enemies, and ended the Ashikaga shogunate. Oda was assassinated in 1582 before he could consolidate his work.

In the chaos of the civil wars, the strict hereditary social ranks lapsed and talented men of humble birth rose to power. The rise of Hideyoshi (1536–1598) was the prime example and without precedent in Japanese history. Born in such a humble family that he had no surname, he rose to power by sheer ruthlessness and ability. Five years after Oda's death, he had consolidated power by killing Oda's young heirs and crushing all foes. After that he adopted the grand surname of Toyotomi, meaning "wealth of the nation!" Subsequently, he ordered a national land survey, assigned fiefs to his supporters, confiscated all weapons from peasants, and, ironically, fixed all people in their social positions and occupations. Ambitious for more conquests and eager to find fresh outlets for his warriors, Hideyoshi set out to conquer the world—meaning China. Before he could attempt to conquer China, however, he had first to control Korea. With an army of

150,000, he overran Korea in 1592, but then was turned back by a Ming army. With Korean "turtle ships," the world's first metal-plated wooden vessels, harassing his supply line, he was forced to retreat. Hideyoshi resumed his attack in 1597, but the invasion was abandoned upon his death the following year. The horrors inflicted on Korea by the invading Japanese left a lasting scar on the victim nation. As much as a third of Korea's population may have perished as a result of the invasion.

Hideyoshi did not have a son until late in life, and had designated a nephew as his heir. When a son was finally born to him, he forced his adult nephew to commit suicide and named his son as successor. As death drew near, he appointed a council of five regents to rule on behalf of his young son. He hoped the regents would check one another's ambitions, thereby enabling the boy to escape the fate of Oda's heirs.

One of the five regents was Tokugawa Ieyasu (1542–1616), a daimyo who did not participate in the Korean campaigns and took advantage of them to expand his power. From his formidable castle at Edo (now the Emperor's palace in modern Tokyo), Tokugawa's forces won the power struggle against his rivals, and he took the title of shogun in 1603. He then killed all Hideyoshi's heirs, organized the government, and enacted new laws that ensured the survival of his family as shoguns until 1868.

To make sure that his heirs to the shogunate would have unrivaled wealth and unchallenged power, he reserved for his family one-quarter of the arable land of Japan, mainly around Edo and Kyoto, as well as all major ports. He surrounded his domains with land awarded to relatives and allies. He ordered many castles torn down and forbade the daimyo to build and even repair old ones without his permission.

Ieyasu required all daimyo to spend alternate years in residence at Edo, and in the off years to keep their principal wives and heirs at the shogun's capital. Like Louis XIV of France, he encouraged the daimyo to build splendid residences, surround themselves with large and sumptuous retinues, and live in lavish style in Edo; many became impoverished courtiers as a result. To forestall plots against the shogunal government, he created a secret service that watched for weapons and scrutinized the secret movements of daimyo wives. To ensure intellectual orthodoxy, Ieyasu encouraged Neo-Confucian studies, banned Christianity, and expelled most foreigners, thereby isolating Japan from a potentially dangerous outside world.

After Ieyasu had done all he could to make his government secure, he retired in 1605 in favor of an adult son. However, he retained the reins of government behind the scene until his death in 1616. In like manner, the second shogun retired in favor of his son. By this means, the younger man learned his job under an experienced father's tutelage. Thus the Tokugawa line was secured. Other laws ensured stability and prevented ambitious officials from seizing power from weak shoguns. As a result, Japan enjoyed two and a half centuries of peace.

Japan Becomes Isolationist

Christian missionaries made an even more powerful impact on Japan than on China. Christianity was introduced to Japan by Francis Xavier, a close friend of Ignatius Loyola, founder of the Society of Jesus. Called the "apostle of the East," Xavier was active in Japan from 1549 to 1551. To many Japanese the Christianity preached by the Jesuits seemed a variant on Buddhism. Noting the deference Portuguese merchants paid to the priests and their tendency to visit ports where missionaries were welcome, many daimyo welcomed the missionaries in order to obtain European goods, especially weapons. Some even converted to Catholicism for that reason and ordered their subjects to do likewise, in the same manner as in Europe where rulers held the power to choose their subjects' religions.

In his attempt to win more Japanese converts, Xavier left Japan for China; he believed that Japanese respect for the Chinese was so great that success in China would lead to massive conversions in Japan. As in China, the Jesuits' success roused the jealousy of the other missionary orders, notably, the Franciscans and Dominicans. By 1582 Christian missionaries had won 150,000 converts in Japan, and by 1615 perhaps as many as 500,000.

Such large numbers of converts caused a backlash among many Japanese, some because they were offended by the Christian intolerance for existing religions. Some Buddhists opposed the Christian missionaries on

Portrait of Tokugawa Ieyasu. This formal portrait of the elderly founder of the Tokugawa shogunate shows a still-imposing man.

Tokugawa Art Museum, Nagoya, Japan

religious principles. Most important, many Japanese leaders equated missionary activities with the expansionist policies of European nations, and they doubted the political loyalty of Japanese converts. Thus Hideyoshi banned Christianity in 1587, but did not strictly enforce his edict. In 1612 all Japanese converts were ordered to renounce Christianity on pain of death, and European missionaries were either expelled or executed. Until 1660 numerous military expeditions searched the countryside for Christian communities, and tens of thousands were killed; as a result, only small clandestine Christian communities on Kyushu Island survived.

In its zeal to isolate Japan from Europe, the Tokugawa shogunate expanded the ban on missionaries to include all Spanish, Portuguese, and English traders as well. The Dutch alone were allowed to send two ships yearly to Nagasaki, because they were not

LIVES AND TIMES ACROSS CULTURES

Determining Political Succession

Succession within the ruling family marked all dynastic rule. Although most cultures had laws regarding succession, some had no clearly defined and accepted practices.

The Moghul dynasty had no definite rules of succession among an emperor's sons by his different wives. Aging Moghul emperors were often challenged by their impatient and ambitious sons; the many revolts and civil wars over succession contributed significantly to weakening the dynasty. For example, the emperor Aurangzeb (reigned 1659–1707) successfully revolted against his father Shah Jahan, imprisoned him for the last seven years of his life, and then murdered his brothers, who had supported their father. As one historian wrote, "his life would have been a blameless one, if he had had no father to depose, no brethren to murder, and no Hindu subjects to oppress." The wars of succession and massive revolts that broke out after Aurengzeb's death ended effective Moghul power.

In China the Ming dynasty strictly followed the practice of primogeniture, and after the successful revolt by the Prince of Yen, fourth son of the founding emperor, no succession struggles marred the dynasty. The Ch'ing dynasty did not follow primogeniture and allowed the ruling emperor to choose among his sons. The nation learned of the choice of the great K'ang-hsi (reigned 1661–1722) only after his death in his final valediction:"My Fourth Son Yin-chen—Prince Yung—has a noble character and profoundly resembles me; it is definite that he has the ability to inherit the empire. Let him succeed me to the throne and become emperor."

In Japan Tokugawa Ieyasu ensured the stability of the shogunate he had founded by choosing an adult son, Hidetada, to succeed him as shogun in 1605. As Ieyasu's biographer stated: "Ieyasu accomplished two things in transferring the shogunal title to Hidetada. First, he established the principle that the shogunal title was the hereditary possession of the Tokugawa family. . . . Second, he shifted a host of tedious administrative and judgemental matters onto Hidetada's shoulders." Ieyasu lived for eleven years after the formal transfer of power. This pattern was repeated by Hidetada with his own son, by which time the line was secure.

Catholics and had not attempted to convert the Japanese; however, the few Dutch who resided in Japan lived in virtual imprisonment on an offshore island. Remarkably, a small number of Japanese continued to learn Dutch and to translate Western books on mathematics, the sciences, and medicine into Japanese during the centuries of isolation. As one late-eighteenth-century Japanese said with admiration:

> In Holland . . . they consider astronomy and geography to be the most important subject of study because unless a ship's captain is well versed in these sciences it is impossible for him to sail as he chooses to all parts of the world. Moreover, the Dutch have the excellent national characteristic of investigating matters with great patience until they can get to the very bottom. For the sake of such research they have devised surveying instruments as well as telescopes and helioscopes with which to examine the sun, moon, and stars.

The isolation of Japan intensified in 1636 when an edict prohibited all Japanese from leaving Japan and those already abroad from returning. Chinese ships were allowed to trade in Japan under license, however, and brought in limited knowledge about the

West. To prevent clandestine departures, shipbuilders were allowed to construct only coastal vessels. Those Japanese already abroad were forbidden to return, the sizable Japanese communities scattered about Southeast Asia were isolated from their homeland, and Japanese trade with Southeast Asia and Europe came to a virtual end. Western interest in Japan soon faded. As a result of this isolation, although the Japanese were as advanced as Europeans in many fields in the sixteenth century, they were well behind the West in technology and industry by the nineteenth.

Feudalism under the Tokugawa Shogunate

Economic growth continued throughout the Tokugawa era. Unlike Europe, where economic growth and political changes in the late Middle Ages had brought feudalism to an end, in Japan, the Tokugawas imposed a centralized and rigidly ordered feudal state and society after they had reunified the country. Unlike Confucian China, where the four hierarchic social classes (scholar, farmer, artisan, and merchant) were fluid and legally not hereditary, in Neo-Confucian Japan (Chu Hsi's Neo-Confucian teachings were proclaimed orthodox in Tokugawa Japan), the four classes (with the samurai replacing the

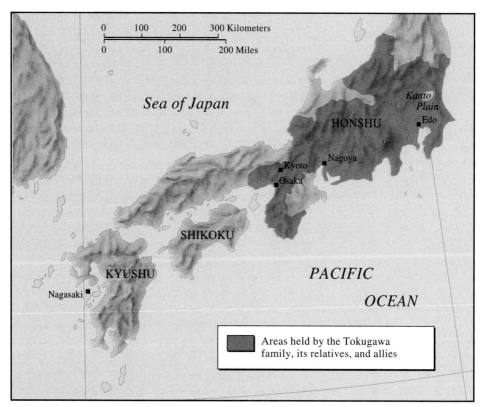

Map 10.6 Japan under the Tokugawa Shogunate. The house of Tokugawa, with its relations and allies, controlled most of the cultivatable lands and cities of Japan and devised laws that restricted the other daimyo. This ensured a period of peace for two and a half centuries.

scholar class) were rigidly divided and hereditary. Japanese social stratification more resembled European social classes under feudalism than Hindu castes, because in both Europe and Japan the divisions were not religiously based, as castes were under Hinduism.

Atop the social structure were the daimyo and their retainers, the samurai, who accounted for about 7 percent of the population, or 2 million people (out of a total of approximately 30 million people at the height of the shogunate, a larger proportion than the aristocracy in feudal Europe). Their incomes were measured in rice equivalents, based on assessments made on the farmers. All samurai bore surnames, lived under a strict code of honor, wore distinctive clothing, were entitled to wear two swords, and were forbidden to engage in manual labor or commerce. They congregated in castle towns of the daimyo or in Edo.

Most daimyo provided schools for educating samurai boys. Their curriculum was divided between the martial arts and the Confucian classics. There were no schools for daughters of samurai. They were taught the womanly arts, including flower arrangement, etiquette and the social graces, music, and practical matters of housekeeping by their mothers and visiting female teachers. Few women learned more than rudimentary Chinese writing; like aristocratic ladies of the Heian age, samurai women of the Tokugawa period learned to write in Kana, the Japanese syllabary form. Samurai were enjoined to be frugal and live hard Spartan lives. With the passage of time, they also took to the same leisure pursuits as townspeople, such as visiting brothels and theaters. Living on fixed incomes, many fell into debt.

Whereas in European feudal society serfs cultivated the land for aristocratic landowners and lived clustered around manors, the bulk of the Japanese were taxpaying peasants (about a quarter were tenants) living in villages and enjoying a large measure of self-government. Some richer peasants, who were descended from samurai but whose ancestors had opted to farm when Hideyoshi allowed them a choice, even bore family names. Many villages had their own schools, often associated with Buddhist temples, and literacy among peasants was high.

Rice was the primary crop, followed by other cereals such as wheat, barley, and millet. Three plants were grown for giving material for textiles: hemp for a linenlike cloth for outer clothing, cotton for daily clothes (at first imported from Korea, grown and manufactured locally after the seventeenth century), and mulberry for silkworms and the luxury silk fabrics. As in China, women were key to the textile industry. Tailoring was simple and was done by women of the household. Garments were merely tacked together, taken apart before each laundering, and resewn afterward. Preoccupied with cleanliness, families either had their own bathhouse or frequently used the communal ones. Woven straw mats covered floors, and shoes were removed upon entering the house.

Farmers paid between 40 and 60 percent of the estimated rice crop in taxes, in addition to other dues and corvée labor. Since taxes increased more slowly after the first half of the seventeenth century than did productivity (partly due to crops introduced from the Americas), so the farmers' standard of living rose.

Unlike the Chinese, who divided the family land among all sons, the eldest son inherited the paternal farm, while younger sons were forced to become farm laborers or to

How to Live and Die with Honor

When they were all seated in a row for final despatch, Sakon turned to the youngest and said: "Go thou first, for I wish to be sure that thou doest it right." Upon the little one's replying that, as he had never seen seppuku performed, he would like to see his brothers do it, and then he could follow them, the older brothers smiled between their tears: "Well said, little fellow. So canst thou well boast of being our father's child." When they had placed him between them, Sakon thrust the dagger into the left side of his abdomen and said: "Look, brother! Dost thou understand now? Only don't push the dagger too far, lest thou fall back. Lean forward, rather, and keep thy knees well composed." Nicki did likewise. . . . The child looked from one to the other, and when both had expired, he calmly . . . followed the example set him on either side.*

The code of honor that governed the lives of samurai dictated that one take one's own life when necessary. This famous true story tells of two young brothers who failed in their attempt to assassinate Tokugawa Ieyasu to avenge wrongs he had inflicted on their father. They were condemned to death, but in recognition of their courage and filial piety, he commuted their sentence to suicide, or *seppuku*. Their youngest brother, only eight years old, was also sentenced to die, in accordance with Japanese tradition (were he allowed to live, he would have to avenge his brothers' deaths). This touching tale tells of how the two older brothers taught the youngest to die like a samurai.

*Inazo Nitobe, Bushido: The Soul of Japan *(New York: Putnam, 1905), p. 121.*

drift to cities. Many families practiced infanticide, euphemistically called "thinning out" (girl infants were more likely to be killed). Abortion was also practiced. In hard times farmers sold extra daughters into what amounted to slavery in the brothels. However, a girl in a brothel or entertainment house could be redeemed either by a patron, to become his wife or mistress, or by her parents. Young women who had worked in brothels or as entertainers were often in demand as wives upon returning to their villages because of their "education" and experiences in the big outside world.

Most accounts about farmers were written by unsympathetic city dwellers who depicted them as crude yokels, or by samurai who portrayed them as near-criminals bent on cheating the samurai out of their rice stipends, or as feckless people prone to rioting. Records show that there were around 1,500 peasant revolts during the Tokugawa era. Most were minor and involved local grievances or were protests against high taxes and other hardships. Leaders of failed peasant revolts were cruelly punished.

Entertainment for country people evolved around family celebrations such as marriages, community projects, and Buddhist and Shinto religious holidays. Early Tokugawa laws prohibited the staging of plays for farmers lest they become discontented from seeing luxurious upper-class living portrayed in plays. Besides, attending performances wasted their time. The law was soon relaxed, however, because it was unenforceable. Watching the sumptuous daimyo processions between Edo and the feudal domains provided free entertainment for those living en route.

Pilgrimages were very popular; the great shrine to the Sun Goddess Amaterasu at Isé was the most favored destination. It was the ambition of most Japanese to visit Isé at least once in their lifetime. Many villages formed Isé associations; all who paid dues were eligible to enter a drawing each year for a trip to the shrine. Those who went represented the whole village and returned with charms and amulets for all. In addition to the shrine, Isé provided a full range of entertainments for the pilgrim, including brothels, restaurants, *kabuki* and puppet theaters, and souvenir shops. Other popular pilgrimage destinations included a hike up the slopes of Mount Fuji.

Cities prospered during the centuries of Tokugawa peace. Edo had almost a million people by the early eighteenth century, Osaka and Kyoto each had about 300,000. Merchants, artisans, and laborers thronged to the cities to serve the needs of the rulers and one another.

The socially lowly but economically well-off merchants dominated urban culture. Their wealth made them the objects of both envy and hate by the samurai; many samurai became indebted to merchants. Several groups of merchants were conspicuously successful, the *sake* (the ubiquitous rice wine) dealers, the rice exchangers, shippers, and pawnbrokers. Successful merchant families formed diversified business empires. The house of Mitsui, a modern giant conglomerate, had its roots in the Tokugawa period. It began with a woman and her sons who became sake merchants, pawnbrokers, and drapery shop owners. Many merchants attributed their success to frugal living and a good work ethic. One merchant house broke down the reasons for its success as follows: early rising, 10 percent; devotion to family business, 40 percent; working after hours, 16 percent; thrift, 20 percent; and good health, 14 percent. It then warned its members against:

1. Expensive food and women; silk *kimonos* every day.
2. Private carrying-chairs for wives; music or card lessons for marriageable daughters.
3. Drum lessons for sons of the house.
4. Football, miniature archery, incense appreciation, poetry contests.
5. Renovations to the house, addiction to the tea ceremony.
6. Cherry-blossom viewing, boat trips, daily baths.
7. Spending nights on the town, gambling parties, playing indoor games.
8. Lessons, for townsmen, in sword drawing and duelling. . . .
9. Sake with the evening meal, excessive pipe-smoking, unnecessary trips to Kyoto.
10. Sponsoring charity wrestling; excessive contributions to temples. . . .
11. Familiarity with actors and pleasure districts.
12. Borrowing money at more than 8 percent per month.

Despite such warnings, townspeople flocked to the kabuki theater, which featured real-life dramas, presented on revolving stages. Wealthy men went to quarters where *geisha* entertained them with witty conversation, song, and dance, just as the hetaerai in Periclean Athens did. (This was the only situation in an otherwise segregated society where men and women mingled socially.)

Artisans also congregated in cities. They were organized into guilds similar to those in medieval Europe. Boys were apprenticed to learn a craft at a young age. Apprentices lived in the homes of their masters for seven to eight years learning their trade and serving their masters with filial respect. They were expected to serve their masters for six months to a year after completion of their apprenticeship. Then they could become journeymen or set up independent businesses. Like their European, Indian, and Chinese counterparts, people of the same trade tended to live together in the same quarter of the town, which often bore their trade names. People of the same trade also shared a protective deity in the Buddhist or Shinto pantheon and celebrated the same festivals.

Some trades were more prestigious than others. The sword makers were among the most respected, not surprising in a warrior culture. Among workers in the same trade, those who worked for the shogun or daimyo also enjoyed greater prestige. Except for the textile industry, most trades were male preserves. Tradesmen paid taxes. Laborers such as porters and servants ranked below artisans, and were numerous in all cities and towns.

Numerous publishing houses flourished, printing a wide range of books including history, poetry, religious commentary, guide books to amusement quarters, and stories that portray characters set in contemporary Japan. Woodblock prints, called *ukiyo-e* (pictures of the floating world because Buddhism taught that the pleasures of the senses were transitory and therefore floating), depicted famous actors, beautiful geisha, and scenic spots. The prints became the popular art of the day because they were less expensive than original paintings. It was the first Japanese art form esteemed in the West and influenced late-nineteenth-century European artists. Ceramic art also flourished, initially under the impetus of Korean potters brought back by Hideyoshi's soldiers. Local potters supplied utilitarian vessels for daily needs and esthetically refined pieces for tea ceremonies.

In cities and the countryside, among all social classes, men were legally superior to women, and marriages were arranged for both parties. The bride normally went to live with her husband's family, where she was strictly subordinated to her mother-in-law; her status improved after she had borne male children. A family that had no son might adopt a son-in-law into the family. In this situation, the roles were reversed. Except among the daimyo, who might have concubines, marriages were monogamous.

Strains in the Late Tokugawa Era

By the eighteenth century, changing economic, social, and cultural conditions had put the rigid political structure of the Tokugawa shogunate under stress. Even in isolation the Japanese economy had outgrown its feudal restrictions. Paper money and drafts of credit were used in business transactions, rice exchanges at Edo and Osaka quoted daily fluctuating prices, and wealthy merchants, such as the house of Mitsui, dominated commerce. The samurai and daimyo, who lived on fixed incomes calculated in measures of rice, found themselves in straitened circumstances in an increasingly affluent world, and many became indebted to merchants. Some daimyo tried such temporary and arbitrary remedies as enacting laws that canceled their debts to the politically impotent merchants. Others married their sons to rich merchants' daughters for their large dowries. Such measures, however, could not solve the fundamental economic problem, which was that the feudal restrictions had put the economy in a straitjacket.

Although the Tokugawa shoguns gave no political power to the emperors, they did treat them with greater respect and dignity than had previous shoguns and thus inadvertently raised them to the status of potential political rivals. In encouraging Neo-Confucianism with its emphasis on the study of history, the shogunate revived interest in the emperor and the cult of the monarchy. Japanese learned that the emperors had once actually ruled, and some began to believe that they should rule again. Still others developed an interest in Shintoism.

The economic changes, social developments, and intellectual turmoil of the late Tokugawa period all point to the increasing strains to the shogunate. Japan was outgrowing its feudal constraints and was on the threshold of entering the modern age. The pervasive ferment beneath the surface calm made Japan much more receptive to change in 1853, when Western nations forced it to open, than China was in the nineteenth century.

Summary and Comparisons

This chapter looked at Asia region by region from the fourteenth to the eighteenth centuries. In the thirteenth century, much of mainland Southeast Asia came under the domination of Kubilai Khan's branch of the Mongol Empire, though the islands escaped conquest. After the fall of the Mongols, Ming China dominated many parts of the region through its preeminence on land and sea. From the sixteenth century on, island Southeast Asia, lacking any strong, unified governments, attracted European traders and empire builders drawn by its many precious raw materials and products, especially spices, and its potential as an entrepôt for trade with China. Portugal's short-lived control of strategically located ports ended in the sixteenth century, to be succeeded by the Dutch Empire based on Java. Spain colonized the Philippine islands and converted the majority of their peoples to Catholicism. Elsewhere Islam continued its peaceful conversion in Malaya and present-day Indonesia. Buddhism, too, continued to thrive.

Powerful empires ruled in India and China during the early modern era. The Moghul dynasty, with its great administrators, avid builders, and generous patrons of the arts, unified India after centuries of division. Though Muslims, many Moghul rulers allowed their majority of Hindu subjects considerable religious freedom. The empire declined rapidly in the eighteenth century, formally ending in 1857. Portuguese sailors, the first Europeans to reach India, were supplanted by the English, who eventually also replaced the Moghuls as India's ruling power.

In 1368 a Chinese-led revolt expelled the Mongols and created the Ming dynasty. The capable early Ming emperors repaired China's shattered economy, repopulated the land, and restored Chinese pride. Well-educated Ming bureaucrats gave China three centuries of stable government at home, while Ming military and naval power secured many vassal states on China's periphery.

In 1648 a frontier people, the Manchus (or Ch'ing), superseded the Ming dynasty after its long decline. Already deeply influenced by Chinese civilization, the Manchu rulers preserved earlier governmental institutions and patronized learning and the arts. As elsewhere in Asia, Portuguese sailors were the first Europeans to reach China and were eventually restricted to one port, Macao. China enjoyed a favorable balance of trade with Europe because of the appeal of luxury products like silk and porcelain. As in India, Jesuit missionaries converted few but earned deep respect as learned men and cultural ambassadors.

CHRONOLOGY

1300	
	Ashikaga shogunate begins in Japan
	Ming dynasty begins in China
1400	Ming capital established at Peking
	Chinese naval expeditions to South and Southeast Asia
	The Portuguese arrive in India
1500	
	Portuguese establish a trade empire in Southeast Asia
	Moghul conquest of India
	Guru Nanak founds Sikhism
	Portuguese establish trade with China
	The Portuguese introduce Christianity and firearms to Japan
	Akbar rules India
	Era of great Chinese opera and novels
	The Spanish rule in the Philippines
	Jesuit missionaries arrive in China
	The Dutch establish a trade empire in the East Indies
1600	Tokugawa shogunate begins in Japan
	Japan expels foreigners
	Neo-Confucianism adopted in Japan
	European trade in China restricted to Canton
	Ch'ing (Manchu) dynasty begins in China
	Taj Mahal built in India
1700	
	Ts'ao Hsueh-ch'in, *The Dream of the Red Chamber*
	Effective Moghul rule ends in India
	Christian missionary activity ends in China
	British embassy sent to China
	Great Britain acquires Ceylon
1800	Great Britain purchases Singapore

In Japan, after a long period of civil chaos, the Tokugawa shogunate inaugurated a centralized and bureaucratic feudal government in 1603, with the emperors remaining as impotent figureheads. Troubled by the early successes of Catholic missionaries in winning converts and the dangers of European weapons in the hands of potential dissidents, the Tokugawa shogunate banned Christianity and closed Japan to the world in the early seventeenth century. This arrested political and social development and helped to perpetuate the Tokugawa shogunate for two and a half centuries.

The Moghul dynasty in India, the Ming and Ch'ing dynasties in China, and the Tokugawa shogunate in Japan all established unified, prosperous, and long-lasting regimes founded on military strength and cultural advancement. All three stimulated intellectual growth and cultural flowering. The Moghuls and Manchus were both outsiders whose language and religion differed from those of the people they conquered. However, while the Moghuls retained their Muslim faith and the Persian language, the Manchus quickly began to speak Chinese and abandoned shamanism for Buddhism and Confucianism. Thus Moghuls introduced another cultural element into India, while the Manchus continued the development of Chinese culture. By contrast, the Ming and Tokugawa were both indigenous rulers. However, the Tokugawa family was of noble lineage, while the founder of the Ming dynasty came from poor peasant stock and rose through his ability alone.

Unlike the other regions discussed in this chapter, Southeast Asia lacked political and cultural unity, having been heavily influenced by Indian and Chinese cultures. Further complexity ensued as the era progressed. China retained its political influence over parts of mainland Southeast Asia, while European nations built trading and territorial empires in the islands. In the religious realm, Islam continued its spread over the Indonesian islands and in Malaya, while Catholicism became predominant in the Philippines.

Selected Sources

Items indicated with an asterisk (*) are available in paperback.

Allan, John, T. W. Haig, and H. H. Dodwell. *The Cambridge Shorter History of India.* Part II: *Muslim India.* 1958. A concise and authoritative account of Muslim rule from the thirteenth century to the end of the Moghul Empire.

Allyn, John. *The 47 Ronins.* 1970. In this true story, a group of eighteenth-century samurai avenge the wrong their lord has suffered.

Babur. *Babur-Nama (Memoirs of Babur).* Translated by Susannah Beveridge. 1922, reprinted 1970. Fascinating, frank autobiography by an empire builder, keen observer, and lover of nature.

Bernier, Françoise. *Travels in the Mogul Empire* A.D. *1656–1668.* 2d ed. Translated by Irving Brock. 1968. Firsthand account by a Frenchman.

Berry, Mary E. *Hideyoshi.* 1982. A biography of Japan's sixteenth-century unifier.

Beurdeley, Cecile. *Giuseppe Castiglione: A Jesuit Painter at the Court of the Chinese Emperors.* 1971. A beautifully illustrated book on Jesuit influence on Chinese art.

Boxer, C. R. *The Christian Century in Japan, 1549–1650.* 1967. On the rise and fall of Catholicism in Japan.

———. *Four Centuries of Portuguese Expansion, 1415–1825.* 1969. A comprehensive survey.

Chaudhuri, K. N. *Trade and Civilization in the Indian Ocean: An Economic History from the Rise of Islam to 1750.* 1985. Explains how the trade, religion, and cultures of many peoples influenced this region.

Cooper, Michael, ed. *They Came to Japan: An Anthology of European Reports on Japan, 1543–1640.* 1965. Interesting accounts of Japan by contemporary Europeans.

Gascoigne, Bamber. *The Great Moghuls.* 1971. Well-written text with lavish illustrations.

Grewal, F. S. *The Sikhs of the Punjab.* 1998. Traces Sikhism from its beginnings to the present.

Hall, D. G. E. *A History of South-East Asia.* 3d ed. 1968. A standard survey of the whole region.

*Huang, Ray. *1587, A Year of No Significance: The Ming Dynasty in Decline.* 1981. Using an unusual approach, Huang has crafted an engrossing book on the personality of the Emperor Wan-li and the politics of the late Ming.

Hucker, Charles O. *The Traditional Chinese State in Ming Times, 1368–1644.* 1961. A concise, clear summary.

Lall, Janardan S. *Taj Mahal and the Glory of Mughal Agra.* 1982. Wonderful color photos make this volume the next best thing to visiting Agra; well-written text.

Lane-Poole, S. *Babur.* 1957. A fine biography drawing heavily from Babur's memoirs.

*Levathes, Louise. *When China Ruled the Seas.* 1994. A lively account of the era of Chinese naval supremacy in the fifteenth century.

Michael, Franz. *The Origins of the Manchu Rule in China.* 1942. Study of the Manchus from tribal nomads to great power.

Mote, Frederick, and Denis Twitchett, eds. *The Cambridge History of China.* Vol. 7, part 1: *The Ming Dynasty, 1368–1644.* 1988. The definitive reference book on the period.

Nishiyama, Matsunosuke. *Edo Culture: Daily Life of Diversions in Urban Japan, 1600–1868.* 1997. An important work on popular culture and daily life.

Reid, Anthony. *Southeast Asia in the Age of Commerce, 1450–1688.* Vols. 1–2. An authoritative treatment of the impact of early Western trade.

Sheldon, C. D. *The Rise of the Merchant Class in Tokugawa Japan, 1600–1868.* 1958. How the merchants rose to importance despite restrictions placed on them by a feudal government.

Shelov, J. M. *Akbar.* 1967. A fine biography.

*Spence, Jonathan. *Emperor of China: Self-Portrait of K'ang Hsi.* 1974. The life and policies of a great ruler in his own words.

*———. *The Memory Palace of Matteo Ricci.* 1984. A richly descriptive book on a great missionary and the China he worked in around 1600.

Totman, Conrad D. *Tokugawa Ieyasu: Shogun.* 1982. Good biography of the powerful founder of the last shogunate.

———. *Early Modern Japan.* 1993. A well-written history of events from the reunification of Japan to the end of the Tokugawa shogunate.

*Ts'ao Hsueh-ch'in. *The Dream of the Red Chamber.* Translated by C. C. Wang. A perennially popular love story set in a large and aristocratic eighteenth-century household in China.

Waldron, Arthur. *The Great Wall of China: From History to Myth.* 1990. Good short book on the political and strategic reasons for building the walls and how they affected the lives of Chinese and nomads.

Wu, Silas. *Passage to Power: K'ang-hsi and His Heir Apparent.* 1979. A moving book on a great monarch and his problems with his sons.

Wurtzburg, Charles E. *Raffles of the Eastern Isles.* 1954. Well-written biography of Britain's great empire builder in Asia.

Additional resources, exercises, and Internet links related to this chapter are available at the Book Companion Web site:
http://history.wadsworth.com/upshurcompact4/

COMPARATIVE ESSAY 8
The Global Impact of Industrialization

The basis of the industrial revolution was the application of steam power to machinery for purposes first of production and then of transport. . . . This transformation of industrial life—which began in England in the later eighteenth century— . . . spread eastward into Europe. Its impact and repercussions varied according to the conditions and character of each country. . . . The chief way in which industrialism affected government and politics was in its conferring new wealth and power upon the growing middle class . . . and in its creation of a new industrial proletariat.
David Thomson, *Europe since Napoleon* (New York: Knopf, 1964), pp. 95–97.

A further consequence is a greed for material possessions, leading certain members of the new generation into reprehensible practices. Corrupt officials, untrustworthy doctors, dishonest engineers are all too common. . . . This generation is in many ways the first which earns its living by industry and commerce alone and which meets the expenses of contemporary life without the benefit of a private fortune: it is thus inclined to increase its profits by any means available. . . .
Abd al-Fattah Subhi Wahida, "On the Eve of the Industrial Era," in Anouar Abdel-Malek, ed., *Contemporary Arab Political Thought* (London: Zed Books, 1983), pp. 31–32.

The British historian David Thomson describes the sweeping economic and social changes—some positive, some problematic—wrought by industrialization. In contrast, the Egyptian writer Abd al-Fattah Wahida warns of the dangers that industrialization and changing economies pose to traditional societies.

Whatever one's assessment of the overall results of industrialization, there is no doubt that the Industrial Revolution ranks with the Agricultural Revolution as one of the greatest turning points in human development. The continuing progress and spread of the Industrial Revolution have been and continue to be key agents in global integration. It has fundamentally changed the mode of production from dependence on human and animal labor to machines powered by wind, water, coal, petroleum, natural gas, and more recently, nuclear energy.

As noted above, the Industrial Revolution began in the mid-eighteenth century in England, where inventors developed steam power to create cheap and ever-more efficient energy sources to increase productivity. Why did the Industrial Revolution first occur in England? The answer is that only England (later called Great Britain), and later other parts of western Europe, had the prerequisites—economic, intellectual, political, and legal—necessary to bring about the changes.

First, economic conditions: England had most of the essential raw materials for beginning an industrial revolution: abundant water that could be harnessed, coal, iron ore, and wool. It also had an adequate but not overly abundant labor supply. (Ancient Egypt, China, India, and Rome all had an abundance of labor, many of whom were forced to work for the state. This availability of cheap labor may well have smothered the incentive to invent labor-saving devices.)

Second, the intellectual climate: The Reformation of the sixteenth and seventeenth centuries also gave impetus to the scientific and intellectual revolution. In Protestant England, both the liberation of intellectual activities from the control of a restrictive church and the work ethic taught by the Calvinist-influenced Protestant church contributed to the quest for knowledge and wealth creation that fueled the Industrial Revolution. The age of the Reformation was followed by the Age of Reason that reigned in Europe during the seventeenth and eighteenth centuries. The intellectual climate of this era encouraged scientific inquiry and experimentation, which led to innovations in manufacturing and agricultural production. James Watt, a Scotsman who invented the steam engine, is an example of an inventor whose practical application of theoretical formulations led to a major industrial advance.

Other inventions revolutionized the traditional textile industry with labor-saving machines that vastly increased productivity. Improvements in farming increased food production. English farmers invented farm machinery that pioneered new methods of plowing and adopted new crops that provided a surplus food supply to feed a growing urban population. For example, "Turnip" Townsend, an English gentleman farmer, discovered that it was no longer necessary to leave a third of the fields fallow every third year. Instead, those fields could instead grow turnips without depleting the soil. Turnips were a good feed for cattle, which as a result no longer had to be slaughtered in the fall because of lack of food to tide them through the winter. This discovery improved soil management and animal husbandry and increased meat supply. These innovations enhanced productivity, reduced costs, and decreased labor needs. The surplus rural workers then migrated to cities, where they found jobs working in the new factories.

Third, political conditions: People with money are more likely to invest it in wealth-producing enterprises if the political order will protect their investment. In traditional societies where arbitrary governments could confiscate commercial profits at will, people tended to hide their money or spend it on nonproductive activities. In Great Britain and France in the eighteenth century, the governments gave support for and developed partnerships with traders in overseas commercial ventures. When the Industrial Revolution began in those countries, the governments likewise encouraged investment in industry.

In Great Britain, as a result of the Glorious Revolution of 1689 and several centuries of struggle with the crown, Parliament emerged supreme. The limiting of the powers of the monarch and the civil rights guaranteed to all Englishmen by the Bill of Rights, which the Glorious Revolution brought about, protected the people from arbitrary taxation and expropriation of their properties. These freedoms and the liberal political climate in Great Britain allowed entrepreneurs to invest in new industrial and commercial enterprises. This situation was in marked contrast to the earlier political order, which allowed fewer opportunities and guarantees for innovations and investment. The spread of constitutional government and legal protections for citizens to western European countries ensured their peoples similar freedoms, and created conditions conducive to the spread of the Industrial Revolution.

Fourth, the legal framework: Legal structures are closely connected to political conditions. Parliamentary rule and political reforms resulted in the creation—first in Great Britain, then in other European countries—of the legal framework and institutions that protected and regulated private enterprise. Modern law codes enhanced the climate conducive to private investment. In Great Britain, the law of primogeniture that gave the eldest son the bulk of the family inheritance also encouraged younger sons to enter business in order to gain enough money to enjoy the high standard of living that they were reared in but could not otherwise maintain. Younger sons from the aristocracy and gentry were thus disproportionately responsible for the enterprises that fueled the expanding economy of Britain during the Industrial Revolution.

The Industrial Revolution affected virtually all aspects of life in Europe and then around the world, transforming the technology and the economy wherever it spread. Steam energy made it possible to develop large manufacturing facilities in iron, steel, and textiles. This led manufacturers to undertake worldwide searches for the raw materials such as iron ore, coal, copper, petroleum, rubber, and cotton needed to produce a wide variety of products. Merchants sought to enlarge old markets and discover new ones for their mass-produced goods. The need for raw materials and new markets and the accelerating pace of inventions (for example, electricity, the internal combustion engine, and, later, atomic energy and the computer) provided motivation for the industrialized nations to take over territories in imperial conquests worldwide.

In addition, many of the inventions brought by the Industrial Revolution resulted in more effective and lethal weapons, making modern warfare more destructive than had been conceivable in earlier times. The fall of traditional empires and the beginning of a new global order hastened global integration and the spread of the Industrial Revolution in the late twentieth century.

Mass production lowered the price of consumer goods and enabled more people to enjoy the basic comforts of life. The Industrial Revolution and the accompanying scientific and medical advances also changed demographic patterns by lowering infant mortality rates and lengthening life spans; it has produced the population explosion that is yet unchecked in parts of the world. Industrialization also contributed to ecological problems, including air and water pollution and the destruction of rain forests and wetlands.

Cities, some so large that they are called megalopolises, developed because of the technologies generated by the Industrial Revolution. They are vastly larger than any earlier urban centers. In Great Britain, for example, whereas there was only one city with a population over 100,000 in 1700, there were thirty by World War I. Many of the new industrial cities mushroomed from villages or farmlands, changing the landscape. This process began in western Europe; it, too, spread throughout the world.

The Industrial Revolution has profoundly altered the lives of all peoples. It has made the pace of daily life more disciplined because the time clocks of the factory shift have replaced the seasonal rhythms of the farm. The problems and pressures that had always plagued urban life—crime, pollution, overcrowding—were also magnified.

Exploitation of workers, in factories and in the mines and on the plantations and farms that produced the crops that supplied the industrial raw materials, was another evil that resulted from the Industrial Revolution. This problem was especially acute during the early stages of the Industrial Revolution and led to the formation of new social theories and political ideologies designed to transform governments and alter the relationship between workers and capitalists. Marxism is the best-known economic and political ideology spawned by the Industrial Revolution. It advocated violent political revolution to bring about social and economic change, and explained most historical changes as economically motivated.

The process of industrialization continues, as do the problems that remain unsolved, including the depletion of natural resources, population explosion, and pollution. Although some fear that industrialization will destroy traditional customs and values, most peoples in nonindustrialized countries still seek the economic benefits that industrially developed nations enjoy.

The West: 1600–1800

•

Silly, you men—so very adept
at wrongly faulting womankind,
not seeing you're alone to blame
for faults you plant in woman's mind.
After you've won by urgent plea
the right to tarnish her good name,
you still expect her to behave—
you, that coaxed her into shame.
You batter her resistance down
and then, all righteousness, proclaim
that feminine frivolity,
not your persistence, is to blame.
When it comes to bravely posturing
your witlessness must take the prize;
you're the child that makes a bogeyman,
and then recoils in fear and cries.

It's your persistent entreaties
that change her from timid to bold.
Having made her thereby naughty,
you would have her good as gold.
So where does the greater guilt lie
for a passion that should not be:
with the man who pleads out baseness
or the woman debased by his plea?

Or which is more to be blamed—
though both will have cause for chagrin:
the woman who sins for money,
or the man who pays money to sin?*

*Sor Juana de la Cruz, "Recondillas," trans. Alan S. Trueblood, in *A Sor Juana Anthology* (Cambridge, Mass.: Harvard University Press, 1988), pp. 111–113.

These lines were written, not by a worldly-wise woman of the viceregal court in Mexico City, but by a Hieronymite nun, Sor Juana Inés de la Cruz, at the end of the seventeenth century. That a cloistered nun wrote poetry and drama may seem surprising. However, the convent was a woman's only alternative to marriage and offered a place for learning and study as well as religious devotion. An early representative of a developing feminist consciousness, Sor Juana poignantly satirized and lambasted patriarchal Spanish and Mexican society. She provides a glimpse into the structure of colonial society and the role of the church.

In the period covered in this chapter, western Europe witnessed controversy over the nature of government and the role of the sovereign. Increasingly absolutist regimes culminated in the reign of Louis XIV of France. By contrast, in Great Britain constitutional institutions flourished and became the model of government in political struggles from the late eighteenth century on. The period also saw philosophical and intellectual excitement generated by scientific discoveries and the advent of the Enlightenment intellectuals who deified reason as the arbiter of human progress. Several authoritarian monarchs in central and eastern Europe claimed they were guided by the "enlightened" dictates of reason, not tradition, in governing.

This chapter also surveys new forms of Western civilization in Latin America and British North America, especially the constitutional government of the newly independent United States of America. It concludes with the emergence of global trade relations and the onset of the Industrial Revolution.

Absolutism and Constitutionalism in Europe

To assign the right of decision to subjects and the duty of deference to sovereigns is to pervert the order of things. The head [of the nation] alone has the right to deliberate and decide, and the functions of all the other members consist only in carrying out . . . commands. . . . [In a well-run state] all eyes are fixed upon [the monarch] alone, all respects are paid to him alone, everything is hoped for from him alone; nothing is expected, nothing is done, except through him alone. His favor is regarded as the only source of all good things; men believe that they are rising in the world to the extent that they come near him or earn his esteem; all else is cringing, all else is powerless. . . . *

*Louis XIV, "Lessons in Kingship," from his *Memoirs,* trans. H. H. Rowen, in *From Absolutism to Revolution* (New York: Macmillan, 1963), pp. 26–27.

Although Louis XIV (1643–1715) of France may never have spoken the words often attributed to him, *"L'état c'est moi"* (I am the state), his principle of government, stated above, conforms to the sentiments they expressed. As previously noted (see the section on The Centralization of Western European Monarchies in Chapter 9), the so-called New Monarchs had wanted to continue the work of centralizing governments in sovereign territorial states, but were interrupted by the troubles of the fourteenth and fifteenth centuries. This process was thus concluded only in the first half of the seventeenth century, the beginning of the age of absolutism. Although absolutism first appeared in the Iberian states, France under Louis XIV produced its most admired and emulated model.

England ("Great Britain" after the 1707 union of England and Scotland) charted its own course, ultimately embracing the principles of constitutionalism under a sovereign legislature and furnishing the archetype of good government for the United States and other British possessions. This section explains the development of absolutism and constitutionalism in western Europe; a subsequent section of this chapter takes up constitutionalism in the United States.

The Foundations of Absolutism

In the early centuries of modern Europe, absolutism, at least in theory, vested ultimate power in a hereditary monarch, who claimed a God-given right to rule. In practice, however, absolutism in Europe, as in China, was seldom arbitrary. Although the monarch was not subject to any earthly authority, particularly any institution of popular representation, he had to respect the laws of God and the laws of nature.

Royal absolutism drew theoretical justification from many sources, including the scriptural teaching that God sanctified the "divine right" of kings. According to this notion, a hereditary monarchy with its inference of unquestioned obedience on the part of subjects was the only divinely approved form of government. The French bishop Jacques Bossuet (1627–1704), a court appointee of Louis XIV, asserted that kings were justified in exercising absolute power because they derived that power by divine right, that is, directly from God. As God's representative on earth, the monarch's judgment was law and he was accountable to no man. According to Bossuet, whoever challenged the king was in reality challenging God Himself. Many other contemporary political theorists like Thomas Hobbes (1688–1789) of England agreed that a single, absolute authority was needed to impose order on all the people of the state. In Hobbes's view, all people are naturally selfish and ambitious, and unless restrained by strong government would engage in "war of all against all." It was also widely believed that people born to high station were inherently better equipped for ruling. Legal scholars justified royal absolutism by pointing to the example of the ancient Roman emperors.

There were also practical reasons for the success of absolute monarchies. After the century of upheavals accompanying the split in the Christian church, the public was ready to support strong leaders who could ensure order and stability. The Reformation had strengthened the monarchs by weakening or eliminating papal interference in the secular affairs of their states.

Finally, economic developments during the seventeenth century fostered the growth of royal absolutism. Absolute monarchs needed money to sustain their powerful governments; mercantilism, the prevailing economic doctrine in Europe, produced that wealth.

Under mercantilism the government supervised all forms of economic activity in order to increase national wealth and thus make the state more powerful in relation to its neighbors. Governments that practiced mercantilism granted trading companies monopolies in various parts of the world, encouraged the expansion of industries and the establishment of new ones, regulated production, erected high tariff barriers on imports, and built navies to protect trade. Some countries established overseas possessions with a view to exploiting them for their benefit. Accordingly, the mother country tried to retain exclusive trading rights with its colonies as a means of acquiring cheap raw materials and assuring markets for its manufactured goods. The aim of mercantilists was to accumulate wealth, ultimately at the expense of other states.

The Eclipse of Spain

The Spanish Empire was the first European state to embrace fully the tenets of absolutism and mercantilism. Toward the end of the fifteenth century Ferdinand and Isabella had arranged the marriage of their daughter Joanna to the Habsburg Archduke Philip of Austria. The offspring of this union succeeded to the Spanish throne in 1516 and three years later became Holy Roman Emperor as Charles V. The most powerful man in Europe, Charles was the formal leader of the decentralized Holy Roman Empire and ruler over a conglomerate domain that included Castile and Aragon, Naples and Sicily, the Spanish Empire in America, Austria, Bohemia, the Free Country of Burgundy, Luxembourg, and the Netherlands.

Arriving in Spain in 1517, Charles did not endear himself to the people in the early years of his reign. Brought up in the Low Countries, he spoke no Spanish and initially installed his Flemish entourage in key government positions. The Spaniards at first regarded him as a foreign prince who taxed them to support policies in which they had no interest. In 1520 Spanish resentment against the government flared into open revolt, beginning in Toledo and spreading to other cities in Castile. By the end of 1521 the uprising had been suppressed and the monarchy was never again threatened under the Habsburgs. Although the monarchy had become absolute in theory, Charles never sought to impose a centralized imperial system lest he offend his subjects. He did his best to avoid his previous errors, respecting the traditional rights and liberties of his subjects, keeping the administration in Spanish hands and identifying himself with Spanish interests. His devotion to his duties and his robust defense of Catholicism gradually won him the loyalty of his subjects. In 1556 Charles abdicated in favor of his son Philip, to whom he bequeathed most of his empire.

Philip II (reigned 1556–1598) firmly believed in his divine right to govern Spain as an absolute ruler, accountable to no one save God. He developed an elaborate bureaucracy, but was determined to maintain close supervision over his possessions and to make all the major decisions himself. In 1580 he made good his claim to the Portuguese throne, defeating in battle his most serious rival, and uniting the Iberian peninsula under one sovereign. With Portugal's vast overseas domains added to the Spanish Empire, Philip could justly claim to rule more of the earth's surface than any previous sovereign in history. The heavy flow of precious metals, tobacco, cocoa, indigo, and sugar from the

Americas, to say nothing of the expanding colonial market, greatly enriched the Spanish treasury. Yet all the incoming revenue was never enough to meet the needs of the Spanish government.

A substantial part of the government's income went to pay for the cost of Philip's imperial wars. Philip's devotion to the Catholic faith influenced not only his personal conduct but his foreign policy as well. His aim was to rid the Mediterranean of infidels and wipe out the Protestant heresy wherever it existed. One of the most glorious moments of his reign occurred in 1571, when his fleet decisively defeated the Turks at Lepanto in the Gulf of Corinth. His religious crusade against the Protestants, however, was much less successful.

Philip became trapped in a quagmire when he tried to reconquer the rebellious Protestants concentrated in the northern part of the Netherlands. These Protestants had declared their independence from Spain in 1581 and formed the United Provinces of the Netherlands. They then invited a staunch Protestant, William the Silent of the House of Orange, to be their chief executive, or *stadtholder* (his descendants still reign in the Netherlands). The Dutch developed a navy to prey on Spanish shipping and built up a merchant fleet. The fighting dragged on until 1609 when the weary combatants agreed to a truce. The United Provinces, commonly called the Dutch Republic, had won their independence. The Spanish retained control of the southern provinces (present-day Belgium).

One of Philip's major ambitions was to bring England back into the Catholic fold. He first married Queen Mary of England, the daughter of Henry VIII and Catherine of Aragon. Mary was a devout Catholic who fervently attempted to undo the Protestant course her father Henry VIII had set, but she ruled for only five years and died childless. Philip hoped to continue his influence over England by gaining the hand of Mary's half-sister and successor, Elizabeth I. However, Elizabeth rejected his marriage proposal, as she did all others. Other differences arose, particularly Elizabeth's assistance to the Dutch rebels and her support of English privateers preying on Spanish treasure ships returning from the Americas. His patience exhausted, he made plans to invade England. For that purpose he assembled about 20,000 soldiers and 130 ships, the greatest display of naval power the world had ever seen. Sailing from Lisbon, the Spanish Armada swept into the English Channel late in July 1588. Just as the smaller but faster and more maneuverable Japanese ships had wrought havoc on larger ships of the Mongol invaders, English warships inflicted heavy damage on the Spanish Armada. And just as the typhoon destroyed most of the crippled Mongol fleet, storms around the British Isles sank most of the remaining Spanish vessels. The defeat of the Armada safeguarded England from invasion and probably ensured the survival of the Dutch Republic. In more general terms, it dealt such a blow to Philip's navy that maritime leadership passed increasingly to the English. During the first half of the seventeenth century Spain would also lose its lofty position as the dominant continental power, a status that France would assume.

Philip II was followed by weak, self-indulgent rulers with little capacity for government. Since the Spanish monarchs' powers were absolute, weak rulers and poor leadership at the top paralyzed the government. Spain's faltering economy was its greatest underlying weakness, however. Spain itself had little mineral wealth and its poor soil inhibited agricultural production. In these circumstances it desperately needed to develop its industries and create a balanced trade pattern, but such practical business moves clashed with the dominant Spanish nobility's notions of chivalry. In addition, Spain's century-long involvement in most European wars had severely strained the Spanish economy, which never fully recovered. Spain was thus beset by economic stagnation and government mismanagement. Only the annual arrival of treasure-laden ships from its American colonies prevented fiscal collapse.

The Pinnacle of Royal Absolutism: France under Louis XIV

In France the move toward more efficient absolutism was threatened by a religious war that lasted nearly thirty years. Despite state-sponsored persecution, Calvinism had grown steadily in France in the sixteenth century, attracting the rising middle class and nearly half the nobility, many of whom resented the centralizing tendencies of the monarchy. Although the Calvinists, nicknamed Huguenots, probably comprised no more than 12 percent of the total population, their wealth and influence made them disproportionately powerful. Distrust between Catholics and Protestants deepened, breaking out into an armed conflict in 1562. The war was fought with unusual savagery. In 1589 the Protestant leader, Henry of Navarre, proclaimed himself Henry IV (reigned 1589–1610) after his Catholic foe was assassinated. Nevertheless, the fighting continued until 1593, ending only after Henry converted to Catholicism. The next year he was officially crowned king of France, the first in the line of Bourbons. To ensure internal calm, Henry issued the Edict of Nantes in 1598, granting Huguenots freedom of worship and equal civil rights. This landmark decree was the first admission by a major European government that two religions could coexist without endangering the state. Henry spent the ensuing decade restoring royal power and rebuilding French prosperity.

The assassination of Henry IV by a religious fanatic left control of the government in the hands of his power-hungry and politically inept widow, Marie de Medici, who acted as regent for the new king, nine-year-old Louis XIII (reigned 1610–1643). The queen mother's misrule plunged the country into a new and prolonged period of disorder as greedy and ambitious courtiers and nobles exploited the state and feuded with one another. Once Louis XIII grew to manhood he threw off the domination of his mother and in 1624 made Cardinal Richelieu his principal minister. With the unfailing support of the king, Richelieu pursued a twofold policy: to exalt royal authority at the expense of the nobility and to restore French prestige by undermining the Habsburgs.

Richelieu died in 1642 and Louis XIII followed him to the grave six months later. Richelieu's successor, an Italian-born cardinal named Jules Mazarin, remained in office on the accession of Louis XIV (reigned 1643–1715), then a child of five, until his own death in 1661. Mazarin carried forward Richelieu's policies of protecting the monarchical structure and waging war against the Habsburgs. But the nobility regarded him as a foreign upstart and the bourgeoisie resented the high taxes he imposed to continue the war with Spain. The upshot was a serious rebellion from 1648 to 1653. The civil war, known as the Fronde, was a last-ditch effort to reverse the drift toward an absolute monarchy. But divisions and mistrust among the Frondeur leaders doomed the uprising and left the

LIVES AND TIMES ACROSS CULTURES

The Pageantry of Versailles

Since his youth Louis had disliked Paris, the seat of the French monarchy, for, among other things, its narrow streets and turbulent crowds. Accordingly he decided to use his father's hunting lodge as a base on which to construct a new residence outside of Paris that would impress the world with its splendor. Work on the palace ran from 1668 till 1702, though the court moved into it in 1682. Louis employed the best talent to design and decorate the palace. Some 35,000 men worked on the royal residence, the grounds, and the canals that supplied the water for the many fountains.

The finished structure was a quarter of a mile long and could house 10,000 people. It was surrounded by acres of gardens, lakes, fountains, and more than 300 kinds of trees brought from all over France. The interior, though lacking in sanitary conveniences, radiated opulence on a grand scale, furnished as it was with mosaics, paintings, statues, and mirrors. At night, thousands of candles set in immense chandeliers or in massive candlesticks lighted the hallways or ballrooms.

From 1682 on, the king lived and worked at Versailles, isolated from his subjects, with his every whim attended to by an army of servants. Each year France's higher nobility were expected to spend time at court. Here Louis dispensed favors and occupied them in idle pursuits, thus further neutralizing them politically. The once proud nobles were reduced to contemptible parasites, frittering their lives away in intrigue and in search of pleasure. A ritual of daily ceremonies centering on the king evolved, from the moment he rose until he retired. Nobles vied with each other to hand Louis his shirt in the morning or to be allowed to hold a candlestick while he climbed into bed. Despite the superficial and stilted atmosphere of Versailles, it evoked the envy of other kings and princes of Europe, some of whom built smaller versions of the palace and tried to imitate the court life and etiquette of the "Grand Monarch."

monarchy stronger than ever by reinforcing the public's belief that only an absolute ruler could maintain peace and security. Mazarin's domestic triumph was followed by a diplomatic victory that concluded the long war with Spain and marked the end of Habsburg leadership in Europe.

Louis assumed personal control of his government at Mazarin's death in 1661. The king's first public act was to summon the heads of the government departments and announce to them that henceforth he would personally take on the duties of chief minister. A profound believer in his divine right to rule, Louis saw himself as the best person to decide on the needs and interests of the state.

Louis was diligent and conscientious, and he was blessed with a robust constitution that enabled him to endure the most stringent of schedules. Building upon the work of Richelieu and Mazarin, Louis moved ruthlessly to crush any challenge to his authority. He expanded the duties of intendants, royal agents sent to the provinces to supervise and to direct the activities of local officials, many of whom had purchased or inherited their offices. By means of a *lettre de cachet*, an administrative order bearing the royal seal,

Royal Palace at Versailles. This 1688 painting shows the palace of Versailles as the king arrives in pomp and circumstance at the gates (bottom). Note the geometrical layout of the vast palace and its grounds.

disobedient subjects were arrested and, without benefit of a trial, were sent into exile or imprisoned indefinitely.

For Louis, religious uniformity suited his concept of absolutism—"one king, one law and one faith." In 1685 Louis revoked the Edict of Nantes, which had been the basis for religious toleration. Under pain of imprisonment or torture, some Protestants converted to Catholicism, others practiced their religion in secret, but most fled abroad, taking with them their wealth and skills as professionals and businessmen, to the detriment of France.

Influenced by painful childhood memories of the Fronde, Louis considered the aristocracy to be the greatest threat to his own despotic rule. While allowing the nobles to keep their economic and social privileges, he excluded them from the leading government offices. Instead Louis staffed his administration with educated men of middle-class background who were entirely dependent on his favor. Prominent among Louis's ministers was Jean Baptiste Colbert, controller-general of finances. As a mercantilist he was committed to government control and encouragement of industry. His ministry built roads and canals and regulated prices, wages, and the quality of goods. It protected French industry with high tariffs, reduced local tolls to strengthen the domestic market, and promoted France's trade with Europe and its expanding overseas empire. Colbert made no fundamental change in government finances, but by eliminating much corruption, expanding the economy, and keeping taxes high, he was able to increase revenue.

Although Louis had more wealth at his disposal than his predecessors had ever dreamed of, it was never enough to meet royal expenditures for wars, building projects, and maintenance of the court.

Just as Charles V and Philip II of Spain had earlier waged wars of aggrandizement, Louis fought four wars to enhance French power between 1667 and 1713. To prevent French domination and to ensure a balance of power among the many separate states, much of the rest of Europe, led by the Dutch and the English, formed alliances to resist his ambitions. By the end of his reign Louis had added some territory to his northeastern frontier and had placed a Bourbon on the throne of Spain, but at a heavy cost in French lives and treasure.

Louis chose the sun as his emblem and called himself the "Sun King," likening himself to the sun around which everything else orbited. He moved to Versailles, where he built, at tremendous cost, a huge palace as a monument to his vanity. To extol the achievements of his reign, the king became the main patron of all the creative arts. His reign coincided with a renaissance of French culture as he established academies (for painting, sculpture, architecture, and music), in addition to subsidizing and honoring a galaxy of artists. In the second half of the seventeenth century, France produced some of the greatest poets and dramatists in its history. But government sponsorship and supervision of the arts had its negative side. Censorship was freely exercised, inhibiting the development of the artists' individuality and reducing them to adjuncts of the government, which used their works to glorify the king and the state.

As Louis was the most admired and emulated monarch in Europe, French culture had an enormous impact on the Continent. The artistic and literary styles of prominent French painters and writers were slavishly copied. French etiquette, taste, cuisine, and fashion became the fad among the elite. All educated Europeans learned French, which replaced Latin as the language of diplomatic exchange.

Classicism and the Spread of French Cultural Influences

The dominant artistic style at the start of Louis's reign was the baroque, which originated in Italy and was inspired by the Counter-Reformation. Baroque emphasized or exaggerated certain features of Renaissance art. Its artists favored massiveness, lavish decorations, bright colors, and the impression of turbulence to dazzle the spectator. The Flemish artist Peter Paul Rubens (1577–1640) was perhaps the most popular painter of his era. His compositions, marked by swirling lines, figures in intense movement, rich colors, and opulence, are masterpieces of the baroque style. The new musical form, the opera, invented by the Italian composer Claudio Monteverdi (1567–1643), clearly illustrated the baroque passion for pageantry and exaggerated emotion. The theatrical effects of baroque art harmonized the purpose of both ecclesiastical and secular authority: the former saw it as an affirmation of a revitalized Catholic church and the latter as reflecting the wealth and power of absolute monarchs.

The wife of Henry IV, Marie de Medici, had introduced the baroque style to France. It reached its apogee with the construction of the magnificent palace at Versailles. But baroque, for reasons described immediately below, did not come close to achieving the same degree of popularity in France as it did in the other Catholic countries of western Europe.

Louis XIV's insistence on order, restraint, and balance, which he presumed were ideal principles of human behavior in any age, led to the development of classicism, a new aesthetic style. French artists looked to Greek and Roman models for their order and appeal to reason, and imitated their style and subject matter. The work of Nicholas Poussin (1594–1665), a painter primarily of pastoral scenes, is explicitly in the French classical tradition with reminders of Greco-Roman architecture and the balance and order of the landscapes. The tragedian Jean Racine (1639–1699), the most famous writer in the court of Louis XIV, wrote in regular, rhythmic verse, and drew on Greco-Roman mythology for his plots. His heroes and heroines were figures of classical nobility, wrestling with the conflicting claims of duty, honor, and love (or lust). French courtiers liked to see themselves in the noble figures of Racine's plays. In contrast, the French comic playwright Jean Molière (1622–1673) used classical dramatic forms to satirize all classes of French society. His plays remain popular and continue to be produced to this day.

Classicism seemed to many to be a new kind of civilization, but, in fact, it was artificial, lacked warmth and spontaneity, and stifled freedom of expression. Nevertheless it endeared itself to the aristocracy because of its elegance and predictability. Like many aspects of French culture, classicism spread to virtually all parts of Europe.

The Rise of Constitutionalism in England

While Richelieu and Mazarin were laying the foundations of absolutism in France, England was in the grip of a constitutional crisis. The accord between parliament and the monarchy, which had been a characteristic of Tudor rule, broke down with the accession of the Stuart dynasty. A struggle ensued that gradually turned into a conflict to determine whether sovereignty should repose in parliament or the crown. The issue was settled after the Glorious Revolution of 1688 with parliament emerging as the dominant partner in government. Thereafter the monarch was limited in power and subject to control by the House of Commons, the elected house of Parliament.

England had flirted with absolutism under the strong-minded Tudors (1485–1603). But the autocratic rule of the Tudors differed considerably from the absolutism of the Bourbons in France. The Estates General (France's parliament) had only advisory powers and so lacked the means to stem absolutism. In England Parliament emerged from the Middle Ages as an integral part of the machinery of government; its consent was required to give legality to royal acts. By controlling taxation and limiting the income of the ruler, Parliament could influence royal policy.

The Tudors, however, were able to avoid parliamentary interference by finding other ways to replenish their financial resources when regular taxation proved insufficient for their needs. The Tudors were skillful rulers who usually got what they wanted without alienating public opinion or creating constitutional crises. They made no effort to supersede Parliament or flout common law. Instead they worked patiently to establish cordial relations with Parliament, consulting it on major issues, controlling its membership, and respecting the laws of the land. Their success was in no small part due to the fact that their policies coincided with the best interests of their subjects. Tudor rule was absolute, but it was also popular and constitutional.

England attained stability, greatness, and cultural maturity during the long reign of Queen Elizabeth I (reigned 1558–1603), the last of the Tudors. She dominated the English scene in the second half of the sixteenth century just as Philip did in Spain. After the country had shuttled between Protestantism and Catholicism, Elizabeth's compromise settlement of the religious issue was approved by the bulk of the English population. As reestablished, the Anglican church was Protestant in its theology, but much of its ritual and ecclesiastical organization remained Catholic in form.

Elizabeth pursued an active foreign policy and dared the vengeance of the world's strongest power. Her navy's dramatic victory over the Spanish Armada in 1588 secured England and opened the way for her country's domination of the seas. She sent an ambassador to the Moghul court in India to begin trade between the two realms, and granted a charter to the English East India Company, allowing it to monopolize trade in India and points east. She also established relations with the rulers of Russia and authorized the formation of the Muscovy Company, the first in western Europe to trade with Russia.

The Elizabethan Age was also noted for its cultural attainments. The extensive repertoire of historical plays, tragedies, and comedies of William Shakespeare (1564–1616), the greatest English writer, played in the Globe Theater in London alongside those of many other great authors. Music also flourished. English composers wrote religious music for the Protestant liturgy and secular music, to which many of Shakespeare's sonnets were sung.

Elizabeth never married, and after her death in 1603 the crown passed to her cousin, James Stuart, king of Scotland, who became James I (reigned 1603–1625) of England. James was warmly welcomed by his new subjects, but his popularity gradually evaporated. He had a better than average education, knew several languages, and was versed in theology, but, for all his learning, he lacked political wisdom. From the outset he failed to understand that the English Parliament, unlike the weak legislature of Scotland, was a strong institution with a definite role in national government. He unwisely claimed to hold by divine right powers that the Tudors had exercised only by carefully managing Parliaments. By rejecting the Tudor appearance of sharing sovereignty, he gave the impression of defying established law. Parliament retaliated by using its control of the purse strings to defy the king. A wise ruler probably could have undone the damage of James's reign, but his son and successor, Charles I (reigned 1625–1649), was inept and stubborn, so the tension between crown and Parliament continued unabated and even grew worse. In 1628 Parliament, in return for a grant of money, obtained the king's agreement to a statement known as the Petition of Right. In particular, it prohibited the king from imposing taxes without parliamentary consent and from arbitrarily imprisoning people. Like the Magna Carta of the thirteenth century, this parliamentary initiative was a landmark attempt to limit royal authority.

Charles ignored the conditions of the Petition of Right, and when Parliament protested, he dismissed it and for eleven years ruled without a Parliament. But severe religious troubles and a shortage of money forced him to reconvene it, and angry parliamentarians took advantage of his troubles to extort concession after concession. Finally, Charles would concede no more, and following fruitless negotiations, a civil war broke out in 1642.

In the ensuing bitter struggle, parliamentary forces led by a stern parliamentary general, Oliver Cromwell, carried the day. Convicted of treason, Charles was executed in January 1649. Cromwell proceeded to establish a Commonwealth, in theory a republic but in practice a military government. England, it turned out, had merely exchanged one type of tyranny for another. Although Cromwell made England a ranking power in Europe once more, at home his conflict with Parliament and his implementation of what today would be called blue laws offended English moderates. His death in 1658 left the country without a strong leader. By 1660 the republican experiment had clearly failed and the country was eager for a change. Parliament, viewing the return of the monarchy as the only solution, invited the son of the beheaded Charles to return from exile.

The new king, Charles II (reigned 1660–1685), soon realized that absolutism was incompatible with England's national mood and therefore resorted to subterfuge and political patronage in dealing with Parliament. His use of favors and bribes to gain parliamentary support for his policies led to the development of two political groups. Those inclined to defend the Anglican church and to allow the monarchy relatively broad latitude came to be called Tories (Irish robbers) by their opponents. The other faction, derisively nicknamed Whigs (Scottish cattle thieves), favored the subordination of the crown to Parliament and religious toleration of "Dissenters," that is, non-Anglican Protestants. These factions were not yet true parties, because they did not see themselves as actually taking power and because they lacked organization and discipline.

Animosity among the different religious groups in England persisted after the Restoration and brought on another constitutional crisis. Parliament, dominated by Anglican Protestants, placed various restrictions on the rights of the Catholic minority, including barring them from public office. Charles II, who never felt secure about his position, did not reveal that he was a Catholic until he was on his deathbed, but his brother and successor James II (reigned 1685–1688) practiced his Catholicism openly. Furthermore, he dismissed Parliament when it refused to repeal laws that discriminated against Catholics, appointed Catholics to high positions, and issued a Declaration of Indulgence that gave religious freedom to all religious denominations. Many thought, with some justification, that James was going to restore Catholicism as the state religion and was also out to establish an absolute monarchy.

When a son was born to James's Catholic wife, the prospect of a Catholic dynasty galvanized parliamentary leaders of both factions to offer the throne to Mary, James's daughter by a previous marriage, who was a Protestant. Mary accepted after Parliament agreed to make her husband, William of Orange, chief magistrate of the Dutch Republic, her co-ruler. In 1688 William and a small expeditionary force landed in southwest England and moved slowly toward London, gathering support along the way. In panic, James and his family fled to France.

The Triumph of Parliament

The essentially nonviolent events of 1688, known as the Glorious Revolution, marked the final stage of Parliament's triumph over the monarchy. By assuming the authority to depose and appoint monarchs, Parliament had dealt a powerful blow to the concept of the divine right of kings.

Further developments consolidated Parliament's position. Early in 1689 William III (reigned 1689–1702) and Mary II (reigned 1689–1694) jointly accepted the throne from Parliament on terms later embodied in the Bill of Rights. This important document asserted and extended the civil rights of the English people and laid down the principles of parliamentary supremacy. Another law granted freedom of worship to non-Anglican Protestants and marked the first step toward religious toleration in England.

The Bill of Rights

And thereupon the said lords spiritual and temporal and Commons . . . for the vindication and assertion of their ancient rights and liberties declare:

1. The pretended power of suspending laws, or the execution of laws, by regal authority, without consent of parliament, is illegal.

2. That the pretended power of dispensing with laws, or the execution of laws, by regal authority, as it hath been assumed and executed, is illegal. . . .

4. The levying money for or to the use of the Crown by pretense of prerogative, without grant of parliament, for longer time or in other manner than the same is or shall be granted, is illegal.

5. That the right of the subjects to petition the king, and all commitments and persecutions for such petitioning are illegal.

6. That the raising or keeping a standing army within the kingdom in time of peace, unless it be with consent of parliament, is against law.

7. That the subjects which are Protestants may have arms for their defense suitable to their conditions, and as allowed by law.

8. That elections of members of parliament ought to be free.

9. That the freedoms of speech, and debates or proceedings in parliament, ought not to be impeached or questioned in any court or place out of parliament.

10. That excessive bail ought not to be required, nor excessive fines imposed nor cruel and unusual punishments inflicted. . . .

13. And that for redress of all grievances, and for the amending, strengthening, and preserving of the laws, parliament ought to be held frequently.

The said lords spiritual and temporal, and commons assembled at Westminster, do resolve that William and Mary, prince and princess of Orange, be, and be declared, king and queen of England, France, and Ireland, and the dominions thereunto belonging, to hold the crown and royal dignity of the said kingdom and dominions to them and the said prince and princess during their lives.*

Like the Magna Carta, the Bill of Rights was largely specific and negative and did not deal in broad generalities of political theory. Nevertheless, the Bill established the essential principles underlying limited monarchy and remains the closest thing to a formal constitution that the British people have. It also served as an inspiration for republican government. The first ten amendments of the U.S. Constitution (1791) and much of the French Declaration of the Rights of Man (1789) owe a debt to the English declaration of 1689.

*Edward P. Cheyney, Readings in English History (Boston: Ginn, 1922), pp. 545–547.

Mary had no children, and those of her sister and successor Queen Anne (reigned 1702–1714) had died young, a situation that prompted Parliament to provide in advance for a peaceful, Protestant succession. The 1701 Act of Settlement barred James II's Catholic descendants from the throne and specified that royal succession should ultimately pass to Anne's Protestant relatives, the rulers of the German state of Hanover. As it happened, this was the last artificial change in the succession of the British monarchy; the descendants of the House of Hanover have reigned to the present. Two events during Queen Anne's reign need to be mentioned. She was the last sovereign to veto an act of Parliament; and in 1707 Parliament passed the Act of Union that joined England and Scotland, creating the Kingdom of Great Britain.

During the half century following the Glorious Revolution, special circumstances influenced the evolution of the relationship between the still influential sovereigns and the newly powerful Parliament. A cabinet of ministers developed from the old privy council of high officials chosen by the king to advise him on policy. Beginning with William III, monarchs began to choose ministers from the party that controlled a majority in the House of Commons. Both William and Anne were powerful sovereigns, appointing and dismissing ministers and actively participating in cabinet meetings.

The accession of the Hanoverians to the British throne put control of the cabinet into the hands of Parliament. George I (reigned 1714–1727) and George II (reigned 1727–1760) were not very interested in English affairs and rarely attended cabinet meetings. In their absence Sir Robert Walpole, the most influential minister between 1721 and 1742, began to chair cabinet meetings and to act as intermediary between the king and cabinet. Thus he became the first (prime) minister, although the title of prime minister did not become official until later. Thereafter, it became traditional for the monarch to appoint as head of the cabinet the acknowledged leader of the strongest party in the House of Commons. In this way, although the cabinet ruled in the monarch's name, its policies were subject to the approval of Parliament. Walpole resigned when he was defeated in Parliament in 1742. His action established the principle, now practiced in all cabinet-style governments the world over, that a ministry must resign when it ceases to command the confidence of the elected house.

Early in his reign, British-born and British-educated George III (reigned 1760–1820) succeeded in subverting the growing power of cabinet government. Later, however, the disasters associated with the years of George's rule (loss of the thirteen American colonies and a huge increase in the national debt) and his periodic lapses into insanity eroded royal influence and enabled the cabinet to regain the initiative. Ever since, the task of governing Great Britain has belonged to the prime minister and his or her cabinet colleagues, subject to the approval of Parliament.

Life in England in the Era of Constitutional Development

England's dynamic development in many areas, which had begun in the great Elizabethan age, continued in the seventeenth and eighteenth centuries. The English people enjoyed a government that was the most efficient in Europe and, after the Glorious

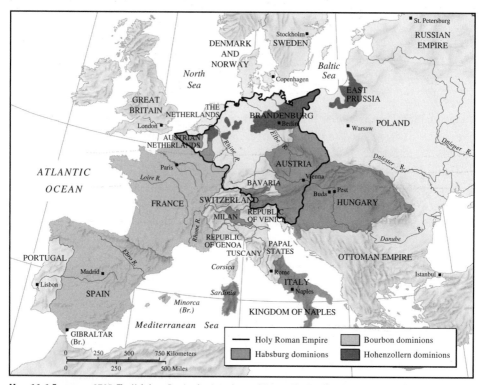

Map 11.1 Europe, c. 1715. The Habsburg Empire dominated central Europe. The Bourbon dynasty ruled both France and Spain but was forbidden to unify the two nations. In northern Germany, the Hohenzollerns were consolidating their disparate lands in a strong centralized state.

Revolution, the freest as well. The events of 1688 vindicated parliamentary government, the rule of law, and the right of revolt against tyranny.

Except for the decades of the mid-seventeenth century, when Puritans ruled and banned the theater and most entertainments as sinful, cultural life was vigorous and urban life flourished. London had half a million inhabitants by the end of the seventeenth century. It was the capital city, a cultural center, and a hub of commerce. Most people lived in villages and hamlets, pursuing not only farming but a flourishing cottage industry of crafts and small-scale manufacture. The medieval open-field method of farming had been replaced by enclosed farms, worked by independent freehold and tenant farmers. Adult males who paid forty shillings in rent or taxes could vote in parliamentary elections. However, a much greater income was required before a man could become a candidate for Parliament.

The countryside also had its poor laborers, paupers, and wandering craftsmen, tinkers, and gypsies. Everyone hunted and snared small game, and the poor and adventurous poached on lands that belonged to the well-to-do. Because roads were very rough and communications poor, few common folk traveled, and local dialects and traditions tended to persist.

LIVES AND TIMES ACROSS CULTURES

Inventing Childhood

Until the seventeenth century, children were generally treated as "miniature adults." At a very young age children entered the workforce, with sons often helping their fathers in the fields or with the animals, and daughters assisting their mothers in household chores or gardening in the family vegetable plot. Well into the twentieth century, children in poorer countries followed these age-old patterns. Clothing and items for children were no more than small replicas of those worn or used by adults.

Across cultures and times toys were universal. Early toys were limited to simple dolls, balls, tops, or carved animals. Toy horses have been uncovered at archeological sites of the ancient Egyptians in Africa, the Chinese in Asia, and Navaho in the Western Hemisphere. But in eighteenth-century Europe, particularly England, as more and more consumer goods were manufactured at decreasing costs, a myriad of items were created solely for children. Parents eagerly bought children's books, games, elaborate dolls, and intricately wrought mechanical toys to amuse their sons and daughters. Some playthings were gender oriented, with dolls for girls and toy soldiers and trains for boys. Others, such as board games, kites, and the hobbyhorse, were for children of either gender.

By the twentieth century, throughout the industrialized world, entire industries revolved around the manufacturing of ever more complex toys, bicycles, skate boards, educational materials, and athletic equipment for the "children's market." Entire theme parks and restaurants catered to children and their parents, and the mass media produced myriads of films, cartoons, and programs aimed solely at children. As a result, childhood became commercialized throughout the industrialized world and parents around the world sought to provide their children with the same toys and highly advertised videos, "spin-off" playthings, and diversions.

Since the days of Elizabeth I, adventurous Britons had sought their fortunes abroad and then returned home to enjoy them. Thomas Pitt, who went to India to trade, rose to be governor of Madras for the East India Company, returned to Great Britain and purchased an estate, and won a seat in Parliament. His grandson, the Earl of Chatham, became prime minister, as did his even more famous great-grandson, William Pitt the Younger.

Many emigrated to the Western Hemisphere. Between 1630 and 1640, 20,000 Puritans settled in New England and about the same number in the West Indies, while Quakers went to Pennsylvania, Catholics to Maryland, and Anglicans to Virginia, the Carolinas, and other colonies. Many went as indentured servants or to escape criminal punishment.

Intellectual and Scientific Developments: The Age of Reason

If we limit ourselves to showing the advantages which have been extracted from the sciences . . . the most important of them perhaps is to have destroyed prejudice and reestablished . . . human intelligence formerly compelled to bend to the false directions forced upon it by . . . absurd beliefs . . . the terrors of superstition and the fear of tyranny.

We may observe that the principles of philosophy, the maxims of liberty, the knowledge of the true rights of men and of their real interests have spread in too great a number of nations, and control in each of them the opinions of too many enlightened men, for them ever to be forgotten again.*

*M. J. de Caritat, Marquis de Condorcet, "Esquisse d'un tableau historique des progrès de l'esprit humain," in O. E. Fellows and N. L. Torrey, eds., *The Age of Enlightenment: An Anthology* (New York: Appleton-Century-Crofts, 1942), pp. 623, 626.

This optimistic account of "the progress of the human spirit" sums up some of the deepest convictions of the eighteenth-century West: the liberating impact of science and reason on the human mind, the importance of human rights, and the inevitable triumph of freedom in the world. The author of these impassioned sentiments, the Marquis de Condorcet (1743–1794), was an enlightened aristocrat and a disciple of Voltaire, the most famous social philosopher of the era. A strong believer in freedom and progress, Condorcet was an admiring student of the experiment in free government undertaken by the United States of America. Ironically, he died a victim of the political terror that accompanied the struggle for survival in the French Revolution. Yet this tract, written shortly before his tragic death, indicates that Condorcet died still confident that in the long run, the political promise of that age of intellectual enlightenment would be realized. The following pages discuss the scientific revolution from which the Age of Reason sprang and thereafter focus on the Enlightenment in Europe and in the European possessions overseas. The section concludes with a summary of developments in the arts during this innovative period. Later sections of this chapter will trace the impact of the Scientific Revolution and the Enlightenment on new forms of Western culture evolving in Latin America and British North America.

The Scientific Revolution

The scientific revolution, contrary to the normal meaning of the word revolution, did not involve rapid, explosive overthrow of traditional authority. Rather, it was a complex movement characterized by gradual and piecemeal change. What was revolutionary was the birth of a new science culture that transformed Europe into a dynamic, rational, and materialistic society.

Beginning in the sixteenth century and reaching full bloom late in the seventeenth, the scientific revolution produced dramatic advances in anatomy, astronomy, physics, and mathematics. Ultimately, rational scientific thought spilled over from pure science into other areas of Western life, notably politics, economics, art, philosophy, and religion.

The evolution of science is best seen against the backdrop of earlier eras in history. In the late Middle Ages, intellectuals had assumed that the universe was the orderly creation of God and that its laws could be explained by rational analysis. They developed in rudimentary form the principles of the scientific method and made crucial advances in mathematics and physics.

The Renaissance witnessed commercial and geographic expansion, which created a demand for more precise instruments of navigation. The resultant technology, in turn, made more accurate measurements possible, something that was central to the new scientific age. The printing press, invented during the second half of the fifteenth century, deserves much credit for later scientific advancements. It facilitated the rapid dissemination of ideas and enabled scientists to profit from each other's work.

Despite such advances, however, Aristotelian concepts still dominated European scientific thinking during the Renaissance. Aristotelian physics posited a world in which all matter was arranged in a hierarchy according to the quality of its substance. Smoke and fire were seeking out their "natural" place in the hierarchy as they moved upwards into the heavens; the same was true as a stone fell to earth or water moved downhill. The different forms of matter had innate properties: smells, sounds, numbers, moods, colors. The entire universe was seen to be alive and arranged in a hierarchy determined by the quality of the material. Such Aristotelian principles were adapted to Christianity by medieval thinkers who argued that the higher an object was located on the hierarchy, the closer its nature was to God.

Ptolemaic astronomy fit in very well with Aristotelian physics because it placed the most important objects in the universe—the earth and humans—in the center of the picture. Christian astronomers then arranged the sun, moon, and planets in an ascending order to God, based on the nobility of their matter.

The medieval/Renaissance hierarchical worldview reinforced the reigning social and political order: members of the nobility were thought to be better than anyone else, regardless of their intellectual, social, or economic abilities. They were by nature more fit to rule because of the composition of their matter. Members of other social strata, including even the wealthy merchant class, were considered unfit for political power because their matter was inferior to that of the aristocracy.

Between 1500 and 1750, scientists developed a new method of inquiry—the "scientific method." Observation and experimentation were followed by rational interpretation of the results. The Englishman Sir Francis Bacon (1561–1626) and the Frenchman René Descartes (1596–1650) rejected traditional abstract approaches and insisted on more empirical methods of discovery. Bacon urged the use of direct observation and collection of data. This emphasis on empiricism, beginning with observable data and building general truths on this foundation, became one of the hallmarks of the new science. Descartes stressed rational understanding as the guarantor of truth. The French philosopher's famous assertion "I think, therefore I am" was the first link in a chain of rational proofs that accounted for the existence, progressively, of humanity, God, and God's universe.

A wide range of sixteenth-century studies that today would fall into the category of magic also helped to create an environment that encouraged exploration and experimentation. The common belief in astrology, which explained earthly affairs by the motions of stars and planets, contributed to interest in astronomy. Alchemy stressed a mystical search for ultimate truth, but alchemists also used laboratory equipment and conducted chemical experiments. Mystical studies of Neoplatonism and of the Jewish religious book, the *Kabbala*, led to a broadening interest in the characteristics of nature and also emphasized the importance of numbers in understanding the way the world worked, a mathematical approach that modern science utilized. The scientific revolution emerged from this stimulating intellectual world.

The New Scientists

The leaders in this scientific revolution included Copernicus, Kepler, Galileo, and Newton. Nicholas Copernicus (1473–1543), who revealed the basic structure of the solar system, is sometimes called the Columbus of the scientific revolution. A Polish churchman with a purely theoretical understanding of astronomy, Copernicus questioned the orthodox Ptolemaic view that the earth stood at the center of the cosmos. In *On the Revolutions of the Heavenly Spheres* (1543), Copernicus declared that the sun was the true center and that the stars and planets orbited around it. The earth, Copernicus dared to suggest, was merely one planet moving around that solar center. His investigations suggested that mathematics is the language of the universe. Johannes Kepler (1571–1630), a German astronomer, offered a much more detailed and exact account of the laws of planetary motion, demonstrating that the planets moved in elliptical orbits around the sun.

Galileo Galilei (1564–1642), a brilliant Italian student of physics and astronomy, made major contributions in both areas. In physics, he challenged Aristotle's theory that objects fall at velocities proportional to their weight. His experiments demonstrated that larger objects did not fall faster than smaller ones; "noble" objects fell at the same rate as a lowly cannonball made out of lead. He established a universally applicable mathematical formula for the acceleration of falling bodies. Galileo replaced Aristotle's qualitative view of the universe with a quantitative one.

In astronomy, Galileo reinforced Copernicus and Kepler's sun-centered theory of the universe by using a telescope, a device newly developed in the Netherlands, for direct astronomical observations. His examination of the moon (see the accompanying box) was a blow to Ptolemaic heavenly hierarchies; instead of a smooth, radiant, material holding one of the noblest objects in its appropriate place in God's celestial hierarchy, Galileo found ordinary matter like that on earth, piled in random peaks and valleys. These revolutionary views brought Galileo a summons from the Inquisition, which forced him to recant his scientific beliefs; however, his ideas long outlived the power of his persecutors.

Once the Aristotelian and Ptolemaic systems were discredited, the question remained: What could explain the workings of the universe? A century and a half after Copernicus, Isaac Newton (1642–1727) tied the achievements of his predecessors together with his crucial formulation of the law of gravity. Gravity was a powerful force that could not be seen, smelled, or heard, yet it exerted a pull on every object in the world. In his *Mathematical Principles of Natural Philosophy* (1687), Newton asserted that every particle of matter in the universe attracts every other particle with a force that varies with the size of the objects and the distance between them. Thus this single force affected everything, from planets in space to apples falling from trees. Newton also explored the nature of light and the laws of optics and defined the general laws of motion in terms of inertia; he declared that for every action there is an equal and opposite reaction. As a result of his long dedication to science, Newton became one of the most honored of all the founders of the scientific revolution. Working separately toward similar ends, Copernicus, Galileo, and Newton had constructed a new, coherent, and increasingly accurate picture of the physical universe.

The First Human Eye to Look upon the Mountains of the Moon

About ten months ago, a report reached my ears that a certain Fleming had constructed a spyglass by means of which visible objects, though very distant from the eye of the observer, were distinctly seen. . . . I succeeded in constructing for myself so excellent an instrument that objects seen by means of it appeared . . . over thirty times closer than when regard[ed] with our natural vision. . . .

Now let us review the observations made during the past two months. . . . Let us speak first of [the] surface of the moon. . . . I distinguish two parts of this surface, a lighter and a darker. . . . From observations of these spots repeated many times, I have been led to the opinion and conviction that the surface of the moon is not smooth, uniform, and precisely spherical, as a great

number of philosophers believe it . . . to be, but is uneven, rough, and full of cavities and prominences, being not unlike the surface of the earth, relieved by chains of mountains and deep valleys. . . .*

Vivid reports like this account of Galileo's discoveries both challenged traditional religious belief that the entire universe was perfect—except for the earth—and fueled the desire for further discoveries about the nature of the universe. Modern societies continue to be fascinated by the formation of the universe and the composition of distant planets. Thus the quest for more knowledge continues in the space explorations of the contemporary era.

*Galileo Galilei, "The Starry Messenger," in Stillman Drake, ed. and trans., Discoveries and Opinions of Galileo *(New York: Doubleday, 1957), pp. 28–29, 31.*

Gradually, the universe came to be seen as an immense and intricate machine that operated according to mathematically formulated laws. Many believed that all matter was composed of atoms, tiny particles whose mass, motion through space, and encounters with other atoms explained everything that happened in nature. To help in these explorations, Francis Bacon advocated the creation of large, state-supported research institutions and correctly predicted that future generations would acquire greater mastery of the material environment than humanity had ever achieved before.

The Enlightenment

The Age of Reason reached its climax in the intellectual movement known as the Enlightenment, a ferment of new ideas important in the growth of modern social, economic, and political thought. The Enlightenment's origins can be found in several major cultural strands from previous centuries, including the Renaissance humanists' reverence for the classics, reactions against the religious intolerance of the Reformation, the impact of the age of discovery, and, above all, the scientific revolution.

Classical education and its emphasis on the literature of the Greeks and Romans, which had been preserved by the Islamic states, provided models for Enlightenment thinkers. French radicals and American revolutionaries alike fancied themselves heirs to that "republican virtue" that had flourished in Rome before the Caesars rose to power. Enlightenment intellectuals also reacted against the widespread religious bigotry that gained momentum during the wars of the Reformation. The new writers demanded not only an end to sectarian intolerance, but a more secular society in general.

Expanded contacts with other cultures, from the Americas to Asia, and the establishment of European empires overseas also influenced writers during the Enlightenment. Eighteenth-century European thinkers were impressed by a wide range of non-European cultural achievements, especially the ancient learning of Confucian China and the native wisdom of preliterate Amerindian cultures. Educated Europeans did not yet know much about these far-flung societies, but the little they did know led them to the recognition that no single continent or culture held a monopoly on truth and encouraged them to develop a greater degree of toleration.

New discoveries in a broad spectrum of scientific fields—biology and chemistry as well as physics and astronomy—also profoundly shaped the thought of the age. Scientific societies such as the British Royal Society were founded to bring scientists and interested laypersons together. Popular books, available to the literate upper classes, explained the scientific worldview. During the Enlightenment many laypeople dabbled in science just as earlier Europeans had patronized the arts during the Renaissance.

Enlightenment writers, influenced by the new thinking about the physical universe, applied the scientific method to the social as well as the natural world. Some posited that human nature was as susceptible to controlling laws as any other part of nature. As the first step in uncovering these laws, Enlightenment thinkers used reason as a means to analyze and expose faults in traditional social institutions. In so doing, they challenged many of the injustices and weaknesses of the ancien régime, as society in this period was later called. Some writers began to dream of a perfect society of the future, designed according to scientific principles, in which all human beings would live a better life. The application of scientific principles to the study of society formed the foundations of the modern social sciences, including political science and economics.

The scientific revolution involved a dangerous political corollary: if nature was not ordered hierarchically, then neither was society. No group or class was "better" than another and should not be favored by laws. Nor should any group monopolize political power because of an accident of birth. The idea spread that society and government should be a meritocracy, where persons were judged by their achievements, not their social background.

The Philosophes

Although the Enlightenment was an international movement, its center was in France, or, to be more precise, in Paris, where its ideas found expression in a unique group of writers known as the *philosophes*. This French word does not denote professional or academic philosophers, but rather social critics who relied on rational analysis to solve the concrete problems of their time.

The philosophes wrote mainly for the aristocracy and the bourgeoisie. Gradually, the ideas of the Enlightenment filtered down to the working classes. Progressive aristocrats, who were eager to keep up with the latest ideas, mingled with the philosophes in a distinctive Enlightenment institution, the salon. At these elegant social gatherings, literary readings, serious conversations, and sparkling wit were to be expected. The salons were often hosted by rich, cultivated women who facilitated the exchange of ideas and introduced various intellectuals to one another.

The writings of the philosophes reached a wide audience among the middle class, who were wealthier, better educated, and more self-confident than ever before. Middle-class readers could identify with the ideas of the philosophes and delighted in their criticism of the gross inequalities of the old regime. Many of the philosophes were of bourgeois origin, and their writings reflected the values and attitudes of their class. Nothing was sacred to these men of letters, who in calling for an intelligent program of reform, held up to public ridicule the stupidity, irrationality, unfairness, and hypocrisy of many existing traditions.

The most successful and famous of the philosophes was François-Marie Arouet (1694–1778), better known by his pen name, Voltaire. He wrote on many subjects and in almost every literary form, including history, philosophical fiction, drama, poetry, popular science, and essays on social questions. Voltaire's voluminous private correspondence alone fills almost ninety-eight volumes. Guests flocked to his home to enjoy good food, wit, and wisdom. A passionate reformer, he turned the sharpest edge of his sword against the Catholic church, frequently mocking its superstition and hypocrisy. Voltaire was no revolutionist, believing that society's evils could be eradicated peacefully through an appeal to common sense and enlightened thinking. As he put it, "the more enlightened men are, the more they will be free." The most widely read of his many books was the comic novel *Candide* (1754), which ridiculed snobbish aristocrats and hypocritical churchmen.

Jean-Jacques Rousseau (1712–1778) was an emotional, deeply serious critic of the social order, occupying a position among writers that was second only to Voltaire's. Rousseau's best-known works are *The Social Contract, Confessions* (autobiographical), and *Emile,* in which he opposed rote learning and championed the development of the individual's innate capacities. Rousseau believed that humans were basically good but that they had become corrupted by the progress of civilization. In contrast to his fellow

A Medieval Solution to the Problem of Earthquakes

The University of Coimbra had pronounced that the sight of a few people ceremoniously burned alive before a slow fire was an infallible prescription for preventing earthquakes; so when the earthquake had subsided after destroying three-quarters of Lisbon, the authorities ... could find no surer means of avoiding total ruin than by giving the people a magnificent auto-da-fé.

They therefore seized a Basque, convicted of marrying his godmother, and two Portuguese Jews who had refused to eat bacon with their chicken; and after dinner Dr. Pangloss and his pupil, Candide, were arrested as well, one for speaking and the other for listening with an air of approval. ... They were then marched in procession ... to hear a moving sermon followed by beautiful music. ... Candide was flogged in time with the

anthem; the Basque and the two men who refused to eat bacon were burnt; and Pangloss was hanged. ... The same day another earthquake occurred and caused tremendous havoc.*

In *Candide,* Voltaire used the historic Lisbon earthquake of 1755 as a means to assault medieval views, anti-Semitism, and the Catholic church. The "crimes" mentioned included violation of dietary and marriage laws (although a godmother is, of course, no blood relation) and the too-free speech for which the philosophes themselves were often punished. To Enlightened thinkers, the practices of much organized religion seemed superstitious, fanatical, and absurd.

*Voltaire, Candide or Optimism, trans. by John Butt (Baltimore: Penguin Books, 1947), pp. 36–37.

philosophes, he held that intuition and emotion were far better guides to the truth than reason. Unlike Voltaire, Rousseau did not achieve wealth or widespread critical acclaim in his own lifetime, but his political ideas, which will be discussed later, had great impact on the course of the French Revolution.

Another leading figure of the Enlightenment was Denis Diderot (1713–1784), chief editor of a multivolume *Encyclopedia* (1751–1772) to which most of the philosophes contributed. Diderot wanted the reference work to sum up and popularize eighteenth-century learning. Thus he sought to apply the methods of science and reason to every area of human knowledge. Although neither the church nor the state was directly attacked, the articles contained veiled criticisms that did not always escape the censor's wrath. Diderot constantly faced the dangers of official censorship and suppression, but he overcame all obstacles and carried the work through to completion.

The role of religion and the existence of a divine being were two of the major questions pondered by Enlightenment writers. Many philosophes became deists and some even moved toward atheism. Deists believed in a rational God who, after creating the world and the laws governing it, refrained from intervening in human affairs. Many also rejected the sectarian divisions between Catholics and Protestants, arguing that all Christians, Muslims, and Buddhists had access to God as they understood the divine being. Public profession of atheism was rare in the eighteenth century, but by 1800 a famous scientist told Napoleon that he had no need of the "hypothesis" of God's existence to explain the universe.

Enlightenment writers also debated the condition of women in society. For centuries women had been regarded as inferiors and denied an education and a professional career; if married, they enjoyed few property rights and could be abused with impunity by their husbands. Although leading writers of the period occasionally decried the legal inferiority of women, they retained the traditional view of women and expected men to dominate marriage and family life. Diderot, who regarded his mistress as his intellectual equal, was among the few to actively support women's rights. He called for improved educational opportunities for women and favored reforms that would accord them the same legal status as men. By the mid-eighteenth century, perceptions began to change as wealthy women organized fashionable salons where the enlightened gathered for free and open discussions. More and more learned women challenged the popular view of their gender. They insisted that women were by nature the equals of men and had been made subservient by artificial laws and institutions. In *Vindication of the Rights of Women* (1792), Mary Wollstonecraft (1759–1797) provided an eloquent statement of female emancipation. Writing at the time of the French Revolution, Wollstonecraft called for a revolt against the tyranny of men and the recognition of women as in every way their equals.

Weary of corrupt absolute monarchies, Enlightenment writers believed that humans, being rational and virtuous, could devise a system of government that was both efficient and benevolent. John Locke (1632–1704), an English philosopher, refuted the defense of divine right and substituted a political theory of his own. He boldly stated that all people are born with equal rights to life, liberty, and property. He argued that the only legitimate government—which could be a constitutional monarchy or an assembly of elected representatives—was one formed by mutual consent between the ruler and the ruled. People invested the government with limited powers in return for the safeguard of their inborn rights. If the government violated the social contract, it forfeited the loyalty of its subjects and could be overthrown. The revolutionary idea that governments were responsible to the sovereign people found an eloquent advocate in Jean-Jacques Rousseau.

In *The Social Contract* Rousseau, in the Lockean tradition, insisted that a government was legitimate only if it had the consent of the governed. He shared the Enlightenment's antipathy for restrictions on individual freedoms, but more than any reformer of his time, he was concerned with the rights of society as a whole. He portrayed the state as a corporate body of citizens whose individual aims must be subordinated to the "general will." This general will always represented what was in the best interest of the entire community and everyone living within it. Those unwilling to conform to the general will must be compelled to do so. Thus Rousseau's doctrine of the general will provided justification for unrestrained government suppression of individual freedoms.

The French aristocracy's resistance to absolute monarchy is symbolized by Baron de la Brède et de Montesquieu (1689–1755). Although an admirer of the British political system, Montesquieu denied that there was a single perfect form of government that was suitable for all people. His solution for avoiding tyranny was a system of checks and balances rather than a social contract. The powers of government should be divided equally among the executive, legislature, and judiciary; each would perform its own functions but be capable of being checked by the other two. This principle was incorporated into the Constitution of the United States and to the present day continues to have a profound effect on the development of liberal democracies throughout the world.

The Enlightenment's faith in reason also led to pressure for social reforms. The philosophes abhorred slavery and the callous treatment of the criminally insane. But nothing stirred them more profoundly than the cumbersome, antiquated judicial procedures and the torture of prisoners. In a legal treatise entitled *Crimes and Punishments,* Cesare Beccaria (1735–1794), an Italian jurist, appealed for the application of reason to the administration of justice. He argued that the aim of punishment was not to extract vengeance but to reform the perpetrators and prepare them for reintegration in society. He maintained that the criminal codes should be clear, that penalties should be applied equally to all classes of society, and that punishments should not only be swift and sure but proportionate to the crime. Widely acclaimed, Beccaria's book was translated into other languages and promoted the cause of penal reform in a number of European countries.

Some philosophes in search of a better life sought to apply the methods of natural law to the study of economics. Rejecting the mercantilist theories that had been held for centuries, early writers concluded that the economy operated best when it was left to its own devices. The most able proponent of the new laissez-faire school was Adam Smith (1723–1790), whose monumental study, *The Wealth of Nations,* published in 1776, became a bible for bourgeoisie capitalism. Smith asserted that a natural law of supply and demand formed the basis of all economic exchanges. If the economy were left free of government regulation, it would respond naturally to public demand, supplying what the people wanted at a price they were willing to pay. Such free-market policies, which were to be widely abused by industrialists in subsequent centuries, would result, according to Smith, in a steady growth in the wealth of all nations. In the twentieth century, the free trade, capitalist, or free enterprise systems of many nations, from the United States to western Europe to Japan, still reflected some of these ideas.

The Arts in the Age of Enlightenment

Enlightenment painting and literature were less innovative than the scientific and social thought of the period, although some new forms and styles emerged. Aristocratic patrons and small, elite groups continued to dominate much of the artistic life during the eighteenth century, but the newly affluent middle class was beginning to demand a role in cultural life and would have an important impact later. Music of the period, performed in large opera houses and concert halls, reached larger numbers of people than ever before. The development of a wider audience was particularly important for the long-term future of the arts.

Neoclassical and rococo styles predominated in the arts during the century. Neoclassicism was a refinement of the classical styles of the past, which required the artist to adhere to the rules and models of the ancients. In contrast, rococo art was light, elegant, and highly decorative. Named for the stone and seashell (*rocaille* and *coquille*) motifs used in its room decorations, the rococo style was lighter than the previous baroque style and more informal than neoclassical.

The growing interest of the middle classes in art led to several major changes in artistic themes and approaches. Interest in the "common people" as opposed to the aristocracy was expressed in paintings of peasants or working people. The depiction of common people often stressed their dignity, piety, and warmth. The English artist William Hogarth (1697–1764) produced satirical printed etchings of the poorest and most disaffected groups with such subjects as *The Harlot's Progress* or *Gin Lane,* which sold many copies.

Middle-class tastes had the greatest impact on prose fiction. The first modern novels, *Robinson Crusoe* by Daniel Defoe (1661–1731) and *Tom Jones* by Henry Fielding (1707–1754), attracted widespread audiences who delighted in the adventurous and even bawdy humor of these novels. *Evelina* by Fanny Burney (1752–1840), one of many female novelists, detailed a girl's discovery of high society. Fictional works like this and shorter stories appeared in many women's magazines, which catered to middle-class preferences for stories stressing feeling and morality.

Perhaps the greatest artistic achievements of the eighteenth century came in music. The German states, particularly Austria, produced many brilliant composers who decisively shaped classical music. From Bach to Mozart, it was one of the great ages in the history of music.

Johann Sebastian Bach (1685–1750) spent a quiet life creating religious music for German church congregations; his compositions embody the very spirit of the Age of Reason. George Frederick Handel (1685–1759), Bach's contemporary, produced dramatic compositions of instrumental and choral music.

Two other Germans, Joseph Haydn (1732–1809) and Wolfgang Amadeus Mozart (1756–1791), dominated the musical world during the second half of the century. Haydn enjoyed the patronage of Austrian royalty and produced an immense volume of compositions. Mozart was a child prodigy who dazzled courtly audiences with his virtuoso playing skills; as an adult, he also earned a more precarious living by composing operas and symphonies and died in debt at the age of only thirty-five. Haydn and Mozart helped to develop the modern symphonic orchestra, and Mozart's operas, especially the often-performed *Marriage of Figaro*, combined comic and tragic themes with intricate composition in works that transcend the age.

Eastern Europe and the Age of Enlightened Despotism

It is certain that among troops one cannot see their equal in the world in beauty, propriety and order; and although along with marching, parading, manual dexterity and the like, goes much that is affected and forced, these are accompanied by so many useful and proper things which belong to the craft itself, that one must say, that not the least thing is missing in the Army and the troops. . . .

All this the King directs, solely and by himself, and besides this he works on public affairs, private affairs, economic affairs and the affairs of his domain with such seriousness that no thaler [Prussian money unit] can be spent without his signature.

He who has not seen it can not believe that one man in the world, of whatever intelligence, could expedite and do by himself so many different things, as one sees this King expedite daily; for which he uses the morning from 3 o'clock to 10 o'clock, but then spends the rest of the day with military exercises. . . .*

*Max Schilling, Quellenbuch zur Geschichte der Neuzeit, trans. George L. Morse (Berlin: 1890), p. 299.

So wrote the Austrian ambassador in 1723 about the Prussian army and the character of Frederick William I, who built the Prussian army into a superb fighting force. A firm believer in absolutism and descendent of a series of competent and hard-working Hohenzollern rulers, Frederick William once declared "Salvation belongs to the Lord; everything else is my affair." Similarly, in the seventeenth and eighteenth centuries the Austrian House of Habsburg rebuilt its fortunes under several able rulers, and isolated and backward Russia emerged as a major power once its own monarchs, most notably Peter the Great, achieved absolute power. All these monarchies sought to follow the pattern set by Louis XIV of France in building and strengthening the machinery of a centralized royal government and in the trappings they instituted at their royal courts.

Enlightened Despotism

In the mid- to late eighteenth century, European absolutism displayed a special set of characteristics that historians now refer to as "enlightened despotism." Inspired by the writings of the Enlightenment philosophes, some monarchs embraced enlightened despotism as a means of reconstructing and strengthening their states during an era marked by recurrent wars.

Enlightened despots believed their own interests could best be served by dynastic internal reforms. Measures designed to promote the development of the economy not only increased the wealth of their subjects but also provided the treasury with more revenues to finance larger armies. By curbing the power of the nobility and church, by building up a corps of trained and salaried officials, and by rationalizing administrative procedures, these monarchs were able to strengthen the central government and increase its efficiency. Other reforms, such as the granting of religious toleration, instituting progressive legal and judicial systems, and improving public health and education, generated greater public support for their rule.

Enlightened despots differed from old-style absolutist monarchs primarily in attitude and style. Enlightened despots rarely spoke of their divine or hereditary right to rule. Instead they focused on their paternalistic roles as heads of state. Denying that the masses were capable of ruling themselves, they claimed their paternalistic government best served the interests of all. Realistically, few enlightened despots actually achieved what they claimed. Collectively, they ignored the philosophes' demand that they accord social equality and individual rights to their subjects, and they refused to institute reforms that damaged their own interests. Of the handful of rulers who embraced the concept of enlightened despotism, the three most outstanding were Joseph II of Austria, Frederick the Great of Prussia, and Catherine the Great of Russia.

Habsburg Revival and Austrian Absolutism

The Thirty Years' War (1618–1648) that ended Europe's religious wars shattered the power of the Habsburg dynasty in central Europe. Surprisingly, however, the Holy Roman emperors of the Habsburg dynasty improved their status during the late seventeenth century and rebuilt their multinational empire. The architect of this revival was Emperor Leopold I of Austria (reigned 1658–1705). A contemporary of Louis XIV, Leopold was an unaggressive, extremely religious prince who had none of the Sun King's self-confidence or skill at public relations. Nevertheless, with the help of brilliant generals, Leopold built up his army and used it to turn back the last great Ottoman invaders of central Europe and to drive them out of Hungary. He then added these new possessions to Austria and Bohemia (modern Czech Republic). Thus strengthened, he reclaimed authority over the German states vested in his role as emperor, and Austria resumed its position as a great power in Europe.

Leopold and his successor Charles VI (reigned 1705–1740) strove to implement centralized absolutist rule, but their efforts were imperfectly realized because of the complex political conditions in central Europe. Unlike Louis XIV, who drew on the French bourgeoisie to assist him in building his centralized absolutist state, the Habsburgs had to rely on the aristocracy, including the non-German Hungarian and Bohemian nobility, as the basis of their power. They had to turn to the aristocrats in part because the Habsburg domains were economically less advanced than France and had few large towns. Large estates owned by conservative aristocrats and worked by serfs predominated in the countryside of the Habsburg possessions. To win the support of the aristocrats, the Habsburgs allowed them to increase their traditional control over their peasant populations, which in effect diluted royal power and enhanced aristocratic influence in the empire.

Powerful provincial assemblies and deep ethnic divisions between the majority Germans and the minority populations of Magyars (Hungarians), Italians, Czechs, and other Slavs also militated against absolutism and allowed for particularism.

The most sincere and least successful of the enlightened despots was Joseph II of Austria (reigned 1780–1790). His cautious mother, Maria Theresa (reigned 1740–1780), had made reforms during the previous reign without offending vested interests. Joseph was well meaning but lacked political wisdom. As a doctrinaire reformer, he was intent on sweeping away anachronistic institutions and creating new ones based on the philosophes' highest ideals of justice and reason, regardless of whether they fitted local requirements. In centralizing the administration of the far-flung Habsburg territories, he curtailed the authority of local assemblies and tried to undermine the power of the nobility. He subordinated the church to the state, stripping it of much of its wealth, ending its control of education, legalizing civil marriages, and granting religious toleration. He made the judicial system more uniform, irrespective of local needs. He made school attendance mandatory for seven years, but did not provide the funds for schools or teachers. He freed the serfs, without making work arrangements for their livelihood. "Joseph always wishes to take the second step before he has taken the first," was the perceptive observation of Frederick the Great. Joseph's reforming whirlwind frightened and alienated almost every segment of society, especially the church and the aristocracy. In the end, most of his reforms failed or fell short of their goal, and he died a broken and disillusioned man at age forty-nine. He summed up his career in an epitaph he composed for himself shortly before his death: "Here lies a prince whose intentions were pure and who had the misfortune to see all his plans miscarry." Most of his reforms were rescinded by his cautious brother and successor Leopold II (reigned 1790–1792).

Hohenzollern Power and Prussian Absolutism

The Hohenzollern dynasty in Prussia provides the most spectacular example of the rise of absolutism in central and eastern Europe. In 1648 the princely House of Hohenzollern governed a string of scattered lands that stretched across northern Germany. The Elector Frederick William I (reigned 1688–1740) wisely used his limited resources to build a powerful and disciplined army, and under his successor the army became the fourth largest in Europe and one of the best. He and his successors also established an efficient governmental bureaucracy.

Collectively, the army and the bureaucracy proved useful instruments that made possible Hohenzollern territorial expansions in the wars of the eighteenth century. Both were staffed by Prussian aristocrats, known as the Junkers, who loyally supported the monarchy in return for increased authority over the peasant populations on their estates. The Junkers remained the backbone of Hohenzollern power until World War I. In 1701 the Hohenzollern rulers acquired the title of king. They then proceeded to transform Berlin, their capital city, into a great metropolis.

To some, Frederick II (reigned 1740–1786), known as Frederick the Great, was the quintessential enlightened despot. This remarkable ruler loved art, literature, and music and was a fervent admirer of the French philosophes, in particular Voltaire, whom he invited to his court. Frederick was a hard worker and called himself "the first servant of the state." Like China's Emperor K'ang-hsi, he rose before dawn and labored at his desk until evening, when he turned to cultural pursuits. No aspect of his government escaped his attention. He visited each part of his kingdom annually and bombarded distant officials with correspondence, periodically sending royal agents to report on their activities. During his rule the Prussian civil service set the standard for efficiency and honesty throughout Europe.

A believer in mercantilism, Frederick tailored his economic and agricultural policies to achieve national self-sufficiency. He also saw to the codification of laws, improved the administration of justice, and extended religious toleration to all except Jews. Torture was eliminated except in cases of murder and treason. He paid judges adequate salaries, thereby reducing the need for them to accept bribes. Under Frederick, justice was made not only simpler and less burdensome but also uniform across his domains.

For all his enlightened reforms, Frederick applied the laws of reason to statecraft only when it suited his interests. He spoke about the value of public education but provided little funding for it. He defended the hierarchical social order and rigidly defined the legal status of the different classes. Because he depended on the aristocracy for service in the army and bureaucracy, he refrained from abolishing serfdom, even though he declared the institution an abomination. He granted only limited freedom of speech and of the press.

Frederick's foreign policy was based on power politics and not on the humanitarian and pacifist ideals of the philosophes. Without any legal or moral justification, he invaded and annexed the rich Austrian province of Silesia, thereby provoking the long and bloody War of the Austrian Succession (1740–1748). Eight years later he was compelled to fight a second conflict, the Seven Years' War (1756–1763), at the end of which he was again allowed to retain his ill-gotten gain. In 1772, in collaboration with Russia and Austria, he participated in the first partition of Poland. He gained West Prussia, which linked East Prussia with the main body of the Hohenzollern state. Thus under his rule Prussia more than doubled in size and population. With its efficient government, sound economy, and superb army, Prussia was the dominant power in central Europe at the time of Frederick's death.

Autocracy in Russia

Strong government was not new to Russia. The Principality of Moscow, the precursor of modern Russia, had an autocratic tradition that reached back hundreds of years. During the fifteenth century, Moscow expanded in every direction. Building on the achievements of his predecessors, Moscow's Prince Ivan III (reigned 1462–1505) subjected other Russian princes to his rule and transformed the Principality of Moscow into the state of Russia. He tripled the territory under his control by annexing several Russian principalities and conquering Novgorod and various Lithuanian-held lands. In addition, he repudiated Mongol authority and stopped tribute payments.

Ivan also identified Russia as the cultural heir of the Byzantine Empire, which had recently been conquered by the Ottoman Turks. He made the Russian church independent of Constantinople and established it as the defender of the true Orthodox faith. The church promoted unity among Slavic Christians and hoped that a strong Moscow might overthrow the Mongol domination.

Ivan III's marriage to Zoe, niece of the last Byzantine emperor, and his adoption of the Byzantine imperial emblem, the double-headed eagle, added political prestige to his military-based state. He now termed himself tsar (caesar or emperor) of all the Russias. Just as Charlemagne considered himself heir to Roman tradition, Ivan saw himself as the successor of the Byzantine emperors and regarded Moscow as the new center of Orthodox civilization, replacing Constantinople.

Ivan III's grandson, Ivan IV (reigned 1533–1584), called Ivan the Terrible, expanded and centralized the Russian state. He won control of the entire Volga River, gained an outlet on the Baltic Sea, and launched expeditions into western Siberia. To weaken the power of the hereditary nobility, Ivan granted newly conquered lands in the form of nonhereditary military fiefs, thus producing a lesser nobility built on service, who in time became the most powerful class in the state. To ensure a supply of workers for those lands and to keep peasants where they could be taxed, Ivan passed a series of laws binding formerly free Russian peasants to the soil for life. Thus serfdom, which had disappeared in England and in other parts of Europe, became a new and permanent institution in Russia.

The autocracy of Ivan III and Ivan IV was followed by the "Time of Troubles," a period of anarchy characterized by popular revolts and invasions by the neighboring states of Sweden and Poland. A new royal dynasty, the house of Romanov, emerged in 1613 and ruled Russia until the revolution of 1917. The first three Romanovs supervised an expansion of the bureaucracy and foreign trade, and most importantly, Russian expansion eastward across Siberia to the Pacific. Nevertheless, throughout the seventeenth century Russia continued to be plagued by peasant and cossack rebellions and by a great schism that split the Russian Orthodox church. Thus, at the beginning of the 1680s, Russia remained a huge backward state at the eastern edge of the European world. It needed a dynamic leader to harness its potentials and transform it into a European power.

Ascending the throne at the age of ten, Peter I (reigned 1682–1725), called Peter the Great, was a major architect of Russian absolutism. He was a human whirlwind, shaking up backward, traditional Russia as it had never been before and would not be again until the twentieth century. Peter was huge, standing nearly seven feet tall. Although illeducated, uncouth, and often brutal, he was nevertheless intelligent, practical, and open to new ideas and possessed an incredible capacity for work. His goal at the outset was to increase his political and military power and bring Russia up to date with the West. In 1697–1698 he traveled through Germany, the Netherlands, and England, observing western practices, technology, and institutions. His return was followed by an imperial policy of westernization that touched almost all phases of Russian life.

For Peter, modernization meant not only introducing new ideas and procedures but also attacking reactionary attitudes. He banned beards and ordered his courtiers and officials to wear Western dress instead of the traditional long robes. Women were summoned to court from their domestic seclusion and encouraged to mingle socially with

The Building of St. Petersburg. Absolute monarchs demonstrated and enhanced their power by building lavish palaces and even whole cities. Here Peter the Great supervises construction of his new capital. Peter, who had worked with his hands in his youth, was a harsh taskmaster, but the city he built is considered by many to be the most beautiful in Russia.

men. Stressing the need for education, he founded schools and institutions of higher learning. He brought in Western technicians in large numbers to help operate new state-subsidized industries, which he protected with mercantilist policies. He adopted a bureaucratic system that in many ways resembled that of Louis IV, to make his authority more absolute. Peter deprived the aristocrats of what political power they had hitherto enjoyed, but rather than reduce them to an idle class, as in France, he compelled them to serve in the government or the army. When the church came out in opposition to some of his reforms, he abolished the office of patriarch and assumed control of religious affairs through an appointed board, the Holy Synod. Moreover, he built a sizable fleet and reorganized the army on the Prussian model.

In foreign affairs, Peter did not achieve all of his objectives, but at least he made Russia a major power. His most important military engagement was a long-drawn-out war against Sweden, from which Russia acquired immense territory, allowing it access to the Baltic Sea. Peter immediately proceeded to build a new capital, St. Petersburg, at the cost of many thousands of workers' lives. He called it his "window on the West." By moving the capital away from isolated Moscow, he opened Russia further to western European trade and cultural influence.

Peter did not really change Russia internally, for few of his reforms survived him. The succession of rulers who followed him were weak or inept. Thirty-seven years would pass before another ruler left an imprint on Russia.

Many historians have viewed Catherine II (reigned 1762–1796), later called Catherine the Great, as another example of an enlightened despot. As such, she owed her reputation more to skillful self-advertising than to her record of accomplishments. A German princess, she came to the throne through a coup in which her husband, Peter III (reigned 1762), was overthrown and subsequently murdered. A crafty ruler, Catherine fancied herself an intellectual, wrote plays, and corresponded with French philosophes. Few of her enlightened ideas, however, were translated into social deeds. Catherine realized early in her reign that the necessary conditions for implementing Enlightenment ideas were not native to Russia. She did, however, carry through such reforms as she thought were politically feasible. She founded orphanages, hospitals, and schools for privileged children and encouraged trade by abolishing internal tolls. Her reforms, such as they were, ended after a violent serf uprising—an episode reminiscent of the abortive slave revolt against Rome led by the gladiator Spartacus in 70 B.C.E. There had been a steady deterioration in the conditions of the serfs so that when Emelian Pugachev, an illiterate cossack, sounded the call to arms in September 1773 they flocked to his banner by tens of thousands. The rebellion became widespread and threatened Moscow before it was crushed. Thereafter the serfs were reduced to the level of chattel slaves with no legal rights against their landlords.

Like Frederick the Great, Catherine pursued an expansionist and unscrupulous foreign policy. As she remarked, "If I could live for two hundred years, all of Europe would be brought under Russian rule." She waged two wars against the Ottoman Empire that gained the north shore of the Black Sea and warm-water—but virtually landlocked—ports. Through three partitions of Poland (1772, 1793, and 1795) Catherine acquired about two-thirds of the once huge Polish state, pushing Russia's western boundary deep into central Europe. Catherine's conquests earned her the title "the Great" and enhanced Russia's position as a great European power.

The Development of Latin American Culture

If [entrance to the city of Cuzco] is not granted at once, I shall not delay for an instant my entrance with fire and sword. . . . I am the only one who remains of the royal blood of the Incas, kings of this kingdom. I have decided to try all means possible that all abuses . . . may cease. . . . My desire is that [tyrannous local officials] shall be suppressed entirely; . . . and that in each province there may be a [governor] of the same Indian nation and other persons of good conscience. . . . It is indispensable that in this city a royal audiencia shall be erected, where a viceroy shall reside as president in order that the Indians may have nearer access to him. I wish to leave to the King of Spain the direct rule which he has had in his possessions. . . . This . . . is not against God or the King, but against the introduction of bad laws. *

*José Gabriel Túpac Amaru, in Lillian E. Fisher, *The Last Inca Revolt, 1780–1783* (Norman: University of Oklahoma Press, 1966), pp. 96, 122.

This is a statement of José Gabriel Túpac Amaru, a descendant of the Inka rulers and the leader of the Amerindian revolt in the Andes, 1780–1783. His words and even his name are a microcosm of eighteenth-century Latin America. His conquered people had been suffering for two and a half centuries under brutal abuses, especially a forced labor system that amounted to slavery. He was determined to destroy the system of local government that fostered this oppression and to give Amerindians a larger role in the political system. Yet at the same time he was also a product of the pervasive impact of Spanish culture in Peru. This mestizo rebel was a devout Catholic, a believer in the justice of the Spanish monarchy, and a firm supporter of the viceroy's rule in Peru, as long as it was supervisory and did not support corrupt and exploitative local officials. Túpac Amaru's rebellion was crushed, and his life ended in an agony of torture and dismemberment.

In the early eighteenth century, 3 million inhabitants of European descent and millions of mixed ancestry lived in Latin America and British North America. European settlers arriving in the Western Hemisphere naturally expected to live in much the same way as they did in their homelands. However, as they experienced the new environment, they dropped or modified inappropriate European practices and adopted new ones more suitable to their current surroundings. This section discusses Latin America, the first part of the world where Western culture as it emerged differed markedly from that of Europe. The next section will take up yet a different version of Western culture, that which evolved in British North America.

A Multiracial Society

The greatest difference between Western civilization as it developed in Latin America compared to Europe was the unique multiracial situation that developed in the Western Hemisphere. The Spanish and Portuguese controlled three-quarters of that hemisphere, an area some forty times larger than their homelands, but only small numbers of Iberians, at first mostly men, settled in the vast conquered areas. By the eighteenth century these whites—Peninsulars (aristocrats from Spain) and Creoles (aristocrats of Spanish descent born in America)—comprising only 2 percent of the population, owned virtually all the mines, ranches, plantations, and manufacturing establishments in the hemisphere. Protected by special privileges and powers, isolated in small groups by great distances and difficult terrain, the elite were surrounded and outnumbered by Amerindian peons, mestizos, African slaves, and mulattos, whose forced labor was the foundation of the economy.

Amerindians remained in the majority in some areas, and throughout the colonial period were the largest single racial group in Latin America. Mestizo descendants from white-Amerindian unions were in the majority in some areas. There was an extensive mulatto (descendants of white and African American unions) population throughout the Caribbean and Brazil.

The realities of multiracial living brought about a somewhat more relaxed attitude about race in Latin America than in Europe or in British North America. The status of the large and increasing mestizo population was in general worked out by a rough color code. A few individuals from wealthy and accomplished families were accepted as mem-

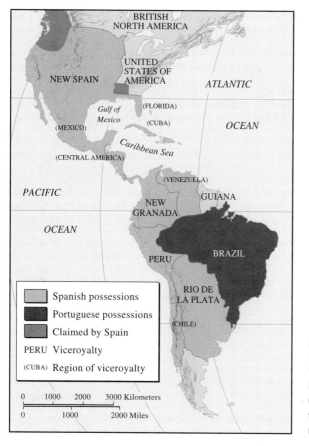

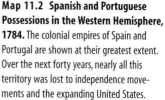

Map 11.2 Spanish and Portuguese Possessions in the Western Hemisphere, 1784. The colonial empires of Spain and Portugal are shown at their greatest extent. Over the next forty years, nearly all this territory was lost to independence movements and the expanding United States.

bers of the white ruling class despite their mixed Amerindian ancestry; others of mixed blood became a part of the small middle class. Some mestizos and lower-class Iberian immigrants filled the need for merchants and artisans.

The Life of the Masses in Latin America

Whatever their ancestry, more than 90 percent of the population—blacks, mulattos, Amerindians, and most mestizos—toiled for the few. Initially, many Amerindians were enslaved; later, the Spanish crown and the Catholic church held that the Amerindians were free subjects of the crown, to be treated as dependent minors. They could be parceled out to work for the benefit of whites, but only on a limited basis, and were to receive religious and vocational instruction. In actuality, whites often worked their "dependents" severely. Masters forced the Amerindians under their control to work in mines and factories, on ranches and farms, and as porters and construction laborers. Often separated from their families, Amerindians frequently labored under brutal conditions that brought premature death. They sometimes rose in revolt, but the uprisings were always crushed. However, by the eighteenth century the more brutal forms of exploitation had disappeared, and the mass of Amerindians and mestizos had become peons, bound to the land by insurmountable debts for shelter, food, and clothing. The local officials who supervised the Indian villages in rural areas often violated the legal rights of the Amerindians by seizing their land and levying fraudulent taxes. These magistrates were the oppressors challenged so vehemently by Túpac Amaru.

Blacks fared even worse than the Amerindians. Whereas most Amerindians at least lived a family life in their villages and continued to practice many aspects of their traditional culture, blacks were torn away as individuals from their home and culture, shipped across the ocean along with other suffering strangers, and put to grueling labor in a strange new land. Since males greatly outnumbered females, most could not even establish families. By law, they held a dual status: as human beings, they were entitled to humane treatment; as slaves, they were chattel, like livestock. In practice, most masters treated their slaves as personal property rather than as human beings. Many slaves were simply worked to death or to incapacity and then replaced by new slaves brought in by the efficient slave-trading companies.

There were a few ways out of slavery. Portugal in particular had provided relatively liberal laws that allowed Brazilian slaves to buy their freedom, and masters found few legal obstacles if they wished to free a slave. In fact, however, few slaves could accumulate the price of freedom, and few masters freed their slaves. Nevertheless, those blacks and mulattos who did gain their freedom legally found that, unlike the situation in British North America, their race was not an absolute barrier to rising in society. Black artisans and mechanics often found acceptance, especially in areas where there were few skilled white workers. In parts of Brazil, where black slaves and freemen overwhelmingly outnumbered whites, even a small degree of white ancestry gave some mulattos the social status of whites.

Blacks resisted their enslavement in several ways. Slaves in the Caribbean sporadically rose in revolt, but always unsuccessfully. Some individuals escaped into unsettled areas, and occasionally runaways banded together and successfully held out against whites, as the Maroons did in the interior of Jamaica. Brazilian slaves often fled into the vast jungle interior. In the seventeenth century, runaway blacks set up the state of Palmares, which lasted thirty years before it was destroyed.

Mercantilist Theory and Spanish American Reality

Like the other colonial powers, the Spanish government followed mercantilist economic doctrine, closely regulating its American colonies until well into the eighteenth century. The crown permitted a group of private companies in Seville and Cadiz to monopolize commerce with Spanish America, while at the same time the Casa de Contratación, the government bureau that managed the economic life of the colonies, collected the crown's share of taxes and monopolies. The Portuguese monarchs were not as rigid as their Spanish counterparts and allowed merchants in Portuguese ports to send their ships to any port in Brazil.

Under the protection of the Spanish navy, two annual convoys stopped at three Caribbean ports in Spanish America, picked up the cargoes waiting there, and then returned to Spain. The Spanish government apparently believed that the convoy system may have been necessary to protect the cargoes of gold and silver. However, forcing all the exportable products scattered across Spain's vast American domains to be gathered at only three ports made it extremely difficult for producers (in most of South America in particular) to get their goods to Spain. By the eighteenth century the convoy policy was strangling Spanish American exports.

Imports posed, if anything, an even greater problem. Under mercantilist doctrine, colonists were to consume the products of the mother country or products from other parts of the world supplied by the ships of the mother country. Colonists were not to buy goods from foreign ships and were not allowed to produce items—metalware, textiles, and wine, for example—that competed with those of the mother country. That was the theory; in fact, by the eighteenth century, Spain was no longer able to supply products needed for everyday life in its colonies. The colonists, desperate for affordable European products, welcomed British, Dutch, and French smugglers. They began to produce their own textiles, metalware, and wine, while Amerindians provided woven goods, pottery, and basketry. The upper classes, however, continued to demand high-quality goods made in Europe.

Church and State in Spanish America

Ministering to the spiritual needs of the millions living in the huge area across the ocean was the responsibility of the Roman Catholic church's widespread colonial organization. The Spanish monarchy selected all clerical officials in America up to the rank of archbishop. Since the church, like the state, reflected the class structure of the time, nearly all the top ecclesiastical appointments (ten archbishops and thirty-eight bishops) went to Spanish aristocrats. Most of the clergymen on the parish or local levels were Spaniards of common origin.

The most important responsibility of the church in Spanish America was to convert the Amerindians. Franciscan and Dominican missionaries accompanied the early conquistadores and converted millions of Amerindians, sometimes forcibly. In the more remote areas, this clergy, now joined by the Jesuits, often replaced the conquistadores as frontiersmen, setting up missions in previously unconquered territories. With the help of army detachments, they rounded up the nearby Amerindians and brought them in to work for the missionaries and to receive Christian instruction and baptism.

The regular clergy were followed by the secular clergy and by the religious orders of nuns. The new orders were specifically sent to organize local parishes, build schools and universities, and found hospitals, orphanages, and poorhouses. Bishops erected cathedrals and other religious edifices with money contributed by rich laity and the government. Many of these buildings were of outstanding architectural and artistic beauty.

As in Spain, Roman Catholicism was the only faith tolerated. The Holy Office (the Inquisition) punished blasphemy by fines and flogging. Unrepentant Protestants, Jews, and atheists faced exile or burning at the stake, although executions were quite infrequent compared to Europe. Amerindians were not subject to the jurisdiction of the Holy Office.

Many abuses and problems attended the transplanting of the Catholic church to the New World. By the eighteenth century the church had accumulated enormous wealth;

that and the huge size of the church organization made corruption inevitable. The Spanish American Catholic church was burdened with idle clerics who congregated in the cities for sumptuous and sometimes debauched living. Up to one-half of city property in the Americas was owned by the church or by the religious orders. The orders often competed with the laity in banking and commerce, taking advantage of their special exemptions from taxation and economic regulation.

The church also faced great problems in the countryside. Many dedicated clerics served their mestizo and Amerindian parishioners faithfully by their teaching, vocational instruction, and spiritual guidance. Some, however, were uneducated and avaricious, exploiting Amerindian labor as brutally as the secular landlords did, while exacting high fees for administering the sacraments and saying mass. Many Amerindians and blacks learned only the external, ceremonial aspects of their new faith. Ironically, some clergy encouraged the exploitation of black slaves in their efforts to protect Amerindians from enslavement and mistreatment.

The political situation in eighteenth-century Spanish America was complex. Up to the middle of the eighteenth century, the administration of Spanish America reflected that of Spain, coupled with some unique features. In Spain the traditional privileges of the nobility and churchmen placed some limits on the power of the monarchy. In America, however, the monarchs had virtually unlimited sovereignty, since the popes had awarded them the Americas as their personal property. With little competition from the aristocrats

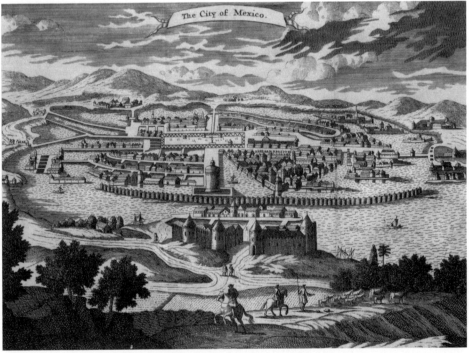

Engraving of Mexico City—1723 by John Clark. Tenochtitlán, conquered by the Spanish 200 years earlier, was built in the middle of Lake Texcoco on an artificial earthen base intersected with canals. The new Mexico City was clearly Mediterranean in its architecture. The approaches to the causeways were protected by turreted fortifications.

and the clerics, the kings quickly set up *cabildos* in Spanish America to buttress royal authority. The cabildo was an appointed city government that administered the surrounding countryside. It was the center of a complex control system that enabled the power of the king to fan out over the islands, jungles, plains, and highlands of the sprawling region. The Spanish monarchs appointed a Council of the Indies and gave that body the authority to act for the king on matters of economic policy, justice, military affairs, and religion.

Viceroys, representing the king in New Spain (Mexico, the Caribbean, and Central America) and Peru (Spanish South America), had great power over local appointments, administration, finance, and the military forces. Their authority was subject to review, however, by judicial-consultative bodies known as *audiencias* and by inspectors sent from Spain. The viceroy also supervised a hierarchical network of officials, including the regional presidents and captains-general, the provincial governors, and local officials. Spain gave most of the important governmental positions to Peninsulars, slighting the Creoles. Only four of the 170 viceroys who governed Spanish America during the colonial period were Creoles. By the early eighteenth century some Creoles were beginning to think of themselves as Spanish Americans rather than as Spaniards and resented the Peninsulars' monopoly of political power and aristocratic privilege. The Creoles, in their turn, were contemptuous of lower-class Iberian immigrants and the mestizo middle class.

Spanish American Culture: Derivation and Innovation

The church controlled education at all levels, and academic training was reserved for the upper and middle classes, who considered it unnecessary and even dangerous to educate the masses. As a result, 90 percent of Spanish Americans remained illiterate. Most women, even of the upper class, were not taught to read and write and were trained only in domestic and social skills.

Until the mid-eighteenth century, intellectual and artistic developments followed the lead of Iberia, which emphasized Aquinas and the scholastics. Innovative thought was discouraged by the Inquisition, with its Index of Prohibited Books. Most Spanish American writers concentrated on literary genres favored in Spain: chivalric romances, lyric poetry, and devotional literature.

However, a few Spanish American writers of the sixteenth and seventeenth centuries contributed to Western literature. These often employed traditional epic and romance formats to portray the struggles between the Spaniards and the Amerindians. An example is the first literary work concerning the Americas, *La Araucana,* an epic poem by Alonso de Ercilla y Zúñiga (1569–1589), which celebrated the heroic resistance of the Araucanian Amerindians of southern Chile.

The greatest poet of Spanish America may well have been Sor Juana Inés de la Cruz (1651–1695), a highly intelligent woman interested in science, mathematics, and writing. Refused admission to the University of Mexico because she was a woman (despite her offer to wear men's clothes!), she went into a convent at sixteen, where she wrote exquisite drama and love poetry while pursuing her studies in other subjects. Her superiors later put a stop to her writing; she sold her enormous library and devoted herself to charity until she died at forty-four.

Histories of the conquest were popular in both Europe and America. Bernal Díaz del Castillo (c. 1492–c. 1581), one of Cortés's soldiers, wrote an influential book entitled *The Discovery and Conquest of Mexico.* Another widely read book on the conquest was the *Royal Commentaries of the Incas,* by Garcilaso de la Vega (c. 1540–1616), son of a Spanish father and an Inka princess. European and Spanish American readers were also interested in descriptions of the Western Hemisphere's strange flora and fauna, such as the *General and Natural History of the Indies* (1535), by Gonzalo Fernández de Oviedo (1478–1557).

By the late eighteenth century, the scientific revolution and the Enlightenment had a widespread impact on Latin America. The ideas of Copernicus and Newton, Bacon and Descartes were taught in Latin America's two dozen universities, particularly those in Mexico City and Lima. Some Spanish American colonists, like their counterparts in the British colonies, corresponded with European scientific societies. Religious toleration remained a problem in Catholic Latin America because the Inquisition could still persecute those advocating radical ideas.

Latin America also became strongly influenced by the social theories of the Enlightenment. Colonial newspapers expressed concern over political abuses, voiced demands for economic and social changes, and spread the ideas of the philosophes. The same new ideas were being discussed by mestizo groups in colonial "economic clubs" and by aristocrats in traditional social gatherings called *tertulias.* No representative assemblies existed in the Latin American colonies, but individual, enlightened Bourbon rulers encouraged social reform. The Enlightenment's belief in reason and social progress and its willingness to challenge traditional authority contributed to the outbreak of the Latin American wars of independence in the early nineteenth century.

Cultural Evolution and Political Independence in British North America

[British] America is formed for happiness, but not for empire: in a course of 1200 miles I did not see a single object that solicited charity; but I saw insuperable causes of weakness, which will necessarily prevent its being a potent state; . . . it appears to me very doubtful . . . whether it would be possible to keep in due order and government so wide and extended an empire; . . . fire and water are not more heterogeneous than the different colonies in North America.

Nothing can exceed the jealousy . . . they possess in regard to each other. . . . In short, such is the difference of character, of manners, of religion, of interest of the different colonies, that . . . were they left to themselves, there would be a civil war, from one end of the continent to the other; while the Indians and Negroes would, with better reason, impatiently watch the opportunity of exterminating them all together. . . . [There] will never take place a permanent union or alliance of all the colonies. . . .*

*Andrew Burnaby, Travels through the Middle Settlements in North America, 2nd ed. (Ithaca: Cornell University Press, 1960), pp. 110–114.

The Reverend Andrew Burnaby, traveling in British North America in the middle of the eighteenth century, was not the only European who foresaw chaos rather than unity for an area so different from Europe. To eyes such as Burnaby's the diversity of British North American society appeared to be a prescription for perpetual disorder. What many observers failed to comprehend at that time, however, was that the heterogeneous, often antagonistic collection of inhabitants that made up British North America were learning how to deal with each other; in the process they were creating a new, more dynamic form of social and political stability.

The Multiracial Basis of British North America

British colonial settlements east of the Appalachians were established more than a century after those in Latin America. The land area and population (about one million) of British North America were both about one-tenth of those of Latin America. Most of British North America had a temperate climate and relatively fertile soil.

In the course of a century and a half of colonial development, settlers in British North America had departed further from European culture than Latin Americans had in almost three. As in Latin America, Europeans arriving in British North America were confronted by Amerindians. The Amerindians were too few in number and too volatile in culture to provide the large sedentary workforce as had the conquered Aztec and Inka people for the Spanish Empire. By the eighteenth century, Europeans settling in North America had virtually exterminated the Amerindians living east of the Appalachians or driven them across the mountains. Thus, before the huge importation of black African slaves began in the eighteenth century, British North America, unlike Latin America, was by population an offspring of Europe.

The status of blacks in British North America varied more than in Latin America. Despite the regimentation and brutality inevitable in slave labor, particularly on the rice plantations of South Carolina, slaves in British North America enjoyed a higher standard of living and lived longer than slaves in Latin America. Slaves in North America also had more family life as the proportion of women relative to men rose through generations of natural increase.

Despite less burdensome living conditions, blacks in British North America, because of their race, were at a greater economic and social disadvantage than Latin American blacks. Northern European settlers had stronger racial prejudices than did Iberians. Slaves were seldom freed, and the few who were had difficulty acquiring property, especially land, or jobs as artisans or mechanics. Free blacks were restricted to the most menial and poorly paid tasks. In contrast to Brazil, racial bias was so strong in British North America that a person with even a small percentage of black ancestry was legally classified by law as black.

A New Economy and Society for the Common Settler

English monarchs began the process of colonial development by granting extensive blocks of land to individual favorites, reserving to the crown a portion of the rent money and all income from precious metals. Grantees were to set up companies, find investors, and put some of England's surplus labor to work on the east coast of North America. These commodity companies were expected to produce profitable commodities that other European nations were finding—spices, silk, precious metals, and sugar. To the chagrin of the English government and the dismay of the grantees and investors, the colonies in North America turned out to be virtually devoid of traditional colonial riches.

Furs were lucrative, but most of the fur-bearing animals were in the northern interior of the continent, an area predominantly under the control of the French before 1763. As it turned out, British North America north of the Chesapeake produced only foodstuffs and a few products of secondary value.

The scarcity of valuable commodities in British North America brought about a radical departure from European economic and social conditions. Abandoning the company/worker format, the English government and its aristocratic grantees began to encourage common folk to settle in North America. The grantees made money by charging the settlers for passage expenses and by dividing up their huge holdings into rental plots.

Unlike Spain, England did not restrict settlement to members of the state church; troublesome English Protestant minorities were often encouraged to emigrate to North America, and some colonies admitted Catholics and Jews. Protestants from the continent were also encouraged to settle. As a consequence, hundreds of thousands of settlers—individuals, families, and religious groups—came to British North America, quadrupling the population between 1700 and 1740.

Most settlers when first arriving undoubtedly believed that society as they knew it in Europe would be replicated in British America. The aristocrats would continue to own the land and the common folk would rent and work it. This idea turned out to be quite erroneous. In fact, absentee landlords found it difficult to collect rent, and some settlers simply seized crown and grantee lands and claimed "squatter's rights"—ownership on the basis that they had improved the property by erecting buildings and tilling the soil. Rather than try to police their distant property, the crown and the grantees found it easier and more profitable to sell off their land in small parcels at affordable prices.

The seller with cheap land was met by the settler with money to pay for it. From its earliest history British North America differed from Europe in having a chronic labor shortage. Although the immigration numbers are impressive, there were nonetheless not enough workers to meet the demands of colonial development. Employers began to abandon European-level wages and indentures (contracts obligating persons to labor for another for a specified period of time) and to compete with each other for scarce labor. By the early eighteenth century employers were offering wages that were so high that commoner families, who would have been lifetime laborers in Europe, had an opportunity in a short time to save enough money to buy land. In most of British North America, high wages continued to be available to white immigrants, but the rice, indigo, and tobacco planters in the southern colonies solved their labor shortages by importing large numbers of black slaves.

As a result of the land and labor situation, by the early eighteenth century, an economic and social revolution was under way. Most commoner families in British North America—unlike their European and Latin American counterparts—owned property or paid a nominal rent. As a consequence, a high percentage of white settler families achieved a rough-and-ready economic security and some measure of social respectability. Compared with the situation in Latin America and Europe, class lines were more fluid in British North America. The mild deference that colonists of the "middling sort" and "lower sort" paid to those of the "better sort" by no means resembled the servile fawning often found in Europe. Individual wealth and merit rather than inherited titles now often determined social status.

Although more numerous than in Latin America, European women in British North America were nevertheless in short supply. This circumstance marginally improved their condition compared with Europe. Although in the colonies, as in Great Britain, the common law defined a married woman as being subject to her husband's authority, the scarcity of women enabled them to make prenuptial agreements giving them some control over their property if widowed. The labor shortage also meant that wives often helped their husbands in business; they sometimes also ran businesses inherited from their husbands.

In contrast to Latin America and Europe, many white families in British North America were able to improve their social standing. With no aristocratic monopoly of property, it was relatively easy for commoners to obtain land, the traditional measure of social status. Laborers who acquired their own farms or shops thus found themselves in the middle class. Those of the middle class who accumulated extensive land or commercial property—or who rose to distinction as professionals, particularly lawyers and clergy—became the gentry, although they were looked on as country bumpkins by European aristocrats.

By the eighteenth century, British North America had developed an extensive international trade along mercantilist lines. The colonists were required to send "Enumerated Articles"—furs, lumber, molasses, naval stores (turpentine, pitch, tar, masts, spars), tobacco, rice, and indigo—to Great Britain, or via Great Britain to other destinations. The northern colonies had built an extensive merchant marine to carry their grain, meat, and fish to the West Indies and the Mediterranean. Colonists north and south had begun to produce iron and iron products, but since they competed with British iron, the British government soon regulated their production. Like their Latin American counterparts, colonists were often forced to sell low and buy high and consequently turned to smuggling.

Great Britain placed fewer controls on its colonies than Spain did on hers. The government restricted trade with the colonies to English (and after 1707 also Scottish) and colonial ships, but it did not limit the trade to a few companies, allowing individual ships to sail in and out of any port. In addition, products not on the Enumerated Articles list could be sold anywhere in the world without regulation.

Religious and ethnic diversity was another distinctive characteristic of British North America. Before 1750, there were English-speaking Anglicans, Congregationalists, Presbyterians, Catholics, Baptists, and Quakers. From continental Europe came Dutch, German, and French Reformed; German, Dutch, and Swedish Lutherans; German Moravians, Mennonites, Dunkers, and Schwenkfelders; and Portuguese-speaking Jews.

Despite the fact that established churches were in place in most colonies by the eighteenth century, efforts to enforce religious uniformity failed in British North America. The English Act of Toleration in 1689 acknowledged England's religious divisions by giving some religious rights to Congregationalists, Presbyterians, and Baptists. About the same time, the English government forced the Congregationalist colonies to allow Anglicans to worship without penalty. Actually, conditions in British North America did more than English laws to encourage diversity. Most colonies needed settlers and unofficially tolerated thousands of adherents of other religions fleeing religious persecution, economic dislocation, and war. Often the new dissenters settled in such numbers that it was impractical for adherents of the established churches to control them or drive them away. Some colonies were founded to protect religious dissenters, further encouraging religious diversity. Catholics, banned from worshipping in England and most colonies, were tolerated in Maryland through most of its history. Catholics and all Protestant groups had full rights in Pennsylvania. Rhode Island went farther, granting full religious freedom to Christians, Jews, and Muslims. Thus, in the early eighteenth century, British North America moved steadily in the direction of complete religious freedom, which in Europe only a few reformers advocated.

A New Political Process

As Iberian monarchies imposed their tradition of expensive, centralized government on Latin America, so too the English government set up its particular brand of frugal, partially decentralized government in its colonies. In England, the lesser gentry had long represented the royal government in local affairs, sparing the crown the expense of a large set of appointed officials. In the colonies, the English government sent a governor only, whose function was to work with an assembly that represented the colonial gentry, who in most colonies also constituted the local government.

The governor of a colony had the power to appoint from the ranks of the colony's gentry a few executive officials and a council, which also served as the upper house of the colonial legislature and performed certain judicial functions. The governor could control the procedures of the assembly and veto its acts. His position was severely weakened, however, because the British government—to save expense—had given the assembly the power to pay the governor's salary from taxes laid on the colonists. Unlike Latin America, the colonists paid no tax money or royal "fifths" to the crown. Nevertheless, many colonial gentry, like many Creoles in Latin America, chafed at what they saw as excessive power wielded by outsiders or by the mother country.

Much of this was soon to change. Partly as a result of broad-scale economic and social change, a new political process, quite unlike anything in Europe, was evolving. Because of the widespread incidence of property holding in British North America, many white males had access to political power. In Great Britain, one of the few nations having some semblance of government by consent, only adult males who owned property and belonged to the state church could vote. This restricted political participation to about 5 percent of the adult males.

When these requirements were brought over to British North America, however, they produced radically different effects in a population where landholding was more widespread with each passing decade. An estimated one-half of the adult white male colonists could vote in the early eighteenth century, and the proportion continued to rise. Many colonists also met the much higher requirements for holding office. Still, only about 10 percent of the eligible voters took advantage of the opportunity. Most had little appreciation for voting practice or its potential. The New England tradition of the local town

The Granger Collection

New England Town Meeting. Although such an intense encounter was exceptional, this public forum is evidence of the new political process under way in British North America.

meeting was a major exception. By and large, however, colonial voters served as no more than a check, occasionally turning out an incompetent gentleman officeholder.

The Enlightenment in North America

By European standards, British North America was as much a wasteland intellectually and culturally as it was geographically. The French scientist the Comte de Buffon and his followers at one time claimed that all species, including humans, degenerated in the New World environment. Certainly, colonists of all class levels, busy exploiting the land's resources, gave little time to the development of scholarship, arts, or letters. Nonetheless, a significant start toward a popular rather than an elite culture had been made. Impelled by the Protestant emphasis on Bible reading and the usefulness of education, many men and some women in British North America learned to read and write. The resources and density of population of the New England towns and the Atlantic seaports provided the means and the will to support schools. Here perhaps two-thirds of the males and one-third of the females were literate by the early eighteenth century, a far higher percentage than anywhere else in the world. To be sure, higher education lagged far behind the great learning centers of Europe and Latin America, but a beginning had been made. By the early eighteenth century, three private colleges, beginning with Harvard in 1636, offered a traditional curriculum designed to train ministers. Seven more colleges would soon be founded.

As it had in Latin America, by the mid-eighteenth century the Enlightenment began to nourish intellectual activity in British North America. Colonial scientists made significant contributions to the fields of biology, physics, astronomy, and other sciences. In the New World, as in the Old, educated persons dabbled in science and met in societies to debate the latest experiments and discoveries.

Benjamin Franklin (1706–1790), the multitalented printer from Philadelphia, is a good example of Enlightenment thinking in North America. One of the founders of the United States, Franklin was noted for his keen enthusiasm for scientific investigations. He experimented with electrical energy and made such practical contributions as the Franklin stove and the lightning rod. Franklin was the founder of a philosophical society, a journal, and an academy that subsequently became a major university. Like a dozen other colonists, Franklin was elected to the Royal Society in Britain.

The political, economic, and social ideas of the Enlightenment also found a warm welcome among the colonists, whose elected legislative assemblies gave them more political power than most Europeans. Merchants and farmers who had come to find greater economic opportunity in North America favored free enterprise. Although religious hatreds remained widespread on the local level, many early American leaders were firm believers in religious tolerance.

Thomas Jefferson (1743–1826), a Virginia landowner, was a latter-day Renaissance man who exemplified the application of Enlightenment thought to political theory and practice. His commitment to political rights and popular sovereignty still lives in the Declaration of Independence and the Bill of Rights. Like Franklin, Jefferson was an avid student of the physical sciences and was also a noted architect; he corresponded with European writers on subjects ranging from science to economics. He was a strong believer in religious toleration and in greater social equality. He opposed slavery of blacks, but failed to support immediate freedom for slaves, preferring a program of gradual emancipation and emigration of blacks to Africa or elsewhere.

Colonial Unrest and Colonial War

After 1763 the British government took the position that the colonists had not borne their proportionate share of the costs of the war against the French and had become too autonomous in their mercantilist relationship with the mother country. Consequently, the British government required the colonists to provide private quarters for the British garrisons and to pay new taxes created by Parliament and enforced by the king. The government imposed new trade regulations and enforced existing ones more stringently. Finally, the government prohibited settlement across the Appalachian Mountains, fearing that settlers would interrupt the deerskin and fur trades and provoke unnecessary wars with the Amerindians. These new policies shocked many colonists in British North

America, who had begun to take autonomy in their local affairs for granted. Because of the new restrictions and exactions, discontent and hostility spread quickly among the colonists in much of British North America during the 1760s. At first the colonists confined their actions to securing the repeal of the new laws and regulations. Colonial lawyers and journalists turned a significant portion of the informed public against the British policies. The colonists' most effective tactic, however, was refusal to sell colonial products to British merchants and to buy British goods. As the colonists had hoped, financially strapped British businessmen persuaded Parliament on several occasions to repeal the offending taxes or regulations.

During the late 1760s and early 1770s, tensions steadily mounted. Radical colonists had begun to question the fundamental constitutional relationship between the colonies and Great Britain. Some denied that Parliament could legitimately regulate colonial affairs and argued that the king was only a symbol of unity and had no constitutional authority to enforce Parliament's policies. By 1774 a number of disruptive incidents instigated by the colonists had provoked the British government into repressive acts. In response, anti-Parliament colonials created the Continental Congress, composed of representatives from the older thirteen colonies (but not the new colonies of Florida and Quebec). The Congress met in Philadelphia and announced a new economic boycott enforced by local vigilante groups. The Congress also encouraged the colonies to organize, equip, and train companies of local militia.

In April 1775 British troops clashed with militia companies at Lexington and Concord, Massachusetts, inaugurating seven years of warfare. Despite the outbreak of fighting, most colonists were still loyal to Great Britain and respected the crown as a symbol of unity. However, George III rejected an appeal by colonists for local autonomy inside the British imperial system. As fighting continued, sentiment crystallized around complete separation from Great Britain. On July 4, 1776, the delegates of the Continental Congress signed a Declaration of Independence stating the reasons for their action.

During the ensuing war for independence, each side enjoyed distinct advantages and suffered from major problems. The British were clearly superior in conventional military forces. They had a winning tradition, a well-trained army, money to buy supplies and allies, and a navy that could land troops wherever desired, giving the British the military initiative. However, Great Britain also faced a new and difficult kind of war. The colonists fought a war of attrition against the large army that their opponents had to deploy across an area four times the size of Great Britain. Communication across the Atlantic was so slow that by the time orders arrived they were often no longer relevant. Supplies and reinforcements frequently were late and inadequate. The British won battles, but the colonists continued to resist, and the British lacked the troops and allies to garrison the hostile countryside. The rebel commander, George Washington, although losing battles, kept his army intact, providing a rallying point for continued resistance.

Although distance, area, time, and sporadic aid from France favored them, the rebels also faced huge problems. Many colonists remained loyal to the crown, and rebel leaders quarreled incessantly, despite Benjamin Franklin's admonition "We must all hang together or we will all hang separately." The rebels were underfinanced, lacked soldiers

"It Is the Will of Heaven for Our Two Countries to Be Sundered Forever"

Yesterday the greatest question was decided which ever was debated in America, and a greater, perhaps, never was nor will be decided among men. A resolution was passed . . . "that these United Colonies are, and of right ought to be, free and independent States. . . . " You will see in a few days a Declaration setting forth the causes which will have impelled us to this mighty revolution, and the reasons which will justify it in the sight of God and man. A plan of confederation will be taken up in a few days.

When I look back . . . and recollect the series of political events, the chain of causes and effects, I am surprised at the suddenness as well as the greatness of this revolution. Britain has been filled with folly, and America with wisdom. . . . Time must determine. It is the will of heaven for our two countries to be sundered forever. It may be the will of Heaven that America shall suffer calamities. . . . But I submit all my hopes and fears to an overruling Providence, in which, unfashionable as the faith may be, I firmly believe.*

John Adams wrote these observations in a letter to his wife Abigail on July 3, 1776, where he expressed a mixture of satisfaction and trepidation. He, as much as any man in America, had brought independence about. The history of independence movements is often a record of heroic idealism on the part of men and women of firm conviction. Though the conditions of revolutions vary from case to case, the willingness to engage, as Jefferson put it, in "dangerous and fateful action" is a common denominator for all of them. The result has been a realignment of political power around the world and also the creation of an enduring creed of liberty and resistance to oppression. That the ideals expressed in that creed have not always been achieved does not diminish the importance of the struggle to realize them.

*John Adams, from Henry S. Commager and Richard B. Morris, eds., The Spirit of 'Seventy-Six: The Story of the American Revolution as Told by Participants (New York: Harper & Row, 1967), pp. 320–321.

willing to abandon cover and fight the British in the open, and were frequently distracted by trouble with the Amerindians. Slowly and painfully, they built a regular army that could fight in the open and reinforce local militias.

By 1777 neither side had made much headway in overcoming their problems. The British controlled only a strip of territory from Philadelphia to New York and had surrendered an army at Saratoga, while Washington and other rebel commanders had difficulty in keeping their fighting forces assembled. As time passed, each side doubted that their supporters could sustain the sacrifices necessary to outlast the enemy and win the war of attrition.

Beginning in 1778, events in Europe transformed the colonial war in the New World. The French, who had been rebuilding their army and especially their navy, watched with interest as Great Britain exhausted itself in North America. Capitalizing on the jealousy and fear of other European powers toward the British, France succeeded in isolating Great Britain diplomatically. Hearing the news of the British defeat at Saratoga, France, followed by Spain and the Netherlands, declared war on Great Britain. The colonial war in North America now expanded to India and the Caribbean. The French gave their most effective aid to the rebels in 1781, when a French army and fleet combined with Washington's army to capture Cornwallis's army at Yorktown, Virginia.

In 1781 the British government, unable to crush the rebellion, gave up their rebellious colonies in North America in order to concentrate their forces in a successful defense of their Caribbean and Indian possessions. At the Peace of Paris in 1783, Great Britain recognized the independence of the United States of America, ceding to the new nation the area south of Canada and east of the Mississippi, except for Florida and the Gulf coast, which went to Spain.

The United States of America

During the first half century of its independence the United States expanded and prospered. The population increased fivefold, and the key aspects of the colonial economy—foodstuffs, fishing, and the maritime trade—continued to flourish. Americans also made a small beginning in manufacturing. An enormous innovation was brought about by a simple technological invention. The cotton gin enabled Americans to grow abundant supplies of short-fibered cotton as the basis for mass-producing cheap cotton clothing. The enormous demand in Europe soon made cotton the most valuable American commodity: as some enthusiastic southerners put it, "Cotton is king!" The huge size of the new nation also placed a premium on improving transportation and communication. Americans, with heavy financial backing from British investors, were in the forefront of constructing or improving canals, roads, steamboats, and, eventually, the railroad and telegraph systems.

Society and politics in the United States continued the trends already under way in the colonial period. The percentage of those owning property continued to rise, as did

The British Surrender at Yorktown, Virginia, October 19, 1781. The victory over the British by rebel colonial forces, aided by French army and navy units, opened the way for independence. In this detail from John Trumbull's somewhat overdramatized painting, General O'Hara, representing the absent General Charles Cornwallis, formally capitulates to General Benjamin Lincoln, representing George Washington.

Yale University Art Gallery, Trumbull Collection

the general standard of living. The passage of time, plus the libertarian influence of the Enlightenment, eased religious animosities and began to create an atmosphere of toleration. Ethnic and religious hostilities persisted, but they lessened as individuals of different backgrounds began to associate and intermarry. Most white Americans learned to read and write, and women rapidly closed the literacy gap between themselves and men. Many colleges opened, mostly sectarian and primarily for men. Some schools reflected the influence of the Enlightenment as they introduced courses in mathematics, science, foreign languages, and history.

Men of property still dominated politics as they had in colonial times, and the officers of the new nation came from the ranks of the upper class. However, the organized political party and the rapid abolition of state religious and property qualifications for voting gradually placed political power in the hands of the mass of white males.

The greatest political achievement of the new nation was the Constitution of 1787 and the Bill of Rights of 1791. These documents fashioned a federal republic in which the national government controlled diplomacy, war, peace, interstate and international commerce, the army and navy, and Indian affairs. The states retained control of the bulk of everyday affairs, including civil and criminal law, education, health and safety, and the militia. The Bill of Rights promised an open, liberal society that would tolerate freedom of religion, speech, and the press. Further, it guaranteed procedural protections and a fair trial for those accused of crime. Most whites did not interpret these provisions as applying to blacks or Amerindians. Nevertheless, the principles of the American revolution, as expressed in the Declaration of Independence, the Constitution, and the Bill of Rights inspired many French revolutionaries in 1789.

Despite its internal prosperity, the United States was an insignificant military power. After 1792 it became enmeshed as a minor party in the long struggle between Great Britain and France. While some Americans were making great sums of money supplying the belligerents, others had their ships seized and some crewmen imprisoned or pressed into naval service by the British and the French. Beyond the Appalachians, the Spanish and British intrigued with the Amerindians and harassed settlers, jeopardizing American interests in the region. When diplomacy and embargo failed to protect its commerce, the United States declared war on Great Britain in 1812, but the struggle was inconclusive.

Although it had great problems in defending its overseas trade, the United States rapidly expanded across the North American continent between 1803 and 1826. U.S. military forces crushed the Amerindians, who thereafter ceased to be a serious obstacle to white expansion. Although the United States failed to take Canada in the War of 1812, it acquired Louisiana and Florida by negotiation, extending its territory to the Rocky Mountains. Beyond the Rockies, the United States laid claim to the Oregon territory from the Rocky Mountains to the Pacific coast.

Despite growing freedom and prosperity in the United States, unresolved problems threatened the unity of the republic. Economic competition between regions had become acute by the 1820s. Many northerners favored a protective tariff to build up American industry and create a home market for agriculture. Most southerners, on the other hand, wanted free trade so they could keep their costs of production down and sell their cotton, rice, and tobacco abroad without fear of foreign tariff retaliation.

The economic competition between north and south was exacerbated by another issue, slavery. Although slavery was declining in the north, the cotton economy had fixed it firmly into the social, cultural, and ideological fabric of the southern states. An increasing number of individuals, mostly in the north, wanted either to restrict slavery to the south for economic reasons or to abolish it for moral reasons. By mid-century, the earlier optimism that the United States was blending its disparate ethnic and social elements into a harmonious society began to fade in the face of increasing sectional rancor.

The Global Contest for Empire and the Onset of the Industrial Revolution

The separating distance was growing less and less. A hundred paces now! Would that grim line of red-coats never fire! Seventy-five!! Fifty!! Forty!! . . . "Ready!—Present!—Fire!!!" . . . the British volleys crashed forth, from right to left, battalion by battalion, all down that thin red line.

The stricken front rank of the French fell before these double-shotted volleys almost to a man. When the smoke cleared off the British had . . . closed up some twenty paces . . . reloading as they came. And now, taking the French in front and flanks, they fired as fast as they could, but steadily and under perfect control. The French on the other hand, were firing wildly, and simply crumbling away under that well-aimed storm of lead. . . . In a vain, last effort to lead them on their officers faced death and found it. Montcalm, . . . told he had only a few hours to live, replied, "So much the better, I shall not see the surrender of Quebec."

Wolfe, with three bullet wounds, also lay dying. "They run; see how they run!" a subordinate shouted. "Who run?" Wolfe demanded, like a man roused from sleep. "The enemy, sir. Egad, they give way everywhere!" Wolfe, turning on his side, murmured, "Now, God be praised, I will die in peace."*

*Thomas Wood, The Passing of New France, pp. 137–148 passim; The Winning of Canada, pp. 138–139. Both in George M. Wrong and H. H. Langton, eds., Chronicles of Canada, vols. 10, 11 (Toronto/Glasgow: Brook, 1914–1921).

On September 13, 1759, on the Plains of Abraham outside the fortress city of Quebec in New France (Canada), the British army led by James Wolfe defeated the French forces of Louis de Montcalm and delivered French North America to Great Britain. Coupled with victories over the French in the Caribbean and India, the conquest of New France gave Great Britain colonial supremacy and dominance of the global trade network. This worldwide confrontation between Great Britain and France had been building throughout the eighteenth century as the great age of seaborne discovery was coming to a close and the age of industrialization was dawning.

Exploration in the Pacific, Competition in North America

In the seventeenth and eighteenth centuries, Europeans continued to expand their knowledge of the world, chiefly through explorations by sea. Commercial gain was as usual the main motive, but there was also a thirst for scientific knowledge that was typical of the Age of Newton. As the explorers discovered areas of the world previously unknown to Europeans, Western traders followed close behind.

Although the Europeans explored the Indian Ocean and other regions, they concentrated on the Pacific during the eighteenth century. The new chronometer, which allowed navigators to calculate the correct longitude in determining a ship's location, was a major aid in the exploring enterprise. Led by the greatest explorer of the age, Captain James Cook (1728–1779) of Great Britain, European ships stopped at Tahiti, Hawaii, and other islands of the central and south Pacific. Following up on earlier sightings and shipwrecks, Dutch and British explorers, chiefly Abel Tasman and Cook, found a land-mass large enough to be classified as a continent; it was later named Australia (Southern Land). Coastal eastern Australia was blessed with a moderate climate that proved suit-able for European settlement. Farther south, Europeans began to detect the frozen conti-nent of Antarctica. In the offshore waters they found sources of future wealth in the whales and seals, whose oil and pelts were in great demand, particularly in China.

Europeans also explored the North Pacific and its North American and Asian shore-lines, finding more whales and seals, as well as sea otters, a new source of wealth. In 1728 Vitus Bering (1680–1741), a Danish explorer in the employ of Peter the Great, found that Asia and North America were separated by a body of water. By 1779, when Cook was killed in a skirmish with the Hawaiians, little was left for Europeans to explore by sea, although the interior of most of the continents still remained unknown to them.

During the eighteenth century, several nations competed vigorously for control of the remote but lucrative furs on the Pacific coast of North America. The Spanish set up mis-sions and forts along the Pacific coast in California and made claims northward as far as Alaska; there they were soon challenged by Russian traders from Siberia looking for sea otter and seal pelts. By the 1790s both Great Britain and the United States were also asserting claims in the Pacific Northwest, based on competing trading posts.

Competing Colonial Systems

The overseas dominions of Spain, Portugal, and the Netherlands expanded only margin-ally during the eighteenth century. Except for its movement north along the California coast, Spain was too weak to do more than doggedly hold on to its sprawling posses-sions. The Portuguese, having lost most of their Asian empire to the Dutch, concentrated on expanding their "second empire" in Brazil. They grew tobacco and sugar in the tropi-cal north, importing ever-larger numbers of slaves from their African possessions. An economic boom came with the discovery of gold and diamonds in Brazil's interior. In the early nineteenth century, as the gold rush faded, the Portuguese turned to producing cof-fee in Brazil's temperate southern uplands.

About 1650 it appeared that the Dutch might carve out the greatest European over-seas empire, but despite having the largest seventeenth-century merchant marine and navy, the Dutch fell victim to their homeland's small size and vulnerable location. They lost three naval wars with the English in the late seventeenth century while at the same time fighting a series of wars against France. Despite these problems, the Dutch in the eighteenth century still held sugar islands in the Caribbean, slave-trading posts on the African coast, settlements at the southern tip of Africa, cinnamon and tea plantations on Ceylon, and clove and nutmeg production in Indonesia; and after 1677 they slowly took control of the pepper and coffee areas in Java and gained footholds in the Spice Islands. During much of their expansion, the Dutch employed the classic divide-and-conquer technique, already used to great effect by the Spanish and other Europeans on the Amerindians and soon to be employed by the British and French in India.

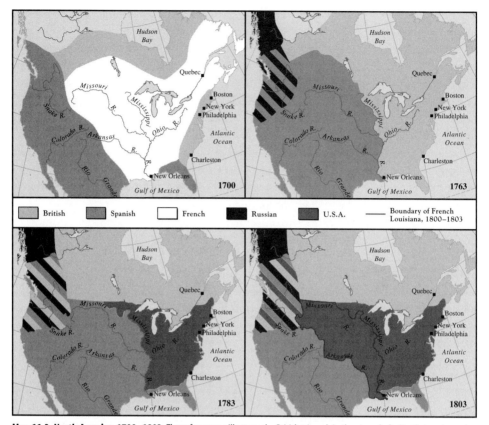

Map 11.3 North America, 1700–1803. These four maps illustrate the British triumph in the struggle for North America and the expansion of the United States at the expense of Great Britain, France, and Spain.

During the eighteenth century, Great Britain and France increased their efforts to control the lucrative colonial trade, redirecting more and more of their economic and military resources from traditional contests on the European continent to new struggles overseas. By mid-century, the fighting in India and the Western Hemisphere had acquired a tempo quite different from that of wars and diplomacy in Europe.

In contrast with the relatively static Portuguese, Spanish, and Dutch colonial regimes, the British and French aggressively expanded their overseas power. In the process, they became embroiled in a long series of international struggles for colonial and continental supremacy (1689–1815). Louis XIV, for example, was as aggressive overseas as he was in Europe; France acquired additional possessions in the Caribbean and trading posts in India.

In North America French pioneers pushing out from New France laid claim to the enormous Mississippi–Missouri–Ohio–Great Lakes basin extending from the Appalachians to the Rocky Mountains and from the Great Lakes to the Gulf coast between Florida and Mexico; they named the whole vast region Louisiana. Meanwhile, French and British traders competed for the profitable far northern fur trade. By 1702 the French had erected a chain of forts from the Great Lakes down the Mississippi to the Gulf coast.

The French now threatened the Spanish possessions in Cuba and Mexico and the British colonies on the Atlantic seaboard, and both nations responded. The Spanish set up several posts in Texas to protect Mexico and one at Pensacola to shield Florida and Cuba. After 1713, however, the new Bourbon dynasty in Spain became an ally of France and later aided the French by attacking settlements in the southern British colonies. The English launched a counteroffensive and conquered Nova Scotia and Newfoundland, prime bases for fishing. British expansion in the Caribbean enabled them to break Spain's trade monopoly with Spanish America.

By the 1750s the British and French were in a critical phase of a worldwide struggle that focused on India, the Caribbean, and North America. In India, British and French trading companies were interested in expanding beyond their original assortment of coastal trading posts. The Indian subcontinent produced valuable spices and textiles, and its huge population was at once a source of cheap labor and an opportunity for profitable taxation. It was also a prospective captive market for European goods that could reverse the drain of European silver going to pay for Indian products. The European-owned East India companies were interested in controlling blocks of territory, where labor could be efficiently organized to produce a higher output of spices and textiles. This arrangement had long been typical of European colonization in the Western Hemisphere, and the Dutch were emulating it in Indonesia.

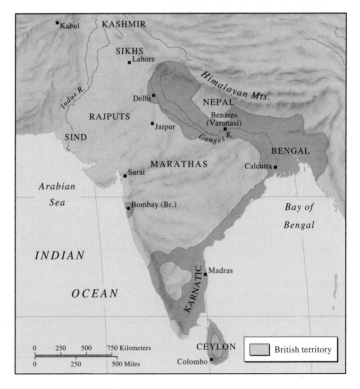

Map 11.4 British Empire in India, c. 1800. After the disintegration of the Moghul Empire and the defeat of France in India in the eighteenth century, Great Britain emerged as the dominant power in India. Further conquests and alliances with Indian princes during the nineteenth century consolidated British supremacy on the subcontinent.

By the mid-eighteenth century, the French and British India companies saw their chance. As the Moghul dynasty of Muslim emperors rapidly dissolved under numerous rebellions and outside attacks, each national trading company supported certain Indian princes against others in return for help in destroying the competing trading company. Once it had eliminated its European rivals, the surviving company could then exploit rivalries among the Indian potentates and expand its economic and political controls over India. By 1751, even while their home governments were at peace, the French and British East India companies were at war. The issue was ultimately decided by the British capture of the key post at Pondicherry in 1761, which effectively eliminated French power in India.

As in India, fighting between the French and British in North America in the mid-1750s preceded hostilities on the Continent. The French took the initiative, building up their military forces in New France (Canada) and along the Great Lakes to the Ohio Valley. In 1754–1755 the French and their Amerindian allies defeated two expeditions mounted against Fort Duquesne (present-day Pittsburgh).

In 1756 a general conflict broke out in Europe and merged with the world war for colonial supremacy already in progress. With France preoccupied on the continent, the British fleet cut off the French in North America and methodically conquered New France. In 1759 James Wolfe defeated the main French army at Quebec, and his successors captured Montreal in 1760. Meanwhile, British naval expeditions wrested away nearly all of the French islands in the Caribbean.

By 1763 Great Britain controlled the largest European colonial empire and the most profitable network of overseas trade; by contrast, the colonial empire of France had been almost totally destroyed. In the Treaty of Paris in 1763, Spain received Louisiana west of the Mississippi, giving it, with its earlier holdings, approximately 40 percent of North America. The British, however, laid claim to New France (thus taking full control of the fur trade), Louisiana east of the Mississippi, and Spanish Florida. Restricted to a few fishery islands off the coast of Newfoundland, the French ceased to be a threat to British colonies in North America.

Although Great Britain was to lose a major part of its empire in North America as a result of the American War of Independence, it continued to expand in other parts of the world. In the South Pacific, the British established a penal colony at Botany Bay (now Sydney) on the east coast of Australia in 1788, soon to be followed by other penal settlements. No other European power considered Australia worth contesting, and Great Britain thus added an entire continent to its dominions.

To the British, however, gaining full control of India was of far greater importance than developing Australia. The process of conquest began in 1757 when Robert Clive defeated a large Indian army at Plassey, obtaining the province of Bengal in northeast India for the British East India Company. Between the 1780s and the 1820s, the efficient and well-equipped forces of the British East India Company seized large additional territories, giving Britain effective control of the subcontinent.

Besides taking over India and Australia, the British made one more major expansion of their colonial empire, seizing some colonies of the Dutch. During the 1790s, revolutionary

France had made the Netherlands a satellite. This gave the British, persistent foes of Revolutionary and Napoleonic France, an opportunity to conquer Dutch possessions that threatened British trade routes to India and East Asia. By 1815, the British had taken over Mauritius Island (from the French), Cape of Good Hope in South Africa from the Dutch, and Ceylon. By the 1820s a major British base at Singapore at the tip of the Malay Peninsula controlled the trade route to East Asia.

The Developing Global Economy

As European explorers charted the world's waterways and fought for footholds and colonies, they built up a global network of seaborne commerce that brought ever-increasing prosperity to Europe. Portugal, Spain, the Netherlands, Great Britain, and France added an extensive colonial commerce to their trade on the continent. Including the smaller colonial trading interests of Hamburg and the Baltic states of Denmark, Sweden, and Prussia, eighteenth-century overseas commerce now rivaled in value the traditional trade patterns inside Europe. Two-thirds of Great Britain's trade now involved areas outside Europe.

Three major trade patterns dominated overseas commerce. The oldest originated when the Spanish began importing gold and silver from Spanish America. The Spanish sent most of these precious metals to Great Britain, France, and the Netherlands in exchange for manufactured products. The Dutch, French, and British then carried this bullion to China and India to exchange for silk and cotton textiles, tea, and spices, which they brought back and sold to Europeans. The new trade routes and the influx of gold and silver from the Western Hemisphere weakened the Ottoman Empire financially as the importance of the overland routes it controlled lessened.

Plantation agriculture in the Western Hemisphere and Asia formed the second, and, by the eighteenth century, most valuable, international trading pattern. Europeans had transformed much of the Atlantic coast of the Americas into plantations. The plantation zone extended 5,000 miles from Chesapeake Bay in North America south through the Caribbean islands and down the northern coast of Brazil. Planters produced a variety of valuable fibers, foodstuffs, drugs, and forest products desired in Europe. Sugar imports alone equaled in value the entire Asian trade. In addition, the Dutch shipped to Europe a variety of commodities from their rapidly developing East Indian plantation system. In a subpattern of this trade, North Americans shipped furs, lumber, and naval stores to Great Britain and France.

The growing commerce in plantation products from the Americas made a third pattern—the trade in slaves—increasingly lucrative. The grueling work under tropical or subtropical conditions and the constantly expanding plantations required a continual flow of fresh labor, and the trade in black African slaves grew increasingly efficient. During the eighteenth century, some 60,000 slaves annually were imported into the Western Hemisphere from Africa. The Portuguese, Dutch, and French had successively taken over the largest share of the slave trade, but by the mid-eighteenth century the British and New Englanders dominated the slaving business outside Brazil, which was supplied by the Portuguese.

The three global trade patterns brought immense prosperity to a few European seaports. Great Britain became the world's foremost overseas trading nation after 1763, and London the world's greatest port, growing rich on Caribbean sugar, Indian cotton, and many other products. Liverpool and Glasgow were fast rising to commercial prominence through their trade in slaves, furs, and tobacco. Until 1763 the overseas trade of France rivaled that of Great Britain in value, with Bordeaux and Nantes prospering from the slave trade, sugar, and Asian goods. Amsterdam, enjoying immense profits from the slave and spice trades, continued to be one of the greatest commercial centers in Europe, although the overall value of Dutch trade had slipped behind that of Great Britain and France. Lisbon and Cadiz were still prosperous cities, although the early colonial trade supremacy of the Iberian states had gone.

The merchants of the great trading centers exerted increasing economic and political power. They had superior management and marketing skills, a knack for cooperating with the banking interests to secure capital and credit, and a sharp eye for technological improvements. Their interests and needs increasingly influenced politics and diplomacy, including decisions on peace and war. Merchants also plowed some of their profits into new manufacturing enterprises, fueling the major socioeconomic transformation known as the Industrial Revolution.

The Beginnings of the Industrial Revolution

Modern industrial society first took shape in Great Britain in the mid-eighteenth century. The changes that industrialization brought were so momentous that historians speak of a "revolution"—not a political upheaval but an "industrial revolution." This revolution

Profiles in Human Misery. By the eighteenth century, the Atlantic slave trade had reached its peak, yielding vast profits to Europeans active in that trade. The brutal inhumanity of the slave ships is graphically portrayed here.

The Granger Collection

may be likened to an explosive chemical reaction. Industry became possible only in the presence of certain essential components: specifically, adequate natural resources and labor, sufficient economic demand, accumulations of capital, technological advances, and entrepreneurship. In the eighteenth century more of these elements were present in Great Britain than elsewhere.

The basic raw materials, iron ore and coal, were found in substantial quantities in central and northern England, either near each other or near water. Entrepreneurs thus found it relatively cheap to bring coal and iron ore together for industrial purposes. The distances from the manufacturing centers to the cities and ports of Great Britain were short, enabling manufactured products to reach both domestic and foreign markets expeditiously.

Another essential element in the Industrial Revolution was increased agricultural production. Eighteenth-century improvements in crop rotation, soil fertilization, and animal breeding boosted British agricultural output, thus increasing the food supply and stimulating a rapid growth in population. The expanding consumption of potatoes, which were more nutritious than corn, led to an increased and healthier population. More efficient agriculture also freed manpower for industrial work. At the same time, landowners were enclosing village lands, dispossessing many peasants and causing them to look for work in the new factories.

The demand for goods that accompanied the increase in population further stimulated industrial production. The prosperity accumulated during centuries of overseas trade also spurred demand; and Great Britain, with its large overseas empire, was the most prosperous nation in eighteenth-century Europe. Improved roads and canals and the absence of internal tolls and tariffs facilitated a profitable flow of goods; after the union of England and Scotland, Great Britain was the largest free trade area in Europe.

Profit from commercial and colonial enterprises also generated investment capital. Great Britain's excellent banks, including Europe's strongest financial institution, the Bank of England, had large amounts of capital to invest. As with the joint-stock companies of an earlier era, limited liability laws also encouraged speculation by restricting an investor's obligation for a firm's debts to the amount of his own investment.

The availability of new sources of energy was a key component in the onset of the Industrial Revolution. The steam engine provided the essential source of power. Steam had long been used in a limited way for pumping water out of coal mines, but in the 1760s a Scottish mechanic, James Watt, designed steam-powered engines efficient enough for other industrial uses. In partnership with Matthew Boulton, an English entrepreneur, Watt produced engines that could do the work of up to twenty horses—the origin of the "horsepower" rating. By the early nineteenth century, steam had replaced water mills as the chief energy source of the booming Industrial Revolution.

Under these favorable conditions, technological advances in industry came rapidly. Inventors and technicians developed new machines specifically to solve recognized industrial problems. Developments in one industry also expanded the technological base from which other entrepreneurs might borrow, furthering even more industrial growth.

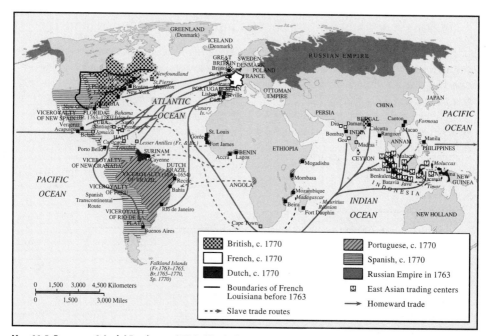

Map 11.5 European Colonial Empires and Global Trade Patterns, c. 1770. After 300 years of exploration and trade outside their continent, European nations had made massive changes around the globe. Nearly all of the Western Hemisphere had come under their control, and they had built up an extensive network of trading centers along the African coast and across much of South and Southeast Asia. Products from four continents poured into the Atlantic ports of five European nations, to be consumed or resold to the rest of Europe. In addition, an enormous trade in African slaves, along with pockets of European settlement, was transforming the Americas racially. The interior of Africa, the Islamic world, and East Asia, at this time lightly touched, faced the power of the European onslaught in the next century.

Additionally, the weakening of the power of the guilds allowed much more rapid innovation than the conservative artisans would have permitted.

Entrepreneurship was another essential catalyst for industrial expansion in Britain. The profits to be made attracted ambitious and ingenious men to industry. The law of primogeniture, which turned a family's entire landed estates over to the oldest son, and the relative lack of prejudice against being "in trade" sent well-educated, self-confident younger sons into business. Such men made a paying proposition out of the new technology and activated the machinery of the Industrial Revolution.

New Industries

The evolution of cotton textile manufacturing well illustrates the dependence of industries on sources of power like the steam engine. Indian imports had already created a growing demand for cotton cloth; Parliament, however, had prohibited the importing of cotton textiles to protect British wool producers, most of whom were peasants with spinning wheels and looms in their cottages. To satisfy the demand for cotton, eager (and

Making Hay while the Sun Shines: Supply and Demand in Industry

We wish you to drop the Sattinets, they are not new here and only fit for two months sale. The Buff stripes ... are not fine enough for People of Fashion.... Arkwright must lower his Twist and he must spin finer....

We want as many spotted muslins and fancy muslins as you can make, the finer the better.... You must give a look to Invention, industry [that is, industriousness] you have in abundance. We expect to hear from you as often as possible and as the sun shines let us make the Hay.*

This correspondence between a late-eighteenth-century British merchant and a manufacturer illustrates how industrial manufacturing in the cotton textile business responded to public demand. When fickle public taste demanded certain dress fabrics, technology was expected to deliver the goods. The entrepreneurial spirit of the early Industrial Revolution is well expressed in the concluding phrase.

*Correspondence between Samuel Oldknow and his London agents, in Charles Wilson, "The Entrepreneur in the Industrial Revolution in Britain," in Sima Lieberman, ed., Europe and the Industrial Revolution (Cambridge, Mass.: Schenkman, 1972), p. 385.

sometimes unscrupulous) entrepreneurs like Richard Arkwright imported raw cotton and began to produce cotton cloth in Great Britain, inventing new machinery in the process.

As the market for cotton fabrics grew, technicians devised machinery to speed up both the spinning of cotton thread and the weaving of the threads into cloth. The new machines, too big and costly for cottage industry, had to be housed in large sheds—the first modern industrial factories—and were driven first by water power and later by the new steam engines.

The immense success of this new industrial system may be measured by the growth of the cotton industry. In 1770 Great Britain had only a handful of cotton manufacturing plants and exported few cotton textiles. By 1830 cotton cloth not only sold widely in Great Britain but also accounted for 45 percent of all its foreign exports, much of it going to protected markets in the British colonies.

Two other industries that were essential to the exploitation of new techniques in many areas of the economy were coal and iron production; both experienced major advances in the eighteenth century. England had burned off much of its forest cover by early modern times and had begun to use coal instead of wood for home heating and for some industrial purposes even before 1700. In the eighteenth century British coal miners developed a number of advanced techniques for extracting coal from greater depth. Steam power was particularly valuable for pumping water out of the deeper shafts of the mines.

Iron production also increased in this first century of the Industrial Revolution. Iron manufacturers learned to use coke (made from coal) instead of expensive charcoal (made from wood) for smelting high-grade iron. Ironmasters like John Wilkinson also learned to work iron precisely and to apply it to many new purposes, from bridges to steam engine boilers.

Summary and Comparisons

Europeans found religious and historical justifications for the absolutist form of government, in part built upon the national-state structure of the preceding era. Charles V and Philip II made the Spanish-Habsburg Empire the foremost absolutist state in Europe in the sixteenth century and imposed a mercantilist economic system on the Spanish Empire. However, Spanish treasure was squandered on mostly unsuccessful wars against the Protestant Netherlands, England, and the German states. After Philip II, an exhausted Spain declined to a second-class power.

Royal absolutism reached full bloom during the reign of Louis XIV of France. Louis reduced the once powerful nobles to frivolous courtiers, ignored the Estates-General, and centralized power in his own hands. Practicing mercantilism, Louis's government developed the French economy, fostered overseas trade, and conquered an overseas empire. It also fought wars to replace Spain as the preeminent European nation. Culture and the arts thrived under Louis's lavish patronage, and everything French—from the Versailles palace to fashion—set the style for the rest of Europe.

The English government evolved from absolutism to constitutionalism during this period. Royal power was decisively checked after a bloody civil war, the execution of one king, and the expulsion of another. Parliament emerged victorious, opening the way for constitutional government.

The conviction that a king should act to eliminate injustice and ensure prosperity and stability of the state led to enlightened despotism, epitomized by Frederick the Great. Frederick saw himself as the first servant of the state and responsible for the welfare of the people in his care.

The Age of Reason, or the Enlightenment, grew out of the scientific revolution of the sixteenth and seventeenth centuries, which had begun with Copernicus's heliocentric theory and climaxed with Newton's formulation of the law of gravity. Meanwhile, seventeenth-century philosophers like Bacon and Descartes developed the scientific method. In the eighteenth century, the philosophes made rational critiques of existing social conventions and proposed new political approaches. Voltaire, Diderot, and Rousseau attacked the abuses of the old regime, and John Locke and Adam Smith urged a new order based on political and economic freedom.

The Enlightenment spread to the Western Hemisphere and affected societies around the world. Other European cultural achievements included the development of the novel and art catering to the tastes of the rising middle class. The Western world was on the threshold of major changes.

Between 1648 and 1740, absolutist governments dominated in central and eastern Europe, as they did in France and Spain. The Austrian Habsburg dynasty used absolutist methods to recover from their loss of power in the Thirty Years' War. The Prussian Hohenzollerns joined the front rank of nations with the help of absolutist techniques and an impressive bureaucracy and army.

By the eighteenth century, the Iberian monarchies had firmly implanted Western civilization throughout an area twice the size of Europe. The impact of Western culture varied

CHRONOLOGY

1500

Copernicus, *On the Revolutions of the Heavenly Spheres*

Philip II of Spain

Galileo Galilei

1600

Garcilaso de la Vega, *Royal Commentaries of the Incas*

Romanov dynasty in Russia

René Descartes

Louis XIV of France

Palace of Versailles built

Harvard University founded

Casa de Contratación

Newton, *Mathematical Principles of Natural Philosophy*

The poetry of Sor Juana Inés de la Cruz

Glorious Revolution in England

1700

Peter the Great begins westernization of Russia

Daniel Defoe, *Robinson Crusoe*

Johann Sebastian Bach

The philosophes

Frederick the Great

Battle of Plassey

Voltaire, *Candide*

Captain James Cook

James Watt's steam engine

1775

Benjamin Franklin

American Revolution

Adam Smith, *The Wealth of Nations*

Catherine the Great of Russia

Destruction of Poland

Thomas Jefferson

The British colonize Australia

U.S. Constitution and Bill of Rights

Joseph II of Austria

Wolfgang Amadeus Mozart

The cotton gin

1800

widely according to region, ranging from strong influence in Mexico and Peru to nonexistent in the Amazon and the southern tip of South America. The impact also varied by social status: the upper classes clung to their Iberian background, while the lower orders were still strongly influenced by their native Amerindian and African cultures. The Iberians established Roman Catholicism as the only faith throughout the colonies. Amerindians "converted" to Catholicism, but on their own spiritual and cultural terms. Three key characteristics of Iberia—paternalistic government, aristocratic social and economic privilege, and mercantilist economics—were substantially replicated in Latin America. Latin Americans also inherited the intellectual, literary, and artistic outlook of Spain and Portugal, though ongoing interaction with Amerindian and African cultures led to new forms of Western civilization.

By the early eighteenth century, the residents of North America had developed a distinct culture that departed more substantially from Europe than did Latin America's. Yet, in some ways, British North America approximated Europe more closely than did Latin America: the area was overwhelmingly European racially and linguistically, and Amerindian culture played an insignificant role. The African impact was also less profound as yet. On the other hand, British North America was fast departing from continental Europe and Latin America in that it demonstrated a strong tendency toward socioeconomic and political liberalization, a tendency that was also getting under way in Great Britain.

Europeans visiting British North America were naturally impressed by the differences rather than the similarities. They commented on the strange landscape, the raw look of both cities and farms, and the lack of monuments or any sign of a living, visible past. They were discomfited by the restless moving about of the population and the cacophony of ethnic groups and religious sects. Above all, Europeans were struck by the individualism at all levels of society and by the absence of servility among the middle and lower orders of whites. Europeans attributed these characteristics to the general prosperity of the population, to education, and to the weakness of the class system. Most visitors went home dismayed by the brawling confusion and the social dislocation, but a few enthusiasts felt they had seen the future of Western civilization.

After 1763 the British attempted to rein in their North American colonists and subject them to new taxes. The colonists resisted and in 1775 fighting broke out; compromise failing, the colonists declared their independence in 1776 and a war of attrition ensued. France and other nations entered the war against Great Britain and in 1783 the British recognized the independence of the United States of America.

A liberal federal republic, the United States enjoyed, in spite of a number of national problems, a vibrant economy and both population and territorial growth. Most of its white citizens owned property, were literate, and participated in politics. By the middle of the nineteenth century, however, dissension between the northern and southern sections brought fears of disunity.

From the late seventeenth to the early nineteenth century, Europeans expanded their knowledge of, and controls over, more of the world. Though they charted the Pacific and discovered Australia, their greatest interest was in the interior and northwest coast of

North America, where several European nations competed for beaver, seal, and otter pelts. The fur trade, however, was only a minor part of an emerging global economy that combined the products of Asia and the Americas and the labor of Africa into enormous wealth for the seafaring powers of Europe and their Atlantic port cities.

While the Spanish, Portuguese, and Dutch were struggling to retain their empires, the French and British rapidly expanded their colonial possessions. The two nations fought each other in North America and India with increasing intensity throughout the first half of the eighteenth century, with the British emerging triumphant in 1763. After Spain was reduced to impotence in India and the Caribbean, Great Britain was by far the greatest colonial power in the world.

The Industrial Revolution was a crucial event in world history, with far-ranging socioeconomic consequences on both sides of the Atlantic. It resulted from a mix of natural resources, an expanding labor force, growing economic demand, the accumulation of investment capital, technological ingenuity, entrepreneurial leadership, and a progressive mindset. Unprecedented manufacturing expansion, first in Britain, thereafter in continental Europe and the Americas, produced new industries and new sources of energy, including iron, coal, textiles, and the steam engine itself in the later 1700s and earlier 1800s. As we shall see in Chapter 12, many nations in Europe and in the New World followed Great Britain's lead.

Selected Sources

Items indicated with an asterisk (*) are available in paperback.

Adam, Antoine. *Grandeur and Illusion: French Literature and Society, 1600–1715.* Translated by Herbert Tint. 1972. Good Survey of the intellectual history of the age; section on classicism particularly well done.

*Artz, Frederick B. *The Enlightenment in France.* 1968. A brief survey of the movement in the land of the philosophes.

Ashton, T. S. *The Industrial Revolution, 1760–1830.* 1968. The English origins of the modern industrial system.

Bannon, John Francis. *The Colonial World of Latin America.* 1982. A useful introduction to Spanish America and Brazil.

*Bernard, Paul P. *Joseph II.* 1968. A concise and balanced treatment of the ill-fated monarch.

Bethell, Leslie, ed. *Colonial Spanish America.* 1987. *Colonial Brazil.* 1988. Both books contain essays concerning Latin America from the conquest to independence. Noted authorities write about rural society and the hacienda, urbanization, and Amerindian cultural matters.

Brading, D. A. *The First America: The Spanish Monarchy, Creole Patriots, and the Liberal State, 1492–1866.* 1990. Stresses the development of an American identity in such Creoles as Simón Bolívar and José de San Martin. Provides good background for the postindependence period.

Braudel, Fernand. *The Mediterranean and the Mediterranean World in the Age of Philip II.* Abridged 1992. Excellent background for understanding Spain and Spanish transplantations in the Americas.

*Bridenbaugh, Carl. *Myths and Realities: Societies of the Colonial South.* 1952, reprinted 1963. A well-written survey of the British North American colonies that most resembled the Caribbean and Brazil.

*Commager, Henry S., and Elmo Giordanetti. *Was America a Mistake?* 1967. A fascinating collection of eighteenth-century attacks on, and defenses of, the New World.

Commager, Henry S., and Richard B. Morris, eds. *The Spirit of 'Seventy-Six: The Story of the American Revolution as Told by Participants.* 1967. An excellent collection of contemporary documents.

*De Madariaga, Isabel. *Russia in the Age of Catherine the Great.* 1981. Meticulously researched biography, sympathetic to Catherine.

*Dumas, Alexander. *The Three Musketeers.* 1844. Famous novel of swashbuckling seventeenth-century soldiers. There are also film versions.

Eccles, William J. *France in America.* 1972. The best study; concise and well written.

Fuentes, Carlos. *The Buried Mirror: Reflections on Spain and the New World.* 1992. Excellent introduction to Spain and the Americas; beautifully crafted with prints, maps, and artwork.

Gardner, Brian. *The East India Company: A History.* 1971. An engagingly written survey of the rise and fall of the greatest trading company in British history.

Gooch, G. P. *Louis XV: The Monarchy in Decline.* 1956. A highly respected study.

Goubert, Pierre. *Louis XIV and Twenty Million Frenchmen.* Translated by Ann Carter. 1970. An analysis of French society under the Grand Monarch.

Hamish, M. Scott. *Enlightened Despotism.* 1990. A good, recent survey of the subject.

Henry, John. *The Scientific Revolution and the Origins of Modern Science.* 1997. A brief survey of the key aspects of the Scientific Revolution.

*Hofstadter, Richard. *America at 1750: A Social Portrait.* 1971. Incomplete at Hofstadter's death, an insightful presentation of society in British North America.

Jensen, Merrill. *The Founding of a Nation: A History of the American Revolution, 1763–1776.* 1968. A long but well-written survey that stresses the complexity of the period.

Kitson, Michael. *The Age of Baroque.* 1966. Beautifully illustrated history of art in Europe in the seventeenth and eighteenth centuries.

*Koyre, Alexander. *From the Closed World to the Infinite Universe.* 1968. Expanding knowledge of the universe, from Copernicus through Newton.

Leonard, Irving A. *Baroque Themes in Old Mexico: Seventeenth-Century Persons, Places, and Practices.* 1966. Although somewhat dated, still an exceptional undergraduate resource. The chapter-length biographies shed much light on class, race, culture, and upper-class mores and ideas.

Lynch, John. *The Spanish-American Revolutions, 1808–1826.* 1973. The best synthesis of a sprawling subject.

Martin, Luis. *Daughters of the Conquistadores: Women of the Viceroyalty of Peru.* 1983. An informative survey, with applications to all of Latin America.

*Massie, Robert. *Peter the Great.* 1980. Highly readable, Pulitzer Prize–winning account.

*Parry, J. H. *Trade and Dominion: The European Overseas Empires in the Eighteenth Century.* 1971. The standard account, stressing the European impact on the colonies.

*Pushkin, Alexander. *The Captain's Daughter.* 1836. Various editions. A colorful Russian novel, set against the Pugachev rebellion.

*Rabb, Theodore K. *The Struggle for Stability in Early Modern Europe.* 1975. Brief, sweeping survey of the "crisis of the seventeenth century," to which absolutism provided partial solution.

*Read, Conyers. *The Tudors: Personalities and Practical Politics in the Sixteenth Century.* 1969. Biographical sketches of the Tudor rulers.

Ritter, Gerhard. *Frederick the Great.* 1968. A useful assessment by a leading German scholar.

Sobol, Dava. *Galileo's Daughter.* 1999. Letters of Galileo's illegitimate daughter, a cloistered nun, reveal much about his struggle to reconcile his scientific discoveries with his Catholic faith.

Trueblood, Alan S., ed. and trans. *A Sor Juana Anthology.* 1988. A bilingual collection with a helpful historical introduction.

*Voltaire, François-Marie Arouet. *Candide or Optimism*. 1759. Many editions. Satirical novel highlighting foibles and hypocrisies of eighteenth-century European and colonial life.

*Wolf, John B. *Louis XIV*. 1968. Monumental biography of the Sun King.

> Additional resources, exercises, and Internet links related to this chapter are available on the Book Companion Web site: http://history.wadsworth.com/upshurcompact4/

COMPARATIVE ESSAY 9
Nationalism: An Emerging Global Force

Our country is our Home; the house that God has given us. In laboring for our own country on the right principle, we labor for Humanity.
Giuseppe Mazzini

Foreigners often compare the Chinese with loose sand because we lack a sense of national cohesiveness. . . . The reason that we have been so long unsuccessful in resisting foreign oppression is because we have not awakened to our dire plight and have not organized our whole race. . . . However, when we do link up and bind together all our 400 million people, then we will not find it difficult to resist foreign aggression.
Sun Yat-sen on his principle of nationalism

Nationalism emerged as a potent force after 1815. Addressing their fellow citizens, the Italian nationalist Giuseppe Mazzini (1805–1872) and the Chinese nationalist Sun Yat-sen (1867–1925) both exhorted them to unify, but they put forth two quite different arguments to justify their calls for national unity. Mazzini used the argument—albeit mythological—that the nation had always existed and was a divine creation. In contrast, Sun Yat-sen stressed that national unity was a prerequisite for the Chinese to maintain their independence and to prevent domination by foreign powers. Numerous nationalist leaders popularized both points of view during the nineteenth and twentieth centuries.

Nationalism may be defined as an emotional loyalty of a people to a given state. The building blocks that help people forge a common national identity include a common language, traditions, history, economic interdependence, belief in a common political and judicial system, hope for a glorious future, and sometimes religion. Although religion has been a unifying force in some nations, in others, such as Ireland, India, and Lebanon, religious or confessional differences have led to long, protracted civil wars and political strife.

Until the end of the nineteenth century, nationalism was a particularly strong force in Europe and the Americas, after which it spread throughout Asia, the Middle East, and Africa. As a worldwide phenomenon, nationalism impelled countless wars of independence and led to the creation of almost 200 separate nations by the end of the twentieth century.

The French Revolution and the Napoleonic wars accelerated the development of modern nationalism, which was also heavily influenced by romanticism. The process began with the transformation of the Estates General into the National Assembly; this new institution represented not three separate classes but the entire nation. The revolution also led to the abolition of class privileges, the destruction of the old, chaotic, provincial government administrations, and, most importantly, the creation of a centralized national governmental system. A constitution made France, like the United States, a nation of free citizens protected by law. The broad participation of the general public in both politics and the armed forces increased the emotional involvement of citizens in the future of their own nations.

Although most political colonial leaders in the United States and Latin America shared the basic ethnic characteristics and cultural values of their European rulers, they nonetheless ousted those rulers when they were perceived to have become both unresponsive and tyrannical. Similarly, during the Napoleonic wars, conquered peoples throughout Europe were willing to pay high costs in life and money to preserve their national and cultural identities. In Spain and Prussia, citizens made enormous sacrifices to throw off alien French rule.

After 1815, national minorities in the polygot Habsburg and Russian Empires and oppressed nationalities in Ireland and the Belgian Netherlands all sought to shake free of foreign domination. In part, both Germany and Italy, as emphasized by Mazzini, were molded into unified nations by recalling—or creating sometimes highly romanticized or mythical—common histories.

There was also a nationalistic awakening among the subject peoples of the Ottoman Empire. In the Ottoman Empire, religion and ethnic-cultural differences as well as dissatisfaction with the increasingly corrupt and ineffectual government led to the growth of separate nationalist groups, first among the Greeks and then among the Arabs, Kurds, Armenians, and others.

In much of Asia and Africa, nationalism was rooted in opposition to Western imperialism and colonial domination. Many Asian and African nationalist leaders were Western-educated and had personally observed the power of nationalism as a driving force in Western nations. For example, the Indian National Congress, the oldest and most powerful nationalist organization in India, was founded in 1885 by British-educated Indians and some Englishmen. Because shared ideals could best be communicated in a common language, the early publications of the Indian National Congress were in English, the unifying language of many educated Indians until the present day. Similarly, in Africa, the Kenyan nationalist leader Jomo Kenyatta and Tanzanian leader Julius Nyerere were both influenced by Western education.

When Sun Yat-sen, father of the Chinese Republic, founded the United League (forerunner to the Kuomintang, or Nationalist Party) in 1905, he made nationalism the first principle of the party's ideology. As noted above, Sun explained that without the glue of nationalism, the Chinese people were like sand, ineffective and doomed to outside domination.

Threats of foreign domination often galvanized nationalist movements. In Japan, already homogenous because of geography and a common history, strong nationalist feelings were easily spread when Western nations threatened economic and cultural domination.

Although nationalism helped to create cohesive unified nations and to provide for conquered people to throw off foreign domination, it also had a number of negative ramifications. The desire for national glory often led to territorial expansion at the expense of neighboring states, thereby inciting major wars. Thus nationalism was a major contributing factor to both World War I and World War II. Nationalism manifested itself in the most brutal form in the totalitarian states that emerged after World War I, in which citizens were taught to worship the state as an end in itself. If the state could do no wrong, it followed that it had the right to expand, even at the expense of other nations. Mussolini, Hitler, and Stalin all manipulated nationalist feelings to exploit popular support and to justify the oppression of their own citizens and the conquest, or even extermination, of other peoples.

Finally, nationalism has also contributed to the continued oppression of national minorities, leading to abuses of human rights and to massacres and the "ethnic cleansing" of rival ethnic or national groups, as in the cases of nations as diverse as India and Sri Lanka in Asia, the states of the former Yugoslavia in Europe, and Rwanda in Africa.

12

The Modernization of the Western World

•

• The French Revolution and the Napoleonic Era •

• Reform and Revolution in the Nineteenth Century •

• Nationalism and Political Conflict in the West: 1848–1914 •

• The Spread of Industrialization and the Appearance of Industrial Society •

• Western Cultural and Intellectual Trends •

• Summary and Comparisons •

It was then that M. de Launay [commander of the forces of the Bastille] asked the garrison what course should be followed, that he saw no other than to blow himself up rather than to expose himself to having his throat cut by people, from the fury of which they could not escape; that they must remount the towers, continue to fight, and blow themselves up rather than surrender.

The soldiers replied that it was impossible to fight any longer, that they would resign themselves to everything rather than destroy such a great number of citizens, that it was best to put the drummer on the towers to beat the recall, hoist a white flag, and capitulate. The governor, having no flag, gave them a white handkerchief. An officer wrote out the capitulation and passed it through the hole, saying that they desired to surrender themselves and lay down their arms, on condition of a promise not to massacre the troops: there was a cry of "Lower your bridge; nothing will happen to you! . . . "

As soon as the great bridge was let down . . . the people rushed into the court of the castle and, full of fury, seized on the troops of Invalides [probably a unit of handicapped soldiers]. . . . Several of these soldiers, whose lives had been promised them, were assassinated; others were dragged like slaves through the streets of Paris. Twenty-two were brought to the Grève [a square in the city], and, after humiliations and inhuman treatment, they had the affliction of seeing two of their comrades hanged. . . . De Launay, torn from the arms of those who wished to save him, had his head cut off under the walls of the Hôtel de Ville [city hall]. . . . De Losme-Salbray, his major, was murdered in the same manner. . . . The head of the Marquis de Launay was carried about Paris by the same populace that he would have crushed had he not been moved to pity. Such were the exploits of those who have since been called the heroes and conquerors of the Bastille.*

*E. L. Higgins, ed., The French Revolution as Told by Contemporaries (Boston: Houghton Mifflin, 1938), pp. 98–100.

The above account by eyewitnesses describes the fall of the Bastille, an imposing medieval fortress once used as a royal prison and a hated symbol of Bourbon despotism. On July 14, 1789, a large crowd, composed mostly of skilled artisans and small shopkeepers, marched to the Bastille in search of arms for protection against a possible counterrevolution. The governor barred the gates and, fearing an attack, ordered his men to fire into the crowd. Enraged by the death of ninety-eight of its members and the wounding of many others, the mob assaulted the fortress and gained entrance after the governor had been persuaded to surrender. The event was an expression of the people's power and provided a catalyst to the French Revolution.

The French Revolution destroyed the old regime and introduced a new era that promised to realize the ideals of the Enlightenment. This chapter focuses on the period from 1789 to 1914, when several powerful trends changed the course of Western history. The French Revolution and the Napoleonic Wars that followed led to other upheavals throughout Europe and to independence movements in Latin America. In the United States the cultural animosity between the northern and southern regions culminated in a civil war lasting four years. The victory by federal forces created an indissoluble union that provided a secure foundation for a constitutional republic. At the same time, the Industrial Revolution spread outside Great Britain and altered European and North American society. New concepts of economics and political theory, such as Karl Marx's socialist ideology, emerged in response to the new economic and social conditions brought on by the revolutionary ferment of the nineteenth century and by the spread of industrialization. The chapter concludes with a survey of nineteenth-century cultural and intellectual developments.

The French Revolution and the Napoleonic Era

The path leading to the scaffold was extremely rough and difficult to pass, the King [Louis XVI] was obliged to lean on my arm, and from the slowness with which he proceeded, I feared for a moment that his courage might fail; but what was my astonishment, when arrived at the last step, I felt that he suddenly let go my arm, and I saw him cross with a firm foot the breadth of the wood scaffold. . . . I heard him pronounce distinctly these memorable words "I die innocent of all the crimes laid to my charge; I pardon those who have occasioned my death; and I pray to God, that the blood you are now going to shed may never be visited on France."

He was proceeding, when a man on horseback, in the national uniform, waved his sword, and . . . the executioners . . . seizing with violence the most virtuous of Kings . . . dragged him under the axe of the guillotine, which with one stroke severed his head from his body. . . . The youngest of the guards, who seemed about eighteen, walked round the scaffold; he accompanied this monstrous ceremony with the most atrocious and indecent gestures. At first an awful silence prevailed; at length some cries of "Vive la République!" were heard. By degrees the voices multiplied, and in less than ten minutes this cry, a thousand times repeated, became the universal shout of the multitude, and every hat was in the air.*

*Abbé Edgeworth, Memoirs (London: Hunter, 1815), pp. 84–87.

This gruesome scene, vividly depicted by a contemporary English observer, was the product of a historical movement inspired, not by a conspiracy to institute a new order, but by men who favored reforming the system. It began with an attempt to solve the financial crisis and then escalated to an attack on the political and social institutions. These economic, political, and social forces converged at a moment when the authoritarian system, its foundations eroded by decades of neglect, inefficiency, and corruption, was ready to succumb. Like the movement of a clock pendulum, the revolution passed through various stages, becoming more extreme and reaching the high tide of radicalism in 1793–1794 before a revulsion in public opinion led to the return of moderate rule. The years of revolutionary activity witnessed the abolition of the monarchy, the end of feudalism, the proclamation of religious and individual freedom, and the legal equality of all Frenchmen. The revolution ended when Napoleon Bonaparte overthrew the government in November 1799 and established a dictatorship.

The French Revolution was one of the pivotal events in the history of the modern European world. It not only repudiated what we now know as the old regime in France but prepared the way for the transformation of Western society. Indeed, even generations later it would inspire uprisings and colonial struggles for independence in Africa and Asia. This section will focus on the period of the revolution and the career of Napoleon Bonaparte.

The Old Regime

The origins of the French Revolution are much disputed among contemporary scholars. If France had been a backward country whose people were brutally governed and miserable, the explanation would be relatively simple. As it happened, France was the center of the Enlightenment, its culture was widely imitated and admired in Europe, it was wealthy, and its underprivileged classes enjoyed a higher standard of living than their counterparts in neighboring states. But it was precisely because they were better off and better informed that they were less willing to tolerate the inequities in the existing institutions.

On the eve of the revolution, France had a population of some 27 million people. The central feature of the government was the absolute monarchy, which had reached full development during the reign of Louis XIV. The king appointed all the high officials in the government, and he alone was responsible for the conduct of the state's foreign policy. As the monarchy was based on the concept of divine right and not on the consent of the people, the king's will was law. The Estates-General, the rough equivalent of Great Britain's Parliament, had not been summoned since 1614 and was, for all intents and purposes, obsolescent. The law courts were riddled with corruption and favoritism. The judges of the supreme courts, the *parlements,* were aristocrats who had bought or inherited their offices. They were mainly interested in using their position to enrich themselves. In cases brought by commoners, the judges always favored their own kind. The inequities inherent in the French system, tolerated in the past, encountered increasing resistance as the ideas of the Enlightenment gained strength.

By custom and law, everyone in France belonged to one of three distinct orders or estates: the clergy made up the first estate; the nobility the second; and everyone else the third. The church in France was practically a state within a state, and, although it was attacked by the philosophes for promoting superstition and impeding reform, it still exerted great influence among the masses. Served by about 130,000 clergymen, it owned about 10 percent of the land. Its annual income, derived from its landed property, tithes levied on crops, and other sources, was immense, estimated to have been half as much as that of the government itself. The church paid no taxes but periodically made a "free gift" to the state—a contribution that was considerably less than direct taxes would have been. A major source of weakness in the church was its deep social divisions. The upper church officials—archbishops, bishops, and abbots—came from the ranks of the aristocracy and lived and upheld the values of their class, while often ignoring their spiritual responsibilities. In contrast, the parish priests and monks were commoners by birth and usually poor. They resented the lifestyle of the upper clergy and served and identified with the interests of the lower classes.

The aristocracy comprised about 2 percent of the population, roughly 400,000 persons, and owned between 20 and 25 percent of the land. They enjoyed special privileges, not the least of which was exemption from direct taxation. The nobility did not form a cohesive social unit but rather varied in fortune and prestige. The one thing that bound them together was a desire to maintain their privileges and regain the political power they had lost under Louis XIV. During the reign of the indifferent Louis XV their aggressiveness in defense of their ancient rights paid off. In the second half of the eighteenth century, the top-level bureaucratic administrators, once drawn mainly from the middle class, were recruited, almost without exception, from the ranks of the nobles. Not content with their virtual monopoly of the highest offices in the government, they looked forward to the day when they would again rule France, just as their ancestors had done in the Middle Ages.

Below the privileged classes stood the commoners—primarily bourgeoisie or middle class, urban workers, and peasants—who comprised about 97 percent of the total population. The upper segment, because of their wealth and education, were the middle class, a varied group that included merchants, bankers, industrialists, intellectuals, professional men, and skilled artisans. Although the bourgeoisie did not face the kind of hardships that the laborers or peasants did, they resented more keenly the abuses of the old regime. What they found especially intolerable was the snobbery of the aristocracy and the second-class status assigned to them by the monarchy. The avenues of social advancement, once open to bourgeoisie who purchased an office that carried with it noble status or gained a high-level position in the army or government, were now full of obstacles because of the aristocratic resurgence. Undoubtedly the desire for social and political advancement was the basic reason why some members of the bourgeoisie challenged the old order. They wanted privileges based on birth abolished and careers opened to talent. For others, imbued by a sense of justice, the motive was more noble. They longed to end royal absolutism and reform France in accordance with the just and rational outlook of the philosophes.

The prosperity of the bourgeoisie was not shared by the petty artisans or unskilled laborers who were concentrated in the major cities, particularly Paris. During the half century before the revolution, prices for consumer goods rose by 65 percent, while wages increased by only 22 percent. Thus workers usually lived on the edges of starvation. The economic depression that gripped France in the late 1780s intensified their suffering and fueled their resentment against the government.

The peasants who tilled the soil made up at least four-fifths of the French population. They enjoyed a unique status in Europe. Serfdom had largely disappeared in France, and peasants owned 30 to 35 percent of the land. Nevertheless, most of their income was siphoned away by feudal and manorial dues, church tithes, and royal taxes. The economic conditions of the peasants worsened during the last decades of the old regime because of poor harvests and high inflation. Yet they remained essentially traditional in outlook, merely desiring relief from taxation and an opportunity to own their land or, if they already did, extend their holdings.

The Last Days of the Old Regime

The glory and prestige that had marked the Bourbon monarchy during the age of Louis XIV began to fade with his passing. Although his heirs lived in great style and claimed to rule by divine right, they were weak and allowed power to slip from their hands. Louis XV (reigned 1715–1774) was intelligent enough, but he was indolent, fickle, pleasure loving, and uninterested in the affairs of state. While seeking new ways to alleviate his boredom, Louis permitted the woman of his current fancy to influence state policy. His haphazard and irresponsible conduct of foreign policy dragged the country into two wars, the last of which, the Seven Years' War, ended in a shattering defeat and the resultant loss of Canada and French India. The immense cost of prosecuting these wars, added to the profligate extravagance at the royal court, cut deep into the nation's finances. Louis left a legacy, best encapsulated in an expression erroneously attributed to him, "Après moi, le déluge."

The new king, Louis XVI (reigned 1774–1792), was twenty years old, well meaning, moral, and anxious to disassociate his reign from that of his discredited late grandfather. But he was also dull and indecisive, lacked intellectual gifts, and suffered from the reflected unpopularity of his Austrian-born wife, Marie Antoinette. The queen's few good qualities were overshadowed by her extravagance, insensitivity, indiscretion, and intrusion in politics. Too often the king ignored the advice of his councilors lest he be subjected to his wife's scorn and ridicule.

Louis XV had made little effort to correct the abuses of the old regime, which had grown more serious by the time his successor ascended the throne. Apart from the mounting social unrest, the government faced a deepening financial crisis. Already high in 1774, the debt would triple over the course of the next fifteen years—largely as a result of France's participation in the American War of Independence. France was a wealthy country, but the crux of the problem was that royal expenditures exceeded income. The only way to remedy the shortfall was to make all classes pay their fair share of taxes. But the nobility and clergy refused to give up their ancient privileges and Louis XVI lacked the backbone to override them. His successive controller-generals had no alternative but to borrow money to cover the deficit. By 1788 half of the state's annual revenue went to service the interest on the accumulated debt of nearly 4 billion livres. In desperation Louis tried to impose a tax on all landowners, but he was challenged by the parlements, which insisted that such a reform required the consent of the Estates-General. Louis's plan to set up new courts to replace the parlements foundered because of popular opposition, leaving him with no option but to summon the Estates-General. The aristocracy was certain that it could control this body and through it protect its privileges and weaken the monarchy. It miscalculated badly.

Forging a New Order: The Moderate Stage

The election of the representatives to the Estates-General took place amid widespread economic suffering. A severe recession had caused a wave of bankruptcies, and unemployment reached staggering levels in the cities. In large parts of the country, hail and drought had reduced the harvest. By the spring of 1789, grain prices had doubled. Because the lower classes spent as much as two-thirds of their income on food, these increases had a particularly devastating effect on their living standards. Riots swept across the country and mobs attacked granaries and bakeries.

In May 1789, one week after a particularly severe riot in Paris, Louis XVI formally opened the proceedings of the Estates-General. Before the delegates turned to the work at hand, a sharp debate broke out over the method of voting. According to tradition, the three estates met separately and voted as individual bodies; that is, each estate cast one vote. Such a system ensured that the privileged estates could always outvote the third estate two to one. The third estate, with its double membership, reinforced by some reform-minded clergy and aristocrats, wanted the three estates to meet as a single body and vote by head. The first and second estates naturally resisted this demand, and a deadlock ensued. The haggling went on for six weeks until finally the third estate took a momentous step. Insisting that it was the only true representative of the nation, it proclaimed itself the National Assembly on June 17 and invited the other estates to join its sessions. When the members of the third estate assembled for their daily debates on June 20, they found the doors of their chamber locked. Carpenters were preparing the hall for a royal speech to be delivered two days later, but the deputies believed that they had been deliberately locked out in an attempt to send them back home. They angrily withdrew to a nearby indoor tennis court where they vowed never to disband until they had given France a constitution. The Tennis Court Oath marks the beginning of the French Revolution. It was an assertion that sovereign power resided with a new body that had no legal authority.

What had begun as an aristocratic struggle to undermine the monarchy had taken an unexpected turn. The nobles became more concerned at the defiant behavior of the third estate, which they saw as a threat to their privileged status. They immediately reversed their long-standing position and joined hands with the king in an effort to stop the incipient social revolution. At the royal session on June 23, the king came down on the side of the nobility, directing the estates to meet separately. The third estate, however, would not budge from its declared purpose. Royal regiments were within call, but the king characteristically vacillated when confronted with a tough decision. On June 27, on learning that a majority of the clergy and some aristocrats had joined the National Assembly, Louis conceded defeat and directed the three estates to sit together and vote by head. His action implied recognition of the right of the National Assembly to act as the highest sovereign power in the nation. The leadership of the revolt had now passed from the aristocracy to the bourgeoisie who represented the masses in the National Assembly.

The king's concession did not reduce the level of tension in Paris. Angry over the increasing cost of food and terrified by the royal regiments concentrating in the vicinity of the city, mobs rioted and broke into gunsmith shops and public buildings in search of arms. Three days of wild disorders culminated with an attack on the Bastille. The day on which the Bastille fell, July 14, is a national holiday in France, celebrated as the birth of freedom and justice.

The disturbances in Paris coincided with a movement in the countryside known as the Great Fear. During the spring of 1789, there were numerous peasant demonstrations sparked by the economic crisis. Galvanized by these mounting disorders, the National Assembly hastily abolished the old feudal privileges, serfdom, ecclesiastical tithes, and all forms of personal obligations formerly imposed on the third estate. It proclaimed the principles of equal taxation and civil equality.

These social changes were supplemented in August by legal guarantees embodied in the Declaration of the Rights of Man and the Citizen. Echoing the U.S. Declaration of Independence, the document proclaimed that men were born and remained free and were equal in rights. It was framed to apply not only to French citizens but to all humans, regardless of their national origin. The universality of the declaration was a challenge to the old regimes throughout Europe and subsequently became a rallying point for champions of human rights around the world.

The king's delay in ratifying the social changes and the Declaration of the Rights of Man and the Citizen fueled rumors that he was planning to use troops to undo the work of the revolution. Amid widespread uncertainty, a large mob of Parisian women marched eleven miles to the royal palace at Versailles and demanded that the price of bread be lowered. The king yielded, and to further appease the women, he agreed to return with them to Paris. After arriving in Paris, the king and his family were installed in the old Tuileries palace. A few weeks later, the National Assembly followed the king to the city. Both the assembly and the king were now subject to the pressure of the Parisian populace.

In Paris the National Assembly, now called the National Constituent Assembly, continued the work of drawing up the constitution. Guided by the philosophes' principles of humanity, rationality, and efficiency, it enacted a series of sweeping reforms that were later incorporated into a single document known as the Constitution of 1791. One of the major undertakings of the assembly was to reorganize the whole ecclesiastical system after it confiscated church property and abolished tithes. To this end, the assembly promulgated the Civil Constitution of the Clergy, which was designed to maintain the clergy and subordinate the church to the state. Clergymen were to be paid by the state and, like other public servants, were to be elected by those they served. Since the pope was denied any authority over the French church, he was left with no choice but to condemn the Civil Constitution. This turned the majority of pious Catholics against the revolution.

In reshaping the government, the Constituent Assembly had confirmed the transferal of power from the privileged orders to the educated bourgeoisie. The constitution preserved the hereditary monarchy, but the authority of the king was reduced in accordance with Montesquieu's formula of "separation of powers." The king still controlled the army and navy and directed foreign policy, but most of the authority over internal affairs was now in the hands of a single Legislative Assembly, which controlled both taxes and expenditures. Suffrage was indirect. Males over the age of twenty-five paying taxes equivalent to three days' wages could vote for electors who chose the deputies. The property requirements for an elector were so high that probably no more than 70,000 Frenchmen had the means to qualify. Nevertheless, the new French political system was more democratic than that of any other European state.

In June 1791 the king, unreconciled to the reforms forced upon him, secretly fled Paris with his family. He hoped to rally loyal supporters in the northeast and to return to power with the support of those European governments alarmed by the revolutionary changes. He was recognized at Varennes near the Belgian border, however, and sent back to Paris under armed guard. After considerable debate, the deputies voted to retain the

LIVES AND TIMES ACROSS CULTURES

Charlotte Corday and the Murder of Marat

On July 9, 1792, Charlotte Corday, a tall, strikingly attractive young woman of twenty-four, boarded a coach for Paris. Born to a noble but poor family in Caen, she was a fanatical follower of a revolutionary faction (Girondins) vying with the more radical elements (Jacobins or Montagnards) for control of the government. Her mission in Paris, which she undertook without anyone's knowledge, was to murder Jean-Paul Marat, whom she had been told was an enemy of freedom and the cause of many of France's woes. Implacable and vengeful, the forty-nine-year-old Marat had been in the forefront of those demanding the execution of the king. Editor of *L'Ami du Peuple* (*Friend of the People*), he attacked a wide range of targets whom he considered enemies of the revolution.

On arriving in Paris, Charlotte took a room in a hotel and then purchased a sharp dinner knife for two francs. On the evening of July 13 she went to Marat's house and gained entry on the pretext that she had important information, which she could only convey to him in person. She found him soaking in a high-walled copper bath, seeking relief from a painful and unpleasant skin disease, which he had contracted hiding in the sewers of Paris. She gave him a report of what was happening in her hometown, revealing the names of men she claimed were plotting against the Jacobins. Marat picked up a nearby pen and began to copy down the names, commenting, "In a few days I will have them all guillotined." Before he could say another word, Charlotte pulled out the knife from the top of her dress and plunged it into his heart. Marat's scream alerted his staff, who ran into the room and captured Charlotte before she could escape. At her trial she did not seek to evade the consequences of her deed and went to her death cheerfully under the illusion that she had saved France from the horrors of a civil war.

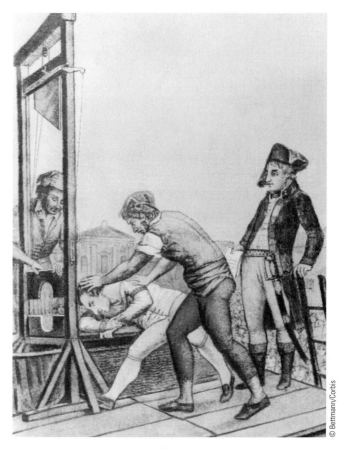

The Guillotine. In keeping with eighteenth-century enlightened thinking about the need to eliminate the torturous punishments practiced during the *ancien régime,* the guillotine was devised as a swifter, more certain, and thus more humane method of execution. As Dr. Joseph-Ignace Guillotin (1728–1814) said when recommending its adoption to the National Assembly, "The mechanism falls like thunder; the head flies off, blood spurts, the man is no more." Though the "machine" is named for the doctor, it was in fact designed and fabricated under the direction of a Dr. Louis, the secretary of the French Academy of Surgery.

© Bettmann/Corbis

monarchy, and when Louis showed himself to be penitent, he was reinstated. In the fall of 1791 the Constituent Assembly disbanded and declared the revolution at an end. Thus far the revolution had ended feudalism, established individual rights and liberties and legal equality, undercut the power of the church, and lessened the authority of the king.

Though launched with great expectations, the constitutional monarchy lasted less than a year. Its demise propelled the revolution from a moderate to a radical stage. The failure of the new system was principally due to three reasons. First, the king was unwilling to accept the modest role he had been assigned under the constitution. Second, the poorer classes in the cities felt cheated by the changes, which had primarily benefited the middle class and the peasants. The bourgeoisie had in effect replaced the aristocracy as the ruling class; the peasants had been freed of feudal obligations, and many of them owned property. Third, the outbreak of war in the spring of 1792 created tension and hysteria. The events in France had alarmed the European monarchs, who feared the spread of revolutionary ideas to their own lands. At the same time, the émigrés (nobles who had fled France) stoked the fires by calling for the destruction of the revolution. Under these circumstances the Austrian and Prussian monarchs publicly supported the use of armed force to restore royal absolutism in France. This move was seen in France as an insult and a threat, and the new Legislative Assembly reacted by declaring war on April 20, 1792.

France was woefully unprepared for war, and early military reverses aroused fear and disturbances in Paris. In August a hysterical mob stormed the Tuileries, convinced that the king was in league with the enemy. The royal family sought refuge in the halls of the Legislative Assembly. Fearful of the mob, the legislators deposed the king and ordered the election of an assembly to draw up a republican constitution. The abolition of the monarchy marked the beginning of the violent phase of the revolution.

From the Reign of Terror to the End of the Revolution

Although the new assembly, called the National Convention, was composed mostly of moderates, its leadership was dominated by Jacobin or left-wing elements. The National Convention held its first session on September 20, 1792, the very day that French troops at Valmy halted the enemy. Free to turn to other matters, the convention formally established a republic and debated the fate of the king. Found guilty of treasonable communication with the enemy, Louis was sentenced to die under the guillotine, now the official instrument of execution. The king's execution on January 21, 1793, sent tremors throughout the capitals of Europe. Ten months later his wife would follow him.

At the time of Louis's death, both external and internal troubles were threatening to destroy the radicals and the revolution itself. After Valmy, French armies took the offensive and occupied the Austrian Netherlands, the Rhineland, and Savoy. However, reverses followed in the spring of 1793 when Great Britain, Spain, Portugal, and several lesser states joined Austria and Prussia in a formidable coalition against France. To make matters worse, a revolt erupted in the Vendée, a region southwest of Paris, where the peasants had remained faithful to the church and the monarchy. The revolution spread to Bordeaux, Lyons, Marseilles, and other important cities.

In April 1793 the National Convention created a Committee of Public Safety with almost unlimited authority to deal with the new perils facing the republic. The most influential member of the twelve-man committee was Maximilien Robespierre (1758–1794), a provincial attorney and rabid exponent of Rousseau's concept of democracy. The committee instituted a reign of terror against a wide range of people perceived to be enemies of the revolution. No dissent was tolerated. All suspected political enemies and all opponents of government policies were imprisoned or guillotined.

While the Committee of Public Safety was ruthlessly crushing its internal foes, the defense of the republic against its external enemies was entrusted to Lazare Carnot, a brilliant soldier and administrator. With the full support of the committee, he mobilized the entire nation for war, instituting universal conscription and placing vital industries under state control. He raised a huge army of keen young conscripts in place of a relatively small army of uninspired riffraff and mercenaries. His officer corps consisted of

Robespierre's Theory of Revolutionary Government, 1793

We shall first outline the principles and the needs underlying the creation of a revolutionary government; next we shall expound the cause that threatens to throttle it at birth.

The theory of revolutionary government is as new as the Revolution that created it. It is as pointless to seek its origins in the books of the political theorists, who failed to foresee this revolution, as in the laws of the tyrants, who are happy enough to abuse their exercise of authority without seeking out its legal justification. And so this phase is for the aristocracy a mere subject of terror or a term of slander, for tyrants an outrage and for many an enigma. It behooves us to explain it to all in order that we may rally good citizens, at least, in support of the principles governing the public interest.

It is the function of government to guide the moral and physical energies of the nation toward the purposes for which it was established.

The object of constitutional government is to preserve the Republic; the object of revolutionary government is to establish it.

Revolution is the war waged by liberty against its enemies; a constitution is that which crowns the edifice of freedom once victory has been won and the nation is at peace.

The revolutionary government has to summon extraordinary activity to its aid precisely because it is at war. It is subjected to less binding and less uniform regulations, because the circumstances in which it finds itself are tempestuous and shifting, above all because it is compelled to deploy, swiftly and incessantly, new resources to meet new and pressing dangers.

The principal concern of constitutional government is civil liberty; that of revolutionary government, public liberty. Under a constitutional government little more is required than to protect the individual against abuses by the state, whereas revolutionary government is obliged to defend the state itself against the factions that assail it from every quarter.

To good citizens revolutionary government owes the full protection of the state; to the enemies of the people it owes only death.*

Strongly influenced by Rousseau's writings, Robespierre was convinced that only through him could the ideals of the revolution be achieved. His obsessive vision of an ideal republic made him indifferent to the human costs of creating it. In this excerpt from a speech he delivered to the National Convention on December 25, 1793, he justifies the extreme steps taken by the revolutionary government as necessary to ensure the survival of liberty.

*George Rudé, ed., Robespierre (Englewood Cliffs, N.J.: Prentice Hall, 1967), pp. 58–59.

men who had risen to their position through merit rather than birth. This energetic policy turned the tide. French troops not only hurled back the forces of the coalition but invaded neighboring nations.

Beyond surmounting the crises and saving the revolution, the committee wanted to make France even more democratic. Robespierre and his associates sought to create a "Republic of Virtue" in which citizens, uncorrupted and fervently dedicated, would practice exemplary behavior. To keep the cost of living down, the committee imposed wage controls and set prices for essential commodities. It abolished imprisonment for debt, slavery in the colonies, and primogeniture. All titles were eliminated, and "citizen" and "citizeness" became the proper form of address. A new "rational" standard of weights and measures, the metric system, was established. It proved so convenient that most of the nations of the world eventually adopted it.

Pushing beyond political and social changes, the ruling Committee of Public Safety launched a movement to de-Christianize France. Churches were converted into temples of reason, where deists like Robespierre and his associates could worship the Supreme Being. A new calendar was introduced that eliminated Sundays and all church holidays and designated the birth of the republic, rather than the birth of Christ, as the beginning of Year 1. It was never popular with the masses, however, and was quietly shelved in 1806.

The work of the committee ended abruptly when Robespierre and his close supporters were overthrown. The republic that Robespierre created bore no resemblance to the utopian one he had tried to establish at the outset. It was in fact a brutal dictatorship, supported by only a small minority of the population and sustained through censorship and terrorist methods. Certain elements in the National Convention, fearing that they would become Robespierre's next victims, denounced him when he made an ill-tempered speech before the convention and stampeded the other members into ordering his arrest. He was executed on July 28, 1794, along with his closest collaborators.

The fall of Robespierre sparked a reaction against the excesses of the Terror, known as the "Thermidorian Reaction" (Thermidor was the month of July in the new revolutionary calendar). The change in public attitude led to a relaxation of tensions, and the government returned to moderate constitutionalism dominated by the urban middle class. The Terror was discontinued, freedom of speech and the press were restored, Catholic churches were reopened, and a laissez-faire economy was reinstated. Finally, the convention drew up a new constitution that provided for an executive board of five directors and a two-house legislature. In October 1795 the National Convention dissolved itself to give way to the new government.

The new regime, called the Directory after its executive board, inherited a sagging economy and other problems from the National Convention. Badly divided and burdened by a war, the government was unable to respond effectively to the task at hand and thus aroused much internal unrest and disorder. It was forced to rely on the army to crush insurrections in Paris and to deal with a dangerous royalist threat. French military reverses in Italy and Germany bred still more popular discontent with the Directory. The unstable internal conditions and collapsing economy, together with the army's defeats, provided an opportunity for Napoleon Bonaparte, a rising, popular general, to seize power.

Women and the French Revolution

The revolution did not afford women the same opportunities and benefits as men. Yet from the outset women of different backgrounds had taken an active role in the revolution. They organized political clubs, were present during the storming of the Bastille, engaged in street demonstrations, and, in their famous march to Versailles, forced the royal family to return to Paris. A few like Jeanne Roland, the wife of a government official, moved close to the center of political power and helped shape policy for their revolutionary factions.

In the emerging new order, women became more militant as they were no longer content to make vague statements about equality. In a spate of pamphlets, feminists called for suffrage, equal partnership in marriage, greater access to education, and better-paying jobs. In 1790 a small group founded the *Cercle Social* (social circle), which launched a campaign to end sexual inequality. Among the great figures of the period, none was more vocal in advocating women's emancipation than the Marquis de Condorcet. He refuted many of the traditional arguments against women and insisted that they should have the same political rights as men, that domestic authority should be shared, and that positions should be opened to both sexes. But his was virtually a lone voice in the wilderness.

The various legislative assemblies, for all their talk of equality and civil rights, were not keen on lifting restrictions against women. On the few occasions when the matter of granting women political rights arose, it was greeted with widespread ridicule and disbelief. Deputies left no doubt that the social role of women was to stay home, obey their husbands, raise the children, and keep out of public affairs. Only minor concessions were made, although they did improve women's private life. Piecemeal legislation between 1790 and 1794 guaranteed the right of women to share equally with male heirs, set the age of majority for women the same as for men (twenty-one), and admitted women as witnesses in civil suits. Moreover, women were to have the same standing as men in divorce cases as well as a voice in the administration of their own property and in the rearing of their children. Unfortunately, most of these gains were rescinded by Napoleon's codes a decade later and were not reinstated until the twentieth century.

The Rise of Napoleon

Napoleon Bonaparte (1769–1821) owed his rapid rise to good fortune and ability rather than to social position or wealth. He was born in 1769 on the French-controlled island of Corsica, the son of an impoverished noble of Italian origin. He studied at military academies in France and at the age of sixteen became a sublieutenant of artillery. Without a title or a powerful patron, Napoleon would not have risen high in the army of the old regime, but the downfall of the monarchy, the flight of many royalist officers, and the European war threw open the gates of opportunity. A general by the time he was twenty-five, he received his first battlefield command two years later in 1796 when he was put in charge of the French army in Italy.

Napoleon's brilliance as a tactician, thoroughness in planning his campaigns, and ability to make quick decisions and inspire his troops led to a series of spectacular victories. Once the war was over in Italy, he returned to France, where he had become a national hero. Anxious to increase his newly won popularity, he decided on a campaign to Egypt, then part of the Ottoman Empire, in order to destroy British commerce and naval predominance in the Mediterranean and ultimately British power in India. Along with his army, Napoleon took many scholars to study the culture of ancient Egypt. Although his forces initially enjoyed military success against the divided government in Egypt, the British fleet dealt him a decisive defeat at the battle of the Nile. Napoleon's dreams of conquering the eastern Mediterranean were crushed. Hearing of French defeats in Europe, he left for France, leaving most of his army stranded in Egypt.

The short-lived conquest of Egypt by French forces had more dramatic consequences in Europe than in the Ottoman Empire. The chance discovery of the Rosetta Stone during the campaign provided the key to deciphering ancient Egyptian hieroglyphics. Travelers' memoirs and scholarly studies of the culture of ancient Egypt excited enormous curiosity among Europeans. This interest later stimulated a lucrative tourist trade as Europeans and Americans traveled to the eastern Mediterranean to see the wonders of the ancient world. As for the Egyptians themselves, a few members of the upper class were influenced by the ideas of the French Revolution and Western scientific developments; however, most Egyptians who came into contact with the French were repulsed by the drunken behavior of the soldiers and resented Napoleon's imperialistic aggression in their country.

Arriving in France in October 1799 Napoleon was greeted with a hero's welcome. The people had heard only of his victories in Egypt and were convinced that he was the man of the hour. Within a few weeks of his return, he joined a conspiracy that was plotting to overthrow the unpopular Directory. On November 9, with the aid of loyal troops, Napoleon compelled the legislators to resign and to turn power over to him and his group.

The coup d'état was soon followed by the promulgation of a constitution that established a dictatorship under the guise of parliamentary government. Napoleon took the title "first consul" (recalling the chief magistrate of republican Rome) and, as chief executive for ten years, held the reins of power. Two other consuls shared the executive but possessed only nominal authority. By means of a plebiscite, the public overwhelmingly endorsed the constitution. Weary after ten years of chaotic revolutionary experiment, the French turned to a strong man whom they believed would restore civil and economic order and guarantee the gains of the revolution.

The Consulate

Napoleon brought to completion the centralizing process begun by Richelieu and Mazarin and provided France with an honest and efficient government. Although he professed to sympathize with the principles of the French Revolution, he was above all a realist, not an ideologue. He continued certain reforms of the revolution that were popular with the nation and that also served his own purpose. On the other hand, he reversed some of the revolutionary gains by suppressing all forms of free expression and by instituting a new form of absolutism. He truly believed that political and social liberties would undermine good government and lead to anarchy. His regime had many of the characteristics of enlightened despotism, which France had eluded in the eighteenth century.

Napoleon wanted to end the war with the other European nations so that he could consolidate his position at home. A combination of brilliant military maneuvers and skillful diplomacy broke the coalition by 1801, leaving Great Britain alone at war with France. Exhausted and isolated, the British were receptive to peace overtures and the following year signed the Peace of Amiens. For the French it was a generous settlement, allowing them to retain most of their European conquests.

The short period of peace enabled Napoleon to concentrate on achieving domestic and financial stability. One of his chief concerns was to heal the breach between church and state that had been created by the Civil Constitution of the Clergy. After protracted

Napoleon's Views on Religion

Conversation with General Gourgaud, August 28, 1817:
"I have been reading the bible," [said the Emperor]. "Jesus should have been hanged like scores of other fanatics who posed as the Prophet or the Messiah. . . . I prefer the religion of Mohomet: it is less ridiculous than ours."*

Conversation with General Bertrand, March 21, 1821, followed by the latter's comment:
"I am very glad that I have no religion," the Emperor remarked. "I find it a great consolation, as I have no imaginary terrors and no fear of the future. . . . " In actual fact the Emperor died a theist, believing in a rewarding God, the principle of all things. Yet he stated . . . in his will . . . that he had died in the Catholic religion because he believed that to be [the right thing to do in terms of] public ethics.**

Conversation with Comte Roederer, August 18, 1800:
"Morality? There is only one way to encourage moral-ity and that is to reestablish religion. Society cannot exist without some being richer than others, and this inequality cannot exist without religion. When one man is dying of hunger next door to another who is stuffing himself with food, the poor man simply cannot accept the disparity unless some authority exists which tells him 'God wishes it so. There have to be both rich and poor in this world: but in heaven things will be different.'"***

Napoleon understood that France was fundamentally Catholic and that reconciliation with the church would be beneficial both to the people and for his own policy. Personally irreligious, he pretended to be a Catholic in France and a Muslim while he was attempting to establish control over Egypt, and he once claimed that if he had occasion to govern a nation of Jews he would rebuild Solomon's temple.

*G. Gourgaud, St. Helena Journal, 1815–1818, trans. S. Gillard (London: Bodley Head, 1932), p. 259.
**General H. G. Bertrand, Napoleon at St. Helena: Journal of General Bertrand (Garden City, N.Y.: Doubleday, 1952), pp. 133, 181.
***M. Vitrac, ed., Autour de Bonaparte: Journal du Comte P. L. Roederer, trans. M. Hutt (Paris: H. Daragon, 1909), pp. 18–19.

negotiations he concluded an agreement, the Concordat of 1801, with Pope Pius VII (reigned 1800–1823). Under the terms of the Concordat, the pope agreed to give up all claims to church property confiscated during the revolution (which the state had broken up and sold mostly as small plots to the peasants) and to allow the state to appoint French bishops. In return, the state recognized Catholicism as the religion of the majority of French citizens and agreed to pay the salaries of the clergy. Napoleon thus not only removed a counterrevolutionary threat, but earned the gratitude of pious French Catholics and owners of former church property.

The Consulate also put the economy on a sound basis. The national debt was handled by issuing bonds bearing 5 percent interest to replace the various existing obligations. In 1800 Napoleon established the Bank of France (on the model of the Bank of Great Britain) for the purpose of lending money to businessmen as well as freeing the government from reliance on private credit. These measures, together with the systematization of tax collection and strict economies in all branches of government, made it possible to balance the budget in 1801–1802. Within two years Napoleon had succeeded in solving the financial problem that had precipitated the revolution and continued to vex the various governments throughout the 1790s.

Napoleon's most enduring domestic achievement was the codification of the laws. In the 1790s the revolutionary governments had taken the first steps in this direction, but it remained for Napoleon to bring the work to completion. The First Consul introduced the civil code in 1804, the first of five codes collectively called the Code Napoleon. The Code Napoleon preserved many of the revolutionary principles such as equality of all men before the law, religious toleration, equality of inheritance, abolition of serfdom, and the right to choose one's occupation. Still, in some respects the code was more reactionary than the laws of the revolutionary era. For example, it discriminated against illegitimate children, protected the interests of the employer by outlawing trade unions and strikes, and subordinated wives to the authority of their husbands. Whatever its faults, the code was an enormous improvement over what had existed before the revolution. Outside of France it greatly influenced the legal systems of Italy, Belgium, parts of Germany, Spain, a number of Latin American nations, and even Louisiana.

Like Caesar Augustus, Napoleon sometimes undermined the institutions he professed to be upholding. His primary concern was to strengthen his regime, not preserve the ideals of the Enlightenment and the French Revolution. That was apparent when he founded the Legion of Honor to reward civil as well as military merit. All decorations and symbols for meritorious service had been abolished during the revolution, but Napoleon recognized that everyone loved distinctions. In creating an aristocracy of merit he would add luster to his rule as well as bind the recipients closer to his person. In overhauling the educational system, Napoleon followed a similar pattern. He made provisions for a nationwide system of public education, creating a network of primary and secondary

The Granger Collection

Coronation of Napoleon and Josephine. Jacques Louis David's painting shows Josephine kneeling to be crowned empress by Napoleon. Moments earlier, Napoleon, defying tradition, had seized the crown from the pope and placed it on his own head. The pope resignedly accepted the indignity and paid the emperor back in kind by withdrawing while Napoleon read the constitutional oath.

schools and institutions of higher learning. However, Napoleon's aim was not so much to bring literacy to the masses as to groom competent administrators and instill moral and patriotic values in the citizenry.

Napoleon undoubtedly would have fulfilled the philosophes' ideal of an enlightened despot, but the reforms that he instituted in France were achieved at the high cost of suppressing liberty and restoring absolutism. Yet he enjoyed popular support from all classes except the diehard royalists and left-wing republicans. As a rule, his subjects were prepared to accept restriction of individual freedoms in exchange for order, prosperity, and the security of property.

Napoleon's Empire: From Triumph to Collapse

In 1802 Napoleon, taking advantage of his rising popularity, declared himself first consul for life. His ambition increased with each addition to his power, and in 1804 he crowned himself Napoleon I, Emperor of the French. Fearful of Napoleon's imperial designs on central Europe, Great Britain declared war on France once again in 1803. Britain was soon joined by the other continental powers. British warships under Lord Nelson (1758–1805) annihilated a French fleet off Cape Trafalgar on October 21, 1805, forcing Napoleon to postpone his scheme for invading Great Britain indefinitely. However, on land, where Napoleon could display his genius as a military commander, it was a different story. Between 1805 and 1807 he defeated in succession Austria, Prussia, and Russia, thus becoming the virtual ruler of continental Europe.

Napoleon extended to conquered lands the reforms he had already instituted in France. New legal codes were introduced, class distinctions abolished, peasants freed from serfdom, and the church subordinated to the state. The middle classes in these territories initially welcomed the French as liberators, but they became less enthusiastic when they discovered that Napoleon's imperial rule also brought political repression and financial exploitation.

By 1808 Napoleon was at the apex of his power, but British resistance had not been broken. Napoleon's inability to knock out Great Britain, the main obstacle to his dream of complete hegemony over Europe and the world beyond, led him to resort to economic strangulation. In laying down his new policy, called the Continental System, Napoleon prohibited the nations of continental Europe from importing British goods. He calculated that by depriving the British of their main export market, he would ruin their trade and commerce and ultimately secure an advantageous peace. The Continental System hurt Great Britain economically but failed to cripple it, principally because its sea power enabled it to develop new markets overseas and smuggle goods to old customers on the Continent. At the same time, his ban caused widespread antagonism to Napoleon's regime on the Continent. A heavy strain was placed on the economies of European nations dependent on Great Britain, not only for cheap manufactured goods, but also as a market for their food and raw materials. Many ships lay idle in ports, hundreds of industries closed down and unemployment rose sharply.

The Continental System not only produced economic distress in Europe, but Napoleon's attempts to enforce it also caused him unexpected difficulties. When Portu-

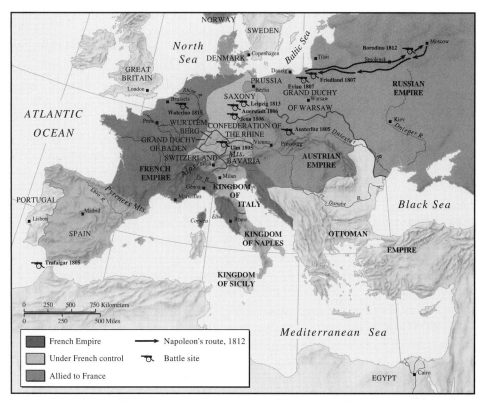

Map 12.1 Napoleon's Grand Empire. Besides pre-1789 France, Napoleon's empire included Belgium, the Netherlands, German lands to the Rhine and eastward to Hamburg, Italian towns down to Rome, Corsica, and the Illyrian provinces (in present-day Yugoslavia). Surrounding the empire were satellite states: the Confederation of the Rhine, the Grand Duchy of Warsaw, the Kingdom of Naples, Switzerland, and Spain. To the north and east were the allied states of Prussia, Austria, Russia, and Denmark.

gal, as an old ally of Great Britain, defied the Continental System in 1807, Napoleon's army poured into the Iberian Peninsula and entered Lisbon without resistance. French troops remained in Spain to protect the lines of communication and supply and ignored official requests to withdraw. Determined to retain control over Spain, Napoleon ousted the Bourbon dynasty and appointed his older brother Joseph to the vacant throne. His action provoked a popular uprising throughout Spain. The Spanish rebels waged guerrilla warfare against the French troops in the spirit of a holy war. The Peninsular War dragged on, draining Napoleon's treasury and tying down 400,000 French troops. "It was the Spanish ulcer," Napoleon later complained, "that ruined me."

Napoleon's assessment may have been an overstatement, but there is no doubt that his disastrous campaign into Russia in 1812 marked a crucial turning point in his fortunes. An almost exclusively agricultural country, Russia had suffered extreme economic distress when it was no longer able to exchange its surplus grain for British manufactured products. Weary of the hardships caused by the Continental System, the Russian tsar, Alexander I (reigned 1801–1825), decided to open his ports to British ships. Napoleon, rather than see his system collapse, decided to punish the tsar.

In June 1812 Napoleon began the long march into Russia with an army of 600,000 men, the largest yet assembled under a single command. Reluctant to face Napoleon in a single great battle, the Russians retreated steadily inland, destroying homes and burning crops as they withdrew. Napoleon advanced over 500 miles before he fought a major engagement, at Borodino, about 75 miles from Moscow, on September 7. Both sides suffered heavy losses, but the French won out and a week later entered Moscow. Almost immediately a fire broke out and destroyed much of the city, leaving the invaders to face a Russian winter without housing and supplies. Napoleon waited five weeks for a surrender that never came, and it was not until October 19 that he ordered a retreat along the same route. The delay had catastrophic consequences. Lack of food and an early, severe winter turned the withdrawal into a rout. Discipline broke down and the once proud Grand Army dissolved into a horde of desperate fugitives struggling to stay alive. When the French army regrouped near the Russian border in mid-December, it contained about 50,000 men. The rest, over half a million, had died of battle wounds or frost or famine or had been captured by pursuing Russians.

The defeat destroyed the myth that Napoleon was invincible, and one by one the European nations joined against him in another formidable coalition. After a complex ebb and flow of military victories and defeats, Napoleon was driven back into France in 1814 and agreed to abdicate. He was exiled to the Mediterranean island of Elba, but returned to France in 1815 and resumed imperial power for a last brief interlude of glory known as the Hundred Days. At the Battle of Waterloo on June 29, 1815, he was decisively beaten by a combined Anglo-Prussian military force led by the "Iron Duke," the British Duke of Wellington. Forced to abdicate once more, Napoleon was sent to a lonely exile on the bleak Atlantic island of St. Helena, where he died in 1821.

Napoleon's defeat can be attributed to a number of interrelated factors. Perhaps his greatest mistake was to neglect his navy, which prevented him from striking directly at Great Britain and effectively enforcing the Continental System. Other factors include the sheer exhaustion of France after twenty years of almost uninterrupted warfare, the backlash in Europe against his rule caused by growing nationalism, and his massive ego, which betrayed him into undertaking unsound schemes such as the invasion of Russia.

Napoleon's career has been the subject of endless debate. Determining the balance between good and harm done by Napoleon is difficult. He was in many ways a thorough reactionary, and the cost of his wars in terms of death, destruction, and human misery was incalculable. Throughout his career he remained convinced that the end justified the means. Yet his accomplishments in the sphere of domestic reform cannot be matched in any other comparable period in French history. His major legal and administrative reforms survived his fall and became part of the machinery of government and society, not only in France but in many other European nations as well. Perhaps the best brief characterization of Napoleon is that of the eminent French historian Alexis de Tocqueville: "He was as great as a man can be without virtue."

Reform and Revolution in the Nineteenth Century

The Kings of Württemberg and Denmark arrived before any of the others . . . but the ceremony which by its pomp and splendor was evidently intended to crown the series of wonders of the Congress was the solemn entry of Tsar Alexander and the King of Prussia. . . .

From the moment Vienna assumed an aspect which was as bright as it was animated. Numberless magnificent carriages traversed the city in all directions [the imperial stables held fourteen hundred horses at the disposal of the royal guests]. . . . The promenades and squares teemed with soldiers of all grades, dressed in the varied uniforms of all the European armies. Added to these were the swarms of the servants of the aristocracy in their gorgeous liveries. . . . When night came, the theatres, the cafés, the public resorts were filled with animated crowds, apparently bent on pleasure only. . . . In almost every big thoroughfare there was the sound of musical instruments discoursing joyous tunes. Noise and bustle everywhere. . . . Hence it is not surprising that the extraordinary expenses of the fêtes of the Congress, during the . . . months of its duration, amounted to forty millions of francs.

Doubtless, at no time of the world's history had more grave and complex interests been discussed amidst so many fêtes. A kingdom was cut into bits or enlarged at a ball; an indemnity was granted in the course of a dinner; a constitution was planned during a hunt; now and again a cleverly placed word or a happy and pertinent remark cemented a treaty. . . . *

*Comte A. de la Garde Chambonas, *Anecdotal Recollections of the Congress of Vienna,* ed. Comte Fleury (London: Chapman and Hall, 1902), pp. 1–3, 12, 29.

In the autumn of 1814, a brilliant gathering of kings, princes, and statesmen assembled in the animated capital of the Habsburg Empire to draw up a peace settlement. As host to the treaty makers, the Austrian government sponsored extravagant festivities, operas, and balls. For ten months, rulers and diplomats, when not dining or dancing, worked to remake the map of Europe. As a rule, they tried to restore conditions as they had been before the French Revolution. They took precautions against a possible renewal of French aggression, returned legitimate monarchs to their thrones whenever feasible, established a balance of power in Europe, and set up a mechanism to crush revolutionary outbreaks at their source before they could spread.

In the aftermath of the Congress of Vienna, most European regimes pursued conservative policies. Monarchies, supported by the aristocracy and clerical hierarchy, resisted the demands of the bourgeoisie and workers for constitutional government or national independence. The inevitable clash between the proponents of the old order and those of change produced a rash of revolutions in Europe in the decade after 1820. The continental powers, in particular Austria, played a central role in preserving the status quo. By maintaining stability and suppressing dissent at home they were able to shore up less secure authoritarian regimes elsewhere. The revolutions were stamped out nearly everywhere in Europe. This was not the case in Latin America, however. Restless South Americans, inspired by the American and French revolutions and benefiting from liberal versus conservative struggles in Europe, seized the opportunity to secure their independence and founded new nations.

By mid-century, however, new historical trends—nationalism and industrialization—had changed the social and economic conditions of life. New political philosophies challenged the traditional systems of governance. The revolutions of 1848, though they failed to curtail the abuses of absolutist governments, were harbingers of more effective and permanent reform movements to follow.

Restoration and Conservatism versus Reform and Revolution

At the Congress of Vienna, the delegates of the major powers—Great Britain, Austria, Russia, and Prussia—formed an inner circle and decided the most important questions, rarely bothering to consult with the representatives of the lesser states. Prince Klemens von Metternich (1773–1859), the foreign minister of Austria, dominated the inner circle. Metternich was determined to inaugurate an era of stability in Europe by suppressing liberal ideas and restoring the balance of power.

The first objective of the peacemakers was to guard against renewed French aggression. France's boundaries were pushed back essentially to where they had been before the outbreak of the revolutionary wars. To contain France within its frontiers, strong buffer states were established around it. Next, Metternich and his colleagues tried to restore the status quo before the French Revolution, returning legitimate monarchs to their thrones and establishing a balance of power in Europe. The Bourbon monarchy, for example, was restored to the French throne in the person of Louis XVIII. The Congress of Vienna also made every effort to distribute the spoils of war fairly among the victors

Map 12.2 Europe after the Congress of Vienna. The boundaries established at the Congress of Vienna were intended to prevent any one state from dominating continental affairs. France was reduced to its pre-1792 borders. Great Britain, despite its key role in overthrowing Napoleon, received only a few naval bases. The Netherlands acquired Belgium, and Prussia gained the Rhineland and much of Saxony. Russia obtained Finland and considerable Polish territories.

or to compensate them for lost territory; thus some territories came under foreign domination once again.

Although the representatives at the Congress of Vienna could not undo the impact of the French Revolution and the era of Napoleon, they did formulate a settlement that helped to preserve the general peace in Europe for almost a century; in that sense the Treaty of Vienna stands as one of the better treaties of the modern era. At the same time, by ignoring democratic and nationalist sentiments, the statesmen at Vienna opened the door to popular unrest and revolution in some European nations. After 1815, many Europeans were determined to regain the social and political advantages they had lost at Vienna; others, once again living under alien governments, were equally determined to throw off foreign domination.

On the heels of the congress, Austria, Russia, Britain, and Prussia joined in the Quadruple Alliance, committing themselves to police the peace settlement for twenty years and to meet regularly to discuss common problems. Metternich was determined to use the league as an international police force to suppress liberal and nationalist movements before they could lead to general war. In 1818 France, having shown good behavior, was admitted into the group, which then became the Quintuple Alliance. This instrument to regulate international conduct, known as the "Concert of Europe," was in some ways a forerunner of the League of Nations. During its early years, it functioned successfully, stamping out popular uprisings in Naples, the Kingdom of Sardinia, and Spain. The system was weakened in 1824 when Great Britain, to protect its vital interests, withdrew from the alliance (see the next section).

Metternich's Conservative Credo

There is besides scarcely any epoch which does not offer a rallying cry to some particular faction. This cry, since 1815, has been Constitution. But do not let us deceive ourselves.... Everywhere it means change and trouble....

Governments having lost their balance, are frightened, intimidated, and thrown into confusion....

We are convinced that society can no longer be saved without strong and vigorous resolutions on the part of the Governments.... By this course the monarchs will fulfill the duties imposed upon them by Him who, by entrusting them with power, has charged them to watch over the maintenance of justice and the rights of all....

The first principle to be followed by the monarchs ... should be that of maintaining the stability of political institutions....

The first and greatest concern for the immense majority of every nation is the stability of the laws....

Let them be just, but strong: beneficent, but strict.

Let them maintain religious principles in all their purity....

In short, let the great monarchs strengthen their union, and prove to the world that if it exists, it is beneficent, and ensures the political peace of Europe ... that the principles which they profess are paternal and protective, menacing only the disturbers of public tranquility.

Metternich's statement of his political principles, written in 1820 at the request of Tsar Alexander I, was designed to justify his policy and refute the ideas that had spawned the revolution.

*Richard Metternich, ed., Memoirs of Prince Metternich, vol. 2 (New York: Harper, 1881), pp. 322–337.

After 1815, most European governments followed policies that were compatible with Metternich's conservative ideas. In France, the monarch, Charles X (reigned 1824–1830), in a bid to restore royal absolutism, canceled the constitution instituted by his predecessor, Louis XVIII. His action set off a popular uproar, and angry Parisians erected barricades in the streets. After three days of fierce fighting, the rebels drove the royal troops from the city, prompting Charles to abdicate. Representatives of the people offered the crown to Louis Philippe, the Duke of Orleans and a relative of the Bourbons, who promptly accepted it. In open defiance of the settlement of 1815, a popular revolt had driven a legitimate monarch from the throne.

The French rebellion of 1830 sparked revolutions elsewhere in Europe. The Belgians overthrew Dutch rule and established an independent constitutional monarchy. The Poles were less fortunate in their struggle against Russia. They fought heroically, but by 1831 the much stronger Russian army had broken their resistance.

After 1830 Metternich's system operated with reduced effectiveness. France, like Great Britain, became committed to a more moderate foreign policy. In contrast, Austria, Prussia, and Russia were firmly resolved to prevent any more breaches in the Vienna settlement. In 1833 they formally pledged to render joint assistance to any monarch threatened by revolution. The forces of nationalism and democracy, however, reinforced by new ideologies, were too powerful to be repressed for long.

Revolt and Independence in Latin America

The aftershocks of the French Revolution and the era of Napoleon were also felt in Latin America. At the beginning of the nineteenth century, Spain, with its huge block of possessions in the Western Hemisphere, rivaled Great Britain as a major European colonial power. The Spanish Empire in America, however, along with Portugal's, soon crumbled under the twin pressures of upheavals at home and revolt in the colonies.

For centuries, Spanish and Portuguese colonists had chafed under economic deprivations, and many Creoles had resented the political power of the Peninsulars sent to govern them. Influenced by the republican political principles instituted in the United States of America and by the reforms of the French Revolution and Napoleon, some Creoles hoped to create comparable liberal institutions in Latin America, at least for the upper classes. Some of the more radical wanted to disestablish the Roman Catholic church and tax or confiscate its property. Few gave much thought to the needs of the masses of workers and peasants.

The revolutionary era was launched, however, not by Creoles but by black slaves and mulatto freemen. In the 1790s, black slaves in the French Caribbean colony of Saint Dominique (Haiti) revolted and drove out white authority. Toussaint L'Ouverture, the rebel leader, created a disciplined army and fended off attacks by other European nations and revolts by mulatto factions. He abolished slavery before the republican government of France belatedly terminated it in all French possessions. Napoleon, however, flirting with thoughts of recreating the old French empire in the Western Hemisphere, decided to restore white rule in Haiti and the old plantation system in the French Caribbean. He sent an army to subdue Haiti, but the climate, yellow fever, and the resistance of blacks destroyed the French in a struggle punctuated by racial massacres. L'Ouverture was captured, however, and died in a French prison. In 1804 Jean Jacques Dessalines proclaimed the independence of the new nation of Haiti, proclaiming himself emperor. The success of the blacks of Haiti disturbed conservative nations in general and slaveholding nations in particular. Haiti was shunned in diplomatic circles for decades.

The main struggle for Latin American independence began in 1807–1808. When Napoleon deposed the Bourbon monarchy in Spain, royal authority throughout Spanish America weakened. Argentina removed itself from royal control in 1810 and formally proclaimed independence in 1816. Rebels in Venezuela pronounced their liberation in 1811. Simón Bolívar (1783–1830), a Venezuelan aristocrat who had taken an oath to free his country from Spain, became the hero of Latin American independence movements. For seven years Bolívar's fortunes fluctuated from splendid victories to humiliating defeats and exile. Finally, his forces decisively defeated the Spanish in Colombia in 1819 and in Venezuela in 1821. The triumphant rebels hailed him as "Liberator." Meanwhile, in 1817, José de San Martin made a spectacular surprise crossing of the high Andes passes from Argentina into Chile and drove out the Spanish in 1818. With the aid of the British and Chileans, he built a navy and in 1821 landed in Lima, Peru, the heart of the Spanish authority in South America. Bolívar moved south in 1822 through Ecuador to join forces with San Martin against the remaining Spanish army. San Martin returned to Argentina, and Bolívar, taking command of the combined armies, crushed the last remnants of Spanish authority at Ayacucho, Peru, in 1824. Ironically, it was victory over the Inkas in the same Andean highlands three centuries earlier that had given the Spanish control over most of South America.

The Spanish were not the only threat to the South American revolutionaries. Conservative nations in Europe had smashed a liberal revolution in Spain in 1822 and restored the deposed monarch. Some of these nations also considered sending troops to Latin America to eradicate the rebellion there against the Spanish monarchy, and perhaps pick up some territory of their own in the Americas. The British government, however, opposed European intervention, realizing that independence had opened up an entire continent to trade and investment. Since the British navy could block any expedition across the Atlantic, the invasion scheme was dropped. Wishing to strengthen its own influence in the hemisphere, the United States, after consulting with Great Britain, issued the Monroe Doctrine (1823) to voice its opposition to European interference. However, the attitude of that weak nation was virtually irrelevant at the time.

The Granger Collection

The Liberator. This portrait of Simón Bolívar depicts a remarkable man. On a dozen battlefields, he liberated one-third of South America from Spanish rule.

Whereas independence movements in South America had essentially been struggles among members of the European-descended upper classes, Mexico's path to independence was marked by class revolution and even race warfare. Various Creole groups and Peninsulars engaged in confused maneuverings from 1808 until 1810, when the upper classes were confronted by an uprising of mestizo and Amerindian peasants initially led by Father Miguel Hidalgo under the banner of the dark-skinned Virgin of Guadalupe. Hidalgo's demands for civil rights for the peasants alarmed the upper classes; liberal and conservative Creoles joined to crush the rebellion, and the revolutionary movement dissolved into guerrilla warfare. The 1820 liberal revolution in Spain inspired conservative Mexican Creoles to rebel. Agustín de Iturbide, a military adventurer, drew up the Plan of Iguala, which called for independence and promised something for all the elite groups in Mexico, without basic social and economic change. Iturbide had such overwhelming support that the Spanish were forced to concede the independence of Mexico in 1821. Social revolution was to recur in Mexico, however, as the twentieth century would show.

Compared with the wars and revolutions in Spanish America, Brazilians won their independence from Portugal relatively easily. While the Portuguese royal family was ruling in exile in Brazil, it opened the territory to free trade, encouraged immigration and industrial production, and formally confederated Brazil with Portugal as a joint kingdom. After King John VI returned to Portugal in 1820, leaving his son Pedro as regent, the Portuguese legislature began to strip Brazil of its status and repealed John's reforms. The exasperated Brazilians persuaded Pedro to support a break with Portugal and to proclaim an independent state in 1822. Portugal capitulated and recognized Brazilian independence in 1825. By that year the only European colonies remaining in the Western Hemisphere south of Canada were the Caribbean islands (except Santo Domingo) and a few small enclaves on the coasts of Central and South America.

By the 1830s nineteen new states had emerged in Latin America. Although each had its distinct social and political personality, their similarities, especially their common colonial heritage, far outweighed their differences. These new nations were dependent on the export and sale of agricultural and mineral raw materials. They imported manufactured goods from European nations and also became indebted to them for investment capital. Their own industrial output was low, and their outmoded production techniques, still dependent on cheap hand labor, resembled those of central and eastern Europe.

Despite these economic negatives, Latin America nonetheless had significant economic attractions, although not necessarily of benefit to the general population. The area contained abundant raw materials, and in some areas there were large populations that could be turned into lucrative markets. Latin American governments augmented these economic opportunities by offering tax breaks and other investment incentives. With the British in the vanguard, Europeans began to invest heavily in Latin America during the nineteenth century. European businessmen combined labor-saving technology with cheap labor to create enormously profitable plantations and mines and later factories, roads, railroads, telegraph networks, and petroleum refineries.

The social and political characteristics of the Latin American states also reflected colonial conditions. Rich property holders and the Catholic church continued to wield eco-

Bolívar Ponders a Suitable Government for Spanish America

The diversity of racial origin will require an infinitely firm hand and great tactfulness to manage this heterogeneous society, whose complex mechanism is easily ... disintegrated by the slightest controversy....

It is a marvel that the [federal] prototype in North America endures so successfully and has not been overthrown at the first sign of adversity or danger.... But ... never ... compare the position and character of two states as dissimilar as the English-American and Spanish-American. We [are] not prepared for such good. ... Our moral fiber [does] not ... possess the stability necessary to derive benefits from a wholly representative government....

Thus I recommend ... the study of the British Constitution ... for that body of laws appears destined to bring about the greatest possible good for the peoples that adopt it; but ... I only refer to its republican features; and indeed can a political system be labeled a monarchy when it recognizes popular sovereignty, division and balance of powers, civil liberty, freedom of conscience and press, and all that is politically sublime? ... [It serves] as a model for those who aspire to the enjoy-

ment of the rights of man and who seek all the political happiness which is compatible with frailty of human nature.*

Writing in 1819, when the future of the independence movement was still in doubt, Simón Bolívar recommended a house of representatives elected by a restricted franchise and a hereditary senate of specially trained and educated members. He also suggested an elected chief executive, reelectable for long terms, and an independent judiciary. Influenced by his readings in Enlightenment thought and by the limitations placed on him because he was a Creole, Bolívar was a radical, demanding equality before the law. He favored limiting political power to the middle and upper classes for the foreseeable future until the masses were educated and their economic condition uplifted. By 1826 the final divisive struggle for independence and the rampant factionalism after independence had made Bolívar more conservative. He created a government for Bolivia that resembled the authoritarian state under Napoleon.

**"Address to the Second National Congress of Venezuela," trans. L. Bertrand, in Selected Writings of Bolívar, ed. Harold A. Bierck (New York: Colonial Press, 1951), pp. 174–197, passim.*

nomic and political power in Spanish America; they were now joined by the national military establishments of the new nations. Independence brought few economic improvements for the masses, who continued to work for the elite. Like the eastern European peasantry, the peons received little pay and lacked decent housing, adequate food, proper sanitation, and basic education.

On paper, the constitutions of Spanish American states were influenced by revolutionary France and the United States. They set up liberal republics with elected officers, civil liberties, equality before the law, and varying degrees of religious toleration. In reality, however, these ideals were difficult to realize in societies composed of a tiny elite at the top and an impoverished and uneducated mass at the bottom. Civil rights were not extended to the masses, and political involvement was limited to a few opportunistic individuals and cliques. Politics was often tainted by fraud and corruption, and elections were frequently overturned by the armed forces, who installed dictators. Two groups emerged in most nations—the conservatives and the liberals: the conservatives stood for preserving the prerogatives and powers of the upper classes and the church, whereas the liberals wished to break down these privileges so that the small, mostly mestizo, middle class could share economic and political power.

1848: The Year of Revolutions

In 1848 an outburst of revolutionary activity occurred throughout much of Europe. Among the major European powers, only Great Britain and Russia were relatively unaffected. The causes of the upheavals varied, but economic distress, nationalism, and liberalism were all potent factors.

As in the past, upheavals in France stoked the fires of revolution through the rest of Europe. A severe economic crisis in 1846–1847 increased working-class opposition to the monarchy and led to a protest campaign that culminated in the overthrow of Louis Philippe. For the second time in a generation, constitutional monarchy had failed in France. In the last days of February 1848 political power passed to a provisional government that proclaimed France a republic and ordered the writing of a new constitution. The government was dominated by moderate elements, but included several socialists led by Louis Blanc, who organized national workshops to provide employment for the poor. The national workshops were public projects that never developed into self-supporting

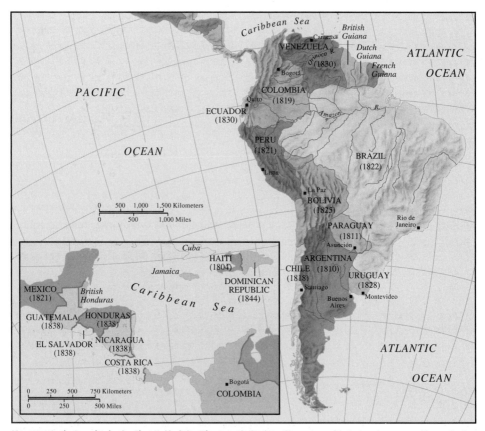

Map 12.3 Latin America in the First Half of the Nineteenth Century. The nations of Latin America appeared in two basic stages. Ten nations achieved independence from Spain and Portugal between 1810 and 1822. The rest appeared when regional issues in the infant nations resulted in secessions between 1825 and 1844.

industrial enterprises as Blanc had intended; instead, they degenerated into a straight dole for unemployed workers.

In April the French voters elected a Constituent Assembly that was much more conservative than the provisional government. One of the first acts of the new Assembly was to dissolve the workshops. Violent reaction to this legislation was brutally crushed and thousands of rebels were executed or deported to penal colonies overseas.

By the autumn of 1848, the Assembly had completed a constitution for the Second French Republic. It declared property inviolable and scrapped a proposed "right to work" clause. It acknowledged free speech, freedom of the press, and security from arbitrary

Map 12.4 Principal Centers of Revolution, 1848–1849. The uprisings all over Europe in 1848 ultimately failed, not only because of the strength of the conservatives but also because hostile national minorities fell out with each other and antagonisms developed between the anticapitalist urban workers and the bourgeoisie. The reactionary regimes responded quickly and quenched the flickering flames of liberty and nationalism in the insurgent countries.

arrest. It provided for a president vested with strong executive powers and a single leg-islative body elected by universal male suffrage (women continued to be excluded from the political process). Thus France emerged from the 1848 revolution as a middle-class rather than a worker's republic.

Reforms in France inspired groups in Prussia and Austria to demand more representa-tive governments and the abolition of remaining feudal practices. In western Europe, where constitutional government had already been achieved, liberals wanted political power extended to all classes. A general economic crisis heightened the tensions of 1848 and fed popular discontent.

The revolutions of 1848 did not spring only from demands for political and economic reforms. Nationalistic ideals inspired Germans and Italians, who were divided among many political entities, to make a bid for national unity. Nationalist fervor also provoked the subject peoples of the Austrian Empire to seek political independence.

Inspired by noble aims, the revolutionary movements of 1848 began with great prom-ise, but in most cases ended in defeat and disappointment, particularly in central and eastern Europe. The revolutionaries gained the upper hand in the opening stages because the European governments were reluctant to use their superior armed forces.

Revolutionary Fighters Resisting Royal Forces, Berlin, March 18–19, 1848. Most of the insurgents were artisans, but merchants and students also participated in the fighting. The victorious Berliners forced King Frederick William to go through a grotesque ceremony of saluting the corpses of slain revolutionaries. Recalling the incident in later life, Frederick William remarked, "We all crawled on our bellies."

Another element explaining the failure of the revolutions was the disintegration of the alliance between middle-class liberals and urban workers. In general, the various groups seeking political concessions made uneasy allies. The middle class favored reforms that would give them a fair share of political control but were unsympathetic to the workers' demands for social and economic change. Finally, long-established ethnic rivalries often divided nationalist movements in central Europe. Eventually, the reactionary governments regained the initiative and moved quickly. Using military force, and often playing one ethnic group off against another, the established order crushed the uprisings.

Although the 1848 revolutions failed to achieve many of their goals, they left their mark on Europe. France adopted universal male suffrage; serfdom was abolished in the Austrian Empire; and parliaments were established in all the German states, though most were not democratic. After 1848 many reformers became convinced that violence was not the best way to reshape society and placed their faith in the British example of gradualism and peaceful change. Others, most notably the Marxists (see next section), continued to struggle for revolutionary transformation of existing political and social systems.

Nationalism and Political Conflict in the West: 1848–1914

Standing erect, his gaze firmly fixed on those who were awaiting him, the image of venerable nobility, the aged monarch [William I] ascended the dais where he would be crowned. . . . There he stood on the very place once occupied by Louis XIV's chair of state, dressed in the uniform of his First Regiment of Foot Guards, adorned with the ribbon of the Order of the Black Eagle as well as a number of other orders, . . .

The Crown Prince energetically commanded, "Remove your helmets to pray!", whereupon Rogge, the court chaplain, recited the liturgy according to Prussian military usage, followed by a performance of a soldier's choir. . . .

Then Bismarck, his face pale, wearing tall riding-boots so that he looked like a giant, bowed deeply before the approaching Emperor. On his shoulders he wore the epaulettes of a lieutenant-general, for he had just been promoted to that rank. In his left hand he held his massive helmet, in his right hand the coronation charter, which he read. . . . Then I heard the Grand Duke von Baden shout in a loud voice. "His Majesty Wilhelm the Victorious, long may he live!" Three times a thundering "Long live the Emperor!" issued from innumerable throats . . . ; flags fell, sabers were drawn from their sheaths, helmets were waved in the air. Again and again the soldiers roared "Hurrah's," almost drowning out the three regimental bands playing "Hail to thee in the victor's wreath!" as loud as they could.*

*Wilhelm Stieber, *The Chancellor's Spy: The Revelations of the Chief of Bismarck's Secret Service* (New York: Grove, 1979), pp. 211–212.

This scene in the Hall of Mirrors in Versailles on January 18, 1871, marked the culmination of the German people's quest for a unified German Empire. It also symbolized the replacement of France by Germany as the most powerful continental European nation. A decade earlier the Italians had also realized their dreams for national unification. Similarly a number of Christian Slavic peoples in the Balkan Peninsula achieved nationhood at the expense of the crumbling Islamic Ottoman Empire. However, the nationalistic aspirations of the Slavs in the Austro-Hungarian Empire remained unfulfilled. Non-Russians in the Russian Empire likewise remained victims of the official policy of Russification.

Newly unified Italy and Germany, together with Great Britain and France as well as the multinational Austro-Hungarian and Russian Empires, shared in varying degrees the social problems caused by the Industrial Revolution. At the same time, the better-educated and increasingly vocal populations in these states demanded political reforms. This section will explore these major themes.

The Second Napoleonic Empire

France continued its turbulent quest for a viable political structure throughout the nineteenth century. When the 1848 revolution overthrew the Orleanist monarchy of Louis Philippe, a Second Republic was briefly established, but it in turn was overthrown in an almost bloodless coup by the popularly elected president, Louis Napoleon Bonaparte. In 1852 Bonaparte established the Second Empire, giving himself the title of Napoleon III (reigned 1852–1870); all his actions were then duly ratified by a plebiscite. Although the governmental structure during the early years of the Second Empire retained the outward forms of a parliamentary system, the emperor had almost unlimited authority, controlling the army, foreign affairs, legislation, and finance. The Legislative Assembly, which was elected by male suffrage, lacked the power to initiate or amend bills. It could only vote for or against the emperor's proposals, and elections were often rigged to return government-sponsored candidates.

Napoleon III did much to develop the French economy and industry, to beautify Paris, and to make France the cultural center of Europe. Eager to emulate the military glory and conquests of his uncle, Napoleon I, he engaged in an active foreign policy, which initially was successful. He joined Great Britain and the Ottoman Empire against Russia in the Crimean War (1853–1856), fought alongside the British against China (1858–1860), and battled the Austrians (1859) to help the Italians in their drive for national unification.

Up to 1860 most Frenchmen did not object to Napoleon III's benevolently despotic government, which offered them order, prosperity, and glory. After 1860, however, his popularity and authority began to crumble, as a result of successive failures in foreign policy. His attempt to create an empire in Mexico was a fiasco that eroded his prestige and damaged French interests, as did the diplomatic setbacks he then experienced in German affairs. Napoleon countered with wide-ranging concessions in an attempt to save his tottering throne. Under the new, "liberal" phase of his empire, Napoleon relaxed press censorship, legalized strikes, and even allowed an opposition to form in the Legislative Assembly. As of 1870 France under Napoleon III apparently remained the leading power on the European continent.

The Triumph of Nationalism in Italy

Italy had not known national unity since the fall of the Roman Empire. It was a patchwork of petty states, or as Metternich had once contemptuously remarked, "a geographical expression." The revolutions of 1848–1849 had failed to unify Italy, leaving Austria more firmly entrenched in the north. After these events, the prospect of Italian national unity seemed more remote than ever. Yet not everything had been in vain. Sardinia, a kingdom comprised of Piedmont and the island of Sardinia, emerged from the conflict with an enhanced prestige because of its liberal constitution and its gallant stand against Austria. More and more Italian patriots looked to the ruler of Sardinia, Victor Emmanuel II (reigned 1849–1878), as the natural leader. Victor Emmanuel was neither inspiring nor a first-class statesman, but he had a good deal of common sense. He showed much wisdom when he selected as his prime minister Count Camillo di Cavour (1810–1861), who was to play a vital role in the unification drama. Cavour, a practitioner of cool, tough-minded statecraft, dominated Italian politics from 1852 until his premature death in 1861. In the early years in office, he strengthened Sardinia with numerous domestic reforms that made it the model Italian state.

The main barrier to Italian unity was Austria, which controlled Lombardy and Venetia in the northeast and dominated the Italian reactionary states. Cavour realized that Sardinia was too small to tackle Austria without allies. Thus he sought to gain favor with Great Britain and France by participating on their side in the Crimean War. Subsequently, he met Napoleon III and promised to cede the Sardinian provinces of Nice and Savoy to France in return for his help in a future war against Austria.

With French military aid assured, Cavour provoked Austria to declare war on Sardinia in 1859. Napoleon, true to his word, quickly moved his troops into Italy and,

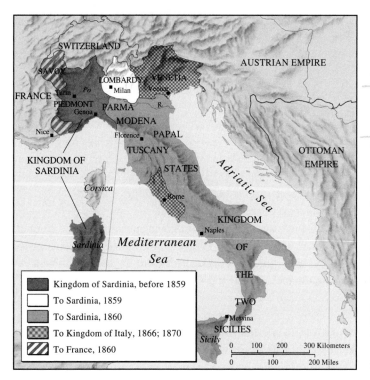

Map 12.5 The Unification of Italy. With the help of France, Sardinia (which included Piedmont) acquired Lombardy in a war against Austria in 1859. Soon afterward, revolutionaries seized power in Modena, Tuscany, Parma, and Romagna (one of the papal states) and voted to join with Sardinia. The nationalist movement spread south and culminated in a new Italian state that included all of the peninsula except Venetia and Rome. Italy received Venetia as a reward for being Prussia's ally in the Seven Weeks' War and took possession of Rome in 1870 when France withdrew its garrison.

Garibaldi Calls on Italians to Fight for Unity

Italians! . . . It is the duty of every Italian to succor [the Sicilian rebels] with words, money, and arms, and above all, in person. . . .

The misfortunes of Italy arise from the indifference of one province to the fate of others.

The redemption of Italy began from the moment that men of the same land ran to help their distressed brothers. . . .

Let the inhabitants of the free provinces lift their voices in behalf of their brethren, and impel their brave youth to the conflict. . . .

A band of those who fought with me the country's battles marches with me to the fight. Good and generous, they will fight for their country to the last drop of their blood, nor ask for other reward than a clear conscience.

"Italy and Victor Emmanuel!" . . .

At this cry . . . the rotten Throne of tyranny shall crumble . . .

*To arms! Let me put an end, once and for all, to the miseries of so many centuries. Prove to the world that it is no lie that Roman generations inhabited this land.**

Giuseppe Garibaldi, the author of this manifesto issued from Sicily in 1860, was a romantic adventurer and the embodiment of Italian military nationalism, as Cavour was its civilian genius. The self-educated Garibaldi was a sailor in his youth and in 1833 joined the cause of Italian unity. He was condemned to death and fled to Latin America, where he was involved in civil wars in Brazil and Uruguay. He returned to Italy during the revolutions of 1848 and fought for Sardinia against Austria.

In 1849 Garibaldi and a volunteer legion tried but failed to defend a republican uprising in Rome against French and Austrian forces; once again he fled for his life, this time to the United States, where he became a citizen. In 1854 he returned to Sardinia. After turning over his forces to Victor Emmanuel in 1861, Garibaldi temporarily retired. In 1862 and 1866 he raised a third and a fourth set of volunteers and twice marched on Rome with the goal of incorporating it into the Italian kingdom. He was defeated both times, first by Victor Emmanuel (who did not want to antagonize the French), then by papal and French forces; taken prisoner twice and released twice. In 1870 Garibaldi, now sixty-three, and his two sons fought as volunteers in the French army against Prussia. In the years before his death in 1882, he became a supporter of socialism.

*"Proclamation for the Liberation of Sicily," Public Documents, The Annual Register, 1860 (London, 1861), pp. 281–282; in Perry M. Rogers, ed., Aspects of Western Civilization: Problems and Sources in History, 2d ed. (Englewood Cliffs, N.J., 1992), 2.225–226.

along with the Sardinians, drove the Austrians out of Lombardy. French military and economic costs were high, however, and Napoleon, without consulting Cavour, concluded a separate peace in which Austria gave up Lombardy but not Venetia. The Sardinian leaders considered the settlement inadequate, but their disappointment was only temporary. Sardinia's victory over Austria had spurred nationalistic uprisings that expelled unpopular rulers from the small states on the upper peninsula and brought all of northern Italy except Venetia into union with Sardinia. In return for Napoleon's acquiescence to the union, Cavour turned over Nice and Savoy as called for in the original agreement.

At this point a firebrand nationalist, Giuseppe Garibaldi (1807–1882), decided to complete the unification process. He raised a volunteer army and headed for Sicily, where a revolution had broken out against the reactionary Bourbon ruler of the Kingdom of the Two Sicilies. Garibaldi landed on the island on May 11, 1860, with 1,000 untrained volunteers (later called the Thousand) dressed in bright red shirts. Gathering strength as he campaigned, Garibaldi and his Red Shirts first conquered Sicily (see the accompanying box) and then crossed over to the mainland. He advanced on Naples, the capital of the kingdom, and, with the Bourbon ruler in flight, entered the city to the joyful acclaim of the populace. Garibaldi threatened to create a crisis when he proposed to march on Rome. Such a move, Cavour believed, was bound to offend France, which since 1849 had stationed a garrison in Rome to protect the pope. To head off Garibaldi, Victor Emmanuel personally led an army south and on the way seized all the papal lands save for Rome and its environs. Just north of Naples, he met Garibaldi, who agreed to give up his command and turn over his conquests. On March 17, 1861, the Kingdom of Italy was proclaimed, with Victor Emmanuel as king. When Cavour died three months later, only Venetia and Rome remained outside the new nation.

Cavour's political heirs completed Italian unification. During the Seven Weeks' War (Austro-Prussian War) in 1866, Italy allied itself with the victorious Prussians and gained Venetia. The outbreak of the Franco-Prussian War in July 1870 compelled Napoleon to recall the French troops from Rome. On September 20, 1870, Italian troops took possession of Rome, except for the few square miles enclosing the Vatican City. Rome was annexed to Italy and became its capital.

The Unification of Germany

Germany, like Italy, had not been a unified state in modern times. German unification came about in a manner strikingly similar to the process that created the Kingdom of Italy. It was essentially the work of one man, who led the strongest and most prosperous of the interested states. The process was achieved in stages through a combination of complex political maneuvering and war. Here, too, the chief victim was Austria, which was ejected as completely from Germany as it had been from Italy.

During the revolutions of 1848, liberal nationalists from the various German states had met at Frankfurt and attempted to create a unified Germany. Their effort was unsuccessful. In 1849 the conservatives regained power throughout Germany, dismissed the Frankfurt Assembly, and nullified its acts. In the aftermath of this failure, frustrated nationalists rejected vague abstractions and misty romantic ideals in favor of cynical realism and power politics. They had been influenced by Cavour's common-sense approach and became convinced that only Prussia was strong enough to play the role Sardinia had assumed in bringing about Italian unity.

Throughout the middle decades of the nineteenth century Prussia's economic infrastructure—industry, banking system, roads and railroads—grew by leaps and bounds. As a result, Prussia became the strongest of the German states, now joined in the *Zollverein* (customs union). In contrast, Austria, which had been excluded from the Zollverein, lagged behind in economic development; this undercut its traditional titular leadership of the German Confederation, a league created chiefly to provide a means of common defense against foreign attack.

During the 1860s the Hohenzollern ruler, King William I of Prussia (reigned 1861–1888), wished to build up the Prussian army. Stung by a recalcitrant Prussian legislature that opposed the new taxes needed to raise the requisite revenues, William was on the verge of abdicating when he appointed Otto von Bismarck (1815–1898) as minister-president. A consummate practitioner of *Realpolitik* (the pursuit of policy by any means), Bismarck, later known as the Iron Chancellor, stated bluntly how he proposed to conduct state

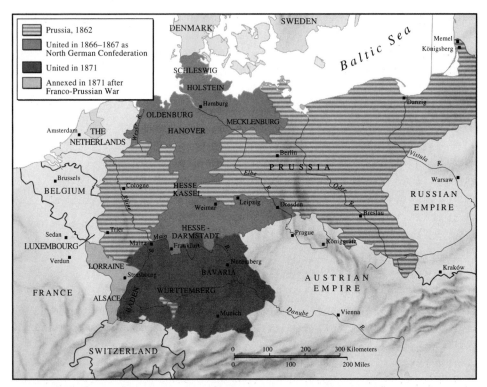

Map 12.6 The Unification of Germany. Prussia, under Bismarck's leadership, unified Germany in three stages. In 1864 Prussia and Austria defeated Denmark over the Schleswig-Holstein issue. Prussia then crushed Austria in a short war in 1866 and then set up the North German Confederation, headed by the Prussian king. Following Prussia's victory over France, the South German states joined the North German Confederation, which, together with Alsace and Lorraine, completed the formation of the German Empire.

business: "The great questions of the day are not to be decided by speeches and majority resolutions . . . but by blood and iron." When parliament continued to resist the proposed taxes, Bismarck ordered them collected anyway. By successfully defying parliament, Bismarck severely undermined the ideals of constitutionalism and liberalism and ensured that the monarchy and the military would dominate Germany's political life for decades to come.

Bismarck engineered three wars to complete German unification under Prussian leadership. The first was a short war against Denmark, in which Prussia and Austria fought together to prevent the Danes from annexing the duchies of Schleswig and Holstein, which had a large German population. After Denmark's defeat, Austrian and Prussian troops occupied the two duchies. Problems in setting up the administration of Schleswig and Holstein prompted Bismarck to harass Austria and maneuver it into declaring war against Prussia. Prussia had new and better weapons and a superb railway system that transported troops and supplies to any front with unprecedented speed. Victory came so quickly that the Austro-Prussian conflict was known as the Seven Weeks' War.

In the treaty that followed the war, Prussia gained territory in north Germany that closed the gap between Prussia's eastern and western provinces and added 5 million people. The treaty also dissolved the German Confederation and excluded Austria from German affairs in the future. In its place Bismarck welded the twenty-two German states north of the Main River into the North German Confederation under Prussian domination. German unification remained incomplete, however, because the four Catholic states of South Germany remained outside. These giant steps toward German unification squelched liberal parliamentary opposition to Bismarck's extraconstitutional methods.

To induce the South German states to join a Prussian-dominated Germany, Bismarck needed a common enemy to unite them. France, led by the vainglorious Napoleon III, was the obvious choice. Bismarck's opportunity came when the vacant Spanish throne was offered to Prince Leopold of Hohenzollern, a distant relative of King William I. Alarmed at the prospect of being encircled by Hohenzollerns, Napoleon protested so vehemently that William persuaded Leopold to withdraw his candidacy. Not content with his diplomatic victory, Napoleon sent his ambassador to the bathing resort of Ems to seek assurances from William that Leopold's candidacy would not be renewed in the future. William firmly but politely refused the French request and later wired an account of the interview to Bismarck, who was in Berlin. Bismarck saw an opportunity, as he described it, to "wave a red flag" before "a Gallic bull." He edited the king's telegram, which has become famous as the Ems Dispatch, to make it appear that the French ambassador and the Prussian king had insulted each other, and then leaked it to the press. The public in both nations were furious, but the French were more openly belligerent and the French government declared war first, in July 1870.

As Bismarck had anticipated, the Franco-Prussian War brought the divided Germans together. Portraying the struggle as a national war and whipping up patriotic sentiment, Bismarck drew in the South German states, and the combined German armies poured into France in three great columns. The battle-tried Prussians overwhelmed the poorly prepared and badly led French troops. Within six weeks the Germans encircled the main French army, commanded by Napoleon himself, and compelled it to surrender. They went on to lay siege to Paris, which was starved into submission on January 28, 1871.

Ten days before Paris capitulated and the French acknowledged defeat, William I was proclaimed German Emperor in the palace at Versailles. The new empire included the states of the North German Confederation, the South German states, and the former French provinces of Alsace and part of Lorraine, which were ceded to Germany by the peace treaty that formally ended the war in 1871.

The United States Creates an Indivisible National Union

At the time Latin Americans were expressing their sense of nationalism by winning independence, citizens of the United States, who had become independent two generations earlier, were beginning to confront the contradictory concepts of nationalism embodied in their federal form of government. Intensifying cultural animosity between the northern and southern regions of the country brought about decades of political, economic, and racial strife during the middle of the nineteenth century, culminating in a brutal civil

"Preserve, Protect, Defend"

I hold, that in contemplation of universal law, and of the Constitution, the Union of these States is perpetual. . . .

It follows from these views that no State . . . can lawfully get out of the Union . . . that resolves and ordinances to that effect are legally void, and the acts of violence, within any State or States, against the authority of the United States, are insurrectionary or revolutionary.

I therefore consider that, in view of the Constitution and the laws, the Union is unbroken; and to the extent of my ability, I shall take care, as the Constitution itself expressly enjoins upon me, that the laws of the Union be faithfully executed in all the States. . . . You have no oath registered in Heaven to destroy the government, while I shall have the most solemn one to "preserve, protect and defend" it.*

The mystic chords of memory, stretching from every battle-field, and patriot grave, to every living heart and hearthstone, all over this broad land, will yet swell the chorus of the Union. . . .

Four score and seven years ago, our fathers brought forth on this continent, a new nation, conceived in lib-

erty, and dedicated to the proposition that all men are created equal.

Now we are engaged in a great civil war, testing whether that nation, or any nation so conceived and so dedicated, can long endure. . . .

We here highly resolve that these dead shall not have died in vain—that this nation, under God, shall have a new birth of freedom—and that the government of the people, by the people, for the people, shall not perish from the earth.**

In these famous addresses, and in many other communications in the first half of the Civil War, Abraham Lincoln, employing both reason and emotion, stressed the nationalist concept of the indissoluble union as the main reason for fighting the war. Later, as in his Second Inaugural, Lincoln, perhaps because of the enormous suffering embodied in the conflict, took the more radical position that slavery, or possibly God's punishment of both sides for permitting slavery, was the basic cause of the war.

*First Inaugural Address, March 4, 1861, in Roy P. Basler, ed., The Collected Works of Abraham Lincoln, vol. 4 (New Brunswick, N.J.: Rutgers University Press, 1953), pp. 264–268 passim.

**Gettysburg Address, November 19, 1863, in Roy P. Basler, ed., The Collected Works of Abraham Lincoln, vol. 7 (New Brunswick, N.J.: Rutgers University Press, 1953), p. 23.

war. Out of this turmoil came a new, more active sense of nationalism in the minds of most Americans. By the turn of the century, many Americans would express their sense of nationalism in the same kind of superior, jingoistic terms that were commonplace among the other great powers, drawing the United States into the worldwide imperialist competition of that era.

From its inception, the Constitution of 1787 contained a deep ambiguity about the nature of the government of the United States. Men of equal talents and insights, such as Thomas Jefferson and Alexander Hamilton, could, and increasingly did, see their federal, two-level form of government quite differently. Some, increasingly centered in the southern states, believed that the separate states were the sovereign entities in the union. The states had created the national government and the states could dissolve it, or, failing that, individual states could withdraw from union with other states. In this view the great bulk of the regulation of personal behavior and property rights, so-called domestic matters, rested in the hands of the states. Radical thinkers along this line, such as John C. Calhoun, believed that the national government was in effect merely an "agent," an employee whose duty was to protect the domestic institutions of the individual states, particularly slavery. The authority of the national government was limited to a few areas where the collective authority was more effective than that of individual states: diplomacy and treaties, war with foreign states, fiscal and monetary policy, and interstate commerce.

At the same time, some Americans, increasingly centered in the North, had come to believe that the American people as a whole, not the states, had created the union. The states collectively could not dissolve it, nor could individual states secede from it. (Such "unionists," while tending to give greater scope to the power of the national government, agreed with their constitutional opponents that most personal and property concerns, as well as civil rights and liberties, were essentially in the domain of state authority; by and large, Americans did not look to the national government to regulate domestic matters until the twentieth century.)

This great difference in constitutional outlook intensified the economic and social differences that increasingly divided the United States into two distinct cultural regions after 1820. At first the focus of the struggle was economic, centering on the protective tariff, which many Southerners viewed as an unconstitutional policy to enrich the North and impoverish the South. Then, after the tariff issue was to some extent compromised, the focus turned to the issue of the enslavement of African Americans in the southern states, a domestic institution that raised a gamut of constitutional and moral issues.

During the 1850s, Southerners and Northerners increasingly saw the other region as a hostile aggressor; many Southerners feared that the northern majority wanted to destroy slavery and bring on a race war; many Northerners believed there was a slave power conspiracy to extend slavery into the North and throughout the Western Hemisphere.

In the months after Abraham Lincoln was elected president in November 1860 on an antislavery platform, eleven southern states seceded from the union and formed a new

The Aftermath of Battle. Confederate dead piled up at Antietam, Maryland, indicate the terrible losses of the Civil War. Out of this carnage a new, stronger union was forged.

government, the Confederate States of America. Lincoln, a unionist, believed that secession was fundamentally unconstitutional and that, in more general terms, state sovereignty concepts represented a threat to the survival of constitutional republics everywhere. He called on Americans to take up arms to force the secessionist states back into the union.

In the Civil War (1861–1865) that followed, the United States conquered the Confederate States, thus creating an indissoluble union that provided a secure foundation for a constitutional republic. The growing perception among U.S. citizens that the United States was a single national entity is shown by the shift between the 1870s and the 1890s from the plural verb reference to the nation ("The United States are determined to proceed in this matter") to the singular verb ("The United States is determined to proceed in this matter").

Although the Civil War brought a unified nation, the United States had not yet become a centralized nation or a truly liberal nation. During the Civil War and the period of Reconstruction that followed (1865–1877), the national government took over a number of governmental powers previously exercised at the state level, especially in protecting the rights of African Americans; after 1877, however, the national government exercised less power in regulating the conduct of citizens. As civil and political rights continued to be reserved for adult white males, the United States was not yet a truly liberal republic, although it was more democratic than any of the major states of the late nineteenth century. Although the unification of the United States into a truly national state had major long-range consequences in world history, it had little effect in Italy or Germany, where the final stages of national unification were just getting under way.

Austria-Hungary and Russia: Multinational Empires

Not all national groups succeeded in their quest for self-determination. Most dissatisfied groups lived as subjects of either the Austro-Hungarian or Russian Empires. The frustrations of the ethnic and religious groups in the Austro-Hungarian Empire contributed to international instability and helped to cause World War I.

In the aftermath of the revolution of 1848–1849, the new Habsburg emperor, Francis Joseph I (reigned 1848–1916) of Austria, and his advisors had attempted to quell ethnic unrest by tightening and centralizing the government's absolutist control. These measures, however, only provoked sharp nationalist resentment, most of all among the Magyars (Hungarians), the largest non-German group.

Austria's embarrassing defeat by Prussia in 1866 made clear that the continuation of the Habsburg monarchy depended on the goodwill of the Magyars. Thus an *Ausgleich* (Compromise) was reached in 1867; the Magyars were recognized as equal partners with the Germans within the empire, thus transforming the Habsburg Empire into the Dual Monarchy of Austria and Hungary. The two parts of the empire shared the head of the House of Habsburg as the sovereign and the ministries of foreign affairs, defense, and finance. Otherwise, each unit was autonomous, with its own constitution, parliament, and official language.

The new settlement satisfied the wishes of the Magyars, but it offered few concessions to the other subject nationalities, who together made up a majority in each half of the Dual Monarchy. Although Austria attempted to make concessions to satisfy some of the demands of its non-German peoples during the next half century, the dominant Magyars made no pretense at conciliating their subject Slavic peoples in Hungary. The Austro-Hungarian Empire survived, sustained by the loyalty of its army, the support of the Catholic church, and the deep-seated veneration its people felt for the long-reigning emperor. Ethnic discontent within the empire, however, remained a time bomb waiting to explode.

Compared with Austria-Hungary, the Russian government had tighter and more effective control over its minority ethnic groups, in part because Great Russians remained the overwhelming majority of the population. Russian conquests during the eighteenth and nineteenth centuries had incorporated into the empire Poles, Jews, Finns, Turkic Muslims, and other nationalities. Tsar Alexander III (reigned 1881–1894), adopting the motto "autocracy, orthodoxy, and nationalism," carried out a vigorous policy of Russification of minority groups. For example, Finns were deprived of their constitution and Finnish was replaced by Russian in schools. Constantine Pobedonostsev (1827–1907), procurator of the Holy Synod (chief lay official of the Russian Orthodox church), and a trusted advisor of Alexander III, used coercive and often brutal methods to convert the subject peoples to Russian Orthodoxy. The Jews suffered severely from periodic state-encouraged pogroms (mob attacks on persons and property) that killed many and forced tens of thousands to seek asylum in the United States and elsewhere.

Austria-Hungary and Russia were rivals in the Balkans, where both hoped to acquire territory at the expense of the rapidly weakening Ottoman Empire. The fate of the Ottoman Empire, then known as the Eastern Question, will be taken up in Chapter 13. Russia was eager to gain warm-water ports and access to the Mediterranean. Austria particularly feared Russia's claim to be the protector of Slavs under Ottoman rule. In 1877 Russia intervened to counteract Turkish atrocities against Christians in Bulgaria, and within months its soldiers were on the verge of overrunning Istanbul, the Ottoman capital. In the Treaty of San Stefano, the Ottoman Empire agreed to the creation of a large autonomous Bulgarian state under Russian protection, and gave complete independence to Romania, Serbia, and Montenegro.

Greatly alarmed at the expansion of Russian power, the other major European nations convened an international conference, the Congress of Berlin (1878), to reconsider the Treaty of San Stefano. The ensuing Treaty of Berlin confirmed the independence of Serbia, Romania, and Montenegro. Russia gained Bessarabia and several districts in the Caucasus, and Austria received the right to administer two Ottoman provinces, Bosnia and Herzegovina. Independent Bulgaria was reduced by two-thirds and deprived of access to the Aegean Sea. In a separate treaty, Great Britain received Cyprus from the Ottoman Empire, and in return pledged to aid the sultan if he were attacked.

The Treaty of Berlin aggrieved Russia and Bulgaria and reduced the Ottoman Empire's European holdings to small, exposed fragments. Because the newly independent states had disputed boundaries and ethnic minorities within their territories, the Balkans remained an unstable region, a hotbed of militant nationalism, seething with intrigues, rivalries, and disorders. The Balkans became known at that time as the Tinderbox of Europe, and have remained so to the present day.

European Political Developments to 1914

Nationalism was not the only major catalytic agent affecting Europe in the nineteenth century. Several western European nations developed democratic political systems and institutions. In Great Britain an evolutionary process of peaceful political reforms forestalled the revolutionary upheavals that periodically afflicted the Continent. Still, that nation remained a virtual oligarchy as late as the middle of the nineteenth century. In the aftermath of the Great Reform Bill of 1832 (which enfranchised more males and reformed parliamentary districting), only one adult male in eight could vote for members of the House of Commons; Parliament remained essentially an undemocratic body. From 1832 to 1867 the landed gentry and the upper middle class worked together to control the government, and there was little to choose between the two national parties, the Conservatives and Liberals.

As the old-guard politicians began to pass from the scene, their place was taken by men of widely different temperament and values. The second generation of political figures, who emerged during the reign of Queen Victoria (reigned 1837–1901), was dominated by William Gladstone (1809–1898), the Liberal leader, and his Conservative counterpart, Benjamin Disraeli (1804–1881). The two men alternated in the office of prime minister, and their personal rivalry stimulated reform. The practice of purchasing commissions in the armed forces was ended; the secret ballot was introduced; and corruption at the polls was suppressed. The Second and Third Reform Bills (1867 and 1884,

---

An Argument for Reform

I take my stand on the broad principle that the enfranchisement of capable citizens, be they few or be they many—and if they be many so much the better— give an addition of strength to the state. The strength of the modern state lies in the Representative System . . . and of the State of this country in particular. . . .

I say this is not a perfect bill with regard to the franchise. . . . No, Sir; ideal perfection is not the true basis of English legislation. We look at the attainable; we look at the practicable; and we have too much of English sense to be drawn away by those sanguine delineations of what might possibly be attainable in Utopia, from a path which promises to enable us to effect great good for the people of England. . . . *

Prime Minister William Gladstone made this speech when he introduced the Franchise Bill (Third Reform Bill) of 1884. When it passed, 2 million more voters, mainly agricultural workers, were added to the register, so that four out of five adult British males could participate in elections. Gladstone's speech shows both his belief that governments based on broad popular support made a modern country strong, and his pragmatism as a politician—he went after the attainable rather than dreaming about the perfect state. These characteristics made him a great British leader.

*Hansard's Parliamentary Debates, 3d ser., vol. 285 (London, 1884), p. 107.

respectively) extended suffrage to practically all adult males. Henceforth the industrial proletariat would share political power with the other groups.

There was a lull in domestic activity after the departure of Gladstone and Disraeli, but at the start of the twentieth century the reigning Liberals initiated a bold program of social change. The Liberal party devised legislation that deprived the House of Lords of the right to veto measures approved in the lower chamber (the House of Commons) in three successive sessions. Known as the Parliament Act, it was another step toward democratic government, granting the elected representatives of the people the final decision in legislative matters.

The Liberals, who prided themselves on ameliorating inequality, were much less accommodating to women. Women marched, staged hunger strikes, assaulted politicians, and employed other tactics to draw public attention to their demand for voting rights. The Liberal leadership was unsympathetic, however, partly because the suffragists resorted to violence and partly because these women dared to reject the Victorian idea of separate spheres for men and women. The government's attitude changed during World War I, when women played an active and significant role in the war effort. In 1918 the franchise was extended to all men over twenty-one and all women over thirty. Ten years later British women secured the vote on the same terms as the men.

In France, Napoleon III's defeat in the Franco-Prussian War ushered in a new era. News of his catastrophic surrender in 1870 at Sedan triggered a riot in Paris that swept away the Second Empire. A republic was proclaimed, and survived by default because

Topical Press Agency/Getty Images

Suffragists Escorted by Police in 1914 after a Demonstration outside Buckingham Palace. When arrested and put in jail, many suffragists (called suffragettes at the time) went on hunger strikes. The government, anxious not to have them die in jail, adopted so-called cat-and-mouse tactics. Kept in jail until they were exhausted, the suffragists were released, allowed to recover, and then arrested again.

the monarchists, who dominated the Constituent Assembly, were divided over which claimant to put on the throne.

The constitution of the Third French Republic set up a government that resembled the British, substituting a figurehead president for a constitutional monarch. Unlike the British two-party system, French politics was characterized by a large number of loosely organized political factions. Since no one group commanded a majority in the Chamber (lower house), all ministries were necessarily weak and unstable coalitions subject to frequent changes. Nevertheless, in its turbulent early history, the Third Republic crushed the revolt of the radicals in the Paris Commune, overcame the threat of a takeover by a colorful general, survived scandals, and made France a secular state. During the years from 1910 to 1914 France was more stable than it had been at any time since 1871. The republic was achieving unity in time to meet its greatest challenge.

Italy was a constitutional monarchy whose political situation resembled that of France. Most Italians were illiterate and poor, and until 1912 most males were ineligible to vote. Mass corruption at the polls made a sham of elections, and the weak political parties produced by the voting were unable to govern effectively or to solve the nation's pressing social and economic problems.

In central Europe, the governments of the German and Austro-Hungarian Empires were a compromise between democratic and authoritarian principles. The constitution of the German Empire provided for a federation of twenty-five states under Prussian leadership. The upper house of the bicameral legislature consisted of appointed members who represented the states. The *Reichstag* (lower house) was elected by universal male suffrage, but it was essentially a consultative body. Unlike government ministers in Great Britain or France, the German chancellor was responsible not to parliament, but to the emperor, who appointed and could dismiss him. Bismarck was the author of this system, and it reflected his autocratic philosophy and his conviction that a strong centralized monarchy was the best guarantee of unity for the new German nation. He was, however, perceptive enough to understand that to govern effectively he needed the participation of political parties, which he attempted to control. When the Social Democratic party, chief critic of the government, won a resounding victory at the 1912 election, strong demands rose for constitutional reform and democratic changes. The outbreak of World War I, however, put a temporary halt to the calls for reform.

Ethnic problems limited political change in the Austro-Hungarian Empire. Reforms in the Austrian half of the empire did give the non-Germans many rights and culminated in universal manhood suffrage in 1907, with the result that they gained a majority in the *Reichsrat* (parliament). Parliamentary debates were so heated, however, that they frequently degenerated into fist fights and unruly demonstrations, which made it impossible for the legislature to carry on business. The emperor had to resort to his emergency powers and rule by decree, sometimes for years at a stretch. Chaos and deadlock in Austria seemed to indicate that political democracy could not function in a nation of such diverse and divided peoples. In Hungary, the Magyars made no effort to conciliate the Slovaks, Rumanians, Serbs, Croatians, and other subject minorities. Although they comprised less than half of the total population, the Magyars monopolized almost all the seats in parliament. The result of this repressive policy was persistent restlessness and disaffection among the non-Magyar peoples. The Serbs and Croats in particular clamored for union with independent Serbia and turned increasingly to their co-nationals outside the empire for support.

In Russia, Alexander III's successor, Nicholas II (reigned 1894–1917), could not maintain the tight lid on antigovernment sentiments. Political parties were formed, including the Constitutional Democratic (Cadet) party, which favored peaceful reforms and constitutional monarchy, and the Marxist-oriented Social Democratic party. The Social Democrats split in 1898 into two factions, one moderately reform-minded and the other revolutionary. Later these two factions became solidified as the *Mensheviks* (minority), who advocated a broad democratic party that included other socialists, while the *Bolsheviks* (majority) preferred a small, tightly knit party under authoritarian leadership. Directed by Vladimir Ilyich Ulyanov (1870–1924), whose underground alias was Lenin, the Bolsheviks insisted on immediate dictatorship of the proletariat, ruling out cooperation with socialists and the liberal bourgeoisie.

Antigovernment groups asserted themselves in 1905 when the Japanese badly defeated Russia's army and sank its navy during the Russo-Japanese War (see Chapter 13). Widespread demonstrations, a general strike, and mutiny among some military units compelled Nicholas to agree to undertake reforms. He promised to adopt a constitution, guarantee individual freedoms, and extend legislative authority to a Duma (parliament) that would be elected by a broad suffrage.

Any hopes for a constitutional monarchy in Russia were dashed, however, after the tsar made peace with Japan and regained his authority. Nicholas proceeded to reinstate his autocracy, rescind most reforms, and reduce the Duma to a mere consultative body. A ruthless secret police sent most political opponents either to jail or to Siberian exile. A few, like Lenin, fled abroad. To make matters worse, the royal family came under the spell of a power-hungry illiterate monk, Gregory Rasputin, who wielded an evil and corrupting influence over national policy. Repressive, inefficient, and corrupt, the tsarist government drifted toward catastrophe.

The Spread of Industrialization and the Appearance of Industrialized Society

At the face the cutters had gone back to work. They often shortened their lunch time so they wouldn't stiffen, and their sandwiches, eaten in ravenous silence so far from the sun, seemed like lead in their stomachs. Stretched out on their sides, they hacked harder than ever, obsessed by the idea of filling as many carts as possible. . . . They no longer felt the water that was trickling over them and swelling their limbs, or the cramps caused by their awkward positions, or the suffocation of the darkness in which they faded like plants that have been put into a cellar. Yet as the day went on, the air became more and more unbreathable, heated by the lamps, by their own foul breaths, by the poisonous firedamp fumes. It seemed to cling to their eyes like cobwebs, and it would only be swept away by the night's ventilation. Meanwhile, at the bottom of their molehill, under the weight of the earth, with no breath left in their overheated lungs, they kept hacking away.*

*Émile Zola, *Germinal* [1885], trans. S. Hochman and E. Hochman (New York: New American Library, 1970), p. 42.

This description of men at work in a nineteenth-century coal mine was written in 1885 by Émile Zola, a French novelist famous for his on-the-spot research and realism. Working men and women like the ones he described labored through exhausting days under brutal conditions during the early stages of the Industrial Revolution. They, as much as the inventors or the shrewd business entrepreneurs, were integral parts of that revolution.

The diffusion of industry triggered the most astonishing economic expansion the world had ever seen. As a result, the Western nations in a short time acquired more material wealth than any earlier civilization. The Industrial Revolution also produced a whole new society. In addition to stimulating rapid growth of population and large cities, it significantly intensified the differences among social classes. The breakdown of the family and a growing sense of alienation among many people in modern society were side effects of such change. This section will survey the expansion of industrialization in Continental Europe and the Americas in the nineteenth century. It will further examine the socialist theories of Karl Marx, and discuss the rise of big business, the emergence of severe social problems, and the reforms undertaken to remedy those problems.

The Spread of Industrialization

From its origins in Great Britain in the eighteenth century, the Industrial Revolution spread to continental Europe, the Western Hemisphere, and Asia in the nineteenth century, as new methods of production were adopted in France, Belgium, the German states, the United States, and Japan. By 1900 industrialization had also taken hold in southern and eastern Europe, and in some Latin American countries. In these newer industrial nations, capital was sometimes provided by government or by foreign loans rather than by local investors.

Meanwhile transportation and communication revolutions continued apace, as steam power contributed to the new ways of traveling and communicating among cities, nations, and continents. The steam locomotive in particular revolutionized passenger travel and freight haulage. George Stephenson's *Rocket,* the first practical locomotive, took to the rails in Britain in 1830, chugging along at twelve miles an hour. Within forty years, 900,000 miles of track crisscrossed western Europe, and the United States and Canada laid rails from the Atlantic to the Pacific.

Robert Fulton's paddle-wheel steamboat, the *Clermont,* first sailed on the Hudson River in the United States in 1807. Shortly after mid-century, screw propellers and more efficient steam engines led to regular transatlantic voyages. By 1900 iron and steel steamships with ten or twenty times the carrying capacity of wooden sailing ships plied the sea lanes of the world.

The new methods of production and transport and the new society they created spread from one European nation to another during the 1800s. Belgium, building on manufacturing traditions going back to medieval times and on large deposits of coal, became the Continent's first industrialized nation. Belgian industrialists produced large quantities of iron and cotton textiles and the first complete railroad network on the Continent. France began industrialization during the French Revolution and the Napoleonic era. Standardized weights and measures, a national investment bank, an excellent system of roads, bridges, and canals, and the world's best engineering school—the Polytechnic in Paris—made France an industrial power.

Germany's political division into dozens of separate small states seriously hampered industrial growth during the first half of the nineteenth century. Industrial products often had to cross several tariff barriers to reach larger international markets through North Sea and Baltic port cities. In 1818, however, the North German customs union, or Zollverein, established a "common market" of German states. Political unification under Prussian leadership in 1871 made the new German Empire a leading industrial nation. By 1900, Germany was overtaking Great Britain as Europe's most productive industrial power.

Governments played a part in bringing the Industrial Revolution to many European countries by sponsoring protective tariffs, subsidies, and large-scale capital investment. However, several factors limited industrialization in parts of the Continent: southern Europe lacked capital as well as essential natural resources (iron and coal); eastern Europe was relatively poor and technologically backward and lacked a large, aggressive commercial middle class.

Nowhere were such problems more important than in Russia under the Romanov tsars. This backward colossus of eastern Europe had never developed a large, dynamic middle class, and the absence of commercial wealth severely limited Russia's fund of private investment capital. Count Serge Witte, minister of finance to Alexander III and Nicholas II between 1892 and 1903, was instrumental in bringing Russia into the industrial age. He promoted the development of the railway system, particularly the enormous Trans-Siberian railroad that linked European Russia with the Pacific across nine time zones. He encouraged industry through government subsidies, protective tariffs, and guaranteed dividends. By placing Russia on the gold standard, Witte attracted much foreign capital, especially from France. Between 1885 and 1900 Russia's index of industrial production tripled: the nation ranked fourth among the world's iron producers and second in petroleum production, an increasingly important power source.

Industrialization also began to spread to the new American republics in the nineteenth century. This was particularly true of the growing North American powerhouse, the United States, which benefited from vast natural resources, including iron, coal, and petroleum. The United States moreover had a fast-growing population, in part because waves of immigrants were arriving from Europe and elsewhere. Investment capital, much of it initially supplied by Great Britain, was relatively plentiful. As in Great Britain, government played a secondary role in U.S. industrialization, although Congress did enact protective tariff laws for American industry and made land grants to railroads. Flamboyant and shrewd entrepreneurs such as Andrew Carnegie, John D. Rockefeller, and Edward H. Harriman built successful financial empires as they led America's industrial growth.

By 1900 the United States, already a leader in agricultural production, had become the world's largest industrial producer. As railroads spanned the continent, great industrial cities had spread from New England across the Midwest. U.S. exports challenged European goods on the world market. Latin America especially was coming under the economic influence of industrialized North America.

Some Latin American nations also began to develop industry in the later nineteenth century. As in North America, a combination of natural resources with foreign capital—first from Great Britain, later from the United States—fueled industrialization in these nations. Nitrates in Chile, tin in Bolivia, and the discovery of petroleum in Mexico at the end of the century all drew eager foreign investors. Argentineans enjoyed a boom based on producing and processing wool, beef, and wheat and other agricultural commodities.

By and large, however, industrialization proceeded at a slower pace in Latin America than in North America or Europe. One reason was the widespread poverty and consequent lack of both domestic demand and domestic capital. Most Latin American nations followed their traditional pattern of exporting raw materials and agricultural products to developed nations in Europe and North America. Rather than constructing industrial economies of their own, they imported manufactured goods from abroad.

New Industries in the Nineteenth Century

The industrial system first formulated in the eighteenth century expanded in new directions during the nineteenth. While industrialists continued to mine coal and produce iron and textiles in increasing quantities, entrepreneurs set up steel and chemical manufacturing combines, generated hydroelectric power, and sponsored amazing advances in transportation and communication.

Steel, a much stronger and more flexible material than iron, became cheaper to produce when technicians learned to combine iron with carbon and such alloys as tungsten or manganese. It was used in a wide variety of products, from sewing machines to ocean-going steamers to superstructures for skyscrapers made possible by the new elevator technology. The Eiffel Tower in Paris was a spectacular example of a tall structure made of steel.

The use of chemicals in industry also increased dramatically. Scientists created artificial dyes for synthetic textiles and adapted alkalis for a range of products from textiles to soap. Whole new industries appeared as chemical industrialists and technologists spearheaded the development of photography and the manufacture of cheap paper for magazines and newspapers.

In the later nineteenth century, inventors like Thomas Edison harnessed electricity for industrial purposes. Water and steam turbines made possible the generation of large quantities of electrical power. The new energy source was soon powering trolley cars and lighting cities with the incandescent lamp. Even more striking, electricity made possible virtually instantaneous communication, when Samuel Morse tapped out the first telegraph message (from Washington to Baltimore) in 1844. Undersea cables linked Great Britain with continental Europe in the 1850s, Europe with North America in the 1860s. Telegraph lines soon joined the cities and nations of the whole world.

Other technological breakthroughs heralded some of the mass-produced manufactured products of the twentieth century. The development of the combustion engine, for example, inaugurated the automobile age. New techniques of petroleum refining would make gasoline and diesel fuel available for cars and trucks. New metal alloys made possible better and more varied tools as well as machine parts. The creation of rayon fabrics and chemical dyes in the laboratory led to the use of synthetic materials in the manufacture of clothing. The canning of food, perfected by the mid-nineteenth century, transformed food preservation; refrigeration, invented in the second half of the century, would revolutionize food storage in the twentieth century.

The Rise of Big Business

The Industrial Revolution had begun in Great Britain in the government-regulated environment of mercantilism. Many of the entrepreneurs who guided the early stages of industrialization felt this government paternalism was a hindrance rather than a help. They agreed with Adam Smith, the eighteenth-century founder of modern economics, that free competition at home and free trade abroad would lead to a great increase in the wealth of nations. Accordingly, these early industrialists agitated for an end to mercantilist economic controls, and in the early nineteenth century their efforts began to pay dividends. Great Britain, the leader in the Industrial Revolution, also became the first country to adopt free trade. Soon other governments ceased to support the traditional monopolies and allowed freer competition in major markets.

From the 1820s into the 1870s, free competition came to dominate much of the European economy. Old and new power sources, industries, and manufacturers competed freely. In cloth making, coal mining, and other industries, thousands of small to medium-sized firms competed for business in a relatively unregulated market. "Competition," business leaders commonly asserted, "is the life of trade and the law of progress."

The new system, like the old, entailed difficulties, however. Competition could be brutal and often led to bankruptcies. Many firms went under, especially during the periodic business depressions of the nineteenth century; business owners were sometimes saddled with lifelong indebtedness. In time, some businessmen began to wonder if limited or controlled competition might better serve their interests.

Not all industries had competition. For instance, city governments often granted monopolies to public utilities and urban streetcar lines. In central and eastern Europe as well as in Japan, the national governments frequently capitalized and owned railroads. Inventors who obtained a patent on a key part or process could enjoy a de facto monopoly in many parts of Europe.

In the last quarter of the nineteenth century, however, monopolies began to appear in other areas of the industrial economy. New methods of controlling the market were established by businesses themselves. Two innovative types of "industrial combination" were the corporation and the cartel. A corporation was formed by the merger of several smaller industrial firms into a single gigantic company. Aggressive entrepreneurs would buy out weaker rivals, strengthening their own position against other competitors, which might then be absorbed in their turn. Such an industrial combination might include a number of firms in the same line of business; horizontal combinations such as the Nobel Dynamite Trust Company in Europe and Andrew Carnegie's U.S. Steel Corporation in the United States controlled manufacturers of the same product.

Another form of industrial amalgamation was the vertical combination of companies in related businesses, often stages of the same process. An impressive combine engineered by German industrialist Albert Krupp illustrates this form. Krupp began as a steelmaker, but then bought up iron and coal mines and such user enterprises as railway manufacturers, shipyards, and the arms factories for which Krupp industries became famous.

In a cartel, by contrast, companies did not merge, but simply formed a loose alliance based on a cartel agreement. Major manufacturers, for example, might form a cartel and agree to fix minimum prices. They would then divide the market among themselves or set a maximum total output and then agree on quotas for each member. Such agreements undercut free competition as effectively as monopolistic industrial combinations. Giant corporations could easily manipulate the market for whatever they produced. Attitudes toward cartels varied. In Great Britain and America, they were often considered illegal "conspiracies in restraint of trade," but in Germany they were legally enforceable accords.

Social Classes in the Industrial Age

Although the society that emerged under the impact of the Industrial Revolution showed continuities with the past, it also differed in several key respects. Population growth, urbanization, and class conflicts, for instance, were not new; yet all three greatly intensified during the eighteenth and nineteenth centuries.

The rapid population growth of the last three centuries is one of the most striking features of modern history. The following figures give a sense of this population explosion. The population of Great Britain, for instance, probably around 5 million in 1710, had increased to 9 million by 1800 and to 32 million by 1900. Moreover, the population of Russia, the largest of the great powers, nearly tripled in the nineteenth century, from 36 million to 100 million people. Western Hemisphere populations grew even more rapidly. The population of the United States, less than 4 million in 1790, was pushing 100 million by 1900.

This sudden population surge had a number of causes. The Industrial Revolution, for example, created many new jobs, making it possible for young people to marry earlier and have more children. Innovations in agricultural techniques and such new crops as the potato supported increasing numbers of people. Then, too, modern medicine and sanitation increased life expectancies by lowering the rates of death from infectious diseases like smallpox and tuberculosis.

The population increase gave the Western world many more workers to mine ores, lay rails, and labor in factories. Many more people began to live in modern industrial cities. Rapid development transformed villages into towns and towns into cities. Workers flocked to the cities seeking jobs in the new factories, which employed both adults and children.

The industrial cities of the nineteenth century were overcrowded and filthy with polluted water and thick industrial smoke. Factories were the scene of many industrial accidents. Workers lived in slum tenements, where whole families were jammed into a single room. The slums were fertile breeding grounds for crime and disease. Industrial depressions threw many out of work. North America's industrial working class, like Europe's, suffered brutal hardships in the early stage of industrialization. As late as 1900, New York's Hell's Kitchen matched the horrors of London's East End slums.

Coketown

It was a town of red brick, or of brick that would have been red if the smoke and ashes had allowed it; but as matters stood it was a town of unnatural red and black like the painted face of a savage. It was a town of machinery and tall chimneys, out of which interminable serpents of smoke trailed themselves forever and ever, and never got uncoiled. It had a black canal in it, and a river that ran purple with ill-smelling dye, and vast piles of buildings full of windows where there was a rattling and a trembling all day long, and where the piston of the steam-engine worked monotonously up and down like the head of an elephant in a state of melancholy madness. It contained several large streets all very like one another, and many small streets still more like one another, inhabited by people equally like one another, who all went in and out at the same hours, with the same sound upon the same pavements, to do the same work, and to whom every day was the same as yesterday and tomorrow, and every year the counterpart of the last and the next.*

The above description of "Coketown," an English industrial city, is from Charles Dickens's novel of the Industrial Revolution, *Hard Times* (1854). This perceptive author vividly depicted many of the problems of urban, industrialized society, including air and water pollution, the ugliness of early industrial cities, and the psychologically crushing monotony of labor controlled by the rhythm of the machines and the discipline of the factory whistle.

*Charles Dickens, Hard Times for These Times (New York: New American Library, 1961), pp. 30–31.

If not the most comfortable places to live, nineteenth-century cities were certainly the most exciting. In cities could be found shops, theaters, cafés, horsecars, and later the electric tram, gas and then electric lights, and the telephone. The charms of earlier periods and the wonders of the new age were concentrated in London, Paris, New York, and Buenos Aires, the capitals of the new industrial civilization.

Before the Industrial Revolution, social divisions had traditionally been based on race, religion, lineage, and legal rankings. In the new industrial society, however, class distinctions corresponded more directly to position in the economic structure. By expanding the opportunities to accumulate great wealth, the Industrial Revolution increased the disparity between the upper and lower classes. The magnitude of the economic changes affected the social order, promoting tensions and even class conflict.

European society was dominated by a small, wealthy elite comprising the landed aristocracy and the commercial and financial magnates of the upper middle class. Although not as powerful as in the past, the aristocracy continued to enjoy status and financial stability throughout most of the nineteenth century. Land maintained a high value, but increased competition from cheaper overseas grain and a reluctance to change the old ways reduced profits. As their income from land declined, some aristocrats were able to make the transition to modern capitalist agriculture or industrialization. The new economy created a group of aggressive and vigorous entrepreneurs who amassed vast fortunes that enabled them to gain control over their nation's economy and government. Increasingly, they established common bonds with the aristocracy. Their sons were admitted to the elite schools that formerly only the children of the aristocracy had attended. Sometimes the wealth of business tycoons and noble titles came together through mutually advantageous marriages. More and more, wealthy industrialists purchased landed estates in the country and emulated the manners and attitudes of the aristocracy. During the latter part of the nineteenth century, the aristocracy and the upper middle class became indistinguishable.

Standing below the wealthy elite were mid- and lower-level bourgeoisie. In the mid-level middle class, such traditional groups as lawyers, physicians, and relatively prosperous businessmen were joined by new groups created by the expansion of industry. These included upper management and the new professionals such as architects, scientists, engineers, and accountants. Small shopkeepers, along with teachers, nurses, and white-collar employees—clerks, secretaries, salespeople, and lower bureaucrats—formed the lower middle class. Although their lifestyles varied somewhat, mid-level and lower bourgeoisie shared the same values and attitudes. They were active churchgoers and professed to follow Christian moral strictures, strove for greater status and income, and understood the importance of science and progress.

The vast majority of Europeans, about 80 percent, still earned their livelihood through physical labor. Many of them were landowning peasants, sharecroppers, and agricultural workers. The latter lived in extreme poverty; their wages averaged less than half the salary of factory workers. The living conditions of the first two groups ranged from deep poverty in much of southern and eastern Europe to relative prosperity in western Europe. These country people were socially conservative and remained loyal to regional customs and old social and religious authorities. They resented government exactions, including high taxes, but resorted to open rebellion only in the hardest of times.

During the latter part of the nineteenth century, urban workers constituted the largest single social group in most western and central European nations. The urban labor force was even more diverse than the middle class. At the top of the hierarchy were the highly skilled workers—machine tool specialists, shipbuilders, metal workers—who were reasonably well off, enjoying steady employment and wages that were at least twice as high as those in industries requiring little or no skill. These workers had middle-class aspirations and sought good housing and education for their children. Those toiling in semi-skilled occupations such as masonry, carpentry, and bricklaying earned about a third less money than the skilled workers. The lowest wages went to the unskilled workers, including domestic servants and the day laborers who had no regular employment.

The standard of living for the urban working class advanced after 1870. During the last three decades of the nineteenth century, new industrial and agricultural techniques kept the price of clothing, shoes, and food down, while real wages rose by 37 percent. Many workers earned wages above the subsistence level. This meant that they now could afford to buy more clothes, move into better housing, and add meat, dairy products, and vegetables to a diet that previously had consisted almost entirely of bread and potatoes. Life expectancy among members of the lower class increased, slowly at first and then more rapidly.

Although some of the patterns of industrial society in Europe were repeated in the Americas, the class divisions and problems of the masses of people in the new nations across the Atlantic were significantly different. Notable differences also existed between the class structures of North and South America.

In Latin America landed aristocrats remained very powerful, owning vast farms and much of the mineral wealth. Landless peasants, including Amerindians, blacks, and mestizos, continued to be bound to the owners of the landed estates by peonage. An urban middle class, however, emerged in the cities of South America. This business bourgeoisie included many exporters of the agricultural products and raw materials of the great landowners. An urban working class was also recruited to build and operate seaports, railways, and similar facilities connected with the export industries. These workers, often immigrants from Europe, began to organize unions and to become politically active by the end of the nineteenth century.

North American social patterns evolved along different lines. In the United States, the landed gentry of the South and the cattle barons of the West never gained the national preeminence enjoyed by the aristocracy in Europe or Latin America. The pre–Civil War black slaves became tenants and sharecroppers after the war. Immigrant farmers often suffered great hardships on the frontier, but did not become the sort of tradition-bound peasantry found in Europe or Latin America. During the nineteenth century, the middle class gradually became the ruling elite. With the great industrial expansion of the post–Civil War period, business leaders acquired enormous wealth, political power, and social prestige. Although some condemned the wealthiest as "robber barons" for their aggressive and often shady tactics, others hailed them as "captains of industry" for their resourcefulness and success.

Women's Work and the Family

The Industrial Revolution and the subsequent movement of large numbers of people to the cities had a significant impact on the life of women and their place in the labor force. Traditionally, members of a household had clearly defined duties based on their age, gender, and position in the family. In rural areas the men worked in the fields as the chief family wage earner. The wives managed the home, raised the children, and in addition engaged in seasonal work such as tending to a garden or working in the fields at planting or harvest time. Single women were sometimes employed as seamstresses, weavers, or domestics; all or part of their wages supplemented their parents' income.

In the second half of the nineteenth century the emergence of large industrial plants and big businesses, together with the expansion of government services, opened new employment opportunities for women. They were hired to work in such heavy industries as mining and metalwork as well as in the textile mills and the garment industry. Unskilled women were paid higher wages than they could have received elsewhere, but they labored long hours in unhealthy and dangerous conditions at wages lower than those paid to adult male workers. They were often excluded from highly skilled and better-paying jobs and were seldom allowed to join early labor unions. In Germany and Great Britain, laws were passed to limit the exploitation of women (and children) in the factories and mines, but these were not enforced and had only marginal impact.

Besides manual work, many women found careers in teaching, nursing, and other white-collar positions. Many of these became rapidly identified as female occupations. The new positions, except for teaching and nursing, required few skills and minimal training. The work was routine and boring, and the wages were low, because employers assumed that their women employees had other sources of income. Women who supported themselves independently had a difficult time finding jobs that paid an adequate wage.

As a rule, women in the new occupations were young and single, and many were from rural areas, drawn to the city both to find higher-paying jobs and to escape parental supervision. For the single woman away from home, lonely, and unable to earn enough money to support herself, the logical move was to find a husband, but marital aspirations were not always fulfilled. In the absence of supervision by parents, the local community, and the church, premarital sex, illegitimate children, and common-law marriages increased dramatically. Because there were always more women seeking employment than there were jobs available, some were forced to enter prostitution or to exchange sexual favors for food in time of scarcity.

Most women did marry, however. A substantial number withdrew from the regular labor force after the birth of their first child but did not stop working altogether. While rearing their children, they favored part-time work that could be pursued at home, often an extension of their household duties. Such work could involve animal husbandry, sewing gloves or clothing, taking in infants to nurse, washing clothes, or assisting their husband in his profession. Work of this type was an important contribution to the family economy.

For a woman, marriage meant that she no longer had to contribute part of her wage to her parents' household. When women married, they transferred to another family and assumed new responsibilities, but they carried the practices and values of their mothers with them. Although women were denied suffrage and were inferior under the law, they tended to prevail in the domestic sphere. The key to their power lay less in the management of household duties than in control of the purse strings. Women kept household accounts, purchased food from the marketplace, made financial decisions, and in some cases even determined the weekly allowance their husbands received.

Marx Predicts the Triumph of Socialism

While revolutions and independence movements were altering political conditions in the early nineteenth century, industrialization was profoundly changing economic and social conditions. From its very beginning, the Industrial Revolution had transformed the lives of the working masses. Workers no longer practiced skilled crafts in small shops or their own cottages. Instead, they labored for long hours in large factories or mines. Women and children were widely employed in factories, especially in the booming textile industry, where alertness and dexterity were more important than physical strength. Women and even small children could thus add a few shillings a week to an impoverished family's income. Their earnings hardly offset the suffering caused by long hours and poor working conditions in the early industrial age.

Industrial working conditions and the political revolutions that had rocked the Western world stimulated innovative thinkers to formulate new theories about economics and society. Socialism, which developed in reaction to the abuses of the Industrial Revolu-

Marx Exhorts the Masses to Revolt

The history of all hitherto existing society is the history of class struggles....

In the earlier epochs of history, we find almost everywhere a complicated arrangement of society into various orders, a manifold gradation of social rank. In ancient Rome we have patricians, knights, plebeians, slaves, in the Middle Ages, feudal lords, vassals, guildmasters, journeymen, apprentices, serfs ...

The bourgeoisie has subjected the country to the rule of the towns. It has created enormous cities.... Just as it has made the country dependent on the towns, so it has made barbarian and semi-barbarian countries dependent on civilized ones, nations of peasants on nations of bourgeois, the East on the West....

We have seen ... that the first step in the revolution by the working class, is to raise the proletariat to the position of ruling class, to win the battle of democracy....

In the most advanced countries the following will be found pretty generally applicable:

1. Abolition of property in land....
2. Graduated income tax.
3. Abolition of all right of inheritance.
4. Confiscation of property of emigrants and rebels.
5. Centralization of credit in the hands of the State....
6. Centralization of the means of communication and transport in the hands of the State.

7. Extension of factories and instruments of production owned by the State; the bringing into cultivation of waste lands....
8. Equal liability of all to labor....
9. Combination of agriculture with manufacturing industries; gradual abolition of the distinction between town and country....
10. Free education for all children in public schools....

The proletarians have nothing to lose but their chains. They have a world to win.
Working men of all countries, unite!*

In *The Communist Manifesto*, Karl Marx and his collaborator, Friedrich Engels, outlined their program for worldwide revolution and a future socialist society. Although the *Manifesto* appeared too late to have an impact on the revolutions of 1848, it became one of the most influential tracts of all time, providing direction for twentieth-century revolutionaries from Russia to China to Cuba. Marx's ideas for revolution and radical change were the direct opposite of Metternich's support for conservative, divine-right monarchy and political stability. The struggle between conservatives wishing to maintain the status quo and revolutionaries seeking to change societies along radical lines continued to be a major trend throughout the twentieth century.

**Karl Marx and Friedrich Engels,* The Communist Manifesto *(New York: Modern Reader Paperbacks, 1968), pp. 2–62.*

tion, was among the most radical of the new doctrines. Although socialist thinkers did not always agree, most advocated abolishing private ownership of the means of production—factories, raw materials, agricultural land, and means of transportation—in favor of some form of public ownership.

Socialism was especially attractive to the educated people of middle-class origin, who had been dismayed and infuriated by the poor working conditions and low wages in the newly industrialized Western nations. Although some socialists attempted to rally peasants in overwhelmingly agricultural nations like Russia, their central concern was with the factory hands, railroad employees, miners, and other workers in the fast-growing industrial sector of the economy. At this time, socialist leaders were not concerned with the poor peasants and miners in Asia, Africa, or South America, the majority of whom came under Western imperial domination and worked for companies owned or dominated by Westerners.

Living in a time of sweeping economic change, Karl Marx (1818–1883), perhaps the most influential social theorist, believed that economic forces shaped the course of history. For Marx, how people earned their living determined how they lived, what they believed, and what role they played in history. Although Marx did not discount the importance of religion, politics, or nationalism, he argued that economic forces such as labor, capital investment, economic booms, and depressions were the primary forces shaping human events. According to Marx, economic forces had always created two conflicting social groups—the "haves," who owned the means of production, and the "have nots," who were forced to sell their labor to the haves in order to survive. Class conflict ultimately was the most important factor in human history. Marx foresaw a worldwide revolution that would end class conflict and create a society in which the means of production were owned by all. In addition, he believed that religion and nationalism were "opiates" used by the ruling classes to keep the impoverished masses drugged and too passive or preoccupied to revolt against the capitalist system.

Other socialists, including Robert Owens and the Fabians in Great Britain, strongly disagreed with Marxian analysis, and by the end of the nineteenth century, many had abandoned Marx's revolutionary ideology. They pointed out that, contrary to Marx's prediction, the living standard of the workers was steadily improving and the bourgeois state was gaining in strength as it became more democratic. Instead of trying to overthrow the state, many socialists sought to cooperate with capitalist and nationalist political parties to move the state in the direction of socialism in a moderate step-by-step fashion.

Industrialization and Social Reforms

As industries spread across Europe and North America, workers everywhere experienced the same problems of low wages, poor working conditions, and long hours. They tried to improve their lives by forming labor unions and using collective bargaining and strikes as their weapons. They also sought political action to improve their lot and joined Marxian and other socialist movements. Still others became anarchists in the belief that all governments were evil and should be abolished through violence.

In nations where there was a trend toward representative institutions, governments often responded to worker needs by enacting reforms that forestalled revolution. In Great Britain the great Reform Act of 1832 ushered in an era of government commissions to study abuses, which were followed by reforms enacted by Parliament. Great Britain led the way in abolishing slavery in its colonies, lowering food costs by introducing free trade, and enacting laws that reduced working hours and improved working conditions. Government inspectors enforced the expanding network of laws that checked abuses. Other laws established free and compulsory education, legalized unions, and improved public health. The era of reform in Great Britain reached a climax with the victory of the "New Liberals" in the election of 1905. They believed in using the power of the state to aid the underprivileged. During the next decade, with the support of the newly formed Labour party, the New Liberals enacted the Workers' Compensation Act, the Old Age Pension Act, and the National Insurance Act, and others that laid the groundwork for a welfare state. A progressive income tax and a heavy tax on unearned income exacted money from the rich to pay for the welfare programs. Such measures would become commonplace in industrialized nations in the twentieth century.

As we have seen, the Industrial Revolution had begun later in Germany than in Great Britain, but once under way, it progressed with astonishing speed. A Socialist Democratic party was formed in Germany to champion the cause of workers. Chancellor Bismarck, who equated socialism with anarchy, outlawed the Socialist Democratic party. At the same time, however, he sponsored a paternalistic social reform program designed to undercut the appeal of the socialists. In the 1880s, parliament passed laws providing for compulsory sickness benefits and accident and old age insurance that were the most comprehensive to date.

In France the heavy indemnity paid to Germany and the loss of Alsace-Lorraine resulting from the Franco-Prussian War of 1870–1871 had retarded its economic growth. The working class was smaller and less influential than its British and German counterparts with the result that French political authorities were slow to come to grips with the social and economic problems of the industrial age. Nevertheless, during the generation after 1871 successive governments enacted laws that legalized labor unions, protected workers and permitted them to strike, and introduced social and accident insurance. However, the ruling class drew the line at the advanced legislation the workers called for. In reaction, an important segment of workers embraced the revolutionary doctrines of syndicalism (from the French word *syndicat,* meaning "trade union"). The goal of the syndicalists was to make trade unions the most powerful institution in society, replacing the state as the owner and operator of the means of production; they intended to do so through strikes and violence. But most workers and socialists were prepared to operate within the parliamentary process. In 1905 various groups combined to form the United Socialist party, which immediately controlled a significant block of seats in the National Assembly (lower house), where social welfare measures comparable to those in Germany and Great Britain soon won passage.

The last major European country to industrialize, Russia, was also most backward in social reforms. Rapid industrialization brought to the Russian working class the same extreme hardships and miseries so common in western Europe. But as the workers had no political representation and were not permitted trade unions, they had no effective way to voice their discontent. The government did try to improve their lives with new laws, but did not have an adequate bureaucracy to enforce them. Russia's numerous peasants lived in dire misery as well. They were burdened with high taxes and heavy redemption payments for their plot of land when they won emancipation from serfdom. Farming methods were primitive, though still effective enough to yield surpluses for exportation (something the Soviet system consistently failed to achieve). Reforms introduced after 1905 legalized trade unions, reduced the workday, and began an insurance program for factory workers; furthermore, they canceled the remaining redemptive payments for peasants (allowing them to own their land outright) and assisted them with credit. An additional purpose of the reforms—to create grassroots support for the throne—was thwarted by the assassination of their author, Peter Stolypin (1863–1911), and by the outbreak of World War I.

In the United States, where the ethos of the rugged individual was prevalent, collective forms of action developed more slowly than in Europe. In the later nineteenth century, farmers' organizations were moderately effective, but labor unions were only just beginning to organize. Only the skilled craft unions had made much headway in wresting concessions from employers. Not until well into the twentieth century did American labor unions become an effective factor in improving working conditions of the labor force.

Western Cultural and Intellectual Trends

The voyage of the Beagle *has been by far the most important event of my life, and has determined my whole career. . . . The glories of the vegetation of the Tropics rise before my mind at the present time more vividly than anything else; though the sense of sublimity, which the great deserts of Patagonia and the forest-clad mountains of Tierra del Fuego excited in me, has left an indelible impression on my mind. . . . Many of my excursions on horseback through wild countries, or in the boats, some of which lasted several weeks, were deeply interesting: their discomfort and some degree of danger were at that time hardly a drawback, and none at all afterwards. I also reflect with high satisfaction on some of my scientific work, such as . . . the discovery of the singular relations of the animals and plants inhabiting the several islands of the Galapagos archipelago, and of all of them to the inhabitants of South America.*

As far as I can judge of myself, I worked to the utmost during the voyage from the mere pleasure of investigation, and from my strong desire to add a few facts to the great mass of facts in Natural Science. But I was also ambitious to take a fair place among scientific men,—whether more ambitious or less so than most of my fellow-workers, I can form no opinion. *

*Francis Darwin, ed., *The Life and Letters of Charles Darwin*, vol. 1 (New York: Appleton, 1887), pp. 82–83.

The nineteenth century witnessed a tremendous advance in the extent of scientific knowledge. The career of Charles Darwin is one of the best examples of that advance. His service for five years as a naturalist aboard the HMS *Beagle* laid the foundations for the great works on natural selection and evolution that he wrote later in his career. Meticulous observation, constant study, and a fearless readiness to follow the evidence wherever it might lead enabled Darwin to revolutionize our view of life on the planet and earned him "a fair place among scientific men."

This section looks at some of the main cultural and intellectual currents in the West in the nineteenth century, when Europeans and Americans were increasingly prosperous, free of major wars, and expanding their global empires. Although movements like romanticism and materialism and towering intellects like Darwin threatened most of the cherished beliefs and values of this immensely successful society, intellectual and artistic rebellion was actually a sign of strength. Nineteenth-century society in Europe and the Americas was powerful and confident enough to tolerate the heretical ideas of its most gifted citizens, who were free to follow the advice of the poet William Blake: "Drive your cart and your plow over the bones of the dead." In so doing, they enriched our intellectual lives.

The Romantic Movement in Literature, Art, and Music

In the late eighteenth century, the Enlightenment gradually gave way to romanticism, a movement that stressed that the empathetic and intuitional faculties ("emotion") could give insights unobtainable by the logical faculties ("reason"). Aristotle's assertion, dear to the philosophes, that "man is the rational animal" was answered by Wordsworth's romantic declaration that "our meddling intellectual misshapes the beauteous form of things: we murder to dissect."

In the late eighteenth century, some writers began to rebel against the rigid rules for writing laid down by seventeenth-century classicism and eighteenth-century neoclassicism. They felt an urge to express their emotional responses in literature, rather than

LIVES AND TIMES ACROSS CULTURES

Classical Greece: A Perennial Source of Inspiration

The rich legacy of classical Greece has been a perennial source of inspiration to the Western world, during the Romantic era as in other periods. Knowledge of Greek and Roman history, literature, philosophy, and art formed a common bond among educated people in Europe and the Americas.

Two examples from the rich repertoire of poetry of the Romantic period well illustrate the legacy of Greek civilization. John Keats (1795–1821) was the son of a stable keeper. Apprenticed to a surgeon, he abandoned a medical career to write poetry. Keats suffered from ill health worsened by caring for a dying brother and an unhappy love; he died while convalescing in Rome. His odes rank among the most tender of Romantic poems. The "Ode on a Grecian Urn" was inspired by the timeless beauty of ancient Greek painted pottery he had seen in the collections of the British Museum. Its last stanza is quoted below.

O Attic shape! Fair attitude! with brede
Of marble men and maidens overwrought,
With forest branches and trodden weed;
Thou, silent form, dost tease us out of thought
As doth eternity: Cold Pastoral!
When old age shall this generation waste,
Thou shalt remain, in midst of other woe
Than ours, a friend to man, to whom thou say'st,
"Beauty is truth, truth beauty,"—that is all
Ye know on earth, and all ye need to know.

The second selection is from a long poem, *Don Juan*, by Lord Byron (1788–1824). Born to a noble family, Cambridge-educated, and widely traveled, Byron wrote prolifically while leading a notoriously dissolute life. Like many other Englishmen of his time, Byron passionately championed the cause of Greek independence against the Ottoman Empire. Byron died of malaria while in Greece during its war of independence.

The mountains look on Marathon—
And Marathon looks on the sea;
And musing there an hour alone,
I dream'd that Greece might still be free;
For standing on the Persians' grave,
I could not deem myself a slave.

Byron is referring to the Persian invasion of Greece and the victory won by democratic Athens against a force two or three times its size at the Plain of Marathon in 490 B.C.E.

offering only rational analysis, balanced judgments, or sardonic wit. These new writers became known as *romantics,* a name derived from "Romance," the medieval tale of adventure, love, and often magic and fantasy.

Romantics felt out of place in the new industrial society of nineteenth-century western Europe. As an expression of this discontent, romanticism offered new ways of writing, painting, and composing music, but also challenged the basic attitudes of Europeans toward society and themselves. Strong feelings stood at the center of the romantic worldview. Personal love in particular dominated romantic poetry, plays, and fiction, and the love poem became a primary romantic form.

Romantic poets favored short lyric poems over long epics or philosophical poems. They also invented their own forms of poetry or drama instead. Many rejected the old-fashioned "poetic" language prescribed by classicists, insisting on words used by real people, especially humble country people rather than educated city folk. This tendency was present already in the work of the Scottish poet Robert Burns (1759–1796):

> *O, my luve is like a red, red rose,*
> *That's newly sprung in June.*
> *O, my luve is like a melodie,*
> *That's sweetly play'd in tune.*
>
> *As fair art thou, my bonie lass,*
> *So deep in love am I,*
> *And I will luve thee still, my dear,*
> *Till a' the seas gang [go] dry.*

These writers often "romanticized" settings like North Africa, the Arab world, or even the forests of the New World, as well as colorful past periods of history, like the medieval era or the Renaissance. *The Hunchback of Notre Dame* (1831) by Victor Hugo (1802–1885) and *Ivanhoe* (1819) by Sir Walter Scott (1771–1832), for example, illustrate the enthusiasm for medieval times.

The heroes of romantic poetry, plays, and prose fiction tended to be rebels, outcasts, great lovers, wanderers in the world, and bearers of dark secrets; they were supreme egoists, glorifying the individual at the expense of society. Some romantic writers were themselves rebels: the romantic poet George Gordon, Lord Byron (1788–1824), lived a scandalous life, engaged in radical politics, and died while still young, in the Greek War of Independence from Turkey.

Nature was another powerful theme in romantic writing; poets like William Wordsworth (1770–1850) felt an almost mystical communion with trees, fields, streams, mountains, and oceans, as in these lines from his moving ode, "Intimations of Immortality from Recollections of Early Childhood":

> *And O, ye Fountains, Meadows, Hills, and Groves,*
> *Forebode not any severing of our loves!*
> *Yet in my heart of hearts I feel your might;*
> *I only have relinquished one delight*
> *To live beneath your more habitual sway.*

When I Was Young

(1)

All thoughts, all passions, all delights,
Whatever stirs the mortal frame,
All are but ministers of Love,
And feed his sacred flame.

Oft in my waking dreams do I
Live o'er again that happy hour,
When midway on the mount I lay,
Beside the ruin'd tower.

The moonshine, stealing o'er the scene,
Had blended with the lights of eve;
And she was there, my hope, my joy,
My own dear Genevieve!....

(2)

Verse, a breeze 'mid blossoms straying,

Where Hope hung feeding, like a bee—
Both were mine! Life went a-maying
With Nature, Hope, and Poesy,
When I was young!*

These extracts from poems by the English romantic poet Samuel Taylor Coleridge develop a number of typical romantic images. The first poem is dedicated to the "sacred flame" of romantic love. The second begins with "verse" or "poesy" (poetry)—one of the arts most influenced by romanticism. Both conjure up romantic natural scenes: a moonlit mountain with ruined tower, a breeze-blown flower. Youth, also a major romantic enthusiasm, is implied in the first and emphasized in the second extract. Such phrases as "Nature, Hope, and Poesy" almost sum up the emotional creed of the romantic poets.

*Samuel Taylor Coleridge, "Love" and "Youth and Age" in Arthur Quiller-Couch, ed., The Oxford Book of English Verse (Oxford: Clarendon Press, 1953), pp. 670, 673.

I love the Brooks which down their channels fret,
Even more than when I tripped lightly as they;
The innocent brightness of a new-born Day
Is lovely yet;
The Clouds that gather round the setting sun
Do take a sober colouring from an eye
That hath kept watch o'er man's mortality;
Another race hath been, and other palms are won.
Thanks to the human heart by which we live,
Thanks to its tenderness, its joys, and fears,
To me the meanest flower that blows can give
Thoughts that do often lie too deep for tears.

Like Rousseau—a precursor of the movement—romantic writers preferred the natural world to the artificial sophistication of cities.

The supernatural, dismissed as superstition by eighteenth-century "enlightened" thinkers, found an important place in the romantic view of life. Johann Wolfgang von Goethe (1749–1832), Germany's greatest writer, brought the Devil himself on stage in his *Faust* (1808). The original "Gothic" novels were full of haunted castles and other horrors, as in *Frankenstein, or the Modern Prometheus* (1818) by Mary Shelley (1797–1851), whose husband was the romantic poet Percy Bysshe Shelley (1792–1822).

Painters, like writers, rejected the classical rules for the arts, using richer colors and deeper shadows than neoclassical artists. They aimed for violent motion instead of balance, often in past times and "exotic" locales; an example is *The Entrance of the Crusaders into Jerusalem,* a painting by the French artist Eugéne Delacroix (1798–1863). J. M. W. Turner (1775–1851), the English painter of seascapes, produced dazzling swirls of color in sunsets and storms at sea.

As musical composers, romantics turned away from the rules of composition developed over the past two centuries, preferring to let strong feeling and free-flowing musical imagination give their work its conviction. French composer and conductor Hector Berlioz (1803–1869) created a rich integration of orchestra with solo and choral voices in his *Romeo and Juliet* and *The Damnation of Faust.*

The romantic ego is also realized in the heroic symphonies of Ludwig van Beethoven (1770–1827), as well as in the brilliantly melodic piano compositions of Frederic Chopin (1810–1849), a Pole who lived in Paris. Virtuoso soloists and famous conductors were hailed as archetypal artistic geniuses; Italian concert violinist and composer Niccolò Paganini (1782–1840), for instance, played so brilliantly that his audiences sometimes burst into tears, yet lived so colorful a life that some said he had bought his talent by selling his soul to the Devil!

Taken as a whole, the romantic movement signified a deep cultural revolt with long-range consequences. Romantic artists—and many of their readers—felt out of place in the new industrial society of nineteenth-century Europe. They had no use for science, preferring to be entranced by the beauty of nature rather than analyzing it. The primacy of the emotions had superseded the glorification of reason. The romantics were early explorers of cultural alienation and nonrationalism, both of which would haunt the modern world throughout the nineteenth and twentieth centuries.

Materialism and Realism in Philosophy and Literature

As romanticism began to fade about the middle of the nineteenth century, materialism, a new view that had its roots in the physical sciences rather than the arts, emerged. Many scientific discoveries contributed significantly to knowledge of the physical universe and added to the prestige of the scientific approach to understanding the world. Scientists explored the structure of matter. The molecular theory explained solids, liquids, and gases (understood to be the three states of matter) in terms of clumps of atoms called molecules in rapid motion. Soon after 1900, subatomic physics penetrated the structure of the atom and revealed miniature solar systems of protons, electrons, and neutrons. Nineteenth-century scientists also developed the cell theory of living tissue. Cells—which had been found in plants as early as the 1600s—were discovered in animals as well. Life itself, it seemed, had a purely material basis. Scientists also formulated the germ theory of the causation of disease: Louis Pasteur (1822–1895) and others discovered that tiny organisms, which they called germs, were the cause of many diseases. Medicine was thus put on a truly scientific basis.

The resurgence of the sciences in the nineteenth century also produced new "isms." One, materialism, was the philosophical belief in matter as the basic causal agent in the universe, to the virtual exclusion of spiritual things. To some extent, this rejection of the ancient, universal belief in a spiritual world beyond this material realm came from both scientists and philosophers. Geologists, for instance, asserted that the earth had not been created by divine decree a few thousand years ago, as Old Testament chronology would have it. Rather, the globe had taken millions of years of slow development to reach its present state.

To the most thoroughgoing materialist philosophers, the cosmos had no place for spirit. Religion was an illusion. God was made in man's image, to serve human psychological needs in times of trouble. The human soul was no more than an individual personality and would die along with the body.

Positivism, an outgrowth of materialism, was primarily concerned with how people could know the truth about the world. Positivists believed that scientific methods should be applied in all academic disciplines. By counting and calculating, by accumulating hard data, historians and economists, like physicists or chemists, could go beyond vague impressions and arrive instead at objective knowledge. Love and appreciation of artistic or natural beauty were merely subjective illusions. As for religion, positivists maintained that Christ was at best a wise teacher and perhaps no more than a myth, like Apollo or Zeus. Systematic biblical criticism and the fledgling discipline of archaeology were stimulated by this attitude. For much of the second half of the nineteenth century, materialism and positivism were enthusiastically supported by many advanced thinkers.

These materialist and positivist trends are best illustrated by the French thinker Auguste Comte (1798–1857), also known as the founder of modern sociology. Comte's "positive philosophy" defined three stages in attempts to understand the world. Early humanity, Comte said, made sense out of the world by supposing gods, spirits, or other humanlike supernatural creatures to be in charge of nature. Later, gods were replaced by principles—philosophical abstractions—governing nature, like the purposive force in nature proposed by Aristotle. Finally, modern empirical science had enabled humans to draw "positive" conclusions about the world from the observation of the material world itself. For Comte and his successors, the last-named way alone was the road to truth.

In the second half of the nineteenth century, painters and novelists often reflected the current fascination with the material world. Reacting vigorously against romantic "prettifying" of the natural world, "realists" insisted on depicting life as it really was. Gustave Courbet (1819–1877), for instance, painted a peasant funeral in meticulous detail, from the bored priest and expectant gravedigger to the country people gossiping throughout the service in the background. He said he did not paint angels because he never saw one.

One group of realist painters who emerged in France in the 1870s, the impressionists, dedicated themselves with scientific zeal to recreating the impact of light and color on the human eye—painting an "impression" of reality rather than the subject itself. Their investigations of light led them to break up subtle shades of color into basic primary colors and set these pigments side by side on the canvas, allowing the eye of the observer to do the mixing. The result was a rough, unfinished-looking picture if one stood close to it, but a brilliant composition if viewed from the proper distance. Claude Monet

(1840–1926) found in the shifting reflections of light off water-lily pools or the Seine River an ideal subject for experiments in the impact of light on the human optic nerve.

Realist writers were as strongly influenced by scientific trends as romantics had been by love and nature. Later nineteenth-century novels bring society to life with remarkable vividness and sociohistorical accuracy. Émile Zola (1840–1902) produced a series of novels about all levels of French society in the last third of the century, treating such grim subjects as alcoholism, prostitution, and the tragic impact of a miner's strike. In England, Charles Dickens (1812–1870) portrayed with meticulous detail such characters as Oliver Twist and David Copperfield against the background of industrial England, especially gritty, lower-class London. Readers of *War and Peace* (1865–1872) by Leo Tolstoy (1828–1910) and *Crime and Punishment* (1866) by Fyodor Dostoyevsky (1821–1881) learn an immense amount about both the aristocracy and the lower classes of Russia. The realist style continued to be cultivated in the early twentieth century, for example, in the work of the Egyptian novelist Naguib Mahfouz (see Chapter 14).

"Survival of the Fittest" in Science and Society

While romanticism and materialism in general challenged the values of nineteenth-century Europeans, Darwin's exploration of the origins of humankind had especially disturbing effects. Charles Darwin (1809–1882), an English naturalist, set out to account for the infinite variety of species of living things. After long years of studying fossils, animal breeding, and hybrid plants around the world, Darwin published *On the Origin of Species* (1859) and *The Descent of Man* (1871), books as important in the history of science as Newton's *Principles of Natural Philosophy* 200 years earlier.

Darwin declared that all species, including humans, were the product of a long biological evolution involving two crucial factors: variation and competition for survival. All individual members of a given species, Darwin said, differed from one another, and these variations in characteristics could be passed to their offspring. There was never enough of the necessities of life for all living creatures. The result was "natural selection," an intense struggle for existence in which those individuals who had the characteristics best fitted for the particular environment survived. These survivors then passed on their particular characteristics to succeeding generations.

In time, unsuitable variations disappeared and a new species, better adapted to its environment, took shape. This Darwin called the "survival of the fittest." For example, the fastest gazelles would escape the tiger, until speed became a primary characteristic of the species. The human race itself, Darwin declared, was also the product of an evolutionary process. Accordingly, both humans and modern apes were descended from common primate ancestors that lived millions of years ago.

Social Darwinists took the scientific concept of survival of the fittest from the world of nature and applied it to human society. For example, they used the theory to account for the fierce, fang-and-claw competition among businessmen and to explain the dominant position of the middle class. They defended the new wave of European imperial conquest (see Chapter 13) as the triumph of the superior—more fit—white race. War itself could be seen as an inevitable form of natural selection.

Facts Which Cannot Be Disputed?

(1)

The main conclusion arrived at in this work, and now held by many naturalists who are well competent to form a sound judgment, is that man is descended from some less highly organized form. The grounds upon which this conclusion rests will never be shaken, for the close similarity between man and the lower animals, in embryonic development, as well as in innumerable points of structure and constitution . . . are facts which cannot be disputed.*

(2)

Mr. Darwin . . . declares that he applies his scheme . . . of natural selection to man himself, as well as to the animals around him. Now, we must say at once that such a notion is absolutely incompatible not only with . . . the word of God . . . but . . . with the whole . . . moral and spiritual condition of man. . . . Man's derived supremacy

over the earth . . . man's gift of reason; man's free will and responsibility; man's fall and man's redemption; the incarnation of the Eternal Son; the indwelling of the Eternal Spirit—all are equally and utterly irreconcilable with the degrading notion of the brute origin of him who was created in the image of God. . . .**

Charles Darwin, in the first extract, claimed the scientific evidence of embryology and anatomy supported his view that human beings had evolved from "some less highly organized form" of life. Bishop Samuel Wilberforce, a leading opponent of Darwinian evolution, responded by pointing in horror to the "moral and spiritual" implications of evolution. Darwin's "facts which cannot be disputed" convinced the large majority of biologists, yet are still debated today, mostly because of the religious and moral implications that so disturbed Wilberforce.

*Charles Darwin, The Descent of Man, in Darwin, ed. P. Appleman (New York: Norton, 1979), p. 196.
**Samuel Wilberforce, review of Origin of Species, in B. D. Henning et al., Crises in English History, 1066–1945 (New York: Holt, 1957), p. 451.

Many people opposed Darwinism. The theory of a struggle for survival, of "nature red in tooth and claw," had little in common either with the Enlightenment vision of a system of harmonious natural laws or with the romantic emphasis on the beauty and divinity of nature. Further, Christian morality was affronted by the efforts of social Darwinists to justify war and unbridled competition as socially healthy for the species despite the pain inflicted on the individual.

Most disturbing to nineteenth-century sensibilities, however, was Darwin's contention that human beings were only very clever animals. Evolution seemed to deny religious notions of the "soul" and a divinely created universe; science seemed to dethrone human reason from its central place.

Darwin helped launch a powerful new secularism around the globe. This amoral outlook, especially attractive to intellectual and political leaders, displaced traditional ideas of man's place in the universe. The new ideology, stressing concepts of intrinsic inferiority and superiority, was to have important repercussions in the twentieth century.

The Development of Culture in the Americas

The cultural life of the new American nations followed its own course in the nineteenth century, although it continued to be heavily influenced by Europe. Both romanticism and literary realism, for instance, had their devotees across the Atlantic. The American poet and short-story writer, Edgar Allan Poe (1809–1849), displayed the romantic's fascination with the emotions, the supernatural, the bizarre, and the macabre, as in this passage from his short story, "The Tell-Tale Heart," in which a madman murderer describes the moments just before his grisly crime:

I scarcely breathed. I held the lantern motionless. I tried how steadily I could maintain the ray upon the eye. Meanwhile the hellish tattoo of the heart increased. It grew quicker and quicker, louder and louder every instant. The old man's terror must have been extreme! It grew louder, I say, louder every moment!—do you mark me well? I have told you that I am nervous: so I am. And now at the dead hour of the night, amid the dreadful silence of that old house, so strange a noise as this excited me to uncontrollable terror.

In the later years of the nineteenth century, American authors like Hamlin Garland (1860–1940) depicted with uncompromising realism the drab loneliness and hard work as well as the strength of spirit of midwestern pioneers and farmers. The muckraking social novels of Frank Norris (1870–1902), which exposed the seamier side of American business and politics, were directly influenced by the works of Zola.

Nineteenth-century American painters were mostly influenced by European artists. The seascapes of Winslow Homer (1836–1910) have a strongly romantic feeling for nature. The impressionist Mary Cassatt (1845–1926) was so deeply involved in French impressionism that she moved permanently to Paris. Distinctively American subjects did attract some artists, however, including the romantic painters of the Hudson River school and George Catlin (1796–1872), who painted American Indians.

The United States in its first century also produced some "isms" of its own. The transcendentalist movement of the pre–Civil War period showed a distinctively American confidence in the divine essence of each individual. Henry David Thoreau (1817–1862) and Ralph Waldo Emerson (1803–1882) preached freedom, individual conscience, and self-reliance as typically American virtues. During the Gilded Age of American industrial growth after the Civil War, William James (1842–1910) expounded another characteristically American philosophy: pragmatism. James defined the truth of an idea in terms of its practical usefulness. Truth, he said, is what works—an idea that suited many people in the bustling, not overly idealistic United States of his time.

Some of the United States' most famous writers were striking individuals not easily classified according to European literary trends. *Moby Dick* (1851) and other novels of the sea by Herman Melville (1819–1891) explored fundamental aspects of individual experience. The humorous narratives of life along the pre–Civil War Mississippi and on the western frontier by Mark Twain (Samuel Clemens, 1835–1910) had no parallel in Europe. The exquisite lyrics of Emily Dickinson (1830–1886) explored her own soul and the spiritual dimensions of simple things. The passionate *Leaves of Grass* (1855) by the poet Walt Whitman (1819–1892) hymned the potential greatness of a whole people, as in these lines from his "When Lilacs Last in the Dooryard Bloom'd":

Lo, body and soul—this land,
My own Manhattan with spires, and the
    sparkling and hurrying tides, and the ships,
The varied and ample land, the South and the North
    in the light, Ohio's shores and flashing Missouri,
And ever the far-spreading prairies cover'd with grass and corn.

Although Latin American scholars and writers drew heavily on European cultural sources, they used these to help them achieve their own cultural and intellectual independence from the Old World. An underlying concern of much of this writing was the desire to explore and establish a genuinely Latin American culture, distinct from those of Europe and the United States. By condemning their European ancestors and glorifying their Amerindian ones, by evoking such clearly South American phenomena as the gaucho of the pampas, these writers strove to achieve a sense of their own cultural uniqueness. Latin American men of letters also frequently combined literature with political affairs or even armed struggle. José Marti, for example, Cuba's most honored writer, was a poet who died fighting in Cuba's rebellion against Spain in the 1890s.

© Bettmann/Corbis

Emily Dickinson. The American poet is depicted here as a young woman. Despite a narrowly circumscribed life in the small town of Amherst, Massachusetts, Dickinson's creative genius could encompass the broadest of human concerns.

Although romanticism had a longer and deeper influence in Latin America than in North America, it was adapted to local cultural needs. South American writers had little enthusiasm for the towering romantic ego of Byron or for the supernaturalism of the Gothic romance. They seized on the romantic glorification of freedom, the primacy of emotion, and the superiority of the primitive over the artificial or sophisticated. Glorifying the free life, for instance, the Argentine poet José Hernandez (1834–1866) praised the freedom-loving gaucho, the cowboy of the pampas. Mexican poets honored the memory of the ancient Aztecs, and Brazilians celebrated their Amerindian ancestors.

Realism, naturalism, and positivism also appeared in Latin America in the last decades of the century. Writers documented the worst abuses of the old Spanish colonial regime and the materialistic inhumanity of the Industrial Revolution in western European nations. Chilean realist Alberto Blest Gana depicted a money-grubbing society in novels like *Arithmetic in Love* (1860). The Brazilian novelist Euclydes da Cunha (1866–1909), in his *Rebellion in the Backlands* (1902), powerfully evoked primitive backwoodsmen in revolt against an oppressive government.

Summary and Comparisons

The French Revolution was a great watershed in European history. Like the Protestant Reformation, it inaugurated widespread changes in Western society. Though the underlying causes of the French Revolution are difficult to disentangle, its immediate source was

CHRONOLOGY

1775	
	The French Revolution
	Napoleon Bonaparte
	Robert Fulton's steamboat
	Ludwig van Beethoven
1815	Battle of Waterloo
	Congress of Vienna
	Latin American independence movements: Simón Bolívar
	Romantic poetry: Wordsworth
	The Great Reform Act in Britain
	Samuel Morse and the telegraph
	Revolutions of 1848
	Karl Marx, *Communist Manifesto*
1850	
	Second French Empire: Napoleon III
	Henry David Thoreau, *Walden*
	Charles Darwin, *On the Origin of Species*
	The Unification of Italy
	U.S. Civil War
	Charles Dickens
	Leo Tolstoy, *War and Peace*
	The unification of Germany
	The Paris Commune
1875	
	Impressionist painting: Claude Monet
	Gladstone and Disraeli dominate British politics
	Thomas Edison and the electric light
	Louis Pastuer and germ theory
	Tsar Alexander III
	The internal combustion engine
1900	
	Euclydes da Cunha, *Rebellion in the Backlands*
	John D. Rockefeller
	Mary Cassatt, American impressionist painter
1920	

the growing national debt, which in turn triggered the collapse of the old regime. The pre- and early revolutionary phases dominated by the aristocracy, seeking to retain privileges and political authority at the expense of the monarchy. Initially the nobles scored a victory when they forced the king to summon the Estates-General in the spring of 1789, but they lost the initiative to the middle class, which transformed France into a constitutional monarchy.

The threat of counterrevolutionaries and a war with the rest of Europe propelled into power the radical Jacobins, who abolished the monarchy and imposed a reign of terror. A reaction followed, as the middle class made a short-lived attempt to reassert its authority. The revolution ended in November 1799 when Napoleon Bonaparte established a military dictatorship.

In many ways Napoleon emulated the best features of enlightened despotism and continued reforming France: finances were put on a sound footing, laws were codified, and the educational system was reorganized. But politically he was a reactionary, reinstituting the very sort of absolutist state the French people had rebelled against. Napoleon moreover indulged his natural instincts for conquest and glory. He did not massacre innocent civilians and raze towns in the manner of Genghis Khan or Timurlane, but his victories were achieved at a high cost in blood and treasure. Those who initially welcomed him as a liberator soon realized they had exchanged one absolute ruler for another. Although he came closer than any man to imposing a political unity on the European continent, he was ultimately defeated at Waterloo.

In the aftermath of Napoleon's downfall, a mood of uneasiness and disillusionment—like that following the Thirty Years' War—permeated Europe. This pessimistic outlook was in part attributable to the peace settlement reached at Vienna in 1815. Metternich, the dominant voice both then and for many years after in European politics, was determined to destroy the forces of nationalism and liberalism released by the French Revolution. He created a system that kept such movements in check, but advocates of radical change again burst forth in the revolutions of 1830 and 1848.

By contrast, Latin American nationalists succeeded in ousting the Spanish and Portuguese and created new independent states. In the first three decades of the nineteenth century, colonists in part of the Caribbean and throughout Latin America won independence. Though most of the new nations were liberal republics, they maintained their common colonial culture in which a small elite controlled the masses and a stagnant but potentially rich economy.

Back in Europe, the revolutions of 1830 succeeded only in the countries where the insurgents formed a large segment of the population. In the revolutions of 1848, the liberals fought for constitutions while revolts in eastern Europe for a time threatened the conservative Habsburg Empire. The failure of the 1848 revolutions heightened the nationalism at work around the world in the second half of the nineteenth century.

In the United States, nationalism was expressed through a momentous civil war that clarified the nature of the American union. The constitution of 1787 was fundamentally unclear as to whether the government of the United States was a confederation of sovereign states or a perpetual union. Economic and cultural differences between the northern and southern sections of the country, especially regarding the enslavement of African Americans, imperiled the young nation. To defend slavery, eleven southern states seceded in 1860–1861. In the ensuing civil war, the state sovereignty doctrine was defeated, and the United States entered the twentieth century as an indissoluble union.

Even more dramatically than in the United States, nationalism in Italy and Germany involved a forcible union of disparate elements into centralized states. The process of political unification in Italy was piloted by Cavour with the Kingdom of Sardinia as its focus, and in Germany by Bismarck under Prussian hegemony. Independence for many Christian peoples in the Balkans, formerly subjects of the Ottoman Empire, marked another victory for nationalism. Not all peoples realized their nationalistic dreams, however, most notably Slavic subjects in the Austro-Hungarian Empire and non-Russians in the Russian Empire. The frustrations of those still denied freedom, and the instability in the new states created a volatile political climate in eastern Europe.

Another continent-wide trend during this era was the development of democratic institutions, smoothly and through an evolutionary process in Great Britain and in lurches and amidst turmoil in France. Germany and Austria-Hungary made concessions to democratic institutions, but their governments retained authoritarian characteristics. Russia remained a despotic empire into the twentieth century and had no meaningful representative institutions.

The Industrial Revolution was as significant in the advancement of humanity as the development of agriculture during the Neolithic period. It began in Great Britain with the widespread use of mechanical power in factories and spread first to the European continent and then to the United States, with far-reaching economic and social consequences. Steam power was harnessed to new forms of transportation, the railroads and steamships, and electrical energy to new means of communication, especially the telegraph.

During this era, many socialists advocated public ownership of the means of production to ensure a more even distribution of wealth and improvements in the living standards of the poor. Followers of Karl Marx believed that class struggle would lead to a world revolution and the seizure of power by the proletariat and an eventual classless society.

The Industrial Revolution transformed Europe's economic institutions. The new business leaders opposed government economic controls and succeeded in destroying the mercantilist system. The unfettered free competition of the mid-nineteenth century, however, gave way after 1870 to a new form of control of the economy by giant corporations and cartels.

Industrial society had several striking features. The population explosion multiplied the sheer number of Western people. An unprecedentedly high proportion of them lived in the new industrial cities. Finally, the middle class became the dominant element in Western society and the industrial masses emerged as a challenging new force. In all these ways, industrialism fostered new European and American societies during the late eighteenth and the nineteenth centuries.

The culture of the nineteenth century was complex and often challenged conventional beliefs and values. Romanticism in the first half of the century and materialism and Darwinism in the second half pervaded the European mind. In the Americas, these and other themes influenced the cultures of the new nations.

Romanticism in literature, painting, and music asserted the superiority of the emotions over reason and exalted nature, underdeveloped cultures, faraway places, and colorful periods of the past. Romantic artists also rejected the classical rules for the arts, insisting instead on the free play of the imagination. As a cultural revolt, romanticism expressed a growing alienation from the vulgarities of nineteenth-century industrial civilization and once more stressed emotion over intellect.

Materialism concluded from the progress of the physical sciences that only the material world existed. Dismissing religion as an illusion, this world view insisted on positivistic knowledge, derived exclusively from empirical observation. Realists attempted to describe this material world in paint or prose. Impressionists tried to paint light as the eye sees it, naturalists like Zola to describe human beings as mere biological organisms, without spiritual or moral dimensions.

Charles Darwin explored the animal origins and instinctive drives beneath human reason. Darwinian evolution stressed the struggle for existence and the transformation of all living creatures through natural selection. His theories led to an intense and unending intellectual debate. As a rule, scientists supported Darwin in contrast to most theologians and the devout, who decried the idea of any direct relationship between man and higher primates as a repudiation of the account of the creation in the biblical book of Genesis.

The cultural history of the Americas reflected both European influences and New World concerns. The growing United States produced some writers influenced by romanticism and realism, but also gave birth to such distinctive schools of thought as transcendentalism and to such unique talents as Mark Twain, Emily Dickinson, and Walt Whitman.

Latin American culture in the nineteenth century struck closer to European models, from romanticism to naturalism and positivism. But Latin American writers used these forms and ideas to define the uniqueness of their culture, lauding freedom and their Amerindian heritage and condemning their Spanish colonial past and the industrializing present.

Selected Sources

Items indicated with an asterisk (*) are available in paperback.

Bloom, Harold, and Lionel Trilling, eds. *Romantic Prose and Poetry.* 1973. A good, representative reader.

Bosher, J. F. *The French Revolution.* 1988. A superb study of the revolution.

*Brinton, Crane. *The Anatomy of Revolution.* 1938, revised ed. 1965. Useful comparison of English, American, French, and Russian revolutions. A good starting point for the understanding of revolution.

*Chevalier, Louis. *Laboring Classes and Dangerous Classes in Paris During the First Half of the Nineteenth Century.* 1981. Working-class misery and resentment in the early Industrial Revolution.

Clark, Kenneth. *The Romantic Rebellion: Romantic versus Classic Art.* 1973. Well-written and illustrated essays on important artists by a leading art historian.

*Crankshaw, Edward. *Bismarck.* 1981. A lively, rather critical account of the Iron Chancellor.

*Dickens, Charles. *A Tale of Two Cities.* 1859. Numerous editions. Colorful, sometimes moving novel based on the French Revolution. Skillfully captures the atmosphere of the revolution.

Doyle, William. *The Oxford History of the French Revolution.* 1989. Insights into a major event in world history. The author rejects the theory of a bourgeois revolution, arguing that this group and the aristocracy shared similar views and interests in the pre-1789 era.

Droz, J. *Europe Between Revolutions, 1815–1848.* 1968. An overview of the period.

*Eiseley, Loren. *Darwin's Century: Evolution and the Men Who Discovered It.* 1958. Thoughtful and readable account of the early evolutionists.

*Herold, J. C. *The Age of Napoleon.* 1963. A well-written popular history.

*Howard, Michael. *The Franco-Prussian War.* 1961. A fascinating and meticulously researched study by a leading British military historian.

Korg, Jacob, ed. *London in Dickens' Day.* 1961. Brief contemporary glimpses of everyday life, from pubs to clubs, parks to prisons.

Landes, David S. *The Unbound Prometheus.* 1969. Survey of industrial development from the eighteenth to the twentieth centuries, especially good on technology.

Levy, Darline G., et al., eds. and trans. *Women in Revolutionary Paris, 1789–1795.* 1979. A useful collection of documents on women in the era.

*Lichtheim, George. *Marxism: An Historical and Critical Study.* 1982. Excellent critique of nineteenth-century Marxism.

*Lindemann, Albert S. *A History of European Socialism.* 1983. Particularly good on comparison of socialist and syndicalist movements.

*Marx, Karl, and Friedrich Engels. *The Communist Manifesto.* 1848. Many editions. Brief presentation of Marx's view of history.

The Molly Maguires. Ritt, Martin, dir. 1970. Film about a workers' rebellion in the Pennsylvania coal fields, with vivid images of life in the mines and company towns.

Norton, Rictor, ed. *Gothic Readings: The First Wave, 1764–1840.* 2000. Contains many Romantic instances of the gothic subgenre.

*Palmer, R. R. *The Age of Revolutions.* 2 vols. 1964. Interesting thesis that the French Revolution was part of a general revolutionary movement in the West, by one of the foremost scholars in the United States.

Popkin, Jeffrey D. *A Short History of the French Revolution.* 1997. A well-written survey, with a discussion of the various interpretations of the origins of the revolution and its broader impact.

Porter, Glenn. *The Rise of Big Business, 1860–1910.* 1973. Good survey of big business in the United States.

Ruis, Eduardo del Rio. *Marx for Beginners.* 1976. Humorous yet informative cartoon book with historical overview. See also *Trotsky for Beginners* and *Cuba for Beginners.*

Schama, Simon. *Citizens: A Chronicle of the French Revolution.* 1989. An excellent study of the revolution from a sociological vantage point.

Smith, Denis Mack. *The Making of Italy, 1796–1870.* 1968. A scholarly overview of the Italian problem in the nineteenth century.

*Stavrianos, Leften S. *The Balkans, 1815–1914.* 1962. Good survey of the troubled area.

*Stearns, Peter. *1848: The Revolutionary Tide in Europe.* 1974. A sound general study, with special emphasis on social conditions.

*Sutherland, D. M. G. *France, 1789–1815.* 1985. An interpretation of the revolutionary period, stressing the connection between social and political conflict.

*Tolstoy, Leo. *War and Peace.* 1865–1869. Numerous editions, complete or abridged. Classic novel about Napoleon's invasion of Russia. (Also a film.)

Ward, Barbara. *Nationalism and Ideology.* 1966. Puts modern nationalism in the broadest context of evolving human loyalties.

Wheen, Francis. *Karl Marx.* 1999. A richly entertaining biography that humanizes the father of historical materialism.

 Additional resources, exercises, and Internet links related to this chapter are available at the Book Companion Web site: http://history.wadsworth.com/upshurcompact4/

COMPARATIVE ESSAY 10
Total War

The great strides which civilization makes against barbarism and unreason are only made actual by the sword.
Heinrich von Treitschke, *Politics*, vol. 1 (New York: Macmillan, 1916), p. 65.

The first shock at the news of war—the war that no one, people or government, had wanted— . . . had suddenly been transformed into enthusiasm. There were parades in the street, flags, ribbons, and music burst forth everywhere, young recruits were marching triumphantly, their faces lighting up at the cheering.
Stefan Zweig, a noted Austrian literary figure, describing the scene in Vienna on the outbreak of war in August 1914. Marvin Perry, Joseph R. Peden, and Theodore von Laure, eds., *Sources of the Western Tradition*, vol. 2 (Boston: Houghton Mifflin, 1987), p. 231.

In three days, on a front of about 200 yards, we lost 909 men, and the enemy casualties must have amounted to thousands. The blue French cloth mingled with the German grey upon the ground, and in some places the bodies were piled so high that one could take cover from shell fire behind them. . . . Don't ask about the fate of the wounded! Anybody who was incapable of walking to the doctor had to die a miserable death; some lingered in agony for hours, some for days, and even for a week. . . . There are moments when even the bravest soldier is so utterly sick of the whole thing that he could cry like a child.
Richard Schmeider, a German student in philosophy writing from a trench near Vaudesincourt, March 13, 1915. Perry M. Rogers, ed., *Aspects of Western Civilization*, vol. 2 (Englewood Cliffs, N.J.: Prentice Hall, 1992), pp. 284–285.

However much we may sympathize with a small nation confronted by a big and powerful neighbor, we cannot in all circumstances undertake to involve the whole British Empire in a war simply on her account.
British Prime Minister Neville Chamberlain in a broadcast to the nation during the crisis over Czechoslovakia. Neville Chamberlain, *In Search of Peace* (Freeport, N.Y.: Books for Libraries Press, 1971), p. 175.

The decade before World War I witnessed a surge of militarism in Europe. This attitude was particularly strong in Germany, where writers like Heinrich von Treitschke gloried warfare as a great adventure that was essential to human progress. In August 1914 the citizens of the belligerent nations, conditioned by years of nationalistic propaganda, greeted their respective government's declaration of war with almost carnival gaiety, cheering and showering flowers and gifts on soldiers departing for the front. After trench warfare set in at the close of 1914, the rapturous mood turned first to disillusionment, then to bitterness as the fighting dragged on for four years, exacting a horrendous toll in human lives. It was the haunting memories of the slaughter in World War I that led statesmen in western European democracies, such as Neville Chamberlain, to embrace a policy of conciliation with Hitler and Mussolini in the 1930s that came to be known as "appeasement."

The wars of both 1914–1918 and 1939–1945 were fought as much at home as at the front. The term *total war* emerged during World War II and is traditionally associated with the two global wars of the twentieth century. Broadly defined, total war required a belligerent nation to mobilize all its resources, both human and material, for the purpose of waging war.

Under these criteria, it would seem that instances of total war predate the twentieth century and that some earlier military conflicts had key features of total war. As an aggressor nation, the ancient Mongols, no less than the modern Nazis, practiced total war against an enemy by organizing all available resources, including military personnel, noncombatant workers, intelligence, transport, money, and provisions. More recently, during the French Revolution, the government in Paris introduced conscription, took control of industries vital to the war effort, managed the economy, and restricted individual rights.

Conversely, targets of aggression were compelled to wage total war to survive as nations or to stave off annihilation. During the Third Punic War, the entire population of Carthage was involved in a desperate effort to resist the Roman siege. Noncombatants toiled feverishly to forge new weapons of war and to strengthen the defenses of the city, while the women gave their hair to be made into strings for bows and catapults. Similarly, the city of Tyre did all it could to resist the siege of Alexander the Great but failed.

The spread of the Industrial Revolution in the nineteenth century revolutionized weapons, tactics, and the ability of nations to mobilize their resources. The totality of warfare was foreshadowed in the U.S. Civil War and in the Franco-Prussian War and the subsequent siege of Paris (1871). In each case, combatants and noncombatants became indistinguishable in the face of the threat to their survival.

When opposing coalitions proved unable to end the war quickly, World War I added a number of novel features to the practice of total war. For the first time governments attempted to integrate completely all elements of a nation in arms, making the home front an integral part of the fighting front. Belligerent nations not only had to put huge armies in the field but also had to devise the means to supply them with weapons, ammunition, replacements, clothing, and food. Simply to remain in the war required a national commitment on a scale never before contemplated. To that end, the government had to control and manage the economy and maintain the nation's morale and its will to go on fighting. The degree to which the belligerent governments succeeded in harnessing their resources varied from nation to nation, but few people were not affected by the war.

Among the most important changes the war imposed on civilians was the great increase in the power of the state to exercise control over all aspects of political, economic, and social life. All able-bodied men, sometimes even those in war-related industries, were drafted into the army. Governments temporarily set aside free market capitalism and moved toward planned economies. They set up agencies to convert industrial machines to military production, allocate raw materials, ration food supplies and essential materials, regulate wages and prices, and nationalize transportation systems and vital industries. Some governments sponsored scientific research and efforts to devise synthetic substitutes for some goods that were simply unattainable. Industries called upon women to replace the men sent to the front.

As the war dragged on with no end in sight, warring governments resorted to propaganda to maintain civilian morale and generate enthusiasm for the war. One way to do this was to foster hatred for the enemy. Both sides portrayed the other as the lowest form of vermin, guilty of heinous crimes and entertaining diabolical war aims. Moreover, the need for national unity precluded dissent of any kind. Thus all governments accompanied their propaganda with censorship.

World War II required an even greater commitment on the part of the belligerents. Fighting was more widespread, weapons more destructive, and civilians more directly exposed to the war. Victory was likely to go to the side better able to mobilize its home front.

As was the case in the 1914–1918 conflict, the power of the central government after 1939, even in democracies, expanded over all facets of national life. Since many of the World War II leaders had gained experience in administration during World War I, they were able to avoid many of the mistakes of the earlier conflict. For example, at the beginning of World War II, they established the full set of regulations that had only come in the last stages of World War I. Once again a national system of rationing, allocation of raw material, and price controls was set up to put the economy under government direction. Women left their homes to work in factories or serve in the armed forces. Propaganda was used to greater effect in the second conflict than in the first. As the struggle took on ideological overtones, warring powers mobilized the press, radio, and film to whip up national sentiment. Science played a crucial part in the war. Scientists were active in all fields, devising ways to escape damaged submarines, planning precision bombing, and improving weapons.

After 1945, nuclear weapons, with their capacity to destroy the world in a matter of hours, if not minutes, made the concept of total war obsolete. As nations stockpiled arsenals of ever more powerful nuclear weapons, the former balance between nations became a balance of terror. A sardonic acronym for this grim "balance of terror" was MAD (Mutually Assured Destruction). Yet these awesome weapons have led to less rather than more death and destruction in recent decades. They have forced nations to seek alternatives to war, or at worst, less destructive forms of warfare to attain their goals. Since World War II, limited, rather than total, warfare has become the norm between nations unable or unwilling to resolve their differences at the negotiating table.

13

The Race for Empire and World War I

•

• Causes of Imperialism and the Partition of Africa •

• Western Imperialism in the Middle East and Asia •

• Japan and the United States Become World Powers •

• The Causes and Course of World War I •

• Postwar Settlements and the Interwar Years •

• Summary and Comparisons •

Take up the White Man's burden—
Send forth the best ye breed—
Go bind your sons to exile
To serve your captives' need;
To wait in heavy harness,
On fluttered folk and wild—
Your new-caught, sullen peoples,
Half-devil and half child.

Take up the White Man's burden—
Have done with childish days—
The lightly proffered laurel,
The easy, ungrudged praise.
Comes now, to search your manhood
Through all the thankless years,
Cold, edged with dear-bought wisdom,
The judgment of your peers!*

*Rudyard Kipling, Rudyard Kipling's Verse: Definitive Edition (New York: Doubleday, 1940), p. 321.

In "The White Man's Burden," Britain's best-known imperialist writer, Rudyard Kipling, represented empire building as a duty, a thankless job, rather than as a naked expression of economic and political power. Kipling earnestly believed in the mission of the white races to bestow the blessings of their higher culture and superior civilization on "backward" societies. He called upon the United States to join Great Britain in this vast civilizing movement. Given that the United States' population had surpassed Great Britain's and its industrial strength was increasing at an unprecedented pace, he felt the time had come for Americans to shoulder the responsibility of a great nation and accept their destiny.

Western, industrialized nations entered the twentieth century confident of their scientific, technological, and cultural superiority. By the end of the nineteenth century, the industrialized nations had become imperialistic, and successfully moved to extend their domination over Africa, Asia, and Latin America. But World War I ended the industrialized world's boundless faith in its own superiority and irrevocably changed the course of history around the world. Attitudes about the continued progress of Western civilization were permanently changed, and society at large no longer believed in the absolute ability of rational thought, as manifested in science and technology, to solve all human problems.

The cost of the war in human and financial terms far exceeded anyone's predictions. Western imperial powers, shaken by the war, would never recover total control over their far-flung territories. Likewise, political and economic systems, particularly in the West, were permanently altered. This chapter begins with a discussion of the causes of imperialism and traces the pattern of Western and Japanese imperialism around the world. It then describes the course of World War I and the far-reaching impacts of the war. Finally, postwar developments in the Western democracies and the worldwide financial crisis of the Great Depression will be described.

Causes of Imperialism and the Partition of Africa

At midday on Tuesday, June 22, 1897, Queen Victoria of England, Defender of the Faith, Empress of India, ruler of the British Dominions beyond the Seas, arrived at St. Paul's Cathedral to thank God for the existence of the greatest Empire ever known.

The representatives of an imperial caste awaited her there. Bishops of the Church of England fluttered hymnal sheets and remembered half a century of Christian effort—the suppression of slavery, the conversion of heathen tribes, mission stations from Niger to Labrador. Generals and admirals blazed with medals and remembered half a century of satisfactory campaigning. . . .

There were poets, musicians, and propagandists. . . . Behind these marshals, soldiers from every part of the Queen's Empire honored the royal presence. The Chinese from Hong Kong wore wide coolie hats. The Zaptiehs, Turkish military policemen from Cyprus, wore fezzes. The Jamaicans wore white gaiters and gold-embroidered jackets. There were Dyaks from Borneo, and Sikhs from India, and Canadian Hussars, and Sierra Leone gunners . . . and Maltese, and South Africans, and a troop of jangling Bengal Lancers. . . . [These soldiers represented] nearly 400 million subjects living in all five continents, honoring a thousand religions, speaking a thousand languages—peoples of every race, culture, stage of development.*

*The Horizon History of the British Empire (New York: American Heritage, 1973), pp. 9, 11.

This account of the Diamond Jubilee, a ceremony celebrating the sixtieth year of the reign of Queen Victoria, describes the high-water mark for the British Empire, the largest and most powerful imperial power of the age. In the nineteenth century a new form of imperialism swept the world. This new imperialism, or extension of one nation-state's domination or control over territory outside its own boundaries, differed from the empires of the fifteenth and sixteenth centuries in that the industrialized nations of the Western world did not generally seek to colonize or to settle territories with their people; rather, they sought to control faraway lands for a complex variety of economic, political, national, and social reasons.

Imperial Motivations

Nineteenth-century imperialism built on many of the same foundations as the earlier imperialism, but its impact on societies and economies around the world was much more intrusive and in many cases more disruptive. This was particularly true in Africa, where the firepower of Western armies and navies overwhelmed the swords and spears of non-Western peoples. Western steam-powered gunboats, rifled artillery, and machine guns could dominate any area of the world. Railroads and river streamers, built by local labor but owned by the Western interests or nations, could transport valuable commodities and raw materials from remote inland regions to industrial centers; conversely, these same transport systems could carry manufactured goods to new markets around the globe. New telegraph lines laid overland and under oceans facilitated rapid communications that previously might have taken months. From modern ports in Africa and Asia, the new oceangoing ships, made of iron and powered by steam-driven screw propellers, carried larger cargoes to their destination faster and more safely than the old wooden sailing ships. Engineers designed and Egyptian laborers dug and constructed the Suez Canal, and later the United States constructed the Panama Canal. These new canals enabled navies and shipping lines to cut in half the length and time of the journey from Great Britain to India or New York to San Francisco.

New economic forces also propelled imperialism. The industrialized nations constantly sought new markets and cheap raw materials. They needed supplies of coal, iron ore, copper, other industrial ores, and (later) rubber and petroleum. As domestic markets in industrial nations became saturated, manufacturers looked for new markets abroad. Nigeria, Egypt, China, and India, with large and growing populations, offered enticing possibilities to industrialists looking for new purchasers of their manufactured goods. These nations also offered a potential supply of cheap labor. In the late nineteenth and early twentieth centuries, as labor unions in the West grew and secured higher wages and better working conditions, many industrialists sought to evade higher costs by transferring their businesses abroad where labor was largely unorganized and where people in need of jobs would accept poor working conditions and low wages.

Some economists such as J. A. Hobson (1858–1940) and Marxists such as V. I. Lenin argued that it was inevitable that the capitalist, industrialized nations would become imperialistic. Hobson and Lenin, among others, stressed that capitalists constantly sought to increase their profits, and as these profits grew, large amounts of capital became available. Thus fortified, capitalists would seek to extend their economic control over the markets, resources, and labor of the rest of the world. This analysis intrigued many Western intellectuals, but, with the possible exception of Japan, the capitalist dynamic does not seem to have been the major, overwhelming factor behind imperialism in the nineteenth century.

Some industrialists even opposed their governments' annexing of new colonies on the grounds that they were too expensive and troublesome. At the same time, many people with no economic interest at stake favored imperialism. In Great Britain, for example, support for imperial expansion tended to be bipartisan; both the conservative and liberal parties—in spite of differing economic policies and outlooks—backed imperial endeavors. Although economic considerations were and still are major factors for imperialism, it is simplistic to attribute all of nineteenth-century imperialism to economic motivations. For example, economic reasons cannot explain why France, one of the least industrialized great European powers, more than doubled its imperial holdings between 1815 and 1870 or took over the landlocked, impoverished regions in Africa.

Certainly, the quest for empire led to a marked increase in nationalist rivalries among European powers. Nationalism, particularly for the average citizen of industrialized Western nations, was a major motivating factor behind imperialism. The desire of industrialized nations to have the biggest and most powerful empire often led them to acquire new territories even when they provided no economic benefit, as, for example, in the case of the French takeover of Chad in Africa, which proved an economic drag on the French economy.

Nations in the late nineteenth century also seized areas for strategic reasons, especially to provide naval bases to protect the sea lanes between the key colonies and the colonial powers. The Hawaiian Islands, the Suez Canal, and Aden on the Arabian coast are examples of such strategic locations. The imperial powers also took the islands in the Pacific and Atlantic oceans for ports and strategic communication lines between the powers and their valuable land territories in Asia, such as India or Indochina.

The desire of nations to impose their culture on others was another major motive for imperialism. With new technology and growing economic and military strength, Western peoples were convinced that theirs was the "best of all possible worlds." They believed that as "superior" people in possession of the best culture, they had been chosen to bring good government, Christian religion, and light to the rest of the world. Most confused scientific and technological superiority with cultural superiority. This misconception—Europeans called it the white man's burden—impelled Western powers to recreate the rest of the world in their own image. As one imperialist writer put it, "We are imperialists in response to the compelling influences of our destiny . . . we are imperialists because we cannot help it."

Westerners evolved two influential doctrines to rationalize their domination over non-Western, nonwhite, and non-Christian civilizations. One was social Darwinism. Some misinterpreted Darwin's theories regarding the survival of the fittest through adaptation to mean that some human groups were intrinsically "fitter" than others. These social Darwinists, typified by the English writer Herbert Spencer (1820–1903), propounded the notion that select human groups would and should flourish and rule over those that were less "fit."

Accepting the misconceptions of social Darwinists, some racists extolled a doctrine of the superiority of the white race. Writers like the English poet Rudyard Kipling (1865–1936) reinforced this belief with emotional and romantic images of whites bringing a better life to their poor, inferior "brown brothers." In effect, most Westerners were sure that their conquests of other peoples conformed to the laws of God and nature. As they saw it, the conquered groups would benefit by being brought under the tutelage of a superior culture and would naturally want to discard their backward ways. Because these inferior peoples were not expected to grasp the essence of Western civilization, they would have to remain under Western rule. Nineteenth-century Westerners were so certain of their superiority that when traveling around the world they tended to see exactly what they wanted or expected to see. Western literature, art, and music depicted the African, Arab, and Asian worlds as exotic, erotic, mysterious, and slightly threatening. To a great extent, many of these "Orientalist" images of Asian and African cultures continue to permeate Western perceptions and culture to the present day.

Nineteenth-century missionaries, explorers, and adventurers were also imbued with attitudes of cultural superiority, and they, too, helped to foster the imperial spirit. The desire to gain converts to Christianity was a key factor in the spread of imperialism. Up to this point the Roman Catholic church had generally taken a far more active and successful role in securing converts than had the Protestant denominations, but this situation changed during the nineteenth century. The aggressive efforts of the French government to spread Catholicism in Africa, Asia, and Polynesia were matched by the vigor with which Protestants from Europe and the United States sought to convert "heathen" peoples under British or U.S. control.

Nineteenth-century Westerners were also interested in exploring formerly inaccessible and remote parts of the globe. In this they were in some ways similar to twentieth-century astronauts. As early as 1788 the British African Association had financed expeditions to West Africa. Ambitious and wealthy Europeans vied to be the first to find the fabled city of Timbuktu or the source of the Nile River. It did not seem important to most of these adventurers that powerful African societies had built Timbuktu or had lived along the Nile River since the beginning of human history. For the most part, historians, and later archaeologists and anthropologists, did not publish serious scholarly studies on African cultural accomplishments until the twentieth century. As a result, most Westerners learned about Africa from the written exploits of explorers like Richard Burton, John Speke, Samuel and Florence Baker, and Henry Stanley, who were all famous for their African journeys.

Explorers also brought back stories of precious metals, valuable goods, and industrial raw materials. Their tales encouraged other adventurers and entrepreneurs to launch enterprises in Africa, South America, and Asia, where many fortunes were made. For example, mining magnate Cecil Rhodes became one of the richest men in the world from his interests in South Africa and Zimbabwe, which he renamed Rhodesia. An astute politician, Rhodes was also instrumental in pushing the British government to construct a Cape-to-Cairo railroad to connect South and North Africa. Although this dream was never realized, Rhodes succeeded in extending British imperial holdings in eastern and southern Africa. Similarly, a company headed by King Leopold of Belgium came to control the entire Congo River basin. Later, after considerable maneuvering, Leopold, who had run the Congo as a private fiefdom, was forced to turn over control of the Congo state, eighty times larger than Belgium, to the Belgian government. Finally, as new advances in tropical medicine controlled some previously incurable diseases, such as malaria, the African interior became more attractive to European settlers.

Motivated by these diverse factors, the European powers raced to grab territories in a so-called scramble for Africa. Until the late nineteenth century, European holdings in sub-Saharan Africa were restricted to coastal regions in West and East Africa and South

Africa. Then, in less than twenty-five years, European nations claimed most of the continent; in 1875 they had controlled less than 10 percent of Africa; by 1900 that percentage had increased ninefold. Great Britain gained almost 5 million square miles; within the British domain, Cecil Rhodes alone controlled almost 3.5 million square miles. By the beginning of World War I, only Ethiopia, which had successfully fought off the Italians, and Liberia, which had been established by the United States and was dominated by U.S. interests, remained independent.

Once the colonies were established, Great Britain and France, the two major colonial powers, adopted radically different policies toward the governing and education of their subjects. British imperialism tended to be based on social exclusiveness. The British did not generally mix or assimilate with the indigenous peoples of their empire. At the same time, the British generally did not attempt to destroy indigenous cultures or languages; they chose instead to train small elite groups for bureaucratic and commercial jobs within the empire. In short, the British tended to believe that foreign peoples could not possibly become "British" in culture or language, and therefore it would be counterproductive to try to assimilate the majority of the peoples under their domination. In the Indian subcontinent, the small number of British working there made such a transformation impossible in any case. The British referred to their imperial policy as "indirect rule."

In contrast, the French believed firmly in the importance of their "civilizing mission." In most of its colonies, France adopted policies of assimilation and encouraged all peoples to learn French culture and language. However, even in places like Algeria, where

---

"Dr. Livingstone, I Presume?"

[Livingstone:] When my spirits had fallen into utter depression, the good Samaritan was already very near. One morning Suzy came running toward me and breathlessly announced: "An Englishman! I saw him!" and she darted away to meet him. The American flag at the head of the caravan showed the stranger's nationality. When I saw the bales of supplies, the tin wash-basins, the pots and large pans and all the rest, I thought: "There's a traveller who has at his disposal all facilities, not a poor devil like myself. . . ."*

[Stanley:] I pushed back the crowds, and passing from the rear walked down a living avenue of people, till I came in front of a semicircle of Arabs, in front of which stood a white man. . . . As I advanced slowly towards him I noticed he was pale, looked weary. I would have run to him, only I was a coward in the presence of such

a mob—would have embraced him, only, he being an Englishman, I did not know how he would receive me; so I did what cowardice and false pride suggested was the best thing—walked deliberately to him, took off my hat, and said: "Dr Livingstone, I presume?" "Yes," said he, with a kind smile, lifting his cap slightly.**

These firsthand accounts describe the famous meeting in 1871 between the Scottish missionary David Livingstone and Henry Stanley, an American of English birth. At various times in his life Stanley was a journalist, adventurer, businessman, and explorer. Financed by a U.S. newspaper, Stanley set out to find Livingstone, who was supposed to be "lost" somewhere in Africa. In fact, Livingstone was not lost, but was merely out of touch with the Western world.

*David Livingstone, The Last Journals of David Livingstone in Central Africa (London: Horace Walles, 1874), in Africa Then: Photographs, 1840–1918, ed. Nicolas Monti (New York: Knopf, 1987), p. 21.

**Henry Morton Stanley, How I Found Livingstone (New York: Scribner's, 1872), in Christopher Hibbert, Africa Explored: Europeans in the Dark Continent, 1769–1889 (London: Allen Lane, 1982), p. 288.

many French colonists settled for more than a century, assimilation of inhabitants never succeeded, because native Algerians resented the suppression of their local languages, religion, and cultures. Most people in Algeria remained devout Muslims, and Islamic culture persisted.

Europe Partitions Africa

The scramble to annex African territories often led to intense rivalries among the European nations, but in general, European governments sought, whenever possible, to avoid direct military confrontations in Africa. Instead, they called international conferences, negotiated binational agreements, and used diplomacy to obtain African lands. At the Berlin conference in 1884, fourteen European nations and the United States discussed how to divide Africa; at a second conference in Brussels in 1890 the Western nations agreed to King Leopold's ownership of the Congo. No Africans were invited to attend these conferences at which their lands were parceled out among the European powers.

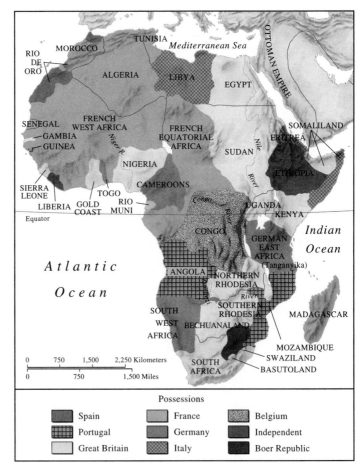

Map 13.1 Africa in 1914, after Partition. Almost all of the African continent was held by European powers by the outbreak of World War I. Great Britain and France held huge contiguous blocks of territory and some smaller possessions as well. Portugal, the oldest colonial power, had consolidated its string of trading posts into three colonies, while the late-arriving Germans and Italians had to settle for small, scattered holdings.

In a sort of giant monopoly game in which nations "traded" properties, European powers sometimes agreed to establish "spheres of influences" or monopolies over specific African territories. For example, in 1881–1882, France and Great Britain agreed that France should establish control over Tunisia, while the British should control Egypt. In western Africa, European nations expanded their control from coastal port cities northward into the interior; in the process they created long, narrow territorial strips that cut across ethnic lines and often put warring or rival fishing peoples from the coast, agriculturalists from the savanna, and nomads from the arid northern region together under one centralized government. Present-day West African nations, like Nigeria, reflect these anomalies and continue to be troubled by them.

The British and French clashed over control of the Sudan and the vital Nile water resources. After defeating the last of the Mahdist forces, in 1898, General Herbert Kitchener immediately sought to extend British control over the southern portions of the Sudan. Simultaneously, French forces, led by Captain Jean-Baptiste Marchand, who had marched from western Africa clear across the continent, had laid claim to the territory. Kitchener and Marchand met "eye-ball to eye-ball" in the remote Sudanese village of Fashoda, but Marchand was greatly outmanned, and Kitchener held the military balance of power. Seeking to defuse a crisis that threatened to turn into open warfare, French and British diplomats quietly met in Paris and London to settle control over the Sudan. Public opinion during the Fashoda crisis was whipped to a fever pitch; a belligerent music hall song expressed the mood in Great Britain:

We don't want to fight,
But by Jingo! if we do
We've got the ships,
We've got the men
And got the money, too!

World War I might have started in the Sudan had the British and the French come to blows. Those in each country who advocated going to war were known as "jingoists" and a new word for extreme and militant nationalists was added to the English language. Calmer minds prevailed in the Fashoda crisis, and a diplomatic settlement was reached whereby the British gained control over the Sudan and, in compensation, the French secured some small territories in West Africa. Similarly, competition between France and Germany over control of Morocco was settled by diplomacy and negotiations, and Morocco was ceded to France as a protectorate in 1912. Morocco was the last African territory taken over by Europe prior to World War I.

African Resistance

African societies did not accept outside domination without a struggle, and they often launched massive resistance movements against European intervention. Many Muslim African societies in particular led well-organized and effective struggles against foreign invaders. In the early nineteenth century, prior to European domination, a number of Muslim crusaders in West Africa had waged highly successful jihads or "holy wars"

(Left) Time Life Pictures/Getty Images (right) Michael Nicholson/Corbis

The Mahdi and General Gordon. The Mahdi, the Sudanese national hero, in an engraving by a European artist; juxtaposed is his archenemy, General Charles George Gordon, a British imperial hero, killed by the Mahdi's forces when they took the city of Khartoum in 1885. The British subsequently determined to avenge Gordon's death by eradicating the Mahdist movement and adding the Sudan to their imperial holdings.

against African nonbelievers. One of the most successful of these militant Muslims, a Fulani named Usuman dan Fodio, commanded an empire in northern Nigeria and Cameroon that still existed when the British invaded that region in the 1890s. Usuman's brother, Abdullah, was an intellectual and poet who captured the religious fervor of the movement when he wrote: "The face of religion had become white after its nadir. And the face of unbelief has become black after dawning brightly. And religion is mighty, and on a straight way. Unbelief is in disgrace." The jihads in West Africa presaged Muslim reform and resistance movements in Libya, Sudan, and the Arabian Peninsula of a later era. Likewise, they are analogous to many militant Islamic movements in the contemporary age.

Muslim zealots in Algeria (discussed later in this chapter) and the Sudan led two of the most protracted struggles against European domination. In the Sudan, Muhammad Ahmad Abdullah (d. 1885), who declared himself the Mahdi (rightly guided one), unified Sudanese tribes under the banner of Islam to attack Ottoman, Egyptian, and British invaders. The Mahdi was both a religious and a Sudanese nationalist leader. His forces inflicted several humiliating defeats on the British and in 1885, after a protracted siege, took the Sudanese capital of Khartoum and beheaded the British commander, General George "Chinese" Gordon. Gordon, who had remained in the Sudan in spite of orders to

King Shaka Questions a European Envoy

The King told his visitors about the glories of his realm. His vast wealth in cattle of which they would get an idea on the morrow and the following days. His regiments which were the terror of all his enemies. The magnificence of his capital, Bulawayo. Then he very pointedly asked if Farewell and his companion had ever seen a more orderly governed State than his Zululand, or subjects who were more moral and law-abiding....

Thereafter he made many inquiries about King George, the size of his army, the nature of his govern-

ment and country, the size of his capital and the number of his cattle and wives. He applauded the wisdom of his "brother" King in having only one wife. "That accounts for his advanced age; but he would have been wiser still to have none at all like myself."*

This passage from a biography of Shaka describes the first meeting between a British envoy, Lieutenant Farewell, and Shaka, the Zulu king. The meeting took place in 1825.

*E. A. Ritter, Shaka Zulu (Harmondsworth: Penguin, 1955), pp. 278–279.

retreat, became a martyr to the British imperial cause, and the British government vowed to avenge his death.

The Mahdi did not live long enough to enjoy or to consolidate the fruits of his victory; he died in 1885. His followers attempted to carry on the struggle but were weakened by drought, economic hardships, and internal divisions. In 1898 the British General Kitchener, a hero of several imperial campaigns, launched the successful invasion of the Sudan that led to the Fashoda crisis. Thousands of Sudanese were killed in the fighting. Kitchener eradicated the Mahdist movement, and the vast Sudanese territories were incorporated into the British Empire.

The Ethiopians were more successful in repelling foreign invasions. In 1896 they soundly defeated the Italian invasion forces at Adowa. By cleverly playing off rival European nations, the Ethiopian emperors managed to secure arms and avoid any subsequent partition or takeover of their ancient nation. Ethiopia remained independent until the 1930s, when it fell to a new wave of Italian invaders.

The Zulus in South Africa also resisted foreign domination. In the early nineteenth century King Shaka, the able political and military Zulu leader, led his skilled warriors to subdue other tribes. At its zenith the Zulu kingdom was as large as all of western Europe. Although he often dealt with his enemies in a brutal fashion, Shaka was known for his sound political judgment. The Zulu kingdom expanded at the expense of weaker tribal groups, and for many who came under Zulu domination, Shaka's reign was known as the Mfecane, or "the time of troubles."

As a result of his successes, Shaka had the military power to deal with Western envoys as equals. He expressed a keen interest in the Western world and was initially eager to establish mutually beneficial ties between his realm and Western nations. Like many absolute rulers, though, Shaka failed to create a peaceable system of succession. Thus, after his assassination by rivals, the Zulu kingdom was torn apart by internal disputes, which in turn weakened its ability to oppose Dutch and British expansion in South Africa.

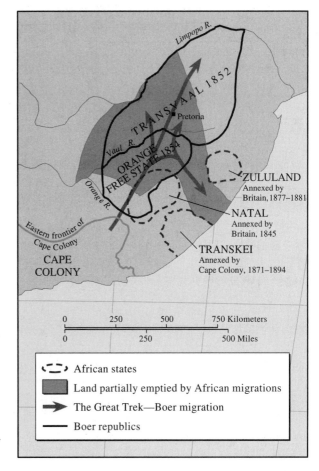

Map 13.2 Conflicting Claims in South Africa. A number of Bantu peoples lived in South Africa, but during the eighteenth century Dutch settlers, known as Boers, moved into the region and struggled with African tribes for control of the land. Then, in the 1800s the British began to incorporate valuable portions of South Africa into their empire. The Boers opposed the British, but were defeated by their enemy's superior military might.

The Boer War

The major military confrontation in Africa prior to World War I was not between European and African forces but between the British and the Dutch Boers in South Africa. This confrontation led to the Boer War (1899–1902). Great Britain had seized the Cape of Good Hope from the Netherlands in 1806 and gained permanent control of the land in 1815 at the end of the Napoleonic Wars. The Dutch settlers, or Boers (farmers), as they were called, resented both British domination and British emancipation of their African slaves. Seeking to evade British domination, in the 1830s and 1840s the Boers began a Great Trek, or mass migration, out of areas under British jurisdiction. In the 1850s the Boers created two independent nations, the Transvaal and the Orange Free State, which Great Britain did not recognize.

Attracted by fertile agricultural land and the discovery of gold and diamonds, increasing numbers of British settlers moved into the coastal areas and subsequently moved northward. The Boers opposed British expansion, discriminated against English settlers in their midst, and resorted to hit-and-run guerrilla tactics against British garrisons. Earlier these same guerilla tactics had been employed by the Zulu in their long but unsuccessful struggle against the Dutch settlers. Soon a full-scale war was in progress.

British forces, joined by units from Australia and commanded by General Kitchener, crushed the Boers' resistance by destroying their villages and rounding up families from entire districts and putting them into internment camps, thereby cutting off civilian support for the Boer fighters. Kitchener's tactics would subsequently be applied by others confronting guerrilla warfare, such as the French against the Algerians and the United States against the Viet Cong. Although the British failed to secure support from other Western nations in the war, they ultimately defeated the Boers. By 1902 the British had won, and in 1908 they incorporated Boer territories and English colonies in southern Africa into the Union of South Africa, granting it self-government within the British Empire.

Africa was not the only continent to be dominated by Western imperial nations, however. Imperial powers also sought to extend their control over Ottoman territories in western Asia and well as India, China, and Southeast Asia. The next section will describe how Western nations established empires in those far-flung regions.

Western Imperialism in the Middle East and Asia

Education, if it is good, produces perfection from imperfection, and nobility from baseness. If it is not good it changes the basic state of nature and becomes the cause of decline and decadence. This appears clearly among agriculturalists, cattle raisers, teachers, civil rulers, and religious leaders. . . .

This is why every people who enter into decline, and whose classes are overtaken by weakness, are always, because of their expectation of Eternal Grace, waiting to see if perhaps there is to be found among them a wise renewer, experienced in policy, who can enlighten their minds. . . .

There is no doubt that in the present age, distress, misfortune, and weakness besiege all classes of Muslims from every side. Therefore every Muslim keeps his eyes and ears open in expectation—to the East, West, North, and South—to see from what corner of the earth the sage and renewer will appear and will reform the minds and souls of the Muslims, repel the unforeseen corruption, and again educate them with a virtuous education. Perhaps through that good education they may return to their former joyful condition.*

*Jamal al-Din al-Afghani, "Commentary on the Commentators," in An Islamic Response to Imperialism: Political and Religious Writings of Sanjid Jamal al-Din "al-Afghani," ed. and trans. Nikki Keddie (Berkeley: University of California Press, 1968), pp. 123–129.

As in Africa, the spreading influence of Western politics, economics, and culture also threatened indigenous cultures in the Middle East and Asia in the nineteenth century. This crisis of identity was particularly intense in Islamic societies, where religious leaders and intellectuals grappled with the problems posed by Western mores and culture. In the above excerpt, Jamal al-Din al-Afghani (1839–1897), a Persian who spent most of his academic career in Egypt, described how Islamic societies felt threatened by Western advances. Al-Afghani was one of the many writers who sought to synthesize Islamic and Western cultures. Like many other writers in Asia, he placed particular emphasis on education as a means of spiritual and political renewal.

Ottoman Reforms and Territorial Losses

Western advances and technology particularly challenged the Ottoman Empire. By the nineteenth century the formerly great empire was in serious decline, and Tsar Nicholas I of Russia dubbed it the Sick Man of Europe. Extensive corruption on the highest levels was only one cause of Ottoman weakness. Officials often secured high positions in the bureaucracy, not through ability but by personal connections and bribery. The system of tax-farming, or hiring individuals to collect taxes, had resulted in many of the poorest and least powerful peasants paying absurdly high taxes, while wealthy landowners evaded payment by providing "kickbacks" to key officials or the tax collectors. At the same time, European nations, particularly Russia, the Austro-Hungarian Empire, and even Great Britain and France, sought to wrest territories along the Black Sea, in the Balkans, and in Africa from Ottoman control.

Mahmud II (reigned 1808–1839) attempted to stem the tide by instituting a series of sweeping internal reforms. He reorganized the army in 1826 and brought in many foreign advisers, especially Germans, to train and to equip the Ottoman army. After 1870 the newly unified German government welcomed the opportunity to assist the Ottoman army. Exchanges between Germany and the Ottoman Empire increased German influence and presence in Ottoman territories. In particular, the Germans were eager to construct a Berlin-to-Baghdad railroad to link their capital with Ottoman territories in Europe and Asia. Like the Cape-to-Cairo railroad in Africa, however, the railroad was never completed. It would have facilitated the extension of German commercial and military interests throughout the Ottoman Empire and, importantly, would have given Germany access to the vital Persian Gulf waterway and points further east in Asia. Not surprisingly, the British and French governments, which both wanted to stem German imperial expansion, staunchly opposed German attempts to build a railroad through Ottoman territory.

By 1839, under pressure from France and Great Britain, the Ottomans issued the Declaration of the Rose Chamber, which guaranteed the security of minorities within the empire and launched widespread domestic reforms. From 1839 through 1876, Ottoman leaders initiated a series of reforms known as the Tanzimat: new legal codes were devised, education was encouraged, and local administration, particularly the collection of taxes, was altered along Western lines. These reforms were reiterated and widened under another formal declaration in 1856.

However well intended, Ottoman efforts at reform were hampered by two major difficulties: they were instituted from above and did not enjoy grassroots support; and they were often forced on the Ottomans by European nations and were, therefore, based on European political and social institutions. As a result, the reforms failed to take into consideration deep-seated religious and cultural attitudes of the predominantly Islamic population. Consequently, Ottoman reforms during the nineteenth century tended to affect only the minorities, particularly the Christians and Jews within the empire, or the elites in urban centers. Despite support from most of the intelligentsia and elites, who were often Western educated, the reforms had little or no impact on the vast majority of the rural population within the Ottoman heartland of the Anatolian Peninsula or the distant

Arab provinces. As a result, the Ottomans were unable to regain their former strength. As the Ottoman Empire crumbled, European imperial powers continued to take over territories in the Middle East and Africa.

The British and French both took Ottoman territories in Africa. In 1830 the French moved into Algeria, which, although nominally an Ottoman territory, had historically been ruled by beys (provincial governors), who exercised considerable autonomy. Under Abdel Kader, a charismatic Muslim political and religious leader, the Algerians tenaciously fought French domination, but by 1847 they were forced to surrender to the superior French forces. Abdel Kader was exiled; he ultimately moved to Syria, where he heroically saved many Christian Syrians during riots in 1860.

Many European nations maneuvered to gain control of Egypt for its strategic geographic location. In Egypt, the French retained cultural and economic ties with Muhammad Ali, a janissary of Albanian origin, who had broken with the Ottomans to establish an autonomous government. When Muhammad Ali, with his newly equipped and trained army, defeated Ottoman forces in several decisive battles and moved to extend his authority over Palestine and Syria, the sultan obtained British and French assistance to perpetuate Ottoman rule in the eastern Mediterranean. In 1840, with French and British assent, Muhammad Ali and his heirs were recognized as the khedives or rulers of Egypt in exchange for withdrawing from Palestine and Syria; they also agreed to nominal recognition of Ottoman suzerainty over Egypt. His heirs continued to act as the real or titular rulers of Egypt until the monarch was overthrown in the 1952 revolution.

Muhammad Ali embarked on an ambitious program of industrial and agricultural development, for which he has often been called the founder of modern Egypt. Subsequent Egyptian khedives continued Muhammad Ali's plans to model the Egyptian economy, educational system, and building programs along Western lines. The Suez Canal was the result of the long-standing cooperation between the French and the Egyptian ruling family.

Ferdinand de Lesseps, a French engineer and financier, had long dreamed of building a canal to connect the Red Sea with the Mediterranean; with the political and financial support of the Egyptian khedive, de Lesseps constructed the canal using Egyptian labor and moneys secured from the sale of private shares in the Suez Canal Company. Although the British initially opposed the construction of a canal, after it was completed in 1869 and began to carry heavy traffic, the British government realized the canal's commercial and strategic importance. When huge expenditures for grandiose development schemes, including the Suez Canal, and personal extravagance by the khedive brought Egypt to the brink of bankruptcy, the British stepped in and took over Egyptian finances.

In 1882, the British military crushed a revolt led by nationalist Egyptian army officers. After some negotiations, the French agreed to the British occupation in exchange for British assent to French occupation of Tunisia in North Africa. Great Britain retained the khedive as the nominal ruler, but through political advisers and a continued military presence, the British controlled the Suez Canal and ruled Egypt. Under Muhammad Ali, Egypt had developed sufficient economic infrastructure to move it close to becoming an industrialized nation. The British, however, were primarily interested in Egypt for strategic reasons and secondarily for its agricultural materials, especially cotton. In an important reversal, they enacted economic restraints that essentially stopped the process toward industrialization; as a consequence of British policies Egypt remained primarily an agricultural country. The loss of Egypt was also a major defeat for the Ottoman Empire and demonstrated its pervasive weakness.

The Eastern Question

To the European powers, the issue of what should become of the ailing Ottoman Empire was known as the Eastern Question. Although the British and French both incorporated former Ottoman provinces into their own empires, they generally acted to keep the Sick Man alive in the eastern Mediterranean. With Austrian support, they protected the Ottoman sultan, not because they were close allies of the Ottomans but because they did not want the Russians to gain territorial advantages in the Black Sea or eastern Mediterranean. The British, and to a lesser extent the French, were particularly anxious that Russia, already in control of the northern shores of the Black Sea that had formerly been held by the Ottomans, not secure warm-water ports and control over the vital Dardanelles and Istanbul, which would increase its influence in the eastern Mediterranean. The Austrians, with imperial ambitions of their own in the Balkans, were also anxious to constrain Russian advances. On the other hand, Russia was anxious to see the Sick Man on his deathbed so that it could expand into eastern Europe and the Mediterranean.

Ottoman leaders recognized the intense rivalries among the European powers and frequently played European governments against one another in order to protect their own imperial interests. Ottoman relations with the various European powers regarding eastern Europe, the Black Sea, and the Dardanelles can be divided into three main phases. In the first phase, from approximately 1702 to 1820, the Eastern Question centered primarily on Russian expansion around the Black Sea. Russia successfully moved into the Black Sea region in 1772 and from that time onward looked toward the Mediterranean. Russian aims in the region alarmed Great Britain. When Napoleon conquered Egypt in 1798, the importance of the Middle East came into sharp focus for the British.

In the second phase, as the Ottoman Empire weakened, the interest of European nations turned to the Balkans, whose predominantly Orthodox Christian peoples, often the victims of Ottoman misgovernment, became increasingly nationalistic during the nineteenth century. The Greek Revolution of 1821 marked the beginning of the long and often bloody struggle for independence by the diverse peoples of the Balkans. Although poorly organized militarily, the Greeks enjoyed the support and sympathy of many Europeans, who admired and felt indebted to ancient Greek culture. The poet Byron and many others publicized and worked for Greek independence; indeed, Byron went so far as to enlist in the Greek struggle. The Greek war against the Ottomans dragged on until 1830, when Greece finally secured its independence along with guarantees for protection by the major European powers. Ottoman decay also enabled European imperial powers and ambitious local leaders to increase their power and influence in Ottoman territories. As previously noted, during the 1820s and 1830s Muhammad Ali had established an autonomous government in Egypt.

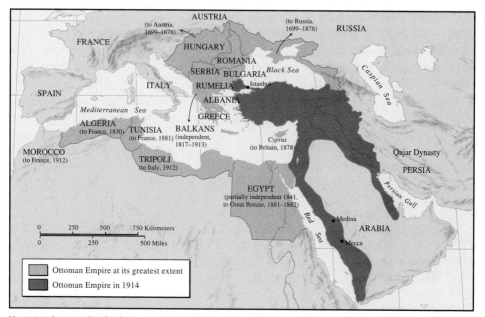

Map 13.3 Ottoman Territorial Losses, 1699–1912. The Ottoman Empire had lost most of its territories by the outbreak of World War I: North Africa to European powers, Black Sea areas to Russia, and the Balkan nations to independence movements. By 1914 the Ottoman Empire had shrunk to a small piece of Europe around Istanbul, the Anatolian Peninsula, the Arab provinces including Greater Syria and Iraq, and the holy cities of Mecca and Medina in the Arabian Peninsula.

The third phase of the Eastern Question culminated in the Crimean War (1853–1856). Conflicting French and Russian aspirations over Christian holy sites in Palestine led to bitter disputes; as ruler over the territories and peoples in question, the Ottoman sultan should have settled the issue, but he was far too weak. It was during this dispute, when asked about the weakness of the Ottoman Empire, that Tsar Nicholas I remarked, "We have on our hands a very sick man."

When the dispute remained unresolved, Russia declared war against the Ottomans, and Great Britain and France joined in on the Ottoman side. Although the Russians won several decisive battles, high casualties on all sides, heavy costs, and bad weather combined to make the war increasingly unpopular. During the war Florence Nightingale (1820–1910), shocked by the high death rate among soldiers, personally went to the battlefield. Appalled by the lack of even rudimentary hygienic practices, she instituted modern nursing techniques that drastically reduced the death rate and marked the beginning of the Red Cross. After the death of Tsar Nicholas I, the new Tsar, Alexander II (reigned 1856–1880), agreed to peace negotiations. Great Britain, Austria-Hungary, and France agreed jointly to guarantee the political independence and territorial integrity of the Ottoman Empire. This great power protection helped the Ottoman Empire to survive until World War I.

Imperial Gains in Asia

At the same time the Europeans were expanding into Ottoman territory, they had also been continuing to extend their influence into the rest of Asia. Compared with the rapid takeover of Africa, European domination over Asia took more than four centuries to accomplish. Europeans initially went to India, China, and Japan to trade. Eventually, however, Western governments began to establish more direct controls over Asian territories. In the nineteenth century, superior British military forces defeated the independent princes of India, while the Russian armies conquered the principalities of central Asia. Persia and the great Chinese Empire, torn by internal disputes, were crumbling under foreign attacks.

The Qajar dynasty, which ruled Persia (present-day Iran) from 1779 to its overthrow in the 1920s, reacted to Western pressures and incursions in similar ways to the Ottoman sultans. Like Mahmud II in the Ottoman Empire, some Qajar shahs attempted internal reforms and supported modernization along Western lines. Western education was encouraged, and elite Iranians traveled, studied, and copied the West. Also like the Ottomans, however, the Qajars were often caught between the conflicting imperial ambitions of the British and the Russians. The Russians sought to expand along their southern border into the potentially rich oil fields of northern Iran. Distribution of crude oil from northern Iran had become a small industry by the end of the nineteenth century. As the industrialized nations converted to the use of internal combustion engines for transport systems, petroleum became a crucial source of energy and, in the twentieth century, was to become a crucial raw material for industries and transportation systems around the world. By 1914, when World War I began, the petroleum industry was already well established in Iran.

Great Britain was also interested in Iran both for the petroleum reserves and in order to maintain a presence in southern Iran as a protective buffer zone for British possessions further east, particularly India. Nevertheless, with its relatively more isolated geographic position vis-à-vis Europe, Persia at the end of the nineteenth century was subjected to less intense Western pressure than the Ottoman Empire. In 1907 the British and the Russians agreed to avoid a direct confrontation by dividing Persia into a Russian sphere of influence in the north and a British sphere of influence in the southeast.

India: The Jewel in the Crown of the British Empire

After 1603 the English East India Company began trading in India under permit from the Moghul Empire. When that empire dissolved, the (by-then) British East India Company virtually completed the conquest of the Indian subcontinent and controlled about 250 million people. In 1857 British control was challenged when company sepoys (native soldiers) rebelled over religious issues. Rebellion then spread in northern India for economic and political reasons and took fourteen months of heavy fighting to suppress. British control was not again seriously threatened until Mohandas K. Gandhi's civil disobedience campaigns in the 1920s. The British government took control of the Indian territories from the company in 1858, ruling 60 percent of the subcontinent directly and the rest indirectly through Indian princes or maharajahs who were supervised by British

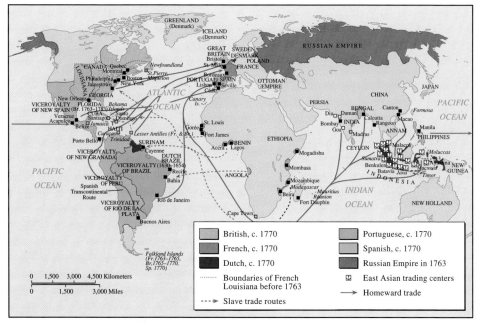

European Colonial Empires and Global Trade Patterns, c. 1770

After 300 years of exploration and trade outside their continent, European nations had made massive changes around the globe. Nearly all of the Western Hemisphere had come under their control, and they had built up an extensive network of trading centers along the African coast and across much of South and Southeast Asia. Products from four continents poured into the Atlantic ports of five European nations, to be consumed or resold to the rest of Europe. In addition, an enormous trade in African slaves, along with pockets of European settlement, was transforming the Americas radically. The interior of Africa, the Islamic world, and East Asia, at this time lightly touched, faced the power of the European onslaught in the next century.

Latin America in the First Half of the Nineteenth Century
The nations of Latin America appeared in two basic stages. Ten nations achieved independence from Spain and Portugal between 1810 and 1822. The rest appeared when regional issues in the infant nations resulted in secessions between 1825 and 1844.

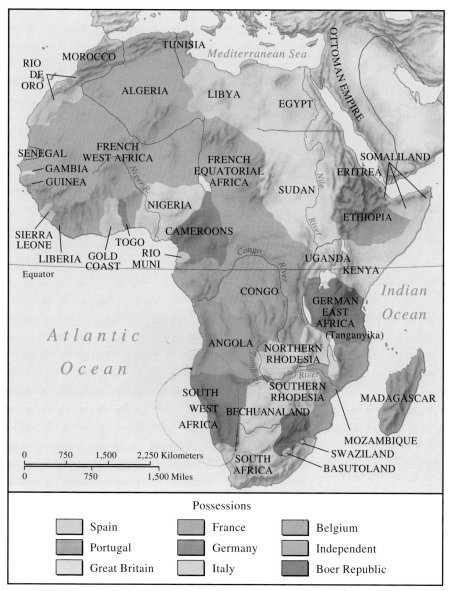

Possessions

Spain	France	Belgium
Portugal	Germany	Independent
Great Britain	Italy	Boer Republic

Africa in 1914, after Partition

Almost all of the African continent was held by European powers by the outbreak of World War I. Great Britain and France held huge contiguous blocks of territory and some smaller possessions as well. Portugal, the oldest colonial power, had consolidated its string of trading posts into three colonies, while the late-arriving Germans and Italians had to settle for small, scattered holdings.

Europe in 1914
The map shows the alliance systems before the war. German, Austria-Hungary, and Italy formed the Triple Alliance, while France, Russia, and Great Britain made up the Triple Entente. Italy refused to join Germany and Austria-Hungary in August 1914, ultimately selling its services to the highest bidder—the Entente.

representatives. India became the centerpiece of the British Empire, symbolized in the proclamation of Queen Victoria as Empress of India in 1876. A special ministry, the India Office, supervised the governing of the Indian subcontinent.

Control of India brought the British vast wealth, which contributed to a substantial rise in the living standards in England. British- and Indian-owned plantations produced indigo, jute, cotton, and tea. To exploit these products, the British built modern textile and steel mills in India and an extensive railroad network and later trunk roads and telegraph lines. India was perhaps more crucial to Great Britain as an importer of British goods than as a supplier of raw materials, however. Hundreds of millions of Indians bought British manufactured products, which entered India duty-free. Consequently, as in Egypt, British domination impeded the industrialization of India.

Several hundred thousand Britons controlled India, with a population of approximately 350 million in the early twentieth century. With its kaleidoscope of ethnic groups, languages, and religions, India was a geographic expression rather than a unified culture; it was further divided by historic animosities, especially between Hindus and Muslims. Thus the British found it relatively easy to persuade Indians of one background or religious affiliation to help them subdue or control Indians of another sect or group. Nepalese Gurkha troops were generally reliable, and many Bengalis and Sikhs, as well as others, aided British rule and received preferential treatment in return.

India also had a major impact on Great Britain. Events in India affected the lives and livelihoods of millions of Britons who never saw the subcontinent. Hundreds of thousands of Britons served in the military or government, and visited for business or pleasure. Many Indian words—bungalo and pajamas, for example—entered the English vocabulary; likewise, Indian foods such as curry became part of regular British cuisine.

Many Britons felt themselves racially and culturally superior to the Indians, as they did with other Asians and Africans; even the maharajahs were viewed as inferiors, capable of learning only the outer forms of Western culture. Rarely appreciating the philosophical, religious, and artistic contributions of India, British officials diligently sought to eradicate social abuses, especially the subjugated status of women. They eliminated the thuggees (a religious cult whose members killed and robbed as a religious act), banned suttee (the burning alive of widows), and tried to eliminate the practice of child brides. A few sympathetic Britons came to admire Indian culture and learning. After discovering Sanskrit's affinity with European languages, some began its scientific study, initiated archaeological investigations, and undertook the preservation of historic relics. These specialists in ancient Indian culture were called Indologists.

Thus, for Indians, as for Africans, British occupation had mixed results. Prior to British rule, the masses of Indians had lived an impoverished and illiterate life toiling for the benefit of their rulers; now they were often forced to toil for two sets of masters. As India was integrated into the world market economy, landlords planted cash crops, which meant less food. By improving sanitation and introducing public health measures, the British contributed to a population explosion. This further reduced the per capita food supply and contributed to periodic famines. A similar population growth, with parallel economic results, also occurred in Egypt.

Western civilization had a distinct impact on India. The great majority readily accepted Western science and technology, such as railroads and telegraph lines, but only a tiny minority embraced European culture. A few, such as Gandhi, also rejected much Western technology and argued that home-based "cottage industries," such as spinning cotton, would be a better way to raise the economic and social status of the poor. Those that chose to copy the British learned English, attained a rudimentary Western education, and adopted British dress and social customs. A small number of upper-class Indian males attended Western-style universities founded in India or were sent to Great Britain to attend elite schools and universities.

British-educated Indians argued that Great Britain should apply its principles of liberty in India. Some of them formed the Indian National Congress in 1885. At first, the Congress was primarily a debating and lobbying society, but after 1905 it began to organize mass demonstrations and boycotts against the British.

Christian missionaries had been active since the arrival of the Portuguese in 1498, but gained few converts; less than 2 percent of the population was Christian by 1900. A few Western-educated Hindus sought to reform regressive social aspects of Hinduism and organized societies to promote its reform. As in Africa and the Middle East, Muslims in India firmly resisted conversion, but formed organizations for social and political reforms later than the Hindus. Nevertheless, by the early twentieth century, Indian Muslims had also begun to advocate social reforms, Western education, and political organization.

Protecting India: Imperialist Confrontations in Asia

Much of Britain's imperial policy revolved around the protection of India. With that objective in mind, the British seized control of such strategic islands and ports as Ceylon (present-day Sri Lanka) and Aden to safeguard the trade routes between the subcontinent and Great Britain. By the end of the eighteenth century the British had eliminated the French threat to India, which was replaced in the nineteenth century by fear of Russian expansion in southern and central Asia.

In 1840 the French annexed Cochin China and by the end of the nineteenth century expanded its control over Cambodia, Laos, and the rest of Vietnam. The French thereby secured rubber, tin, and rice and in the process sought to spread Catholicism and French culture. This revival of French aspirations in Southeast Asia drew a quick British response. To create a buffer zone between India and French-controlled territories in Asia, the British took over Burma (present-day Myanmar) and expanded from Singapore onto the Malay Peninsula. Although conflicting imperial ambitions of the British and French overlapped, they avoided war by using Siam (present-day Thailand) as a buffer between their empires.

To the north and west of India, the British Empire faced the threat of expansionistic tsarist Russia. The Russians had moved steadily in Siberia and the southeastern steppes of central Asia during the nineteenth century and had incorporated the Muslim khanates near the Indian frontier. The Russians were also interested in Afghanistan and Iran as means of access to the Persian Gulf and Indian Ocean. Britain and Russia came close to war over Afghanistan, but the Boer War (1899–1902) and the Russo-Japanese War (1904–1905) forestalled the confrontation.

British Settlement of Australasia

British imperialism in Australia and New Zealand paralleled the pattern in British North America. The British conquered the Maori native population of New Zealand and pushed aside the Australian Aborigine people by the end of the nineteenth century. The British initially used parts of Australia as penal colonies, but most of coastal Australia and much of New Zealand were temperate areas that attracted many settlers from the British Isles and Europe. They originally came for sheep ranching and farming but quickly developed a mixed economy, including mining and manufacturing.

Remembering its North American experience, the British government granted its colonists in Australasia self-rule, unified the six Australian colonies into the self-governing Commonwealth of Australia in 1901, and created the equivalent for New Zealand in 1907. Labor governments brought in the welfare state in both nations, and women secured the vote by the 1890s, much earlier than in Europe or the United States.

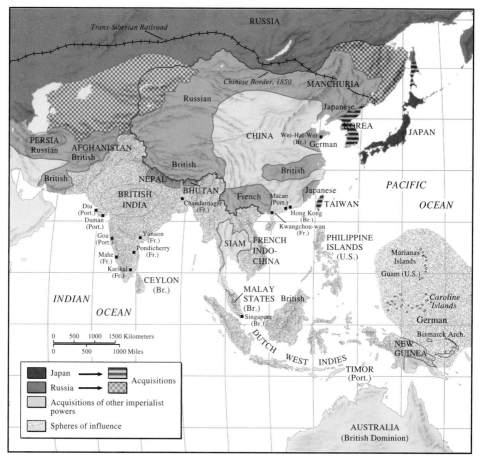

Map 13.4 Asia in 1914. Much of Asia was now controlled by imperial powers. Many areas of South and Southeast Asia were colonial possessions of the European nations and the United States. Independent states like Persia and China came under the control of foreign nations, which divided parts of those countries into their spheres of influence. Japan, the new imperialist power in Asia, had annexed Korea and the island the Japanese called Formosa (Taiwan); Japan also obtained a sphere of influence in China.

Great Britain, Germany, and the United States sought to extend their control over the Pacific, even though the economic value of the scattered islands of the area was slight, and most of them had little strategic value. By 1914 nearly all of the islands and coral atolls in the Pacific Ocean flew the flag of one of the imperialist nations.

The European Onslaught on the Ch'ing Empire in China

As discussed in Chapter 10, the Western nations became rivals for control over the vast Chinese Empire, the one great prize that had eluded them. Whereas Western traders sought tea, silk, porcelain and other commodities, there was little that the Chinese wanted except payments in gold, silver, and furs. Trade with the West was a profitable but minor part of the Chinese economy, and the Manchu or Ch'ing Empire, like the Ming dynasty before it, permitted Westerners to trade only in the Canton area of South China.

In the nineteenth century, several major factors led to the accelerated decline of the Manchu dynasty: dynastic problems of leadership, rapid population increases that led to mass impoverishment and rebellions, spreading addiction to opium (a drug introduced by Westerners), and increasing Chinese resentment of ineffectual Manchu rule. Westerners and the Japanese began to see China not only as purchasers of manufactured goods but also as a source of coal, iron ore, and other industrial raw materials. The Chinese, unaccustomed to borrowing from other cultures, had done little to industrialize or to build up modern armed forces.

By the nineteenth century, powerful European nations had the military strength to defeat the Chinese, but mutual rivalries prevented any of them from annexing major parts of it. In a series of wars beginning in 1839 and ending in 1885, victorious British, French, German, and Russian forces defeated the Chinese Empire. The Chinese government was forced to accept a series of unequal treaties that compelled it to open ports, accept trade on Western nations' terms, permit the import of opium, cede territories, pay indemnities, and establish diplomatic relations with the victors.

The defeated Chinese had to surrender areas in central Asia, Manchuria, and the northeast Pacific coast to Russia. The British took Hong Kong and established a leading role in trade and shipping. France forced China to give up its overlordship of Vietnam, while Japan gained influence in Korea. Loss of territory on the fringes of the empire was secondary, however, compared with three disastrous impositions that the West forced on the Chinese: spheres of influence, fixed tariffs, and extraterritoriality (freedom of citizens of Western countries from Chinese laws). By the end of the century Great Britain, France, Germany, Japan, and Russia had divided most of China into spheres of influences. Each European nation and Japan had the exclusive right to secure and sell materials and commodities, build railroads, and develop ports in its sphere. Their gunboats patrolled the coasts and rivers of China to secure the spheres against competitors and to intimidate the Chinese into compliance. China was saved from partition only by fear among the Western powers and Japan that such attempts would lead to war with one another.

Chinese Opposition to the Drug Trade

During the commercial intercourse which has existed so long, among the numerous foreign merchants resorting hither, are wheat and tares, good and bad; and of these latter are some who, by means of introducing opium by stealth, have seduced our Chinese people, and caused every province of the land to overflow with that poison. . . . Moreover, the great emperor hearing of it, actually quivered with indignation, and especially dispatched me, the commissioner, to Canton, that in conjunction with the viceroy and lieut.-governor of the province, means might be taken for its suppression!

Every native . . . who sells opium, as also all who smoke it, are alike adjudged to death. Were we then to go back and take up the crimes of the foreigners, who, by selling it for many years have induced dreadful calamity and robbed us of enormous wealth, and punish them with equal severity, our laws could not but award to them absolute annihilation.

We find that your country is distant from us about sixty or seventy thousand miles, that your foreign ships come hither striving the one with the other for our trade, and for the simple reason of their strong desire to reap a profit. . . .

We have heard that in your own country opium is prohibited with the utmost strictness and severity—this is a strong proof that you know full well how hurt-ful it is to mankind. Since then you do not permit it to injure your own country, you ought not to have the injurious drug transferred to another country. . . .

Your honorable nation takes away the products of our central land, and not only do you thereby obtain food and support for yourselves, but moreover, by reselling these products to other countries you reap a threefold profit. Now if you would only not sell opium, this threefold profit would be secured to you: how can you possibly consent to forgo it for a drug that is hurtful to men, and an unbridled craving after gain that seems to know no bounds! . . .

P.S. We annex an abstract of the new law, . . . "Any foreigner or foreigners bringing opium to the Central Land, with the design to sell the same, the principals shall most assuredly be decapitated."*

In a letter that ironically foreshadows the drug problem in the modern West, commissioner Lin Tse-hsu, an official in the Chinese government, wrote to Queen Victoria in 1840 to denounce the British government for permitting its merchants to sell opium to China. Lin's letter is also revealing for its blunt discussion of the economic relationships between China and Great Britain.

**Chinese Repository, vol. 8 (February 1840), pp. 497–503, in Modern Asia and Africa, ed. William H. McNeill and Mitsuko Iriye (New York: Oxford University Press, 1971), pp. 111–118.*

Western nations carved out "concessions" in Chinese ports, where their laws prevailed. Christian missionaries flocked into China to convert the Chinese. As in India, few Chinese converted, but Christian educators became an important force in changing China.

The unequal treaties were a humiliation to the heirs of a proud civilization. Anti-Western sentiment came to a head in 1900, when the Boxers, xenophobic people who practiced shadow boxing and hated Westerners and Westernized Chinese, took control of Peking. Supported by the ruling Dowager Empress Tz'u-hsi, who also hated foreigners, the Boxers besieged the foreign diplomatic section of the city, killing many, until an international relief expedition drove them off. As a result of the Boxer Rebellion, China was forced to pay an indemnity and make other concessions. The accumulated humiliations convinced many Chinese that the Manchu dynasty had to be replaced by a government strong enough to end foreign domination and lift China to equality among nations.

Like the Japanese earlier, progressive Chinese believed that China would have to develop Western technology and educational institutions. Chinese students went to the United States, Europe, and Japan to study, and some of them began to plan a revolution to overthrow the Ch'ing Empire and to establish a republic that would make sweeping changes. The next section will discuss the emergence of Japan and the United States as major imperial powers and their quest for empire in the Western Hemisphere and Asia.

Japan and the United States Become World Powers

*I am willing to admit my pride in this accomplishment for Japan. The facts are these: It was not until 1853 that we began to study navigation from the Dutch in Nagasaki; by 1860, the science was sufficiently understood to enable us to sail a ship across the Pacific. This means that about seven years after the first sight of a steamship, after only about five years of practice, the Japanese people made a trans-Pacific crossing without help from foreign experts. I think we can without undue pride boast before the world of this courage and skill. . . . ***

*Eiichi Kiyowka, *The Autobiography of Yukichi Fukuzawa* (New York: Columbia University Press, 1966), quoted in Peter N. Stearns, ed., *Documents in World History,* Vol. 2 (New York: Harper & Row, 1988), p. 60.

In his autobiography, the noted Japanese educator Yukichi Fukuzawa shows his pride in the rapid industrialization of Japan and its success in adopting Western technology. The founding president of an important university, he had contributed to this progress. As Japan and the United States became world powers in the nineteenth century, their growing pride and worldwide economic interests would cause them first to compete and later to clash over dominance in the Pacific and Asia.

The emergence of Japan as a world power was more disturbing to the Europeans than the rise of the United States. In one generation, Japan succeeded in transforming from a technologically backward state to one of the world's great powers. It then expanded in East Asia at the expense of China, Russia, and Korea and in competition with both the European nations and the United States.

Confronted in the 1850s by U.S. naval power and forced to open its ports and to sign unequal treaties, the Japanese leaders quickly realized that they would lose their independence unless they built up an industrial base and a modern military. Japan's cultural traditions permitted borrowing and adapting from other societies. More than a millennium earlier it had incorporated many aspects of Chinese culture; it now looked to adopt the best from the West.

In 1868 the Tokugawa shogun, whose government could not resist Japan's forced opening, was overthrown by new leaders who proclaimed loyalty to the young Meiji Emperor. They destroyed the power of the old military elite and embarked on a massive program of modernization. Japanese missions were sent to Europe and the United States to study Western technology, education, and government. Industrialists and entrepreneurs were encouraged to establish modern enterprises, becoming the new elite of the nation. Benefiting from government policies, private firms such as Mitsui expanded into zaibatsu, or vast conglomerates. To forestall labor unrest, the government also enacted welfare programs. Importantly, most Japanese workers were intensely loyal to their employers and, in contrast to workers in the West, rarely moved from job to job. In return, companies provided their employees with numerous social and welfare benefits. The Meiji government also established a universal education program that stressed loyalty to the emperor and nation. After studying governmental systems in the West, it adopted a constitution modeled after that of Germany.

By the end of the nineteenth century, Japan had built a powerful industrial base, a modern transportation system, and a large merchant marine. New schools had all but eliminated illiteracy and provided broad technological and vocational education to undergird their industrialization. Modern universities prepared the brightest young men for government service and managerial positions; women's colleges trained young women for modern professions in medicine, nursing, and teaching. Japan also constructed a large fleet of warships like Great Britain's and adopted conscription for an army like Germany's. Japan was the first Asian country that successfully pressured the Western powers to relinquish the unequal treaties.

The Japanese people paid a high price for the government's successes. They were subjected to a grinding discipline of long hours, low pay, heavy taxes, and a standard of living below that of the more affluent nations of the West. As in Great Britain, population increases had made Japan dependent on imported foodstuffs, and Japanese factories needed raw materials from abroad. As in the West, Japan's growing industrial output led it to seek overseas markets where it could sell its goods.

Japanese Imperialism

In an age of imperialism, Japanese leaders sought international recognition through expansion. Japan attacked China in 1894 in a dispute over Korea, a Chinese tributary state, and defeated it easily on land and sea. China was forced to give up overlordship of Korea, which allowed Japan to pursue its aggressive designs there; and to cede to Japan its island province of Taiwan (Formosa). In 1900, Japanese forces joined an international expedition sent to Peking to put down the Boxer Rebellion.

By 1904, Japan was ready to confront Russia. Russia had established a sphere of influence in northeastern China, in a region called Manchuria, where it had a naval base and an extension of the trans-Siberian railroad. Japan launched a surprise attack that destroyed the Russian Far Eastern fleet in 1904 and then drove the Russian army out of southern Manchuria. Later, in the Battle of Tsushima Straits, the Japanese navy inflicted a devastating defeat on the Russian Baltic fleet as it arrived off the Japanese coast. These victories astonished Western observers and earned their respect, but more importantly the Japanese defeat of a major Western power electrified other Asians and gave them hope that Western imperialism was not invincible. In the peace treaty that ended the Russo-Japanese War (brokered by U.S. president Theodore Roosevelt), Russia ceded to Japan southern Sakhalin Island and its spheres of influence in southern Manchuria. It also agreed to keep its hands off Korea. Japan annexed hapless Korea in 1910.

The Rise of the United States

By the nineteenth century, Americans had become one of the most affluent peoples on earth. The United States was virtually self-sufficient in food and led the world in agricultural exports, iron ore and coal output, iron and steel production, and railroad mileage. Its manufacturing output had increased so markedly that it was rapidly catching up to the leading European industrialized nations.

However, the economic boom also created new social problems. Periodic labor strikes and boycotts led to increased unionization among American workers; farmers also organized politically and formed the Populist party to push forward their demands for social change. Racism and opposition to new immigrants from eastern Europe also continued to divide the society. Urban and rural reformers sought to institute welfare projects that were often rejected by the more conservative courts. The Progressive movement, which advocated a number of reform measures, also attracted numerous supporters in the early

Technological Imperialism. The Panama Canal, here shown under construction, was the engineering marvel of the early twentieth century. Cut through a mountain range and operated by means of a system of hydraulic locks, it was a much greater technological feat than the Suez Canal, which was essentially a ditch through flat terrain. The Panama Canal, opened in 1919, was the realization of centuries of hope by those in international commerce for a direct connection between the Atlantic and the Pacific.

twentieth century. Progressive leaders wanted to increase the powers of state and national governments while regulating big business and the economy. The progressive movement was instrumental in obtaining the graduated income tax, the regulation of food and drug standards, and improved public services.

The United States Becomes an Imperialist Power

By 1900 the United States stood on the threshold of great-power status. It was the fourth most populous nation, and its residents were the most literate and longest-lived in the world. In general, the average U.S. citizen's standard of living equaled that of the citizens of the major powers of western Europe. The government, relatively stable, was dominated by white males who enjoyed suffrage and constitutionally protected individual rights.

Despite its self-sufficiency in many areas, the United States was typical of other rapidly industrializing nations in that it increasingly looked overseas for raw materials, consumer products, and markets. Protected by two oceans from would-be enemies, the United States possessed only a small army. However, to protect its expanding overseas commerce, it built the third-largest navy in the world. Many Americans opposed overseas expansion, but by 1900 those favoring expansion were in the ascendancy.

The Caribbean Becomes a U.S. Lake

Mexico, the Caribbean, and South America were the first regions to feel the effects of U.S. expansionism. As an imperialist power, the United States was primarily interested in dominating the Western Hemisphere. U.S. policy had three goals: prevent European domination over the Caribbean, obtain land for a canal across Central America, and dominate trade with Latin America and Canada. The United States was able to achieve its goals because no nation in the Americas was strong enough to oppose it, and most European nations, preoccupied with imperialist ventures in Asia and Africa, chose not to interfere with U.S. interests in the Western Hemisphere.

In the five years between 1898 and 1903, presidents William McKinley and the staunch imperialist Theodore "Teddy" Roosevelt took control of the Caribbean. In a "splendid little war" brought on by tensions over Cuba, where declining Spanish power was challenged by local unrest, the United States defeated Spain and forced it to give up Cuba and Puerto Rico, its two last possessions in the New World. Whereas the United States retained Puerto Rico and built naval installations there, it allowed Cuba nominal independence but turned it into an economic and political protectorate, extracting from Cuba a perpetual lease of the strategic Guantánamo Bay for a naval base.

These new bases in Puerto Rico and Cuba enabled the United States to become the major naval power in the Caribbean by 1901. Great Britain agreed to withdraw its naval forces from the Caribbean in return for a U.S. pledge that the British would have unencumbered rights to use any future canal across Central America.

In 1903 the United States supported a separatist movement in the Colombian province of Panama. Once freed, Panama promptly granted the United States the right to complete a canal started earlier and abandoned by a French company, and also granted the United States the further right to control in perpetuity a thirteen-mile strip on either

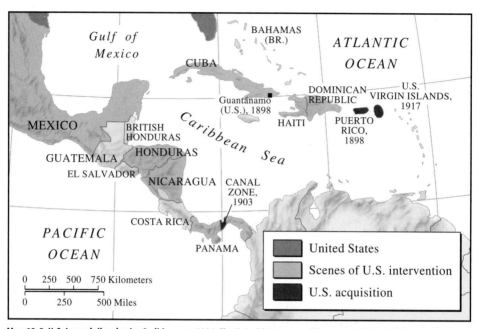

Map 13.5 U.S. Imperialism in the Caribbean to 1934. The United States secured firm control of the Caribbean region during the early twentieth century. By acquiring bases in Cuba and Puerto Rico and controlling the Panama Canal, the United States strategically dominated the region and enforced its supremacy by intervening in or occupying for varying periods most Latin American nations in the area. Some, like Nicaragua, were taken over several times.

side of the Canal. The new Panama Canal, opened to international traffic in 1914, was an impressive multilock project cut through mountains. U.S. medical authorities also eliminated the scourge of yellow fever in the canal zone.

Although many Americans viewed the Caribbean as *mare nostrum,* "our sea," the United States was not completely secure in the Caribbean, as was demonstrated when a combined European fleet led by Germany bombarded Venezuela in 1902 for violating its treaty and defaulting on its loan obligations to them. Fearing more European interference in Latin America, the United States modified its 1823 Monroe Doctrine, which opposed European expansion into the Western Hemisphere. The new Roosevelt Corollary to the doctrine stated that if Latin American nations exhibited "chronic wrongdoing," the United States would exercise international police power and intervene to make financial reforms and restore order. European nations would thus have no legitimate reason to intervene. The Roosevelt Corollary succeeded in its purpose. European nations avoided any future interventions and did not challenge U.S. military control over the region.

The United States increased its share of trade and investment in Latin America through its "Dollar Diplomacy," whereby Latin American governments were pressured to support U.S. business interests in their nations. U.S. businessmen accordingly made extensive investments in Latin American petroleum, copper, coffee, fruit, rubber, tin, sugar, and other products. By 1913 the United States had displaced Great Britain as the leading exporter to Latin America. With many valuable investments and markets, U.S. businessmen were eager to maintain orderly, pro-American governments in power in the region, an example being the compliant dictator Porfirio Diaz in Mexico.

Sometimes having friends in high places was not enough. Thus when periods of disorder swept Latin American nations, the U.S. government would intervene militarily. Between 1903 and 1934 it sent armed forces one or more times into six nations in the Caribbean, occupying three of them for more than a decade.

U.S. wealth and power generated fear and hatred throughout the Caribbean. To many upper-class Latin Americans, Yankee Imperialism by the Colossus of the North was an affront and an injury to their national sovereignty. By openly backing dictators, the United States also became a party to the exploitation of the masses. Consequently, many Latin American reformers and revolutionaries viewed the United States as an enemy to domestic social change and revolution.

The United States and Canada

The United States also periodically showed interest in expansion north of the border. Ever since the War for Independence many Americans wished to bring Canada into the Union. In 1867 the British Parliament passed a bill that united its colonies in North America and the Hudson's Bay Company into a federation called the Dominion of Canada. Through a process called devolution, early in the twentieth century Great Britain allowed Canada to assume control of its external affairs. U.S. businesses continued to invest heavily in Canada, accounting for almost one-quarter of its foreign investments in 1914. Great Britain, however, still remained Canada's major trading partner.

U.S. Expansion in Asia

From its inception, the United States had been interested in the China trade. By 1900 the United States had assumed a major role in the Pacific, with possessions that extended from Alaska to Samoa, including a string of island stepping-stones leading from the west coast of the United States through the Hawaiian Islands (annexed in 1898) to the Philippines. Like the Cubans, the Filipinos had begun to fight a guerrilla war for independence from Spain during the Spanish-American War. The United States, for a mixture of strategic, economic, and cultural reasons, refused to allow the Filipinos independence and acquired the islands from Spain at the end of the war. President McKinley even went so far as to announce that God supported U.S. control over the Philippines.

In 1899 Filipino nationalists revolted against U.S. rule and waged a protracted guerrilla war at an enormous human and economic cost; but they lost. The United States established its largest overseas naval base at Subic Bay in the Philippines to safeguard its Asian interests.

Because the United States was interested in maintaining its share of the China trade, it proposed an Open Door policy of equal trading opportunity for all foreign nations in

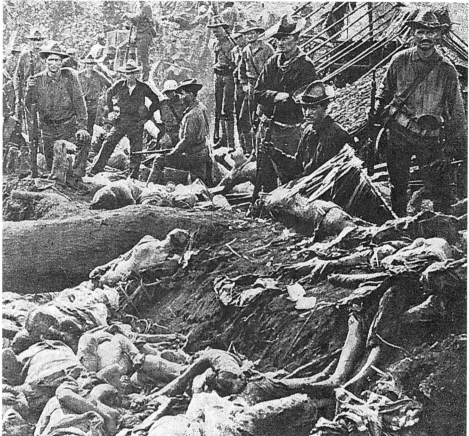

Imperialism in Asia. U.S. troops engaged in suppressing the insurrection in the Philippines are shown after a massacre of lightly armed Filipinos. The insurgents had originally been fighting for their independence against the Spanish; when they found that the United States was going to hold the Philippines rather than grant independence, they also fought the Americans, but were eventually defeated.

China in 1899. The European nations and Japan did not formally agree to the Open Door, but for fear of offending the United States, none openly rejected the principle. U.S. businessmen, engineers, and missionaries became increasingly active in China in the twentieth century, and U.S. gunboats patrolled China's major rivers to protect them. Unequal treaties imposed on China allowed Americans to enjoy the same extraterritorial immunity from Chinese laws as did the Europeans. Similarly, Westerners enjoyed immunity from local laws in Persia and the Ottoman Empire.

By the twentieth century, peoples under imperial control began to form political and economic organizations to combat foreign domination and to achieve national independence. Later chapters will describe the mounting opposition by Asian and African peoples to Western and Japanese imperial domination.

The Causes and Course of World War I

In Flanders Fields the poppies blow
Between the crosses, row on row,
That mark our place; and in the sky
The larks, still bravely singing, fly
Scarce heard amid the guns below.

We are the Dead. Short days ago
We lived, felt dawn, saw sunset glow,
Loved and were loved, and now we lie
In Flanders Fields.

Take up our quarrel with the foe:
To you from failing hands we throw
The torch; be yours to hold it high.
If ye break faith with us who die
We shall not sleep, though poppies grow
*In Flanders Fields.**

*John McCrae, *Punch,* December 6, 1915.

This haunting poem, written in the spring of 1915 by a Canadian physician at the front, evokes the terrible loss of life that occurred during World War I (then called the Great War). Months earlier most countries had greeted the outbreak of the war with relief and

Map 13.6 Europe in 1914. The map shows the alliance systems before the war. Germany, Austria-Hungary, and Italy formed the Triple Alliance, while France, Russia, and Great Britain made up the Triple Entente. Italy refused to join Germany and Austria-Hungary in August 1914, ultimately selling its services to the highest bidder—the Entente.

enthusiasm. Almost everyone expected a short conflict like the Austro-Prussian War of 1866 and more recently the wars in the Balkans. Economists strengthened this line of thinking by predicting that the heavy cost of modern war could not be borne by any participant for very long. No one dreamed that the war would last four years, drain the energies of the belligerents, and ultimately involve many nations outside Europe. Nor did anyone foresee that the war would wreck the order and stability of Europe, leaving its people to face a forbidding future.

The Underlying Causes of the Conflict

The origins of World War I are complex and cannot be explained solely on the basis of the events that immediately preceded it. Fundamentally, the Great War was the product of destructive forces whose roots go far back into history. Among the deeper causes of the war were nationalism, the arms race and militarism, and the alliance system.

Nationalism, with its roots in the era of the French Revolution, had increased significantly during the second half of the nineteenth century. While the Germans and Italians had achieved nationhood, other groups had not. The divisive effect of ethnic nationalism was particularly evident in the Habsburg Empire. The Dual Monarchy of Austria-Hungary kept the Slavs in the empire subordinate to the German Austrians and the Magyars of Hungary. By the turn of the century, Slavic nationalists, having concluded that their people would never acquire equal status, intensified their efforts to secede from the Austro-Hungarian Empire. Such an event would permit some Slavic elements like the Czechs to set up their own independent state and others like the South Slavs (Croats, Slovenes, and Serbs) to join the national state of their kin, Serbia, across the border. Freed from Ottoman rule in 1878, Serbia had dreams of a greater Serbia that would include the South Slavs not only in Austria-Hungary but in Bosnia and Herzegovina as well. Since Serbia was weaker than Austria-Hungary, it launched a covert campaign of agitation and subversion designed to undermine and ultimately destroy the integrity of the Dual Monarchy.

The atmosphere of suspicion and fear after 1870 gave rise to a bitter and costly armaments race. In the name of national security, Western states vied with one another in strengthening their armies and navies. Huge sums were spent on military equipment and ships, and all the major powers, except Great Britain and the United States, adopted conscription. German and Austrian military spending doubled between 1910 and 1914, and the expenditures of other powers increased markedly. By 1914, Germany and France each had about 800,000 men in uniform with millions of trained reservists. The military buildup on land was accompanied by a naval race between Great Britain and Germany. When, in 1906, Great Britain launched a new, superior class of battleships with the *Dreadnought*, Germany followed suit. Such contests not only drained national reserves but stirred hostility and distrust.

The arms race also led to growing militarism—a spirit that exalts military virtues and ideals—which conditioned people to view war as a glorious adventure essential to human progress. Such an outlook profoundly affected foreign policy, as political leaders more frequently sought and took the advice of army and naval officials. This was particularly evident during the summer of 1914, when governments, confronted by the inflexibility of their generals, often made decisions based on military rather than political considerations.

Besides strengthening their military capability, the European powers forged alliances among themselves in the hopes of deterring aggression and preventing war. But belonging to an alliance carried unforeseen risks and increased the chances that a local conflict would spread into a general war.

Bismarckian Diplomacy

Chancellor Otto von Bismarck of Germany originated Europe's system of alliances. Fearing that France might try to retaliate for its humiliating defeat in the Franco-Prussian War, Bismarck tried to keep France weak and diplomatically isolated. To that end, in 1873, he engineered a major alliance, composed of Germany, Austria-Hungary, and Russia. Known as the League of Three Emperors, it committed the signatories to maintain friendly neutrality in the event one of them was at war with a fourth power. That combination never worked well because of the growing rivalry between Austria and Russia as each sought to expand in the Balkans at the expense of the declining Ottoman Empire. In 1879 Bismarck negotiated a defensive military agreement, the Dual Alliance, with the Habsburg government of Austria-Hungary. Two years later the partnership was expanded into the Triple Alliance when Bismarck brought in Italy, which deeply resented French occupation of Tunis in North Africa, where it had designs of its own. When the League of Three Emperors finally broke down because of new tensions in the Balkans, Bismarck managed to retain the friendship of Russia by signing the Reinsurance Treaty (1887), which provided for the neutrality of each power should the other become involved in a war. By a complex system of alliances as well as by maintaining cordial relations with Great Britain, Bismarck had cut off France from any potential allies.

The Post-Bismarck Era

After 1890 the alliance system drove Europe toward war rather than preserving the peace. The impetuous new German emperor, Kaiser William II (reigned 1888–1918), dismissed Bismarck, changed the direction of Germany's foreign policy, and allowed the Reinsurance Treaty to lapse. This unexpected turn of events prompted France to solicit the friendship of the Russians, offering, as an inducement, arms and large loans. The resulting rapprochement led to a defensive pact between France and Russia in 1894.

France scored another diplomatic triumph ten years later when it buried its differences with Great Britain and signed the Entente Cordiale. This accord was a friendly understanding to reconcile points of contention and not a formal military alliance. The next logical step for the French was to bring together Britain and Russia, two traditional enemies. The timing was propitious. Badly defeated by the Japanese, the Russians wanted to reestablish their position in Europe. The British, with the threat of Russian aggression in Asia removed, were more concerned about Germany's uncertain aims. The upshot was the Anglo-Russian Entente of 1907. Again, no provision was made for mutual military assistance, but the parties' conciliatory attitude made cooperation easier.

The agreement completed the three-power bloc of France, Russia, and Great Britain, which came to be known as the Triple Entente.

Conflicts and Compromises, 1907–1914

Between 1907 and 1913 crises resulting from suspicions and national rivalries threatened to embroil the major European powers in a general war. Although in each instance solutions were found and major warfare avoided, these crises tended to solidify the alliance systems and to widen the gulf separating the two camps.

In 1911 Germany protested France's penetration of Morocco, and for a time the two powers stood on the brink of war. The Germans had raised similar objections six years earlier, but an international conference at Algeciras, Spain, had ruled in favor of France. This time the Germans held their ground, and at the eleventh hour the French backed down. They gave the Germans a slice of the French Congo in return for recognition of their rights to Morocco.

The other hot spot was in the Balkans. In 1908 Austrian annexation of Bosnia and Herzegovina infuriated both Serbian nationalists, who hoped to create an enlarged Slavic state, and the Russian government, which had imperial ambitions of its own in the region. When Germany came to Austria's support, Serbia and Russia were forced to yield. In 1912 four Balkan states joined forces to oust the Ottoman Turks from the region in the First Balkan War. They won a succession of victories and were about to overrun Istanbul when the great powers intervened to prevent the total collapse of the Ottoman Empire. At the peace conference, the Ottoman Empire was stripped of all its territory in Europe except Istanbul and its environs. The ink on the treaty was barely dry when the victors clashed over the distribution of the spoils. The Second Balkan War erupted in 1913 and, although it was over quickly, the Balkans remained a politically unstable region.

Rather than inducing the European powers to exercise greater caution, these recurring crises convinced them that they should take all steps to avoid a repetition of past failures. By 1914, national rivalries, sharpened by the feverish arms race, had brought tensions in Europe to a highly combustible state. Only a spark was needed to set off the explosion.

Archduke Francis Ferdinand's Assassination Leads to War

On June 28, 1914, the Archduke Francis Ferdinand, heir to the Austrian throne, and his wife were shot to death as their motorcade drove through the streets of Sarajevo, capital of Bosnia. The assassin, Gavrilo Princip, was the tool of a secret Serbian terrorist society, the Black Hand, dedicated to unifying all South Slavs under Serbian rule. The Archduke became a victim of the Black Hand because it was widely believed that he wanted to place the Slavs on the same autonomous footing as the Germans and Magyars within the Habsburg Empire. Such a policy would have caused the South Slavs in the Austrian Empire to lose their enthusiasm for union with Serbia. The murder plot had been hatched in Belgrade, the Serbian capital, and was the brainchild of the chief of intelligence of the Serbian army. Though not directly involved in the conspiracy, members of the Serbian government knew of it but took no effective steps to foil it or to forewarn Austrian authorities.

The Austrians saw the assassination as a chance to settle accounts with Serbia once and for all. Before taking punitive action, they sought support from their ally, Germany. The kaiser and his advisers believed that Austria required the complete support of Germany if it was to survive as a great power and be an effective partner in the alliance. They urged the Austrians to take vigorous action against Serbia even though it could lead to a European war. They believed a major war was inevitable and that Germany was in a better position to fight now than it would be in several years when Russia and France would be stronger as a result of army reforms. Fortified by Germany's "blank check," Austria delivered an ultimatum to Serbia, couched in terms calculated to make its rejection certain. The Serbians were unexpectedly conciliatory, but Austria deemed the reply unsatisfactory and on 28 July declared war on Serbia. The Austrians wanted to localize the conflict, hoping that Germany's unqualified support would deter the Russians from helping Serbia.

Austria's Reaction to the Serbian Reply

The Austrian Ambassador to the British Foreign Office, July 27, 1914:

The Royal Serbian Government has refused to agree to the demands which we were forced to make for the lasting assurance of those of our vital interests threatened by that Government, and has thus given evidence that it is not willing to desist from its destructive efforts directed toward the constant disturbance of some of our border territories and their eventual separation from the control of the Monarchy. We are therefore compelled, to our regret and much against our will, to force Serbia by the sharpest means to a fundamental alteration of her hitherto hostile attitude. That in so doing, aggressive intentions are far from our thoughts, and that it is merely in self-defense that we have finally determined, after years of patience, to oppose the Greater Serbia intrigues with the sword, is well known to the Imperial German Government.

It is a cause of honest satisfaction to us that we find both in the Imperial German Government and in the entire German people a complete comprehension of the fact that our patience was of necessity exhausted after the assassination at Sarajevo, which, according to the results of the inquiry, was planned at Belgrade and carried out by emissaries from that city; and that we are now forced to the task of securing ourselves by every means against the continuation of the present intolerable conditions on our southwestern border.

We confidently hope that our prospective difference with Serbia will be the cause of no further complications; but in the event that such should nevertheless occur, we are gratefully certain that Germany, with a fidelity long proven, will bear in mind the obligations of her alliance and lend us her support in any fight forced upon us by another opponent.*

In the days following Austria's ultimatum, Great Britain took the lead among European states in pressing the Habsburg government to refrain from attacking Serbia. In this note, authorities in Vienna seek to justify the coming invasion of Serbia. The Austrians were worried about the attitude of Great Britain, which, as yet, had refused to give any firm pledge to assist the entente in case of war. The hint of full German backing was evidently intended to dissuade the British from abandoning their position of neutrality.

*Max Montgelas and Walter Schücking, eds., Outbreak of the World War: German Documents Collected by Karl Kautsky, trans. Carnegie Endowment for International Peace (New York: Oxford University Press, 1924), no. 268, p. 249.

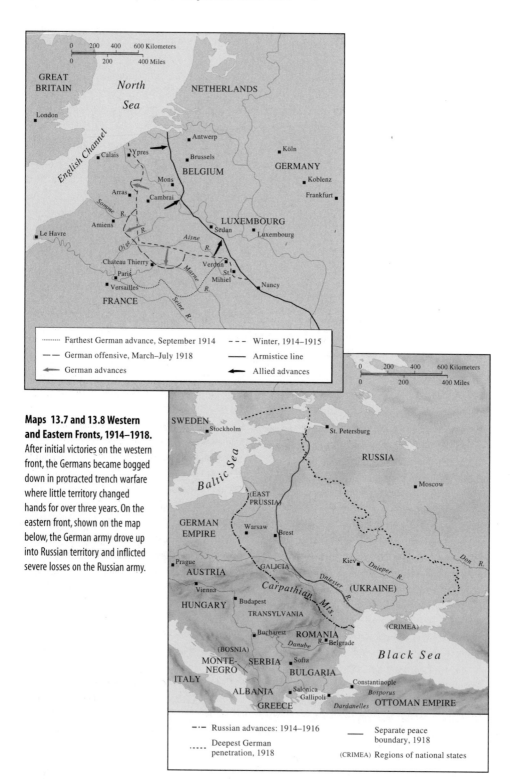

Maps 13.7 and 13.8 Western and Eastern Fronts, 1914–1918. After initial victories on the western front, the Germans became bogged down in protracted trench warfare where little territory changed hands for over three years. On the eastern front, shown on the map below, the German army drove up into Russian territory and inflicted severe losses on the Russian army.

.... Farthest German advance, September 1914

– – – Winter, 1914–1915

– — German offensive, March–July 1918

——— Armistice line

German advances

Allied advances

–··– Russian advances: 1914–1916

.... Deepest German penetration, 1918

——— Separate peace boundary, 1918

(CRIMEA) Regions of national states

Within a week, however, Austria's military initiative brought about a general war. Russia, assured of French support, ordered immediate full mobilization because it required more time to get its military machine into operation than did either Austria or Germany. For the Germans, Russia's mobilization was equivalent to an act of war. Germany's Schlieffen plan—devised by Count von Schlieffen, chief of the general staff from 1891 to 1906—envisaged a two-front war against Russia and France. It called for a holding action against the slowly mobilizing Russians while the bulk of the German army drove through Belgium in order to outflank France's frontier defenses, encircle Paris, and fall behind the French forces in the south. The full strength of the German army could then be directed against the Russians. Thus Germany could not permit Russia to mobilize first. When the tsar refused to heed a warning from Berlin to stop military preparations, Germany declared war on Russia on August 1. Two days later, the kaiser's government declared war on France, having concluded that France was almost certain to come to the aid of its Russian ally.

At this point, Italy and Great Britain hesitated to enter the conflict. Italy claimed that its obligations to the Triple Alliance did not include supporting a war of aggression. Great Britain was not legally bound to help France or Russia but did so when Germany violated a long-standing international treaty guaranteeing Belgium neutrality. If Germany could

Life in the Trenches

Patriotism, in the trenches, was too remote a sentiment, and at once rejected as fit only for civilians, or prisoners. A new arrival who talked patriotism would soon be told to cut it out. . . . Great Britain . . . included not only the trench-soldiers themselves and those who had gone home wounded, but the staff, Army Service Corps, lines-of-communication troops, base units, home-service units, and all civilians down to the detested grades of journalists, profiteers, "starred" men exempted from enlistment, conscientious objectors, and members of the Government. The trench-soldier, with this carefully graded caste-system of honour, never considered that the Germans opposite might have built up exactly the same system themselves. . . .

Hardly one soldier in a hundred was inspired by religious feeling of even the crudest kind. It would have been difficult to remain religious in the trenches even if one had survived the irreligion of the training battalion at home. A regular sergeant at Montagne . . . had recently told me that he did not hold with religion in time of war. . . . "And all this damn nonsense, Sir—

excuse me, Sir—that we read in the papers, Sir, about how miraculous it is that the wayside crucifixes are always getting shot at, but the figure of our Lord Jesus somehow don't get hurt, it fairly makes me sick, Sir." *This was his explanation why, when giving practice fire-orders from the hill-top, he had shouted, unaware that I stood behind him: "Seven hundred half left, bloke on cross, five rounds, concentrate, FIRE!" . . . His platoon, including the two unusual "bible-wallahs" whose letters home always began in the same formal way: "Dear Sister in Christ," or "Dear Brother in Christ," blazed away.**

This passage from the memoirs of a British infantry captain, who later gained fame as a writer, reflects the contempt of fighting soldiers for those who did not serve with them in the trenches. That emotion had no great effect in Great Britain, but it had a major impact in Italy and Germany after the war. The passage also reveals the decline in religious belief among those who witnessed the barbarities of World War I.

*Robert Graves, Good-bye to All That, rev. ed (Garden City, N.Y.: Doubleday, 1957), pp. 188–189.

dominate the Netherlands and Belgium, directly across the English Channel, England would be in jeopardy. Hence Great Britain declared war against Germany on August 4.

The two conflicting groups were known as the Allies and the Central Powers. Initially the Allies consisted of Great Britain, France, Russia, Serbia, and Belgium. Japan, partly to honor its treaty commitments to Great Britain, entered the conflict late in August 1914. Italy remained on the sidelines until 1915 when it reversed sides and joined the Allies, as did the United States two years later. Germany and Austria-Hungary were joined by the Ottoman Empire late in 1914 and Bulgaria in 1915. Eventually the war involved more than thirty nations and some 65 million fighting men.

The Controversy over Responsibility

Few topics in modern European history have generated more heated debate than the question of who was most at fault for the outbreak of World War I. Soon after the fighting broke out, the governments of the various belligerent nations hastened to publish diplomatic documents relating to the July crisis in 1914. They selected only those that

Trench Warfare on the Western Front. For nearly four years the two great armies were cramped in a double line of trenches from which futile attacks to dislodge the enemy were repeatedly launched. Life for the common soldier was a hell of boredom in rat-infested trenches, horrifying battle experiences, bad weather, sniper fire, and the loss of comrades. Trench warfare left terrible psychological as well as physical scars on many of those who survived.

Imperial War Museum, London

portrayed their action in a favorable light and cast their enemies in the role of aggressors. The Allies, the eventual victors, went so far as to write a clause in the peace treaty blaming the war on Germany and its associates. Historians began to challenge that harsh assessment in the 1920s and instead apportioned blame to all the initial participants.

The next generation of historians, benefiting from documents made available after World War II, rejected both interpretations. While acknowledging that no nation was wholly to blame, historians judged certain governments and individuals more responsible than others. One thing is certain: Germany urged Austria forward during the critical period, knowing that doing so was likely to lead to a general war. If Germany is to be singled out as the chief culprit, then Austria-Hungry, Serbia, and Russia are not far behind. France follows, with Britain bearing little if any responsibility. To this day there is no consensus on the exact degree to which each power was responsible for the war, in part because information on disputed points is missing. But undoubtedly all the involved nations made errors in judgment during the tense weeks after the assassination, and none, with the possible exception of Great Britain, is entirely free of blame.

Stalemate on the Western Front

Both sides had based their plans on a lightning offensive campaign that would overwhelm the opposition and produce a quick victory. The first phase of the Schlieffen plan worked with almost clockwork precision. The German army smashed through Belgium, poured into northeastern France, and by early September was within forty miles of Paris. In the meantime the French drove into Alsace-Lorraine, only to be hurled back after some of the fiercest fighting in the war. The French redeployed northward and westward to meet the invading Germans. Aided by a small British contingent, they counterattacked along the Marne River. The Germans, who were exhausted and bewildered, were halted and driven back. The First Battle of the Marne dashed Germany's hopes for a quick victory over France and compelled it to fight a protracted war on two fronts.

Thereafter the fighting in the west changed from a war of movement to a war of position. The opposing armies tried to outflank one another but only succeeded in extending the front northward. By the end of 1914 the combatants faced each other along a 500-mile line of trenches from the Swiss border to the North Sea. Flanking movements were no longer possible, and the greatly increased firepower of modern weapons, especially machine guns, and fortified trench networks gave the defense a clear advantage against frontal assaults. Behind barbed wire entanglements, defenders repelled attacking waves with scorching fire, mowing the attackers down in swaths.

Baffled by the new type of warfare, unimaginative generals concentrated men and artillery against a sector of the enemy's line, confident of breaking through and resuming the war of movement. As a result, millions of young men were recklessly squandered in a futile effort to pierce the enemy's defenses. The French army lost 1,430,000 men in various attacks in 1915. The Germans abandoned the five-month siege of Verdun (1916) after their killed and wounded approached 300,000. The French defenders sustained slightly heavier casualties. Over 57,000 British infantrymen were killed or wounded on the first day of the Battle of the Somme (1916), the heaviest loss Great Britain ever suffered in a single day's battle. All this carnage served absolutely no purpose. Despite the introduction of new weapons such as poison gas, flamethrowers, and tanks, the battle lines established at the close of 1914 changed little in three and a half years.

The Eastern Front

In contrast to the stalemate in the west, the war in the east was fluid, with frequently shifting battle lines that resulted in huge blocks of territory won and lost. When war began, the Russians completed mobilization quickly and mounted ill-prepared invasions of German and Habsburg territory. With most of the German army tied up in the west, the Russians made unexpected gains, advancing well into Germany's easternmost province. Alarmed German authorities appointed General Paul von Hindenburg (1847–1934) to direct the operations with the brilliant General Erich Ludendorff (1865–1937) as his chief of staff. Although outnumbered, von Hindenburg won major

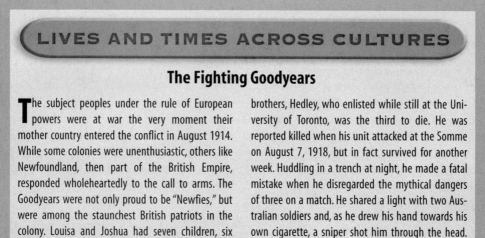

LIVES AND TIMES ACROSS CULTURES

The Fighting Goodyears

The subject peoples under the rule of European powers were at war the very moment their mother country entered the conflict in August 1914. While some colonies were unenthusiastic, others like Newfoundland, then part of the British Empire, responded wholeheartedly to the call to arms. The Goodyears were not only proud to be "Newfies," but were among the staunchest British patriots in the colony. Louisa and Joshua had seven children, six boys and a girl. Five of the boys volunteered for the army and the girl, Kate, served in the nursing corps. Raymond, the youngest, wanted to go to war with his brothers, and twice tried to enlist, only to be retrieved each time by his father. Although still slightly underage, he got his wish early in 1916 and in the fall joined the Newfoundland Regiment manning the line outside of Ypres. In his first battle, a shrapnel shell ripped open his waist, killing him instantly. A year later his brother Stan, athletic and deemed indestructible, tempted fate once too often and was killed by an artillery blast while racing through a firefight to bring munitions to his unit near Langemarck in Belgium. The oldest of the brothers, Hedley, who enlisted while still at the University of Toronto, was the third to die. He was reported killed when his unit attacked at the Somme on August 7, 1918, but in fact survived for another week. Huddling in a trench at night, he made a fatal mistake when he disregarded the mythical dangers of three on a match. He shared a light with two Australian soldiers and, as he drew his hand towards his own cigarette, a sniper shot him through the head. The remaining two brothers, Joe and Ken, suffered serious wounds and were invalided home.

For Kate, who attended to the wounded at St. Luke's hospital in Ottawa, and the other surviving members of her family, the war did not end in 1918. Her great-nephew wrote that for the next seventy years the normally reserved Kate would sometimes pause in the midst of a sentence, particularly at the thought or mention of Hedley, whom she adored, as tears welled up unexpectedly in her eyes. Kate Goodyear and millions like her lived with their losses, mindful always of the void that could never be filled, and of what might have been had their loved ones lived to return home.

victories, first at Tannenberg at the end of August and two weeks later at the Masurian Lakes. In these two battles the Germans killed or captured 250,000 Russians.

The Russians fared better against Austria, occupying most of Galicia before the arrival of four German army corps from the western front checked their drive. In the spring and summer of 1915 a combined Austro-German thrust forced the underequipped Russians to abandon Galicia and most of Poland and inflicted some 2 million casualties. Remarkably, the Russians not only stayed in the field after these incredible losses but mounted an offensive the following year. They opened a wide gap in the Austrian lines and took several hundred thousand prisoners but were unable to sustain the drive. A German counteroffensive cost the Russians all the territory they had gained and a good deal more. Russia lost another million men and sank into a state of apathy from which it never recovered. These defeats, food shortages, and the inefficiency and corruption of the government bred discontent among the civilian population. In March 1917 popular outbreaks forced the tsar to abdicate, and a provisional government was created. When the government attempted to continue the war effort, it was overthrown by Marxist revolutionaries who immediately negotiated a peace treaty with Germany. In March 1918 Russia signed the Treaty of Brest-Litovsk and dropped out of the war.

The War outside Europe

Although the main battles were fought in Europe there were subsidiary operations elsewhere involving forces from many countries of the world. Instinctive loyalty to Great Britain prompted the self-governing dominions to pledge their support the moment the British government declared war. Canada sent 640,000 men to fight overseas, Australia 329,000, and New Zealand 117,000. As the war expanded, Britain drew on India and other colonies for manpower. For its part France raised 270,000 men from its North African colonies alone. African losses in the various campaigns likely amounted to at least 300,000 men.

Allied command of the seas sealed the fate of Germany's colonies in Asia and Africa. To the Japanese, the war offered an opportunity to consolidate and expand their empire in East Asia. In September 1914 their forces landed on the Shantung Peninsula of China and in a brief, hard-fought campaign took the German port of Tsingtao. The Japanese then forced the Chinese government to transfer to them all German possessions in Shantung, as well as commercial rights in southern Manchuria and elsewhere in China. During November 1914 Japanese soldiers occupied the Marianas, the Marshalls, the Carolines, and other German-held North Pacific islands. South of the equator, New Zealand and Australia had raced ahead of Japan to acquire the German colonial islands of Samoa and New Guinea, respectively.

Similarly, German colonies in Africa fell one by one to the Allies. In 1914 British and French troops seized Togoland and, within a year and a half, the Cameroons. In 1915 Great Britain's dominion of South Africa invaded and occupied German Southwest Africa. In German East Africa, British, Indian, and South African forces took possession of most of the colony, although the resourceful German commander, Lettow-Vorbeck, kept his badly outnumbered army in the field right up to war's end.

The war in West Asia was of greater magnitude and consequence than in Africa. By joining the Central Powers, the strategically located Ottoman Empire posed grave problems for the Allies, particularly Great Britain. In 1915 the British landed an army on the Gallipoli Peninsula with the object of knocking the Ottoman Empire out of the war and bringing aid to the beleaguered Russians. Blunders in planning and execution forced the British to withdraw after suffering heavy losses. The British sustained another major defeat in Mesopotamia, where they had undertaken to advance on Baghdad with insufficient strength. Halted and then surrounded at Kut, British-Indian forces withstood a six-month siege before surrendering in April 1916. Great Britain had more success against the Turks in Syria and Palestine. A British force advancing from Egypt found invaluable allies in the Arabs, who were advised by British officers, including the famous T. E. Lawrence (1888–1935)—later romanticized as Lawrence of Arabia. Roused by the British, the Arabs fought the Turks to secure an independent state after the war. The conquest of Jerusalem and southern Palestine by the end of 1917 was followed by a vigorous drive into Syria in 1918 that led to the capitulation of the Ottoman Empire.

The war outside Europe had wide ramifications. In Asia, Japan's increased power and aggressive policies in China set the stage for future trouble. Within the British dominions, the war had stirred strong national feelings and demands for more say in shaping their foreign policy. Indian nationalists like Mohandas K. Gandhi had backed the British war effort in the expectation that victory would hasten the independence of India. In the Middle East, the Arabs had aided the Allied cause in exchange for freedom. But in the Balfour Declaration of 1917 Britain had pledged to establish a national home for the Jewish people in Palestine, thereby violating promises made to the Arabs (the impact of the conflicting agreements will be described in the next chapter). All these forces set in motion created many problems after the war.

The Home Front

World War I was the first total war in modern history to impose burdens on all the citizens of the participating states. Gone were the days when wars were fought by professional armies while the average civilians at home went about their usual business.

In August 1914 the belligerents anticipated a brief war and lacked the resources and contingency plans to meet long-term production needs. As the war dragged on, all governments had to confront the vital questions of matériel, food, and manpower. The demands of total war led to the increased centralization of political authority, the imposition of economic controls, and the restriction of civil liberties.

In the euphoria that accompanied the outbreak of war, the general public and all political parties rallied behind their respective governments. In France, the president appealed for a "sacred union" of all French to defend the homeland. The kaiser, in a speech before parliament, exclaimed "I know parties no more. I know only Germans." "I am in perfect union with my united people!" said Tsar Nicholas II. In the name of national security, governments indulged in practices that the press and opposition parties would never have tolerated in time of peace. In Russia progress toward sharing political responsibility ended when the tsar suspended the Duma for the duration of the war. During 1917 and 1918 the Hindenburg-Ludendorff team in Germany had replaced the imperial government with a military dictatorship, controlling diplomatic and economic as well as military policy. Even in France and Great Britain, greater power was concentrated in the hands of the prime minister and the cabinet.

The stress of total war also produced tight control in the economic organization of the belligerent nations. The economy had to be managed so that human and material resources were employed in the most efficient manner. Everywhere priorities were set for military versus civilian needs. Germany, which was short on raw materials, was the first to introduce economic regimentation, establishing a War Raw Materials Department to allocate raw materials on a priority basis. In the United States, Bernard Baruch, a Wall Street financier, was given sweeping powers to harness the nation's industrial capacity. Laws passed between 1914 and 1916 empowered the British government to requisition factories and control production, discard trade union rules, outlaw strikes, and introduce conscription.

The regulation of economic life and the need to maintain the nation's unity and its will to go on fighting placed restrictions upon the freedoms of citizens. All governments, even those of democracies, passed laws to intern people suspected of being enemy agents or sympathizers and prohibited defeatist activities. Houses were searched without warrants, public meetings were prohibited, and persons making antiwar speeches were liable to receive prison sentences.

Along with censorship, all governments actively used propaganda to achieve their goals. Newspapers were censored, and all items that were critical of the government or provided aid and comfort to the enemy were deleted. In trying to win over neutral states, each side tried to discredit the other while trumpeting the righteousness of its cause. Allied propaganda effectively highlighted Germany's brutal conduct in Belgium, sinking of merchant ships, and misusing of civilians in occupied countries. It became common in Great Britain to refer to the Germans as Huns. At home propaganda was designed to breed confidence in victory and to engender hatred of the foe. The German people were shielded from the truth and until practically the end they were told they were winning the war. In the Allied countries, the kaiser was a favorite target of cartoonists. With his spiked helmet and with gleaming eyes and oversized upturned mustache, he was depicted as the incarnation of the devil or as a mad fiend bent on world domination. Such ideas and images deepened hatreds and created illusions that were difficult to set aside when the time came to arrange a peace.

Women and the War

The war provided women with an opportunity to assume new roles and to contribute to the war effort in various ways. In Great Britain newly established women auxiliary forces attracted thousands of volunteers. These women lived in camps, wore khaki uniforms, and drilled, but worked mostly as secretaries and kitchen help. The Russian government organized battalions of women to help maintain order in the cities.

All nations relied on volunteer aides along with professional nurses to serve in understaffed hospitals. Many unpaid volunteer nurses from wealthy families worked side by side with salaried nurses from more modest backgrounds. In an atmosphere where all pulled together for the nation's survival, class divisions were blurred. All toiled long hours to mitigate the sufferings of soldiers under primitive conditions that exposed them to infections and disease. Those in medical facilities immediately behind the front were also exposed to the dangers of artillery bombardment and possible capture. One of the best-known incidents of the war involved a British nurse, Edith Cavell, who worked with the Red Cross in German-occupied Belgium. Tried for helping British and French soldiers caught behind enemy lines to escape, she was found guilty of espionage and shot. The worldwide revulsion that followed provided another propaganda triumph for the Allies.

In the cities, employers were compelled to turn to women as replacements. In some nations special agencies solicited and assigned women for war work. Women by the thousands took over jobs previously denied them. They drove trucks, delivered mail, swept chimneys, and worked in mortuaries and especially in factories. In Great Britain women eventually comprised 60 percent of all those employed in the armament industry. Only a handful of women were employed in the Krupp Armament Works in Germany before the war, but by 1917 their numbers had climbed to 12,000. The percentage of women in the industrial force in Moscow rose from 39.4 percent in 1913 to 48.7 percent in 1917. In rural areas, women managed family farms, plowed the land, and made business decisions.

Although women held all sorts of jobs formerly reserved for men, they were paid less than men doing the same work, and few reached positions of authority. In the munitions factories, for example, women earned only about half of what men received. Some governments tried to intercede on behalf of women workers. In France the government established minimum wages for women in certain industries and then outlawed discrimination on the basis of sex. Although women made more as a result of government regulations, their wages by war's end still lagged behind those of their male counterparts.

The war had an impact on the social behavior of women. Economic independence ensured them the personal freedoms they desired. More women lived on their own. Even their appearance was transformed: they cut their hair, wore shorter skirts and less constraining clothes—many abandoned the corset—went out unescorted in public, and put on makeup, a practice traditionally associated with prostitutes. Women enjoyed greater sexual freedom as well. The high risks for young men going to the front encouraged couples to become intimate more quickly.

Men generally acknowledged the essential contributions women made to the war effort and conceded their right to participate in the political process, a notable reversal of prewar attitudes. In 1917 the provisional government in Russia even allowed women to vote. In February 1918 the British parliament granted the suffrage to women over thirty. Immediately after the war, women in Austria, Germany, and the United States were similarly enfranchised.

Women workers suffered setbacks after the war ended, however, when demobilized soldiers reclaimed their jobs. Nearly all the gains made during the war were reversed. In the postwar period, males reverted to traditional attitudes and demanded that women return to their homes.

American Entry and the Collapse of the Central Powers

The highly touted German High Seas Fleet was reluctant to challenge Britain's domination of the seas. It remained in port except for one sortie in May 1916 when it suffered a defeat in a running battle with a British squadron off the coast of Jutland. Thereafter the Germans relied on a deadly new naval weapon, the submarine, to break the crippling British blockade. As a highly industrial nation, Germany depended on overseas imports of raw materials and especially food in order to survive.

As early as 1915, the German government had declared the waters surrounding Great Britain a war zone in which Allied merchant ships would be torpedoed without warning. In May the British liner *Lusitania*, which was carrying war matériel, was torpedoed with the loss of 1,200 passengers, including more than a hundred Americans. Strong protests from Washington compelled the German government to modify its policy, and the crisis passed. By the beginning of 1917 the Allied blockade was having a serious effect on Germany, strangling its industry and causing widespread food shortages. The German High Command considered defeat inevitable if the war lasted much longer. Thus in a desperate bid to starve Great Britain into submission, the German authorities decided to resume unrestricted submarine warfare, even at the risk of adding the United States to their growing list of opponents. Germany believed, however, that the United States was militarily unprepared and incapable of putting a sizable army in the field before Great Britain was defeated.

The outrage in the United States was great. President Woodrow Wilson (1856–1924) suspended diplomatic relations with Germany but did not immediately ask Congress for a declaration of war. The sinking of several American ships was followed by revelations that Germany was plotting to entice Mexico to attack the United States, promising to restore Mexico's "lost provinces" of Texas, Arizona, and New Mexico in return for its support in case of war between Germany and the United States. Appearing before Congress on April 2, Wilson declared that U.S. intervention would make the world "safe for democracy." Congress approved a declaration of war four days later. Although American troops did not arrive at the front for a year, the United States did supply the war-weary Allies with immediate financial, material, and naval aid.

At first Germany's unrestricted submarine campaign exceeded the expectations of its planners, but as the months passed Great Britain developed increasingly effective countermeasures, including depth charges, hydrophonic detectors, mine barrages, and the convoy system. By the close of 1917, it was clear that the submarine campaign had failed. Facing economic strangulation, Germany was forced to seek a decisive breakthrough on the western front.

In the spring of 1918, with reinforcements from the Russian front, General Ludendorff launched the first of five offensives that nearly won the war for Germany. Ludendorff not only possessed superiority in numbers, but he also counted on new tactics pioneered by General Oscar von Huetier: rather than attack on a broad front after an intense artillery barrage, the idea was to push highly trained shock troops, organized into small fire teams, through weakly defended areas, leaving follow-up units to reduce the strong points. Achieving strategic surprise, Ludendorff pierced the Allied line and within three months stood on the Marne, some forty miles away from Paris. In this crucial hour, the Allies took the long delayed step of creating a unified command under a French general, Ferdinand Foch (1851–1929), to coordinate their operations. Ludendorff's great offensive ultimately stalled owing to the exhaustion of his soldiers and the timely arrival of American forces. The last German offensive in July lacked strength after the initial surge. With the Americans arriving at the rate of 250,000 a month, time had run out for the Germans.

On July 18 the Allies counterattacked along the whole front, driving the Germans back from their gains of the previous spring. On August 8, the "black day of the German army," British tanks smashed through the German lines near Amiens; the Allies now pressed on relentlessly, with the Americans bearing the brunt of the fighting. German morale began to crumble, and on September 29, Ludendorff, almost in a panic, advised the kaiser to seek peace. While Germany entered into negotiations to achieve a cease-fire, its allies dropped out of the war one by one. On November 8 the Allies presented their armistice terms to a German commission. At 11.00 A.M. on November 11, 1918, the guns fell silent on the western front.

The Great War was one of the greatest calamities to befall Western civilization. Not since the Black Death in the mid-fourteenth century had so many people died in so brief a time. The war killed about 10 million soldiers and wounded twice that many. Civilian losses from air raids, bombardments, submarines, and the blockade totaled at least another million. A whole generation of European youth had been wiped out. The war also destroyed the wealth the European states had accumulated during the preceding century and left them heavily in debt. It caused the collapse of the German, Austro-Hungarian, Russian, and Ottoman Empires. It was the beginning of the end of Europe's political domination of the rest of the world.

Survivors of the Great War were left with a sense of despair and futility. The senseless mass destruction of life and property by nations thought to be the most advanced in the world shook the confidence of Western men and women in the basic tenets of rationality and progress. It was hoped that the peace settlements would be the first step in the reconstruction of Europe's social, political, and economic order.

Postwar Settlements and the Interwar Years

So far as possible . . . it was the policy of France to set the clock back and to undo what, since 1870, the progress of Germany had accomplished. By loss of territory and other measures her population was to be curtailed; but chiefly the economic system, upon which she depended for her new strength, the vast fabric built upon iron, coal, and transport must be destroyed. If France could seize, even in part, what Germany was compelled to drop, the inequality between the two rivals for European hegemony might be remedied for many generations.*

*John Maynard Keynes, *The Economic Consequences of the Peace* (New York: Harcourt, 1920), pp. 35–36.

In this discussion, the leading postwar economist, John Maynard Keynes, inaccurately outlines France's plans to destroy future German power and its attempts to inflict a final defeat on its old enemy at the peace table. Keynes knew little about French policy, and his views were shaped by his own guilt as a pacifist over having participated in Great Britain's war effort. There is no evidence that France was seeking hegemony, revenge, or anything beyond security against a third German invasion. Keynes's book was slanted, but given his international reputation, it was accepted as gospel in English-speaking countries. As a result, Keynes helped to create the myth that the peace settlements were instruments of Allied vengeance that prepared the way for a future war.

The Paris Peace Conference and the Versailles Treaty

In January 1919 delegates of the victorious nations gathered in Paris to decide the fate of Germany and its associates. The Central Powers were not represented, nor was Russia, which had dropped out of the war and was currently in the midst of civil strife. Taking a lesson from the 1815 Congress of Vienna, where the loser (the French) had participated and exploited the divisions among the victors, the Allies decided that they would meet

Wilson's Fourteen Points

I. Open covenants of peace, openly arrived at, after which there shall be no private international understandings of any kind but diplomacy shall always proceed frankly and in the public view.

II. Absolute freedom of navigation upon the seas, ... alike in peace and in war.

III. The removal, so far as possible, of all economic barriers and the establishment of an equality of trade conditions among all the nations....

IV. Adequate guarantees given and taken that national armaments will be reduced to the lowest point consistent with domestic safety.

V. A free, open-minded, and absolutely impartial adjustment of all colonial claims, based upon a strict observance of the principle that in determining all such questions of sovereignty the interests of the populations concerned must have equal weight with the equitable claims of the government whose title is to be determined.

VI. The evacuation of all Russian territory....

VII. Belgium ... must be evacuated and restored.

VIII. All French territory should be free ... the wrong done to France in the matter ... of Lorraine ... should be righted.

IX. A readjustment of the frontiers of Italy should be effected along clearly recognizable lines of nationality.

X. The peoples of Austria-Hungary ... should be accorded the freest opportunity of autonomous development.

XI. Rumania, Serbia, and Montenegro should be evacuated, occupied territories restored.

XII. The Turkish portion of the present Ottoman Empire should be assured a ... sovereignty, but the other nationalities which are now under Turkish rule ... [should have] autonomous development.

XIII. An independent Polish state should be created which should include the territories inhabited by indisputably Polish populations, which should be assured a free and secure access to the sea....

XIV. A general association of nations must be formed under specific covenants for the purpose of affording mutual guarantees of political independence and territorial integrity to great and small states alike.*

Wilson knew what he wanted the conference to do, but many of his Fourteen Points were maddeningly vague. He hoped to overcome any problems that arose through the force of his own personal popularity and through the new power of the United States. Wilson relied perhaps too heavily on influencing the other Allied leaders by flexing America's economic muscle. He failed to understand that there were things money could not purchase. Not even a shack had been destroyed in the United States during the war, but in France alone 4,000 towns had been obliterated. For Clemenceau, France's security had no price tag. He proposed to protect France not with vague Wilsonian principles but with practical measures that would cripple Germany.

*Speech of President Woodrow Wilson to a joint Session of Congress, January 8, 1918, Congressional Record, 56 (1918), pt. I, 680–681.

first without the Germans present. The victors would thus agree on the broad outlines of the peace and require Germany to sign that "preliminary" peace before holding a general peace conference with Germany's participation. As matters turned out, the preliminary peace became the final peace, and the Germans never had the opportunity to present their case.

The major decisions in Paris were made by an inner council of four: President Wilson of the United States and Prime Ministers Georges Clemenceau of France, David Lloyd George of Great Britain, and Vittorio Orlando of Italy. In theory, all sovereign states had the same rights. In reality, the lesser states were consulted only in cases involving their direct interests. Since the "Big Four" powers would have the responsibility of carrying out the treaty provisions, their agreement was vital.

The Allied leaders were eager to lay the foundations of a lasting peace, but they differed on the means to achieve their goal. Wilson alone made no territorial or financial claims on the defeated nations. His idealistic vision of a just and enduring peace, embodied in the Fourteen Points, would obviate defeated Germany's desire for revenge and permit the building of a better and safer world order. In November 1918 the Allies had tacitly agreed to make peace on Wilson's terms, excluding only two offending points regarding freedom of the seas and reparations.

Yet when the actual peace negotiations got under way, the Fourteen Points were often conspicuously disregarded. The European leaders, whose people had fought and suffered through a long war, demanded indemnification from the Central Powers. They were bound by secret treaties and agreements, and each had his own ulterior motives. Clemenceau, nicknamed the Tiger, wanted above all to ensure France's security, which he felt could only be accomplished by crippling Germany. He viewed Wilson with extreme cynicism. The Tiger reportedly quipped that since mankind had been unable to keep God's Ten Commandments, it was unlikely to do better with Wilson's Fourteen Points. Besides coveting certain German and Ottoman territories, Lloyd George wanted to prevent any one power from dominating Europe. Orlando concerned himself chiefly with gaining territories from the former Austro-Hungarian Empire. When it became clear that all his demands would not be met, he left the conference in a huff, and the Big Four became the Big Three.

The Paris Peace Conference lasted from January to May 1919 and was marked by bitter wranglings and threats of a breakup. The most serious disagreement was over the future of the Rhineland, German territory on the left bank of the Rhine River. As protection against a new invasion from Germany, Clemenceau wanted the area turned into a buffer zone, preferably under French control. But Wilson, backed by Lloyd George, resisted the demand, and Clemenceau was driven to accept its demilitarized status. One by one, important issues were settled by reconciling clashing viewpoints, and a draft treaty was drawn up and handed to a German delegation.

The Germans protested the severity of the treaty's terms, but the Allies made no substantive changes in the document and warned the Germans that failure to accept it would mean renewal of the war. Germany's delegates signed the treaty on June 28, 1919, in the Hall of Mirrors at Versailles.

The Versailles Treaty weakened but did not destroy Germany as a great state. Still, Germany lost about 10 percent of its population and territory in Europe. It ceded Alsace-Lorraine to France, small areas of land to Belgium and Denmark, and much of Prussia, including a corridor to the Baltic Sea, to Poland. The Saar Valley was placed under international control for fifteen years, after which a plebiscite was to be held to determine whether the population wished to be under France or Germany. Germany gave up all its colonial possessions to the Allies as mandates (trusteeships) nominally under the supervision of the League of Nations. Germany's reparations bill, as determined by an Allied commission in 1921, was set at about $33 billion.

The treaty sought to prevent a resurgence of German militarism by reducing its army to 100,000 volunteers and severely limiting its weaponry and the size of its navy. Germany had to accept the demilitarization and military occupation of the Rhineland. The kaiser and other leaders were to be tried for violations of international law and customs of war. But the kaiser, who had abdicated on November 9, 1918, was not brought to trial. The government of the Netherlands, which granted him sanctuary, refused to allow him to be extradited.

The Settlements with the Other Central Powers

Treaties with the other defeated nations were signed in 1919 and 1920; all were closely modeled on the Versailles pact, with provisions for reparations and reduction of armed forces. The treaties with Austria and Hungary dissolved the Habsburg Empire and created independent Czechoslovakia, Poland, and Yugoslavia from its former domains. Austria was also forbidden to enter into union with Germany. Bulgaria surrendered territory to Romania, Greece, and Yugoslavia, losing its outlet to the Mediterranean.

A first treaty with Turkey in April 1920 stripped it of lands occupied mostly by Arabs and partitioned the Turkish heartland of Anatolia. The harsh terms produced a vehement Turkish reaction, and nationalists found a leader in a World War I hero, Mustafa Kemal (1881–1938), later Atatürk ("chief Turk"), who organized resistance and drove Allied forces from the Anatolian Peninsula. In 1923 the Allies reluctantly negotiated a new treaty, by which Turkey kept all of the Anatolian Peninsula, Istanbul, and the European territory around the city. Turkey under Atatürk also successfully resisted Armenian demands for an independent state carved out of Anatolia.

The Arab territories in the Ottoman Empire were divided as mandates between France and Great Britain, with France receiving Syria, including present-day Lebanon, and Great Britain securing Palestine, Transjordan, and Iraq (these divisions and nationalist reactions to them will be detailed in Chapter 14). Territories in the Arabian Peninsula, including the Muslim holy cities of Mecca and Medina, achieved independence and later formed the Kingdom of Saudi Arabia under Abd al-Aziz ibn Saud.

Evaluation of the Peace Treaties

Few peace treaties in modern times have provoked sharper criticism or controversy than those hammered out in Paris in 1919 and 1920. The treaties were denounced by the defeated nations, as was to be expected. But in the victor nations as well, many critics

Atatürk Addresses the Turkish Assembly

Let us return to a closer examination of the facts....

Morally and materially, the enemy Powers were openly attacking the Ottoman empire and the country itself. They were determined to disintegrate and annihilate both....

Now, Gentlemen, I will ask you what decision I ought to have arrived at in such circumstances....

1. *To demand protection from England.*
2. *To accept the United States of America as a mandatory Power....*
3. *The third proposal was to deliver the country by allowing each district to act in its own way and according to its own capability....*

The results of the Lausanne Conference, which lasted for eight months in two sessions, are known to the world at large....

The debates were heated and animated. No positive results regarding the recognition of Turkish rights were noticeable....

The Ottoman Empire, whose heirs we were, had no value, no merit, no authority in the eyes of the world. It was regarded ... as it were, under the tutelage and protection of somebody else.

We were not guilty of the neglect and errors of the past.... It was, however, our duty to bear responsibility for them before the world. In order to procure true independence ... for the nation we had still to submit to these difficulties and sacrifices.... Our greatest strength and our surest point of support was the fact that we had realized our national sovereignty, had actually placed it in the hands of the nation and had proved by facts that we were capable of maintaining it.*

In this speech to the Turkish assembly in October 1924, Atatürk explained how Turkey managed to avoid partition and retain its independence. Once in power, Atatürk embarked on a series of reforms that swept away old Ottoman institutions, including the sultanate and the Islamic institution of the caliphate.

* William H. McNeill and Marilyn R. Waldman, eds., The Islamic World *(New York: Oxford University Press, 1973; reprint, Chicago: University of Chicago Press, 1983), pp. 432–438.*

charged that the Paris settlements were unduly harsh and violated many of the Fourteen Points. John Maynard Keynes, whose book *The Economic Consequences of the Peace* (1919) shaped public opinion in the United States and Great Britain, asserted that the Versailles Treaty was ruinous, immoral, and unworkable. He likened it to a "Carthaginian peace" (like those ancient Rome dictated to defeated Carthage), arguing that the proposed reparations would cripple Germany's economy and bring economic ruin to Europe.

More recently, some scholars have taken exception, noting that Germany, unlike ancient Carthage, had not been destroyed, but remained politically united, with its industrial strength relatively intact. They claim that Adolf Hitler's rise to power was due less to the Versailles Treaty than to Allied unwillingness to enforce it and point out that had Germany won the war, it would almost certainly have imposed much harsher terms on the Allies. No one can be sure whether a conciliatory peace would have prevented World War II.

A more relevant question is whether a conciliatory peace was possible. Wilson's idealistic vision was ill-suited to the realities of 1919. Moreover, none of the Big Four was a free agent. They were all bound to interpret and execute the will of their public and legislatures back home. Trapped in their own rhetoric and propaganda, they could not disavow the hopes and expectations they had raised at home without creating an electoral backlash that would drive them out of office. The upshot was an unsatisfying compromise between Wilson's high moral principles and Clemenceau's nationalistic aims. It was neither harsh enough to cripple Germany forever, as the French had wished, nor generous enough to conciliate the vanquished in the postwar era.

In short, it is perhaps unfair to judge the peacemakers of 1919 too harshly for the treaty's shortcomings, given the complex and multiple issues that had to be faced and the time limitations and other difficulties under which they worked. It is unlikely that any peace treaty, however carefully drawn, could have preserved the peace. Colonel Edward House, Wilson's chief adviser, summed it up neatly in his diary entry on the day he left Paris: "Looking at the conference in retrospect there is much to approve and much to regret. It is easy to say what should have been done, but more difficult to have found a way of doing it. . . . While I should have preferred a different peace, I doubt whether it could have been made, for the ingredients of such a peace . . . were lacking at Paris."

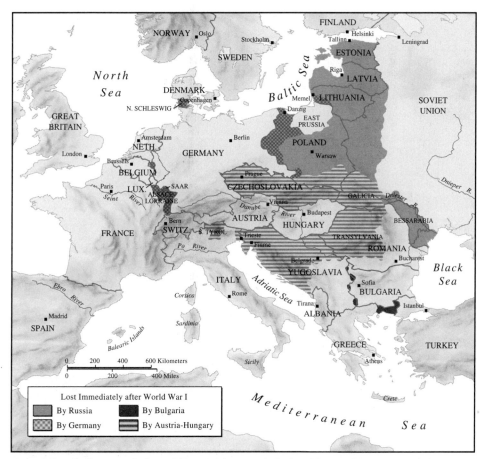

Map 13.9 Europe after 1919. The post–World War I settlements radically altered the map of Europe. Germany had to return Alsace-Lorraine to France, while Bulgaria lost its coastline to Greece. Italy acquired South Tyrol, Trieste, and Istria. The greatest changes occurred in eastern Europe, where seven new, fully sovereign states were created. The Habsburg Empire was broken up, and the independence of Czechoslovakia, Poland, and Yugoslavia was recognized. On the Baltic the subject nationalities of the Russian Empire—namely, the Finns, Estonians, Latvians, and Lithuanians—also gained their independence.

The League of Nations

All the treaties contained the covenant (charter) of the League of Nations, Wilson's top priority for postwar rehabilitation. Wilson sacrificed a number of his cherished principles to gain its acceptance, but he was confident that once the League began to operate, it would correct the mistakes and make good the deficiencies in the peace treaties. However, there was no agreement on precisely how the League would do its work.

The League of Nations was established in 1920, with headquarters in Geneva, Switzerland. It consisted of two deliberative bodies, the assembly and the council. All member nations were represented in the assembly, where each had a vote. The council was made up of the four great powers (Great Britain, France, Japan, and Italy) as permanent members, together with four other nations chosen periodically by the assembly. The third organ, the World Court, with international jurists elected by the assembly, adjudicated international quarrels.

The primary function of the League was to provide the machinery for a peaceful resolution of international disputes. Members had to respect the territorial integrity of other members and seek arbitration should regular diplomatic methods fail to resolve a dispute. If an aggrieved nation deemed the arbitration result unsatisfactory, it could not resort to war until at least three months after the decision had been rendered. Failure to abide by these terms could result in the League imposing economic sanctions against the offender or, if that proved inadequate, taking military action with troops provided by member states.

League membership came from every part of the globe, reaching its peak of fifty in 1924. Tragically, the United States did not join the League. Wilson was unable to allay

The League of Nations. The League of Nations was weakened by the refusal of the United States to join and by a lack of commitment on the part of its members. League members struggled but failed to keep the general peace.

isolationist fears in the U.S. Senate that membership in the League might lead to involvement in foreign quarrels. Russia, under Bolshevik rule, was kept out until 1934. Nor were the defeated powers immediately permitted to join. Japan, Germany, and Italy later resigned to pursue their respective courses of aggression. Only Great Britain and France remained members throughout the League's existence.

The League was judged to have been a failure because it was unable to prevent aggression and preserve the peace. One cause of the failure can be traced to the peacemakers themselves, who deprived the League of the mantle of impartiality by associating it with the treaties ending World War I. A second factor was the absence of some of the great powers, in particular, the United States, in the international organization. Third, even among the members, there was a reluctance to agree to arrangements that would limit their sovereignty. Last, decisions in the council on crucial issues required unanimity, which was almost impossible to obtain among states motivated more by self-interest than moral considerations.

The League did, however, successfully promote international cooperation in economic and technical areas. It was most effective in social projects such as aiding and settling refugees, providing drugs and vaccines, and generally improving health care in less advanced countries. The World Court successfully mediated a number of disputes between small, weak nations. As a rule, however, large, powerful nations opted to settle disputes on their own terms rather than rely upon decisions by a panel over which they had little control.

Germany under the Weimar Republic

The kaiser's government collapsed just before the armistice and was replaced by a provisional government committed to the establishment of a republic. The men in charge of Germany's affairs held elections for a National Assembly, which met in the town of Weimar and drafted a constitution for what would become known as the Weimar Republic. The democratic constitution, approved in July 1919, provided for a president and a two-house legislature.

The Weimar Republic led a precarious existence from the very beginning. Although the government conformed to democratic principles, conservatives dominated the new republic through control of the army, judiciary, bureaucracy, and educational systems. Antidemocratic elements were strengthened when the government signed the unpopular Versailles Treaty.

Weimar Germany suffered from a troubled economy and the $33 billion reparations bill assessed by the Allied Reparations Commission. The German government, unable to make the scheduled payments, tried to meet its obligations by printing more and more currency. The result was disastrous inflation. The mark fell from 4.2 to the U.S. dollar in 1914 to 62 to the dollar in May 1921 and 270 to the dollar by the end of November. When Germany defaulted on its payments in 1923, France (the chief recipient of reparations) and Belgium retaliated by occupying the entire Ruhr region, the main center of German industry. But the move caused a patriotic reaction in the Ruhr, where the workers engaged in passive resistance, refusing to enter the mines and factories. The 5 million inhabitants of the Ruhr had to be fed and supported; to do this, the German government printed more money, triggering more inflation. By September 1923 the mark had fallen to 100 million to the dollar, by October to more than 1 trillion, and by November to 4.2 trillion. Wages and prices had to be revised daily, even hourly. Like most inflations, it had only a slight effect on the rich, who owned apartment buildings and factories, which retained their value regardless of currency convulsions. It hit the lower middle class hardest, quickly wiping out savings and pensions. These bitter and impoverished Germans later became Hitler's most fanatical followers.

The turning point came in August 1923, when Gustav Stresemann became chancellor of a coalition of moderate parties. He ended the policy of passive resistance in the Ruhr, pledged resumption of reparation payments, and took drastic steps to halt inflation and stabilize the currency. Stresemann worked to restore Germany to equality with the other great powers and to bring about a treaty revision. Two committees of experts were formed to draft a plan to reduce the annual German payment and provide loans to speed up German economic recovery. In 1924 France evacuated the Ruhr.

Stresemann's successful policies restored stability and prosperity to Germany. During the second half of the 1920s, Germany benefited enormously from a massive infusion of foreign investment and loans, mainly from the United States, where the postwar boom had created surplus capital. German industry modernized its equipment and, by adopting methods of mass production and scientific management on the U.S. model, regained the lead in Europe that it had held before the war. The Weimar Republic appeared politically healthy and economically prosperous.

The Quest for International Security

In 1919 most Allied nations felt optimistic about lasting world peace. The task of peacekeeping became a secondary concern as most nations focused on rebuilding their society and economy. The United States rejected the treaty and reverted to isolationism. Great Britain, burdened with economic and imperial problems, wanted to limit its involvement in European affairs and wavered between a stern attitude and leniency toward Germany. Russia under communist rule was an outcast. Thus the responsibility for enforcing the peace and maintaining stability rested primarily with France.

The central concern of the French government was the containment of Germany. France felt deserted by its wartime allies and did not look to the League of Nations as an instrument to preserve peace. Instead it relied on diplomatic and military policies to secure its own protection. It concluded alliances with Poland, Czechoslovakia, Romania, and Yugoslavia in the 1920s, but few French deluded themselves into thinking that they could replace the pre–World War I alliance with Russia as a counterbalance to Germany.

In 1925 Stresemann, now Germany's foreign minister, sought to allay French fears by offering to respect the western frontiers established at Versailles. The outcome of his proposal was the Locarno Pact, signed in December of that year. With Great Britain and Italy as guarantors, France, Germany, and Belgium agreed to respect one another's existing frontiers. Interestingly enough, Germany did not provide the same assurances to Czechoslovakia and Poland on its eastern borders. Still, the Locarno Pact engendered a mood of goodwill and conciliation dubbed the Spirit of Locarno. Germany was now admitted to the League of Nations, ending its period of isolation. At the Washington Naval Disarmament Conference in 1921–1922, the powers established a ten-year naval holiday, during which no new capital warships would be built. Furthermore, they set up a system to limit the size of navies: the British and U.S. navies would be equal, the Japanese navy would be three-fifths that size, and the Italian and French navies one-third the size of the first two.

In 1928 the French foreign minister, Aristide Briand, and U.S. Secretary of State Frank Kellogg prepared a document in which the signatories, which ultimately totaled sixty-two nations, formally renounced war as an instrument of national policy. In reality, the agreement merely fostered the illusion of peace, for no machinery was set up to enforce the ban on war. But on the positive side, the agreement further contributed to the relaxation of European tensions. There followed several additional diplomatic pacts, one of which provided for the evacuation of Allied troops from the Rhineland (completed in 1930, four years ahead of schedule).

Although the second half of the 1920s was an interlude of stability and good feeling, it had produced no real reconciliation. The basic cause of friction remained. Germany wanted to revise features of the Versailles Treaty it found objectionable. The French for their part were haunted by fears of facing a revenge-minded Germany alone and were adamant about collecting their share of reparations to cover the cost of rebuilding their war-ravaged country. Thus the spirit of international cooperation never struck deep roots. It ended abruptly with the advent of the depression.

The Victorious Democracies in the 1920s

The return of peace presented the victorious democracies with social and economic problems of unprecedented magnitude and complexity. These myriad problems could not be solved through conventional methods; they called for vigorous and creative leadership, which was conspicuously lacking. As a result, critics charged that liberal democracy was too slow, obstructive, and inefficient to resolve the urgent postwar problems and espoused totalitarian dictatorships.

Generally speaking, governments on both sides of the Atlantic showed little concern for social reform in the 1920s. The United States resumed "business as usual," viewing the war as an unpleasant interruption. The Republican majority in the Senate enacted Prohibition (against alcohol consumption) and sought to lessen the power of organized labor. In Europe, the focus on achieving economic stability, coupled with resistance by entrenched interest groups, checked any impetus toward social reform. The annihilation of a whole generation of young men in the war had allowed the older generation, fearful of everything from Bolshevism to Americanization, to maintain its hold on business, government administration, education, and the army. In France only the threat of massive strikes prompted the government to enact the eight-hour workday. The sole notable legislative victory in Great Britain was the broadening of the franchise to include women.

Besides destroying a great deal of the housing, industrial plants, and transportation and communication facilities in northeastern France, Belgium, and northern Italy, the war caused a major loss of foreign markets. Conversely, business interests in the United States expanded into overseas markets formerly monopolized by European manufacturers.

Great Britain, heavily dependent on foreign trade, suffered grievously and never fully recovered.

The decade following the peace treaties may be divided into two parts. The first period, from 1919 to 1924, was a time of psychic exhaustion and economic hardship mingled with cynicism and a general lack of direction. In multiparty states like France and Italy, the fragility of party coalitions led to notoriously short-lived governments unable to implement long-term economic and political programs. Still, both Great Britain and France, unlike Italy, survived their crises without sacrificing their democratic institutions.

Between 1925 and 1928, western Europe experienced a sort of Indian summer, marked by economic recovery and political stability. Europe's share of total world production returned to prewar levels, monetary systems stabilized, and living standards improved. The United States doubled its industrial production over the decade, and the value of stocks and bonds skyrocketed on the Wall Street stock exchange.

Beneath the surface prosperity of the era, however, important segments of Western society were still mired in poverty. Miners in the United States and elsewhere were badly hurt by the postwar decline in demand for their products. International competition caused agricultural prices to fall, forcing farmers into debt. In France inflation and weak government finance hampered the reconstruction of the devastated regions. In Great Britain massive unemployment remained endemic.

The social customs of the Roaring Twenties, as the press sometimes called the decade, were markedly more liberal than before. Young women in particular broke with traditional social mores and gender stereotypes. Short skirts and bobbed hair were symbols of the greater freedom of women, even in Japan and China, to hold jobs, live independently, and assert their general social and moral emancipation. The automobile liberated "flaming youth" of both sexes to seek entertainment away from home, and drinking, smoking, and recreational sex became chic.

Each nation had its peculiar problems. The United States experienced a "Red Scare," when Marxists and other radicals were harassed, arrested, and, if aliens, deported. A prewar trend toward racism and hostility to recent immigrants resulted in new, tighter immigration laws to limit the numbers of entries into the country. There was also a new wave of anti-Semitism and a resurgence of bigotry against African Americans typified by the revival of the Ku Klux Klan.

Great Britain struggled with the perennial Irish demands for independence. After an unsuccessful Easter Rebellion in 1916, the Sinn Fein (Gaelic for "we ourselves"), or Irish Nationalist party, employed guerrilla tactics and terrorism in an effort to achieve complete independence from Great Britain. Finally, in 1921 the British government signed a treaty with moderate Irish republicans. It divided Ireland into a northern part, Ulster, which was predominantly Protestant and remained united with Great Britain, and a self-governing dominion called the Irish Free State, comprising the remainder of Ireland. In 1937 the Irish Free State gained complete independence and changed its name to Eire. The division of Ireland created a problem that persists to the present.

French policy was dominated by the quest for security against Germany. Accordingly, France maintained a large standing army and formed military alliances. It also built a massive row of fortifications, called the Maginot Line, across its eastern frontier as an impregnable barrier against German invaders.

All in all, the latter part of the 1920s encouraged many people to face the future with optimism. The physical damage to property had been largely repaired, immediate postwar problems had been solved, unemployment had been reduced, and increased harmony characterized international relations. The prosperity evident in most European countries, however, rested on a shaky base, dependent as it was on the continued voluntary flow of funds from the United States to Germany.

The Great Depression

The roots of the global depression of the 1930s lay in the fundamental financial weaknesses of the postwar world. Because the economies of most African, Asian, and Latin American nations were tied to those of the industrialized Western nations, they, too, felt the impact of the economic crisis. The Great Depression, which began in the United States in 1929, soon spread around the world, creating a crisis for all and an opportune climate for the rise of totalitarian dictators in the 1930s.

The United States emerged from the war as the richest nation in the world, having converted itself from a net debtor to a net creditor. With its mass markets and rapid technological advances, profits and production reached new heights over the next decade. During the economic boom, many individuals speculated in the soaring stock market, often on credit and amassing debts far beyond their ability to pay. In 1929 there was an economic slowdown. An exceptionally good harvest in Europe cut demand for American agricultural products, decreasing the purchasing power of U.S. farmers. Simultaneously there was a reduction in exports of American raw materials and fuels. Overproduction led to depressed prices and unemployment. As a reflection of the slumping economy, the stock market was hit by a wave of panic selling on October 24, 1929. As the value of stocks tumbled, many investors panicked and rushed to sell, thereby causing further drops in prices. Those who could not repay their debts lost everything;

Devastating Dust Bowl Destroys Crops and Family Farms

In the middle of the night the wind passed on and left the land quiet. The dust-filled air muffled sound more completely than fog does. . . . All day the dust sifted down from the sky, and the next day it sifted down. An even blanket covered the earth. It settled on the corn, piled up on the tops of the fence posts, piled up on the wires; it settled on roofs, blanketed the weeds and trees.

The people came out of their houses and smelled the hot stinging air and covered their noses from it. And the children came out of the houses, but they did not run or shout as they would have done after a rain. Men *stood by their fences and looked at the ruined corn, drying fast now, only a little green showing through the film of dust. The men were silent and they did not move often. And the women came out of the houses to stand beside their men—to feel whether this time the men would break.**

John Steinbeck in his moving novel *The Grapes of Wrath* vividly describes the dust bowls of Oklahoma that destroyed crops and forced farmers to travel west to California in search of better lives.

*John Steinbeck, The Grapes of Wrath (1939; reprint, Baltimore: Penguin, 1979), pp. 3–4.

A Homeless Family during the Depression. The abject poverty and misery of the underprivileged are vividly captured in this portrait taken during the depression. Note that the woman and her children are living in a tent.

Library of Congress

demand for goods dropped, and overstocked factories closed, throwing many workers out of jobs. Because the unemployed could not afford to purchase goods, a vicious cycle of further surpluses and factory closings was set in motion. Consequently, the economies of even unindustrialized countries like China, which were largely dependent on supplying raw materials and agricultural goods to the industrialized world, were severely undermined.

By 1931 the full effects of the depression in the United States were evident in Europe. The most immediate result was the withdrawal of American capital, which caused banks and businesses to fail. Throughout the world, trade declined and unemployment rose. A few figures give an indication of the impact caused by the economic collapse. By 1932, production in France was down 28 percent from predepression levels, in the United States 30 percent, and in Germany 50 percent. A quarter of all U.S. workers were unemployed, and the percentage was even higher in Germany. In the United States the shantytowns filled with jobless people were called "Hoovervilles," after President Herbert Hoover.

The Great Depression, or world slump, shook the governments of the Western world and Japan. While the United States and Great Britain responded to the economic crisis within the framework of their democratic institutions, other nations, such as Germany, turned to totalitarian solutions. The United States took effective countermeasures to combat the depression after President Franklin Roosevelt (1882–1945) assumed office in 1933. A New York aristocrat with a keen sense of humor, Roosevelt, although crippled by polio, had enthusiasm and determination. With the help of his politically concerned and active wife, Eleanor, and a team of reforming advisers dubbed the "brain trust," he immediately launched his New Deal.

The New Deal was a comprehensive program of national planning, economic experimentation, and innovative reforms that went far toward pulling the nation out of the depression. New laws and government bureaus provided relief payments for the hungry, low-cost mortgages, business loans, public works jobs for some of the unemployed—especially the young—and assistance for hard-hit farmers. Additional legislation monitored business and finance to prevent a repetition of the stock market collapse. Wages, hours, and conditions of labor were also regulated by new laws similar to those already enacted in many European nations. Most important, the New Deal began to build a welfare state in the United States by instituting the Social Security system.

Unlike the United States, Great Britain, France, and other Western democracies did not respond vigorously to the depression. The Conservative government in Great Britain tried to get by with the "dole," relief payments for unemployed workers, and subsidies to farmers. In France, the socialist premier Léon Blum tried to end the economic crisis by introducing reforms reminiscent of the New Deal, but his coalition government did not survive long enough to make a difference.

Latin America felt the crisis very severely because its economies were heavily dependent on exports. Likewise, global demand for Japanese exports dropped 50 percent from 1929 to 1931. Farmers were particularly affected by falling prices, and unemployment reached an all-time high. The Japanese people blamed the politicians and the rich bankers and industrialists for the economic crisis, and many argued that only an authoritarian regime headed by the military could solve the problems. As a result, Japanese democracy, which was not deeply rooted, collapsed. Although Japan was among the first industrialized nations to recover from the depression, conservative military and authoritarian forces gained widespread popularity and support as a direct consequence of the crisis. In foreign policy, these groups advocated conquest and expansion to solve Japan's economic and population problems.

The Great Depression was the primary cause or catalyst of the radical swings from liberal and leftist governments to rightist, totalitarian, or authoritarian regimes in much of Europe, Japan, and Latin America. These totalitarian regimes adopted radical measures to remedy the problems caused by the economic disaster; in Hitler's Germany and elsewhere, the totalitarian rulers seemed more successful than the democratic ones in achieving economic recovery. Furthermore, the Great Depression reinforced demands by nationalists in West and East Asia and Africa for both economic and political independence. The Soviet Union pointed to the depression as seeming proof of the inherent weaknesses of the capitalist system. Anti-imperialist struggles, revolutionary Marxism in the Soviet Union, and the emergence of totalitarian regimes during the interwar years will be described in the next chapter.

Summary and Comparisons

From 1800 till 1914, European nations, the United States, and Japan dominated Africa, Asia, and Latin America. Demands for raw materials and markets and a variety of strategic, cultural, and nationalistic motives propelled the powerful nations of the world to dominate weaker states and peoples. Twentieth-century imperialism differed from previous conquests in that most imperial powers did not incorporate their new territories into their own states or settle them with colonists; rather, they were more interested in the natural resources, markets, and national glory that empire provided.

European imperialists overran Africa in one generation. Although Africans resisted conquest and often revolted against European domination, European military superiority was too great. Through international conferences and diplomacy, the European nations avoided conflict with one another as they partitioned the continent.

Similarly, the weakened Ottoman Empire, in spite of internal reforms, lost territory to Russia and western European nations. The Persian Empire under the Qajars was threatened by Russian and British expansion. In Asia, Great Britain was chiefly concerned with controlling India. Meanwhile, European powers defeated the Chinese Empire, dividing it into spheres of influence where the victors monopolized raw materials and markets and generally exercised control over Chinese internal affairs.

By adopting Western technology and modern military techniques, Japan also became an imperialist power. Japan expanded in East Asia by defeating Russia and China. The United States, already a major economic power, also became imperialistic. Beginning in 1898, it took military and economic control of the Caribbean and extended its economic domination over South America and Canada, while annexing the Philippines. Thus, by the first decade of the twentieth century, most of Africa, Asia, and Latin America had come under either direct or indirect imperial domination.

During the years before 1914, nationalism, the arms race, and the system of alliances all contributed to rising international tensions. None of the participating powers wanted a general war, but it is equally true that none did all they could to prevent the conflict. The assassination of the Archduke Ferdinand by a Serb nationalist provided the spark for the war. Taking for granted the complicity of the Serbian government, Austria declared war against its neighbor. When that happened, the system of alliances and the exigencies of military planning and mobilization schedules instantly dragged the major European powers, save one, into the conflict.

In August 1914 the belligerents went into battle confident that the war would be over in a few months. The French attack broke down completely, while the Germans almost reached Paris before they were halted. A stalemate ensued, and both sides dug in for a long period of trench warfare. In the east the Germans handed the Russians one defeat after another and eventually knocked them out of the war. Unrestricted submarine warfare by Germans against any ships carrying goods to the Allies helped to bring the United States into the conflict. The involvement of the United States counteracted the loss of Russia and helped boost Anglo-French morale. In the spring of 1918 the Germans made a desperate effort to win the war before the Americans could arrive in France in force. When Germany's drive failed, its leaders agreed to an armistice that went into effect on November 11, 1918.

CHRONOLOGY

1775	
	Britain settles Australia
	King Shaka's Zulu kingdom
	Greek war of independence
	Muhammad Ali in Egypt
	Britain settles New Zealand
	Ottoman Empire declining
	Britain defeats China in Opium War
	Abdel Kader in Algeria
	Decline of the Manchu dynasty
1850	
	United States opens Japan
	Christian missions in Africa
	Direct British rule in India
	Opening of the Suez Canal
	Meiji Restoration; modernization of Japan
	European partition of Africa
	African resistance to imperialism
	Beginning of shifting European alliance systems
	Stories of Rudyard Kipling
	Spanish-American War; United States annexes Philippines
	United States proposes "Open Door" policy in China
	The Boer War
	The Boxer Rebellion in China
1900	
	The Russo-Japanese War
	Arms stockpiling and war plans by European nations
	United States domination in Latin America; the Panama Canal
	World War I
	Paris Peace Conference
1920	
	Formation of the League of Nations
	The Weimar Republic in Germany
	The Great Depression
1930	

At the peace conference, which met in Paris in the first half of 1919, separate treaties were arranged with each of the defeated nations. Only the winners participated in the discussions at Paris, unlike the earlier Congress of Vienna, where the losing French had been allowed to attend. Moreover, at Vienna the issues had been resolved by Europeans alone, whereas at Paris nations from around the world, including the United States and Japan, participated. In 1815 the winners had been very lenient toward the French, but at Paris the Allies came down hard on Germany and its associates, stripping them of much wealth and territory.

Whether the Central Powers were treated unjustly has long been a matter of debate. The purpose of both the Paris and Vienna meetings was to redraw the boundaries of Europe and ensure a lasting peace. In both cases there was no common blueprint and the settlements were decided by the leaders of the great powers. The Congress of Vienna produced an agreement that provided nearly a century of general peace in Europe. In contrast, the Paris accords, far from preserving peace, fostered resentment, particularly in Germany and Italy, and contributed to both the economic depression of the 1930s and World War II.

The return of peace confronted the Western democracies with numerous complex problems, but none as daunting as the Great Depression, which was triggered by the Wall Street crash in October 1929. The West tried various experiments to cope with the depression. The United States abandoned economic liberalism when it embraced the New Deal, opening the way for government participation in the economy. Great Britain declined to put the economy further under state control and essentially left the task of recovery to industry itself.

The French government made many significant reforms, but political instability inhibited economic recovery. The major nations in the West recovered from the depression at varying rates and degrees, but full recovery was not achieved until World War II.

Selected Sources

Items indicated with an asterisk (*) are available in paperback.

*Achebe, Chinua. *Things Fall Apart*. 1978. A fascinating novel about the clash between African and Western cultures; by a noted Nigerian author.

Beasley, W. G., ed. *The Rise of Modern Japan: Political, Economic and Social Change since 1850*. 2d ed. 1995. A clear and comprehensive look at Japan's modern transformation.

Brading, D. A. *The First America: The Spanish Monarchy, Creole Patriots, and the Liberal State, 1492–1866*. 1990. Stresses the development of an American identity in such Creoles as Bolívar and San Martín. Provides good background for the postindependence period.

Brittain, Vera. *Testament of Youth: An Autobiographical Study of the Years 1900–1925*. 1933; reprinted 1980. A moving account of what the war meant to an entire generation. See also *Testament of Experience* on World War II.

Carrington, Charles. *Soldier from the Wars Returning*. 1965. Carrington, who was a company officer in World War I, a military historian in the years between the wars, and a general staff officer in World War II, brings multiple perspectives to his study of the war years.

*Collins, Robert O., ed. *Historical Problems of Imperial Africa*. Rev. ed., 1992. An overview of key issues, including education, nationalism, and colonial rule and its impact on African societies.

Dedijier, Vladimir. *The Road to Sarajevo*. 1966. The author had access to Serbian sources and defends the conspirators.

Elegant, Robert. *Mandarin*. 1983. A novel depicting the interplay of traditional and Western culture in late nineteenth-century China.

Eyck, Erich. *A History of the Weimar Republic*. 2 vols. 1962. The best overall study of Weimar.

*Fairbank, John K. *The United States and China*. 4th, enlarged ed. 1983. A good analysis of Chinese history and U.S. involvement in China.

*Fischer, Fritz. *Germany's Aims in the First World War.* 1967. A controversial account, stressing German responsibility in bringing on the war.

*Forbath, Peter. *The River Congo.* 1977. A dramatic account of Western exploration and exploitation of central Africa; with maps and illustrations.

*Forster, E. M. *Passage to India.* 1924. A novel about English men and women in India and their interaction with Indians. Also a film.

Fussell, Paul. *The Great War and Modern Memory.* 1975. A study of the literary tradition of the war and of what the war meant to contemporaries.

*Galbraith, J. K. *The Great Crash.* 1929; reprinted 1979. An account of the Wall Street stock market panic by a well-known economist.

The Grapes of Wrath. John Ford, director. 1940. A dramatic rendition of Steinbeck's famous novel on the Dust Bowl and its human victims.

The Great Depression. Public Broadcasting System. A six-part series with extensive documentary footage and moving narrative.

*Joll, James. *The Origins of the First World War.* 2d ed. 1992. A well-written and capable analysis of the evidence and divergent interpretations of a controversial question.

Keegan, John. *The First World War.* 1999. A lively recent account.

Kerr, Ian J. *Building the Railways of the Raj, 1850–1900.* 1995. An account of the largest transfer of technology in the nineteenth century.

*Kindleberger, Charles P. *The World in Depression, 1929–1939.* 1975. A good survey of the global economic crisis.

Lauderdale Graham, Sandra. *House and Street: The Domestic World of Servants and Masters in Nineteenth-Century Rio de Janeiro.* 1990. A well-written social history.

*Lyons, Alan. *The Versailles Settlement: Peacemaking in Paris, 1919.* 1991. An accurate and insightful study.

Lyons, Michael J. *World War I.* Rev. ed. 2000. A fine overview with an annotated bibliography.

Macfarlane, David. *Come from Away: Memory, War, and the Search for a Family's Past.* 1991. A poignant and well-written account of one family's war.

*Marks, Sally. *The Illusion of Peace: International Relations in Europe, 1918–1933.* 1976. A sound summary of the diplomatic history of the 1920s.

*Miller, Susan Gilson, ed. and trans. *Disorienting Encounters: Travels of a Moroccan Scholar in France in 1845–1846: The Voyage of Muhammad As-Saffar.* 1992. This firsthand account of a visit to France by a Moroccan official provides a rare, unromanticized, and unprejudiced glimpse into Arab/Muslim reactions to the West.

Morgan, C. Wayne. *America's Road to Empire.* 1968. A description of the motives of U.S. imperialism.

*Remarque, Erich Maria. *All Quiet on the Western Front.* 1929. The preeminent novel of the war, distinctly antiwar in tone.

*Taylor, Stephen. *Shaka's Children: A History of the Zulu People.* 1994. A readable narrative about Shaka Zulu and his historical impact on South Africa.

*Tuchman, Barbara. *The Proud Tower.* 1966. In a series of essays, Tuchman evokes the period before the war.

Waley, Arthur. *The Opium War through Chinese Eyes.* 1958. A sympathetic account of China's attempt to deal with opium.

Wohl, Robert. *The Generation of 1914.* 1979. What the war did to the youth of the European nations.

 Additional resources, exercises, and Internet links related to this chapter are available at the Book Companion Web site: http://history.wadsworth.com/upshurcompact4/

COMPARATIVE ESSAY 11
Anti-imperialism

There are some who say we have no right in Africa at all, that "it belongs to the natives." I hold that our right is the necessity that is upon us to provide for our ever-growing population—either by opening new fields for emigration, or by providing work and employment which the development of over-sea extension entails. . . . While thus serving our interests as a nation, we may, by selecting men of the right stamp for the control of new territories, bring at the same time many advantages to Africa.

Captain F. D. Lugard, *The Rise of Our East African Empire*, vol. 1 (London: Blackwood, 1893), pp. 379–382, 473, reprinted in Dennis Sherman, *Western Civilization: Sources, Images, and Interpretations*, vol. 2: Since 1660 (New York: McGraw-Hill, 1995), p. 184.

Europe undertook the leadership of the world with ardor, cynicism, and violence. Look at how the shadow of her palaces stretches out ever further! . . . If we want to turn Africa into a new Europe, and America into a new Europe, then let us leave the destiny of our countries to Europeans. . . . But if we want humanity to advance a step further . . . we must invent and we must make discoveries. . . . For Europe, for ourselves, and for humanity . . . we must turn over a new leaf, we must work out new concepts, and try to set afoot a new man.

Frantz Fanon, *The Wretched of the Earth,* trans. Constance Farrington (New York: Grove Press, 1963), pp. 311, 315–316.

In the first passage, Lord Lugard, a British soldier and colonial administrator, justifies Great Britain's quest for empire. Lugard and many others argued that empires were economic necessities for industrialized powers, but that, properly governed, they could also bring benefits to poor, less "developed" peoples. In contrast, Frantz Fanon, a French-educated psychiatrist from the island of Martinique, speaks for the oppressed who struggled to free themselves from imperial domination in the twentieth century. Fanon became an active member of the Algerian Liberation Front (FLN), which fought a long and bloody war to achieve independence from France. Fanon's writings epitomize the often idealistic dreams for the creation of new societies in a postimperial world that many youth in the so-called Third World championed during the era from 1950 through the 1970s.

In the nineteenth century in Asia and Africa, the prospects for successful resistance to Western domination were not promising. The Indians waged an unsuccessful uprising against British rule; similarly, the Boxers in China attempted and failed to expel foreign intruders in 1900. In Africa European forces defeated the followers of the Mahdi in the Sudan and the Zulu in South Africa. Only Ethiopia was able to retain its independence in Africa. Although most of China, Persia, and the Ottoman Empire were not ruled directly by the Western imperial nations, they were indirectly but very effectively dominated by them. During the nineteenth and early twentieth centuries, Japan was the only non-Western nation to transform its economy from an agricultural to an industrial one. After 1895 Japan also emerged as a major imperialist power with a growing empire in Asia.

In the twentieth century, subject peoples adopted new methods to oppose imperial powers and, as a result, overthrew empires to establish many new nations. Paradoxically, the seeds for future independence movements were germinating just as the forces of imperial oppression seemed at their zenith.

In Asia, Africa, and Latin America, societies were subjected to humiliation, economic exploitation, and social and cultural dislocations. However, Western domination also brought some benefits, including improved health care, new education and legal institutions, and modern transportation and communication systems. In the process, societies under imperial control were introduced to such Western concepts as nationalism, individualism, and various forms of parliamentary systems. The elites in many Asian, African, and Latin American societies eventually adopted and adapted these concepts in their struggles against imperialism.

Children of elite families around the world went to school in Europe and North America, where they learned about Western politics, education, and military affairs. They also learned the value of mass political action and propaganda methods. They then adopted these techniques to good effect in their homelands to mobilize the masses and exert political and economic pressure on the colonial governments. At the same time, those with modern education filled the lower-echelon civil and military posts in colonial administrations, thereby gaining the experience needed to run their governments after they achieved independence.

In 1885 Western-educated Indians formed the Indian National Congress to pressure the British government to grant increased self-government, which would lead to independence. Under the leadership of Mohandas K. Gandhi, the Congress developed techniques of strikes, economic boycotts, and nonviolent civil disobedience. Egyptian nationalists used similar methods to oppose the British. Gandhi's tactics of noncooperation and mass campaigning contributed to winning Indian independence. His ideals were later adopted by the leaders of the civil rights movement in the United States and initially by the African National Congress in South Africa. World Wars I and II also weakened the economic, political, and military might of most European nations.

People in many other nations, such as Vietnam, Algeria, Kenya, and several in southern Africa, had to resort to armed struggles to achieve independence. In these nations, nationalist leaders used guerrilla warfare tactics and protracted armed rebellions to oust the imperial powers. By the 1970s most nations in Asia and Africa had achieved independence, and by the 1990s even South Africa had achieved full political rights for all of its citizens.

In Latin America many nations continued to struggle against the indirect economic and political domination of the United States. When Latin American nations threatened to move too far outside the orbit of the United States, Washington invoked Theodore Roosevelt's adage, "Speak softly but carry a big stick," intervening militarily or in covert actions in nations as diverse as Chile, Panama, and Grenada.

The Soviet Russian Empire was the last to collapse, but during the 1990s the former Soviet republics finally broke away from Russian domination. The collapse of the Soviet Union was generally bloodless and resulted in a number of newly independent nations in eastern Europe and western Asia. As a result, as the century drew to a close, the traditional imperial systems had been dismantled, and nationalism seemed to have triumphed everywhere.

14

Twentieth-Century Political and Cultural Ferment

•

Late in the evening of the ninth day in his new home, Ford brought a primitive, toylike engine into the kitchen. Its cylinder consisted of a one-inch diameter gas pipe fitted with a piston and connected to a flywheel made from an old lathe. It was Christmas Eve, and as [his wife] Clara bustled about preparing dinner for a host of relatives expected the next day, Henry clamped the engine to the sink. Since the house was on direct current, he was able to split the electric wire and use it to provide a spark. Beckoning to Clara, he had her drip gasoline into the cylinder from a can. As he spun the flywheel, the engine exploded into life. Spurting flame, popping wildly, filling the house with smoke and fumes, it shook the sink and brought coughing protestations from Clara.

Henry was elated. It was a beginning. *

*Robert Conot, *American Odyssey* (New York: Morrow, 1974; reprinted New York: Bantam, 1975), pp. 145–146.

Henry Ford's home experimentation with the internal combustion engine in 1896 was indeed a beginning. The American industrial genius had soon built factories to mass-produce automobiles by the assembly-line method; in 1913, the firm showed a profit of $27 million. But far more significant than the balance sheet of the Ford Motor Company was the all-pervading impact of motorized transport in the twentieth century, on everything from Hitler's blitzkrieg tactics to expressway travel and the modern suburban lifestyle.

The tremendous increase in speed of transportation was paralleled in other spheres of activity; indeed, it has been said that in the past century change itself changed. This has been true in global political developments, with the end of colonialism, the emergence of new nations, and revolutionary changes in government; in the economic realm, with the rise of multinational corporations; in social dynamics, with the alteration of the traditional family structure; in science, with the advent of the atomic (and subatomic) age; in information technology, with the proliferation of computers, electronic mail, and the Internet. And all of this at an astounding pace that has led some to speak of "future shock."

This chapter begins with the story of people living under the sway of imperialism fighting back with increasing determination. For some, as in China, this meant adapting Western science and technology to their own traditional cultures and religions. Others, such as the leadership in Turkey or Iran, rejected their traditional cultures as outdated and oppressive and fully embraced the Western system. Still others, like Gandhi in India, shunned Western scientific discoveries in favor of a traditional, religious way of life. The desire for economic and political independence fueled anti-imperialist struggles around the world. This chapter also discusses a number of the major nationalist movements in Africa and Asia as well as the sweeping revolutionary changes in Mexico and Russia. It concludes with an overview of many of the scientific, technological, economic, and cultural developments that have made the twentieth century, for better or worse, an era of rapidly accelerating innovation and achievement.

Independence Movements in West Asia, Africa, and Mexico

- *I am an Arab, and I believe that the Arabs constitute one nation.*
- *The Arabs: All who are Arab in their language, culture, and loyalty.*
- *The Arab Homeland: It is the land which has been, or is, inhabited by an Arab majority, in the above sense, in Asia and Africa.*
- *Arab Nationalism: It is the feeling for necessity of independence and unity which the inhabitants of the Arab lands share.*
- *The Arab Movement: Its motive force is her glorious past, her remarkable vitality and the awareness of her present and future interests.*
- *The Arab National Idea: It is a national idea which proscribes the existence of racial, regional, and communal fanaticism. It respects the freedom of religious observance, and individual freedoms such as the freedom of opinion, work, and assembly, unless they conflict with the public good.* *

*"First Arab Students' Congress, 1938," in *Arab Nationalism: An Anthology*, ed. Sylvia G. Haim (Berkeley: University of California Press, 1962), pp. 100–101.

This Arab manifesto of 1938 typifies the ideas and statements of nationalists throughout Africa, Asia, and South America. Emulating the liberal, secular nationalism of the West, Arab leaders and their contemporaries under imperial domination throughout the world at the turn of the century sought to oust the imperial powers and to create independent, progressive nations. By 1900, the various people within the Ottoman Empire—like those under or threatened by imperial domination around the world—had become nationalistic. Because the development of nationalism in West Asia is closely interrelated with World War I and the postwar era, the emergence of national movements and the dismemberment of the Ottoman Empire into a number of separate nations are discussed in its entirety in this section.

Prior to the onset of World War I in 1914, a group of highly Westernized Turkish officials and army officers organized the so-called Young Turk movement to seize control of the authoritarian, corrupt sultanate. In 1908 the Young Turks forced Sultan Abdul Hamid II (reigned 1876–1909) to restore the old constitution of 1876 and to institute reforms. The Young Turks centralized the administration and educational institutions

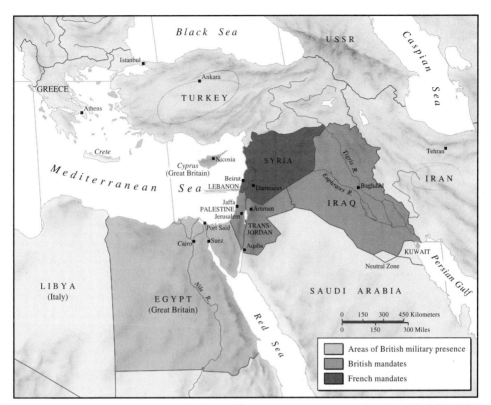

Map 14.1 Spheres of Influence in West Asia after World War I. After World War I the British and French divided the Arab provinces of the former Ottoman Empire into separate states, which they controlled either indirectly or as mandates.

under their control. They believed that by emphasizing the importance of Turkish history, culture, and language, they could save the crumbling empire from final destruction. In reaction to their attempts, Arab nationalist feelings intensified.

The non-Turkish people in the empire, Kurds, Armenians, and especially Arabs, who formed the single largest component of the populace, all opposed the programs to enforce Turkish as the language of the empire or to teach history from a solely Turkish perspective in the schools. Efforts to make Turkish the main language of instruction in schools were particularly unpopular. In the years prior to World War I, both Kurdish and Armenian national movements were crushed, and the Armenians suffered from massive persecutions and massacres. When the Young Turks joined the war effort in 1914 on the side of the Central Powers, many nationalists in the region seized the opportunity to further their goals for independent nationhood.

Three Conflicting Agreements Regarding the Arab World

World War I was a decisive turning point in Arab history. The various deals and agreements made by the British government, the Arabs, and the Zionists (Jewish nationalists) during the crucial years of 1914 to 1920 set the stage for many of the problems facing the region and the world until the present day.

The British were interested in the Arab world for military, political, and strategic reasons. They already controlled Egypt with the vital Suez Canal and most of the coastal areas along the Arabian Peninsula, and they wished to secure indirect—if not direct—influence over the Arab territories of the eastern Mediterranean. Recognizing that the Ottoman Empire, which had joined the German side in the war, would be dismembered after the war ended, the British were determined to become the dominant force in the region.

The Arabs also believed Ottoman participation in the war would bring about its final collapse. They saw the war as an opportunity to secure big power support for the creation of an independent Arab nation. Consequently, the British, who were anxious to secure whatever support possible to assist in the war effort against the Central Powers, therefore negotiated three separate agreements with regard to the Arab territories in the eastern Mediterranean: one with the Arabs, one with the French, and one with the Zionists.

The British negotiated the Sherif Husayn-McMahon Correspondence, the first, and in many ways the most complicated of these agreements, in a series of letters with Sherif Husayn, a key Arab leader in the holy city of Mecca. Henry McMahon was the British high commissioner in Egypt. Sherif Husayn, from the important Hashemite tribe, could trace his ancestry back to the Prophet Muhammad, and he became the self-appointed spokesperson for Arab nationalism. In 1915 Sherif Husayn proposed that the Arabs rise up against the Ottomans and fight on the side of the Allies in the war in exchange for an independent Arab state when the war was over. Husayn proposed that the borders of the

Emir Faysal. Sherif Husayn's son, Faysal (center), tried but failed to persuade the great powers at the Paris Peace Conference to accept the creation of one independent nation. Lawrence of Arabia (in British military uniform and Arab headdress and standing behind Faysal to his left) had participated in the Arab revolt and acted as an adviser to Faysal at the conference. Subsequently, Faysal, with British support, was made king of Iraq.

Imperial War Museum, London

new Arab state include all of the Arabian Peninsula and the territories of Iraq and greater Syria to the southern border of what is today Turkey and along the eastern Mediterranean to the Red Sea.

Although the British were delighted with the idea of having yet another ally in the war effort, they did not accept the proposed borders. The British knew there was oil in Iraq, and they had strategic interests in Palestine along the eastern Mediterranean; in addition, the French had imperial ambitions in Lebanon and Syria. Consequently, the British delayed settlements on Iraq and Lebanon. Sherif Husayn agreed in 1916 to raise the standard of revolt in exchange for an independent Arab state that would not include the territories of Iraq and Lebanon. Importantly, no specific mention was made of the territories that now comprise the nations of Jordan and Palestine (present-day Israel), which did not exist as separate entities at the time. It was assumed—at least by the Arabs—that those regions, which were overwhelmingly Arab in population, would be included within the Arab nation.

In June 1916 the Arabs revolted against the Ottoman Turks and fought alongside the British for the rest of the war. The British, however, had simultaneously negotiated with the French over what should become of the Arab territories after the war. In the Sykes-Picot Agreement of May 1916, the British and the French secretly agreed to divide up the old Ottoman Empire. The French got present-day Lebanon and Syria, and the British Iraq and present-day Israel and Jordan.

In the course of the war, Great Britain also made a public agreement with the Zionists, or Jewish nationalists, regarding Palestine. Under the public Balfour Declaration in 1917, the British government announced that it would "view with favor" the establishment of a Jewish homeland in Palestine. The wording of the Balfour Declaration was purposely vague, but the Zionists contended that it constituted British support for the creation of an independent Jewish nation in Palestine. Thus the three wartime agreements contradicted one another over control of Palestine. The British justified the agreements on the grounds that these were pragmatic deals necessary to bolster the Allied war effort and that any conflicting claims could be resolved after the war.

At the Paris Peace Conference the various parties with interests in West Asia came to present their cases. Sherif Husayn sent his son Faysal, who was the great favorite of Lawrence of Arabia, one of the British "advisers" to the Arab war effort. The Arabs were optimistic because President Wilson had strongly supported the idea of self-determination. Sherif Husayn even wrote to President Wilson requesting U.S. support. The Zionists sent the President of the World Zionist Organization, Chaim Weizmann, who had excellent contacts in the West and who had been instrumental in securing the Balfour Declaration, to represent them at Paris. In the end, however, the imperial interests of France and Great Britain triumphed.

Although it was no longer possible in an era of increasing nationalist fervor for the victors to annex lands of defeated powers as colonies, the victorious Western powers sought to retain or expand their imperial influence by devising a stratagem of issuing "mandates" under which the League of Nations would exercise nominal control over territory actually governed by Western nations. As a result, France secured mandates over what is today Lebanon and Syria. Great Britain got control over Iraq and present-day Jordan and Israel. The French also agreed that Great Britain would retain the major interest or "sphere of influence" over the territory of the Arabian Peninsula that comprises present-day Saudi Arabia. As no one knew there was petroleum in the peninsula, the imperial powers did not demand direct control over the largely desert territory. Thus the Arab world was divided into several states under British or French domination.

The French had a very difficult time in establishing control in their mandated territories and in fact ruled in Syria only by military force. Although the French succeeded in putting down the revolts, the Syrians were never reconciled to the French presence. In Lebanon, the French established a patron-client relationship with the Maronite Christian population, with which they had a long historic relationship; they also gave additional Syrian territory to Lebanon. French policies in Lebanon laid the foundations for the "confessional" system whereby political power was meted out on the basis of one's religious affiliation. As in Ireland, the confessional system has caused many of the ongoing problems in present-day Lebanon.

The British decided the fate of their Arab empire at the Cairo Conference in 1921. Led by the then colonial secretary, Winston Churchill, the British decided that the most efficient and cheapest method of rule would be to install, wherever possible, quasi-independent Arab leaders. In spite of a massive rebellion by tribal groups and nationalists in Iraq, the British installed their favorite, Amir (prince) Faysal, as king of Iraq. That monarchy continued to rule Iraq until it was overthrown in a military-led revolution in 1958.

When Egyptian demands for "complete independence" were refused, in 1919 the Egyptians launched a full-scale revolt in which all sectors of Egyptian society participated. When many of the male leaders were jailed and exiled by the British, Egyptian women stepped in to fill leadership roles and to lead the opposition. Finally, in face of continued strikes, riots, boycotts, and protests, Great Britain granted Egypt limited independence under a constitutional monarchy in 1922. However, the British continued to maintain a large military presence along the Suez Canal and directly interfered in Egyptian politics whenever British interests were threatened. The Egyptian monarchy lasted until it was overthrown in a popular revolution in 1952.

In Jordan, which had traditionally been ruled from Damascus as part of greater Syria, the British selected Sherif Husayn's eldest son, Abdullah, to become amir and ultimately king. That monarchy continues to reign; the present King Abdullah was named for his great-grandfather.

The British viewed Palestine as a strategic buffer zone to protect the Suez Canal and therefore installed direct military, political, and economic controls there. At the same time, it attempted to balance the conflicting nationalist demands of the Zionists, who wanted an independent Jewish state, and the Palestinians, who wanted an independent Arab state. When the British gained the mandate over Palestine, the Jewish population constituted approximately 10 percent of the total populace; in spite of Palestinian Arab opposition, the British permitted increased Jewish immigration. A tricornered struggle among the British, Zionists, and Palestinians for control of the territory continued until the British withdrew, and the Zionists proclaimed Israel an independent Jewish state in 1948.

Modernism versus Traditional Thought in Islam

Hasan Al-Banna: Spokesperson for Tradition

When we observe the evolution in the political, social, and moral spheres of the lives of nations and people, we note that the Islamic world—and, naturally, in the forefront, the Arab world—gives to its rebirth an Islamic flavor. This trend is ever-increasing. Until recently, writers, intellectuals, scholars, and governments glorified the principles of European civilization, gave themselves a Western tint, and adopted a European style and manner; today, on the contrary, the wind has changed, and reserve and distrust have taken their place. Voices are raised proclaiming the necessity for a return to the principles, teachings, and ways of Islam, and, taking into account the situation, for initiating the reconciliation of modern life with these principles, as a prelude to a final "Islamization."

The Western way of life . . . has remained incapable of offering to men's minds a flicker of light, a ray of hope, a grain of faith, or of providing anxious persons the smallest path toward rest and tranquillity.*

Taha Hussein: Spokesperson for Modernism

The subject to be treated in this discourse is the future of culture in Egypt. . . . Many people in various parts of the world have found their freedom and independence to be meaningless and unproductive. . . . There is no use in regretting what is past, for we cannot do anything about it.

Like every patriotic educated Egyptian who is zealous for his country's good reputation, I want our new life to harmonize with our ancient glory. . . .

The controlling factors in Egypt's destiny are its geographical situation, religion, artistic heritage, unbroken history, and the Arabic language. To defend our country, with its geographical situation, against aggression necessitates adopting European weapons and technique. Our religion, I feel, will be best maintained by doing as our ancestors did and keeping it responsive to contemporary needs.**

These excerpts from al-Banna and Hussein typify the arguments over modernism versus traditional thought made by Muslim Arab intellectuals and activists in the twentieth century. Although Western ideas and institutions heavily influenced most anti-imperialist leaders, some, like Hasan al-Banna (1906–1949), rejected Western culture and advocated the creation of a society based on Islam and traditional mores. An Egyptian, Al-Banna established the Muslim Brotherhood, which attracted members throughout the Islamic world. The Brotherhood opposed secular governments and worked for the creation of states based on religious law. Offshoots of the Brotherhood have continued to demand the creation of states based on Islamic law and principles to the present day.

Al-Banna's ideas contrast sharply with the secular approach of another Egyptian, Taha Hussein (1889–1973). Although secular leaders dominated the first generation of nationalists, in the second half of the twentieth century, religious leaders and their followers would become increasingly powerful in Iran, southern Lebanon, and elsewhere in the Islamic world.

*Hasan al-Banna, in Peter N. Stearns, ed., Documents in World History, vol. 2 (New York: Harper & Row, 1988), p. 176.
**Taha Hussein, in William H. McNeill and Marilyn Robinson Waldman, eds., The Islamic World (Chicago: University of Chicago Press, 1973), pp. 412–421.

In those regions not taken over directly by the European imperial powers, independent nationalist leaders rose to power. These leaders differed markedly in their domestic policies and programs for future development. Modernizing approaches were particularly evident in Turkey and Iran, while in Saudi Arabia the government adopted a policy of retaining traditional culture and Islam as the basis of the nation.

Modernism versus Tradition

After the war, Turkey and Iran were led by military dictators committed to destroying old traditional institutions, while Saudi Arabia was led by a monarchy based on tradition

Mustafa Kemal, or Atatürk.
Atatürk traveled widely throughout Turkey to popularize his programs for modernization. As seen here, he sometimes brought a portable blackboard along and used it to teach the new alphabet to villagers in the countryside.

Stock Montage

and puritanical Islamic law. Both Mustafa Kemal, or Atatürk, father of the Turks (1881–1938), in Turkey and Reza Khan (1878–1944) in Iran were determined to westernize their nations as rapidly as possible. Atatürk toppled the old Ottoman monarchy and successfully led his forces against the Allied attempts to partition Turkey. A popular national hero, Atatürk saved Turkey from foreign domination; he then used his charismatic personality and national reputation to push through a series of sweeping reforms calculated to destroy the last vestiges of the Ottoman Empire and to make Turkey as European as possible. Hating both religion and the Ottoman regime, Atatürk abolished both the sultanate and the caliphate and personally developed a parliamentary constitutional state that by law was secular. Although he forced the creation of a two-party system, in actual fact, Atatürk controlled the political life of the nation until his death in 1938.

Atatürk's reforms also extended into the social sphere. He abolished wearing the fez, the traditional Ottoman headdress for men, and the veil for women and pushed such Western social activities as ballroom dancing. Encouraged by women's movements elsewhere and by Atatürk's social reforms, Turkish feminists organized to demand greater legal rights in the 1920s and even dropped leaflets from an airplane to attract attention to their cause.

Atatürk encouraged the development of modern state-owned industries and changed the Turkish alphabet from the old Arabic script to Western script. Although he was a dictator, Atatürk never amassed a personal fortune and, importantly, he bequeathed a tradition of parliamentary and secular government to Turkey. Atatürk has often been viewed as the personification of a "benevolent" dictator.

Similarly, in 1923 Reza Khan, a professional soldier, overthrew the Qajar dynasty in Persia. He abolished the old monarchy and embarked on a massive program of modernization, which included building roads, reforming the military and financial administration, and encouraging Western, secular education. He, too, attempted to lessen the power of religion and in particular sought to destroy the authority of the mullahs, the established Shi'i clergy. In contrast to Atatürk, Reza Khan amassed a huge personal fortune. He also created a new royal dynasty, the Pahlavi, with himself as the first shah. In 1935 he formally changed the nation's name from Persia to Iran. The failure to establish lasting parliamentary institutions, the attacks against the clergy, and the continuation of the monarchy all had long-lasting impacts on Iranian political and social development.

The political development of Saudi Arabia offers a marked contrast to that of Iran and Turkey. During the nineteenth century, the House of Saud had linked forces with Muhammad ibn Abd al-Wahhab, a puritanical reformer who wanted to purge Islam of worldly deviations that had crept into the religion over the centuries. As in the early centuries of Islamic development, the merger of a political and military force with religious reform proved a potent combination. As the house of Saud and the Wahhabi followers spread their brand of Islamic puritanism across the Arabian Peninsula, they were repeatedly attacked by tribal rivals and by the Ottomans. The Wahhabi movement was militarily defeated several times, but each time, like the proverbial phoenix, it came back to life stronger than ever.

In Abd al-Aziz ibn Saud, king of Saudi Arabia (reigned 1932–1953), the movement found a charismatic, energetic champion. During the first decades of the twentieth century, Abd al-Aziz ibn Saud steadily enlarged his territories and defeated his rivals. After World War I, he moved against Sherif Husayn, his main rival in the Arabian Peninsula. Sherif Husayn's forces were no match for the committed and zealous Wahhabis, and by 1926 Abd al-Aziz ibn Saud had ousted Husayn's supporters and had taken over the holy cities of Mecca and Medina. King Abd al-Aziz promptly proceeded to forge a kingdom, Saudi Arabia (named after his family), based on strict adherence to puritanical Islam. Although the legitimacy of King Abd al-Aziz's rule rested primarily upon his commitment to maintaining the kingdom as an Islamic state, he did not reject modern technological innovations. He brought cars, radios, and telephones into the kingdom. The first telephone link in the nation was between Abd al-Aziz's palace and his beloved sister's home. With the discovery of huge petroleum reserves in the peninsula and the subsequent influx of large amounts of money after World War II, Saud's kingdom was soon awash with consumer goods. Abd al-Aziz's sons have continued to rule Saudi Arabia to the present day. The kingdom is representative of those states that have attempted to amalgamate modern technology with fundamentalist religion and traditional culture. How successful that amalgamation will prove remains uncertain.

Chilembwe Rouses His People to Action

You are all patriots as you sit.... This very night you are to go and strike the blow and then die. I do not say that you are going to win the war at all. You have no weapons with you and you are not at all trained military men even. One great thing you must remember is ... love [of] your own country and country men, I now encourage you to go and strike a blow bravely and die.

You must not think that with that blow, you are going to defeat whitemen and then become Kings of your own country, no.... I am also warning you strongly against seizing property from anybody. ... Another

order I want you to remember, is about women and young children, do not, in any way, do anything to them, treat them as innocents, what you are to do with them is to bring them over peacefully, and afterwards send them back.... Be of good courage, and strike the blow and die.... *

John Chilembwe led an abortive revolt against British coffee and tobacco plantation owners in Nyasaland in 1915. Before the battle, Chilembwe delivered the rousing patriotic speech quoted above.

*The Horizon History of Africa (New York: American Heritage, 1971), p. 472.

African Revolts against Foreign Domination

As in West Asia, numerous armed revolts against European domination in Africa occurred during the first quarter of the twentieth century. Specific ethnic or tribal groups generally dominated these revolts or religious movements that rallied mass support against foreign occupation. Without exception, the Europeans, with superior military power, were able to defeat these movements, but at enormous human cost to their African opponents. In a very real way, these revolts presaged many of the successful armed struggles launched around the world against imperial domination following World War II.

Like the Boxer Rebellion in China, the revolts in Africa were motivated by distrust and hatred of foreign occupation, anger over the destruction of local economies, and the determination to protect indigenous cultures from destruction. Owing to their relative military weakness vis-à-vis the Europeans, who possessed both technologically superior weapons and the will to use them, all the African revolts against European domination at the beginning of the twentieth century failed. The British succeeded in putting down strong resistance by the Ashanti in the Gold Coast in 1900. The Herero revolts in German South-West Africa (present-day Namibia) from 1904 to 1906 and the Maji Maji Revolt (1905–1907) in German East Africa (present-day Tanzania) are other examples of armed struggles by Africans against European domination. The Germans so brutally defeated these movements that the Herero people were nearly destroyed. The last Zulu revolt in South Africa occurred in 1906, and it, too, was defeated. Likewise, the Portuguese put down widespread rebellions in Angola in 1913, though the Tutsi, cattle-owning people, and the Hutu, mainly farming people, in present-day Burundi and Rwanda continued to resist both the British and Germans from 1911 until 1917.

As in much of the Islamic world, African opposition to foreign domination often took religious forms. For example, John Chilembwe in Nyasaland (present-day Malawi) established his own separatist religious mission. A product of Protestant missionary education, Chilembwe had lived in the United States, where he had become involved in the political activities of African Americans seeking the unity of blacks and a return to Africa. Angered by the favoritism shown to white settlers and increased prices and shortages brought about by World War I, Chilembwe led a rebellion against the settlers and British domination in 1915; his revolt was crushed, however, and Chilembwe was ambushed and assassinated.

In North Africa, resistance movements were able to organize and maintain more protracted and far bloodier struggles. Under the leadership of Muhammad Abd al-Krim, the tribes in the Moroccan Rif Mountains organized an efficient and effective opposition to Spanish domination. In 1921 Krim's forces inflicted a devastating military defeat on the Spanish at Anual; several years of bloody confrontations ensued. Determined to defeat Krim's forces, successive Spanish leaders reinforced their troops. Francisco Franco, the future dictator of Spain, began his rise to power by leading Spanish forces fighting in North Africa.

As Krim's rebellion spread, it was opposed by France, which held the protectorate over the portion of Morocco not held by Spain. Although successful in repelling the weak and dispirited Spanish army, Krim's forces were no match for the French. By 1926 Krim was forced to surrender to them and was sent into exile on the island of Réunion in the Indian Ocean. Moroccan independence from Spain and France would not be achieved until after World War II.

During the 1920s Omar Mukhtar's struggle against Italian occupation of Libya had a similar outcome. The Libyans fiercely opposed the Italian occupation, but, once in power, Mussolini was equally determined to incorporate Libya into his new Italian Empire. Using bases in desert oases, the support of the people, and superior knowledge of the terrain, Omar Mukhtar launched guerrilla warfare against the Italian troops in the 1920s. After suffering several humiliating defeats, the Italians began rounding up Libyans, killing many, placing women and children in concentration camps, cutting off supplies from the outside, and attacking with planes and superior military armaments. In 1931 Mukhtar was captured, summarily tried, and publicly executed by Italian forces. The struggle in Libya presaged similar confrontations against the Italians in Ethiopia in the 1930s, and were an indication of postwar resistance movements against the European imperial powers. Meanwhile, Africans took their nationalist struggles into political arenas as well.

The Emergence of African Political Organizations

As noted in Chapter 13, World War I had a major impact on Africa. Not only had hundreds of thousands of Africans died in the war, but the imperial powers, particularly the British and French, had increased taxes and commercial controls in their African possessions in order to help pay for the war. After the war, the British and French sought to hold on to their African possessions for as long as possible and to make them increasingly profitable. Because these policies stimulated opposition, it can be said that the war hastened the development of African political organizations. Many of the early African political movements were influenced by a pan-African approach and had international components. Three very disparate personalities dominated the pan-African movement, and they adopted widely different approaches to the problems of people of African descent around the world.

Dr. W. E. B. DuBois, an African American, was one of the foremost intellectual leaders of the pan-African movement. Influential in the United States, DuBois organized a pan-African congress in Paris to coincide with the Paris Peace Conference in 1919. He called for improved racial, economic, and political reforms and called attention to the problems facing blacks. Early pan-Africanists had often been influenced by négritude, a literary movement extolling the virtues of black Africa. In a very real way, writers and politicians like Leopold Senghor (1906–1993; see the final section of this chapter) sought to compensate for racism and ethnocentric Western attitudes regarding Africans and African culture.

Initially, DuBois enjoyed the support of Blaise Diagne from Senegal; however, the two leaders disagreed over what course African relations with the imperial powers should take. In short, Diagne and others believed that Africans should seek to attain parity with the Europeans within the imperial framework. The French encouraged this approach by advocating assimilation, and, when that policy was attacked, a program of association. To implement this approach, France granted citizenship to the Senegalese and allowed them to elect a deputy to the French National Assembly. In 1914 Diagne was elected to this post, which he held until his death in 1934. Diagne used his influential position to push for improved relations between the French and black Africa. When DuBois became more strident in calling for African independence and economic freedom, Diagne denounced him for holding pro-Marxist ideas. Diagne continued to believe that only France would give equal political and social treatment to Africans.

A flamboyant Jamaican, Marcus Garvey, was perhaps the most popular pan-African leader. Operating from Harlem in New York City, Garvey campaigned for a return to Africa by all blacks in the Western Hemisphere. African Americans from the United States, the Caribbean, and South America flocked to his calls, but political problems in Liberia, where many African Americans planned to return, prevented a major emigration from the West. Nonetheless, Garvey's political platform and his publication in 1920 of a "Declaration of Rights of the Negro People of the World" influenced a future generation of African leaders, including Kwame Nkrumah of Ghana (formerly known as the Gold Coast).

Other Africans also began to form political organizations aimed at securing independence in specific African nations. For example, in 1917 a number of educated West Africans established the National Congress of British West Africa; led by J. E. Casely Hayford, a journalist and lawyer from the Gold Coast, members of the congress traveled to London in 1920 to demand an elected legislature with the power to impose taxes, equal opportunities for Africans and Europeans in the civil service, the foundation of a university, and autonomy for local chiefs. After some protracted negotiations in the 1920s, the British allowed the creation of some legislative councils, dominated by Europeans, in Nigeria and Ghana.

Anticolonial political organizing began early in South Africa. Established in 1912, the South African Native National Congress was the first political organization of its type in Africa. Later, it changed its name to the African National Congress (ANC) and continued to lead the protracted struggle for African political rights in South Africa. Similarly, in eastern Africa, opposition to land appropriations by whites led to the formation of the East Africa Association and the Kikuyu Provincial Association led by Harry Thuku. The Kikuyu, who were generally farmers, had been particularly affected by white settlers, who in the 1930s began to expand their farms by ousting the Kikuyu from rented land the Kikuyu regarded as their own. The settlers then took on the displaced Kikuyu as hired hands.

None of these political organizations called for complete independence; rather, they all sought to secure domestic reforms and improved economic status. Prior to World War II, African organizations had little success in altering European imperial policies or in improving the day-to-day standard of living in their nations.

While black Africans were expanding their demands, whites in South Africa also organized to perpetuate their dominant social, economic, and political positions. In 1934 the Afrikaners, led by Generals Jan Smuts and James Hertzog, organized the United party. The United party remained the preeminent white political organization until it was superseded by the Afrikaner National party, which adopted even more rigid policies of racial segregation and white supremacy. The tendency toward government policies of racial segregation was apparent even in the United party's 1936 Natives Representation Act. Under this law Africans lost their political rights, but coloureds (people of Asian or mixed racial heritage) kept the right to vote on the common roll in the Cape Province. Thus, while the Union of South Africa allowed for democratic representation of whites, the majority of the nation was denied any political rights. In the decades to follow, segregationist policies were extended and further entrenched into government policy by the Afrikaner minority.

Social Revolution in Mexico

Unlike events in West Asia and Africa, the revolution that swept through Mexico in 1911 was not a revolt against direct colonial rule; Mexico had been independent since 1821. It was, however, the first social revolution of the twentieth century in which the masses of peasants and urban workers were an active force. It was also the first time in the modern history of the Western Hemisphere other than Haiti that persons of part or full Amerindian descent improved their position in a region where persons of European descent dominated nations.

In 1911, after thirty-four years in power, Porfirio Díaz's dictatorial rule came to an abrupt end in Mexico. The reign of the dictator had touched every aspect of Mexican life. Díaz's policies were designed to achieve political stability by centralizing power and to modernize the economy by building a modern technological infrastructure and increasing exports. In pursuit of these goals, Díaz's regime allowed the *haciendados*, the large landowners, to increasingly take over small farms and Amerindian communal property in order to consolidate large tracts of land for raising products for export, such as sisal, hemp, sugar, and meat. He excluded most of the developing middle class and northern elites from political power and harshly suppressed urban workers who wished to organize for better working conditions and workers' rights. These policies were characterized by the phrase *pan o palo*—"bread or a club."

Mexico's Favorite Revolutionary. The collapse of Francisco Madero's administration sparked unrest in the Mexican countryside. Emiliano Zapata, pictured here, led rebellious Amerindians against wealthy landowners in southern Mexico, making demands of his own for land reform.

Brown Brothers

Foreign capital and finance paid for Mexican modernization, and the Díaz regime allowed non-Mexicans unprecedented holdings in mining, transportation, communications, electricity, and petroleum. By linking local economies to larger markets, modernization also linked the peasantry to the volatile whims of the global market. Railway intrusion into the countryside spurred the commercialization of agriculture; wherever railroads were built, demand for land increased and so did takeovers. The new developments in communications and transportation also gave Díaz stronger political control over larger areas and allowed his rule to reach the farthest corners of Mexico.

As Díaz's regime widened and centralized, it also weakened. When Diaz extended his power to isolated, localized regions, he installed political officials of his choosing, thereby excluding from the power structure, and alienating, local elites who were used to a large degree of self-rule. As a result, coalitions opposed to Díaz's centralization began to form.

Initial opposition arose in the northern section of Mexico, which, ironically, was one of the chief beneficiaries of Porfirian modernization. The north was experiencing an unprecedented growth in economic prosperity, which gave rise to an urban middle class. Both this middle class and the economically powerful desired access to political power.

In 1910 Francisco Madero, one of the northern elite, challenged Díaz, having taken him at his word when, in an interview with a journalist from the United States, Díaz promised to allow opposition candidates in the upcoming elections. Madero wrote an influential work regarding the elections that promptly landed him in jail as an opposition spokesperson. Madero escaped and fled to San Antonio, where he and his supporters put together a political platform. They issued the Plan of San Luis Potosí, which proclaimed Madero provisional president of Mexico, declared Díaz's rule null and void, and called for an uprising set for November 20, 1910. At this point, no significant mention was made of any social programs or reforms, other than a brief mention of the restitution of illegally acquired lands to the peasantry. Madero's "Revolt from Abroad" prevailed; Díaz fled the country in 1911 with the parting words: "Madero has unleashed a tiger; let us see if he can control it."

Díaz's departure was followed by six years of bloody civil war. Madero became president, but soon fell victim to a counterrevolution by conservative forces, who in turn soon fell to the legendary figures in Mexican history, Pancho Villa and Emiliano Zapata. Villa was a bandit and popular hero of the lower classes in northern Mexico. He was a staunch supporter of Madero, and after Madero's death formed his own "Division of the North" to carry out the revolution. Zapata was a small landowner in the state of Morelos, south of Mexico City. Zapata reflected the agrarian nature of the revolution; he was a leader of *campesinos* (peasants) fighting against exploitation. His Plan of Ayala called for the restitution of lands to all peasants who had suffered losses to large landowners and illegal landgrabbers.

By 1917 the Constitutionalist faction had gained the upper hand in the civil war and convened a constitution-drafting body that contained representatives of most of the competing factions. They produced a constitution that set up the most socially and nationalistically radical basis for government in the Western world. The constitution called for the redistribution of land to the peasantry and to all persons requiring it. Land and subsoil rights (ores, gas, and petroleum) were to be the property of the nation and its peoples. Other provisions guaranteed sweeping workers' rights, including a minimum wage, eight-hour workdays, regulation of child and female labor, safety standards, and the right to strike. The constitution also deprived the Catholic church in Mexico of much of its wealth, power, and influence over the masses.

Most of the bloody revolutionary infighting ended by 1920, and political stability was solid enough for elections to be held. With the end to revolution, reconstruction of the nation began, with a new constitution, a new sense of nationalism, and a new generation of political elites. From 1927 on, the Institutional Revolutionary party (PRI) ruled Mexico, allowing no major formal opposition. The party was not rooted in one political philosophy but rather was composed of all members of the political spectrum and worked solely to perpetuate its own power and rule. One unemployed general snorted that "the revolution has now degenerated into a government."

The revolution did, however, make great strides during the presidency of Lázaro Cárdenas (ruled 1934–1940). His administration bore many similarities to the New Deal programs of U.S. president Franklin Roosevelt. The popular Cárdenas actively sought information about the plight of the Mexican peasantry by visiting villages. He expedited land reform by restoring land to Amerindians and by shifting it from the wealthy *hacienderos* to the destitute farmers. Cárdenas also took an interest in building schools and improving industrial working conditions in the cities. Another development of these years was the nationalization of the railroads and petroleum companies. The government ran the national oil corporation more effectively than foreign owners had run the former private corporations. Though large foreign consumers of Mexican oil in the United States and Europe raised objections, the Cárdenas administration channeled much of the increased flow of oil into important new domestic projects.

Besides changing the social and economic structures of the country, the revolution brought a change in the Mexican self-image. The Latin element in Mexican civilization was emphasized in favor of stressing Amerindian history and culture. Mestizos, after all, were now a major element in the racial mixture of Mexico. Books, paintings, and the mass media featured themes from contemporary Amerindian life and informed the populace about the great achievements of the Aztec and Mayan cultures.

The revolution lost its momentum in the 1940s. Despite land redistribution policies, the *hacienderos* were still in possession of half the cultivable land in the country, while a third of the Mexican people still lived in virtual serfdom. Governmental corruption also impeded many of the reforms initiated by Cárdenas. Nonetheless, Mexico had traveled a long way from the dictatorship of Porfirio Díaz.

In retrospect, the Mexican Revolution appears to have been an indigenous phenomenon. Its leaders sought unique Mexican solutions to Mexican problems; they did so without applying any of the ideologies that motivated many European revolutionaries. From a decade of civil chaos, a consensus among disparate groups and a political party capable of concerted action emerged slowly. The profound changes in economics, society, and culture that the revolution set in motion still remained to be consummated.

As in West Asia, Africa, and Mexico, nationalists in East and South Asia also fought for increased control over their own national identities in the interwar years. The organization of Asian nationalist movements and their conflicts with imperial forces are treated in the next section of this chapter.

Struggles for Independence in South and East Asia

Salt suddenly became a mysterious word, a word of power. The salt tax was to be attacked, the salt laws were to be broken. . . . As people followed the fortunes of this marching column of pilgrims from day to day, the temperature of the country went up. . . .

I went to see Gandhiji [Indians add "ji" to name endings to indicate respect; Gandhiji is thus a respectful way of referring to Gandhi]. . . . We spent a few hours with him there and then saw him stride away with his party to the next stage in the journey to the salt sea.

It seemed as though a spring had been suddenly released; all over the country, in town and village, salt manufacture was the topic of the day. . . . We knew precious little about it. . . . It was really immaterial whether the stuff was good or bad; the main thing was to commit a breach of the obnoxious salt law, and we were successful in that, even though the quality of our salt was poor.

I was arrested on the 14th of April. . . . That very day I was tried in prison and sentenced to six months' imprisonment under the Salt Act.

When I heard that my aged mother and, of course, my sisters used to stand under the hot summer sun picketing before foreign cloth shops, I was greatly moved.

Many strange things happened in those days, but undoubtedly the most striking was the part of the women in the national struggle. They came out in large numbers from the seclusion of their homes and, though unused to public activity, threw themselves into the heart of the struggle. The picketing of foreign cloth and liquor shops they made their preserve. Enormous processions consisting of women alone were taken out in all the cities; and, generally, the attitude of the women was more unyielding than that of the men.*

*The Autobiography of Jawaharlal Nehru (London: John Day/Bodley Head, 1941), in *Modern Asia and Africa,* eds. William H. McNeill and Mitsuko Iriye (New York: Oxford University Press, 1971), pp. 224–229.

In his *Autobiography,* Indian nationalist leader Jawaharlal Nehru described his participation in the struggle for independence from British rule. Nehru wrote his *Autobiography* while in British prison during World War II, serving one of several prison terms to which he was sentenced for his involvement in the nationalist movement. For many Asian and African nationalists before and after World War II, a prison sentence was the price they paid for the independence struggle for their homelands.

All of Asia came under some degree of European political and economic domination. In South and Southeast Asia, all nations except Thailand were fully incorporated into Western empires. In the Indian subcontinent and on mainland and island Southeast Asia, militant organizations developed with the primary goal of ousting imperial control and winning national independence.

British Rule and the Birth of Modern India

In Asia as in Africa, Great Britain was not so much concerned with either assimilation or elimination of indigenous cultures as with maintaining control over its territories. While Britain ruled most of India directly, it nevertheless retained many of the native princes or maharajas in power in their ancestral domains. Even in these native states, however, British officials supervised the administration.

Although Great Britain did not work actively to subvert local culture and traditions in India and its other colonial holdings in Asia, British policy did suppress certain local practices such as child marriages. Some traditionalist Hindus objected strenuously to these attempts because they tampered with old traditions and religious rules; others reacted by reexamining their traditions to reform outmoded practices. Although Hindus and Muslims were allowed to retain their religious beliefs in the civil law code, the British administration gradually superimposed British legal concepts in criminal law, and also instituted modern commercial codes. British banking and commercial institutions, modern roads, and the telegraph gradually transformed India and integrated it into a global economy.

As early as the 1830s, British authorities in India had begun to establish modern English-language schools and universities and also encouraged religious institutions and other bodies to open private Western-style schools. These schools educated the children of Hindu upper and middle classes, as well as those who traditionally had no opportunity to obtain an education, notably girls and lower-caste Hindus. Some of the brightest boys went on to attend schools and universities in Great Britain. Civil service exams recruited the best to join the prestigious Indian Civil Service. Upper-caste Hindus who tradition-ally revered education eagerly grasped these educational opportunities. Many Muslims, however, felt aggrieved because Britons had replaced them as the ruling class. They were thus reluctant to send their children to Western-style schools. As a result, the number of Muslims with a modern education was small in proportion to their total population; consequently, Muslims played a lesser role in the modern sector than their proportional numbers warranted.

British policy tried to maintain a balance and tolerance for all the religions in the sub-continent, particularly Islam and Hinduism. Great Britain did not encourage conversion of members of either religious community to Christianity. Christian religious missionar-ies made few converts, but medical and educational missionaries were highly successful in introducing modern medicine and technology through education. English was used in the new schools and so became the common language of a growing urban middle class, bridging regional and linguistic barriers among Indians.

Indian Nationalist Awakening

The growth of national consciousness was the most important phenomenon of modern India because it culminated in independence for the subcontinent. It was also the fore-runner of other independence movements throughout the colonial world. The Indian National Congress, formed in 1885 by seventy modern educated Indians and Britons, was the first major secular nationalist organization in India. Meeting in annual conven-tions, the Congress from the beginning had two main goals: developing self-government by means of representative institutions, and promoting educational, social, and other reforms. A modern press in English and vernacular languages began to demand the extension to Indians of the same political rights enjoyed by Britons in their own country, as well as social reforms, including the emancipation of women.

Although membership in the Indian National Congress was open to all, few Muslims joined. As the Congress's lobbying efforts won increasing respect from British leaders, Muslims became fearful of the implications of representative government: as the minority community, they would lose any elections. In 1905 Indian Muslim leaders organized the All India Muslim League, which had the twin goals of representative government and separate electorates for Muslims (that is, Muslims would vote for Muslims for designated Muslim seats in any elections). Although the Congress opposed separate electorates, they were granted to Muslims in 1909 when the British parliament passed the Morley-Minto Reforms, which granted limited suffrage to male Indians and created advisory represen-tative bodies.

As in the African colonies, India also played an important part in the British Empire's war effort during World War I. After the war, Indians demanded increased participation in their own government. In 1919 the British Parliament responded by enacting the Government of India Act, which expanded the franchise (women were granted the right to vote on the same terms as men in 1925) and the powers of the elected legislatures. Separate electorates for Muslims were retained at the insistence of the League. Indian nationalists maintained that the concessions were insufficient and began to agitate for complete independence.

After World War I Mohandas K. Gandhi (1869–1948) reenergized the mass struggle for Indian independence. The son of a prosperous Hindu family and a London-educated lawyer, Gandhi had won great respect among Indians for his use of nonviolent techniques to champion Indian rights against discrimination by whites in South Africa. Returning to India from South Africa in 1915, Gandhi emerged as the spiritual head of the Indian nationalist movement by perfecting the techniques of nonviolent protest and by widening the appeal of Congress to millions of ordinary Indians. Gandhi taught that whatever the grievance, violence was wrong. He also taught Indians that because Indian acquiescence had made British rule possible, Indians could force Britain to leave India if they withheld their cooperation. He therefore organized nationwide nonviolent, noncooperation campaigns similar to strikes that shut down the government and all its services. When the strikes and demonstrations turned violent, Gandhi would call them off, because, he maintained, two wrongs did not make a right. For this reason, some Indians anxious to win independence immediately and at any price accused Gandhi of retarding the achievement of Indian independence.

Gandhi also championed social reforms such as the right of Hindu widows to remarry, the ending of child marriages, and above all the end of untouchability, which made millions outcastes from Hindu society. He sought to attain his goals not by legislation but by his own saintly example and by touching the hearts of friends and adversaries

Gandhi Revitalizes the Congress

Gandhi . . . brought about a complete change in its [the Congress's] constitution. He made it democratic and a mass organization. Democratic it had been previously also, but it had so far been limited in franchise and restricted to the upper classes. Now the peasants rolled in, and in its new garb it began to assume the look of a vast agrarian organization with a strong sprinkling of the middle classes. . . . Industrial workers also came in, but as individuals and not in their separate, organized capacity.

Action was to be the basis and objective of this organization, action based on peaceful methods. Thus far the alternatives had been: just talk and passing resolutions, or terroristic activity. Both of these were set aside and terrorism was especially condemned as opposed to the basic policy of the Congress. A new technique of action was evolved which, though perfectly peaceful, yet involved non-submission to what was considered wrong, and as a consequence, a willing acceptance of the pain and suffering involved in this. . . .

The call to action was twofold. There was of course the action involved in challenging and resisting foreign rules; there was also the action which led us to fight our own social evils . . . which involved the solution of the minority problems, and the raising of the depressed classes and the ending of the curse of untouchability. . . .

He sent us to the villages, and the countryside hummed with the activity of innumerable messengers of the new gospel of action. The peasant was shaken up and he began to emerge from his quiescent shell. The effect on us was different but equally far-reaching, for we saw, for the first time as it were, the villager in the intimacy of his mud hut and with the stark shadow of hunger always pursuing him. We learned our Indian economics more from these visits than from books and learned discourses.*

Jawaharlal Nehru was Gandhi's disciple, a leader of the Congress, and first prime minister of independent India. Here he commented on Gandhi's effect on both the elite leadership of the Congress and on Indian masses.

*Jawaharlal Nehru, The Discovery of India, ed. Robert I. Crane (Garden City, N.Y.: Anchor Books, 1946), pp. 276–279.

alike. Gandhi also taught his followers the dignity of labor and sought to avoid the abuses of industrial society by advocating handicrafts. He gave up wearing Western clothes, spun and wove cloth for his own clothes, and insisted that all men and women of the Congress do likewise. Thus the spinning wheel came to symbolize the Indian nationalist movement. Later, independent India would reject Gandhi's idyllic notions of a nonindustrial society. Nevertheless, he continued to be revered in India and worldwide as the gentle apostle of peace and as a nonviolent crusader for social change. Because of his exemplary life and the humanitarian causes he championed, Gandhi came to be called the Mahatma (Great Soul). Gandhi's philosophy of nonviolent resistance to wrongs and immoral laws influenced U.S. civil rights leader Martin Luther King Jr. and South Africa's Nelson Mandela.

During the 1920s and 1930s, the Gandhi-led nonviolent protest movements filled British jails and baffled British officials, who had no precedent in dealing with such a saintly adversary. Public opinion forced the British to negotiate and make concessions to Gandhi's demands, thus advancing the Indian nationalist movement. By the mid-1930s Gandhi's massive civil disobedience campaigns against British rule compelled the British government to advance the time frame for its withdrawal from India. As the prospect of independence drew nearer, however, Muslim fear of Hindu domination also intensified. In India communal differences, or identification by religious affiliation, were old and intense, and became more so between Hindus and Muslims as independence drew closer. The tensions arose because all modern Indian nationalist movements sought to establish democratically elected governments after independence. The majority Hindus foresaw political dominance as rightfully theirs, but that prospect frightened the Muslims, who would become a permanent minority under Hindu domination.

During the 1930s the British government conferred with Gandhi in London and held a series of conferences over the timetable and conditions of independence. In 1935 the British parliament passed the India Act, which made India a federation of provinces and princely states under a British-appointed governor-general, who shared power with representatives of a bicameral legislature of elected and appointed members. The franchise was further enlarged, Muslims retained separate electorates, and reserved seats were guaranteed for women, depressed classes, and minority communities. At the national level, this act was the last transitional step before the full attainment of self-government. On the provincial level, an elected government comprised of Indians controlled all affairs, with the British-appointed provincial governor retaining only emergency powers. This plan gave wide powers to the provinces and princely states and was an attempt to reconcile the fears of the Muslims and accommodate the special needs of the princely states. As expected, the elections held under the India Act returned Congress majorities to predominantly Hindu provinces and League majorities to provinces where Muslims predominated.

Mohammed Ali Jinnah (1876–1948), a British-educated lawyer and founder of the Muslim League, led the Muslim community in demanding a separate identity for Muslims. Jinnah epitomized Indian Muslim separateness in a speech he made in 1940 at the annual meeting of the Muslim League:

Hindus and Muslims belong to two different religious philosophies, social customs, literature. . . . To yoke together two such nations under a single state, one as a numerical minority and the other as a majority, must lead to growing discontent and final destruction of any fabric that may be so built up for the government of such a state. . . . The only course open to us all is to allow the major nations separate homelands for dividing India into "autonomous nation states."

Following this speech the Muslim League passed the Pakistan Resolution, which called for the creation of a separate state called Pakistan ("Land of the Pure" in Urdu, the language of many Muslims in northwestern India) in areas of the Indian subcontinent where Muslims formed a majority.

In contrast to 1914, when Indians followed Great Britain to war without protest and made major contributions to the Allied cause, in 1939 the Congress protested India's automatic involvement in World War II on behalf of the British Empire. Congress leaders argued that an India that was itself unfree could not join in the effort to fight against Nazi and Fascist tyranny. They demanded the immediate granting of full independence by Great Britain, and promised that as a free people, they would gladly join in the Allied war effort.

Great Britain responded by dissolving the Congress-controlled provincial governments and imprisoning the key Congress leaders, including Gandhi. Jinnah and the League declared the closing of Congress-dominated provincial governments a "Day of Deliverance and Thanksgiving." The League and the provinces it controlled cooperated with the British war effort, thereby gaining administrative experience and improving the Muslims' political position.

Several British missions came to India to negotiate with Indian leaders during the war. They suggested formulas for power sharing, but all failed because of the irreconcilable differences between the Congress and the League and conflict over the timetable for granting complete independence. Despite these unresolved problems, India and Indians played greater roles in World War II than in World War I. The Indian Army increased from 182,000 men in 1939 to over 2 million in 1945. Indian units served with distinction in North Africa, West Asia, Italy, western Europe, and Southeast Asia and defended India from threatened Japanese invasion. India's abundant resources were also put to full use in aiding the Allied war effort.

A Changing Indian Society

With improved medical care and technology, India's population reached 400 million people by 1945. However, the standard of living for most Indians, especially in the rural sectors where 80 percent of the people lived, remained pitifully low. After particularly severe famines in 1896 and 1901, the British government responded by establishing famine relief funds and by founding agricultural colleges, a department of agriculture, and agricultural cooperative services. It also began various major irrigation projects to bring more land into production and to increase agricultural yield.

The British government also emphasized the need to expand the economy by establishing industries, beginning with textile, iron, and steel industries. The two world wars assisted in rapid industrialization. The development of industries led to legislation to regulate the conditions of labor. India's first Factory Act was passed in 1911. It regulated working hours and conditions for women and children and was the forerunner of other factory legislation that set minimum wages and allowed unions and legalized strikes. The labor movement, however, was hobbled by the abundance of labor, generally poor standard of living, and lack of adequate enforcement.

The status of women steadily advanced. Ameliorative measures included several laws beginning in the early twentieth century to increase the minimum marriageable age for girls (and boys too). In 1923 a Women's Indian Association was founded; it operated children's homes and performed other social services. In 1924 a Birth Control League was established in Bombay. In 1914 the All-India Muslim Ladies Conference was organized; among its goals was the abolition of polygamy. The Women's Suffrage Movement, founded in 1917, reflected the growth of women's political consciousness. As a result of its lobbying and in accordance with a worldwide trend, women gained the right to vote under the same conditions as men in the 1920s, and the India Act of 1935 reserved a number of seats in all legislatures for women. In 1925 a woman activist and poet, Sarojini Naidu, was elected president of the annual meeting of the Indian National Congress (she later became the first woman provincial governor). Other women leaders of international renown followed her. An All-India Women's Conference was established in 1926; it became an auxiliary organization for the Indian National Congress, just as similar women's organizations in Egypt had made important contributions to the nationalist cause.

The changes in women's role in society matched those in the political realm. Women began to come out of seclusion; many entered the professions, especially as elementary school teachers. By the 1940s government agencies recommended that the same educational facilities be provided for both girls and boys. The actual status of women continued to be subordinate, however, because ancient traditions held fast in the conservative countryside.

Both Hindus and Muslims worked to bring about a cultural renaissance in their communities and a general awakening of the nation. The Brahma Samaj (Brahman Society) and Arya Samaj (Aryan Society) were foremost among Hindu organizations in reexamining and reforming traditional Hindu values, while the Aligarh Movement did the same for Islam. They all promoted education, a popular press, and social service. There was a new appreciation of traditional arts, and literature in many vernacular languages flourished. Despite excellent universities and schools, literacy remained low because of poverty and the high birthrate. Yet literacy did rise from 8 percent in 1931 to 12 percent in 1941.

Nationalist Opposition in Southeast Asia

In Burma (present-day Myanmar) as in India, the British faced mounting opposition to their continued imperial domination. Anti-British riots in the 1930s forced the British to separate Burma from India and to grant it limited autonomy. As the Japanese moved closer to occupying Burma during World War II, many Burmese nationalists sided with the Japanese, who, they mistakenly hoped, would grant them full independence.

Similarly, a robust nationalist movement developed in the Dutch East Indies, named Indonesia after independence. In 1908 a largely student-led cultural and religious society became the vanguard nationalist movement against the Dutch, who maintained a highly paternalistic regime there. In 1926 a Communist-led revolt shook Dutch complacency. This revolt was followed by the creation of the Indonesian Nationalist party (PNI) in 1927 by Achmed Sukarno (1901–1970), a Dutch-educated engineer who was known by the single name Sukarno. Like Gandhi in India, Sukarno advocated a policy of noncooperation with the Dutch, who responded by imprisoning him and other PNI leaders in 1929. Sukarno spent thirteen of the next fifteen years in exile or prison. In reaction to Dutch repression, many Indonesians welcomed the Japanese when they invaded the islands in 1941.

Early in the twentieth century, independence movements also emerged in French Indochina, especially in Vietnam. Vietnamese Communists, led by Ho Chi Minh and Vo Nguyen Giap, both committed Marxists, protested French domination. France crushed all pro-independence uprisings and imprisoned or exiled nationalist leaders. After the Japanese occupation in 1941, Ho and Giap organized guerrilla resistance against the Japanese. Later, they used these same techniques against French and U.S. forces. Although none of these movements succeeded, they laid the foundations for protracted but successful struggles for independence after World War II ended.

The Chinese Nationalists Triumph

By the late nineteenth century, many educated Chinese had concluded that, like the Japanese a generation earlier, they would have to adopt Western technology, science, government, and military techniques if the nation was to survive as an independent entity (see Chapter 13). As more Chinese went to the United States, Europe, and Japan to study, many were converted to work toward overthrowing the Manchu dynasty, now widely regarded as incapable of leading them to modern statehood.

Western-educated Dr. Sun Yat-sen (1867–1925) became the leader of an anti-Manchu republican movement that proclaimed a program for the regeneration of China called the Three People's Principles. The principles were nationalism (anti-Manchu dynasty and anti-Western imperialism), democracy, and people's livelihood (social reforms). An uprising in 1911 led to the abdication of the last Manchu boy emperor and the establishment of Asia's first republic. Sun served briefly as president of China, but, lacking a powerful military force, he and his revolutionary organization, renamed the *Kuomintang* (Nationalist party), were unable to hold power, and Sun was forced to resign in favor of a leading general.

The young Chinese republic soon fell into chaos as rival generals or warlords staked out their respective territorial domains, as had occurred after the fall of earlier powerful dynasties in China, and in India following the decline of the Moghul dynasty. The warlords were local leaders, who took advantage of the weakened Manchu dynasty and the infant republic to raise private armies with which they challenged the authority of any central government. Unlike previous eras of chaos, however, it was no longer sufficient

Sun Yat-sen's Formula for Revitalizing China

If we today want to restore the standing of our people, we must first restore our national spirit.... Therefore, ... besides arousing a sense of national solidarity uniting all our people, we must recover and restore our characteristic, traditional morality.... First comes loyalty and filial piety, then humanity and love, faithfulness and duty, harmony and peace.

What are the newest discoveries in the way of exercising popular sovereignty? First, there is suffrage, and it is the only method practised throughout the so-called advanced democracies.... The Second ... is the right of recall.... These two rights give the people control over officials and enable them to put all government officials in their positions or to remove them from their positions.... What powers must the people possess in order to control the laws? If the people think that a certain law would be of great advantage to them, they should

have the power to decide upon this law and turn it over to the government for execution. This third kind of popular power is called the initiative. If the people think that an old law is not beneficial to them, they should have the power to amend it and to ask the government to enforce the amended law.... This is called the referendum and is a fourth form of popular sovereignty.*

Sun Yat-sen was the founder of the Kuomintang and father of the Chinese republic. Educated in Honolulu and trained as a medical doctor in Hong Kong, Sun Yat-sen devoted his life to making a new China. His vision for China was to combine what he considered to be the best of its traditional morals and virtues with the best democratic methods of government that he had learned from the West.

*Sun Yat-sen, lecture 6, pp. 51–52, 143–145, in Sources of Chinese Tradition, ed. William T. de Bary (New York: Columbia University Press, 1960), pp. 771, 773–774.

for a charismatic leader to assume the mandate of heaven and create a new dynasty. An ideology that could lift China from impotence and fit it into the modern world had become essential. Sun Yat-sen had an attractive ideology but no army. Thus he had been powerless to oppose the warlords until he sought and received aid from the new Marxist government of the Soviet Union in 1923, on condition that he accept members of China's infant Communist party into his Kuomintang.

Although he advocated a moderate socialist approach to China's economic woes, Sun Yat-sen also sought to absorb the Chinese Communist party into his own. Because Sun died from cancer in 1925, it is uncertain whether he would have succeeded in the effort. After Sun's death, his brother-in-law (the two men had married sisters of the powerful Soong family), Chiang Kai-shek (1887–1975) became the leader of the Nationalist party. A professional military officer, Chiang was not so firmly committed to democratic institutions and socialism as his mentor had been. Between 1926 and 1928, Chiang built up a modern military force for the Kuomintang and led a military expedition that defeated many warlords and unified China.

Between 1928 and 1937, the Nationalist government modernized and expanded modern education and built industries, roads, and railways. It also implemented numerous reforms, including new legal codes that gave equality to women. The legal reforms were partially aimed at ending the extraterritorial rights wrested from China by imperialist nations on the grounds that Chinese legal codes did not conform with Western standards. The Nationalist government succeeded in regaining tariff autonomy and other

LIVES AND TIMES ACROSS CULTURES

Nontraditional Schools

Illiteracy has been widespread in poor, premodern nations. During the twentieth century, innovative programs to eradicate illiteracy and other social problems have been tried in China, India, and other countries.

In Ting Hsien (a county in North China near Peking) in the 1920s and 1930s, a successful experiment in mass literacy, improved public health services, and agricultural reform was led by American-educated James Yen and other idealistic men and women with various skills. Because there were few trained teachers in the villages, Yen and his associates promoted a system of "chain teaching" using the "little teacher" method. Their slogan was "each one teach one," whereby schoolchildren would go home and teach their family members. Older students were used as "student guides" or teacher's assistants. As Charles Hayford said in his book *To the People: James Yen and Village China:* "The approach was not to substitute raw talent and unfocused enthusiasm in the role of the professional, but to develop a system in which roles were carefully and creatively designed to be filled by the people available."

Ting Hsien was proclaimed a model county; its successful programs were emulated in other regions.

The experiment was halted by the Japanese invasion and World War II and ended after the Communist victory in China in 1949. In 1948 Yen persuaded the U.S. Congress to found the Sino-American Joint Commission on Rural Reconstruction. After 1949 the commission moved to Taiwan, where it oversaw many rural improvement projects and contributed to the Taiwanese "economic miracle." The Philippine government invited Yen to form the Philippines Rural Reconstruction Movement, which became the basis for the International Rural Reconstruction Movement that he headed in 1952.

In India after World War I, Mohandas K. Gandhi advocated "basic schools" in the villages to foster mass education; they were cheaper to establish and operate than conventional schools because they employed local people, who taught village children to read and write and to become skillful in useful, marketable crafts. Gandhi promoted basic schools and village industries to play complementary roles in uplifting the people. It is a testament to his foresight that basic schools continue to operate in every state in India.

concessions from Western nations. However, Great Britain, France, and the United States and increasingly powerful Japan refused to give up their remaining privileges.

The Twin Challenges of Communism and Japanese Imperialism

Although the Nationalist government had instituted some improvements for the middle and upper classes, it failed to implement the type of sweeping agrarian reforms necessary to improve the lot of the Chinese peasants. The Chinese Communists played upon these failures and gained peasant support by making violent and dramatic land reforms in areas they controlled, similar to the land reforms made during the early years of Communist power in the Soviet Union. The Kuomintang, determined to prevent the Chinese Communists from gaining power, empowered Chiang to launch all-out attacks on them.

In the 1930s a new leader emerged in the Chinese Communist movement. Unlike many Nationalist leaders and the founders of the Chinese Communist party, who came

Mao Tse-tung. A young Mao, left, led the Chinese Communists on the Long March to Yenan and subsequently to victory over the Chinese Nationalist government under Chiang Kai-shek.

Earl Leaf/Rapho

from middle-class families and had studied in the West or Japan, Mao Tse-tung (1893–1976) was the son of a wealthy farmer, had only attended normal school, and had not been educated in the West. Classical Marxism called for the urban proletariat to wrest power from the bourgeoisie, but China's urban proletariat was too small to play that role. Thus Mao argued that the peasants in China and other agrarian countries held the key to seizing political power.

By 1934, however, the Chinese Communists were clearly being defeated by Chiang. To escape destruction, Mao Tse-tung (Zedong) led the Communists on a 6,000-mile circuitous march from southern China to Yenan in the northwest. The Long March began with almost 100,000 people. One year later only about 20,000 were left, but they included Mao and other key leaders. It was a rare feat of survival and came to symbolize the Communist struggle against the Nationalists. The Communists survived in Yenan thanks to the difficult terrain of that isolated region, and, more importantly, the Sino-Japanese War that began in 1937.

Unlike China, Japan had successfully modernized and westernized its society and economy. It was the first and up to that time the only Asian country to transform itself into a powerful nation. Determined to prove its equality with Western nations, Japan embarked on expansion at the expense of its neighbors (see Chapter 13). By defeating China in 1895, Japan annexed its first colony, Taiwan (Formosa). After defeating Russia in 1905, Japan annexed Korea. When Western nations ceased expanding at China's expense, Japan stepped in to fill the vacuum. A weak and divided China was crucial to the Japanese imperialistic dream of expansion on the Asian continent. Conversely, the threat of Japanese imperialism drove the Kuomintang government to accelerate its program of uniting and strengthening China.

To forestall Chinese unity, Japan invaded and seized northeastern China (called Manchuria in the West) in 1931. Unable to resist Japan unaided, China appealed to the League of Nations and the United States for help, but in vain. Japanese military success in Manchuria doomed both parliamentary government in Japan (because Japanese civilian leaders were less imperialistic than the military but proved unable to control it) and the League of Nations as international peacekeeper. Ultimately, Japan's success encouraged Fascist Italy and Nazi Germany to flout the League of Nations in launching aggressions against other sovereign states.

Militarily, Chiang Kai-shek was correct when he maintained that weak China's only hope of successfully resisting Japan lay in first achieving domestic unity. Thus he saw the destruction of the remnant Communists as his first task; but public opinion was opposed to continuing a civil war in the face of the Japanese threat. The Nationalists were forced to call off the anticommunist campaign and forge a united front with the Chinese Communist party to resist Japan. To the Chinese Communists, war with Japan was their salvation, both because it would end the Nationalist attempt to eliminate them and because they knew that a prolonged war with Japan would weaken the Nationalist army and government.

Mao Explains the Global Nature of Communism

Comrade Norman Bethune, a member of the Communist Party of Canada, was around fifty when he was sent by the Communist Parties of Canada and the United States to China; he made light of travelling thousands of miles to help us in our War of Resistance Against Japan. He arrived in Yenan in the spring of last year [1938], went to work in the Wutai Mountains, and to our great sorrow died a martyr at his post. What kind of spirit is this that makes a foreigner selflessly adopt the cause of the Chinese people's liberation as his own? It is the spirit of internationalism, the spirit of communism, from which every Chinese Communist must learn....

We must unite with the proletariat of all the capitalist countries, with the proletariat of Japan, Britain, the United States, Germany, Italy and all other capitalist countries, for this is the only way to overthrow imperialism, to liberate our nation and people and to liberate the other nations and peoples of the world. This is our internationalism, the internationalism with which we oppose both narrow nationalism and narrow patriotism.*

In 1939, the Chinese Communist leader Mao Zedong gave a speech in memory of Norman Bethune, a Canadian doctor who had traveled to China to assist the Communist revolution. On this occasion, Mao emphasized the global aspects of the conflict in China.

*Mao Zedong, speech of December 21, 1939, in Selected Works of Mao Tse-tung, vol. 2 (Peking, 1965), pp. 337–338, reprinted in Modern Asia and Africa, ed. William H. McNeill and Mitsuko Iriye (New York: Oxford University Press, 1971), pp. 240–241.

After 1932 Japan's technologically superior armed forces seized additional territory in North China, and the military-dominated Japanese government became more aggressive toward the Chinese government. Japanese imperialism became the catalyst that fueled Chinese nationalism, while intensifying Chinese nationalism fueled Japanese militarists' demand for a full-scale war to subdue China before it succeeded in unifying. The all-out Japanese invasion of China in 1937 led the Nationalists and the Chinese Communists to abandon their civil war temporarily and form a united front against the Japanese. Japan initially expected to defeat China in six months. Despite heavy losses, China fought on. In 1941, the Sino-Japanese war became a part of World War II when Japan attacked the United States at Pearl Harbor and in the U.S.-held Philippines, as well as British and Dutch possessions in Asia.

A Changing Chinese Society

Much of the chaos China suffered in the nineteenth and early twentieth century seemed a repetition of earlier eras of dynastic change. However, a change in attitude toward science, technology, and values introduced by the West marked this period as different from previous eras.

The Beginning of Women's Emancipation

In my childhood I used to sleep in the same bed with my oldest sister. One night I was awakened by the sound of chirping sobs; I saw her sitting up with the quilt over her shoulders, holding her feet in her hands and weeping, her face streaked with tears. . . . I asked her what was wrong. She replied in a low voice, "My feet have been bound by Nanny Ho. Although during the day it makes walking difficult, I can still bear the pain. But at night my feet get hot under the quilt, and I can't sleep with the cutting pain. What am I to do?" . . .

At daybreak, I went to Mother's bedroom and tearfully told her about Elder Sister's suffering. I earnestly beseeched her to permit Sister to unbind her feet. I also vowed, "I would rather no one showed any interest in me all my life than try to curry favor injuring the body my parents gave me." . . .

My mother put on her clothes and got up out of bed. She patted me on the head and said with a nod, "What you say is quite right. Let's wait for the right opportunity."

Two years later, the American missionary Dr. Gilbert Reid founded the Society for Natural Feet in Shanghsien

Hall in Shanghai. My father was the first to support this, and he sent us the society's rules and regulations and its literature promoting natural feet. I was overjoyed and begged my mother to print hundreds of thousands of copies to distribute all over. I led my aunts and sisters in liberating their feet, and never tired of talking to anyone about the harmful effects of footbinding and the advantages of natural feet, as evident in all the advanced countries of the world.*

Chang Mo-chun (1884–1965) wrote this passage in her autobiography. The daughter of a prominent father and a poet mother, she, like all wealthy girls of her era, was expected to have her feet bound to make her attractive. Her revolt against the time-honored practice had her mother's passive and later her father's active support. Nevertheless, the moving force behind the "natural feet movement" was a U.S. missionary. Chang later joined Sun Yat-sen's anti-Manchu society, participated in the 1911 revolution, and had a long and distinguished career as a women's leader and educational administrator.

**Yu-ning Li, ed. Chinese Women through Chinese Eyes (Armonk, N.Y.: M. E. Sharpe, 1992), pp. 125–127.*

Western science and technology were irresistible, and China needed to master them to survive. But Western science and technology were premised on Western philosophy, institutions, and values, and China needed to learn them, too. When the 2,000-year-old imperial system collapsed, so did the Confucian philosophy that was its foundation. Although the Chinese often floundered about in their quest for a new and viable political system, all contenders ruled out a return to the monarchial past. Most articulate Chinese wished to establish a modern Western-style government; some advocated a Marxist-type government.

When the Confucian political system fell, so did the other foundations that Confucianism was built upon: submission of youth to age in a patriarchal family, and women to men in society. "Mr. Science" and "Mr. Democracy" became the catchwords of the educated young as they sought to adopt Western individualism and establish a modern civil society. A social and sexual revolution was beginning in China.

Since the nineteenth century, Christian missionaries had been busily trying to convert the Chinese, opening missions, schools, hospitals, and charitable establishments to do so. As in India, however, few Chinese converted to Christianity. Nonetheless, also as in India, Christian schools and hospitals revolutionized Chinese thinking and society. Christian missionaries opened the first schools for girls and spoke out against the ancient and pernicious custom of foot binding for middle- and upper-class girls. Earlier efforts by the Manchus had failed to persuade the Chinese to give up foot binding, but by the early twentieth century the "natural foot movement" was sweeping China.

Not surprisingly, Western-educated young men and women flocked to Sun Yat-sen's revolutionary movement. A women's battalion fought alongside men during the revolution in 1911. A women's delegation demanded equality at the first meeting of the parliament of the republic, but were denied a hearing. Nevertheless, the movement for equality gathered inexorable force, and women gained legal equality in the new codes promulgated in the 1930s; for example, daughters now had equal inheritance rights with sons. Men and women demanded and won the right to choose their marriage mates and the right to divorce them, and men were no longer allowed to take concubines.

By the early 1920s, almost all Chinese universities had become coeducational, and by the mid-1930s a quarter of college students were females. Increasing numbers of women entered government service, teaching, and the professions. As in India, a lively modern vernacular literature developed to reflect the changes in society. Western literature as well as scientific and technological works were translated into Chinese. Shanghai, the most cosmopolitan city, had a flourishing film industry.

The changes sponsored by the nationalist movement in China mostly affected a relatively small Western-educated or Western-influenced urban middle class. As in India, the new laws and ideas had little effect on the majority of the tradition-bound rural people. Nevertheless, in winning these rights and in obtaining economic independence in the modern cities, many young men and women in the middle class had freed themselves from dominance by the traditional patriarchal family, and as will be seen, they paved the way for more fundamental changes later.

The Soviet Union, 1917–1939

Down in front of the Soviet palace an autotruck was going to the front. Half a dozen Red Guards, some sailors, and a soldier or two, under command of a huge workman, clambered in and shouted to me to come along. . . . A three-inch cannon was loaded. . . . Occasionally a patrol tried to stop us. Soldiers ran out into the road before us, shouted "Stoi!" and threw up their guns.

We paid no attention. "The devil take you!" cried the Red Guards. "We don't stop for anybody! We're Red Guards!" and we thundered imperiously on.*

*John Reed, Ten Days That Shook the World (New York: Random House, 1960), pp. 308–309.

This description by the U.S. revolutionary John Reed captures some of the excitement and energy that spilled out into the streets of Petrograd, the Russian capital, during the 1917 revolution that swept the old regime from power and instituted massive revolutionary changes. The Russian Revolution was one of the major events of the twentieth century and was to have an enormous impact on much of the rest of the world.

Imperial Russia in the middle 1800s was an autocracy, an empire in which the tsar, or emperor, had total power with no restraint from a parliament or constitution. The tsar exercised authority through the nobility, whose wealth came from large estates worked by serfs. By the early nineteenth century, serfdom had disappeared in the rest of Europe but remained entrenched in Russia. As late as 1850, almost half of Russia's population lived in conditions close to those of slavery. Stung by the poor showing of serf-soldiers in the Crimean War and eager to avert a revolution, in 1861 Tsar Alexander II promulgated decrees that led to the emancipation of the serfs. Although liberated from servitude to their noble masters and allotted a small parcel of land, the newly freed slaves gained only limited freedom (as their activities were supervised) and they were burdened with heavy annual "redemption" payments to the government. Emancipation did not transform the peasants into contented, loyal citizens.

The Last Years of the Tsarist Regime

At the dawn of the twentieth century, Russia was the most politically authoritarian and economically backward of the great powers. The Romanov dynasty headed by Nicholas II (reigned 1894–1917) still regarded itself as a divine right monarchy, ruling with the help of a large bureaucracy and an army that could be used against rebellious subjects as well as against foreign enemies. A secret police that had made Siberia notorious as the site of Russian penal colonies kept down dissent.

The people of imperial Russia faced major problems in the last years before World War I. The peasant population increased more than 50 percent between 1861 and 1900, mostly as a consequence of the high birthrate and declining death rate. This meant a reduction in individual peasant land holdings, which were too small in the first instance to maintain a family adequately. In the latter stages of the nineteenth century, Russia experienced the growth of large-scale machine industry, resulting in the emergence of a small, urban working class. Since industrialization was new to Russia, its workers labored under conditions reminiscent of the early factories in Great Britain. In 1904–1905 Russia's imperial designs for expansion into eastern Asia culminated in a disastrous war against Japan, which brought the accumulated troubles to a head. As defeat followed defeat and evidence of inefficiency and corruption in high circles came to light, a wave of strikes, disturbances, and riots swept across the land and blossomed into a full-fledged revolt in 1905.

The tsarist government managed to restore order in the fall of 1905 after agreeing to make constitutional reforms. In October 1905, a month after the Treaty of Portsmouth ended the war with Japan, the tsar issued a manifesto that promised full civil liberties, a constitution, and the creation of a Duma—an elective legislature with the power to enact laws. The October Manifesto was supposed to transform autocratic Russia into a constitutional monarchy. But once the revolutionary crisis had passed, the government returned to its reactionary ways and restricted the authority of the Duma.

World War I hastened the decay that had been eating away at Russia for decades. As described in Chapter 13, the Germans inflicted several crushing defeats on the Russians and sent them reeling back into Russia. In the fall of 1915 Tsar Nicholas II unwisely took personal command of the Russian armies, marking him in the public eye as the cause of Russia's defeats. Effective control of the government fell into the hands of Empress Alexandra and her confidant, Gregory Rasputin, a dissolute and self-proclaimed holy man. Ministers were appointed and dismissed on a word from Rasputin, while inefficiency

Abdication of the Russian Throne

In the midst of the great struggle against a foreign foe, who has been striving for three years to enslave our country, it has pleased God to lay on Russia a new and painful trial. Newly popular disturbances in the interior imperil the successful continuation of the stubborn fight. The fate of Russia, the honor of our heroic army, the welfare of our people, the entire future of our dear land, call for the prosecution of the conflict, regardless of the sacrifices, to a triumphant end. The cruel foe is making his last effort and the hour is near when our brave army, together with our glorious Allies, will crush him.

In these decisive days in the life of Russia, we deem it our duty to do what we can to help our people to draw together and unite all their forces with the State Duma. We therefore think it best to abdicate the throne of the Russian State and to lay down the Supreme Power. Not wishing to be separated from our beloved son, we hand down our inheritance to our brother, Grand Duke Michael Alexandrovich, and give him our blessing on mounting the throne of the Russian Empire....

We call on all faithful sons of the Fatherland to fulfil their sacred obligations to their country by obeying the Tsar at this hour of national distress, and to help him and the representatives of the people to take the path of victory, well-being, and glory.

May the Lord God help Russia.
March 15, 1917, 3 P.M. *

Nicholas chose to abdicate out of patriotic motives: to avoid the disintegration of the Russian army, which would have led to a humiliating defeat. If his foremost concern had been to preserve his throne, he would have arranged a settlement with Germany and used his frontline troops to crush the internal disturbances. Nicholas also abdicated on behalf of his sick son, passing the crown to his brother Michael. The leaders of the Duma, however, warned Michael that if he accepted the throne a violent rising was certain to erupt and, without reliable troops on hand, they could not guarantee his personal safety. Thereupon Michael renounced the throne.

*"Abdication of The Tsar" in Frank A. Golder, ed., Documents of Russian History, 1914–1917, trans. Emanuel Aronsberg (New York: Century, 1927), pp. 296–297.

and corruption in government reached new heights. Fearful for the survival of the monarchy, three members of the high aristocracy murdered Rasputin in December 1916. But by then all public confidence in the tsar had disappeared.

The Provisional Government Succeeds the Tsar

Three years of war had shattered Russia's armies and devastated the home front. Enormous casualties, shortages of food, fuel, and housing, government inefficiency and corruption, and rumors of treason in high places had turned the people against the crown. On March 8, 1917, a spontaneous outbreak of strikes and riots convulsed the capital, now called Petrograd (the new name was meant to replace the German-sounding name of St. Petersburg). Troops ordered to fire upon the crowds chose instead to join them, and in succeeding days demonstrations against the government spread rapidly to other cities. Alone and helpless, Nicholas followed the advice of his generals and abdicated on March 15. Thus the long reign of the Romanovs ended abruptly in a leaderless and nearly bloodless revolution.

Nicholas was replaced by a provisional government, headed first by a liberal nobleman, Prince Georgi Lvov, and later by a moderate socialist, Alexander Kerensky. The new regime proclaimed civil liberties, announced plans for social reforms, and promised to summon a constituent assembly. It faced many massive problems, but two stood above the rest—the peasants' hunger for land and the nation's overwhelming desire for peace. Lacking clearheaded leadership, the provisional government failed to address the urgent domestic issues and thereby played into the hands of an emerging Marxist revolutionary group, the Bolsheviks, led by Vladimir Ilyich Ulyanov, better known by his underground alias, Lenin.

Lenin and the Bolsheviks Seize Power

The course of the revolution began to change when Lenin returned to Russia in mid-April 1917. A professional revolutionary since the 1880s, Lenin had spent the war years in exile in Switzerland. There he lived a miserable and lonely existence, all but abandoning hope that he would live to see a socialist state patterned on Marxist ideology. His opportunity came after the sudden fall of the imperial regime. Impatient to return to Russia, he received help from an unexpected source. The German High Command, calculating that Lenin's agitation would disrupt and weaken Russia's war effort, arranged to transport him in a sealed train through Germany and Scandinavia. Back in Russia, Lenin was soon joined by Leon Trotsky (1870–1940), as well as other fellow Marxists, whom the tsar had formerly imprisoned or forced to flee abroad.

The Bolsheviks were a small socialist group, but like the Jacobins in 1792, they alone, in the face of confusion and despair, had a clear program. In speech after speech, Lenin repeated the familiar themes of Marxism; under the benevolence of a Bolshevik regime, he promised, Russia would see the emergence of a new, happy society, resting upon equality, without rich or poor. His promise of land, peace, and bread—three things that the provisional government had been unable to provide—had a wide appeal to the land-hungry peasants, the soldiers sick of the war, and the workers threatened with starvation. Throughout the summer of 1917, the Bolsheviks increased their party membership and gained control of the revolutionary councils, or soviets, in Petrograd, Moscow, and other cities and towns. Spontaneously created at the local, provincial, and national levels, the soviets consisted of elected delegates representing soldiers, workers, and peasants. As the war continued to go badly and conditions at home worsened, Lenin demanded that power be transferred to the soviets, which he claimed, with justification, were more representative of the people than the provisional government. Of course, Lenin realized that his party's only chance to gain control of the government was to use force. While he laid plans for an armed insurrection, his lieutenants organized a workers' militia called the Red Guards in Petrograd and other cities.

The Bolshevik takeover proved relatively easy, given the weakness of the provisional government. On the evening of November 6, the Red Guards, supported by sympathetic regular army units, quietly seized railroad and communication centers, post offices, electric power plants, and other key points in Petrograd. At noon the next day they stormed the Winter Palace, seat of the provisional government, and arrested or put to flight all the cabinet ministers. Kerensky escaped in a car borrowed from the U.S. embassy and eventually settled as an exile in the United States. In less than a day the Bolsheviks had successfully carried out their revolution with a minimum of bloodshed.

On the afternoon of November 7, Lenin announced to the National Congress of Soviets (representing local councils from all over the country) in Petrograd that he was transferring sovereignty to that body. Lenin's seemingly selfless display was a mask for his real objective, the dictatorship of the Bolshevik party. He maneuvered the Congress into accepting the Council of Peoples' Commissars as the executive of the new government.

Lenin Speaks. V. I. Lenin addresses a rally in Moscow in 1917. In later years Communists, like other totalitarian parties, organized large-scale parades and public spectacles as expressions of solidarity and loyalty to the party.

The Bolsheviks occupied the top positions in the council. Lenin took the post of chairman with Trotsky in charge of foreign affairs and Joseph Stalin (1879–1953) as commissar for national minorities. Lenin pledged to build a socialist state and to end the war with Germany.

The Bolshevik Regime, 1918–1924

In the first months, the Bolsheviks built the rudiments of a new order, while struggling to hold on to power. A series of decrees nationalized the economy, distributed confiscated land to the peasants, and turned over management of mines and factories to the workers. All imperial institutions were dismantled, and a venomous campaign was unleashed against the church, which the Bolsheviks regarded as an ally of the tsar and an enemy of change. The debts incurred by the tsarist administration were repudiated to the fury of foreign governments that had provided funds to Russia before and during the war.

Confident that a majority of the public would confirm their policies, the Bolsheviks allowed elections for a constituent assembly to be held. To their shock and disbelief, their main adversaries, the Social Revolutionaries, won twice as many seats as they did. But Lenin and his associates had come too far to be thwarted by a mere popular verdict. When the constituent assembly met in January 1918, Bolshevik troops disbanded it as part of a calculated policy to establish a one-party dictatorship. Combating all counter-revolutionary activity was the newly established secret police, familiarly called the Cheka (later known by other names, including the KGB), which would become a dreaded symbol of Bolshevik oppression.

Next to staying in power, Lenin's most cherished goal was to conclude hostilities with Germany. In December 1917 he opened peace negotiations with the Germans, who, realizing Russia's helplessness, demanded, among other things, Finland, Ukraine, Poland, and the Baltic provinces—more than a million square miles of territory, including a quarter of Russia's population, a third of its arable land, and much of its natural resources. Lenin balked at making such concessions, but the resumption of the German advance, coupled with the disintegration of the Russian army, left him no option but to yield. The treaty signed at Brest-Litovsk in March 1918 was a harbinger of the fate of the Allies had they lost the war.

Lenin was not overly troubled at the exorbitant price of peace, trusting that a socialist revolution would soon spread to Germany and invalidate the treaty. But real peace, which Lenin needed to consolidate his regime at home, would prove elusive. No sooner did hostilities against Germany end than Russia sank into civil war.

As 1918 wore on, groups hostile to the Bolsheviks, who now called themselves Communists, emerged from every quarter of Russia. These counterrevolutionaries, collectively called "Whites," were led by former tsarist officers and included members of the outlawed nobility, former landowners, supporters of the tsar, and rival revolutionary parties. The Allies intervened in the civil war. The Japanese occupied Russia's far eastern provinces, while the French, Americans, and British sent supplies as well as troops to aid the White forces. The Allies were eager to see the Whites win, not only to prevent the spread of communism but also because they hoped that under different leadership Russia would reenter the war. To meet the new danger, the Communists hastily formed the Red Army in the summer of 1918. Under the leadership of Trotsky, now war commissar, it became a well-organized and disciplined fighting force.

The conflict was the bloodiest phase of the revolution, with neither side asking or giving quarter and both sides committing the most gruesome atrocities. Although close to defeat in the early stages of the conflict, the Red Army reversed the tide and succeeded in defeating its enemies one by one, until by 1920 its victory was assured. A number of factors enabled the Communists to triumph over seemingly hopeless odds. The Whites were unable to cooperate effectively with each other, partly because of deep political differences and partly because their forces, moving in from the periphery, were separated by vast distances. By contrast, the Communists, single-minded in their sense of purpose, had the advantage of interior lines that allowed them to shift troops rapidly from one front to the other. Finally, the Allies gave the White elements only halfhearted support. Once Germany was beaten, they were less concerned about what kind of regime ruled Russia and withdrew their troops in 1920, except for the Japanese, who stayed in western Siberia until 1922.

The Communists were equally successful in crushing political opposition in the territory under their control. Following a failed attempt to assassinate Lenin, the Communists initiated a "Red Terror" to eliminate suspected counterrevolutionaries and terrorize the rest into accepting their rule. The Cheka, repeating the worst excesses of the French Revolution, brutally carried out its task, summarily executing anyone known or suspected of being hostile to the revolution. The most famous victims were the former tsar, Nicholas II, and his entire family, who were executed in Ekaterinburg. All other political parties were outlawed so that no organized opposition could develop. The Communists had converted Russia into a one-party dictatorship.

At the end of the civil war, the Communists faced probably their most severe crisis. The ravages of a disastrous general war, two revolutions, and a savage civil war were followed by a severe famine. Lenin and his colleagues had exacerbated the hardships during the civil war by seeking to socialize the economy and requisitioning food from the peasants. In most industries and mines, chaos resulted because workers lacked experience in management. The output fell until by 1921 it was only 17 percent of the 1913 level. Many workers moved from cities to rural areas seeking work. Agricultural production also experienced a sharp decline. The practice of requisitioning food so alienated the peasants that many grew only enough food for their own immediate needs. By 1921 only about 62 percent of the farmland was under cultivation. Shortages of grain and manufactured articles caused prices to rise inordinately. Transportation broke down, and the value of exports shrank to a fraction of the 1917 level. Russia, it seemed, was on the verge of a complete collapse.

A mutiny by the sailors at Kronstadt, once the shock troops of the revolution, induced the pragmatic Lenin to make an ideological retreat. In 1921 he adopted the New Economic Policy, better known by its initials as NEP, which was a compromise

Map 14.2 Union of Soviet Socialist Republics (USSR). Under the 1924 constitution, the USSR became a federated nation of republics that, in fact, had exceedingly limited autonomy. This map shows the various republics with Russia as the dominant power.

between socialist and capitalist practices. Lenin spoke of it as "a step back in order to go forward," a temporary measure that would be abandoned as soon as the economy stabilized. Under the NEP the state retained control over large industries, transportation, and foreign trade. It did, however, permit private local trade and restored small shops and factories to their former owners. A fixed tax in kind replaced the forcible requisitioning of produce and allowed the peasants to sell their surplus crops on the open market. Concessions were offered to foreign entrepreneurs to exploit mines and oil wells in Russia. By 1927 these measures had restored output in both agricultural and nonagricultural areas to prewar levels. Without the NEP it is doubtful that the Communist revolution would have survived.

While coping with a myriad of problems, the Communists formalized their authoritarian rule in the constitution of 1924. The Soviet Union, or Union of Soviet Socialist Republics (USSR), officially came into being as a federated union consisting of territories, regions, nominally autonomous states, and republics. Originally there were four republics, with Russia the largest and most influential; the number would rise to eleven by 1936, either by carving states out of Russia or by upgrading autonomous areas.

Under a veneer of democratic procedures, the Soviet Union was in fact a dictatorship. The constitution granted the franchise to all productive workers over age eighteen but not to the bourgeoisie or to those closely identified with tsarism and the church. Despite the election of various soviets, congresses, and committees, real power rested with the Politburo, the high command of the Communist party, which made all the major policy decisions for both the party and the government.

The Deadly Struggle for the Succession to Lenin

On January 21, 1924, at about the same time the constitution was promulgated, Lenin died after a series of paralytic strokes that had left him incapacitated. Because Lenin had not designated a successor, a desperate power struggle ensued between Trotsky and Stalin, two of his chief associates. Both men were ardent revolutionaries, but they differed on matters of policy. For example, Trotsky stood for an unceasing effort to promote revolutionary uprisings throughout the world, whereas Stalin maintained that communism must consolidate its power at home before it could be established elsewhere. A gifted orator, intellectually brilliant and idealistic, Trotsky enjoyed a popularity with the public that was second only to Lenin's. Abler than his rival, he disdained petty backstairs maneuvering, and his aloof manner, interpreted as arrogance, often offended his comrades.

Stalin lacked polish and formal education, but he was relentless and cunning, excelled as an infighter, and profited from his position as general secretary of the Communist party. As such, he was able to place his henchmen in key positions so that he essentially controlled the party apparatus by the time Lenin died. Stalin emerged victorious and had Trotsky expelled from the Politburo and the party. Forced to leave the Soviet Union in 1929, Trotsky entered a period of exile that would take him to distant Mexico, where he was assassinated in 1940 by a Stalinist agent.

The Stalin Dictatorship

Stalin's triumph ended whatever democratic practices had existed in the Communist party and government. Lenin had sanctioned police-state methods as a means of survival, but he had permitted freedom of discussion within the party itself. Stalin wanted no rivals who might challenge his scheme to transform the political structure of the country into a personal dictatorship. By a most skillful and ruthless campaign, he forced old Bolshevik adversaries out of key positions and replaced them with his followers in the Politburo, in the party organizations in the cities, and in the organs of the central government. Thereafter, Stalin's advance toward complete authoritarianism was unstoppable.

Stalin proposed to use his power to transform his backward, agricultural nation into a modern industrial state. Lenin had been forced to retreat from socializing the economy because of the chaos of the civil war. Although the NEP had rescued the Soviet Union from a major economic crisis, Stalin remained committed to the old Communist dream of effacing capitalism. In the process he altered the daily life of the Soviet people to a far greater extent than did the first Bolshevik revolution.

In 1928 Stalin marked the end of the NEP by launching the first of three Five-Year Plans. Their object was to eliminate all elements of capitalism, increase agricultural production through mechanized collective farming, and develop large-scale industries. Implementing the first goal meant dispossessing the property of the *kulaks* (prosperous, landowning peasants) and the *nepmen*, who operated small businesses. Simultaneously, the Communists undertook to merge the many small holdings into mechanized state-run farms that were expected to increase productivity significantly. Peasants relocated on the collectives were to share in the profits according to their original (forced) contribution in land and livestock as well as the amount and quality of their work. By and large, though, the peasants cherished their own plots of land and wanted no part of collectivization. Pandemonium broke out in the countryside. Many were killed outright or sent off to forced-labor camps in Siberia. Nevertheless, peasants continued to resist collectivization by burning their crops, smashing their equipment, and destroying their livestock. By 1933 agricultural production had actually declined, and the total number of cattle, sheep, and goats had fallen to half of the 1928 level. In that half-decade, executions and deportations, together with a severe famine, had claimed no fewer than 5 million lives.

The drive to expand Russia's industrial output was more successful. Production quotas were fixed, and plans were laid to accelerate mining operations, extend or improve railways, and rapidly construct power plants, refineries, large factories, and steel mills. The emphasis was on heavy industry, not consumer goods. Such difficulties as shortages of workers, inexperienced management, inadequate equipment, and an inefficient transportation system prevented some of the government's objectives from being met. Even so, between 1928 and 1939 overall production rose sevenfold, a phenomenal achievement. On the eve of World War II, the Soviet Union ranked third among the world's industrial powers, behind only the United States and Germany. Yet Soviet industrial expansion was achieved at a heavy cost. To fund the acquisition of technical expertise and heavy equipment from the West, the government kept workers' wages low and exported grain at the expense of its ill-fed and often starving population.

The imposition of a socialized economy enabled the state to tighten its grip on the masses. But the hardships caused by Stalin's program provoked opposition even from within his own party. Beginning in 1934, Stalin undertook sweeping purges of his opponents, real or imagined. After initially targeting potential political rivals and other Communist bosses, the purge extended down to the lower ranks of the party and ultimately spread to virtually all branches of government, the army, and the secret police itself. By 1939 millions had been executed, jailed, or sent to forced-labor camps. With the elimination of all rivals, Stalin had cemented his power.

At the height of the terror in 1936, Stalin promulgated a new Soviet constitution that guaranteed universal suffrage, the secret ballot, and freedom of speech, assembly, and the press. As a piece of propaganda, it was very effective, fooling Western liberals ready to be duped. In reality, the new constitution marked no change from Stalin's rule of force. The existence of a one-party system obviously precluded the establishment of democracy.

Life and Culture in the Soviet Union

The creation of a new classless society along Marxian lines meant a repudiation of traditional religious values and social institutions. Once in firm control, the Communists tried to destroy the Russian Orthodox church. They closed churches, confiscated church property, persecuted the clergy, decreed that only civil marriages were legal, forbade religious instruction in schools, and encouraged atheism. But in time it became apparent that the antireligious campaign was counterproductive. Most Russians, especially peasants, were devout Orthodox Christians or affiliated with other religions. Stalin relaxed his campaign in the mid-1930s, in part because he needed the support of the Christian West.

From the beginning, the Bolsheviks aimed to achieve a classless society, rewarding each "according to his needs." That philosophy did not survive the first Five-Year Plan, because economic equality robbed workers of all incentive and kept able individuals from accepting positions of responsibility. The Communists were compelled to return to some of the bourgeois values they had previously denounced. Wage differentials were introduced with factory managers, engineers, and scientists receiving preferential treatment. Even among ordinary workers, those who were especially productive were rewarded with higher wages and paid vacation trips.

Although Soviet society embraced aspects of capitalism, it did develop distinctive features of its own. While the standard of living for workers was far below that of their counterparts in the industrialized West, the Soviet government was unique in guaranteeing the right of employment. The state also provided extensive welfare programs such as free medical care and nurseries for children of working mothers and subsidized housing and food. An extensive program of compulsory free education covering all levels was launched in 1928; it reduced illiteracy from about two-thirds to a fifth of the population. The quality of education was uneven, however. Soviet universities produced good scientists and engineers, but courses in the liberal arts were peppered with propaganda, and the truth was often deliberately distorted. As proponents of equality between the sexes, the Communists granted women the franchise as well as equal educational and professional opportunities. Although women worked in all occupations—from street cleaner to scientist—they rarely reached the highest political or economic positions.

As in education, the Soviet government controlled the arts in order to shape the fundamental beliefs of its subjects. Artists, writers, and composers were expected to conform to Marxian ideology, to serve the interests of the party, and to integrate their work into the everyday lives of the masses. "Art belongs to the people," Lenin remarked; "it must have its deepest roots in the broad masses of the workers. It must be understood and loved by them." Few well-known artists and writers of the older generation were prepared to come to terms with the Communists; most of the disillusioned allowed their creative talents to languish or went into exile. But young artists, who shared the utopian revolutionary zeal of the new regime, put on poetry readings and concerts for workers and created artistic works that extolled revolutionary heroes or glorified the social aims of the government. By and large the literature, art, and music produced, particularly under Stalin, tended to be for propaganda effect and had little creative value.

Soviet Foreign Policy

When the Bolsheviks toppled the provisional government in 1917, they expected anticapitalist revolutions to break out in Europe within a matter of months. As Marxists, they believed in the inevitability of world revolution and in the triumph of the proletariat. Accordingly, they took steps to exploit the unrest caused by the war, inspiring a few futile social uprisings in central Europe. In March 1919 they founded the Third Internationale, known thereafter as the Comintern, which eventually included Communist parties from various parts of the world. With headquarters in Moscow, its avowed purpose was to promote and direct revolutions throughout the world. But the Western democracies survived the trials of the immediate postwar period, and world revolution failed to materialize. The Comintern's policy of subversion only served to create fear abroad and to make the Soviet Union a pariah among nations.

After the advent of the NEP, the Soviet Union adopted a more conciliatory attitude toward the West. Since the Soviet economy could not recover without foreign trade and capital, the Communist leaders were anxious to resume normal relations with the rest of the world. The Western powers, wanting to believe that the new Soviet regime was about to revert to capitalism, responded positively to the friendly overtures. In the early 1920s Russia signed commercial treaties with such countries as Poland, Turkey, and Great Britain. By 1924 most of the powers had recognized the Soviet Union, although the United States held back until 1933.

Cooperation between the Soviet Union and the West broadened after 1928. The success of the first Five-Year Plan depended heavily on Western equipment, machines, and technical experts. The rising threat of Japan and Nazi Germany was another factor in pushing the Soviet Union closer to the Western democracies. To promote friendly relations, Stalin stressed the idea of conciliation rather than world revolution and clamped down on the activities of the Comintern. In 1934 the Soviet Union was admitted into the League of Nations, and the following year it concluded military agreements with France and Czechoslovakia. But the outward collaboration did not dissipate the distrust between the capitalistic states and the Soviet Union. The ideological differences separating them were too great to be bridged by trade agreements or alliance treaties.

Twentieth-Century Scientific, Technological, and Economic Developments

I vow to strive to apply my professional skills only to projects which, after conscientious examination, I believe to contribute to the goal of co-existence of all human beings in peace, human dignity and self-fulfilment.

I believe that this goal requires the provision of an adequate supply of the necessities of life (good food, air, water, clothing and housing, access to natural and man-made beauty), education, and opportunities to enable [people] . . . to work out for [themselves] . . . [their] life objectives and to develop creativeness and skill in the use of hands as well as head.

I vow to struggle through my work to minimise danger; noise; strain or invasion of privacy of the individual; pollution of earth, air or water; destruction of natural beauty, mineral resources and wildlife.*

*Meredith Thring, "Scientist Oath," in New Scientist (1971), reprinted in From Creation to Chaos: Classic Writings in Science, ed. B. Dixon (Oxford: Blackwell, 1989), p. 220.

The sentiments expressed in this scientist's version of the Hippocratic oath of medical doctors are certainly praiseworthy, and modern science may rightfully claim to have alleviated much human misery. But science in the twentieth century has also made it possible to unleash previously unimagined destructive forces, such as the atomic bomb, nerve gas, and biological weapons. And, by probing the mysteries of life itself, "genetic engineers" have not only opened new vistas for good, but also posed difficult moral and ethical questions. In short, those who have made the crucial scientific and technological advances in this century have not always had the goals of the "scientist oath" in the fore-front of their minds. The repercussions of these advances—for good and for ill—have been profound.

Despite such catastrophes as World Wars I and II, the Great Depression, and the Cold War, there has been outstanding material progress in the present century. The overall economic trend for industrialized, high-income nations has risen to a level of affluence unmatched in history. Scientific and technological advances have yielded a productive capacity unequaled in quantity, intricacy, or quality. Socially, new wealth and the new technology have brought unprecedented levels of health, education, and material welfare to those who can afford it.

This section surveys the progress of knowledge in several branches of scientific study. It also looks at technological advances of the twentieth century and the economic and social changes they have entailed.

Scientific Advances in the Age of Einstein

The scientific achievements of the past century have been enormous. Scientists have split the atom and probed the depths of the human psyche, speculated on the evolution of the universe and learned many of the secrets of life itself. Like the age of Isaac Newton, the century of Albert Einstein has impressively expanded understanding of our world, par-ticularly in the fields of physics and astronomy.

Physicists in the twentieth century have uncovered many mysteries and have begun at least to formulate some answers. Even before 1900, for example, scientific experiments raised seemingly unanswerable questions about the nature of light. Light behaved some-times as waves, sometimes as though it were quanta (a series of separate pulses of energy). Similar challenges to common sense resulted from exploration of the phenome-non of radiation. In her experiments with radium, Marie Curie (1867–1934) discovered that this rare element lost weight as it gave off radiant energy. Mass was being converted into energy; this defied the traditional scientific distinction between the material and the immaterial.

The theory of relativity proposed by Albert Einstein (1879–1955) challenged scientific common sense even further. Einstein insisted that physical phenomena were not absolute, independent entities, but were relative to one another. The basic nature of any-thing, he asserted, is fundamentally determined by its relationships to other things. He defined a four-dimensional space-time continuum with length, breadth, depth, and a "fourth dimension"—time.

Physicists formulated broad new conclusions about the relationships of matter and energy. They discovered, for example, that the "indivisible" atom is really composed of still smaller particles, called protons, neutrons, and electrons. Subsequent research multi-plied the kinds of particles and offered a much more complex image of their motions; this made the billiard-ball atomic models of the seventeenth century and the crude philosophical materialism of the nineteenth look very simplistic indeed.

The Newtonian vision of a single law of gravity has also been upset by twentieth-century scientists. Einstein suggested that gravity is not a force of attraction linking any two objects but a field of forces through which objects move. This gravitational field affects the motions, not only of material things, but of such manifestations of pure energy as light itself. The work of Curie and others on radiation made it clear that gravity was not the only fundamental force affecting the behavior of the universe. In this century, three basic forces have in fact been distinguished: gravity, the "strong force" holding the atomic nucleus together, and the "electro-weak force" revealed in electromagnetism and radioactivity. The formulation of a "unified field" theory that would reduce these three governing forces to a single underlying principle has been a great, elusive goal of modern physics.

Twentieth-century astronomers have greatly expanded our detailed knowledge of the universe, in part through the development of new instruments for probing the farthest reaches of space. Bigger and better telescopes, including ones stationed in space (outside the earth's atmosphere), gathered in the light of distant, previously undetected stars. After many initial problems that were corrected in a record-setting five days of repairs by crews operating in space, the Hubble Space Telescope in 1994 permitted scientists to see farther into space than ever before and has continued to expand and enrich our knowledge since.

In the aftermath of the Cold War, international, cooperative space probes and shuttles including crews of Americans, Russians, Europeans, Saudi Arabian, and other experts have continued to provide new information about the universe. Many women scientists and astronauts are leaders in these exciting new fields of exploration; in the United States Space program (NASA) women hold key leadership and administrative roles.

Spectroscopes make possible the analysis of light to determine the elemental composition of stars. Radio astronomy facilitates the study of radiation outside the visible spectrum. Space probes took human beings to the moon and have transported cameras to other planets to collect photographic data.

Astronomers have mapped the outer reaches of space and analyzed the flaming interiors of stars. They have discovered that the cosmos is composed of immense collections of millions of stars called galaxies and proposed such intriguing possibilities as "black holes"—burned-out stars with gravitational fields so strong that nothing, not even light, can escape from them.

New cosmological theories about the origin, history, and ultimate fate of the universe have also emerged. The "big bang" theory, for example, asserts that perhaps 15 billion years ago all the matter and energy in the universe was condensed in a single, unimaginably dense "cosmic fireball." This ball then exploded, producing the big bang with which the universe as we know it was born. The history of the cosmos since has been the story of the expansion and cooling of the fragments of matter and energy thus unleashed. Some scientists believe that the expanding universe will gradually run out of energy, until all the stars are burnt out and the cosmos itself is left dead and cold. Others foresee gravity slowly reining in the scattered fallout from the primal explosion and pulling it all back together again. This may in turn be followed by another big bang and another expansion and contraction; ours may thus be a "pulsating" universe, cyclically reborn again and again.

Major Trends in Biology, Anthropology, and Psychology

Charles Darwin's theory of biological evolution through natural selection remains central to twentieth-century biology. However, biologists have modified Darwin's basic evolutionary theory (see Chapter 12); some have argued that evolution is not a process of small changes adding up to large transformations over long periods, but rather of relatively rapid change interspersed with long, static periods of little change in any given species. Botanists and zoologists, especially those seeking to increase and improve the world's food supply, have accelerated the "natural selection" process. Hybrid corn, for example, now produces more than twice the yield in a shorter growing season than was possible fifty years ago.

Major new biological discoveries are revealing much about the genetic base of life and the ecological interaction of many species in a system of related life forms. At the microscopic level, biologists discovered DNA (deoxyribonucleic acid), which controls the chromosomes composing the nucleus of the living cell. DNA molecules twisted around each other in a complicated "double helix" pattern, program living tissue to develop and reproduce itself through cell division—that is, to perform all the basic processes of life. Among the results of the Human Genome Project will be a better understanding of the genetic origins of disease and clues to their cures.

At a different level of organization of life, ecologists have studied how species of animals and plants interact with each other and with other aspects of their common environment. Through their discoveries of the interrelatedness of all living matter, ecologists have warned that what humans do to their common environment profoundly affects the lives of other species on the planet.

The science of anthropology developed in the wake of Charles Darwin's discoveries about human biology. Physical anthropologists study the biological differences among the racial subdivisions of the human species. Cultural anthropologists investigate the beliefs and ways of life of peoples who lived in older and simpler forms of society. Some anthropologists work with archaeologists and biologists to learn about our prehistoric ancestors; by piecing together bits of bone and crude stone tools, they have reconstructed the story of early human life on earth. Investigators like the Leakey family— Louis, Mary, and their son Richard—accumulate evidence on the nature and development of prehistoric humanity, and have proved that the human race and its precursors goes back millions of years.

Some anthropologists did field work by living with the isolated, technologically primitive peoples they were studying in order to understand them better and to learn about cultural evolution. Margaret Mead (1901–1978), for example, became famous for her observations about adolescent sexuality and guilt-free sexual practices in some South Pacific island societies. Some anthropologists have also applied their findings to more "advanced" societies, as Mead did when she wrote about the generation gap in the contemporary United States.

Anthropologists seek to judge each society or culture by its own standards, rather than by any supposedly universal set of standards. They contribute to an attitude of cultural relativism now widespread among serious students of history. Many anthropologists argue that norms of right and wrong are specific to a given society, and that cultures and peoples have different but equally valid standards of behavior.

Sigmund Freud (1856–1939), the founder of psychoanalysis, and Ivan Pavlov (1849–1936), the pioneer of behaviorism, originated theories and procedures that provided a fundamental basis for the science of psychology in the twentieth century. Freud explained that all human attitudes and actions are rooted in the unconscious mind. The basic human drive, he believed, is libido, controlling not only the sexual instinct but also a broad range of human desires. Freud further developed and applied his ideas of unconscious instincts shaping thoughts and behavior, and postulated not one but two basic human impulses, a life-affirming urge related to the libido, and a "death instinct" that could drive the human race to destroy itself in holocausts like the First World War. Freud also applied his theories to the most fundamental achievements of the past, explaining religion and civilization itself as products of psychological needs and conflicts.

Several disciples of Freud's developed their own psychological theories, explaining behavior by other unconscious instincts than those Freud had proposed. Alfred Adler (1870–1937), for instance, saw an aggressive urge to achieve superiority as the central human motive and explained many psychological problems as the result of "inferiority complexes." Carl Jung (1875–1961) developed such basic psychological types as "introvert" and "extrovert" and found deep psychological meaning in the symbols of the great world religions. Others, like Freud's daughter, Anna Freud (1895–1982), and Melanie Klein (1882–1960), applied Freudian doctrines to new areas such as the psychoanalysis of children.

The chief rival of Freudianism was the behaviorist school founded by the Russian psychologist Ivan Pavlov (1849–1930). Pavlov and his successors, particularly the American B. F. Skinner (1904–1990), explored their subject not in the psychiatrist's office, but in laboratories. They maintained that human actions, like those of other animals, were caused by "conditioned reflexes." Behavior that earns rewards—from nature, from society, from the authority figures of laboratory experimenters—tends to be repeated to earn further rewards. Behavior met by punishment tends not to be repeated and soon disappears. Child rearing, commercial advertising, and government propaganda all depend on such conditioning to manipulate human behavior. For behavioral psychologists, free will is a delusion, and human conduct (response) is shaped not by unconscious instincts but by the conditioning impact (stimulus) of the external environment.

New Trends in Technology

Underlying the fluctuations in economic prosperity and the new forms of economic organization in this century was the accelerating advance of technology, especially in heavy industry. Even before 1900, iron and coal were giving way to steel and petroleum as the essential materials of industrialization. Steamships and railroads continued to be the most important means of transportation until World War II, but from then on, automobiles, trucks, and airplanes increasingly replaced them.

Important breakthroughs in manufacturing included the assembly line, automation, and the use of efficiency studies to increase productivity. Henry Ford (1863–1947) used assembly lines to great advantage in his automobile factories. By the 1980s, computer electronics made it possible to put entire manufacturing facilities under robotic controls, all but eliminating the human industrial worker. Efficiency studies, pioneered by Frederick Taylor early in the century, detected wasted time and motion in the plant or office, showing where improvements could be made. All of these developments speeded up the processes of industrial production, making goods less expensive to manufacture and more affordable to purchase.

Americans and Russians became the global leaders in heavy industry. The United States led in the production of oil, steel, and other heavy industrial products for more than half the century. Cities like Pittsburgh and Detroit became internationally known for their steel mills and automobile factories, and forests of oil derricks put Texas on the industrial map. The Soviet Union developed heavy industries after 1928 principally through the large-scale, centralized state planning that was the core of the Soviet system. Hydroelectric dams and industrial complexes like Magnetogorsk, Russia's "steel city," sprang up in impressive numbers beginning in the 1930s. Industrialization also changed the architectural face of modern cities, as twentieth-century builders used structural steel, poured concrete, and plate glass, combined with the electric elevator, to fill cities with skyscrapers.

A Ford Model T. Mass-produced automobiles like this famous Ford car gave middle-class Americans a new freedom of movement in the 1920s. These women have paused in their touring to draw water from a well, perhaps to replenish the auto's radiator.

The development of efficient agricultural equipment—the tractor and various harvesting machines—proceeded rapidly in the twentieth century. The use of chemical fertilizers and insecticides and the perfection of new and inexpensive varieties of seeds produced hardier, more abundant crops, to the point that we may speak of a "green revolution."

Technology brought remarkable transformations in the manufacture of food products and clothing, household implements, and recreational devices. Useful objects of all sorts were now made of plastics (complex organic compounds produced by polymerization), and a broad range of clothing was woven of synthetics or of a mix of synthetic and natural fibers. These artificial "raw materials" enabled manufacturers of consumer goods to fabricate products with the durability, toughness, resistance to heat, and other properties that met the demands of increasingly selective consumers. In western Europe, Japan, and the United States, the new consumer technology produced a culture of waste. Cheap discardable items such as tin, glass, paper, and plastic created a "throw-away" economy.

Twentieth-century technology made a host of labor-saving household appliances commonplace. Though invented earlier, both gas and electric ovens first came into wide use after World War I. Electric washing machines, vacuum cleaners, refrigerators, and freezers (and thus frozen foods) were more recent inventions. Telephones were invented as early as 1876, but were not widely available until after 1900.

The automobile was made economically available to the masses through Henry Ford's assembly-line manufacturing techniques after 1908. In 1913, a million cars were on American roads; by 1970, over a hundred million. Goods were delivered by trucks over networks of highways, and developers laid out business districts and residential areas on the assumption that shoppers and homeowners would own automobiles.

In the affluent West, luxury recreational or entertainment items became virtual necessities. Motion picture theaters spread to countless cities and even small towns beginning in the 1920s. Millions of families bought radios during the first half of the century and televisions in the second half. Whole industries, such as those devoted to musical records, tapes, and compact disks, have grown up to satisfy the demands of consumers for entertainment. The United States has been the leader in mass production of consumer goods, although today Japan, western Europe, and the Pacific rim area are striving to overtake it.

Technology advanced at a much faster rate in the twentieth century than in earlier ages. Individual inventions, small in themselves—like the vacuum tube or the microchip—had remarkable consequences in many fields, and the science fiction of earlier times became the hard science of the present.

Medical scientists, building on such earlier discoveries as anesthetics, antiseptics, and the microbe theory of the causation of disease, carried both surgical and chemical medicine to unprecedented levels. Researchers discovered vaccines for yellow fever, tuberculosis, diphtheria, polio, measles, and other diseases. Vitamins and the science of human nutrition provided cures for rickets, beriberi, and similar disorders. Sulfa, penicillin, and many other antibiotic "wonder drugs" saved countless lives.

Surgery also made astonishing advances. The use of X rays greatly improved diagnostic methods, and radiation treatment for various forms of cancer is common. Tissue and organ transplant surgery and the use of surgical lasers became commonplace. Medical scientists devised and improved mechanical support systems for failing lungs, livers, and hearts.

From the 1980s onward, the computer revolution has ushered in major changes in communications, business practices, and human interactions. Computers operate much more rapidly than the human brain, instantly processing immense quantities of information. Computers have been applied to an expanding variety of tasks, from recording airline reservations to guiding artificial satellites and shuttlecraft in their orbits. The Japanese and others "robotized" entire factories with computers. At present, Japanese and American scientists are in a friendly competition to produce even more powerful computers.

Computer technology has enabled societies around the world to store, order, and retrieve vast amounts of knowledge. As the decades pass, raw data piles up in records repositories, on paper and film, on tapes and computer disks. Collections of statistical data alone furnish mountains of information unimaginable in the past. But in many ways, the resulting flood of knowledge has often been overwhelming. The twentieth century has become an age of specialization—a century of experts. As a result, people even in the same society or nation often do not share a common body of knowledge or cultural values. Thus at the very time that technology has made it far easier to transmit and share knowledge, the cultural values and belief systems of many societies have become increasingly fragmented and diverse.

As always, the latest technology was increasingly applied to military weaponry. World War I saw the widespread use of machine guns, submarines, and aircraft as well as the introduction of the flame thrower, poison gas, and tanks. With World War II came amphibious landing craft, radar, and incendiary bombs. Scientists learned to use subatomic particles to split other atoms; the United States won the race to produce the atomic bomb, which was then used to level Hiroshima and hasten the end of World War II. After 1945, scientists expanded the arsenals of the great powers to include napalm, rockets, military helicopters, jet bombers, intercontinental missiles, and laser weapons.

Technology also made the twentieth century the age of flight. In 1903, Orville and Wilbur Wright flew a propeller-driven heavier-than-air craft for the first time. Aviators in small airplanes conducted reconnaissance missions and dog fights in World War I and carried the mails between the wars. In World War II, the multiengine bombing plane came into its own. After the war, jet-propelled airplanes became prevalent in both military and commercial aviation.

Space exploration began in 1957, when the Soviet Union put the first artificial satellite, called *Sputnik,* into orbit. In 1961, a Russian cosmonaut, Yuri Gagarin, circled the earth in an orbital space vehicle. In 1969, an American astronaut, Neil Armstrong, became the first to set foot on the surface of the moon. In the 1980s, American spacecraft landed on Mars, and Voyager II photographed the outer planets and their moons.

The entire age of flight, from Kitty Hawk to the moons of Uranus, has taken place within a single human lifetime.

Twentieth-century technology also brought great dangers. Modern industry polluted the air and water; "acid rain" defoliated large forest areas. Automobiles put a whole society on wheels; yet road accidents also injured millions and killed tens of thousands annually. High technology also raised the specter of earth-orbiting, high-tech "Star Wars" weaponry. Atomic weapons, stockpiled in huge quantities by the superpowers, posed a very real threat of global annihilation.

An especially momentous breakthrough in technology was the peaceful use of nuclear energy, which now produces substantial proportions of the electricity consumed in industrial societies. But this, too, is a mixed blessing. Although atomic power plants provide cheap energy, the peril of accidental damage to reactors and the leaking of radiation is considerable. The explosions at the Chernobyl nuclear power plant in the Soviet Union in 1986 raised radiation levels in many parts of Europe and had dire long-term consequences.

Changing Patterns of Economic Organization

The overall economic picture in the twentieth century has been one of upward surges and downward slides. World War I produced an economic boom that generally lasted through the 1920s; it was followed by the Great Depression in the 1930s. In the United States, World War II brought another great upsurge in production and affluence. After the war, this prosperity spread to western Europe and Japan. In the early 1970s, a huge rise in the price of petroleum triggered a major economic downturn or recession that lasted into the 1980s. Today, recovery from that crisis has meant generally strong economic conditions in most developed nations of the world, which now include nations of the Pacific rim of Asia.

The twentieth century witnessed remarkable changes in the patterns of industrial activity for both management and labor. Already in the 1880s, a fundamental shift had begun with the "managerial revolution." Today, major enterprises are rarely run by their owners. Capitalist ownership of big companies is spread among many stockholders, who may vote on major issues affecting their companies. Professional executives, trained in business schools and moving from one firm to another, control daily operation and long-range planning of their companies. Computer-controlled robotic machinery has replaced many factory workers. A growing percentage of the labor force is now employed in "white collar" office jobs. Automated farms and factories have meant a shortfall in the number of production jobs available and a general change toward employment in service industries.

In the industrialized world, more people have entered "service" occupations, from hotel or restaurant work to jobs in hospitals, schools, and the public sector. Although they use the new industrial technology, from microwave ovens to X-ray machines in their work, these service workers do not manufacture anything.

Despite efforts to restrain the growth of big business in the twentieth century, huge corporations and international cartels, developed during the preceding century, continue to dominate economic life. In addition, such recent innovations as conglomerates, franchising, and multinational corporations have loomed larger on the business scene.

The growth of conglomerates has reflected the increasing complexity of big business. A conglomerate does not bring together production stages in a single process, as old-fashioned vertical combinations did, nor does it unite competitors in the same line of business, as horizontal combinations do. Instead, the conglomerate brings producers in a broad spectrum of different fields under a single corporate umbrella. It might thus buy up firms manufacturing soap flakes, books, and pharmaceuticals, and then perhaps add television stations or vacation resorts to the mix. Such firms sacrifice the expertise that goes with specialization, but they gain economic balance and the freedom to move into profitable areas of investment wherever they might be found.

The trend toward franchising has been particularly strong in service industries. A parent company leases to a local operator the right to use a particular trademark or to sell a particular product. Hotels, fast-food restaurants, automobile dealerships, and real estate companies are often franchise operations. Individuals with limited capital but good knowledge of local business conditions gain from the name recognition, purchasing power, and quality control furnished by the central organization. The McDonald's restaurant chain is perhaps the most visible example worldwide of a successful franchising organization.

Multinational firms have played a big role in post–World War II business life. These huge corporations own and operate subsidiary companies or factories in a number of nations. Such firms headquartered or created in developed Western countries often build factories in less developed lands, where labor is cheap. This practice has also enabled the multinational to avoid tariff barriers, since the goods are not produced inside any such system of protective tariffs. Thus many U.S. factories have been opened in Europe, Asia, and Latin America since World War II. More recently, Japanese manufacturers have begun to set up factories in the United States.

As in earlier periods, governments after World War II continued to play an important part in economic life, both stimulating and regulating business enterprise. In western Europe, North America, Japan, the Pacific rim area, and most of Latin America, private capital still owns most businesses, and private business people make most operating decisions. In the 1920s and 1930s, however, the government of the Soviet Union took over most of that nation's economic institutions in a form of state capitalism. Other eastern European communist nations nationalized many industries in the 1940s and 1950s, when they became client states of the Soviet Union. Western European governments, recovering from World War II, invested public capital to rebuild industry. Newly independent countries like India, which lacked private capital, also established government-run industries and marketing boards to stimulate their economies. Most capitalist nations, in fact, have developed some nationalized industries, from airlines and electronic media to banks or steel mills.

A key feature of twentieth-century government involvement in economic life was central planning. In communist nations, an elaborate bureaucratic structure set goals and allocated resources for all parts of the economy. In western European nations and Japan, government boards now investigate the international market, encourage research in potentially profitable areas, and generally help private capitalists to be competitive. With the collapse of the Communist regimes in eastern Europe in the late 1980s and the disintegration of the Soviet Union, former Communist nations now seek to privatize and move toward full economic integration with their capitalist Western neighbors as quickly as possible. This rapid decline of the communist, state-run economies has resulted in massive social and economic dislocations that will be described in Chapter 17.

At the international level, post–World War II groups like western Europe's Coal and Steel Community helped businesses in member nations to plan and regulate the production of these vital commodities. Another important task of government economic organizations has been to coordinate the roles of private capital and the state. Government regulation in the public interest has extended from labor conditions and the purity of food and drugs to stock market and banking practices, land usage, and pollution control.

Societal Changes and Women's Rights

The material lives of ordinary human beings during the twentieth century have been changed by technological advances but also in many other ways, including the size and distribution of population, the level of health care and education, and the state of public welfare in general.

Population growth has continued at an accelerated pace. World population numbered some 1.5 billion in 1900. Because of technological advances and improved health care, world population in 1990 rose to over 5 billion with almost 2 billion of the world's people in China and India alone. Western Europe had over 350 million inhabitants, and in Latin America, Brazil had a population of more than 150 million, and Mexico almost 89 million, while Asian nations continued to have the largest populations.

In most nations, the population explosion is a huge problem. In the advanced Western states, Japan, and recently the Pacific rim area, however, population has remained relatively stable, growing at a rate of slightly more than one-half of 1 percent a year. In Europe, indeed, many nations have achieved zero population growth (births almost exactly balanced by deaths). The problem has been more serious in Latin America, where the growth rate is comparable to that in Asia and Africa—between 2.5 and 3 percent a year. At these rates, the estimated world population in the year 2000 was 7 billion people.

The trend toward urbanization is another feature of twentieth-century demographics. Russia, for example, was a nation of peasants in 1900, but by the 1970s 50 percent of the people lived in cities. Most of the worldwide growth in urban population is the result of rural migration, which has brought Egyptian *fellaheen* (peasants) to Cairo, *campesinos* (country folk) into São Paolo, and African Americans from the rural south to Detroit.

Rapid urbanization brought problems in sanitation, health care, education, crime, and especially housing, as slums sprang up around the city centers. Since World War II, some Western governments have built public housing projects or "new towns" to house the urban poor. Small towns have metamorphosed into new cities throughout Europe

Women Demand the Vote

The only recklessness the Suffragettes have ever shown has been about their own lives and not about the lives of others. It has never been, and it never will be, the policy of the women's Social and Political Union recklessly to endanger human life. We leave that to the men in warfare. . . . There is something that Governments care far more for than human life, and that is the security of property and so it is through property that we shall strike the enemy.

Be militant each in your own way. Those of you who can express your militancy by going to the House of Commons and refusing to leave without satisfaction, as we did in the early days—do so. Those of you who can express militancy by facing party mobs at Cabinet Ministers' meetings when you remind them of their falseness to principle—do so. Those of you who can express

your militancy by joining us in our anti-Government –by-election policy—do so. Those of you who can break windows—break them. . . . And my last word is to the Government: I incite this meeting to rebellion.*

The agitation to secure voting rights for women in Britain entered a militant phase when Mrs. Emmeline Pankhurst founded the Women's Social and Political Union in 1903. As the members of the group adopted drastic measures to publicize their cause, others responded in varied ways, from support to amusement to hostility. Although the suffragists succeeded in raising public awareness of "women's issues," women did not secure the vote in Western nations until after World War I.

*Mrs. Emmeline Pankhurst's Address to Suffragettes on October 17, 1912.

and the United States. In the United States, the suburb has provided pleasant living areas for middle- and upper-class citizens who work in the cities.

The growth of the welfare state has changed the lives of almost all Western peoples. The goal of welfare legislation has been to provide such goods and services as unemployment relief, child care, public health and geriatric facilities, and low-cost housing to the citizenry. The economic and technological capacities of the industrialized world have brought these goals within reach. In the 1930s, totalitarian leaders attracted support by promising many forms of social services. The Great Depression led democratic governments in Europe and the Americas to offer relief for the unemployed and other forms of "social security." Only after World War II, however, did communism in eastern Europe and welfare capitalism in western Europe, North America, Canada, and Australia bring basic care to most Western people.

The welfare state has its critics. Some believe that too much security makes people less hardworking. Others claim that, especially during economic downswings, even wealthy nations simply cannot afford the full range of welfare benefits.

A good education has never been more essential than in the present technologically sophisticated age. Governments the world over have offered more years of formal education and specialized training to their citizens, although some are too poor to live up to their aspirations. In 1900, most European nations provided free elementary education to boys and girls, and two-thirds of the American states had some form of public grade-school education. Today, virtually all North American and European children attend elementary school, as do most Latin Americans. Four-fifths of North Americans, two-thirds of Europeans, and one-third of Latin Americans go on to secondary school. In the

United States, almost half the population has access to some sort of higher education. European nations accomplish in their secondary schools what is normally completed in the United States in the first two years of college. Less than a fifth of the young people in European nations pass the rigorous examinations for college entrance. In Latin America lack of financial and educational resources has held the figure down to 5 percent. Japan and the Asian Pacific rim countries, heirs to centuries-old traditions of respect for learning, have among the best and most rigorous educational systems. These have played a major role in the rise of these nations to economic prosperity.

A striking feature of the expansion of education the world over is its spread across segments of society traditionally excluded from much schooling. Public education means that education is available to the poor as well as to the rich. The relaxation of ancient sexist taboos has given women access to learning at the highest levels in most parts of the world—and to the careers that are open to those with advanced training; however, in poorer nations preference in economic allocations and societal traditions continues to favor men over women. As a result, women in poor nations may receive inferior or little or no schooling, and many are forced to drop out after only two or three years of primary education.

In the West, major changes occurred in the relationships between urban workers and the established middle and upper classes. The urban proletariat organized to improve wages, hours, and working conditions through labor unions and collective bargaining. When the middle and upper classes, anxious to placate unrest, extended the franchise, workers used the vote as a means to further their cause. In Europe, and to a lesser extent in the United States, they supported moderate socialist parties dedicated to bringing public ownership of the means of production by peaceful, constitutional methods. A minority of workers around the world embraced the radical doctrines of revolutionary Marxism, syndicalism, and anarchism. The capitalist leaders of national governments tried to preempt the advance of socialism by enacting significant measures to promote the welfare of the masses.

The status and role of women also changed. By 1900, women in the industrialized world and from the upper classes in the areas under imperial control were already integrating into many phases of the economy and society. In the West, during the nineteenth century, women had been incorporated into the labor force in major industries such as textiles and garment manufacturing. They had also established their claims to professions in teaching and nursing.

Today, women comprise one-third of the workforce in western Europe, the United States, and Japan, and almost half in the Soviet Union and Taiwan. Women now enter prestigious legal and medical professions in increasing numbers: one-quarter of the doctors in Great Britain and more than half of those in the Soviet Union are women. Women have succeeded only very slowly in securing top business management positions, however, and continue to be paid less than men. Nevertheless, a trend to equal participation by women in the economic life of the industrialized world has been established.

A variety of factors combined to expand women's roles. Both world wars drew women into heavy industry, replacing men drafted into the armies. Technological advances also played a part. Labor-saving devices freed women from onerous housework, and modern

NOW and ERA. Members of NOW interrupt Senate proceedings in 1970 to demand hearings on an equal rights amendment (ERA). In 1972, with the new feminism gathering momentum, the ERA finally cleared Congress. The amendment was later declared dead when it failed to win the approval of the necessary thirty-eight states.

contraceptive techniques allowed parents to limit family size. Finally, ideology has also played an important part. Liberals and feminists from industrialized and traditional societies and communist regimes in eastern Europe all supported—or at least paid lip service to—women's demands for equal treatment.

In 1900, only women in Australia and New Zealand had the right to vote. Prior to World War I, British women led the way in demanding voting rights. To bring public attention to their cause, suffragists (those who struggled for women's suffrage) in Britain chained themselves to lampposts, started fires in mailboxes, and smashed department store windows. When jailed, many suffragists went on hunger strikes. These tactics failed to secure the vote, which was granted after World War I largely owing to women's contributions toward the war effort. In 1918, the franchise in Britain was extended to all males over twenty-one and all women over thirty. Ten years later, British women received the vote on the same terms as the men. Women in the United States secured the vote in 1920 and during the interwar years, the vote was extended to women in most European nations, although French and Swiss women did not receive the vote until after World War II.

Similarly, upper- and middle-class women in Africa and Asia led movements to improve the status of all women. Women were particularly active in nationalist movements to secure independence. A women's corps fought in the Chinese nationalist revolution in 1911. In 1919, Chinese female students were active in the May 4th Movement that led to an intellectual revolution. In Egypt, women played a leading role in opposition to continued British domination. In India, Gandhi's passive resistance movement attracted many women followers. In Turkey and Egypt, urban feminists threw off the veil and demanded more social and civil rights. Egyptian feminists, led by Huda Sharawi, joined others at the International Feminist Meeting in Rome in 1923, which was a prelude to many future conferences on the status of women.

After World War II, the role and treatment of women around the world continued to be hotly debated. Simone de Beauvoir (1908–1986), a French novelist and existentialist thinker (see the next section of this chapter), published her ground-breaking book, *The Second Sex,* in 1949 (English translation 1953), and gave intellectual substance to the accelerating quest for fairer treatment of women. In the English-speaking world, which took the lead in the fight for gender equality, the women's liberation movement found provocative, powerfully eloquent, and persuasive voices in books such as Betty Friedan's *The Feminine Mystique* (1963), Germaine Greer's *The Female Eunuch* (1970), and, in a more literary vein, Mary Ellman's *Thinking about Women* (1968) and Kate Millett's *Sexual Politics* (1970); these works provided a catalyst for changing how many women thought about themselves and their role in the family, the workplace, and society in general. Gloria Steinem created an open forum for the airing of feminist concerns by founding *Ms.* magazine in 1972; this periodical, whose circulation rose as high as 500,000, has introduced the work of such important writers as Alice Walker, Erica Jong, and Mary Gordon and has provided a forum where such pressing issues as sexual harassment, domestic violence, and the crisis in child care have been discussed and debated.

In the United States and other Western, industrialized nations, women organized into groups like the National Organization for Women (NOW) to demand and secure equal rights in hiring, pay scales, and laws governing marriage and divorce and for protection against physical assault and abuse. For most of the twentieth century, the struggle for gender equality has been a persistent and ongoing challenge in societies around the world.

Twentieth-Century Social and Cultural Patterns

The models of development that the West and East offer us today are compendiums of horrors. Can we devise more humane models that correspond to what we are? As people on the fringes, inhabitants of the suburbs of history, we Latin Americans have arrived at the feast of modernity as the lights are about to be put out. . . . We have not been able to save even what the Spaniards left us when they departed, we have stabbed one another. . . . Despite all this, and despite the fact that our countries are inimical to thought, poets and prose writers and painters who equal the best in the other parts of the world have sprung up here and there, separately but without interruption. Will we now, at last, be capable of thinking for ourselves? Can we plan a society that is not based on the domination of others and that will not end up like the chilling police paradises of the East or with the explosions of disgust and hatred that disrupt the banquet of the West?*

*Octavio Paz, The Other Mexico: Critique of the Pyramid, trans. L. Kemp (New York: Grove, 1972), pp. viii–x, in Peter N. Stearns, ed., Documents in World History (New York: Harper & Row, 1988), vol. 2, p. 190.

This passage by the noted Mexican essayist and Nobel laureate Octavio Paz (1914–1998) describes the problems of many Latin American, African, and Asian writers and artists who have sought to create innovative and unique works of art independent of outside influences. Despite the appearance of a truly global civilization in the twentieth century, cultural and social diversity has been one of the hallmarks of the era. This section will discuss some of the many cultural currents, historical trends, and social developments that have contributed to the modernist revolution around the world.

Philosophic Trends: Secularism, Pragmatism, Existentialism

The most influential philosophical thought, particularly in the Western world, has focused on the material world, on how best to understand and get along in it. Contemporary philosophers have given comparatively little attention to absolute truths or mystical revelations. Instead, such attitudes as secularism, pragmatism, and more formal schools of thought such as existentialism have predominated.

The secular attitudes of later nineteenth-century materialism have spread widely around the world in the twentieth century. Many have come to believe that whereas science has discovered verifiable truths about this material world, religious convictions about the spiritual world are matters of opinion rather than of fact. The real world, for secularists, is the world of matter known to the senses and studied by scientists.

Modern institutions have reflected this prevailing secularism. Most Western democracies have also institutionalized the separation of church and state. Totalitarian countries typically discourage religion, in part because they see it as a rival to their official ideology.

Cultural and moral relativism has also accompanied secularism. Relativists have argued that a particular belief or practice should not be judged right or proper in absolute terms, but only in terms of its own culture. Behavior considered immoral in one society might be quite moral in another. Cultural anthropologists have increasingly endorsed this view. Pragmatists have encouraged a more active, positive attitude toward this world without certainties. For example, John Dewey (1859–1952) insisted on judging ideas by their social usefulness; Dewey's instrumentalism saw ideas as tools, means to an end, valid if and to the extent they worked in society. This pragmatic, can-do attitude, originally associated with optimistic Americans, was widely admired in China after World War I and has become common in many parts of the world.

In contrast, the existentialists reacted against the materialistic or secular world view. Existentialists trace the roots of their world view to such nineteenth-century thinkers as Nietzsche, who proclaimed the "death of God" in the materialistic age. The French writer Jean-Paul Sartre (1905–1980) expressed the existential mood of the mid-twentieth century in his play *No Exit* and novel *Nausea*. Sartre defined existentialism with the pithy phrase "existence precedes essence," meaning that material existence is the fundamental reality, and essences or spiritual beings are only myths. For existentialists, the harshest thing about human existence is its sheer meaninglessness or even absurdity. For a generation that had survived the horrors of the Great Depression and World War II, absurdity and anguish seemed fitting responses to the age.

Secularism versus Religion

Conflict between secularism and religion has been another continuing trend during the twentieth century. Although some devout Christians and Jews in the West attempted to merge religion and secular materialism, others pushed for increased spirituality and greater religious influence in governmental and educational institutions. Fundamentalists have also often opposed what they perceived to be the moral decline and laxity of modern Western society.

Some Hindus in India and Confucians in China also tried to reconcile Western institutions and values with their own religious and moral beliefs. Likewise, modernizers like al-Afghani and Muhammad Abdu in the Muslim world argued that traditional Islam and Western values and technology were not mutually exclusive but could be fused with one another. In contrast, traditionalists in India and the Muslim world not only rejected Western secularism but also severely criticized their coreligionists for accepting foreign secular ideas. The Muslim Brotherhood, which began in Egypt and expanded through much of the Arab world, is one example of a dynamic organization that sought to establish independent governments based on strict, fundamentalist interpretations of Islam. In part, the legitimacy of the Saudi Arabian monarchy has been based upon its strict adherence to puritanical Islamic government and law.

For the first half of the twentieth century it appeared that the Western secularists were the dominant force in the conflict between materialism and spirituality. Initially, even those traditional societies that achieved independence from the imperial powers following World War II adopted Western governmental forms and largely separated the functions of church and state. However, during the latter part of the century, militant Christian, Muslim, and Jewish movements in Iran, the Arab world, India, Israel, and even the United States gained support and influence. Thus no resolution of the conflict over the relative importance and role of religion in all societies has yet been achieved.

Social Thought in the Contemporary Era

Twentieth-century theories about politics and society have drawn heavily on nineteenth-century ideologies: in particular, nationalism and internationalism, conservatism, liberalism, socialism, and communism. Of these, nationalism has undoubtedly had the greatest impact around the world. After World War II, passionate loyalty to individual nation-states declined somewhat in Europe but remained exceedingly strong in the Americas and in Third World areas struggling to gain independence. Allegiance of citizens to their nations, newly freed from Western domination, remained a powerful force in Asia and Africa. In contrast, the relative success of international organizations like the United Nations and the Common Market in Europe have encouraged many to adopt more global perspectives in dealing with political, social, and economic issues.

Conservatism, an ideology dedicated to preserving traditional institutions, has sought to defend the best features of ancient political principles and time-tested institutions. Thus religious principles have remained central to its philosophy. However, twentieth-century conservatives have gradually ceased to champion the old monarchies and hereditary aristocracies and have become dedicated to the preservation of the free enterprise, capitalist economic system. In many nations, conservatives have also reluctantly accepted many features of the welfare state.

Liberalism has also retained some of its original ideas while adding new notions. By 1900, liberal doctrine had evolved toward the belief that government should be by and for all people. Concern for the political rights of all led to such major breakthroughs as

Differing Worldviews

The truth is that the contemporary spirit came to an end with the outbreak of the Great War, in other words the moment 20th Century man discovered that the ideals of the revolutionary democrats—who had put their faith in science and believed that world progress was the . . . consequence of scientific advance—were grossly over-optimistic. The Western camp then split into three groups. The first of these turned back to Christianity . . . and can now be called conservative.

The second group is composed of those who, having despaired of democratic ways, turned away from the Church. . . . This group then rallied to the Communist doctrine. . . .

Finally, there is a third group, people whom Christianity and Communism have not been able to satisfy—people who are looking for a solution to that which the church has disdained and the [Communists] left unanswered. In the West, some of them are awaiting a magician who will provide what neither Hitler nor Mussolini could give them. Others turn to existentialism, which, in the end, is not a solution.

Doubtless, the West still possesses considerable intellectual and spiritual resources; but I defy anybody . . . to deny that there is, in the West today, an attempt to go back to first principles in order to make a stand against the prevailing intellectual and moral chaos. Therefore let us not shun our own fundamental origins, made up of faith in freedom, pride in reason and unchanging values.

Above all, we owe it to ourselves to keep before our eyes the goal we are working towards; namely to serve our society, elevate it, promote its self-awareness and infuse it with the determination to defend its rights and do its duty.*

The above passage, written in 1952 by the Moroccan nationalist Alal al-Fasi, provides an analysis of how many Third World peoples view the intellectual and cultural crisis of the Western world; al-Fasi and many other writers have attempted to assimilate the ideas of modernization with their own indigenous cultures and traditions.

*Alal al-Fasi, "The Problems of a Contemporary Approach" (1952), in Contemporary Arab Political Thought, ed. Anouar Abdel-Malek (London: Zed Books, 1970, rev. 1980), p. 98.

the American civil rights movement in the 1960s, when the civil disobedience campaign of Martin Luther King Jr. (1929–1968) helped win civil liberties for African Americans. In economic spheres liberals like British economist John Maynard Keynes (1883–1946) advocated government intervention in such times of crisis as the Great Depression of the 1930s.

In the twentieth century, socialism moved in two directions. Western European socialists moved toward social democracy and the democratic welfare state. Prior to World War II and during the Cold War, the Soviet Union, and much of eastern Europe after the war, moved in the opposite direction, toward the totalitarian regimes of communism. As previously noted, the collapse of the Communist regimes in Europe narrowed the differences between eastern and western European economic systems.

Modernism and the Arts

Nineteenth-century romanticism and materialism and certain aspects of non-Western cultures in Asia and Africa have all influenced twentieth-century culture. Each of these factors has enriched the arts in its own unique way.

From romanticism, modern artists inherited an emphasis on the value of the emotions over that of the rational mind. In this tradition, many writers and artists have glorified love, sex, suffering, and violence and have delved deeply into such emotional experiences as dreams, drugs, and madness. Like their romantic predecessors, recent artists

Frida Kahlo and Diego Rivera.
This self-portrait shows Kahlo and her husband Rivera in 1931. Both Rivera and Kahlo were well-known twentieth-century artists. From Mexico, Rivera was renowned for his large, brightly colored, and finely detailed murals. As a socialist, he often used political themes and messages in his work; consequently, his murals were sometimes criticized or even destroyed by political opponents. In contrast, Kahlo's work, as revealed in this portrait, was more self-analytical and emotional in nature.

Frida Kahlo, Frida and Diego Rivera 1931. Oil on canvas. 39 1/2" x 31". San Francisco Museum of Modern Art, Albert M. Bender Collection; gift of Albert M. Bender

have often felt alienated from their own societies. They have also been fascinated by the grimy underside of modern life, vividly depicting criminal, immoral, and hypocritical behavior. Freud's writings led many to seek truth in the depths of the unconscious mind.

Western artists were often heavily influenced by non-Western traditions and styles. Paul Gauguin (1848–1903) left Europe for the South Seas where, with a vision heavily clouded by "Orientalism" or his own version of what traditional societies should be, he wrote that, "I have all the joys of free life, both animal and human. I am escaping from fakery, I am entering into Nature." His brilliantly colored paintings depict lush landscapes and romanticized native women.

Pablo Picasso (1881–1973), the most famous twentieth-century painter, was influenced by African art and owned a large collection of African masks that he used for inspiration. Picasso's most famous style, cubism, divided real objects, as in his naked Ladies of Avignon, into fragmentary shapes, which he then recombined. Many of Picasso's paintings show remarkable parallels to African sculpture. Likewise, African wood carvings influenced the works of the Romanian-born French abstract sculptor Constantine Brancusi (1876–1957) and the British sculptor Henry Moore (1898–1986), best known for his semiabstract sculptural depictions of the human figure.

Creators of much modern music and dance deliberately attempted to break with traditional Western forms and to suffuse their creations with non-Western themes and modalities. American jazz represented a mixture of African, Latin, and American music. Other musicians such as the Hungarian Béla Bartók (1881–1945) used traditional or "folk" songs as the basis for new renditions. Similarly, modern Arabic singers such as Um Kalthoum or Fairuz adapted Western instrumentation to Arabic improvisational music.

In the field of literature cross-cultural exchanges became commonplace. In Latin America, scholars and writers drew heavily on European cultural sources, but used them to achieve their own cultural statements. Latin American writers often sought to explore and establish a genuinely Latin American culture, distinct from that of Europe. By condemning their European ancestors and glorifying their Amerindian ones, by evoking such clearly South American phenomena as the gaucho of the pampas, these writers achieved a sense of their own cultural uniqueness.

The Egyptian writer Naguib Mahfouz (1911–), used the novel, a Western creation, as his form of expression while describing in vivid terms life in urban Egypt. Léopold Senghor of Senegal, a Catholic married to a French woman, admitted the great influence of Western, particulary French, literature. Yet during the 1930s he led the movement celebrating

Léopold Senghor Laments the Decimation of Africa

Lord God, forgive white Europe.
It is true Lord, that for four enlightened centuries, she
    has scattered the baying and slaver of her mastiffs
    over my lands
And the Christians, forsaking Thy light and the gentle-
    ness of Thy heart
Have lit their camp fires with my parchments, tortured
    my disciples, deported my doctors and masters of
    science.
Their powder has crumbled in a flash the pride of tatas
    and hills
And their bullets have gone through the bowels of vast
    empires like daylight, from the Horn of the West to
    the Eastern Horizon.
They have fired the intangible woods like hunting
    grounds, dragged out Ancestors and spirits by their
    peaceable beards,
And turned their mystery into Sunday distraction for
    somnambulant bourgeois.
Lord, forgive them who turned . . .
My household servants into "boys," my peasants into
    wage-earners, my people into a working class.

For Thou must forgive those who have hunted my chil-
    dren like wild elephants,
And broken them in with whips, have made them the
    black hands of those whose hands were white.
For Thou must forget those who exported two millions
    of my sons in the leperhouses of their ships
Who killed two hundred millions of them.
And have made for me a solitary old age in the forest of
    my nights and the savannah of my days.
Lord, the glasses of my eyes grow dim
And lo, the serpent of hatred raises its head in my
    heart, that serpent that I believed was dead.*

Senghor was a leading spokesperson for an African cultural renaissance and in 1960 became president of independent Senegal. Educated in France, Senghor wrote this poem in French but sought to fuse African and European artistic expressions. This poem also highlights Senghor's sorrow and anger over the tragic impact of Western invasions into Africa and the human tragedy of the slave trade.

*Léopold Sédar Senghor, Selected Poems, trans. John Reed and Clive Wake (Oxford: Oxford University Press, 1964), reprinted in William H. McNeill and Mitsuko Iriye, eds., Modern Asia and Africa (New York: Oxford University Press, 1971), pp. 280–281.

Négritude, or "the sum total of the values of the African world." His poetry focused on Africa, its people and traditions. In addition to being a poet of some renown, Senghor led the nationalist movement in Senegal and was elected the first president of the independent republic in 1960, a position he held till 1980.

Popular Culture

While many artists and writers have gone their own ways in the twentieth century, the rise of the electronic media with their ability to reach large groups of people created a popular culture with a mass following around the world. Sound recording, radio, film, and television brought music, drama, and much more to whole populations on a scale never before imagined.

The history of popular music illustrates how the United States has become the center for much popular culture. Although some of the most successful performers, like the Beatles and the Rolling Stones, came from Great Britain, and many new rhythms and dances such as the tango, samba, reggae, or lambada originated in Latin America or the Caribbean, internationally popular musical forms such as jazz and rock came from the United States. Rock and roll has become the predominant form of popular music around the world. Rock drew heavily on African-American rhythms, as well as on the country and folk music of the rural southern United States. The African-American composer and singer Chuck Berry was a shaping influence on the new form, but Elvis Presley (1935–1977) became the first rock superstar.

Musicians around the world have fused their own traditional forms with elements of Western pop, jazz, and reggae. "Highlife" music by Fela Anikulapo Kuti (1938–1997) and others in Nigeria, and "Rai" from Algeria have become enormously popular among youth in search of their own identities.

Relying on a strong beat, the electric guitar, electronic amplification, and dazzling staging and lighting, rock musicians have sold out their concerts to thousands of fans and circulated millions of copies of their records around the world. Some, like the Jamaican reggae artist Bob Marley (1945–1981), and Bob Dylan (1941–) from the United States, have addressed political controversies and thereby helped to fuel the social protest by youth in the latter half of the twentieth century.

Film and television have also been major factors in creating popular culture. Both as a theatrical form and adapted for the home television screen, moving pictures are the most universally appealing of modern arts. Home videos have made them even more accessible and popular. Film produced its own array of artistic geniuses: director D. W. Griffith (1875–1948) invented many basic techniques of filmmaking, and Charlie Chaplin (1889–1977) brought artistic sensitivity to his portrayal of "the little tramp" victimized by the modern world. Filmmakers like Luis Buñuel (1900–1983) of Spain, Federico Fellini (1920–1993) of Italy, Ingmar Bergman (1918–) of Sweden, Satyajit Ray (1922–1992) of India, Akira Kurosawa (1910–1998) of Japan, and Stanley Kubrick (1928–1999), Martin Scorsese (1942–), Spike Lee (1957–), and Quentin Tarantino (1963–) of the United States have all experimented with new techniques and subject matter. The motion picture also produced a long series of stars whose immense popularity was rooted in personal qualities portrayed on the screen. Marlene Dietrich (1904–1992),

John Wayne (1907–1979), Robert De Niro (1943–), Meryl Streep (1949–), and Tom Hanks (1956–) are a few examples.

Television, widespread after 1950, opened up new realms of popular entertainment. From radio, television inherited the serial program format, in which the same central characters had new adventures every week. Television evolved the more flexible miniseries form, in which one story, often derived from a successful novel, is told in installments adding up to many hours in length. Films and television both had broad popular appeal, transporting viewers out of their humdrum daily lives into mansions and penthouses, steaming jungles, or distant wars. Torrid love scenes, wild automobile chases, and violence have become parts of the imaginary lives of millions. Fans in Bogotá, Tokyo, and Rome all eagerly watch the latest crisis on *ER, NYPD Blue,* or *Baywatch,* while satellite transmitters provide instant images of events to viewers around the globe.

Finally, the Americanization of popular culture throughout the West and around the globe has been a notable feature of the postwar world. Many social commentators have noted the widespread influence of American jazz, rock and roll music, films, and television programs. However, this popularization of American culture has also been a source of tension as many peoples around the world have sought to maintain their individuality and traditional cultural expressions in the arts, music, literature, architecture, and even dress.

Summary and Comparisons

During the twentieth century, peoples in Africa and Asia organized nationalist revolts against foreign domination. After World War I, despite British promises to support independence, the Arab provinces of the old Ottoman Empire were divided between the British and the French. Atatürk in Turkey and the Pahlavi Shah Reza in Iran led their nations toward independence and westernization. In contrast, leaders like King Abd al-Aziz ibn Saud in Saudi Arabia adopted Western technology and Western material goods, but sought to retain traditional ways and to observe Muslim precepts. This tension between the "modernizers" and "traditionalists" was quite pronounced and sometimes violent.

In Africa, superior European military forces quelled a number of nationalist revolts. India and Southeast Asia, too, witnessed protracted struggles for national independence. In India, Gandhi led the Congress in a struggle of passive resistance against the British.

In China, the Nationalist party embarked on reforms and created the first republic in Asia. However, the Chinese Communist party led by Mao Zedong called for the establishment of a communist regime. In the 1930s, Japan moved to expand its empire into China, launching World War II in Asia.

Thus most nationalist movements in Africa and in both West and East Asia failed to secure complete independence prior to World War II. Sweeping changes in Europe brought about a second global conflict and the ultimate collapse of Western empires.

In the Russian Revolution of 1917, Lenin and the Bolshevik party instituted revolutionary changes to create a socialist state. After Lenin's death, Stalin purged the regime of all rivals, collectivized agriculture, and embarked on an ambitious program to industrialize the Soviet Union; Soviet industrial productivity grew dramatically, but at enormous

CHRONOLOGY

1885	Indian National Congress
1900	Nationalism in Asia and Africa
	Freud, *The Interpretation of Dreams*
	African resistance movements
	Marie Curie's Nobel Prize in physics
	Chinese Republic: Sun Yat-sen
	Díaz dictatorship overthrown
	Wright brothers at Kitty Hawk
	Einstein's theory of relativity
	Assembly-line production
	Conflicting interests of Arabs and Zionists in West Asia
	Constitution of 1917 in Mexico
	The Russian Revolution
	Du Bois and pan-Africanism
	Women's suffrage
	Motion pictures
1920	Rise of Gandhi, Ali Jinnah
	Atatürk modernizes Turkey
	Reza Khan westernizes Persia (Iran)
	King Abd al-Aziz in Arabia
	Chiang Kai-shek unites China
	Stalin in power in USSR
	Indonesian and Vietnamese nationalism: Sukarno, Ho Chi Minh
	Institutional Revolutionary party in Mexico
	Afrikaners in South Africa
	Stalin's first Five-Year Plan
	Civil war between Kuomintang and Communists in China
	Modernism in art: Pablo Picasso, Henry Moore
	Négritude literary movement: Léopold Senghor
	Cárdenas reforms in Mexico
1940	Existentialism: Jean-Paul Sartre
	Television
1950	
	Rock and roll music
	DNA research
1960	
	Novels of Naguib Mahfouz
	Rise of feminism
1970	

human cost. The Russian Revolution, like the French Revolution, swept away the old regime, destroyed the power of the church, and altered the fabric of society. In both cases political change outlived social and economic reforms.

During the twentieth century, stupendous and rapid advances were made in all areas of physical science, from astronomy to physics to biology and chemistry. Information gained in the theoretical sciences was applied to medicine, space research, and such fields as psychology, archaeology, and anthropology.

The material lives of most people, especially in the Western world, improved by leaps and bounds. Synthetic materials added to the array of goods; new sources of energy expedited travel and the growth of cities. In many countries heavy smokestack industry gave way to high-tech and service industries. Conglomerates, large corporations, and government-owned enterprises replaced small companies. Wars and changing economic conditions brought women into the workforce and increased demand for political rights and an equitable share of economic prosperity.

Advances in knowledge in many fields globalized twentieth-century cultural life. New ideologies addressed changing conditions around the world. The most influential, rooted in the nineteenth century but maturing in the twentieth, were nationalism, socialism, conservatism, liberalism, and fascism.

Modernism typified twentieth-century artistic developments in painting, sculpture, and music. Rapid communications expedited cross-cultural exchanges of ideas and techniques among many different cultures. Although cultural and economic transmissions had been a constant fact of human history, modern technology and communication systems sped up these exchanges tremendously. Popular culture flourished, with the United States setting trends in music, film, television, "pop" idols, and literature around the world.

Selected Sources

Items indicated with an asterisk (*) are available in paperback.

Afigbo, A. E., et al. *The Making of Modern Africa.* Vol. 2, 1986. Timely, scholarly accounts of independence movements throughout the continent.

*Barrett, William. *Irrational Man: A Study of Existential Philosophy.* 1958. Good overview, from nineteenth-century origins to Sartre.

Bass, Thomas A. *Reinventing the Future: Conversations with the World's Leading Scientists.* 1994. Lively interviews with eleven scientists, including biologists and physicists.

The Beatles. *Sergeant Pepper's Lonely Hearts Club Band.* 1967. An album of rock music made popular by this group.

*Borges, Jorge Luis. *Labyrinths.* 1977. Short fictions by the dean of Latin American modernist writers.

Chadha, Yogesh. *Gandhi: A Life.* 1997. A readable biography of a compelling personality.

Chekhov, Anton. *Peasants and Other Stories.* Ed. Edmund Wilson. 1956. Gives insight into the lives and problems of Russian peasants before the revolution.

Conquest, Robert. *The Harvest of Sorrow: Soviet Collectivization and the Terror-Famine.* 1986. Somewhat marred by the author's mistaken belief that the famine in the Ukraine was an attempt at genocide, but it is still one of the best books available on collectivization.

*Crossman, Richard, ed. *The God That Failed.* 1960. Ideological commitment and disillusionment of the left in the 1930s.

Doctor Zhivago. David Lean, dir. 1965. This super-epic film is worthy of Boris Pasternak's novel in following one life through the 1917 revolutions and the civil war. Also see *Lawrence of Arabia* (1962), Lean's epic film of the Arab revolt.

Drees, Willem B. *Beyond the Big Bang: Quantum Cosmologies and God.* 1980. A discussion of the complementary roles of science and religion as guides to an understanding of the nature of the cosmos.

Eisenstein, Sergei M. Films directed by Eisenstein are important not only for their historical elements but also for their cinematic value. Note especially *Potemkin* (1925) on the Revolution of 1905 and *Ivan the Terrible,* Parts I (1944) and II (1945). In the latter, Eisenstein tries to create an analogy between what Tsar Ivan did in the 1500s and what Stalin was doing.

*Fisher, Sydney N., and William Ochsenwald. *The Middle East: A History.* 2 vols. 5th ed. 1997. A readable survey with fine chapters on the region during the nineteenth and twentieth centuries.

*Friedan, Betty. *The Feminine Mystique.* 1963. An influential work that served as a catalyst for the women's movement in the 1960s and 1970s.

*Gandhi, Mohandas K. *An Autobiography: The Story of My Experiments with Truth.* 2d ed. 1940, reprinted 1983. Gandhi's frank account of his life, ideas, and actions.

Gandhi. Richard Attenborough, dir. 1984. An evocative film on the father of Indian independence and the twentieth-century prophet of nonviolence.

"The History of Flight." Video on development of aviation with footage on the Wright brothers and Charles Lindbergh. [Merit Audio Visual.]

Howard, Jane. *Margaret Mead: A Life.* 1984. A readable biography of a leading anthropologist.

Hsu, Immanuel C. Y. *The Rise of Modern China.* 6th ed. 2000. The standard textbook on nineteenth- and twentieth-century China.

The Hunt for Pancho Villa. PBS Video. 1994. Dramatic account of often violent clashes along Mexican-U.S. border during the Mexican civil war.

*Khalidi, R., et al., eds. *The Origins of Arab Nationalism.* 1993. A collection of short essays on Arab national leaders and writers.

Khapoya, Vincent B. *The African Experience: An Introduction.* 2d ed. 1998. A short, engaging overview of African nationalist movements and leaders.

Knight, Alan. *The Mexican Revolution.* 2 vols. 1986. A thorough analysis and definitive account of the revolution from 1910 to the constitution in 1917; Knight argues that the revolution was agrarian and social, begun and sustained by the peasantry.

*Laqueur, Walter Z. *History of Zionism.* 1972. Detailed discussion of the philosophical and historical roots of Jewish nationalism.

Li, Yu-ning, ed. *Chinese Women through Chinese Eyes.* 1992. On and by Chinese women, ancient and modern.

Lion of the Desert. Moustapha Akkad, dir. 1980. An epic film on Omar Mukhtar's struggle against Italian aggression in Libya with Anthony Quinn in the starring role.

*Macfie, A. L. *Ataturk.* 1994. Concise and well-balanced biography of the charismatic Turkish leader.

Mahfouz, Naguib. *Palace Walk.* 1990. *Palace of Desire.* 1991. *Sugar Street.* 1992. The "Cairo Trilogy" of novels by the Egyptian Nobel laureate focuses on family life in Cairo during the twentieth century.

*McLuhan, Marshall. *Understanding Media.* 1965. Pithy commentary on the mass media and their impact on audiences.

"The Meiji Period (1868–1912)." Video on the modernization of Japan prior to World War I. 52 minutes. [Films for the Humanities and Sciences.]

*Nehru, Jawaharlal. *The Discovery of India.* 1946. An Indian nationalist leader and prime minister looks back on Indian history.

Pipes, Richard. *A Concise History of the Russian Revolution.* 1995. An abridgement of the author's two-volume study of the dramatic changes that occurred in Russia from 1917 to 1924.

Reds. Warren Beatty, dir. 1981. An interesting film about the experiences of the American journalist John Reed (see below) during the Russian Revolution.

Reed, John. *Insurgent Mexico.* 1914. The classic journalistic account of the revolution. Reed, who spent a year with Pancho Villa's "Division of the North," presents a sympathetic and engrossing account of the enigmatic Villa.

*———. *Ten Days That Shook the World.* 1919. Sympathetic study by a left-wing U.S. journalist who was in Petrograd during the Bolshevik Revolution.

*Sartre, Jean-Paul. *No Exit and Three Other Plays.* 1955. The existential worldview presented in dramatic form.

*Schiffrin, Harold Z. *Sun Yat-sen and the Origins of the Chinese Revolution.* 1970. A good work on Sun's formative years.

Schram, Stuart. *Mao Tse-tung.* 1966. An excellent biography of Mao, excluding his last years.

*Shattuck, Roger. *The Banquet Years.* 1968. Colorful profile of Paris culture in the Bohemian end-of-the-century years.

*Sheridan, James Z. *China in Disintegration: The Republican Era in Chinese History, 1912–1949.* 1975. On China's struggle toward modern nationhood.

*Sholokov, Mikhail. *And Quiet Flows the Don.* Trans. Stephen Garry. 1934, reprinted 1966. The first volume of the author's epochal narrative of the effect of the Soviet state on the Cossacks.

*Stromberg, Roland N. *After Everything.* 1975. Stimulating, brief survey of cultural trends in the twentieth century.

*Tergeman, Siham. *Daughter of Damascus.* 1994. This highly personal memoir vividly describes family life in an Arab Muslim household during the early part of the twentieth century.

*Trotsky, Leon. *The Russian Revolution.* 1932. A study by one of the major participants; readers should remember that he liked Lenin and loathed Stalin.

Tucker, Robert C. *Stalin in Power: The Revolution from Above, 1928–1941.* 1990. An excellent analysis of the period.

Wolff, Bertram D. *Three Who Made a Revolution.* 1948. A triple biography of Lenin, Trotsky, and Stalin.

Womack, John. *Zapata and the Mexican Revolution.* 1968. The best analysis and interpretation of Emiliano Zapata and the Zapatista movement from 1910 to Zapata's death.

Woolman, David. S. *Rebels in the Rif: Abd el Krim and the Rif Rebellion.* 1968. Dramatic account of Moroccan revolt against the Spanish.

Additional resources, exercises, and Internet links related to this chapter are available at the Book Companion Web site: http://history.wadsworth.com/upshurcompact4/

15

The Interwar Years, World War II, and the Cold War

•

• Militarism, Fascism, and Nazism •

• Aggression In Asia and Europe •

• World War II and Postwar Settlements •

• Cold War in Europe •

• Summary and Comparisons •

Someone was standing up and had begun to talk, hesitatingly and shyly at first. . . . Then suddenly the speech gathered momentum. I was caught, I was listening. . . . The crowd began to stir. The haggard grey faces were reflecting hope. . . . Two seats to my left, an old officer was crying like a child. I felt alternately hot and cold. . . . It was as though guns were thundering. . . . I was beside myself. I was shouting hurrah. Nobody seemed surprised. The man up there looked at me for a moment. His blue eyes met my glance like a flame. This was a command. At that moment I was reborn. . . . Now I know what road to take. . . .

Hitler's words were like a scourge. When he spoke of the disgrace of Germany, I felt ready to spring on any enemy . . . glancing around, I saw his magnetism was holding these thousands as one. . . . I was a man of 32, weary of disgust and disillusionment, a wanderer seeking a cause . . . a yearner after the heroic without a hero. The intense will of the man, the passion of his sincerity, seemed to flow from him into me. I experienced a feeling that could be likened only to a religious conversion. . . . I felt sure that no-one who heard Hitler that night could doubt he was the man of destiny. . . . I had given him my heart. *

*Perry M. Rodgers, ed., *Aspects of Western Civilization* (Englewood Cliffs, N.J.: Prentice-Hall, 1992), vol. 2, p. 361.

Adolf Hitler possessed an uncanny ability to sway masses with his demonic oratory, not so much by what he said as how he said it. His voice shaking with emotion in the manner of a fanatical fundamentalist preacher, he offered his audience propaganda based on ideals of patriotism, a greater Germany, and race mastery. Many were moved as if by a spiritual conversion, rather than a political experience. The above excerpts by two such converts illustrate this phenomenon.

In the aftermath of the Nazis' rise to power, Germany underwent profound social and political changes. Between the two world wars a similar transformation occurred in Italy and Japan under authoritarian, militaristic regimes. All three countries undertook major shifts in foreign policy as well.

During the 1930s, the aggressive regimes in Japan, Italy, and Germany victimized weak nations to satisfy their appetites for empire and domination. Japan's successful conquest of Manchuria from China in 1931 and the failure of the League of Nations to intervene encouraged further aggressions, culminating in an all-out war against China in 1937. The Sino-Japanese War expanded to World War II in Asia in 1941 when Japan launched attacks on the U.S. naval base in Hawaii and western colonies in Southeast Asia.

In Europe, Fascist Italy attacked Ethiopia and, like Japan, defied the League of Nations. Hitler's annexation of Austria and Czechoslovakia finally discredited appeasement. When he attacked Poland in 1939, Great Britain and France declared war against Nazi Germany. The Soviet Union and the United States later entered the war against the Axis. Despite their initial advantages, the brutality of the Germans and Japanese spurred their victims in Europe and Asia to determined resistance. Finally, the Allies triumphed, but at the cost of tens of millions of lives and devastation on an unprecedented scale.

This chapter will also detail the postwar settlements with Germany and Japan, the emergence of the United States and the Soviet Union as leaders of two antagonistic blocs, and the beginning of the Cold War.

Militarism, Fascism, and Nazism

The best state constitution and state form is that which, with the most unquestioned certainty, raises the best minds in the national community to leading position and leading influence. There must be no majority decisions, but only responsible persons, and the word "council" must be restored to its original meaning. Surely every man will have advisers by his side, but the decision will be made by one man. This principle—absolute responsibility unconditionally combined with absolute authority—will gradually breed an elite of leaders such as today, in this era of irresponsible parliamentarianism, is utterly inconceivable.

As regards the possibility of putting these ideas into practice, I beg you not to forget that the parliamentary principle of democratic majority rule has by no means always dominated mankind, but on the contrary is to be found only in brief periods of history, which are always epochs of the decay of peoples and states.

But it should not be believed that such a transformation can be accomplished by purely theoretical measures from above, since logically it may not even stop at the state constitution, but must permeate all other legislation, and indeed all civil life. Such a fundamental change can and will only take place through a movement which is itself constructed in the spirit of these ideas and hence bears the future state within itself.

Hence the National Socialist movement should today adapt itself entirely to these ideas and carry them to practical fruition within its own organization, so that some day it may not only show the state these same guiding principles, but can also place the completed body of its own state at its disposal. *

*Adolf Hitler, *Mein Kampf (My Struggle)*, trans. R. Manheim (Boston: Houghton Mifflin, 1943), reprinted in Peter N. Stearns, ed., *Documents in World History*, vol. 2 (New York: Harper & Row, 1988), pp. 113–114.

In 1924, in his meandering, often illogical book, *Mein Kampf*, Adolf Hitler set forth his future plans and purposes in explicit detail. In this selection, Hitler describes his concept of dictatorship, which he proposed to put into practice on assuming power.

After World War I a number of governments fell under a variety of dictatorial regimes. Disillusioned by the horrors and unfulfilled promises of the war and fearful of continued economic crises, peoples in Asia, Latin America, and Europe often turned toward opportunist dictators who promised easy answers to the overwhelming problems facing the postwar world. In Latin America, which had a long tradition of military interference in politics, most of these dictators were led by or supported by army leaders. In Japan the militarists, supported by conservative rightist groups, also gradually acquired control over the political system. Likewise, a large number of European nations moved from democratic forms to authoritarian, dictatorial regimes. In contrast to "totalitarian" dictators like Joseph Stalin and Hitler, who sought to control not only the state, but the private lives of its citizens, authoritarian dictators controlled the political institutions of the state, but not necessarily every aspect of the society. This section begins with the emergence of militarism in Japan and then turns to the growing power of the Fascists and Nazis in Europe and concludes with a discussion of the dictators in Latin America.

Militarism in Japan

In Japan the years between 1913 and 1926 are called the period of Taisho democracy, after the reign title of the Taisho emperor. Party government by the winning political parties in the elections became the rule. For many Japanese, the defeat of autocratic Germany and the Austro-Hungarian Empire in World War I proved the superiority of liberal institutions and democratic governments. Western mass culture became popular in urban Japan; young Japanese were attracted to Western music, movies, cafés, and sports. As in Western countries, the "flapper" symbolized the modern young woman (called the *moga* in Japanese, the abbreviation for "modern girl").

Emperor Hirohito (reigned 1926–1989), known in Japan by his reign title, Showa, ascended the throne in 1926. Soon after, Japan began to turn to militarism, ultranationalism, and increasingly more ruthless imperialism. The role of the Showa emperor in these changes is unclear and still debated, but Japanese who favored the changes called the new policy and era the Showa Restoration.

Japan's economy had expanded rapidly during World War I but could not sustain its gains in the postwar years and was severely affected by the Great Depression of 1929. Ordinary Japanese workers and farmers bore the brunt of the hard times. As a result, many Japanese turned against the democratic West and toward ultranationalism and militarism. They blamed their troubles on Western discrimination against Japanese goods and the unwillingness of Western nations to accept Japanese as equals. They were particularly angered by President Wilson's refusal to accept Japan's demand for a clause on racial equality in the Covenant of the League of Nations.

Nationalism and militarism found natural champions in the army and navy, especially among zealous young officers, whose narrow military education had not exposed them to liberal influences from the West. Ultranationalist officers joined organizations such as the Black Dragon Society, which advocated military expansion in continental Asia against China and the Soviet Union. Insisting that they truly represented the imperial will, they claimed that expansion would solve Japan's population and economic problems and that Japan had a mission to dominate Asia. They also maintained that Japan's security had been undermined by the politicians who favored a moderate foreign policy and international cooperation.

The change from a civilian to a military-dominated government occurred without abolishing the Meiji Constitution of 1889, because under that constitution the civil government had no authority over the army and navy, which were commanded by the emperor. As the army and navy defied the civilian government and the emperor did not object, the military gradually gained the upper hand. Middle-level and junior military officers took many policy matters into their own hands and forced their superiors and the civilian leaders to accept the consequences. In some cases, these zealots assassinated superior officers, government leaders, and captains of industry. This outbreak of terrorism culminated in the February Rebellion of 1936 (it occurred on February 26), when fanatical officers assassinated many key government officials. When the courts tried these murderers, the public tended to sympathize with them; when the defendants were sentenced to die, they were viewed as martyrs and became objects of public adulation. As a result of the rebellion, civilian leaders of political parties lost the last vestiges of political influence; the military thereafter dictated foreign policy.

In another form of direct action, the military began to make vital decisions without government authorization. Most notably, on September 18, 1931, army officers launched an all-out offensive against Manchuria in northeastern China. The Japanese army proceeded to conquer Manchuria despite government orders and League of Nations resolutions calling for a cease-fire and restoration of the territory to China. The Japanese public acclaimed the conquest with wild enthusiasm, the cabinet fell, and Japan resigned from the League of Nations. Japan was the first great power to defy the League; its defiance showed that the League could not enforce international law.

The army's triumph against both China and the civilian government marked the victory of pro-militarist forces in Japan. After 1931 censorship laws were enforced with vigor, military police helped ordinary law enforcement officers weed out potential troublemakers, independent-minded professors were dismissed from teaching posts, and their books were banned; hundreds of labor leaders, socialists, and students were thrown into jail. The government revised textbooks to reflect fervent nationalism and used radio and movies to indoctrinate all citizens. Individualism and democracy were denounced, and such previously popular Western practices as ballroom dancing were discouraged as immoral. Ironically, no one demanded the abandonment of Western technology. Even such ancient Confucian virtues as the brotherhood of all humans were reinterpreted to mean worldwide Japanese domination.

Thus Japan's short experiment with some semblance of representative government ended with the triumph of ultranationalist militarism. Most Japanese people, lacking a long democratic tradition, submissively and even enthusiastically embraced the military's dominance over political life. Unlike the Fascists in Italy and the Nazis in Germany, Japanese militarists won without a mass party, a charismatic leader, or a clearly articulated ideology.

In the late 1930s, Japan signed agreements with totalitarian Germany and Italy, forming an Axis alliance that seemed bent on global domination and that threatened both the Soviet Union and the United States. The Axis alliance soon forced wars on the Western democracies and their empires.

Totalitarian Regimes in Europe

Totalitarian government aimed at total control of society—politics, the economy, and the social lives of the people. The totalitarian leaders of the interwar years had massive bureaucracies and employed modern technologies to exert control more effectively than any absolute monarch or despot of the past. They depended heavily on mass communication—radio and motion pictures—to secure public favor during their rise to power.

In addition, totalitarian regimes relied on their political parties. The Fascists in Italy and the Nazis in Germany were organized political parties before they were governments. They offered uniforms, rallies, careers, and a sense of membership for all, irrespective of class. Above all, totalitarian parties offered a clear political alternative to the disillusioned and demoralized during the interwar era. While fascism in its early existence was really an anti-movement, Nazism drew heavily on the racist nationalism of the late nineteenth century, and communism built on the ideas of Karl Marx. All the totalitarian regimes modified and simplified ideas with slogans and battle cries that aroused mass support. Like nineteenth-century reformers, totalitarian dictators aimed to change society.

Fascism in Italy

Italy under Benito Mussolini (1883–1945) was the first European state to espouse fascism. Mussolini rose to power against a background of government inaction in the face of a collapsing economy, widespread unemployment, and violent social unrest in industrial centers at the end of the war. The son of a blacksmith, Mussolini had embraced socialism as a youth, but broke with the party because of its pacifistic position in 1914. After serving in the army, Mussolini formed the Fascist party (from *fasces,* the bundle of rods with an axe that was the ancient Roman symbol of authority), which at first combined socialist demands with nationalism and anticlericalism. Early electoral setbacks convinced him that he needed to move his party farther to the right.

With increasing financial support from industrialists and large landowners, Mussolini recruited a number of restless and disillusioned men, many of whom were ex-soldiers and unemployed youths. As Il Duce (The Leader), he dressed them in black shirts, subjected them to military discipline, and paraded them through the streets. He had no detailed program or coherent set of principles. Not until after he gained power did his party begin to develop a philosophy to fit its needs. As Mussolini himself admitted, "Fascism was not suckled on a doctrine in advance around a table. It was born of a need for action, and it was action. It was not a party, but in the first two years it was an anti-party and anti-movement."

In his many speeches the charismatic Mussolini told his audience what they wanted to hear, railing against Communists and appealing to the wounded pride of nationalists who felt Italy had been cheated at Versailles. Frequently resorting to violence, Fascists broke up socialist and Communist meetings, smashed their printing presses, broke up strikes, and intimidated workers. The weak Italian constitutional monarchy was unable to stop them. In October 1922 Mussolini, after denouncing the ministry in power, sent his blackshirts to Rome by the thousands to take over the administration by direct action. After they flooded into the city, a bewildered King Victor Emmanuel III (reigned 1900–1946), fearful of civil war, summoned Mussolini and asked him to become the new Italian premier.

Although Mussolini achieved power legally, he had contempt for democratic institutions and wanted to rule Italy as a dictator. Initially, though, he headed a coalition government and made every effort to operate within constitutional limits. He requested and received from parliament dictatorial powers for one year to enable him to restore order. The results were seen almost immediately; strikes were called off or broken up, street fighting subsided, and government services operated with increased efficiency. The public's confidence in Mussolini was evident in 1924 when the Fascists won 63 percent of the vote in the general elections. Backed by a parliamentary majority, Mussolini could proceed to consolidate his authority. In 1925–1926 a series of laws instituted press censorship, forbade strikes, outlawed rival political parties, and gave Mussolini the authority to rule by decree. Like Lenin, Mussolini acted as both chief of state and head of the party that controlled the legislature and administration.

Mussolini further strengthened his position by making peace with the Roman Catholic church. By the Lateran Treaty in 1929, the papacy recognized the Italian state and in turn gained sovereignty over the Vatican City in Rome, received large reparations from the Fascist government for the loss of the papal states (during the unification process), and retained control over education in Italy. Through these concessions, Mussolini gained a freer hand over the political and economic life of the nation. The grateful pope called Mussolini a "man sent by Providence" and generally refrained from criticizing the Fascist regime.

Brown Brothers

Adolf Hitler and Benito Mussolini. The totalitarian rulers of Germany and Italy both enjoyed reviewing the troops. Militarism was a central feature of most of the authoritarian regimes of the interwar period.

In the early 1930s, Mussolini moved to restructure the nation's economy into a "corporate state." He organized major industries into two dozen "corporations," each run by committees of businessmen, union leaders, and Fascist party officials representing the government. Together the members of the corporations were given the task of determining working conditions, wages, and prices. In general, big business retained a strong voice in these corporations, although Mussolini continued to portray himself as "a man of the people."

During the 1920s and 1930s, Il Duce also surrounded himself with the militaristic pomp that became one of the hallmarks of future totalitarian leaders. Using a variety of "bread and circuses," Mussolini whipped up mass popular support for his regime. The Fascists extolled the glories of ancient Rome. They promised that the Mediterranean would again become an Italian lake and that past victories would be repeated as Italy became an empire once again. Their dreams of reviving the Roman Empire led directly to an expansionist foreign policy in the Adriatic and in North and East Africa.

Nazism in Germany

Next to Russia during the Stalin era, the most vicious and thoroughgoing totalitarian state was Nazi Germany under Adolf Hitler (1889–1945). As a young man, the Austrian-born Hitler tried desperately to become an artist, but he lacked the necessary ability to draw, and the Vienna Academy of Fine Arts rejected his application for admission. Unable to hold a job, he lived like a tramp, eking out a miserable existence from casual manual work and selling postcards. In 1913 he moved to Germany, and when World War I broke out, he joined a Bavarian regiment. Twice wounded in action and decorated, he returned from the front an ardent nationalist. His skill as an orator gradually won him leadership of the National Socialist German Workers' party, familiarly known as the Nazi party, a racist militarist group that opposed the Weimar government. In 1923 Hitler was imprisoned for leading a failed coup, the so-called Beer Hall Putsch, that sought to overthrow the Bavarian government. During his short stay in jail, Hitler wrote the first volume of *Mein Kampf (My Struggle)*, an autobiography that contained his plan to regenerate Germany through the overthrow of parliamentary rule and the persecution of Jews.

In his quest for political mastery of Germany, Hitler used the violent tactics already pioneered by Mussolini in Italy. He terrorized his enemies by using a uniformed paramilitary force of brownshirts. He expertly mobilized public support through mass rallies, radio, and motion pictures. His passionate nationalism and his violent anticommunism made him a favorite with big business, the lower middle classes, and students.

The Nazis made little headway in the 1920s, but the economic crisis that began in 1930 destroyed public confidence in democratic institutions. As unemployment and poverty became widespread, the bewildered Germans began to clutch at ideological straws. In the elections of 1930, the number of Nazi deputies in the Reichstag, the popularly elected house of parliament, rose from 12 to 107. As the Great Depression paralyzed Germany's coalition governments in the early 1930s, the Nazis' strength continued to increase until they became the largest party in the Reichstag. Hoping to exploit Hitler's voter appeal for their own ends, a conservative faction persuaded the aged President

Paul von Hindenburg to appoint Hitler chancellor (prime minister) in 1933. These conservatives were neither the first nor the last to be mistaken about Hitler's real intentions.

Nazi State and Society

Within a year Hitler had achieved his purpose of welding Germany into a centralized national state under the control of his party. Since the Nazis were a minority in the cabinet, Hitler requested new elections so that his party could win a parliamentary majority. Before the elections, unknown arsonists set fire to the Reichstag building. The Nazis blamed the fire on the Communists and, on the pretext that stern measures were needed to safeguard the security of the country, persuaded the president to invoke emergency provisions and suspend civil liberties. This enabled the Nazis to legally institute a reign of terror against the opposition, particularly the Communists and socialists. But even intimidation did not produce a clear majority for the Nazis, although they did obtain 44 percent of the popular vote. Nevertheless, the Nazis were able to retain a majority with the support of the Nationalist party, which had garnered 8 percent of the vote. As a next step, Hitler persuaded or coerced two-thirds of the Reichstag to pass the Enabling Act, giving him the power to rule by decree for four years. Within seven weeks Hitler had risen from chancellor to virtual dictator.

Hitler wasted no time in achieving total power. He abrogated the authority of the federal states so that for the first time Germany became a centralized, unitary state. He took control of the press and radio, forbade public meetings, dissolved rival parties, and sought to subordinate religion to the state. Hitler even purged the Nazi party of his rivals and those he did not trust. Particular targets of this "blood purge" were leaders of Hitler's own brownshirts. He appears to have sacrificed them to win the support of Germany's army officers, who feared the growing influence of the Nazi paramilitary force.

After von Hindenburg's death in 1934, Hitler assumed the powers of both president and chancellor under the title *Der Führer* (The Leader). As supreme commander of the armed forces, he required all officers and men to take personal oaths of allegiance to Der Führer. Hitler's deference toward the military kept the army loyal to his regime while he was consolidating his authority.

No action the Nazis undertook would have mattered if they had not been successful in lifting Germany out of the depression. They did so by skillful economic planning, using a mixture of state ownership and free enterprise, and by strong-arm methods. Specifically, the government granted tax relief to industries; it invested in massive public works programs, including the construction of superhighways (*autobahns*), housing projects, and armament production. All this was bankrolled through forced loans from banks and businesses and intricate financial juggling and controls. Because the Nazis lacked an adequate gold supply, they forged agreements with other nations under which Germany's manufactured goods were bartered for raw materials and foodstuffs.

As a result of the government's economic policies, unemployment, which stood at 6 million in 1932, was eradicated less than six years later. Wages were low, however, and the standard of living for average workers rose only slightly. This was because workers were denied collective bargaining powers to win concessions from big business. In 1934 labor unions were abolished and replaced by a National Labor Front controlled by the state. Strikes were forbidden, and disputes with management were referred to a system of enforced arbitration modeled after the one set up by Mussolini in Italy.

Nazi ideology, like that of Fascist Italy, was expansionist and militaristic. It also aimed at reestablishing an old empire or Reich. For Hitler his Third Reich would exceed Germany's previous two and last 1,000 years—the First Reich had lasted 900 years and the Second less than 50. Building up the country's strength was therefore of paramount importance.

Germany's declining birthrate greatly alarmed the Nazi leaders. Their plans called for a population large enough to supply plenty of soldiers in the future and settlers to occupy the new lands they hoped to conquer. Accordingly, they encouraged large families. This mandated that women stay at home rather than go to work. The regime inveighed against women who sought independence and pursued employment in public life traditionally reserved for men. It cultivated the traditional image of women as homemakers, wives, and bearers of children. As an incentive to reproduction, the state provided marriage loans, child subsidies, and generous family allowances. Moreover, it awarded three types of honor crosses to mothers who proved most fertile—gold for more than eight children, silver for more than six, and bronze for more than five.

In contrast to Mussolini, whose early Fascist program was not racist, Nazi ideology propounded the myth of the inherent superiority of the Aryan or Nordic race, of which Germans were supposedly the prime example. According to Hitler, Aryan stock over the years had degenerated through intermarriage with other races. Hence the basic aim of Nazi racial policy was to "purify" the German race by weeding out inferior peoples; in particular, Jews, whom Hitler had labeled the cause of all of the nation's ills.

Hitler's SS (*Schutzstaffel*) troops and his secret police, the Gestapo, spread a reign of terror among so-called undesirable elements of the population. They arrested, imprisoned, tortured, and ultimately executed hundreds of thousands of citizens. German Jews were singled out from the beginning. Initially, they were deprived of jobs, stripped of their civil rights, and forced to mark their persons and buildings with a Star of David. Later, they were attacked by mobs, murdered, sometimes compelled to emigrate, and finally imprisoned in slave labor or concentration camps. Dissidents, including religious leaders and leftists who opposed the Nazis, were also imprisoned. After World War II began, the Nazi regime executed these political opponents, along with millions of European Jews, Gypsies, and Slavs—all considered inferior peoples by the Nazis. As the Nazi state began to expand aggressively throughout Europe, these racist policies were implemented in the territories that fell under its control.

All cultural activity was subordinated to the state and its purpose. The Nazis insisted that the new Germany be free of "decadent" cultural influences from the Western democracies. They wanted the masses exposed to ideas and images that glorified the Führer and the party, invited worship of the Fatherland, and called for the destruction of the enemies of the Third Reich. Artists with any sense of creativity and objectivity were blacklisted and left with no choice but to change professions or emigrate. To indoctrinate the nation in their ideology, the Nazis held public spectacles. Hitler copied Mussolini's carefully staged mass rallies and mesmerized the crowds with nighttime "shows," in which he worked his audience into frenzies with promises of future glories. Like all totalitarian regimes, the Nazis sought to control and mold the thoughts of the rising generation. They controlled the school curriculum, falsified textbooks, persecuted teachers who protested, and compelled all youth to join Nazi juvenile organizations such as the Hitler Youth.

The majority of Germans gladly accepted Hitler's authoritarian regime. The new order had ended political instability, solved the unemployment problem, and, to all appearances, was pushing Germany along the path to world power status. When witnessing Nazi horrors, they looked the other way and pretended not to notice what was happening.

Authoritarian Regimes in the Iberian Peninsula

Authoritarian regimes also came to power in the Iberian Peninsula. In Portugal an economics professor, Antonio de Oliveira Salazar (1889–1970), was appointed in the early 1930s as prime minister by a military junta seeking political and economic stability. Salazar made himself dictator of Portugal and ruled until his death in 1970. In Portugal and Spain, the landowners, high officials in the Catholic church, and army officers tended to support the authoritarian regimes as solutions to social disorder and possible revolution. Peasants, urban workers, and students who tended to support leftist or more progressive forces were kept under careful watch.

In Spain General Miguel Primo de Rivera (1870–1930) ruled during the 1920s. In 1931, after a decade of military rule, liberal leaders won the elections; supported by urban workers, some peasants, and socialists, the newly elected "republican" government enacted a series of social, political, and economic reforms and abolished the monarchy. In 1936 the disaffected old power elites launched a revolt against the new republican government. A career army officer, Francisco Franco (1892–1975), gradually emerged as the leader of these conservatives, or "Nationalists," as they called themselves. The Spanish Civil War between the legitimate republican government and the Nationalists continued from 1936 to 1939.

Liberal and totalitarian regimes in much of Europe took sides in the Spanish Civil War. Many viewed it as the first battle of World War II in Europe. For many Western liberals, Spain seemed the last chance to stop the aggressions of authoritarian and totalitarian regimes. Although democratic governments in Europe and America declared themselves neutral in the Spanish Civil War, liberals, socialists, and others from many Western nations formed brigades of volunteers to fight on the side of the republican government. The Soviet Union sent military advisers and aided the republican government, which included a number of socialist politicians. Much more help poured in for Franco from Mussolini, who sent tens of thousands of troops, and Hitler, who dispatched air support. Hitler saw the war as a testing ground for his newly reequipped military. The German Condor Legion "terror bombed" Guernica and other towns, intentionally causing heavy casualties to destroy civilian morale. Such terror bombing of civilians had been used by the Japanese against the Chinese since 1937 and became common practice during World War II. Franco won the war in 1939, thanks to the substantial aid he received from Germany and Italy. He proceeded to organize Spain along the lines of Mussolini's Italy.

Personalist Dictatorships in Latin America

Dictatorships predominated in Latin America, particularly in the 1930s. By 1930 most Latin American countries had been republics in form for more than a century, considerably longer than most eastern or southern European nations. But democratic forms had often cloaked autocratic regimes. As on the Iberian Peninsula, authoritarian power in Latin America had traditionally been based on the landlords, church, and armed forces, which dominated the backward and poverty-stricken peasant and Amerindian populations. Since the late nineteenth century, however, urban exporters and their foreign customers, often British or American, demanded stable regimes in the interests of commercial development. Whether to preserve the traditional order or to encourage commercial growth, military rulers frequently installed the autocratic government required.

In the 1930s and subsequent decades, "personalist" dictatorships, often patterned along the lines of the Fascist regimes in Italy and Spain, flourished, especially in the larger and more developed Latin American nations. By combining welfare programs for the working class with law and order and protective tariffs for business interests, these rulers were sometimes popular with urban workers as well as with business leaders. Examples of such regimes include the Vargas dictatorship in Brazil and the Concordancia government in Argentina.

Getúlio Vargas (1883–1954) seized power in 1930 and dominated Brazilian politics for the next twenty-five years. Vargas made opposition parties illegal, often ruled by decree, and sometimes mobilized the army to impose his will. At the same time, he strengthened Brazilian industry and provided guaranteed employment, wages, and pensions for the urban working classes.

Argentina's Concordancia was an alliance of military men, nationalists, and conservatives who seized control in 1930 and governed through the decade. They ruled by fixing elections and ruthlessly crushing opposition. They also, however, helped Argentine industry to move out of small workshops and into sizable factories, a substantial economic advance. In 1943 a group of military officers, including the future dictator Juan Perón (1895–1974), seized power. Perón, who had observed the Nazi rule in Germany and the Fascist regime in Italy, was elected president in 1946 and 1951. Extremely popular among Argentina's working classes, Perón and his wife, Evita, developed a cult of personality, linking their fate to that of the entire nation. Perón instituted a series of social welfare programs but also accrued a massive public debt. Evita ran her own foundation to provide food and jobs for the urban poor, who repaid her with boundless loyalty. After Evita's death in 1952, there was even a campaign to have her declared a saint. Perón continued to rule until he was ousted in 1955. Perónism enjoyed a brief surge of popularity in the 1970s, but it was quashed by a brutal military dictatorship later in the decade.

Thus, during the interwar years, a wide variety of totalitarian and other authoritarian regimes came to power around the world. The chief totalitarian states were Fascist Italy, Nazi Germany, the Soviet Union under Stalin, and Japan. Less rigorous and bloody were the authoritarian governments of eastern and southern Europe and Latin America.

Aggression in Asia and Europe

I described [Britain's] foreign policy as being based upon three principles—first upon the protection of British interests . . . ; secondly on the maintenance of peace, and, as far as we can influence it, the settlement of differences by peaceful means and not by force; and thirdly the promotion of friendly relations with other nations. . . .

If we truly desire peace it is necessary to make a sustained effort to ascertain, and if possible to remove the causes which threaten peace. . . . We are now engaged upon a gigantic scheme of rearmament . . . , indeed, we were the last of the nations to rearm . . . [but] I cannot believe that, with a little good will and determination, it is not possible to remove genuine grievances and to clear away suspicions which may be entirely unfounded.

For these reasons, then, my colleagues and I have been anxious to find some opportunity of entering upon conversations with the two European countries with which we have been at variance, namely Germany and Italy, in order that we might find out whether there was any common ground upon which we might build up a general scheme of appeasement in Europe.*

You know already that I have done all that one man can do to compose this quarrel [between Germany and Czechoslovakia]. After my visit to Germany I have realized vividly how Herr Hitler feels that he must champion other Germans, and his indignation that grievances have not been met before this. He told me privately, and last night he repeated publicly, that after this Sudeten German question is settled, that is the end of Germany's territorial claims in Europe.**

*Prime Minister Neville Chamberlain, *Hansard's Parliamentary Debates,* Commons, 5th ser. (1938), pp. 53, 54, 64, 332, reprinted in George L. Mosse et al., eds., *Europe in Review: Readings and Sources since 1500,* rev. ed. (Chicago: Rand McNally, 1964), pp. 514–516.

**The Times (London), September 28, 1938, p. 12, reprinted in Mosse et al., eds. *Europe in Review,* pp. 514–516.

The international order built up by the Paris peace treaties broke down in the 1930s as Japan, Germany, and Italy resorted to force to achieve their national goals and settle real or imagined grievances. These statements by the British prime minister, Neville Chamberlain, sum up the reasons Western democracies appeased the aggressor nations. First, although he did not say so explicitly, no major power was willing to assist victims of aggression if that action could lead to war. Second, the Western democracies were militarily weak because they had largely demobilized their armed forces after World War I and were only belatedly rearming in the late 1930s. Third, some leaders, including many in Great Britain, believed that Germany had legitimate grievances, and they assumed that Hitler was a reasonable leader who would keep his promises. In addition, most Western nations feared international communism, and some regarded Hitler and Mussolini as better alternatives, and as bulwarks against Soviet expansion. As we shall see, appeasement encouraged aggressive actions by Japan in Asia, Italy in Europe and Africa, and Germany in Europe that culminated in World War II.

Although no nation fully realized its goals through the Paris peace treaties, Great Britain, the United States, and France were largely satisfied. This was not the case for their allies, Japan and Italy. Italy's ambitions in the Balkans were unrealized, while Japan wanted to further bolster its position in China and the Pacific. Among the defeated nations, Germany was especially bitter at the harsh terms in the Treaty of Versailles. It strongly resented the "war guilt" clause, the heavy reparations imposed, the loss of colonies and territory, and the severe limitations placed on its military establishment. The Soviet Union, a pariah nation now shunned because of its withdrawal from the conflict and its postwar talk of exporting Communist revolution, feared the hostility of the capitalist nations and sought to recover territories lost during World War I.

During the 1920s Great Britain, France, Italy, and Japan dominated the League of Nations, which tried to promote international cooperation and achieve international peace. As previously indicated, some positive steps toward peace were taken: the League mediated peace settlements between minor warring nations; naval powers met in Washington in 1921–1922 and signed a naval limitation treaty; the Locarno Pact of 1925 resolved international disputes, particularly between France and Germany; finally, sixty powers signed the Kellogg-Briand Pact of 1928, committing themselves to renounce war altogether. No general arms limitation agreement was reached, however, and France and the small new nations of Europe, fearful of Germany, built up large armies.

In the 1930s Japan, Italy, and Germany began to use armed force to redress their perceived wrongs and satisfy their territorial ambitions. Great Britain, the United States, and France tried to maintain peace at all costs. They found this could be done only by making repeated concessions to the aggressor states. The result was a pattern of aggression by totalitarian nations and appeasement by the democracies.

Japanese Aggression against China

Since the late nineteenth century, Japan had sought to expel Western imperialist nations from Asia and to replace them. It had already annexed Taiwan and Korea and established a sphere of influence in China. Japan had joined World War I as Great Britain's ally in order to seize German-held islands in the North Pacific and the German sphere of influence in China; these conquests had been confirmed by the Allies in the Treaty of Versailles. Japan had also forced weak China to make repeated concessions to Japanese commercial and political demands.

In 1928 the Nationalist party, led by Chiang Kai-shek, succeeded in unifying China for the first time since the fall of the Manchu dynasty. As Chiang began to organize China's first modern government, Japan feared the emergence of a strong China that could effectively resist Japanese imperialism. When many nations tried to combat the world depression of 1928 by imposing high tariffs on foreign imports, Japan became even more fearful for its economic well-being in a potentially hostile world. Leaders of the army and navy began to plan the conquest of Asia to secure essential raw materials and markets for Japan's manufactured products.

Japan especially coveted sparsely populated Manchuria's abundant agricultural and mineral resources. As General Tanaka Giichi, prime minister of Japan, purportedly said, "To conquer the world it is necessary to conquer China first, and to conquer China it is necessary to conquer Manchuria and Mongolia first." As long as they could control the local ruler in Manchuria, the Japanese were willing to allow China to maintain a facade of sovereignty over its northeastern provinces. The Nationalist government in China, however, had targeted Manchuria for economic development and was eager to recover rights already lost to Japan. Therefore the Japanese military decided they needed to strike before the Chinese developed a strong defense.

On September 18, 1931, middle-rank officers in the Japanese army stationed in Manchuria staged a bomb explosion on a Japanese-controlled railway outside Mukden, the chief administrative city of the Manchurian provinces. After blaming the Chinese for the Manchurian or Mukden Incident, as it was called, the entire Japanese army in Manchuria, reinforced by Japanese units stationed in Korea, swung into action over a wide front. When the Japanese prime minister and the civilian cabinet tried to control the army during the next months, the minister of war undermined them by declaring that the military was not subordinate to the political authorities. Public support for the army's insubordination led to the fall of the cabinet.

Because the Chinese army would be no match for the Japanese, China appealed to the League of Nations and nations such as the United States that had signed the Kellogg-Briand Pact to resolve the Manchurian Incident. Ignoring the pleas of the League and the U.S. government to cease military activities, the Japanese army completed its conquest of Manchuria in early 1932. Japan then established a puppet regime, called Manchukuo, in the conquered region. The League dispatched a commission headed by the British diplomat Lord Lytton to investigate. Its findings, known as the Lytton Report, condemned Japanese aggression in Manchuria, branded Manchukuo a puppet state, and called on Japan to restore Manchuria to China. When the League Assembly unanimously endorsed the Lytton Report, Japan resigned from the League of Nations. The U.S. government refused to recognize Manchukuo or the territorial changes that resulted from the aggression. Save for these moral sanctions, nothing was done to restrain Japan.

Japan followed up with other acts of aggression against China. In 1932 the Japanese navy opened a second front by attacking Shanghai, China's major port. Japanese warships shelled the city at point-blank range and killed many civilians, but Chinese defenses prevailed and Shanghai did not fall. After this debacle, the Japanese aggressors were uniformly successful. In 1933 they conquered Jehol, a province adjacent to Manchuria, and added it to Manchukuo. Beginning in 1934, Japan launched a simultaneous military and propaganda campaign aimed at creating a second puppet state to comprise all of North China and be called "North-Chinaland."

Realizing that China was not militarily ready to face the Japanese, Chiang Kai-shek sought to gain time by appeasing Japan with piecemeal concessions. Meanwhile, with the help of German advisers, he hurriedly built up his army and air force. He also constructed railroads, roads, and factories in preparation for war. All along, Chiang insisted that China must achieve "unification before resistance." This required that he defeat the Chinese Communist rebels first. Though militarily sound, this strategy was unpopular with many Chinese, who demanded an immediate response to Japanese expansion. In 1935 university students called for the organization of a National Salvation movement to fight Japan. The concept won widespread popular support and eventually forced Chiang to stop his drive against the Chinese Communist forces and to begin talks for the formation of a united front. The hard-pressed Chinese Communists were happy to begin negotiations. The Soviet Union, busily preparing for war against Nazi Germany, also pressed the

Chinese Communists to accede to the Nationalist terms. The Soviets recognized that a united China could better resist Japan and thereby ease Japanese pressure on Soviet Siberia.

The prospect of a united China worried Japanese militarists and extremists, who now had great influence in their government. A strong China would foil their dream of controlling Asia. Assassinations of key leaders by junior army officers in the February Rebellion of 1936 had cowed the remaining civilian politicians and allowed the military to dominate the Japanese government. Once in power they sought the international isolation of the Soviet Union and closer collaboration with Germany. To this end they signed the Anti-Comintern Pact with Germany in 1936. When Italy joined a year later, the Axis alliance was complete. While preparing for a possible armed conflict with the United States and Great Britain, General Tojo Hideki (1884–1948), then chief of staff of the Japanese army in China (later prime minister), provoked war with China.

Fascist Italy's Aggressions

Since coming to power in 1922, Mussolini's Fascist government had preached strident nationalism. It bombarded Italians with stirring reminders of the greatness of the ancient Roman Empire and prominently displayed archaeological projects undertaken at government expense. To demonstrate Italy's greatness, in 1935 Mussolini launched an invasion of Ethiopia, one of two independent nations left in Africa and one that had repulsed Italian aggression in 1896. The Ethiopians resisted with all that they had, and Emperor Haile Selassie (reigned 1930–1974) made a moving appeal before the League of Nations on behalf of his country.

The League condemned Italy but took no effective steps to check its aggression. Only an embargo of petroleum to Italy would have stopped Mussolini's war machine, but the economically depressed democracies such as Great Britain and France were unwilling to take that step, and the United States, not being a League member, was not bound by its resolutions. British, French, and U.S. oil companies continued to supply petroleum to Italy. As Japan had shown, a determined power could defy the League and not suffer punishment, and, like Japan, Italy resigned from the League. As the Japanese military had done in Manchuria and Shanghai, Italian planes bombed Ethiopian civilian centers.

In 1936, after a brief, one-sided struggle, Ethiopia was incorporated into the Italian Empire, and Italy's King Victor Emmanuel III was declared emperor of Ethiopia. Two years later, in 1938, Mussolini's forces attacked and conquered tiny Albania, a small Balkan nation Italy had coveted but failed to gain at the Paris Peace Conference.

Nazi Aggression in Europe

Meanwhile Adolf Hitler was implementing his own aggressive foreign policies in central Europe. After coming to power in 1933, Hitler moved quickly to restore Germany's self-confidence and military and economic strength. In defiance of the Treaty of Versailles, Hitler promptly began to rebuild Germany's armed forces. He vigorously demanded that central European territories with large German-speaking populations be incorporated into the Third Reich. He was no less insistent on obtaining living space (*Lebensraum*) for Germans, particularly in Slavic areas of eastern Europe, where German peoples had been settling since the Middle Ages.

Having rearmed Germany and strengthened its industries, Hitler successfully implemented his grand designs between 1936 and 1939. His first move was to send the revived German army into the Rhineland in 1936. Although part of Germany, this important industrial region had been demilitarized under the terms of the Treaty of Versailles and served as a buffer zone between Germany and France. A demilitarized Rhineland gave France a measure of security, but was a galling symbol of Germany's defeat in World War I. German commanders worried that the French would send troops to stop the Germans and enforce the treaty, but Hitler guessed rightly that they would not. Thus Germany remilitarized the Rhineland. Hitler had won his biggest gamble thus far, and his prestige soared. The weakened German high command, which had advised against risking French retaliation by militarizing the Rhineland, was subsequently reluctant to challenge Hitler's judgment.

Great Britain and France had the military power to stop Hitler at this stage, but they did not for a variety of reasons. First, the general populace in both countries genuinely abhorred war. The generation that had suffered from the horrors of World War I was now in power. Governments were also reluctant to increase military spending in the face of many unsolved social and economic problems caused by the depression. Many, especially in Great Britain, felt that Germany had been dealt with too harshly after World War I and thought that the German demands for treaty revision were justified; a few in western Europe and the United States liked Hitler and his policies. Hitler moreover had convinced many that he was a reasonable man with limited goals. Most western Europeans also feared the Soviet Union and viewed a strong Germany under Hitler as a bulwark against potential Soviet aggression and against the feared spread of communism in general.

The Munich Conference. At Munich, Germany, September 29–30, 1938, Neville Chamberlain (here seated to Hitler's right) and other Western leaders tried to avoid war by agreeing to Adolf Hitler's demand to absorb the Sudetenland. Hitler went on to seize the rest of Czechoslovakia, and in less than a year Europe was at war. Ever since, the name "Munich" has symbolized pointless appeasement of an aggressor.

Although the isolationist-minded United States viewed the advances of the aggressive totalitarian states with misgivings, it adopted no effective policy to counter them. As we have seen, the United States protested the Japanese aggression against China and refused to recognize their conquests. Understandably, the Japanese were unimpressed and unde- terred. Most Americans viewed their participation in World War I as a mistake and did

Map 15.1 Central Europe, April 1939. This map shows German gains after three years of aggression and consolidation under Adolf Hitler. Italy, Poland, and Hungary also expanded. Although to this point Hitler had enlarged Germany without war, Great Britain and France were now awake to the futility of appeasement, and Hitler's next aggressive move, against Poland, ignited World War II in Europe.

not wish to get embroiled in European problems again. Because they felt that Germany had received harsh treatment at Versailles, most were inclined to be conciliatory to Hitler. They, too, regarded Hitler's Germany as a buffer against international communism. Most Americans devoted their energies to economic recovery from the Great Depression and gave little thought to fascist aggressors. Thus President Franklin Roosevelt's criticism of Hitler's remilitarization of the Rhineland was muted.

Early in 1938 Hitler again violated the Versailles settlement by annexing the German-speaking nation of Austria into his new empire. This move was part of Hitler's ambitious plan to expand Germany by incorporating all adjacent German populations into his Third Reich. Austrian Nazis and many other Austrians supported the century-old notion of greater German unity, and the occupation of Austria was bloodless. The union with Austria, or the *Anschluss*, substantially increased the size and population of Germany.

Having achieved the *Anschluss* without opposition from the Western democracies, Hitler turned his attention to the German-speaking minority in the Sudeten mountain region of Czechoslovakia, which, like Austria, bordered on Germany. Hitler demanded the right to incorporate the Sudetenland into Germany, because 3 million ethnic Germans lived there.

France and the Soviet Union had signed treaties with Czechoslovakia that required them to aid the Czechs in the event of war. Although Great Britain had no treaty ties with Czechoslovakia, it was also concerned about peace in Europe. The democracies' acquiescence in Hitler's dismemberment of Czechoslovakia, a brutal act against a peaceful, sovereign nation, was a shameful episode of appeasement. Many Americans were shocked by what happened to Czechoslovakia, and Roosevelt appealed to Hitler to refrain from attacking other European nations in the future. Hitler ridiculed Roosevelt's appeal and characterized the United States as a degenerate nation that would not fight. Indeed, the U.S. Congress refused to repeal neutrality laws that made it impossible to help victims of bellicose nations; thus the United States remained a spectator as aggressors went unchecked in Europe and Asia.

British prime minister Neville Chamberlain (1869–1940), joined by the French premier Edouard Daladier (1884–1970) and Mussolini, met with Hitler at Munich in September 1938 to address the crisis. Although the Soviet Union had earlier declared its willingness to come to the aid of Czechoslovakia, Great Britain and France decided to appease Hitler. They agreed to allow Hitler to annex the Sudetenland in return for his guarantee that the rest of Czechoslovakia would remain free. Abandoned by its allies, Czechoslovakia decided not to resist the Nazi takeover of the Sudetenland. As a result, it lost about a third of its population, much of its heavy industry, and important defensive fortifications. Chamberlain declared on his return to London that he had achieved "peace for our time." This peace proved illusory, however, for by March 1939 Hitler and the authoritarian leaders of Hungary and Poland had divided the remaining portion of Czechoslovakia.

Hitler then turned his attention to Lithuania and Poland. He took Memel, a Baltic port with a large German population, from Lithuania and demanded Danzig (which also had a German-speaking population) and other concessions from Poland. British and French leaders, at last convinced that Hitler's word was worthless, announced that they would fight to defend the territorial integrity of Poland, but Hitler, with good reason, doubted their resolve.

Hitler also formed alliances with like-minded aggressive states. Agreements in 1936 and 1937 had created the Berlin-Rome-Tokyo Axis, avowedly an anticommunist alliance, but one that was also intended to coordinate the aggressive activities of the three partner states.

Hitler's most startling diplomatic coup was the Hitler-Stalin Pact of August 1939, in which the two archenemies agreed not to attack each other and to remain neutral should either be attacked by a third party. This agreement protected Hitler from a two-front war in case the British and French should finally take up arms against Germany. It gave Stalin the time he needed to build up Soviet military and industrial strength for what he knew would be an eventual reckoning with Hitler, and it also ensured that he, too, would not have to fight a two-front war with both Germany and Japan. A secret protocol divided Poland between the Soviet Union and Germany and recognized Estonia, Latvia, and Lithuania, three independent states on the Baltic coast, as being within the Soviet sphere of influence. On September 1, 1939, one week after signing the pact, Germany invaded Poland, marking the beginning of World War II in Europe.

World War II and Postwar Settlements

Following recent developments at Lukouchiao, the Japanese have by low and treacherous methods seized our cities . . . and have killed many of our fellow-countrymen. There is no end to the humiliation and insults that they have heaped upon us. . . . Since the Mukden [Manchurian] incident on September 18, 1931, the more indignities we have borne, the more we have yielded, the more violent has Japanese aggression become. . . . Now we have reached the point when we can endure no longer; we will give away no more. The whole nation must rise as one man and fight these Japanese bandits until we have destroyed them and our own life is secure. . . .

Soldiers! The supreme moment has come. With one heart and purpose advance! Refuse to retreat. Drive out the unspeakably evil invaders and bring about the rebirth of our nation.*

*Chiang Kai-shek, Resistance and Reconstruction: Messages during China's Six Years of War, 1937–1943 (New York: Harper & Row, 1943), pp. 16, 19.

In 1937 the Japanese army, which had occupied Manchuria six years earlier, struck China again, overrunning its eastern provinces. The head of the Kuomintang (the party that governed China), Chiang Kai-shek, retreated to the interior, where he set up his government. In this excerpt from a speech delivered in 1937, Chiang, appealing to the nationalism of his men, announces that the time has come to take up the challenge to drive the enemy out of China.

Just as Japan meant to dominate East Asia, Hitler's goal was to raise Germany to a preeminent position in Europe. The Western democracies, distracted and on the defensive, took no positive action for fear of causing a major war. But concessions only whetted Hitler's appetite, and it was soon apparent that he was not content with uniting the Germans under his rule. His occupation of Czechoslovakia demonstrated that his appeal for self-determination was in fact a hollow disguise for a brutal policy of expansion. By overreaching himself, Hitler converted the European democracies from appeasement to resistance.

Japan Launches All-Out War against China

War began in Asia on July 7, 1937, when Japanese forces attacked a railway junction near Peking. The action came to be known as the Marco Polo Bridge Incident. The Japanese at first hoped to use the incident to extort political and territorial concessions from China, but an aroused Chinese nation insisted that the government refuse further Japanese demands. Thereupon Japan, without declaring formal war, launched an all-out attack, hoping to score a quick victory. In spite of recent modernizing efforts, the Chinese forces were no match for the Japanese army and navy and could only delay enemy advances. Japanese planes bombed civilian targets indiscriminately, just as the Italians had in Ethiopia and the Germans in Spain. The fall of the Chinese capital, Nanking, was followed by frightful atrocities, including the massacre of an estimated 300,000 civilians. By the end of 1938, the entire Chinese coast was under Japanese occupation.

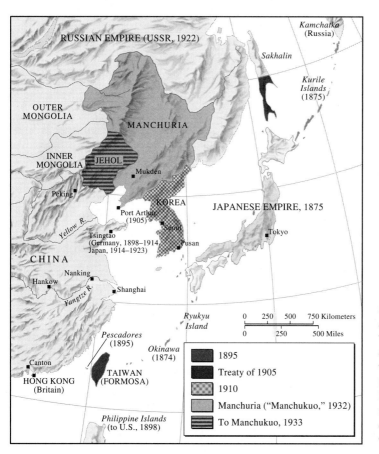

Map 15.2 Japanese Aggression in Asia. Up to 1937 the Japanese were able to conquer large sections of China with little resistance. In that year, however, the Chinese refused to make further concessions, and full-scale war erupted.

United by the common enemy, the Kuomintang and the Communists stopped their civil war and rallied around Chiang Kai-shek. The government moved up the Yangtze River to mountain-rimmed Chungking, in southwestern China, beyond the reach of Japan's mechanized divisions but not Japanese bombs. Millions of civilians trekked to the interior, taking with them dismantled factories, schools, libraries, and equipment. They destroyed much of what they could not take, leaving a scorched earth for the Japanese occupiers. The retreating Chinese paid a high cost in lives, but such tactics as opening the dikes of the Yellow River slowed down the Japanese advance.

The war continued because the Chinese refused to surrender, and Japan would not abandon its efforts to subdue China completely. The bulk of the Japanese army was pinned down in China and would remain there throughout the war. Even with 2 million troops in China, the Japanese could effectively control only cities and major communication lines. Japanese brutality aroused nationalistic fervor among the hitherto politically apathetic peasants, many of whom became guerrilla fighters. The Japanese were equally unsuccessful in luring important Chinese leaders to collaborate with them. They gave no real power to those who did, merely placing them at the head of puppet governments in occupied areas.

China fought alone until Japan's attack on Pearl Harbor in December 1941. Western powers were sympathetic, but Great Britain and France were preoccupied with the Nazi threat in Europe. The United States followed an isolationist policy, but in fact, its trade law benefited Japan by allowing it to buy steel and fuel that aided its operations in China. Only the Soviet Union, which feared Japanese designs on its Asian territories, gave substantial aid in the first years in the form of loans, airplanes, and pilots who helped to organize China's air defense.

The outbreak of war in Europe in 1939 initially made China's position even bleaker: the Soviet Union withdrew its assistance to concentrate on the home front, and Great Britain and France, fully occupied in Europe, bent over backward not to offend Japan. The real turning point was Japan's attack on Pearl Harbor and the U.S.-controlled Philippines and on British possessions in Southeast Asia. The British and U.S. declaration of war against Japan and similar Chinese actions against Japan and its partners incorporated the war in Asia into the worldwide conflict against Axis aggression. China became part of the China-Burma-India war theater, and Chiang Kai-shek became supreme Allied commander of the China theater.

Axis Advances in Europe

As described previously, Germany, along with the other two aggressor nations, had formed the Berlin-Rome-Tokyo Axis in 1937, ostensibly to contain the expansion of communism. Hitler's next alliance stunned the democratic powers. Untroubled by ideological scruples, in August 1939 Hitler and the Soviet Union signed a nonaggression pact that also included provisions for the division of eastern Europe. Secure that he would not be attacked by the Soviet Union, Hitler ordered his troops to invade Poland on September 1, 1939. To Hitler's surprise, Great Britain and France promptly declared war on Germany.

In stark contrast to the static trench warfare of 1914–1918, the Germans in their first major action introduced new tactics called *blitzkrieg*, meaning "lightning war." The first phase was carried out through the air. The German Luftwaffe knocked out the small Polish air force, while German *stukas*, or dive bombers, demolished rearward communications and spread terror among the civilian population by massive bombardments. The second phase was initiated by heavy tanks, followed by lighter armored divisions. After tearing large gaps in the enemy lines, the fast-moving motorized columns streaked across the Polish plain, often several days ahead of the main body of infantry. The antiquated Polish army fought bravely, but it was torn to shreds. With the Soviet Union invading simultaneously from the east and Great Britain and France unable to help, Polish resistance collapsed in less than a month.

Throughout the autumn there was practically no activity on the western front, and as the war dragged on into the winter of 1939–1940, cynics began to call it the "phony war." During this period the British concentrated on building up their armaments, clearing enemy surface vessels from the ocean, and imposing a blockade on Germany. The French army, expecting another long defensive war, waited complacently behind the elaborately fortified Maginot line.

After the Allies had ignored Hitler's peace offer, he struck without warning in April 1940, seizing Norway and Denmark. Having secured his northern flank, he attacked France through Belgium and the Netherlands so as to outflank the Maginot line. Beginning their blitzkrieg against the West on May 10, German forces quickly breached the defenses of the Netherlands and Luxembourg. The Belgians held out longer, as they were supported by French troops and a small British force. Farther south, German armored columns invaded France through the Ardennes forest, which was thought to be militarily impenetrable, and raced to the channel coast, trapping tens of thousands of French, British, and Belgian troops in Flanders. The retreating Allied forces fell back to Dunkirk, where hundreds of British ships, many of them civilian craft, managed to evacuate some 335,000 men, one-third of whom were French and Belgian.

The heroic rescue operation saved the British army for the future and awakened British pride, but it did nothing to relieve the situation in France. With the French reeling under the onslaught, Mussolini, anxious to participate in the division of the spoils, declared war on France on June 10. Four days later the Germans entered Paris unopposed, and the new head of the French government, eighty-four-year-old Marshal Philippe Pétain (1856–1951), one-time hero of the battle of Verdun, believed further resistance was hopeless and requested a cease-fire. The terms, dictated by Hitler personally in the same railroad car in which Germany had agreed to an armistice in 1918, divided France into two zones. The northern half was occupied by German troops, and the rest of the country was placed under a puppet regime with its headquarters at Vichy and headed by Pétain.

Great Britain was left alone to face the might of Hitler's military machine. But under the inspired leadership of Prime Minister Winston Churchill (1874–1965), who took office on May 10, 1940, the British were determined to continue fighting, regardless of the cost. Hitler understood that complete mastery of the air was essential for the safe

"All Behind You, Winston." This cartoon appeared in the London *Evening Standard,* May 10, 1940, the day Winston Churchill took office and formed a national government. Shunned as too rash and controversial a figure in the prewar years, Churchill took an active role in nearly every aspect of the war effort, incessantly demanding more imagination and rapid action from his subordinates. His stirring speeches inspired heroism in the British people standing alone against Hitler's Third Reich.

transport of his invasion force across the channel. After the British rejected a second peace offer, in August 1940 Hitler launched a fierce air attack against Great Britain aimed at destroying the Royal Air Force (RAF).

In the ensuing weeks, the Luftwaffe wreaked massive destruction on the ground but also sustained losses far exceeding those of the RAF. Indeed, the toll on the Luftwaffe was so great that at the start of September the German leaders abandoned their primary objective of bombing air installations and defeating the RAF and began instead to carry out night raids against London and other major southern cities. Some industrial towns like Coventry took a terrible pounding, and parts of London were reduced to rubble, but the exorbitant costs only increased British solidarity and will to resist. By winter, when it was obvious that the air campaign had failed, Hitler postponed indefinitely his plans to invade Great Britain. The battle of Britain was over. The entire nation had played a part in handing Hitler his first military defeat, but none more than the RAF, whose lasting monument was Churchill's eulogy: "Never in the field of human conflict was so much owed by so many to so few."

Frustrated in his air assault on Great Britain, Hitler turned his attention to the Balkans in preparation for his clash with the Soviet Union. By threats and bribes, Hitler had already brought Hungary, Romania, and Bulgaria into the Axis camp in the fall of 1940, but Yugoslavia stubbornly clung to its independence. In the spring of 1941, Hitler's armies quickly subjugated Yugoslavia and unleashed a massive attack against Greece with the object of rescuing Mussolini. In the previous October, Mussolini's armies had invaded Greece, but after initial successes they had been driven back to Albania. In a lightning campaign, the Germans forced the Greeks to surrender on April 23, 1941.

Hitler had found it expedient to sign a nonaggression pact with Stalin, but he had never abandoned his plans for an eventual attack on the Soviet Union as a prerequisite to seizing living space for the German people in the east. Hitler expected to conquer the

Soviet Union by the end of the summer. Like Napoleon, he underestimated the vast distances, the bitterly harsh winters, and the capacity of the Soviet soldiers and civilians to endure untold suffering and hardships. The invasion, originally scheduled for May, had to be postponed a month so that German troops could bail out Mussolini from his plight in Greece. The delay may have meant the difference between victory and defeat.

In the early hours of June 22, 1941, Hitler unleashed 3 million men along the entire eastern front from Finland to the Caucasus. It was the start of one of the most savagely fought struggles in the annals of military history. All the early signs indicated that the German blitzkrieg was enjoying the same success in the Soviet Union as it had elsewhere. German armored columns slashed deep into Soviet territory, encircling the dazed and disorganized enemy forces and capturing hundreds of thousands of prisoners. As the Germans pressed forward, however, they encountered unexpected resistance, and the drives on Moscow and Leningrad, hampered by an early and severe cold, bogged down. Hitler had expected victory before winter set in, so the Germans were unprepared for the arctic weather. The men froze in their summer uniforms and many suffered from frostbite. Guns would not fire and motorized equipment stalled without antifreeze. The German juggernaut ground to a halt just short of complete victory. It would never regain its initial advantage.

During the first week of December, the Red Army, which had secretly brought fresh troops from Siberia, mounted a huge counteroffensive north and south of Moscow. They drove the Germans back until Hitler gave his troops strict orders not to yield any more ground, even if it meant certain death. The Germans regrouped and stabilized the

Churchill Addresses Parliament on May 13, 1940

*I would say to the House, as I have said to those who have joined this Government: I "have nothing to offer but blood, toil, tears and sweat." We have before us an ordeal of the most grievous kind. We have before us many, many long months of struggle and of suffering. You ask what is our policy? I can say: It is to wage war, by sea, land and air, with all our might and with all the strength that God can give us; to wage war against a monstrous tyranny, never surpassed in the dark lamentable catalogue of human crime. That is our policy. You ask what is our aim? I can answer in one word: it is victory, victory at all costs, victory in spite of all terror, victory, however long and hard the road may be; for without victory, there is no survival. Let that be realized; no survival for the British Empire, no survival for all that the British Empire has stood for, no survival for the urge and impulses of the ages, that mankind will move for-*ward towards its goal. But I take my task with buoyancy and hope. I feel sure that our cause will not be suffered to fail among men. At this time I feel entitled to claim the aid of all, and I say, "Come then, let us go forward together with our united strength."*

Churchill assumed the reins of government on May 10 in the worst of circumstances. His inaugural speech to Parliament as war leader three days later was intended to instill confidence in a nation shaken by the fall of Europe. Churchill's greatest contribution to winning the war was his oratory, or to be more precise, his speeches, particularly those which dramatized the events of 1940–1941 when Britain had no hope of winning the war alone and only a slender chance of survival unless help arrived from outside.

*Robert Rhodes James, ed., Winston S. Churchill: His Complete Speeches (New York: Chelsea House, 1974), vol. 6 (1935–1942), p. 6220.

1,000-mile front. The Soviet Union had paid an exorbitant price during the early months of the fighting. The Germans occupied the best farmland in the Soviet Union as well as the most important industrial areas. The Red Army had lost hundreds of thousands of men in combat, and nearly 4 million more had been captured. Nevertheless, Hitler had not defeated the Soviet Union by December as he had planned. Thereafter both sides attacked and counterattacked on an unprecedented scale. The Soviet Union would remain the main theater of war until the Allies invaded France in the summer of 1944.

The United States Enters the War

In 1940 Japan faced a serious dilemma. Its army could neither win the war in China nor extricate itself without admitting defeat. In the meantime U.S. public opinion had become so aroused by events in China that Washington had forbidden shipment of scrap iron and oil to Japan and persuaded the Dutch and British to do the same. With these vital supplies cut off, the Japanese military adopted a southern strategy aimed at conquering Southeast Asia so that they could seize the needed oil and other raw materials produced in that region. Japan had already secured de facto control of French Indochina from the puppet Vichy regime. With Great Britain tied down in its desperate struggle against Nazi Germany in Europe, only the United States could challenge Japan's ambitions in Southeast Asia. Negotiations between the two nations became deadlocked when the United States demanded Japanese withdrawal from China.

Japan decided to gamble on war with the United States. Its militarists assumed that in a general war the United States would first move against Germany. If Germany won, Japan would be safe; and even if Germany should lose, the Japanese would have bought sufficient time to bring China to its knees and to consolidate their empire in Southeast Asia and the Pacific. Japanese militarists were further convinced that the United States lacked the moral fiber to wage a determined war. Thus, without consulting Japan's Axis allies, Prime Minister and General Hideki Tojo ordered a simultaneous surprise attack on the British, Dutch, and U.S. possessions in Southeast Asia and the Pacific. Japanese forces struck on all fronts on December 7–8, 1941. Carrier-based bombers struck Pearl Harbor in Hawaii, crippling the U.S. navy in a single blow. The United States immediately declared war against Japan; Japan and the other Axis powers responded by declaring war against the United States. With the United States and many nations in the Western Hemisphere involved, World War II was now a truly global conflict.

Japanese war aims initially succeeded brilliantly. In quick succession Japanese forces captured British Malaya and the great British naval base at Singapore, the Dutch East Indies, the U.S.-held Philippines, and British Burma. Independent Thailand bowed to Japanese demands in order to avoid conquest and became a subject ally. India and Australia were threatened with invasion. Within six months of Pearl Harbor, Japanese forces had conquered more territory in Asia than had the Germans in Europe. Japan euphemistically called its empire the Greater Asia Co-Prosperity Sphere.

Japan's lightning success dealt an irreparable blow to Western imperialism in Asia. However, "Co-Prosperity" and its slogan "Asia for the Asians" soon proved a cruel hoax; those Asians who had hoped that Japan would emancipate them from European rule and grant them freedom found that they had only changed masters. The brutal Japanese mil-

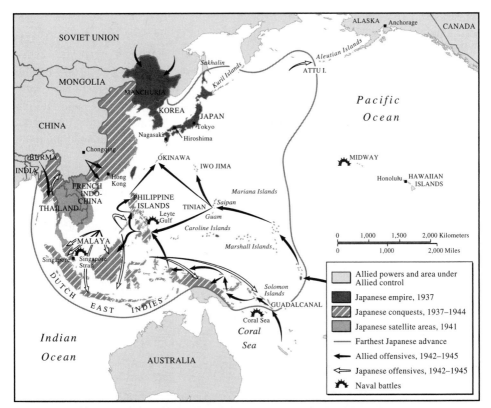

Map 15.3 World War II in Asia and the Pacific. War came to this area in stages, beginning with Japan's invasion of China in 1937. In December 1941 the Japanese attacked British, Dutch, and American possessions. By May 1942, they controlled Southeast Asia and the western Pacific and were even threatening Australia and India. The United States defeated the Japanese by destroying their fleet and bombing their home islands. At the time of surrender, Japanese land forces still held large areas of Asia and the Pacific.

itary rulers felt superior to their conquered peoples and made exacting demands for raw materials and human resources from the conquered regions. As a result, anti-Japanese resistance rose in all the conquered lands and abetted the growing nationalism of these colonial peoples.

Hitler's "New Order"

By the end of 1941, Hitler was at the pinnacle of his power, having acquired the most extensive empire in European history. The administration of the captive states varied, depending on German aims. A number of areas on Germany's borders like Alsace-Lorraine and Luxembourg were annexed outright to the Reich or set aside for future German colonization. Some regions were administered indirectly through puppet regimes such as the one headed by Pétain. Still others in German-occupied territories were ruled by military governors. The satellite states of eastern Europe were more or less left alone, except in the last stages of the war. To a weary and disillusioned Europe, Hitler offered a new order of discipline and purpose, a refashioned Europe in which each nation would be assigned its fitting role. But Hitler's new order, as it eventually evolved, bore no resemblance to the promised ideal.

Hitler's main interest was to subjugate the conquered territories to the immediate wartime needs of the Reich. All countries under the heel of the Germans had to pay for the cost of occupation as well as deliver raw materials and food to the Reich. Since most able-bodied Germans were at the front or holding down a conquered continent, millions of new workers were needed for the fields and factories. The only labor reservoir available to Hitler was in the occupied territories. At first, workers were recruited voluntarily, but as demand soared, the Germans resorted to forced labor drafts. By the end of the war, millions of foreigners had been transported to the Reich as slave labor.

Even more reprehensible was Hitler's racial policy. Hitler had made no secret from the outset of his career that he considered the Germans to be superior to all other groups. During the war people in the subject territories were placed in various categories. Those who fit into the Nazis' conception of the Aryan race, such as the Dutch and Scandina-

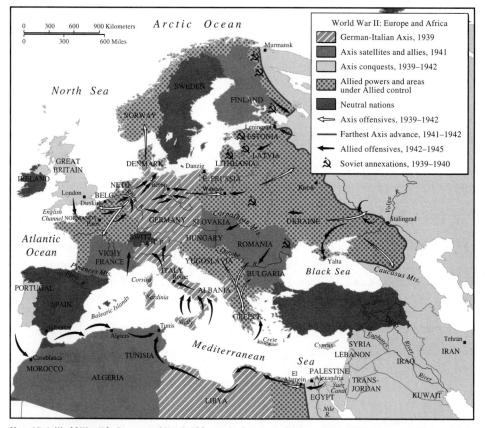

Map 15.4 World War II in Europe and North Africa. In the first phase of the war (1939–1942), Germany and Italy and their allies subjugated most of Europe except for Great Britain and the Soviet Union. In the second stage of the war (1942–1945), powerful U.S. forces arrived in the west and, with the aid of the British, cleared the Mediterranean. They then landed in France and pushed eastward into Germany. Meanwhile, the newly constituted, massive Soviet army drove westward through central Europe and the Balkans, meeting the Western allies in the heart of Germany.

vians, were given preferential treatment, for they were supposedly destined to join the Germans as partners in the new order. The French and Belgians were considered inferior races but tolerated on account of their usefulness in a supportive capacity. In the eyes of the Nazis, the Slavs, classified as subhumans, were fit only for enslavement. Huge numbers of Poles and Russians were herded into camps as forced laborers, condemned to work and live under conditions of filth and misery; many died of exhaustion, starvation, or beatings from guards.

The camps became giant slaughterhouses after Hitler decided to exterminate the Jews, whom he regarded, along with homosexuals and Gypsies, as the lowest species of humanity. Hitler's "Final Solution" was entrusted to the elite SS, which carried out its grisly duties with fanaticism and efficiency. The horrors the Nazis perpetrated were so shocking to the human imagination that even today they can scarcely be believed. In 1941, in Auschwitz, Poland, one of many death camps, the Nazis killed an average of 12,000 people a day. All told, the Nazis murdered 6 million Jews, about 75 percent of the European Jewish population, in the greatest act of genocide in history. It is now referred to as the Holocaust.

The Home Front

To an even greater extent than World War I, World War II required the cooperation of all sectors of the warring societies. All civilians became involved in the conflict in one way or another. It is estimated that almost as many civilians as military personnel died from enemy action. Aerial bombardments, sieges, wide operational sweeps on the ground, and bloody reprisals by invading armies brought the reality of war directly to tens of millions of people in Europe and Asia. Unlike World War I, the men serving at the front bore no resentment toward those who stayed at home. Everyone was considered to be pulling together and sharing the hardships caused by the war.

The war was more widespread and involved more men in the fighting line and greater weapons of destruction than ever before. Millions of men had to be mobilized and equipped, and guns, tanks, and airplanes had to be turned out as fast as humanly possible. In this total war, central governments assumed great powers as a prerequisite to coordinating the national economy, conducting long-range planning, and ensuring cooperation from every sector of society. The Soviet Union, which had a planned economy, quickly mobilized its human and material resources, pressing into service all civilians between the ages of sixteen and fifty-five, imposing severe rationing, and extending hours for workers. Although the British government responded more slowly, it effectively managed its resources and production distribution, regulated wages and prices, and sponsored much scientific research. During the first two years of the war, the German government refrained from demanding all-out sacrifice from its people, and domestic consumption remained relatively high. Only after it was obvious that the war would drag on did Germany mobilize more systematically.

As in World War I, all belligerent nations tried to maintain patriotic enthusiasm among their civilian populations. All news was censored, and governments waged propaganda campaigns that stressed the righteousness of their cause and exhorted their people to hate the enemy, work harder, and make sacrifices. Examples of intolerance

Holocaust in the Ukraine

[Public notice in Kiev:] All Yids living in the city of Kiev and its vicinity are to report by 8 o'clock on the morning of Monday, September 29th, 1941, at the corner of Melnikovsky and Dokhturov Streets (near the cemetery). They are to take with them documents, money, valuables, as well as warm clothes, underwear, etc.

Any Yid not carrying out this instruction and who is found elsewhere will be shot....

They started arriving while it was still dark, to be in good time to get seats in the train. With their howling children, their old and sick, some of them weeping, others swearing at each other, the Jews who lived and worked on the vegetable farm emerged on to the street. There were bundles roughly tied woven baskets, boxes of carpenters' tools.... Some elderly women were wearing strings of onions hung around their necks like gigantic necklaces—food supplies for the journey....

Then the people in charge started giving orders and shouting, making those who were sitting down stand up and moving them on, pushing the ones in the rear forward, so that some sort of straggling queue was formed. Some of the people's belongings were put down in one place, others in another; there was much pushing and shoving....

At that moment they entered a long corridor formed by two rows of soldiers and dogs. It was very narrow—some four or five feet across. The soldiers were lined up shoulder to shoulder, with their sleeves rolled up, each of them brandishing a rubber club or big stick.

Blows rained down on the people as they passed through.

There was no question of being able to dodge or get away.

Brutal blows, immediately drawing blood, descended on their heads, backs and shoulders from left and right. The soldiers kept shouting: "Schnell, schnell!" laughing happily, as if they were watching a circus act; they even found ways of delivering harder blows in the more vulnerable places, the ribs, the stomach and the groin....

The poor people, now quite out of their minds, tumbled out into a space cordoned off by troops, a sort of square overgrown with grass. The whole of this grass plot was scattered with articles of underwear, footwear and other clothes.

The Ukrainian police ... were grabbing hold of people roughly, hitting them and shouting:

"Get your clothes off! Quickly! Schnell!"

Those who hesitated had their clothes ripped off them by force, and were kicked and struck with knuckle-dusters or clubs by the Germans, who seemed to be drunk with fury in a sort of sadistic rage....

[Back in Kiev] ... A fourteen-year-old boy, the son of the collective-farm stableman ... [ran] into the farmyard and was telling the most frightful stories: that they were being made to take all their clothes off; that several of them would be lined up [in a quarry], one behind the other, so as to kill more than one at a time; that the bodies were then piled up and earth thrown over them, and then more bodies were laid on top; that there were many who were not really dead, so that you could see the earth moving, that some had managed to crawl out, only to be knocked over the head and thrown back into the pile....

They packed the hospital patients into the gas-chambers in groups of sixty to seventy, then ran the engines for some fifteen minutes so that the exhaust gases went into the vans. Then the suffocated people were taken out and dropped into a pit. This work went on for several days, quietly and methodically. The Germans were not in a hurry, and took regular hour-long breaks for meals.

*The patients in the hospital were not all mad; there were many who were simply being treated for nervous disorders. But they were all buried in the pits of Babi Yar. Most remarkable of all was that after the first horrible days of Babi Yar the destruction of all the patients in an enormous hospital went practically unnoticed and was even taken as a matter of course.... ***

*A. Anatoli (Kuznetsov), Babi Yar, trans. David Floyd (New York: Farrar, Straus and Giroux, 1970), pp. 91, 93, 97, 105, 106, 153.

occurred even in the United States, where Americans of Japanese ancestry were interned in camps for the duration of the war simply because of the unjustified fear that they might be disloyal.

Nazi Victims at Bergen-Belsen. The British, who liberated the concentration camp in April 1945, were horrified by what they found. The camp had been ravaged by a typhus epidemic and thousands of bodies lay unburied, rotting in the sun. Mass graves were dug and bulldozers were brought up to shovel in the dead.

© Bettmann/Corbis

Even more than in World War I, large numbers of women came out of their homes and into occupations traditionally dominated by men. In the United States, 200,000 women served in auxiliary branches of the armed forces, and 6 million worked in munitions factories. In some of the occupied countries, women fought in the resistance movement. Russia used women not only in the factories, mines, and railroads but also as combatants. Germany was something of an exception in that Nazi ideology forbade women any role outside the home. Thus few were allowed to replace the men in the fields and the factories.

The War in North Africa and the Invasion of Italy

Soon after Italy entered the war, Mussolini made a bid to wrest control of the eastern Mediterranean from the British. From bases in Ethiopia and Libya, he dispatched an army of 500,000 men against the small, poorly equipped British forces in northeastern Africa. One Italian army overran British Somaliland while another invaded Egypt from Libya with the object of seizing the Suez Canal. In December 1940 the British counterattacked and routed the Italian army, capturing 130,000 prisoners (about four times the number of British soldiers involved in the attack). Simultaneously, the British drove the Italians out of Somaliland and Ethiopia.

Once again, Hitler came to the rescue of his embattled ally, sending an elite unit, the Afrika Corps, under Field Marshal Erwin Rommel (1891–1944) across the Mediterranean. Rommel, known as the Desert Fox on account of his audacity and mastery of tank warfare, drove back the British, who had been weakened by the dispatch of some 60,000 troops to the Balkans. Rommel might have seized control of Egypt and the entire Middle East if he had been given sufficient forces, but Hitler could not spare them because he was attacking the Balkans and was about to invade Russia.

Forced to retreat late in 1941, Rommel lashed out with a devastating assault the following spring and advanced all the way to El-Alamein, sixty miles from Alexandria, where overextended supply lines forced him to call a halt. The lull permitted the British to rebuild their strength, and at the end of October 1942, under a new commander, the egotistical but brilliant General Bernard Montgomery (1887–1976), they were able to take the offensive. It proved successful—the first major British triumph in the war. Montgomery's forces smashed through the German defenses at El-Alamein, driving the invaders headlong into Libya. At this point an Allied army under General Dwight D. Eisenhower (1890–1969) landed in Morocco and Algeria. The Germans were eventually trapped between the Allies advancing from the west and the British from the east. In May 1943 the remnant of Rommel's weary army surrendered.

After clearing the Axis forces from North Africa, the Allies moved quickly to knock dispirited Italy out of the war. In July 1943 the Allies landed in Sicily and, facing only token resistance, conquered the island in less than six weeks. The invasion of Sicily proved fatal to Mussolini, who was forced out of office in a bloodless coup. The new Italian administration negotiated an armistice with General Eisenhower on September 3, one day after Canadian and British troops had established bridgeheads on the mainland.

Hitler reacted by sending as many troops as he could spare to prevent Italy from falling into Allied hands. The Allies found campaigning up the rugged peninsula arduous and costly and did not reach Rome until July 1944. The Germans were not completely expelled from Italy until May the following year, only weeks before Germany's final surrender. In the dying days of the war in Italy, Mussolini and his mistress tried to escape to Switzerland, but they were captured by the partisans and executed. Their corpses were hung upside down in a public square in Milan. It was an inglorious end for a man who had long likened himself to a Roman caesar.

Allied Victory in Europe

The Allies (the United States, Great Britain, the Soviet Union, and China) realized that they had to forge a worldwide alliance and agree on strategic priorities if the Axis powers were to be beaten. From 1942 to 1945, Roosevelt frequently met with Churchill and sometimes also with Stalin and Chiang to coordinate strategy. As Japanese planners had expected, the Allies decided to defeat Germany first, because it represented the greatest threat to Great Britain and the Soviet Union.

With both Great Britain and the Soviet Union already exhausted, the enormous productivity of U.S. industry became the backbone of the Allied war effort. The United States truly became the "Great Arsenal of Democracy" and supplied much of the war matériel used by all the Allies as well as arming 12 million soldiers. Government, military, and

LIVES AND TIMES ACROSS CULTURES

What Goes Around Comes Around: Tannenberg and Stalingrad

To check the Russian advance into East Prussia in August 1914, the German High Command sent General Paul von Hindenburg to take charge of the Eighth Army and appointed General Erich Ludendorff as his chief of staff. Ludendorff devised a plan to destroy the Russian army under General Alexander Samsonov invading from the south.

Basing his tactics on Hannibal's spectacular victory at Cannae in 216 B.C.E., Ludendorff moved a corps by rail to the region around Tannenberg to hold Samsonov's army, while sending two corps to envelop it from the flank and rear. Blinded by early Russian successes, Samsonov threw caution to the wind and obligingly walked into the trap. When he attacked, the German center yielded. As he drove ahead, German forces on both sides closed in and virtually encircled his army. The bitter fighting ended three days later with 125,000 Russians dead, wounded, or taken prisoner. Unable to face the tsar, Samsonov shot himself. The battle of Tannenberg offers one of the few examples of the complete destruction of an army. It made popular heroes of Hindenburg and Ludendorff in Germany and, more important, ended Russian plans in East Prussia even more completely than the Marne had stymied German plans in the west.

Thirty years later the Soviet regime avenged Tannenberg. In the spring of 1942 Hitler planned a drive from the Ukraine to Stalingrad on the Volga to prepare the way for his onslaught into the Caucasus, where 75 percent of Soviet oil reserves were located. During the first week in September, the German Sixth Army reached the outskirts of Stalingrad, expecting to take it in short order. The city, renamed after Stalin, was an industrial and transportation center. On orders from Stalin to hold or die, the defenders stood their ground, fighting first over sections of the city, then at close quarters over streets and houses. Casualties on both sides were horrendous. The Germans captured most of the gutted city but could not dislodge about 40,000 Soviet fighters from the industrial section along the Volga.

In mid-November, as the stalled invaders were running short of manpower and munitions, Russian forces under Marshal Georgy Zhukov went over to the offensive. One army attacked to the north of the city while another attacked to the south, the two forming a great pincer. The Germans, led by General Friedrich Paulus, could probably have fought their way out, but Hitler, who had already proclaimed the Soviet Union broken and defeated, would not hear of it. As winter set in, the Germans mounted a rescue operation, but it was halted short of its goal. Isolated, outnumbered, freezing, starving, and half-crazy, the men of the Sixth Army held out for two months. Finally on January 31, 1943 (ironically, the tenth anniversary of Hitler's accession to power), Paulus surrendered what was left of his army—91,000 out of the original 330,000. The Battle of Stalingrad broke the offensive power of the German army. From then on the initiative on the eastern front passed to the Soviet army.

private enterprise closely cooperated to sustain the total war effort. By 1945 U.S. military production was more than double that of the combined Axis powers.

First, the U.S. and British navies cleared the seas of marauding German submarines (also called U-boats) that had preyed on Allied shipping, and as a result, large amounts of supplies began to arrive in Great Britain. Next, British and U.S. bombers, protected by fighter planes, flew missions to bomb military installations, industries, transportation networks, and European cities held by the Axis powers. As German air defenses weakened, Germany was forced to relocate factories underground, but as ground transportation was destroyed, these underground factories could not obtain raw materials or ship their products.

In late 1942 the tide of war began to turn decisively. With British and U.S. air forces inflicting huge damage on the German economy and supply system, Germany could not keep its armed forces adequately supplied. As previously described, British and U.S. units had cleared North Africa of Axis forces by 1943 and followed this victory up by successfully invading Italy. Strengthened by supplies of U.S. and British arms, 6 million Soviet troops began counteroffensives in late 1942. In ferocious fighting that inflicted enormous casualties on both sides, Soviet troops surrounded and then captured German units at the battle of Stalingrad. From that point on, the Soviet forces inexorably pushed the demoralized Germans out of the Soviet Union. They then advanced into Poland and Romania in 1944, with the final goal of invading Germany.

In the summer and autumn of 1944, the Allies began the crucial campaign that ended the war in Europe. On "D Day," June 6, U.S., British, and Canadian forces launched a massive landing on the coast of Normandy in France. German defenders held the Allied forces on the beaches for a month of bitter fighting, but finally were routed. The Normandy landing opened a second front on the European continent. German forces were sent reeling back to Germany from France, Italy, and the eastern front. By the spring of 1945, Germany was caught in a giant vise. While U.S. and British forces crossed the Rhine River and pressed eastward, Soviet troops captured the Balkans and Hungary and eventually invaded Germany itself. As Soviet forces occupied Berlin, Hitler committed suicide on April 30 in his underground bunker. In accordance with terms laid down by Roosevelt and Churchill at Casablanca in 1942, German forces surrendered unconditionally on May 8, 1945. After nearly six years, the war in Europe had come to an end.

The Defeat of Japan

Victory over Japan was not long delayed. In concentrating on defeating Germany first, the Allies had not abandoned the Pacific entirely to the Japanese. The U.S. war effort was turning out enough war matériel and training enough men to press the war in both theaters. In the spring of 1942, six months after the disaster at Pearl Harbor, the U.S. navy stopped the southward Japanese advance at the Battles of Coral Sea and Midway. These battles ended the threat of a Japanese invasion of Hawaii and Australia and marked a turning point in the Pacific war.

Beginning in June 1943, a two-pronged U.S. counteroffensive struck the Pacific islands where Japan's hold was weakest, leaving the major strongholds to wither away without supplies and reinforcements. With this "island hopping" strategy, the U.S. troops avoided having to engage in numerous scattered offensives, but where fighting occurred, they encountered ferocious resistance for every foot of ground. In the Japanese military code, capture was a disgrace, and usually the only way to dislodge Japanese soldiers from their tunnels and pillboxes was with flamethrowers, hand grenades, and dynamite. By mid-1944 Admiral Chester Nimitz (1885–1966), leading one arm of the U.S. advance, had captured the Marshall Islands and Saipan and Guam in the Marianas, bringing land-based bombers within range of Japanese cities. After a remarkable advance

D Day. On June 6, 1944, Allied forces launched the greatest sea-to-land invasion in history, crossing the English Channel from Great Britain to assault German fortifications on the coast of Normandy, France. This opened the western front, which, together with the Soviet drive from the east, overwhelmed the Nazi regime in less than a year.

up the coast of New Guinea, General Douglas MacArthur (1880–1964), commanding the other arm, landed on Leyte in October 1944 to reclaim the Philippines for the United States. In February 1945 MacArthur freed Manila.

In the spring of 1945, the move toward the Japanese home islands was being pressed steadily. In March U.S. troops took Iwo Jima and then converged on Okinawa, which was well situated for staging an attack on Japan's main islands. In desperation Japan sent specially trained and indoctrinated pilots on suicide missions to ram their explosive-packed planes directly into U.S. warships. The Japanese called these *kamikaze* attacks, recalling the "divine wind" that had turned back the Mongol invaders in 1281. This time, however, the winds failed Japan. The capture of Okinawa and Iwo Jima gave the Americans additional bases from which to launch intense air bombardments of Japan's home islands. Japan's position was now hopeless. Its cities were being leveled by napalm bombs, its navy was no longer a factor, and its overseas garrisons were isolated and defeated. Nevertheless, Japanese military leaders wanted to fight to the finish.

Plans for an invasion of Japan were completed before Germany capitulated. Considering the fanatical resistance shown by the Japanese at Okinawa and elsewhere, casualties for the invading force were expected to run as high as half a million men. But the availability of the atomic bomb, which had been successfully tested in New Mexico, made the costly venture unnecessary. On August 6, 1945, an atomic bomb was dropped on

LIVES AND TIMES ACROSS CULTURES

Hollywood and the Two World Wars

Films occasionally shape the public's perception of the past but more often reflect the mood of the society and culture in which they were created. Thus some films have portrayed war in a negative light, while others have seen war as idealistic, courageous, and heroic, providing a powerful medium to mobilize aggressive nationalistic feelings against the enemy.

During the First World War there were no feature movies related to the conflict, only silent news footage shot in war zones. Nearly a decade passed after 1918 before a trend began to take shape—dramatizing and analyzing the war experience in motion pictures. By then the level of disillusionment at the waste and futility of the war in Europe and the United States was significant, and some movies were used to generate revulsion against warfare. No film better conveys the nature of trench warfare and its attendant horrors than *All Quiet on the Western Front* (1930), directed by Lewis Milestone (1895–1980), with Lew Ayres in the starring role. In 1936 Howard Hawks directed *The Road to Glory* (1936), which also graphically portrays the horrific results of the fighting on the western front. A few years later that grim image disappeared from the screen but would return in the post–World War II period. Stanley Kubrick (1928–1999) directed and cowrote *Paths of Glory* (1957), one of the most powerful antiwar movies in the history of Hollywood. With Kirk Douglas in the role of the hero, it is a savage indictment of the French High Command during the First World War.

The only antiwar film made in Hollywood during or after the Second World War, universally depicted as a just and moral conflict, was *Saving Private Ryan* (1998), directed by Stephen Spielberg (1947–). It is so effectively graphic and so emotionally reconstructs the American landing at Omaha beach on D Day that audiences must steel themselves before seeing it. Otherwise, war movies followed a familiar pattern. Movie makers often worked hand in hand with the government to produce movies that not only entertained but were used to build unity through propaganda. Even before the entrance of the United States into the war, there was an effort to overcome the general mood of isolationism by compelling movie audiences to confront the evils of the fascist regime. The films *The Man I Married* (1940), *The Mortal Storm* (1940), *A Yank in the RAF* (1941), and particularly *Underground* (1941) are classic examples. The latter, concentrating on a dedicated group of Germans opposed to Hitler, contains some of the most explicit portrayal of Nazi brutality hitherto seen on the screen.

The early combat films about the Second World War such as *Flying Tigers* (1942), *Pride of the Marines* (1945), and *Bataan* (1943) display a good deal of anti-Japanese feeling. A more evenhanded approach was made in 1970 with the film *Tora! Tora! Tora!* A Darryl Zanuck (1902–1979) production, it is unusual in its recreation of the bombing of Pearl Harbor from the perspective of both the U.S. and Japan. *Midway* (1976) follows a similar line. Most recently, *Pearl Harbor* (2001) uses special effects wizardry to reconstruct the terrible "day of infamy."

Because American troops were absent from the fighting in Europe until the middle of 1944, most of the films involving the Germans came out after the war. The focus is not on vilifying the enemy but on entertaining audiences. Among these are *Twelve O'Clock High* (1950), *Battleground* (1950), *Run Silent, Run Deep* (1958), *The Longest Day* (1962), *The Dirty Dozen* (1967), and *Patton* (1970).

Hiroshima, leveling the city and killing over 50,000 people and maiming 100,000 more. Three days later, while the stunned Japanese still hesitated, a second bomb hit Nagasaki with similar lethal effects. In accordance with its earlier agreement, the Soviet Union declared war against Japan on August 8, just before Japan's surrender and in time to have a voice in the postwar settlement. Soviet troops immediately occupied Manchuria and Korea.

The bombing of Hiroshima and Nagasaki convinced Emperor Hirohito to exert his influence to end the war. On August 14 Hirohito broadcast Japan's acceptance of Allied terms. Germany's government had been dismantled after its unconditional surrender, but the Japanese emperor was allowed to remain to ease the transition and provide for a smooth Allied occupation. Japanese fighting men everywhere obeyed the emperor's command and did not continue to fight as some Allied leaders had feared they might. On September 2 General MacArthur accepted Japan's formal unconditional surrender on the U.S. battleship *Missouri* in Tokyo Bay, ending World War II.

World War II was truly a global war, fought on three continents and on all the oceans. It lasted eight years for China, six for Europe, and nearly four for the United States. It was by far the most destructive war in history. No accurate count can be made of the dead, but perhaps as many as 50 million, both civilians and soldiers, perished. Countless cities in Europe and Asia were flattened or severely damaged. The transportation networks of most belligerent countries were in shambles, and millions of acres of farmland were damaged. The fiscal cost of the war was estimated at $1.5 trillion. The economies of nearly all the belligerents were in ruins, while the survivors were physically and psychologically exhausted.

World War II had an important political consequence as well. It brought to completion a trend that began in 1919—the decline of Europe's power and influence in world affairs. Henceforth global leadership would pass to the United States and the Soviet Union.

Settlements with Germany and Japan

As the victorious Allies began to rebuild their shattered nations, they also had to face the problem of making peace with their former enemies. Since most statesmen were determined not to repeat the error of a quick peace settlement, there was a considerable cooling-off period to allow emotions aroused by the war to subside. Eighteen months passed before even the minor treaties were ready for signing.

Instead of a formal peace conference as after World War I, Allied leaders worked out most issues in a series of conferences during and after the war. These agreements were then formalized in bilateral and multilateral treaties. A consensus on allowing East and West Germany to unify did not occur until 1990. However, territorial disputes between the Soviet Union and Japan remained unsettled.

Regarding Europe, as at Versailles, the victors were primarily concerned with the postwar status of Germany. During the war they had considered permanently dismembering Germany or reducing it to a feeble agricultural region. By 1945, however, the Allies had agreed to retain Germany as a single nation, but they imposed strong safeguards to ensure that it would never again threaten the peace of Europe. Germany was disarmed and divided into four occupation zones: British, U.S., French, and Soviet. The occupying forces were to remain until the German people had been de-Nazified and had set up a government acceptable to all the occupying powers, presumably in three to five years. The victors were initially interested in reparation settlements and agreed that the

heavily ravaged Soviet Union would receive the largest share. Soviet authorities dismantled some remaining factories in their zone of occupation and shipped them to the Soviet
Union as reparations.

Berlin became a bone of contention among the victors. Although Germany's capital
city was situated in the heart of the Soviet zone, the Western powers insisted on sharing
in its control. In an awkward arrangement, Berlin was divided into four occupation
zones separate from the rest of Germany. The Western powers had the right of access to
Berlin by air through the Soviet occupation zone, but they were in a precarious military
situation, because the city was far behind the Soviet lines.

A special court convened by the Allies at Nuremberg during 1945–1946 punished
Nazi leaders for waging aggressive war and for crimes against humanity. Trials of lesser
officials followed. The court set precedents by punishing those responsible for brutal
treatment of prisoners and noncombatants and ruled their excuse of "following orders"
an insufficient defense. Twelve leading Nazis were condemned to death, the most prominent being Hermann Göring, who cheated the hangman by committing suicide. Seven
were imprisoned for terms up to life, and three were acquitted.

The territorial changes mostly affected eastern Europe. The Soviet Union retained the
areas first acquired in 1939–1940 and still in its possession at the end of the war: Estonia, Latvia, Lithuania, portions of Romania and Finland, and the eastern half of Poland.
It also annexed a province of Czechoslovakia and the northern half of East Prussia. As a
result, the Soviet boundary moved dramatically westward. Poland was compensated for
its loss in the east by receiving the eastern quarter of Germany. Hitler's allies, Italy, Finland, Hungary, Romania, and Bulgaria, were not harshly treated. Their territories were
adjusted in minor ways, and they had to pay small reparations. In the west, the German
boundary was altered as well. Alsace-Lorraine was returned to France, and Austria was
detached from Germany.

Unlike Germany, Japan was not directly governed by the Allied occupation forces. It
retained its emperor and government, purged of militarists. U.S. forces occupied Japan
under General MacArthur. Although he was Supreme Commander for the Allied Powers
(SCAP), MacArthur actually took orders only from the U.S. government. Japan lost all
conquests made since the late nineteenth century: the southern Sakhalin and the Kurile
Islands went to the Soviet Union; Taiwan and all other Chinese territories were returned
to China; Korea was to become independent, while the Ryukyu Islands, with the important Okinawa airbase, were to be administered by the United States. Japan also gave up
all its colonial conquests in Southeast Asia and made small reparation payments to its
victims there.

MacArthur carried out the SCAP mandate to change Japan from an aggressive, imperialistic nation to a peaceful, democratic one. Japanese militarists who had waged aggressive war and had ordered atrocities against prisoners and conquered civilians were tried
at the Tokyo International Court; some, Tojo being the most prominent, were condemned to death, while others were sentenced to prison terms. Another agency oversaw
the purge of lesser figures in the government and industrial complex, which had abetted
and profited from aggression. Those singled out were forbidden from participating in

future policy decisions. Further measures led to the dismantling of Japan's armed forces and to the repatriation of former colonial administrators and settlers.

On January 1, 1946, the emperor made a Declaration of Humanity in which he formally renounced his divine status. General MacArthur and his civilian advisers closely supervised the writing of Japan's new constitution, which was promulgated in 1947 and included a bill of rights. Borrowing passages from the U.S. Constitution, the Bill of Rights, and the Gettysburg address, the constitution placed sovereignty in the hands of the Japanese and provided for a government similar to that of Great Britain. One provision renounced war and the right of belligerency forever and declared that "land, sea, and air forces, as well as other war potential, will never be maintained." Women gained the right to vote and to be elected to office. SCAP also supervised widespread economic, educational, and social reforms that restructured the formerly paternalistic and authoritarian society to a more liberal and individualistic one.

Japan regained full independence in the Treaty of San Francisco in 1951. The treaty was signed by forty-eight of the victor nations. The Soviet bloc nations refused to sign. Neither of China's two governments—the People's Republic (Communist), which controlled mainland China, and the Republic (Nationalists), which ruled Taiwan—was included. Separate treaties were signed between Nationalist China and Japan immediately afterward and between the People's Republic of China and Japan in the 1970s.

Cold War in Europe

On March 31, 1948, the Russians ordered that unless inspectors were permitted to examine passengers and luggage, Western military trains would be not merely delayed but would be turned back. An order also was issued that no freight trains could leave Berlin without a Soviet permit.

The next Soviet move was to stop all passenger trains departing from Berlin. About this time, Americans in Berlin seemed to be the only Westerners who were determined to stay there. French officials repeated the familiar remark that not a single Frenchman would vote to fight for Berlin. The British, believing that Berlin's geographical position makes the city indefensible, opposed an outright showdown. . . .

On June 24 . . . the full extent of the Soviet threat became clear when all rail traffic between Berlin and the West was halted "due to technical difficulties."

During the intermittent traffic stoppages prior to the all-out blockade, we had discovered that airplanes could bring in a surprising amount of essentials. The National Security Council therefore decided that we should enforce only our written agreements for use of specific air corridors. That decision became the inspiration for the fabulous Airlift. . . .

One incongruous aspect of the Airlift epoch was the help which black marketeers brought to Berlin. . . . Black marketeers discovered innumerable ways to move desired goods into the beleaguered city. . . . Luxuries flowed in. . . . As one of my aides remarked to me, "We are a capitalist oasis in a socialist desert!" May 12, 1949 marked the end of the Berlin blockade. . . .

By coincidence, the Berlin blockade was lifted on the same day that two other prolonged negotiations in Germany were also concluded. The French Government completed arrangements to merge the economy of its occupation zone with the economy of the American and British zones. . . .

Today [1964] for better or worse, the German-American alliance has become the key to the American military position in Europe. It seems to me that Americans came out of their German experience *as winners on the whole, and the Russians as losers. Even the isolation of Berlin has worked out more in our favor than the Kremlin's. The Russians inadvertently gave us an outpost one hundred miles inside the Iron Curtain, where the inadequacies of the Communist system show up more conspicuously than anywhere else, in full view of everybody in the world.* *

*Robert Murphy, *Diplomat among Warriors* (New York: Doubleday, 1964), pp. 315–323.

The Berlin blockade was the first major crisis in the Cold War. It had the effect of hastening the postwar division of Germany into two separate states—a division that persisted until 1990. In the preceding excerpts from his memoirs, Robert Murphy, a career diplomat with the U.S. State Department, recalled the Berlin crisis in 1948–1949 and its outcome. He was writing from a perspective in which the globe was divided into two warring camps, one dominated by the United States and the other by the Soviet Union. Cold War confrontations and maneuverings between the superpowers dominated global relations after World War II. By 1989 radical changes in the Soviet Union inspired by President Mikhail Gorbachev, crumbling economic systems in the Soviet-dominated eastern European bloc, fears of nuclear annihilation, and *glasnost* (increased openness and communication among the major powers) seemed to mark the end of the Cold War and the beginning of a new, multipolar world.

The Cold War was a complex pattern of competitive, often hostile relationships between the two postwar superpowers—the United States and the Soviet Union—that began in Europe as World War II came to an end and persisted at varying levels of intensity into the 1980s. It involved economic, diplomatic, and military competition between the superpowers and their allies, but never escalated to direct military warfare between the United States and the Soviet Union or to the use of nuclear weapons. During the 1950s and 1960s, the Cold War spread from Europe to Asia, Africa, and Latin America. The United States and the Soviet Union also competed in a global arms race. Eventually, the two powers stockpiled so many nuclear weapons that either could destroy the world in a matter of minutes.

The Beginning of the Cold War: 1945–1949

During World War II, leaders in the United States, Great Britain, and the Soviet Union were already anticipating changes in the postwar world and sought to maximize their respective gains. Great Britain wished to retain its empire and its imperial economic system. The United States wanted not only to maintain its sphere of influence in the Western Hemisphere and Asia, but also to construct a worldwide system of free markets. The Soviet Union had suffered over 20 million wartime dead, and its totalitarian ruler, Joseph Stalin, wanted to dominate eastern Europe and to keep Germany militarily impotent. Moscow also sought to promote Marxism around the world, but without embroiling itself in too many direct involvements or difficulties.

The origins and course of the Cold War continue to be debated heatedly among historians. Whether the United States employed the atomic bomb because it was necessary to win the war or used it primarily to threaten the Soviet Union remains an issue of controversy. Historians and politicians have also differed over whether the United States or

© Bettmann/Corbis

Joseph Stalin. This portrait shows Stalin as robust, alert, strong-willed, and confident, attributes he worked hard to convey to the West and to his own people. In truth, he was short, insecure, paranoid, and one of the most brutal men in history.

the Soviet Union was more aggressive in causing and pursuing the Cold War and whether ideological, military, or economic factors carried the most weight in framing postwar policies.

Relationships among the victorious powers rapidly deteriorated during and after the last two wartime conferences at Yalta and Potsdam in 1945. One major issue was reparations. The United States, whose economy had prospered during the war, was more interested in rebuilding Germany as a potential trading partner than in crushing it economically. In contrast, the Soviet Union, which had been devastated during the war, wished to rebuild its economy mostly with reparations from defeated Germany (along with postwar loans from the United States).

Late in World War II the Soviet army occupied eastern Europe as it drove the Germans out, and Stalin clearly intended to stay there to bolster the Soviet Union's security and strategic position. The Western powers desired the withdrawal of the Soviets and the establishment of democratic governments and free market economies in eastern Europe. To pressure the Soviet Union into opening up eastern Europe, the United States cut off the Lend-Lease program and ended shipments of German industrial supplies to the Soviet Union from Allied occupation zones. The Soviet Union responded by stripping its occupation zone in eastern Germany of industrial plants and materials.

As a result, eastern Europe became the main area of East-West contention in the years immediately after the war. With its occupying troops in the region, the Soviet Union was determined to weld eastern Europe into a buffer zone of friendly nations, or at least friendly governments, to prevent the possibility of future invasions. Despite pressure from the United States to permit free elections and to open up the area to free trade with the Western capitalist nations, the Soviet Union tightened the grip of Communist parties over Poland, Romania, and Bulgaria. A local Communist party also dominated Albania. By 1948 Communist party takeovers had added Hungary and Czechoslovakia to the Soviet sphere. Only Yugoslavia, although Communist, took an independent, nationalistic course under Marshal Josef Tito (1892–1980).

Once in political control, the Soviets began to integrate the economies of the eastern European nations with their own economy. While former British prime minister Winston Churchill charged that an "iron curtain" had fallen between eastern Europe and the West, Stalin told the Soviet people that they were surrounded by enemies and would have to endure more shortages and cutbacks to maintain their military strength.

The possession of the atomic bomb by the United States also affected postwar relationships. The Soviet Union, which did not then have its own atomic bomb, feared the U.S. weapon, but not enough to back down from defending its interests. Meanwhile, the United States presented the Baruch Plan, under which nations would refrain from making atomic bombs and submit to inspection by an independent international agency. Because the United States and its allies controlled the United Nations, and thus the proposed international agency, the Soviet Union rejected the plan.

As the Soviet Union consolidated its power in eastern Europe, trouble developed in the Mediterranean. Turkey, hoping for Western support, refused a Soviet demand in 1946 and early 1947 for joint Soviet-Turkish supervision of the Bosporus, the waterway connecting the Black Sea to the Aegean Sea. At the same time, Greece was embroiled in a brutal civil war between the corrupt royal government and Communist-dominated guerrillas backed by the Communist regimes in the Balkans. The British, who had been aiding the Greek government in order to keep the Soviet Union out of the Mediterranean, were forced for economic reasons to pull out in 1947. These developments brought in the United States to take up where the British had left off.

Economic and Political Divisions

The developments in Greece and Turkey, as well as the situation in eastern Europe, caused the Truman administration to reverse the traditional isolationist policy of the United States in international affairs. In the past, U.S. policymakers had taken the position that the nation's interests were best served by staying out of European affairs. Only when U.S. vital interests were threatened, as in the two world wars, had Americans entered into European conflicts. President Harry Truman (1884–1972) moved to reverse 150 years of isolationist sentiment and replace it with a policy whereby the United States adopted a role of global leadership.

By 1947 Truman, a staunch anticommunist, and most of his civilian and military advisers had concluded that the Soviet Union was planning to destroy the "free" (non-Communist) world. Only by active participation could the United States prevent the Soviets from dominating Greece and Turkey. On March 12, 1947, Truman laid out the new principles of U.S. foreign policy in a speech to Congress. In it he advocated U.S.

economic aid to Greece and Turkey and to any nation that threatened to come under Communist control. The new policy, called the Truman Doctrine, became crucial in the containment of communism during the following decades.

At the request of the president and after intense lobbying, Congress authorized $150 million in aid to Turkey and $250 million to Greece. With U.S. backing the Turkish government continued to hold out against the Soviet Union. Reorganized and better equipped, the Greek army became more effective against the Communist insurgents, who gave up in 1949 after Yugoslavia cut off vital aid.

Trouble in western Europe quickly produced another major policy innovation, the Marshall Plan. By 1947 despite billions of dollars in U.S. loans, the economy of western Europe had not recovered from wartime devastation. France and Italy in particular were plagued with shortages, inflation, unemployment, and inadequate housing. Out of desperation, many French and Italians voted for Socialist and Communist candidates, who consequently held a number of seats in the cabinets of both governments. In the eyes of the Truman administration, this situation demanded effective U.S. economic intervention.

In June 1947 Secretary of State George Marshall (1880–1959) proposed that the nations of Europe consult with one another and with the United States to determine the amount of economic assistance they needed to rebuild their economies. The Soviet Union, fearful of U.S. economic expansion, prevented eastern European nations from participating. With some reluctance, Congress in 1948 created the European Recovery Program, usually referred to as the Marshall Plan, with an initial outlay of $4 billion. By 1951 Marshall Plan aid had totaled over $13 billion. Most of it went to Great Britain, France, and Italy, whose economies recovered rapidly under its impetus.

The Marshall Plan was a political success as well, assuring the decline of Communist political fortunes in Europe, which had begun to fade even before the implementation of the program. In both Italy and France, voters excluded Communists from cabinet positions after mid-1947, and Communist-led strikes were broken by government action. Hoping for a similar success in the non-Western world, Congress funded the Point Four program in 1950. This program aimed at providing foreign aid to emerging non-Western nations to prevent them from turning to communism as a means to solve their economic problems. The vast infusion of funds that flowed into Europe under the Marshall Plan not only laid the foundations for postwar European prosperity and economic integration but also helped the U.S. economy to grow.

Another development that aided the recovery of western Europe was the formation of the European Economic Community (EEC), popularly called the Common Market. Founded in 1957, and initially including France, Italy, West Germany, the Netherlands, Belgium, and Luxembourg, the Common Market was a customs union that reduced competition among its members and turned western Europe into an open market area. The EEC was so successful that Great Britain and other nations, including Greece, Portugal, and Spain, all sought membership and were later admitted. As European economies grew stronger and relationships among the governments became more cordial, plans were approved for the integration of both European governments and economies by 1992; the new union was known as the European Community, or EC.

The new technology generated by World War II revolutionized both agricultural and industrial production in western Europe. The Common Market allowed goods to circulate freely in western Europe, supplying the demand created by a postwar "baby boom." Rapid economic growth and unprecedented prosperity resulted. Prostrate in 1945, western Europe, especially Germany, was a major competitor of the United States in global markets by 1965.

As the Western nations established more friendly relations with their occupied sections of Germany, the Soviet Union grew increasingly fearful that Germany would again be unified and become a strong, potential military threat. Following some initial maneuvers, the Soviets announced in June 1948 that they had closed "for repairs" those railroads and highways in East Germany set aside to supply Western troops and civilians in West Berlin. The Western governments countered by using the air corridors for the Berlin airlift, or "Operation Vittles," to supply more than 2 million West Berliners and Western troops with food, clothing, coal, and other supplies. The Berlin blockade and airlift dragged on for almost a year before the Soviets conceded defeat and reopened the highways and railroads in May 1949. The immediate crisis was over, but Berlin remained a trouble spot.

Map 15.5 Post–World War II European Economic Division. In 1949 the Soviet Union and its eighteen eastern European satellites formed the Council for Mutual Economic Assistance (COMECON), while France, West Germany, Italy, Belgium, the Netherlands, and Luxembourg organized the European Economic Community (EEC). The EEC expanded to include most noncommunist European countries, all of which prospered as a result of membership; the Soviet-dominated COMECON did not fare so well.

In September 1949 the United States and its allies combined the three western zones of occupation in Germany into a German national state as a buffer against the Soviet-controlled eastern sector. Later the western zones became the Federal Republic of Germany (West Germany). U.S., British, and French military forces remained in West Germany, but their role had changed from being anti-German to anti-Soviet.

The Soviet Union countered by organizing its zone into the German Democratic Republic (East Germany). The division of Germany remained in effect for four decades. Thus by the end of the 1940s Europe had effectively been divided into two spheres of influence: one, the Western bloc, was effectively dominated by the United States, and the other, the Eastern bloc, was directly occupied and controlled by the Soviet Union.

By the late 1940s and 1950s, the Cold War had permeated Western and Soviet attitudes. As in other wars, both sides bombarded their publics with propaganda that depicted the other side as bent on destroying their way of life. The mass media, now including television, played a major role. In the totalitarian Soviet bloc, the governments carefully controlled all information received by their citizens, even going to the extreme of jamming outside radio broadcasts. In the Western bloc, the independent press and electronic media generally followed the lead of their governments. Americans were egged on to worry about alleged "subversives," "Commie dupes," "parlor pinks," and "fellow travelers." They became uneasy when the Communists defeated the Nationalist forces in a civil war in China in 1949, and fearful when the new leaders of that nation aided North Korea against the U.S.-supported South Korean government in the Korean War. Congress investigated alleged subversives in the United States and enacted legislation granting government agencies broad powers to combat treasonous organizations. After the mid-1950s, the anticommunist hysteria gradually died down in the United States.

Cold War Military Expansion

The Cold War had a direct military impact on Europe. In 1949 the Truman administration moved to a much more aggressive form of containment when it abandoned its traditional policy of unilateral action and created a system of anti-Soviet alliances and military bases along the Soviet perimeters. Postwar developments that culminated in the Communists seizing power in Czechoslovakia in 1948 and the Berlin blockade in 1948–1949 convinced U.S. leaders that the Soviet Union represented a permanent aggressive threat in Europe that had to be balanced by a permanent U.S. military presence there.

The Truman administration set up a military alliance called the North Atlantic Treaty Organization (NATO). NATO initially included the United States, Canada, Great Britain, France, West Germany, Iceland, Norway, Denmark, the Netherlands, Belgium, Luxembourg, Portugal, and Italy. Member states agreed to come to one another's aid if attacked. NATO seemed to work so well in countering possible Soviet expansion that it was enlarged to include such questionably North Atlantic nations as Greece and Turkey. The national armed forces of the member nations were incorporated into a unified military operation under the direction of a U.S. commander in chief. The U.S. Strategic Air Command (SAC) established airbases in western Europe and in the non-NATO nations of Spain and Libya. From these bases, U.S. bombers could inflict untold damage on the Soviet Union in case of war.

The U.S.-led encirclement of the Soviet Union in Europe created a series of escalating pressures in Europe. The Soviet Union increased the size of its army in Europe until it greatly outnumbered the NATO forces opposing it. This in effect turned western European nations into hostages in a U.S.-Soviet confrontation, because Europe would be the primary battleground for the superpowers and its people the likely victims of any nuclear explosion. Fear of becoming such a battleground led western European nations to restrain the United States in its stance toward the Soviet Union.

The Cold War entered an even more dangerous phase in 1957, when the Soviets, using a powerful new rocket, launched the first satellite into orbit around the earth. Two months later, they launched an intercontinental ballistic missile (ICBM). The space and missile age had arrived. Americans were predictably alarmed. Having prided themselves on leading the world in science and technology, they enthusiastically supported President Dwight D. Eisenhower's decision to pour money into scientific research. A National Aeronautics and Space Administration (NASA) was created to push the United States

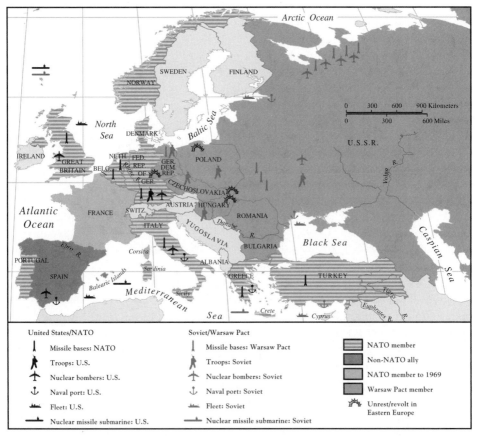

Map 15.6 The Cold War in Europe. After World War II, the division of Europe into spheres dominated by the two superpowers was intensified by the NATO and Warsaw Pact alliances and by the arms race. Rival land forces, backed by arrays of nuclear missiles and bombers, faced each other in central Europe, while surface fleets and missile-firing submarines roamed the Atlantic and the Mediterranean. Despite, or because of, Cold War confrontations and military buildups, Europe remained at peace after 1945.

ahead in the space race. Stung by Democratic charges of a "missile gap," the Eisenhower administration began a major ICBM building program and also constructed submarine-launched missiles (SLM). A U.S. satellite was launched in 1958. By 1963 the United States had 450 missiles and 2,000 bombers capable of striking the Soviet Union versus 50 to 100 Soviet ICBMs and 200 bombers that could reach the United States. The phrases "balance of terror" and, later, "mutually assured destruction" (MAD) came into use.

In 1955 the Soviet Union countered the creation of NATO with its own military alliance system called the Warsaw Pact, which integrated the armed forces of eastern Europe into a unified force under Soviet command. In addition, the Soviets recognized East Germany as an independent state and admitted it into the Warsaw Pact.

People in several satellite nations challenged Soviet hegemony in eastern Europe in the 1950s. Dissatisfaction with living conditions, hopes raised by more liberal policies under new Soviet leader Nikita Khrushchev, and encouragement by U.S. propaganda led to riots and other convulsions in East Germany in 1953 and Poland and Hungary in 1956. When the Hungarians announced widespread reforms, including free elections, and said that they would withdraw from the Warsaw Pact, Soviet troops and tanks poured in and surrounded every large city and every important military installation. The

Map 15.7 Zones of Allied Occupation in Germany and Austria, 1945–1955. After World War II, Hitler's Reich was reduced, redivided into Germany and Austria, and occupied by Allied troops. Separate occupation authorities controlled Germany, Austria, and the city of Berlin. The three Western powers had intended the occupation to last only until the German people had a democratic government and no longer threatened their neighbors. But as the Cold War set in, both the Western powers and the Soviet Union began to view this area of Europe as a buffer zone and "their" Germans as future allies in the ongoing competition. The three western zones were consolidated from 1946 to 1949, becoming the Federal Republic of Germany; the Soviet zone became the German Democratic Republic in 1949. In both cases, foreign troops remained as invited allies. By contrast, all occupying forces left Austria when it became independent in 1955. Berlin remained an occupied entity and a dangerous flash point till the end of the Cold War in the early 1990s.

United States, distracted by the fighting in the Suez (see Chapter 17) and unwilling to go to war over eastern Europe, was sympathetic to the Hungarian rebels but did not move to intervene on their behalf. The Soviet Union ruthlessly crushed the rebellion, executed independence-minded Hungarian leaders, and maintained its domination over eastern Europe.

In the mid-1950s, the superpowers made several attempts to negotiate their differences. Although mutually suspicious, U.S. president Dwight Eisenhower and Soviet leader Nikita Khrushchev met at a summit conference in Geneva in 1955. The two men agreed to end their occupation of Austria, restore it to independence, and guarantee its neutrality. The Soviet Union also recognized the West German government. The talks had been productive, and they opened the way for future, periodic summit meetings between leaders of the superpowers.

After 1960, however, relations took a turn for the worse, and for a time the two superpowers appeared headed toward nuclear confrontation. In May 1960 the Soviet Union shot down a U.S. high-altitude spy plane (U-2) flying over Soviet territory. The subsequent diplomatic furor, to say nothing of the embarrassment to the U.S. government, led to the cancellation of a planned Eisenhower-Khrushchev summit. It further contributed to the election of John F. Kennedy (1917–1963), who promised new programs to restore U.S. prestige.

In 1961 a dangerous crisis flared up in Berlin, a perennial trouble spot. Khrushchev was embarrassed by Berlin, not only because it contained a Western military garrison behind Soviet lines, but also because it was a source of worldwide ridicule, as tens of thousands of East Germans annually fled the Communist regime by crossing from East Berlin into West Berlin. The loss of people was another sore point, causing East Germany severe labor and economic problems. The Soviet Union therefore authorized the East German government to construct the Berlin Wall in August 1961. The wall prevented East Germans from escaping to the West and quickly became the symbol of the Cold War and Communist repression. Tensions mounted and additional U.S. troops were sent into Berlin. President Kennedy traveled to the city to underscore U.S. determination to protect the city, telling an excited crowd, "Ich bin ein Berliner" (I am a Berliner). Although tensions later lessened, Berlin remained a flashpoint, the only spot on the globe where U.S. and Soviet troops were face to face.

Despite these events, Europe saw no major war in the decades following World War II. All nations understood that an attack on a European ally of a superpower meant a general nuclear war. No disastrous miscalculations occurred, because the leaders on both sides had a rather clear idea of each other's interests. As a result, Europeans spent the postwar period worrying that the leaders of the superpowers would lose perspective and destroy them. At the same time, western European economies not only recovered from the devastation of World War II but enjoyed unprecedented levels of prosperity. In comparison, the economies of eastern Europe stagnated, especially in nations with rigid centralized planning. The retreat of Soviet power from eastern Europe resulted in a treaty between the four wartime allies and the two German governments in 1990. The allies agreed to give up their rights in Berlin and Germany and to permit the unification of Germany. Reunited Germany would remain a member of NATO.

Summary and Comparisons

The interwar years saw the rise of totalitarian dictatorships with their doctrinaire ideologies and radical social programs. These regimes varied, yet also shared common traits. Totalitarianism first appeared with the Bolshevik revolution in Russia. Paradoxically, the Soviet regime had much in common with the most anticommunist authoritarian state, Nazi Germany—brutal suppression of dissidents; a single ideology; total domination of the government by the party; a cult of the leader; and an aggressive foreign policy designed to spread the nation's ideology by intimidation or conquest.

The two ideologies, however, were diametrically opposed. Nazism supported an ethnic elite, whereas communism advocated egalitarianism, aiming, at least in theory, for a classless society. The Nazis used their power to induce all classes to cooperate and work in

CHRONOLOGY

1920	
	Fascism in Italy: Benito Mussolini
	Locarno Pact
1930	Japanese militarism and expansionism
	Manchurian incident
	Japan withdraws from League of Nations
	Personalist dictatorships in Latin America
	Nazism: Adolf Hitler becomes chancellor of Germany
	Mussolini invades Ethiopia
	Spanish Civil War: Francisco Franco
	Sino-Japanese War
	Munich Agreement
	Hitler-Stalin Nonaggression Pact
	Hitler invades Poland
1940	
	Japan attacks Pearl Harbor
	The Holocaust: Nazi genocide of Jews
	Atomic bombing of Hiroshima and Nagasaki
	United Nations charter adopted
	End of World War II; beginning of the Cold War
	Truman Doctrine and the Marshall Plan
	Soviet blockade of Berlin
	NATO formed
1950	Warsaw Pact formed
	European Economic Community (EEC) formed in western Europe
1960	
	Construction of the Berlin Wall
1970	

harmony. The Communists, by contrast, sought to eliminate the aristocracy and the bourgeoisie and set up a dictatorship of the proletariat. Finally, the Nazis permitted capitalism and protected the possessions of the landowning class and the industrialists. The Communists suppressed capitalism, nationalizing the land and other means of production.

Among the leading totalitarian states—Japan, Italy, and Germany—the notion grew that armed might could rectify long-standing grievances. Their pact in 1937, the Berlin-Rome-Tokyo Axis, was designed to ensure that each power obtained what it wished, namely, territories to provide space for overcrowding at home as well as badly needed raw materials. As justification for their aggression, they claimed they were out to stop the advances of communism. All respected force and were contemptuous of democratic governments and the League of Nations, which had been set up for the peaceful resolution of international differences.

The first breach in the system of collective security occurred in 1931–1932 when Japan seized Manchuria. The Japanese viewed themselves as superior to other Asians (the same way the Nazis considered Germans the most outstanding people in the world) and believed they were entitled to rule over other peoples. The weakness of the League of Nations was revealed when the democracies took no preventive action and merely scolded Japan.

The failure of the League of Nations to restrain Japan encouraged Italy's Mussolini, who attempted to conquer Ethiopia in 1935 and two years later sent troops to help Franco, an ideological kindred, win the Spanish Civil War. Hitler followed suit, convinced that the time was ripe for a revision of the Treaty of Versailles and for Germany's return to world power status. He first remilitarized the Rhineland, next annexed Austria, and finally dismembered Czechoslovakia at Munich in 1938. In each instance the Western democracies countered totalitarian aggression with a policy of appeasement. Struggling against unemployment and a host of other problems caused by the Great Depression, they were ready to do almost anything to prevent another major war. But appeasement only encouraged further aggression and in the end did not avert war.

World War II differed from World War I in a number of respects. Whereas the underlying and immediate origins of World War I were complex, World War II resulted primarily from the deliberate aggression of the totalitarian states. The first great conflict was static and was fought mainly in the trenches. The second was fully mobile, fought over a greater area of the globe, and more mechanized and scientific in character. In World War I most of the casualties were soldiers, but in World War II as many civilians as troops were killed.

The starting dates for World War II differed in Asia and Europe. Japan struck first by invading China in 1937. China's determined resistance and Japan's inability to bring its campaign in China to a victorious end led to an expansion of the war in Asia. In 1941 Japan's surprise attack on the U.S. fleet at Pearl Harbor in Hawaii and its invasion of British and Dutch colonial holdings in Southeast Asia broadened the war in Asia to include the Western powers.

In the meantime, Hitler concluded a nonaggression pact with the Soviet Union. With his eastern front secure, Hitler attacked Poland in 1939, ignoring British and French warnings that such action would lead to war against them as well. Hitler's military won spectacular successes in eastern and western Europe in 1939 and 1940, until only Great Britain remained. The energetic and inspirational British prime minister, Winston Churchill, was doggedly determined to keep on fighting. Hitler's invasion of the Soviet Union in 1941 and Japan's attack against the United States at Pearl Harbor drove these two nations into the conflict on the side of Great Britain. In arduous campaigns the Allies gradually gained the upper hand, first defeating Italy, next Nazi Germany, and then Japan.

The peacemakers after World War II did not follow the same route as their 1919 counterparts. No one in 1945 appeared with a program remotely similar to Wilson's Fourteen Points. The idealism that had heralded the Paris Peace Conference was conspicuously absent in 1945. Moreover, the victors in 1945 paused to gain perspective, unlike the proceedings in Paris, which began in 1919 within two months of the armistice. After World War II, leading Nazi and Japanese leaders were prosecuted and convicted of crimes against humanity. No such trials occurred after World War I.

The United States and the Soviet Union emerged as the two superpowers at the end of World War II. While the United States led the democratic countries of western Europe, the Soviet Union's forces occupied and dominated eastern Europe. The two blocs confronted each other in the Cold War that followed, divided by an iron curtain of Communist governments established by Soviet forces in eastern Europe. Soviet attempts to oust Western occupation forces in Berlin, destabilize Turkey, and aid Communist rebels in Greece led to determined U.S. responses in the Berlin airlift, the Truman Doctrine, and the formation of NATO, which checked Soviet expansion. Economic aid in the form of the Marshall Plan, followed by the formation of the Common Market, revived western Europe's economy and made communism unattractive to most people in that region. The Soviet Union countered with the Warsaw Pact of eastern European nations.

Selected Sources

Items indicated with an asterisk (*) are available in paperback.

Baer, George W. *The Test Case: Italy, Ethiopia, and the League of Nations.* 1976. A discussion of the failure of international peacekeeping efforts in the face of totalitarian aggression.

*Bell, P. M. H. *The Origins of the Second World War in Europe.* 1987. A clear survey suitable for undergraduates.

*Benedict, Ruth. *The Chrysanthemum and the Sword: Patterns of Japanese Culture.* 1946. A description of Japanese society prior to World War II by a U.S. anthropologist.

*Bullock, Alan. *Hitler: A Study in Tyranny.* Revised ed. 1962. A good account of the Hitler years as well as of the man.

*Butow, Robert J. C. *Tojo and the Coming of the War.* 1961. An excellent study of Tojo's role in leading Japan to war.

*Carr, Raymond. *The Spanish Tragedy: The Civil War in Perspective.* 1977. A thoughtful analysis of the Spanish Civil War and foreign intervention.

*Chang, Iris. *The Rape of Nanking: The Forgotten Holocaust of World War II.* 1997. Excellent book documenting the horrors Japanese soldiers inflicted on the people of Nanking.

*Clark, Alan. *Barbarossa.* 1965. A lively account of the gigantic struggle between the Soviet Union and Germany.

Costello, John. *The Pacific War.* 1981. An authoritative account of the war between the United States and Japan.

Dulles, Foster Rhea. *American Policy toward Communist China, 1949–1969.* 1972. A good analysis.

Feis, Herbert. *Japan Surrendered: The Atomic Bomb and the End of the War in the Pacific.* 1961. A good account of the end of the war against Japan.

——. *From Trust to Terror: The Onset of the Cold War, 1945–1950.* 1970. An important general treatment.

Gilbert, Martin. *The Holocaust: A History of the Jews of Europe during the Second World War.* 1985. A detailed and well-researched account.

*Hemingway, Ernest. *For Whom the Bell Tolls.* 1940. A novel about the Spanish Civil War by one who took part in it. Also a film.

*Hsiung, James C., and Steven I. Levine, eds. *China's Bitter Victory: The War with Japan, 1937–1945.* 1992. Many experts contributed to this multifaceted book on the most devastating war in Chinese history.

*Iriye, Akira. *The Origins of the Second World War in Asia and the Pacific.* 1987. A clear account.

*Keegan, John. *The Second World War.* 1990. A balanced and well-written study with superb maps and plentiful illustrations.

*Monsarrat, Nicholas. *The Cruel Sea.* 1951. An enthralling novel depicting the destroyer-submarine struggle in the Atlantic. Also a motion picture. Should be seen in conjunction with the German motion picture *Das Boot.*

Rowse, A. L. *Appeasement: A Study in Political Decline, 1933–1939.* 1963. A critical look at the liberal appeasement of aggression in the 1930s.

Sih, Paul K. T., ed. *Nationalist China during the Sino-Japanese War, 1937–1945.* 1970. Many experts contributed to this study of China during the war.

*Smith, Bradley. *Reaching Judgment at Nuremberg.* 1979. An insightful look at the corruption of Nazism. Also a motion picture, *Judgment at Nuremberg.*

*Speer, Albert. *Inside the Third Reich.* 1970. A fascinating biography by Hitler's friend, architect, and minister of armaments. Written during the author's twenty-year imprisonment after his conviction at the Nuremberg trials.

*Taylor, A. J. P. *The Origins of the Second World War.* 1962. The controversial assertion by a noted scholar that Hitler was not the prime instigator of World War II.

*——. *The War Lords.* 1977. A description of the men who directed World War II.

Toland, John. *The Rising Sun: Decline and Fall of the Japanese Empire, 1936–1945.* 1971. A classic on Japanese imperialism leading to defeat.

Triumph of the Will. Riefenstahl, Leni, director. 1935. A striking film of a Nazi rally showing the wide support for Hitler among Germans. Regarded by many as the greatest propaganda film ever produced.

*Wiskemann, Elizabeth. *Fascism in Italy.* 1970. A short, well-written analysis of Mussolini's regime.

Additional resources, exercises, and Internet links related to this chapter are available at the Book Companion Web site:
http://history.wadsworth.com/upshurcompact4/

16

Global Conflicts during the Cold War: 1945–1989

•

• The Triumph of Nationalist Struggles for Independence •

• The Cold War in Asia And Africa •

• Conflict in Latin America •

• Shifting World Alliances •

• Summary and Comparisons •

I say to you today, my friends, so even though we face the difficulties of today and tomorrow, I still have a dream. It is a dream deeply rooted in the American dream. I have a dream that one day this nation will rise up and live out the true meaning of its creed—that we hold these truths to be self-evident, that all men are created equal.

I have a dream that one day on the red hills of Georgia, the sons of former slaves and the sons of former slave-owners will be able to sit down together at the table of brotherhood. . . .

I have a dream that my four little children will one day live in a nation where they will not be judged by the color of their skin but by the content of their character. I have a dream today! . . .

When we allow freedom to ring, when we let it ring from every village and every hamlet, from every state and every city, we will be able to speed up that day when all of God's children—black men and white men, Jews and Gentiles, Protestants and Catholics—will be able to join hands and sing in the words of the old Negro spiritual, "Free at last, free at last; thank God Almighty, we are free at last."*

*Copyright 1963 Dr. Martin Luther King, Jr., copyright renewed 1991 by Coretta Scott King.

In his "I Have a Dream" speech, delivered at the March on Washington in the summer of 1963, Martin Luther King Jr., one of the key leaders of the civil rights movement in the United States, movingly summarized the desire of men and women around the world for equal rights and opportunity. King and others in the movement used many of the nonviolent tactics—boycotts, strikes, sit-ins, marches—advocated by Mohandas Gandhi in his struggle for Indian independence a generation earlier. During the 1950s and 1960s many African Americans struggled to end racial segregation and gain equal access to education, the political system, restaurants, transportation, and a host of other services. The refusal of Rosa Parks, exhausted after a hard day of work, to give up her seat on a public bus to a white man in Birmingham, Alabama, in 1955 spurred a wave of protests and galvanized a generation to demand legislative changes to ensure equal rights. Although racism has remained a persistent problem in the United States and elsewhere, the civil rights movement ended many of the worst abuses of segregation and secured legislative guarantees for equal rights. It inspired human rights advocates among women, other people of color, homosexuals, and many others.

King's demands for freedom were echoed throughout Asia and Africa, where most nations gained their independence from Western imperial powers after World War II, unfortunately often only by violent confrontations and warfare. This chapter traces how the realization of independence in Asian and African nations changed the global balance of power. Many of the newly independent nations faced daunting problems of reconstruction and economic development, and many fell to military dictatorships. Many also struggled to maintain their cultural and religious identities while adapting to Western technology. This chapter also describes the Cold War struggles between the superpowers and their involvement in Asia, Africa, and Latin America, where one of the most dangerous Cold War confrontations—the Cuban Missile Crisis—occurred. Finally, it traces the shifting nature of the economic, political, and military relationships between the Western bloc led by the United States and the Eastern bloc dominated by the Soviet Union through the 1980s.

The Triumph of Nationalist Struggles for Independence

Long years ago we made a tryst with destiny, and now the time comes when we shall redeem our pledge, not wholly or in full measure, but very substantially. At the stroke of midnight hour, when the world sleeps, India will awake to life and freedom. A moment comes, which comes but rarely in history, when we step out from the old to the new, when an age ends, and when the soul of a nation, long suppressed, finds utterance. . . . The achievement we celebrate today is but a step, an opening of opportunity, to the greater triumphs and achievements that await us.*

*Jawaharlal Nehru on the occasion of Indian independence, 1947, in Michael Brecher, Nehru: A Political Biography (London: Oxford University Press, 1961), p. 137.

The eloquence of Jawaharlal Nehru (1889–1964), the first prime minister of independent India, was more than political rhetoric. Nehru's statement celebrated the declaration of Indian independence at the stroke of midnight, August 15, 1947. Few realized that this momentous event heralded the end of colonization and the onset of independence for African and Asian nations. In the twenty years that followed, many leaders across Asia and Africa echoed Nehru's sentiments.

Imperialism in Decline

The scope of the postwar independence movement can scarcely be exaggerated. In the three decades after 1945, Western nations lost their empires in Asia and Africa. In a single generation, former colonies, some of which had been ruled by Europeans for nearly five centuries, gained their independence, and dozens of new nations emerged.

There were precursors to the postwar independence movement, particularly in the evolution of the British Commonwealth of Nations since the second half of the nineteenth century. The Act of Westminster, passed by the British Parliament in 1931, made official the de facto independence of white-dominated dominions of Canada, Australia, New Zealand, and South Africa. The voluntary affiliation of these nations in the Commonwealth under a single monarch did not limit their self-rule. France and the Netherlands, however, did not follow suit in establishing a similar arrangement with their colonies before World War II.

The pattern by which former colonies attained their independence was not uniform, but important similarities existed. Western-educated Asians and Africans led most anticolonial movements. Often these nationalist leaders were highly charismatic figures who embraced and utilized Western ideas, institutions, and weapons to oust the imperial powers.

Some independence movements succeeded in a relatively peaceful fashion. Exhausted by World War II, some European nations found it increasingly hard to justify imperialism and were sometimes glad to rid themselves of colonial entanglements with a minimum of struggle. Others refused to abandon their vested interests abroad.

The fiercest resistance to independence tended to come in regions where Westerners had settled in substantial numbers. Thus, in regions such as Rhodesia (present-day Zimbabwe),

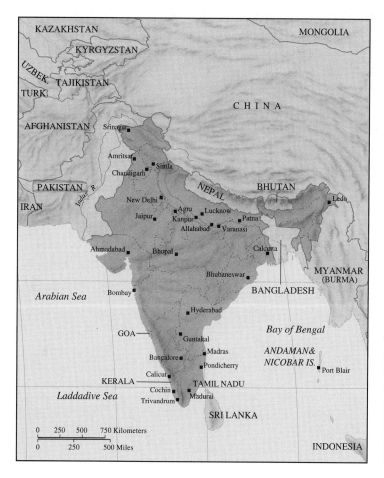

Map 16.1 Present-Day South Asia. In 1947 India and Pakistan obtained independence from Great Britain. Subsequently, Pakistan broke into two separate nations, Pakistan in the west and Bangladesh in the east. The India-Pakistan border remained tense, particularly in the disputed area of Kashmir. China also extended its influence and control along the northern border into Tibet.

Algeria, and South Africa, African nationalist leaders sometimes had to resort to violence such as bombings and guerrilla warfare to gain freedom. In French-ruled Indochina and Algeria, Portuguese-ruled Mozambique, and the Belgian Congo, indigenous peoples fought protracted wars of liberation to throw off the colonial yoke.

The British Empire in Asia Collapses

The Western-ruled empires that encompassed all of South and Southeast Asia (except Thailand) gave rise to some of the world's first post–World War II independence movements. In the Indian subcontinent and in much of colonial Southeast Asia, militant and sometimes violent mass movements were required to expel the Western imperialists.

The inhabitants of British India, the jewel in Queen Victoria's crown a century earlier, were the first to gain independence. Indian demands, first for autonomy and then for complete independence, had intensified during the twentieth century. After World War I, the Indian National Congress, under Mohandas K. Gandhi's leadership, instituted a series of strikes, economic boycotts, and demonstrations against the British. After World War II, the newly elected British Labour government, long opposed to imperial entanglements, negotiated the final transition to Indian independence.

Both the British and Gandhi originally hoped to achieve independence for a united subcontinent. Unfortunately, religious tensions between Hindus and Muslims, long antedating the arrival of the British, made such a postimperial union impracticable. Muslims feared discrimination in a unified state in which Hindus would heavily outnumber them. A virtual civil war erupted, and mass migrations took place as Hindus rushed toward the safety of Hindu-dominated regions and Muslims moved toward Muslim-dominated areas. Gandhi, the spiritual leader of the nationalist movement, and Jawaharlal Nehru, its tactician, eventually had to settle for the establishment of two separate states: India, which was mostly Hindu, and Pakistan, which was created for the Muslims out of predominantly Muslim regions in the northwestern and northeastern sectors of the subcontinent. Finally, on August 15, 1947, the independence of the two states was proclaimed. Only a few months later, in 1948, a fanatical Hindu, who opposed his efforts to negotiate with the Muslims, assassinated Gandhi.

Nehru became the first prime minister of India. He immediately faced the tasks of quelling the continued border strife with neighboring Pakistan and raising the standard of living for the rapidly growing Indian population. Under the provisions of its 1950 constitution, India became a federal republic and the world's largest democracy. Nehru continued as prime minister until his death in 1964, and his Congress party remained the dominant political force for over forty years.

In 1966, two years after Nehru's death, his daughter Indira Nehru Gandhi (1917–1984; no relation to Mohandas K. Gandhi), was elected prime minister. Following a stunning electoral victory in 1971, Gandhi pushed through a number of authoritarian measures and banned opposition political parties for two years. Gandhi and many within the Congress party firmly supported equality for women and struggled against the oppression of women and children, both of whom were frequently exploited as free labor. Such social policies, particularly a massive state-sponsored program for birth control, alienated many Indians. Deeply entrenched traditions and conservatism, particularly

Jawaharlal Nehru and Mohandas K. Gandhi. Here the leaders of India's independence movement enjoy a relaxed moment on the eve of their country's liberation in 1947. Nehru, a longtime follower of the immensely popular Mahatma, adopted a more formal style of leadership as the first prime minister of the new nation.

in the countryside where most Indians continued to live, made implementation of government laws and policies difficult. Gandhi lost the election of 1977, but returned to power in the 1980 elections.

In spite of notable strides toward industrialization and increased agricultural productivity, India, with its growing population, continued to face formidable economic problems and troubling sectarian disputes among its many religious and ethnic minorities, especially the Sikhs. After Indira Gandhi's assassination by her Sikh bodyguard in 1984, her son Rajiv was elected Prime minister, thereby continuing the Congress party's and the Nehru-Gandhi family's domination over Indian politics. Voters disgruntled over charges of corruption, inefficiency, and nepotism voted Rajiv Gandhi out of office in 1989, and he was assassinated by Tamil extremists while campaigning for office in 1990. However, except for the two years that Mrs. Gandhi suspended the constitution, India continued to be governed by democratically elected politicians.

Pakistan, too, was plagued with internal political problems. With the partition of the subcontinent, the new Muslim state consisted of two separate sections, West Pakistan and East Pakistan, separated by India. Different ethnic and language groups with little in common except Islam populated East and West Pakistan. East Pakistan, densely populated and extremely poor, was neglected by ruling West Pakistani leaders, and this fueled its political and economic grievances. Mohammed Ali Jinnah (1887–1948), the father of Pakistan, died before a satisfactory constitution could be devised. His weak successors had to contend with land and border disputes with India and Afghanistan. In the face of these problems, the Pakistani military staged a coup in 1958.

The military, heavily dominated by officers from West Pakistan, made no attempt to redress East Pakistani grievances. As a result, serious riots erupted in East Pakistan; and the Awami League, an East Pakistani political party, moved for secession and independence. Indian intervention allowed the party to form the independent state of Bangladesh in 1971. Since its independence, Bangladesh, one of the poorest nations in the world, has suffered recurring floods, famines, political upheavals, and military takeovers.

Under Zulfiqar Ali Bhutto (1929–1979), Pakistan, now confined only to the western sector, enjoyed seven years of civilian rule during the 1970s, but Bhutto was overthrown and executed in a military coup d'état led by General Zia al-Haq. In domestic policy, General Zia instituted stricter adherence to Islamic law, but in foreign relations he maintained a close alliance with the United States. After Zia died in a mysterious helicopter crash, Bhutto's daughter Benazir, heading the Pakistan People's party, was elected prime minister in 1988. The popular Bhutto moved to liberalize the political life of the nation and to make social and economic reforms, but Pakistan continued to face daunting economic problems. In addition, Bhutto and her family were accused of massive corruption and were ousted from office in the 1990s. Benazir Bhutto was the first female head of government in a predominantly Muslim state; indeed women had been elected to the highest political office in few nations at the time. Subsequently, female prime ministers were also elected to office in both Bangladesh and Turkey, two other Muslim states.

Meanwhile, like India and Pakistan, British colonies in Southeast Asia had secured their independence. Following successful fights against guerrilla nationalists, Great Britain granted independence to Burma (present-day Myanmar) and Ceylon (present-day Sri Lanka) in 1948 and to Malaya (present-day Malaysia) in 1957. The most prosperous of these former colonies was the great port and former British naval base of Singapore at the tip of the Malay Peninsula. Singapore, which had a Chinese majority, acquired independence in 1959.

In sharp contrast to the British, the Dutch attempted to retain control of Indonesia. This proved futile, and following a revolt led by Achmad Sukarno (1901–1970), the Dutch granted independence to Indonesians in 1949. After bloody clashes between the strongly entrenched Communist party and the army, Sukarno was ousted from power by General Suharto (1921–) in 1967 in a bloody coup in which hundreds of thousands were killed. Suharto's military dictatorship continued to rule Indonesia until 1998.

The struggle for independence in Indochina was a long and bloody one. The war in Indochina also became part of the Cold War in Asia and will therefore be discussed later in this chapter.

Unlike the situation in Indonesia or Indochina, the Philippines obtained full independence peacefully from the United States in 1946. In the face of a protracted insurgency by Communist rebels, Ferdinand Marcos, who had been elected president in 1965, established martial law. The Marcos regime engaged in widespread nepotism and corruption, allowing the urban middle class and Marcos supporters to prosper while many Filipinos suffered from mounting poverty. As his health failed in the 1980s, Marcos faced a growing opposition movement led by Corazon Aquino (1933–), the widow of a Marcos opponent who had been assassinated. Following allegations of election fraud and massive demonstrations, a military coup ousted Marcos and democracy was restored under the leadership of Aquino. Subsequently, however, democratically elected governments failed to address the ongoing problems of poverty, land reform, and urban slums.

Finally, many Pacific islands also achieved independence in the postwar years. However, some enclaves of Western colonialism have remained, and France, Great Britain, and the United States have all retained a military and administrative presence on scattered Pacific island chains.

Independent African Nations

As they did in Asia, European nations gradually granted independence to their African colonies following World War II. In 1956, the French, suffering from a recent defeat in Indochina and facing a mounting war in neighboring Algeria, granted independence to Morocco and Tunisia. However, they were absolutely determined to retain control of Algeria, which they had held since 1830 and where many French colonists had settled. The French also sought to retain control over the potential wealth of Algeria's petroleum and mineral deposits.

In 1954, the Algerian National Liberation Front (FLN) launched dozens of attacks against French installations throughout the country, and a long and bloody struggle ensued. The French army responded to Algerian guerrilla attacks and urban terrorism by

"Algérie Française!"

"All-that-France-has-done-in-Algeria" (the hospitals, the roads, the port facilities, the big towns, the beginnings of an industry, and a quarter of the schools that are needed) and "All-that-France-hasn't-done-in-Algeria" (the remaining three quarters of the necessary schools, other industries, and an agricultural plan with the agrarian reform and the technical experts it will call for) form together a sort of explosive compound, to the destructive force of which our accomplishments contribute no less powerfully than our misdeeds.

And now that the good and the evil that we have done have fused to produce one of the most terrifying time-bombs in the world, quite a number of Frenchmen, it must be admitted, cherish the daydream of leaving Algeria and the Algerians to sort out their own problems as best they can. Well, we undertook to solve those problems, and they are still soluble—at an enormous

*effort, but not one beyond our means. Without our aid, what ever happens, they will never be solved.**

In the above excerpt, Germaine Tillion, a French anthropologist and member of the French resistance during World War II, expressed her hopes for a resolution to the long and vicious Algerian war. From 1934 to 1940, Tillion worked on scientific missions in Algeria. Although she recognized the shortcomings of French policies in Algeria, she remained convinced that Algeria was part of France and should remain so for the mutual benefit of the French and Algerian people. In this belief she echoed the rallying cry "Algérie Française," or "Algeria is France," which became the slogan for all those seeking a French victory in Algeria. Nevertheless, protracted negotiations between France under the leadership of General Charles de Gaulle and the FLN led to Algerian independence in 1962.

* Germaine Tillion, Algeria: The Realities (New York: Knopf, 1958), p. 69.

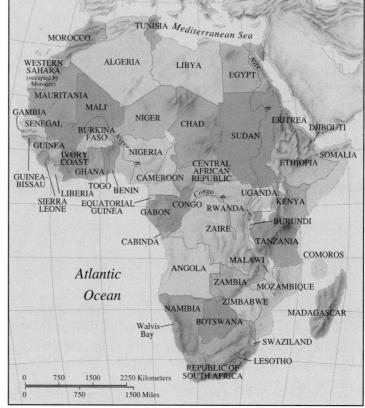

Map 16.2 Africa after World War II. This map depicts the results of the independence movements in northern and central Africa in the 1950s and 1960s and in southern Africa in the 1970s. European powers departed peacefully from their overwhelmingly black colonies, but they had to be pushed out by guerrilla warfare from areas that contained a minority of white settlers. French forces remained by invitation in some former French colonies, and Cuban troops arrived in two instances to support Marxist interests in the Cold War.

bombing villages, removing people from the countryside into fenced camps, and torturing FLN suspects or sympathizers. The French settlers organized their own terrorist group, the Secret Army Organization (OAS), which killed many Algerians.

The French populace was divided over the issue of Algerian independence, as the people of the United States would later be over Vietnam. After General Charles de Gaulle (1890–1970) became leader of France in 1958, he toured war-torn Algeria and concluded that although France might be able to gain a military victory, in the long run Algeria must be accorded independence. He initiated protracted negotiations with FLN leaders, many of whom were in French prisons.

Meanwhile, the fighting continued to escalate as both sides sought to improve their bargaining positions in the field. The negotiations dragged on until 1962, when Algeria gained its independence. The new government, headed by Ahmed Ben Bella (1919–), faced the formidable task of rebuilding a largely devastated nation. A million Algerians had died in the war, while many others had been forcibly uprooted from their homes, which were then destroyed. Although revenues from a growing petroleum industry helped bolster the economy, successive Algerian governments had to cope with a rapidly growing population, high unemployment, particularly among the young, and declining agricultural output. Ironically, France remained Algeria's major trading partner. Internationally, Algeria took a leadership role among Third World nations. In times of crisis its nonaligned leaders often served as negotiators between Western nations and Arab, Muslim, or African states.

The emergence of independent states in sub-Saharan Africa, most of which was ruled by the British, the French, the Portuguese, and the Belgians, differed markedly from the struggles and independence of states in most of Asia. As the imperial powers gained control in sub-Saharan Africa, they had carved out dozens of small states, many of which had not been independent political entities prior to the imperial age. As a result, the independent nations in Africa—in contrast to those in Asia—often were new political creations that did not have the long national history of their Asian counterparts. In addition, in contrast to Asia, whites had settled in some areas of Africa. These settlers often waged protracted and tenacious struggles to retain their privileged positions and to prevent majority black rule. The following description of African independence struggles will in general follow a geographic pattern from largely French-held western Africa to largely British-dominated eastern Africa and then to central and southern Africa, where the struggles for independence were particularly violent and protracted.

The French controlled a wide band of colonies, collectively known as French West Africa and French Equatorial Africa, that ran south of the Sahara from the Atlantic east to the borders of Egypt and the Sudan. By the mid-twentieth century, Africans in these areas were actively pursuing independence. Felix Houphouet-Boigny (1905–1993), a black African planter, doctor, and politician from the small but relatively prosperous Ivory Coast, was one of the most successful and long-lived leaders of the movement for independence in the French colonies. Having served in French governments in Paris, he was an experienced political leader. Together with other African leaders, he organized a West African independence party and worked with liberal and socialist politicians in Paris to end French rule in the area. This objective was achieved with little violence. After a referendum in 1958, the French government under de Gaulle granted limited freedom to most of the colonies, while France retained some political and economic control. The colony of Guinea, under the socialist leader Ahmed Sékou Touré (1922–1984), however, voted for complete independence. In 1960 the rest of French West Africa and French Equatorial Africa secured independence, as did Madagascar, an island off the eastern coast of Africa.

Great Britain's African colonies after World War II consisted of a scattering of territories along the southern edge of French West Africa and a band of colonies down the length of East Africa. With the exception of Kenya, leaders of liberation movements won independence for their countries largely without armed conflict.

Ghana, formerly called the Gold Coast, was the first black colony in Africa to be liberated. Kwame Nkrumah (1909–1972), the leader of Ghana's drive for self-government, had studied in Great Britain and the United States. On his return to the Gold Coast in 1947, he rallied people behind the Convention People's party (CPP), a grassroots, popular African liberation party. Boycotts, strikes, and other measures brought Ghana independence in 1957. Once in power, Nkrumah set the tone for many postindependence

African leaders. He created a cult of personality, becoming president for life in 1960, and made the CPP the only legal party. Increasingly, independent African states became one-man dictatorships, one-party states, or military regimes.

In 1960 Nigeria, a large federated state, gained independence from Great Britain. Its petroleum revenues soon made Nigeria comparatively prosperous economically, but internal divisions culminated in 1967 in the attempt of the Igbo peoples in southeastern Nigeria to secede from the union and form the independent nation of Biafra. A violent civil war raged until 1970, when Biafra admitted defeat, and programs for reconstruction began. As in many former British and French colonies, military coups were punctuated by intermittent returns to democracy, as successive governments of Nigeria grappled with persistent economic problems. (The economic and social problems faced by African nations will be described in Chapter 17.)

Two of Great Britain's holdings in East Africa, Tanganyika (present-day Tanzania; this former German colony had been mandated to Britain after World War I) and Uganda, achieved independence during 1961 and 1962 with relatively little violence. In neigh-boring Kenya, however, the Mau Mau liberation movement was forced to resort to arms in order to dislodge the British settlers who had taken large tracts of the best agricultural land in the Kenyan highlands. Although the Western press greatly exaggerated the extent of the Mau Mau's attacks against the British, mounting violence did hasten Great Britain's moves to withdraw from Kenya. Politically, Kenyan men and women rallied behind Jomo Kenyatta (c. 1897–1978) and the Kenya African Union and sang nationalist songs such as the following:

> The white community are foreigners
> This land they must quit
> And where will you go, their sympathizers
> When all the Kikuyu gather?
>
>   * * *
>
> We are in every place
> The time is flying and never retreats
> Our time is flying and never retreats
> Our cry is for education
> We want our children to learn
> Now when there is time.

Faced with armed and political opposition, Great Britain granted Kenya independence in 1963. Kenyatta, a charismatic political leader and writer, became the first president; he led Kenya until his death in 1978.

The government encouraged racial harmony among the white settler and Indian minorities and the black majority population with slogans like *harambee* (Let us pull together). During the 1960s and 1970s Kenya was also notable among the newly inde-pendent African nations for maintaining its democratic government, but by the 1980s it was dominated by one-party, one-man rule under Daniel arap Moi. Moi's suppression of all political opponents led to numerous popular demonstrations against his regime, but he tenaciously clung to power, claiming that "politics is king."

Independence Must Be Won

Africa will tell the West that today it desires the rehabilitation of Africa, a return to the roots, a revalorization of moral values. The African personality must be expressed: that is the meaning of our policy of positive neutrality. Africa will have no blocs such as you have in Europe....

We have absolutely no intention of letting ourselves be guided by any ideology whatsoever. We have our own ideology, a strong, noble ideology which is the affirmation of the African personality.

We refuse assimilation because assimilation means depersonalizing the African and Africa. So to ally ourselves with this or that bloc, this or that ideology means abandoning our African personality. Never. The imperialists should know that if their policy of assimilating and depersonalizing Africa has succeeded elsewhere, in the other former ... British, Portuguese, and French colonies, it won't succeed in the Congo.... I am convinced that in one month or two you are all going to find honest, capable, competent civil servants throughout the country. There are even some traditional chiefs who are capable; they are illiterate, but tomorrow they will be excellent administrators....

We are going to protect all the citizens. We do not want a bourgeois government that lives at a distance. We are going to go down among the people, speak with the people every time.

Government policy will be none other than that of the people. It is the people who dictate our actions, and we operate according to the interests and aspirations of the people. Independence is the beginning of a real struggle.... Independence must be won for it to be real.*

Addressing the Congolese people, Patrice Lumumba enunciated the national demands for independence from Western imperialists and expressed his inflated hopes for a bright future. Lumumba urged all Third World nations to adopt a neutral course in the Cold War and to avoid foreign entanglements that would limit their own progress. A highly charismatic speaker, Lumumba practiced a fiery brand of nationalism that was opposed by political rivals in the Congo and by foreign powers, including the United States, who feared he would institute socialism in the mineral-rich Congo. Political rivals, with the support of some Western nations, assassinated Lumumba in 1961.

*Patrice Lumumba, La Pensée Politique de Patrice Lumumba (Paris, 1963), reprinted in The African Reader: Independent Africa, ed. Wildred Cartey and Martin Kilson (New York: Random House, 1970), pp. 87–89.

European colonial holdings in central and southern Africa included the huge Belgian Congo, two large Portuguese territories—Angola and Mozambique—and the British colonies of Northern and Southern Rhodesia. The struggles for independence in most of these colonies were protracted and violent. The Belgian Congo (later renamed Zaire), was important for its valuable copper mines in the Katanga province. At the first sign of agitation for independence, the Belgian government, fearful of becoming mired in colonial wars as France and the Dutch had been, pulled out of the Congo in 1960. Belgium had done little to prepare its colony for independence, however, and left no governmental infrastructure in place. Patrice Lumumba (1925–1961) attempted to rally all Congolese around a program of national unity and neutralism (see the accompanying box), but the Congo's vast mineral wealth attracted other industrialized nations and private corporations. Torn by civil war and troubled by interference from European nations, the Soviet Union, and the United States, Congo became the battleground for Cold War competition in Africa (discussed later in this chapter).

In contrast to Belgium's rapid pullout from the Congo, Portugal refused to consider independence for Angola or Mozambique. Guerrilla revolts broke out in both colonies in the 1960s. In the long struggle that followed, the autocratic Portuguese government received assistance from its NATO allies, whereas the Marxist leaders of the nationalist guerrilla forces received aid from the Soviet Union's eastern European satellites and Cuba. Angola and Mozambique received their independence in 1975, aided in part by the collapse of the dictatorial government in Portugal.

In Angola, the struggle continued even after independence; the Marxist-led Angolan Liberation Movement (MPLA) was immediately engulfed in a new struggle for supremacy against other nationalist guerrillas from rival ethnic alignments. Both the Republic of South Africa and the United States supported an opposition group led by Jonas Savimbi, while Cuban military forces moved in to prop up the MPLA. After a negotiated compromise, Cuban forces and other foreign supporters, including South Africa, withdrew in the late 1980s. The continued conflicts in southern Africa and struggle for equal rights in the Union of South Africa will be described in detail in Chapter 17.

During the 1960s a similar armed struggle broke out in neighboring Namibia. This former German colony had been mandated to South Africa after World War I. Although the United Nations revoked the South African mandate over Namibia in 1966 and annually condemned its illegal occupation, the South African government refused to withdraw. As a result, a guerrilla revolt led by the South West African People's Organization (SWAPO) started against South Africa. SWAPO received the support of other indepen-

Namibians Struggle to Vote. In 1989 the first-ever elections in Namibia brought a huge voter turnout; people eagerly cast their votes for the new independent government. Here an elderly woman crawls to the voting place to cast her ballot.

dent black African nations. In the 1970s and 1980s, members of the Communist bloc supported SWAPO, and newly liberated Angola provided bases and support. South Africa moved to crush the guerrillas and conducted armed "destabilization" raids into Angola itself. In the late 1980s, a fragile cease-fire was achieved, and a negotiated settlement was reached whereby all outside forces were to be withdrawn. In 1989 Namibia had its first free elections and moved toward independence under the elected leadership of SWAPO.

The fates of the two Rhodesias were quite different. Like Kenya and Algeria, both colonies had minority populations of white settlers. As in the other areas, British colonists in the Rhodesias lobbied hard against any form of independence that would allow black majority rule. In 1964, however, the British government imposed a democratic constitution on the settlers of Northern Rhodesia; the new constitution led to the election of a black African president and to the creation of the new nation of Zambia.

White settlers in Southern Rhodesia resisted similar efforts by the British government to impose democracy and black majority rule. In 1965 the white settlers declared their own independence under the white supremacist leader Ian Smith. Only South Africa supported this minority regime. In the face of mounting guerrilla opposition against the regime, both Great Britain and the United States sought a negotiated settlement that would grant majority rule. Fifteen years after the whites' unilateral declaration of independence, relatively free elections were finally held, and in 1980 the black African leader Robert Mugabe (1924–) became the first prime minister of the independent nation of Zimbabwe. Thus, by the 1990s independence had been achieved in most of Africa.

The Superpowers and the New Nations

Among other major concerns, the leaders of the world's new nations faced a foreign policy problem of the first magnitude: how to relate to the Cold War confrontation between the United States and the Soviet Union, each of which was supported by a number of allies and satellites. Inevitably, both blocs pressured the recently independent nations to choose sides. The choice presented real difficulties. Both sides claimed to be opposed to imperialism, the United States pointing to its tradition of democratic self-government; the Soviet Union emphasizing the Leninist view that imperialism was a form of capitalist exploitation. Both sides had offered some support to independence movements. The United States pressured its European allies to hasten decolonization, while the Soviet Union provided material support for some guerrilla movements.

Both superpowers wanted the new nations to allow access to their natural resources, to provide sites for military bases, and to render diplomatic support in the United Nations. In return, both superpowers could offer the new nations economic and technological aid, arms, and sometimes military support in their regional struggles. Finally, both could punish nations that rejected their overtures by withdrawing aid or by supporting their enemies.

Most Asian and African countries were fearful of domination by the superpowers and were also disillusioned with both Western capitalism and Soviet communism. Many nations therefore chose to follow nonalignment, the approach taken by India early in the postwar independence era. Nehru, and subsequently the leaders of many of the new states, believed that newly independent and predominantly poor nations were more likely to retain their independence and improve their economies if they avoided firm alliances with either superpower and took stands on international issues on the basis of their own self-interest. Nehru also hoped to pressure the wealthy, industrialized nations into assisting the economic development of the poor nations, thereby achieving a more equitable distribution of goods and services around the world. Thus nonaligned nations, many of which were also part of the Third World bloc, stood apart from the so-called First World of Western nations and the Second World of the Soviet Union and its allies.

The policy of nonalignment and neutrality was formalized with the establishment of the Organization of Nonaligned States at Bandung, Indonesia, in 1955. Thereafter heads of many Asian and African nations and of some Latin American states came together for periodic discussions of common problems. Nehru, Gamal Abdul Nasser of Egypt, and Josef Tito of Yugoslavia became the prominent leaders of the nonaligned movement. In the General Assembly of the United Nations, many Asian and African nations operated as a voting bloc on key issues, where their numbers often outweighed the votes of the industrialized nations.

Some nations, such as India and Egypt, took an officially neutralist stance, but in fact followed a policy that was often pro-Soviet. This infuriated Western leaders like Eisenhower's Secretary of State, John Foster Dulles, who characterized nonalignment as "immoral." During the 1980s Jeane Kirkpatrick, U.S. ambassador to the United Nations, claimed that these nations had a decided tilt against the West and in favor of the Soviet bloc. There was some substance to this charge. India's Indira Gandhi, for example, opposed many U.S. policies and particularly objected to the close relations between the United States and Pakistan. Consequently, she tightened India's alliances with the Soviet Union.

The leaders of former colonies often resented the colonial legacy of the Western nations and indirectly the United States as leader of the Western bloc. Because most of them had no experience with Soviet imperialism, they tended to be less anti-Soviet. Cold War rivalry often moved the United States and the Soviet Union to support opposing sides in the Third World. The Soviet bloc supplied at least some military aid and training, and much rhetorical support, for anti-imperialist guerrilla movements during the 1970s and 1980s. The United States, by contrast, in opposing the expansion of communism, often maintained political and economic ties with conservative, pro-Western regimes. This policy often influenced officially nonaligned nations to favor the Soviet Union. Third World leaders also criticized U.S. support for Israel and for the white minority government in South Africa.

The Cold War in Asia and Africa

In 1949 New China was founded and we peasants became masters of the country. Land reform was carried out, with feudalist land ownership abolished and farmland returned to the tillers.

In 1951 the agricultural collectivization movement got underway in my village. We first got organized into mutual-aid production teams and then into elementary agricultural co-operatives and put our farmland into public ownership. The principle of "to each according to his work" was followed.

Long Live the Victory of People's War!

It was on the basis of the lessons derived from the people's wars in China that Comrade Mao Tse-tung, using the simplest and the most vivid language, advanced the famous thesis that "political power grows out of the barrel of a gun." . . .

So long as imperialism and the system of exploitation of man by man exist, the imperialists and reactionaries will invariably rely on armed force to maintain their reactionary rule and impose war on the oppressed nations and peoples. . . .

The history of the people's war in China and other countries provides conclusive evidence that the growth of the people's revolutionary forces from weak and small beginnings into strong and large forces is a universal law of development of the class struggle, a universal law of development of the people's war.

It must be emphasized that Comrade Mao Tse-tung's theory of the establishment of rural revolutionary base areas and the encirclement of cities from the countryside is of outstanding and universal practical importance for the present revolutionary struggles of all the oppressed nations and peoples, and particularly for the revolutionary struggles of the oppressed nations and peoples in Asia, Africa and Latin America against imperialism and its lackeys.

The Chinese revolution provides a successful lesson of making a thorough-going national-democratic revolution under the leadership of the proletariat.

Ours is the epoch in which world capitalism and imperialism are heading for their doom. . . . The new experience gained in the people's revolutionary struggles in various countries since World War II has provided continuous evidence that Mao Tse-tung's thought is a common asset of the revolutionary people of the whole world. This is the great international significance of the thought of Mao Tse-tung.[*]

In this article, Marshal Lin Piao, minister of defense in China and, at the time, a close ally of Mao Zedong, extolled Mao's contributions to Marxist revolutionary ideology and his impact on Third World revolutions. In the mid-1960s, when this article was written, Lin and most other revolutionaries were convinced that communism would ultimately triumph over capitalism and that peasant-led revolutions would lead to the establishment of independent socialist nations. In both the Soviet Union and China, however, the Communist party established a dictatorial regime that instituted a form of state capitalism rather than a classless society led by workers. By the 1980s both nations were moving toward privatization and free enterprise, although the Communist party retained its control over the government in China.

[*]Lin Piao, article distributed by official Chinese press agency, September 1965, reprinted in Henry M. Christman, Communism in Action: A Documentary History (New York: Bantam Books, 1969), pp. 341–347.

During those years, since everyone worked hard and the government provided the co-operative with preferential loans and farm tools, production grew rapidly. I remember my family got more than enough wheat that year. We lived quite well during those years.

In 1958 we got organized into the people's commune, which brought about some desirable changes. . . .

In 1966, the chaotic "cultural revolution" began. I could no longer collect firewood or grow melons because these were seen as capitalist undertakings. We peasants, unlike workers who have regular wages, had to work in the fields or we would have had nothing to eat. So our agricultural production continued as usual.

In retrospect, my life improved steadily after I began working. But I always thought I could have done much better.[*]

[*]Wang Xin and Yang Xiabing, "A Peasant Maps His Road to Wealth," *Beijing Review*, 27 (November 12, 1984): 28–30, reprinted in Peter N. Stearns, ed., *Documents in World History*, vol. 2 (New York: Harper & Row, 1988), pp. 143–145.

In this reminiscence, a Chinese peasant who survived the upheavals of war and prospered under the Communist revolution described the sweeping changes in social and economic structures Mao Zedong instituted in the decades following the Communist victory in 1949. This rather positive description offers a striking comparison to the more critical account by a son of Chinese intellectuals presented in a box later in this chapter.

Mao's reliance on peasant support became the model for many Third World liberation movements and revolutions. The United States, as champion of capitalist systems, often saw these movements in Cold War terms as positive gains for communism that would benefit the Soviet Union. The United States, therefore, frequently moved to overthrow or defeat Marxist-dominated regimes in Asia and Africa.

Communism Wins in China

On October 1, 1949, Mao Zedong, the victorious Communist leader in China's civil war, proclaimed the founding of the People's Republic of China. Just as World War I had discredited the Tsarist government in Russia and brought about the triumph of communism under Lenin, World War II exhausted and discredited the Nationalist (Kuomintang) government in China and brought the Chinese Communist party (CCP) to power. Mao had expanded Marx's revolutionary theory by stressing that socialist revolutions could triumph in agricultural as well as industrial nations. Peasants as well as the proletariat could be the revolutionary vanguard. Mao worked effectively with the Chinese peasants, attending to their needs while indoctrinating and organizing them to overthrow the Nationalists. As his following grew, Mao was able, with captured Japanese equipment and some Soviet help, to move from guerrilla warfare to conventional battle tactics that finally destroyed Chiang Kai-shek's forces. Chiang went into exile on the island of Taiwan, where he proclaimed the continuation of his Nationalist government and his determination to return to the mainland in order to liberate China from the Communists.

A Young Man Remembers Hard Times

It was in 1960 . . . all China fell on hard times. I was almost seven. Rice, cooking oil, and soybean products were severely rationed, and meat, eggs, flour, and sugar gradually disappeared from the market completely. . . .

Father explained that the rivers and lakes had overflowed and the peasants couldn't grow anything for us to eat. "But you're lucky," he said. "You live in a big capital city, and the Party and Chairman Mao are giving you food from the storage bins. The peasants have to find a way out for themselves."

The situation dragged on and got worse, month after month, until a whole year had passed. . . .

One day Father came home unusually silent and depressed. . . . Finally he told us that in a commune . . . to the South, nearly an entire Production Team had died of hunger, and there was no one left with enough strength to bury the bodies.*

In this excerpt Liang Heng, whose father was a reporter and whose mother was a ranking cadre in the local police, describes life in an urban area during the massive famine that afflicted vast areas of China between 1959 and 1961, the result of Mao's forcing all farmers into communes. An estimated 30 million people died as a result. Liang's memories differ markedly from the more favorable conclusions given by the peasant in the introductory excerpt.

*Liang Heng and Judith Shapiro, Son of the Revolution (New York: Vintage Books, 1984), pp. 17–18.

Jiang Qing on Trial.
Here Jiang Qing, Mao's widow, is shown at her trial in 1980–1981, when she and her three leading supporters, called the Gang of Four, were tried for crimes committed during the Cultural Revolution. She was placed in a bamboo cage with a sign beside her reading, "The Accused."

© Eastfoto

In different ways, both superpowers misunderstood the successful peasant war in China. The United States, fearing the spread of communism, backed the anticommunist but dictatorial Chiang government. After the embittering experience of the Korean War, the United States ignored the most populous nation on earth and refused to recognize Mao's government. Until 1971 the United States vetoed all attempts to seat the People's Republic in the United Nations, hoping that Chiang could make a comeback from his refuge on the island of Taiwan.

The Soviet Union also misjudged the Chinese situation. Soviet leaders after Stalin refused to recognize Mao as the senior leader of the Communist world or to concede his claim to be the leading Marxist theoretician. The Soviet leaders insisted that Moscow should continue to be the sole interpreter of Marxian theory and viewed Maoist ideology as diversionary. The Chinese Communist government responded that it was the only truly revolutionary force and that the Soviet regime had "gone off the tracks" of true Marxism. In addition, the People's Republic demanded that the Soviet Union return the territories the tsars had taken from the Manchus in the nineteenth century. By the 1960s these issues led to growing tensions between the two great Marxist states. In 1980 China refused to renew the 1950 treaty of alliance with the Soviet Union. The Sino-Soviet border, the longest in the world, also became one of the most heavily guarded. As a result, the Soviet Union found itself facing major enemies in both Europe and Asia.

The Sino-Soviet split marked the beginning of radical changes in China. Already, since 1950 China had nationalized private enterprise, collectivized the land, and gathered peasants into communes; China claimed that all these efforts represented more progress toward a Marxist utopia than Soviet collective farms. The Great Proletarian Cultural Revolution of 1966–1969 was an attempt by Mao to keep China in an extreme revolutionary condition. It was marked by massive purges of so-called revisionists that eliminated many of the best-educated and most effective leaders and brought Mao to supreme power at the expense of his more pragmatic colleagues. Mao's thoughts were embodied in the Little Red Book, which became mandatory reading for all Chinese during this period. The Cultural Revolution resulted in a cult of personality around Mao as extreme as Stalin's had been in the Soviet Union.

After Mao's death in 1976, the Communist government purged the "Gang of Four," headed by Mao's wife, who had risen to power during the Cultural Revolution and had sought to keep China evolving along radical revolutionary lines. As part of their effort to improve China's economy and acquire Western technology, the new leaders improved ties with the West, dismantled the collective farms, and increased private enterprise within China. The Communist party, however, retained strict control over the political apparatus and in the late 1980s smashed movements for increased liberalization and democracy (see Chapter 17).

The Korean War

The Korean War (1950–1953) was a conventional Great Power struggle over spheres of influence. As a result of agreements made during World War II, after the war Japan's former colony, Korea, was split into two occupation zones, divided by the 38th parallel. The Soviet zone in the north expanded its presence in Asia, while the U.S. zone in the south protected Japan. Before the occupation forces left, a Communist dictatorship was established in North Korea and an anticommunist dictatorship emerged in South Korea.

In contrast to its role in Europe, the United States was uncertain over the extent of its commitment in Asia. While the U.S. umbrella definitely covered Japan, Okinawa, and the Philippines, it was not clear whether it also extended to Taiwan, South Korea, and Southeast Asia. Believing that the United States did not intend to protect South Korea, the Soviet Union allowed North Korea to invade the south. North Korean forces quickly overran most of South Korea in June 1950 before a counteroffensive was mounted under the command of the United Nations (UN) but with mostly South Korean and U.S. soldiers. The ensuing struggle expanded the Cold War in Asia. Since South Korea and other U.S. allies in Asia were weaker than the allies of the Soviet Union, the United States had to provide both supplies and its own fighting men to prop up its allies, whereas the Soviet Union needed only to give material aid to keep its allies in the field.

As North Korean forces moved forward, the Truman administration decided that it wished to retain South Korea as a buffer to protect Japan. It exploited the temporary boycott of the United Nations by Soviet representatives and obtained UN agreement to send in U.S. troops and those of other nations to help South Korea. Under the direction of General Douglas MacArthur, UN forces, overwhelmingly U.S. and South Korean, drove the North Koreans back northward close to the border of the People's Republic. Fearing the fall of North Korea and a possible invasion of China, Mao sent Chinese troops into Korea. As a result, the UN forces were driven back into South Korea. By

1951 fighting had bogged down near the original border between the two Koreas. It appeared that U.S. forces could not win a conventional, limited ground war against the Chinese, who could only be defeated by the bombing of Chinese bases or by using nuclear weapons. The use of such tactics would have made war with the Soviet Union a distinct possibility.

The Truman administration concluded that U.S. interests on the Asian mainland were not important enough to risk a third world war. The People's Republic was not bombed, and MacArthur, who had advocated massive bombings and the use of nuclear weapons, was fired when he publicly protested. Agreeing to the stalemate, the combatants signed an armistice in 1953. The cease-fire line, which roughly corresponded to the 38th parallel, remained heavily fortified through the 1990s.

The Korean War was part of the containment policy adopted by the United States after World War II. As part of this policy, the United States signed mutual defense treaties with South Korea, Taiwan, and later South Vietnam. It also established the Southeast Asia Treaty Organization (SEATO), a military alliance of the United States, Great Britain, France, Australia, New Zealand, Thailand, and the Philippines; however, SEATO was never as effective as the North Atlantic Treaty Organization (NATO) in Europe. With its series of regional military alliances—NATO, the Central Treaty Organization (CENTO) in West Asia (the Middle East), and SEATO—the Eisenhower administration believed it had walled in "Communist aggression."

This optimistic view proved illusory. During the 1950s the Soviet Union promoted Marxist-led peasant guerrilla conflicts in much of Southeast Asia. Depending on the circumstances, Marxist guerrillas struck at landlords, colonial authorities, and independent governments. Not understanding the causes of such unrest, the United States focused on the elimination of Marxism and sent Truman Doctrine–style military aid and advisers to bolster unenlightened colonial regimes and authoritarian, anticommunist leaders. In combination with other factors, this aid eliminated insurgency in some areas, but Marxist guerrillas continued to operate in Burma, Thailand, and the Philippines.

By the late 1950s and early 1960s, the Eisenhower and Kennedy administrations were coming to realize that while the United States was trying to maintain its global network of pro-U.S. and anti-Soviet allies, it was also facing mounting demands for social and economic reforms around the world. Leaders in the United States began to see that many of the struggles in Asia, Africa, and Latin America were essentially revolts against economic and social deprivation, rather than support for the Soviet Union in the Cold War. The newly independent, predominantly agricultural, peasant nations of the Third World posed a number of questions for the United States that often seemed to have no satisfactory answers. Should the United States, the bastion of free enterprise and private property, interfere in sovereign states and force land reform? Should the United States support regimes that were often oppressive but were always reliable allies in the Cold War and hope that either by force or domestic reforms they would deal with peasant unrest within their nations? If some of these governments, even with U.S. military and economic aid, still failed to stop peasant movements and Marxist-led guerrillas, should the United States send troops to fight the insurgents in order to save an anti-Soviet regime?

Escalating War in Vietnam

Nowhere were the dilemmas just described more clearly manifested than in Vietnam. After losing to the Viet Minh guerrillas under the Communist leader Ho Chi Minh (1890–1969) at Dien Bien Phu, the French military had reluctantly pulled out of Indochina in 1954; France then granted independence to its former colony. The withdrawal was followed by an international conference at Geneva, where the United States was able to prevent Ho from gaining control of all of Vietnam. Four states emerged in Indochina: Laos, Cambodia, Communist-dominated North Vietnam, and pro-Western South Vietnam. The two Vietnams were divided along the 17th parallel, as Korea was divided near the 38th. By the late 1950s, Communist guerrillas were operating in Laos, and South Vietnam had seen the emergence of Marxist-led groups that resisted the repressive but strongly anticommunist government of Ngo Dinh Diem. The anti-Diem guerrillas were supported by a large section of the peasantry, but at first received little more than moral support from North Vietnam and other Marxist nations. Diem, however, claimed that his opponents were all Viet Cong (Vietnamese Communists) and further claimed that he was being attacked by troops from North Vietnam. He asked the United States for assistance under the Truman Doctrine.

Agreeing with Diem's claims, the Eisenhower and Kennedy administrations sent military equipment and advisers to South Vietnam. As a result, the United States became directly involved in a peasant guerrilla war. Despite U.S. aid, by 1963 the Viet Cong, supplied along the mountainous and jungle-covered Ho Chi Minh Trail with Soviet,

Vietnam War. Trying to catch an elusive enemy, U.S. forces in Vietnam transported infantry by helicopter to surprise Viet Cong and North Vietnamese units. The intent was to inflict casualties rather than capture territory, and the attacking forces usually withdrew afterward. Besides helicopter raids, U.S. tactics included patrols, defense of fixed positions, "freefire zones," napalm strikes, and high-altitude carpet bombardment with conventional bombs or Agent Orange used to defoliate the dense jungle.

"Nam"

The mood was sardonic, fatalistic, and melancholy. I could hear it in our black jokes: "Hey, Bill, you're going on patrol today. If you get your legs blown off can I have your boots?" I could hear it in the songs we sang. Some were versions of maudlin country-and-western tunes like "Detroit City," the refrain of which expressed every rifleman's hope:

I wanna go home, I wanna go home,
O, I wanna go home. . . .

The fighting had not only become more intense, but more vicious. Both we and the Viet Cong began to make a habit of atrocities. One of 1st Battalion's radio operators was captured by an enemy patrol, tied up, beaten with clubs, then executed. . . .

We paid the enemy back, sometimes with interest. . . . According to those "rules of engagement," it was morally right to shoot an unarmed Vietnamese who was running, but wrong to shoot one who was standing or walking; it was wrong to shoot an enemy prisoner at close range, but right for a sniper at long range to kill an enemy soldier who was no more able than a prisoner to defend himself; it was wrong for infantrymen to destroy a village with white-phosphorus grenades, but right for a fighter pilot to drop napalm on it. Ethics seemed to be a matter of distance and technology. You could never go wrong if you killed people at long range with sophisticated weapons.*

United States soldiers and marines were unprepared for the ground fighting in Vietnam. They had expected to face their enemy in open battle, as in World War II and in Korea. In Vietnam, there were few battlefronts; helicopters flew in troops to spots where the enemy allegedly were concentrated and after combat flew them out again. After ten patrols up the same trail, one second of carelessness on the eleventh patrol meant sudden wounds or death from an antipersonnel mine. The enemy was nowhere and everywhere; the villagers working in the fields claimed to know nothing, but some tossed grenades into U.S. bivouacs at night. After serving for a few months, burnt-out veterans had to be replaced with fresh, but still unprepared, troops.

*Philip Caputo, A Rumor of War (New York: Holt, Rinehart & Winston, 1977), pp. 227–230.

North Vietnamese, and Chinese weapons and with other war matériel, had gained control of large sections of South Vietnam.

During 1964–1965, two decisions transformed what had been a predominantly civil war among South Vietnamese into a multinational, full-scale struggle. Most U.S. military and civilian leaders believed that the fall of South Vietnam would be the first "domino" in a process whereby all the Southeast Asian nations would fall one by one. As a consequence, the United States sharply increased its support of the South Vietnamese government by setting up huge supply bases guarded by U.S. troops. After U.S. naval ships off the North Vietnamese coast in the Gulf of Tonkin were allegedly attacked, the Johnson administration sent troops into South Vietnam and began bombing the Ho Chi Minh Trail and the southern section of North Vietnam.

In response, the North Vietnamese began to move many units of their army into South Vietnam to support the Viet Cong. Strictly disciplined, the Communist forces waged a war of attrition against U.S. and South Vietnamese troops. They were willing to suffer heavy casualties and extensive bomb destruction for however long it took to inflict enough casualties on the Americans that the United States lost its will to continue the struggle. Once the Americans withdrew, Vietnam would be united by force into a single Communist state.

As in the Korean War, Cold War considerations dictated U.S. military policy. As the struggle in Vietnam escalated, the world powers tacitly agreed to keep the conflict from triggering a devastating nuclear world war. The Soviet Union and the People's Republic confined themselves to sending supplies and refrained from sending combat units to Vietnam. The United States refrained from employing nuclear weapons and from bombing Soviet supply ships or Chinese supply depots in North Vietnam.

On the Korean Peninsula, it had been possible to draw a battle line from coast to coast, but U.S. forces in Vietnam faced a kaleidoscope of shifting battle lines on the edge of an enormous land mass. Despite building their forces to over half a million men by 1968, the Americans failed to make decisive headway in the war. The South Vietnamese peasants were caught in the middle of the conflict. They had little loyalty to the corrupt and repressive South Vietnamese government and none at all to the foreign Westerners who not only backed the government but also had earlier supported the French. Most peasants were not committed to Marxism either, but at least the Marxists were Vietnamese. Most Americans in the war had little knowledge of or respect for the people of Vietnam. Separated by differences in language, culture, and physical appearance, many Americans regarded Vietnamese and other Asians as alien "gooks." Equally important, the Vietnamese Communists were in the long run more effective in controlling the peasant villages through social contacts, indoctrination, and their daily presence than the Americans were with sporadic raids and "resettlement" programs.

The war reached a turning point in 1968. Just as a large segment of the French public had opposed the war in Algeria, so, too, did influential elements of the U.S. public turn against the war. Antidraft and antiwar disruptions steadily increased. The Nixon administration intensified aspects of the war while systematically withdrawing American troops; protracted negotiations with Hanoi ensued. In 1973 both sides agreed to an armistice and the withdrawal of all foreign troops from South Vietnam. U.S. forces left, and in 1975 North Vietnamese forces and the Vietcong launched a major assault, overrunning South Vietnam in a few weeks. Meanwhile, Communist units also took over in Laos and Cambodia. A major Cold War struggle had come to an end in Asia, but others continued in Africa and Latin America.

The Cold War in Africa

As already noted, both the superpowers, either directly or through intermediary nations such as Israel and Cuba, had become involved in various struggles for independence in central and southern Africa. One major instance was the complex struggle for leadership over the newly independent Congo. The leader of the Congolese nationalists, Patrice Lumumba, was appointed the first prime minister, but as a more radical nationalist, he was feared by conservative Africans and by the West and was eventually assassinated (see the box earlier in the chapter). With Western help, mineral-rich Katanga province seceded and remained independent for two years. Finally, the United Nations was called in to restore order, and a military dictatorship under Sese Seko Mobutu (1930–1997) took over the government. Mobutu carefully balanced demands for Africanization of foreign properties with support for foreign mining interests. Although his regime was

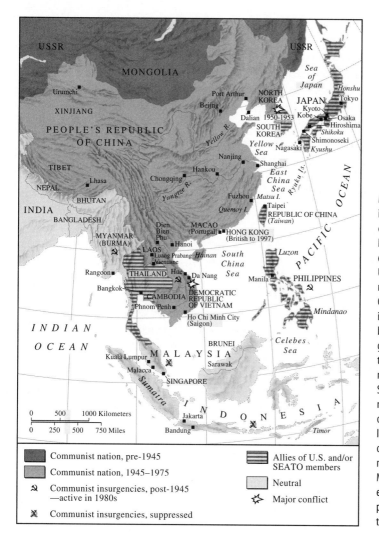

Map 16.3 The Cold War in Asia. After World War II, communism spread into Asia by means of armed struggle, despite resistance by the United States. Communist regimes came to power in China through civil war and in Vietnam, Laos, and Cambodia through armed struggles against the French and the Americans. Only a major military effort by the United States prevented the Communists from taking over all of Korea. Communist guerrillas were also active throughout Southeast Asia; in some nations (for example, Malaysia), the guerrillas were eliminated, but in others, particularly the Philippines, they persisted.

notoriously corrupt, Mobotu proved to be one of the most durable African leaders; he styled himself as "President for Life" of the Congo, which he renamed Zaire.

The superpowers also played out their Cold War rivalry in the Horn of Africa in the eastern section of the continent. Its geographic location along the flank of the petroleum-rich Arabian Peninsula and beside the Suez Canal–Red Sea short route between Europe and Asia made the Horn important to both superpowers. Under Emperor Haile Selassie, Ethiopia had remained a largely feudal nation with close ties to the United States, which established a large radar tracking base there. In 1974, after refusing to institute reforms or to acknowledge widespread famine from drought, the emperor was deposed by a group of left-wing army officers. The new Marxist government promptly closed the U.S. base and established close relations with the Soviet Union. However, the impact of the prolonged drought and starvation was only exacerbated by constant civil and border wars. Ethiopia, whether in alliance with the United States or the Soviet Union, remained one of the world's poorest nations.

Neighboring Somalia was also the scene of superpower rivalry. In Somalia a leftist government had established ties with the Soviet Union; however, drought and starvation resulted in a right-wing coup whose leaders then moved closer to the West. In a 180-degree turnabout, the United States, recently ousted from Ethiopia, then moved to support the new Somali military regime. Here, too, the population continued to suffer the ravages of famine and war with Ethiopia. In the late 1980s, when the Soviet Union under Gorbachev moved to disentangle itself from foreign involvements, it reduced economic and political support for the Ethiopian Marxists, and the regime collapsed. As will be described in the following chapter, the Horn of Africa has remained a region of internal wars and extreme poverty.

Conflict in Latin America

I call upon Chairman Khrushchev to halt and eliminate this clandestine, reckless, and provocative threat to world peace and to stabilize relations between our two nations. I call upon him further to abandon this course of world domination and to join in an historic effort to end the perilous arms race and transform the history of man. He has an opportunity now to move the world back from the abyss of destruction—by . . . withdrawing these weapons from Cuba—by refraining from any action which will widen or deepen the present crisis—and then by participating in a search for peaceful and permanent solutions. . . .

It is difficult to settle or even discuss these problems in an atmosphere of intimidation. That is why this latest Soviet threat—or any other threat which is made either independently or in response to our actions this week—must and will be met with determination. Any hostile move anywhere in the world against the safety and freedom of peoples to whom we are committed . . . will be met by whatever action is needed. *

*John F. Kennedy, in David L. Larson, ed., *The Cuban Crisis of 1962: Selected Documents and Chronology* (Boston: Houghton Mifflin, 1963), pp. 44–45.

On the evening of October 22, 1962, as an anxious American public watched President Kennedy deliver these words on television, the world stood on the brink of atomic holocaust. The two great nuclear-armed superpowers, the United States and the Soviet Union, faced each other in a heart-stopping confrontation issuing out of the installation of Soviet missiles in Cuba aimed at the United States. The Cold War, which had already extended from Europe to Asia, had now shifted its focus to Latin America. In many nations of this region, glaring social inequities had led to domestic unrest. There was also a long-standing resentment of "Yankee Imperialism," a term long applied to U.S. political and economic policies exploiting the resources of Latin America. While some in Latin America supported these policies, many Latin Americans called for social and economic reform at home and for freedom from U.S. economic and political controls. Latin America was therefore fertile ground for the spread of Marxism and for other doctrines that called for social change and for opposition to the United States. From the late 1950s onward, Latin America was often a surrogate battleground for the Cold War superpowers.

Demands for Agrarian Reform

All the peasants want an Agrarian Reform:
so that it is the cows that
are milked . . . not the tenants.
When the sow gives birth
my heart aches;
the son of the landlord
eats my piglets. . . .

The landlord's wife
gave me half a plot (of land);
I did the work
and she took the product.
The boss goes by car
we travel by cart;
these are the delights
of our landlord's rule.

The boss is well-heeled;
we walk about in sandals,
The boss is well dressed;
we are without a stitch . . .

The poor work harder
even than oxen;
the rich do not work
and live like kings.
The priest from my village
told me to wait. . . .
But I cannot endure any more
I want an "Agrarian Reform."*

Song sung by members of the Peasants' Federation in Ecuador, 1975. This song was also sung in Chile in the 1950s and 60s.

*Hazel Johnson et al., Third World Lives of Struggle (London: Heinemann, 1982), pp. 43–44.

Demographic, Economic, and Social Trends

Economically and militarily, Latin America escaped the ravages of World War II, but it continued to suffer from the Great Depression, which caused the prices of its raw exports, mostly foodstuffs and minerals, to drop to all-time lows. The old aristocracy of large landowners and a newly arrived business and professional elite were oriented toward trade with Europe and North America; they exported raw materials and agricultural products in exchange for consumer goods. These leaders gave economic growth, especially industrial output, a high priority after the war. Unfortunately, the interrelated economic, social, and demographic facts of Latin American life made progress very difficult.

Despite a high infant mortality rate, the high birth rate in the region brought a significant population increase to many Latin American nations. In the 1970s the population of Latin America grew at a rate of 2.7 percent per year, compared with 0.9 percent for North America and 0.6 percent for Europe. Those children born into *campesino* (country) families faced a serflike existence of labor on the great Latin American estates. Often there was only seasonal employment for these workers, who received low wages and paid high prices at the landowner's store. They lived in dirt-floor shacks with no running water or electricity and had to cope with a polluted public water supply, inadequate medical services, and primitive sanitation. Of course, they had no education and no political rights.

Latin America experienced rapid urbanization as hundreds of thousands of impoverished peasants fled the misery of the countryside in hopes of better opportunities in the cities. In 1930 only one Latin American city had a population of more than a million; by 1997, 29 cities were near or over 1 million. The influx of campesinos put severe strains on the already overburdened city services, particularly housing, transportation, and sanitation. As in the country, many new arrivals could find only part-time work, and many more no work at all. Tar-paper-shack slums increasingly surrounded most Latin American (and, indeed, most Third World) cities, while the rich barricaded themselves and hired armed guards.

Although Latin America as a whole had a higher per capita GNP than most of Africa or West Asia, it lagged behind the rest of the West in industrial development. Political leaders in some nations such as Mexico encouraged domestic industry and even nationalized foreign holdings from the 1930s onward, but the region remained heavily dependent on fluctuating commodity prices for its manufactured and agricultural goods. Declining prices for the region's resource exports, including the petroleum of Mexico and Venezuela during the petroleum glut of the 1980s, hampered plans for road systems, hydroelectric plants, and housing, as well as for improving the standard of living for the impoverished masses. Development loans, coming due when the Latin American nations could least afford to pay them, pushed such large nations as Mexico and Brazil to the verge of bankruptcy.

The burdened Latin American economies might have had some relief if their fast-growing population had constituted a healthy domestic sales market. Instead, postwar population growth in Latin America far exceeded the increase in economic growth; the unemployed and underemployed masses did not have the income to buy the products turned out by the new industrial facilities, and the economic and social gap between the landholding and urban elite and the peasants continued to widen. Throughout Latin America, workers and miners called for higher wages and better working conditions, and some of the normally passive campesinos began to demand improvements in their living conditions, and even land.

Against this backdrop of economic problems, post–World War II Latin American politics embodied a wide spectrum of responses. In many of the smaller, mostly agricultural Latin American nations, the traditional economic elite, supported by the military leaders and by the predominantly conservative Roman Catholic church, ignored the needs of the masses or made only token reforms. The most repressive regimes, as in Paraguay under General Alfredo Stroessner, often banned or repressed unions and workers' organizations. In more industrially developed nations like Mexico, Venezuela, Brazil, Argentina, and Chile, the political authorities, whether authoritarian or republican, accommodated at least some of the demands of the urban workforce. The earlier "personalist" crypto-fascist governments of Vargas and Péron in Brazil and Argentina have already been discussed. By the 1960s, as unrest intensified and took on some aspects of Marxist urban guerrilla terrorism (see below), modern military dictatorships took over in Brazil, Argentina, and Uruguay. Juntas (cliques) of professional officers ruled a number of Latin American nations. They promised stability and order and sometimes brought economic progress, in terms of gross national product and foreign exports. Usually, however, they protected the traditional landholding and business classes and did little to improve the lot of the campesinos or factory workers. Representative government, with honest elections and changes in party control, had been rare in Latin America both before and during World War II.

Costa Rica, Chile, and intermittently Venezuela and Colombia had histories of republicanism, but even in these nations political parties were merely factions of the elite, little concerned with the plight of the masses. After the war, representative government made headway in Brazil, Argentina, and other nations, but often the republican process succumbed to leftist agitation and military takeovers. Consequently, disaffected campesinos and workers who wished to end the inequities in Latin America began to look to revolutionary action instead of republican government.

One possibility was to follow the path of Mexico. The indigenous social revolution in Mexico had made some headway before 1940, but great inequities still existed there, and in the opinion of many, the gap between the rich and the poor in Mexico was about the same as elsewhere in non-Marxist Latin America, and was increasing. Mexico had the forms of representative government but was in fact a one-party dictatorship. In any case, the revolution in Mexico arose out of circumstances peculiar to Mexico and could not necessarily be duplicated in other nations.

As elsewhere around the globe after World War II, many in Latin America considered Marxism, whether revolutionary or evolutionary, to be the best approach to achieving economic, social, and political justice. However, Leninist communism in the Soviet Union and Maoist communism in the People's Republic of China appeared to many as repellent examples of totalitarianism. Many Latin Americans embraced a broader view of Marxism and worked outside the established Communist parties that were controlled from Moscow or Beijing.

Reform through Marxism was highly problematic in Latin America, however. Not only was it contested by the usual array of economic, social, political, military, and religious

A Revolutionary Credo

Why does our government have to be . . . isolated, and threatened by destruction and death?

They want, simply, to destroy our revolution in order to continue exploiting the other nations of Latin America. . . . they want to destroy us, because we have had the desire to liberate ourselves economically. They want to destroy us because we have desired to do justice. They want to destroy us because we have concerned ourselves with the humble of our land, because we have cast our lot with the poor of our country. . . .

Revolutions are remedies—bitter remedies, yes. But at times revolution is the only remedy that can be applied to evils even more bitter. . . . The Cuban revolution is already a reality for the history of the world.

What is the outcome of a situation in which misery and hunger lead year by year to more misery and

hunger? Can there be any other outcome than that of revolution? . . . This revolution, in the situation of present-day Latin America, can only come by the armed struggle of the peoples. . . .

We want to convert our work to wealth and welfare for our own people and for other peoples. . . . Our country, our people, and our future are important, but still more important are our 230 million Latin American brothers!*

Fidel Castro here gives the Marxist viewpoint on revolution and social change and on the United States' reaction to it. He stresses economic improvement, not political freedom. Castro also expresses his conviction about the inevitable triumph of Marxism, first in Cuba, then throughout the rest of Latin America.

*Fidel Castro, Labor Day Address, May 1, 1960 (Havana: Cooperativa Obera de Publicidad, 1966), pp. 14, 16–17, 21, in Fidel Castro Speaks, ed. M. Kenner and J. Petras (New York: Grove Press, 1969), pp. 151, 159.

elites, it was implacably opposed by the leaders of the United States of America. Most of them did not make fine distinctions among various forms of Marxism; they saw in all Marxists de facto allies of the Soviet Union, and therefore opponents of the United States in the Cold War. Any signs of Marxist power, especially in the Caribbean, essential to the strategic defense of the United States, must be immediately destroyed, or the Soviet Union would enter the Western Hemisphere and outflank the United States to the south.

The United States used a variety of policies to uproot Marxism in the Caribbean and elsewhere in Latin America. It sometimes engaged in economic warfare against leftist governments through blockade and boycott, hoping an impoverished population would rise against its government. The United States also provided covert assistance, including insurgency training, to conservative opponents seeking to overthrow leftist governments; it also trained and deployed counterinsurgency forces against guerrilla opponents of pro-U.S. regimes. In urgent cases, notably to protect its political and economic interests in the Caribbean, the United States resorted to direct military intervention as it had in its earlier twentieth-century phase of imperialism. The Reagan and Bush administrations pursued a wide range of anti-Marxist policies both overtly and covertly. By and large, the United States was successful in keeping Marxism out of Latin America.

As the decades passed after the war, many U.S. leaders saw with increasing clarity that Marxism drew its strength from the misery of the Latin American masses. Hoping to

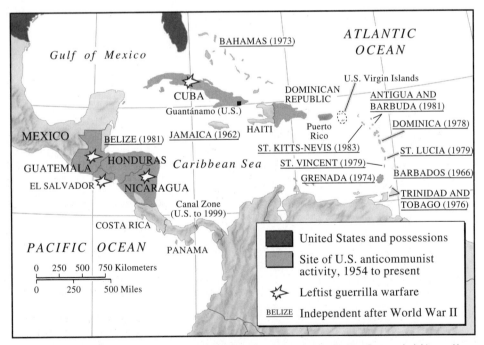

Map 16.4 The Caribbean and Central America after World War II. Two major developments have marked this area. Many colonies of Great Britain became independent, although those held by the French and the Dutch kept their association with the governing nation. At the same time, the United States actively intervened in areas it considered allied with its Cold War rival, the Soviet Union.

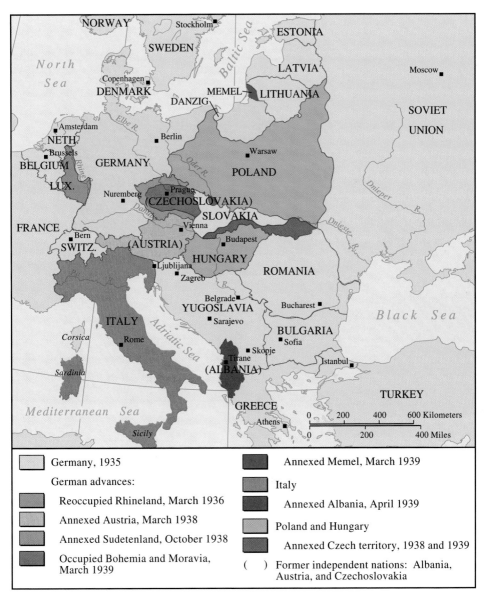

Germany, 1935	Annexed Memel, March 1939
German advances:	Italy
Reoccupied Rhineland, March 1936	Annexed Albania, April 1939
Annexed Austria, March 1938	Poland and Hungary
Annexed Sudetenland, October 1938	Annexed Czech territory, 1938 and 1939
Occupied Bohemia and Moravia, March 1939	( ) Former independent nations: Albania, Austria, and Czechoslovakia

Central Europe, April 1939

This map shows German gains after three years of aggression and consolidation under Adolf Hitler. Italy, Poland, and Hungary also expanded. Although to this point, Hitler had enlarged Germany without war, Great Britain and France were now awake to the futility of appeasement, and Hitler's next aggressive move, against Poland, ignited World War II and Europe.

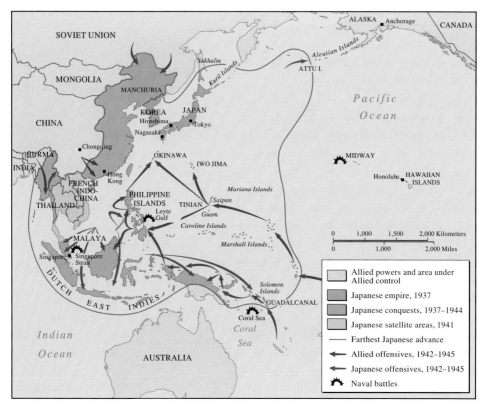

World War II in Asia and the Pacific

War came to this area in stages, beginning with Japan's invasion of China in 1937. In December 1941 the Japanese attacked British, Dutch, and American possessions. By May 1942, they controlled Southeast Asia and the western Pacific and were even threatening Australia and India. The United States defeated the Japanese by destroying their fleet and bombing their home islands. At the time of surrender, Japanese land forces still held large areas of Asia and the Pacific.

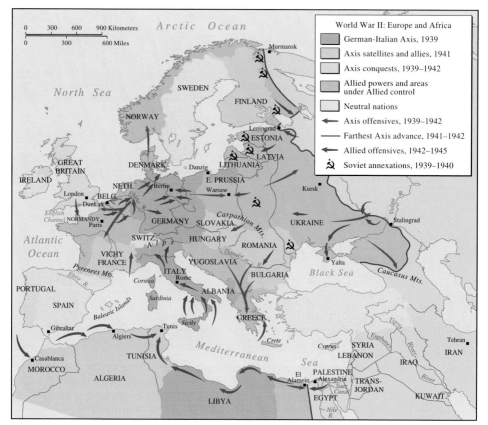

World War II in Europe and North Africa

In the first phase of the war (1939–1942), Germany and Italy and their allies subjugated most of Europe except for Great Britain and the Soviet Union. In the second stage of the war (1942–1945), powerful U.S. forces arrived in the west, and with the aid of the British, cleared the Mediterranean. They then landed in France and pushed eastward into Germany. Meanwhile, the newly constituted, massive Soviet army drove westward through central Europe and the Balkans, meeting the Western allies in the heart of Germany.

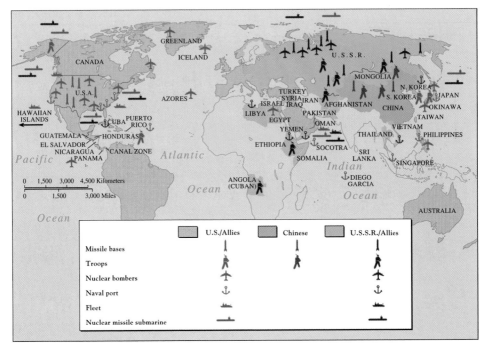

The Global Cold War, 1950s–1980s

This map only hints at the massive, unprecedented outlay of global military power. Both the United States and the Soviet Union spread their forces and weaponry around the globe, challenging each other on the ground in Europe and East Asia, at sea in every ocean, everywhere in the air, including the poles, and even in outer space. China played a secondary "third party" role. The enormous cost of this global confrontation put heavy strains on the United States, and eventually broke down the Soviet economy, bringing the Cold War to an end by the early 1990s.

eliminate the source of Marxist agitation, the United States offered economic aid to entice the governments of Latin America to undertake economic, social, and political reforms. Such programs as the Alliance for Progress and the Inter-American Development Bank failed, however, because most Latin American governments were more fearful of losing power through reform than through Marxist takeover. The United States also moved to shed the image of an old-fashioned imperial power by agreeing in 1978 to give up the Panama Canal Zone and to relinquish control of the canal itself by 2000. Although the latter action was good public relations, U.S. activity in regard to Latin America did little to improve the standard of living for the masses.

Marxism in a Cold War Context: Castro's Revolution in Cuba

The major test for the United States developed during the 1950s when the Cuban government swung abruptly from a moderate right-wing military regime to a left-wing revolutionary dictatorship. Cuba was controlled by Fulgencio Batista, an ally of the U.S. government and of business interests ranging from sugar refining to gambling. Under Batista, Cuban cities enjoyed a relatively high standard of living, but the rural peasantry suffered from seasonal unemployment and inadequate medical and educational facilities. The United States supported Batista because he was strongly anticommunist and pro-United States in domestic and international policies.

In 1959 Fidel Castro, a young Marxist lawyer, gathered enough support to topple Batista's regime. Initially the United States adopted a "wait and see" policy toward Castro's government and hoped that it would institute more liberal reforms and a more efficient government. Castro, however, assumed dictatorial powers and soon announced that his goal was to create a society based on Marxist principles. He nationalized large-scale landholdings, many held by U.S. corporations, closed the casinos (again, many owned by U.S. interests), and made overtures to the Soviet Union for economic aid.

In the climate of the Cold War, the presence of a revolutionary Marxist government close to U.S. borders was unacceptable to the Eisenhower administration, which reacted vigorously against the Castro regime by imposing a total embargo on all Cuban products. Castro then set out to make Cuba a model Communist state in the Western Hemisphere. In the following years, Castro's government established a wide range of social services for the poorest Cubans; these included public housing, education, and medical and sanitary care. His efforts, however, were undermined by his failure to diversify Cuba's economy or to increase and expedite the production of sugar, Cuba's main export. Caught in the grip of the U.S. economic embargo, Castro became increasingly dependent on Soviet aid.

Castro also steadfastly refused to open the political system or to allow any dissent. For many, particularly the middle class and intellectuals, the new system was as repressive as the preceding dictatorships; many fled to the United States. As a militant Marxist, Castro tried to export revolution throughout Latin America through peasant and urban guerrilla warfare. Castro's comrade, Ernesto "Che" Guevara, directed several of these efforts and caught the imagination of leftists everywhere. Most of these efforts failed, however, in the face of strong counterrevolutionary measures. Guevara was killed by U.S.-led counterinsurgency forces in Bolivia in 1967.

A Moment of Marxist Triumph in Latin America. Latin revolutionaries Fidel Castro (center left) and Che Guevara (center right), among others, review a victory parade in Havana shortly after coming to power in 1959. Although Castro clung to power, relentless economic and diplomatic pressures mounted against Cuba by the U.S. government, coupled with poor planning by Castro's government, continued to cripple the living standard of the Cuban people well into the 1990s.

The Cuban Missile Crisis

Besides imposing the economic embargo and breaking off diplomatic relations, Eisenhower, believing that once the Cubans had a taste of communism they would rebel against it, went another step toward toppling Castro. Following a precedent set in overthrowing the leftist government of Guatemala in 1954, Eisenhower authorized the Central Intelligence Agency (CIA) to recruit and train anti-Castro Cubans to invade Cuba and provide a rallying point for the Cuban population to overthrow Castro.

On entering office in 1961, President John Kennedy reaffirmed the plans for invasion, but stipulated that the United States was not to be involved in the landing itself. In April 1961 anti-Castro forces bombed a Cuban airbase and landed at the Bay of Pigs in Cuba. The Cuban campesinos, whose lives had improved under Castro, did not revolt; instead, they rallied behind the new regime. Kennedy vetoed pleas to provide air support to the invaders, and Cuban militia crushed the invasion. Although the U.S. government for many years publicly denied any complicity in the Bay of Pigs fiasco, the invasion's failure hurt Kennedy's prestige and strengthened his resolve to act more vigorously in any future crisis.

The Bay of Pigs debacle led Khrushchev to view Kennedy as a weak leader. More ominously, it tempted Khrushchev to use Cuba to solve some of his own problems: his colleagues were criticizing him for deficient agricultural production and for letting the United States outstrip the Soviet Union in the missile race. Castro, afraid that the United States would try again to topple him, called for additional support from the Soviet Union. Recently declassified documents and statements made by Soviet and U.S. policy makers during 1989 roundtable discussions reveal that Castro's fears were justified. The United States did have plans to topple the Cuban leader during 1962.

Khrushchev decided to send medium-range bombers and missiles to Cuba to help defend Castro and also to threaten the United States. The missiles would also act as a counterweight to U.S. missiles in Europe and Turkey, which were aimed at key targets in the Soviet Union. In October 1962 U.S. spy planes discovered missile sites under construction in Cuba. It is now known that the Soviet Union already had some missiles in Cuba, but they had not been equipped with nuclear warheads.

The Kennedy administration viewed this provocative Soviet move as a direct challenge to its sphere of influence and promptly reacted. Kennedy demanded that the Soviets voluntarily remove the missiles and bombers from Cuba or face their destruction by U.S. air strikes or outright invasion. This was a zero-tolerance matter; the United States was prepared to go to war over the issue. Some Strategic Air Command (SAC) bombers of the U.S. air force were put into the air and others were placed on fifteen-minute alert. President Kennedy also imposed a "quarantine," a peacetime naval blockade of Cuba (by international law an act of war). Latin American nations, at a meeting of the Organization of American States (OAS), supported the blockade. While publicly throwing down the gauntlet, the Kennedy administration was careful not to back the Soviet Union into a corner; it sent word by private channels that in return for Soviet withdrawal, the United States would not attack Cuba, and perhaps would even remove some of its missiles based in Turkey.

For six days people around the world feared war was about to break out between the two superpowers. Fearful of U.S. nuclear superiority, Khrushchev ordered the return of Soviet ships carrying missiles to Cuba. In an exchange of notes, Khrushchev and Kennedy agreed that the Soviet Union would remove the missiles and bombers from Cuba and that the United States would publicly pledge not to invade the island nation. The United States also removed some missiles from Turkey. The armed forces of the two superpowers were ordered to stand down, and nuclear war was avoided. Castro's regime continued into the twenty-first century but became increasingly isolated, impoverished at home, and ineffective abroad.

The United States Combats Marxism throughout Latin America

Marxism in Cuba, with its Cold War associations and risk of thermonuclear destruction, was only the most spectacular instance of U.S.-Marxist confrontation in Latin America. Marxist revolutionary movements broke out regularly throughout Latin America in a twenty-year period from the mid-1950s to the mid-1970s. The big military dictatorships in Brazil, Argentina, and Uruguay, aided in many ways by the United States, crushed Marxism in their own countries.

Besides supporting anti-Marxist governments, the United States also intervened more directly in Latin American nations it perceived as being or becoming Marxist states. The United States intervened covertly in Guatemala in 1954 and militarily in the Dominican Republic in 1965, Grenada in 1983, and Panama (allegedly because of the drug traffic) in 1990.

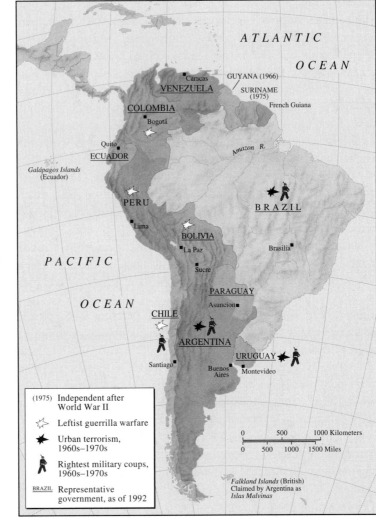

Map 16.5 Political Trends in South America since World War II. South America was swept by a number of shifting political and social trends in the last half of the twentieth century. A wave of Castroite revolutionary struggles, both rural and urban, broke out in several South American nations, but most were suppressed by forces loyal to traditional elites. More economically advanced nations, such as Argentina, Brazil, and Chile, generally fell under the control of military juntas in the 1960s and 1970s, but returned to representative government by the early 1990s, as did caudillo states such as Paraguay.

A striking example of indirect intervention occurred in Chile, which had a long tradition of democracy. A military clique led by General Augusto Pinochet, with U.S. approval and covert support, overthrew the freely elected, left-leaning government of Salvador Allende and killed Allende in 1973. The Pinochet regime brutally purged Allende supporters and imposed strict political and social controls over Chileans. By 1990 representative government had been restored in Chile, and Chileans defeated Pinochet's bid to be elected president.

The main response of the United States to Marxism in Central America, however, centered on the revolutionary government of Nicaragua. In 1978–1979 a broad-based Sandinista guerrilla movement overthrew the dictatorial regime of the Somoza family, which had close ties to the United States. Meanwhile, several Marxist guerrilla groups fought to take over the government of El Salvador, and an intermittent but persistent Marxist uprising continued in Guatemala. President Jimmy Carter recognized and offered aid to the new Sandinista government, which apparently had no ties to the Soviet Union, but his successor, President Ronald Reagan, strongly opposed the Sandinista regime, which by then had implemented a number of socialist reforms. Like Castro in Cuba, the Sandinistas (named after Augusto César Sandino, a Nicaraguan nationalist killed while opposing U.S. occupation of Nicaragua in the 1930s) offered a combination of state socialism and social services to the people. As with Cuba, however, U.S. opposition— and Soviet support—stemmed as much from the politics of the intensified Cold War as from the nature of the Nicaraguan revolution.

The Reagan administration believed the Sandinistas were allied with Castro and the Soviet Union and were supporting guerrilla activities in nearby El Salvador. During the 1980s the United States, as it had in Cuba, applied a number of economic sanctions against Nicaragua. In addition, it sponsored the Contras, an anti-Sandinista guerrilla movement, and supported El Salvador's efforts to suppress the leftist guerrillas in that country. During the late 1980s, Costa Rican president Oscar Arias announced a peace plan to resolve the complex conflicts of the region; the various parties involved expressed varying degrees of support for the plan. Largely as a result of the Arias peace plan, free elections were held in Nicaragua in 1990. To the surprise of many political analysts, Daniel Ortega, the Sandinista leader, lost to opposition candidate Violeta Chamorro, who promised a return to capitalism and national reconciliation. When the Sandinistas turned over the reins of power, the Chamorro regime faced the daunting job of unifying the war-torn nation and implementing economic recovery.

The Marxist presence in Central America continued to wane: in Nicaragua, the Sandinistas remained out of power as they lost elections. In the early 1990s a truce brought an end to the fighting in El Salvador. Guerrilla warfare persisted in Guatemala, where another major issue—the political and cultural oppression of the Amerindian population of the Western Hemisphere (see Chapter 17)—became the focus.

The Rise of Representative Government in Latin America

Marxist struggles did not tell the whole story of contemporary Latin American politics. States like Costa Rica and petroleum-rich Venezuela had long-established representative governments. During the 1980s democratic movements increased markedly in the region. Argentina, Brazil, and other Latin American nations moved away from military dictatorships toward working, though fragile, parliamentary regimes. Peru, however, with a checkered history of both authoritarian and republican governments, endured economic problems and mounting revolutionary upheaval. As the revolutionary Shining Path organization stepped up its attacks in both urban and rural areas, Peru drifted from republicanism toward dictatorship.

Thus democratic governments faced many problems in Latin America. Although some of the new democratic regimes continued to thrive, only time would tell whether representative government could solve Latin America's enormous, chronic social and economic problems.

Shifting World Alliances

There has been much agitation, particularly in the American press; over the past several months. I will say to you that the experience I have had personally over the past 25 years with public reactions in the United States has made me less than surprised with the outbursts that pass for opinion. . . .

The United States . . . possesses nuclear weapons without which the fate of the world would be rapidly settled, and France . . . whatever the current inferiority of its means . . . is politically, geographically and morally, [and] militarily essential to the coalition. . . .

In my opinion, the differences of today stem quite simply from the intrinsic changes which have taken place, . . . in the absolute and relative situation of America and France. . . . The situation in France has profoundly changed. Her new institutions have put her in a position to will and to act. Her internal development has brought her prosperity and has caused her to acquire the means of power. . . .

From the political point of view, it is true that the Soviet Bloc retains a totalitarian and threatening ideology, and that even recently . . . the scandal of the Berlin Wall, and the installation of nuclear weapons in Cuba, have shown that, by this fact, peace remains precarious. Meantime, the human evolution in Russia and the satellites, the important economic and social difficulties in the life of these countries, and especially the beginnings of an opposition which is becoming manifest between, on the one hand, a European empire possessing immense Asiatic territories, and which have made it the greatest colonial power of our time, and, on the other, the Empire of China, its neighbor along a distance of 10,000 kilometers, with a population of 700 million, an empire which is indestructible, ambitious, and denuded of everything—all this can, in effect, introduce some new conjunctures in the concerns of the Kremlin and induce it to bring a note of sincerity to the refrain it devotes to peaceful coexistence.

France, in fact, has believed for a long time that there can come a day when a real détente and even a sincere entente would permit a complete change in the relations between East and West in Europe, and she expects when this day comes . . . to make some constructive proposals with regard to peace, equilibrium, and the destiny of Europe. *

*Charles de Gaulle Press Conference, July 29, 1963, *Discours et messages*, vol. 4, *Pour l'effort, Août 1962–Decembre 1965* (Paris: Plon, 1970), pp. 119–123, reprinted in Charles G. Cogan, *Charles de Gaulle: A Brief Biography with Documents* (New York: St. Martin's, 1996), pp. 205–207.

Thus French President Charles de Gaulle announced France's determination to steer an independent course in the Cold War conflicts between the United States and the Soviet Union. With his profound understanding of political and historical realities, de Gaulle correctly predicted the forthcoming split between the Soviet Union and The People's Republic of China and future changes in Europe. Under de Gaulle, France developed its own nuclear armament program, took independent stances on Asian and African issues, and in 1965 withdrew from NATO, the U.S.-sponsored Western military alliance. His actions illustrated the weakening of the Cold War power blocs in Europe during the 1960s and 1970s. De Gaulle represented a trend in newly prosperous western Europe, which was anxious to be independent from post–World War II tutelage to the United States.

The United States and the Soviet Union, which dominated the globe after World War II, were the most powerful nations in history. They differed strikingly in most respects. Politically, the United States was a nation where citizens enjoyed great freedoms, while the Soviet Union was one of the most authoritarian nations. Militarily, the two seemed to have achieved a rough parity by the 1980s, and both were far stronger than any potential challenger. Despite their might, these two superpowers, like other nations of the Western world, also experienced economic, social, and political problems. Their power was further weakened in the last quarter of the twentieth century by the trend toward independence from superpower domination that spread from western Europe to eastern Europe and the rest of the world. Powerful Asian and European economic blocs also challenged the United States and the Soviet Union.

The United States since 1960

Politically, the people of the United States alternated between support for liberal Democrats and support for conservative Republicans. During the Kennedy-Johnson administrations in the 1960s Americans supported the enactment of liberal legislation, but during Ronald Reagan's two terms in office (1980–1988), many of these trends were reversed.

The 1960s were years of social change in the United States. African Americans spearheaded many of these demands for change. Their leader, Reverend Martin Luther King Jr., advocated tactics of nonviolence, inspired by the teachings of Gandhi, to achieve civil rights. African American advances in civil rights encouraged women, Hispanic Americans, Native Americans, poor Americans, homosexuals, the physically handicapped, and other groups faced with discrimination to make similar demands. The Supreme Court under Chief Justice Earl Warren actively furthered the expansion of civil rights and civil liberties, overturning generations of entrenched discriminatory practice.

LIVES AND TIMES ACROSS CULTURES

Counterculture in the 1960s and 1970s

During the 1960s and 1970s, many young people in the United States and other Western nations dropped out of so-called mainstream society to experiment with a wide range of countercultural lifestyles. Advocates of alternative lifestyles urged students to "turn on, tune in, and drop out." "Hippie" dress styles of jeans with bell-bottoms, dyed T-shirts, beads, and long hair for both men and women became popular. Many experimented with marijuana and hallucinogenic drugs.

Rock-and-roll bands like the Beatles and the Rolling Stones from England attracted millions of fans around the world. The Grateful Dead gave free concerts in San Francisco, and the city became a mecca for those wanting to live the hippie lifestyle. So-called Deadheads followed the band around on tour in a motley array of cars and vans painted in psychedelic colors. The 1970s were heady times of "sex, drugs, and rock and roll."

At the same time, many students became active in political and social movements. Students in both France and the United States propelled the antiwar movements against the wars in Algeria and Vietnam. University campuses became centers of rebellion against the war in Vietnam as students chanting, "LBJ, LBJ [Lyndon Baines Johnson, the U.S. president], how many kids did you kill today?" joined protests across the country. Young people also joined, and often led, civil rights and feminist movements to demand equal rights for all people, regardless of their race, age, creed, or gender.

The Civil Rights Revolution in the United States. In 1965 Martin Luther King Jr. and Coretta King lead a march protesting racial segregation and other forms of discrimination, both in the South and throughout the nation. Although most African Americans followed King and his peaceful approach based on the principles of the African American churches and on M. K. Gandhi's methods, some turned to violence and to the more radical approaches of Malcolm X and Stokely Carmichael.

© Flip Schulke/Corbis

The late 1960s and the 1970s were a discouraging and bewildering time for many Americans. There were bitter antiwar protests against U.S. military involvement in Vietnam, and national self-esteem was further undermined by revelations of criminal abuses of power by President Richard Nixon (1913–1994) in the Watergate affair. The repressive tactics that Nixon used against social and antiwar activists and his "dirty tricks" against leaders of the Democratic party led to the conviction of many of his aides for illegal actions and to Nixon's resignation to avoid impeachment in 1974, a first in U.S. history. In addition, soaring prices for petroleum, accelerating inflation, high unemployment, and economic competition from Japanese and other Asian manufacturers also contributed to mounting economic woes in the 1970s.

During the 1960s and 1970s, many young people also experimented with "far-out" dress and hair styles, rock and roll music, sex, and drugs. Others "dropped out" to live the so-called hippie lifestyle in communes. They not only opposed U.S. involvement in the war in Vietnam, but denounced the commercialization of American culture, calling for a return to nature and the return to simpler ways of living.

Although some changes, particularly more relaxed dress styles and new music, entered the mainstream, for the most part the upheavals of the 1970s were temporary. Following the election of President Ronald Reagan (1911–) in 1980, the United States seemed to embark on a new direction and to recover much of its earlier self-confidence. Reagan, a former film actor, was a skilled public speaker who had an instinct for expressing many of the hopes and fears of the U.S. public. Although Reagan supported conservative policies, not all of them succeeded. His early promise to balance the budget was abandoned in favor of a huge armaments program that doubled the size of the national debt and left a legacy of indebtedness that worried other industrial nations and contributed to economic strains at home. Reagan also cut or abolished government spending for many social programs. Importantly, he appointed many conservatives to judgeships, including the Supreme Court. The Supreme Court's decisions on police practices and abortion in the late 1980s reflected that conservative trend. In international affairs, Reagan took a strongly anticommunist position. His successor, President George Bush (1924–), although conservative, was less ideologically committed and more pragmatic about economic development and international relations, particularly with the Soviet Union.

The Soviet Union from Khrushchev to Gorbachev

The Soviet Union exhibited more outward domestic stability during the quarter century after 1960 than at any time since the 1917 revolution. However, the stability was deceptive, as it masked many problems that became evident after 1985. From the 1960s to the 1980s, under Communist party control, the economic and political life of the nation remained as strictly controlled and planned as under Stalin. Waste, inefficiency, and mismanagement created enormous problems that lowered productivity. A new affluent, but often corrupt, bureaucracy was another drain on the Soviet economy. Yet, despite the unchanging facade of aging Stalinist rulers, political changes did occur in the Soviet Union. The most apparent change was in leadership style from the crude and heavy-handed Nikita Khrushchev in the 1960s to the more sophisticated, youthful, and urbane Mikhail Gorbachev (1931–) after 1985.

After Khrushchev was forced from office in 1964, Communist party General-Secretary Leonid Brezhnev (1906–1982) dominated the state for almost two decades. Politically, Brezhnev supported career men in the party and in the state bureaucracy. He persecuted dissenters and sent them to labor camps, internal exile, or mental institutions.

Soviet heavy industry continued to grow, but living standards only slowly improved. At enormous economic cost, an expensive armaments program brought the Soviet Union to a position of equality with the United States. Agricultural production remained low, however, and the Soviet Union annually had to import grain, paying for it with hard currency earned through the export of raw materials such as petroleum, gold, and diamonds.

Assuming power in 1985, Mikhail Gorbachev initiated a more subtle and flexible style of Soviet leadership. Gorbachev instituted a program of *glasnost* (openness to the West) and allowed more freedoms for Soviet citizens. His charismatic personality and creative political style brought out cheering crowds during his well-publicized tours to Europe and the United States.

Domestically, Gorbachev advocated a new program of *perestroika* (economic restructuring) to revitalize the sagging Soviet economy by increasing industrial and agricultural production, improving living standards by more efficient methods, lessening corruption, and permitting incentives and some privatization. Hard-liners within the Communist party and many Soviet citizens accustomed to decades of planned economy remained skeptical of these reforms. When the reforms failed to produce the promised improvements in living standards, many people within the Soviet Union became openly critical of the regime, and some minority ethnic groups went so far as to advocate secession from the Soviet Union.

By 1990 mounting restlessness among the many ethnic and religious minorities, which collectively exceeded the population of the politically dominant Great Russians, posed a major threat to Gorbachev's political survival. Gorbachev attempted to balance the opening up of the political system to dissent with reforms aimed at eliminating corruption and inefficiency within the bureaucracy, but he failed, thereby helping to pave the way for the collapse of Communist regimes in eastern Europe and the break-up of the Soviet Union. (The demise of the Soviet Union will be described in the next chapter.)

European Political Trends

The revitalization of democratic political institutions has been one of the most impressive trends in the political life of western Europe since 1945. The claim of the European totalitarian leaders of the interwar years that democracy was doomed proved false. After World War II, free elections and civil liberties flourished in western Europe. Between 1949 and 1969, West Germany's conservative Christian Democratic party, led for many years by the aging anti-Nazi and anticommunist chancellor Konrad Adenauer (1876–1956), guided Germany's return to prosperity and international respectability. Free France's wartime leader, General Charles de Gaulle, in power between 1958 and 1969, brought that nation stability and a return to self-confidence. De Gaulle led France away from its postwar dependency on the United States and toward more independent, individualistic domestic and international policies. (See the introduction to this section for an example of de Gaulle's strongly independent, nationalist rhetoric.)

In the years immediately after World War II, the Labour party dominated British politics. Weakened militarily and economically by the war, Britain, as described in earlier sections of this chapter, reluctantly gave up its imperial holdings and began the long, arduous task of rebuilding its economy. After much debate it also moved toward closer political and economic ties with the rest of Europe by joining the European Economic Community (EEC). During the 1980s the Conservative party under Prime Minister Margaret Thatcher (1925–) dominated the political scene. She was the first female British prime minister and became the longest-serving one since the early nineteenth century.

In the 1980s a new political force, sometimes called the Greens, emerged to challenge the old policies of both the conservative and socialist parties in many European nations. The Greens demanded disarmament, legislation to protect the environment (forests, the ozone layer, and wildlife), and large-scale programs to improve the quality of life. The new party had many active and politically mobilized women in leadership roles and enjoyed growing popularity particularly among the young.

In contrast to the success of the centrist political parties, both Communists on the left and old-fashioned authoritarian regimes of the right were compelled to moderate their ideological programs. Communist parties remained popular in Italy and France, but because of the stigma of their ties to Moscow were unable to win power in national elections. As a result, leaders declared their parties nationalist organizations free of international communism. In Greece, the reign of a military junta, "the colonels," was replaced with a democratic regime. Authoritarian Spain and Portugal were transformed from fascist dictatorships into democracies after the deaths of the aged dictators, Franco and Antonio Salazar, in the 1970s. Spain, under a democratically oriented king, Juan Carlos, who faced down right-wing military rebels gun in hand, and who worked with a Socialist prime minister, provided a striking example of the flexibility, variety, and vitality of political life in Europe.

Until 1989 Soviet military power sustained Communist governments in Soviet satellites in eastern Europe. The Soviets had crushed violent outbreaks in East Germany in 1953 and in Hungary in 1956. In 1968 Brezhnev sent Russian troops into insurgent Czechoslovakia to overthrow a reformist government, but by 1981 Soviet domination over eastern Europe began to fade.

Economic Recovery and Prosperity

A high level of prosperity was the most striking feature of many industrialized nations after World War II. The integration of the economies of the western European nations under the aegis of the European Economic Community (EEC), or Common Market, and, to a lesser degree, of eastern Europe's COMECON was an important element of European economic resurgence.

Although the European Economic Community had originally aimed for full economic integration among its members by 1992, the collapse of the Soviet Union and the resulting economic problems delayed full union; however, the potential economic clout of a unified Europe was tremendous.

During the late 1970s and the early 1980s, Europe suffered from the same global economic decline that already affected the United States. Soaring petroleum prices hurt many European economies, except those of Great Britain and Norway, which derived petroleum from the North Sea. Unemployment rose to unprecedented levels in such wealthy and productive nations as West Germany. Heavy indebtedness to Western banks, meanwhile, pushed several Eastern bloc nations like Poland and Romania to the brink of economic collapse. The failure to provide full, productive employment in peacetime was an ongoing problem for both capitalist and socialist economies until the end of the twentieth century. Neither the conservative remedies of privatization applied by Prime Minister Margaret Thatcher in Great Britain nor the socialist policies of France's President François Mitterand (1916–1996) brought the hoped-for rapid recovery or full employment.

Both Europe and the United States faced formidable competition for world markets from the Pacific rim economic powerhouses of Japan, South Korea, Taiwan, Hong Kong, and Singapore. After World War II, Japan made a phenomenal economic recovery. Under U.S. military occupation, Japan was forced to adopt a democratic constitution patterned on U.S. and British models, and the emperor was forced to renounce his divine status. From the 1950s onward, the conservative Liberal Democratic party dominated Japanese politics and provided extraordinarily stable conditions and state support for economic growth.

Work Regulations in a Japanese Factory

Orientation starts at 8:30. Today, we learn the most important rules:

WORK REGULATIONS:

- Don't divulge secrets learned during work.
- Try hard to increase efficiency and productivity.
- Follow instructions concerning your duties.
- Go to bed early, get up early, and be cheerful.
- Be properly and neatly dressed.
- Try to get acquainted with your surroundings quickly.
- Pay attention to your safety and security, and follow instructions and regulations.
- Ask someone between you to start the work if you don't know it well.

I arrived yesterday, January 7, 1980, the first working day of Toyota's new year.... A big sign in the hall showing "The Number of Toyotas Produced up to the Present" lights up quite impressively. Its electronic panel displays a long row of figures: 29,894,140.... This is the total number of vehicles since Toyota shipped out its first real automobile in 1935.... Of course, this figure is only as of 11:15 A.M. As I watch, the last digit continually increases. Timing it, I realize that the number is changing every six seconds.... The 20 millionth came in July 1976.... Watching the figure increase with each pass-

ing second, I feel all choked up. I can see it: the conveyor belts moving along mercilessly; the workers moving frantically as they try to keep up. I can hear their sighs. One vehicle every six seconds. The conveyor belts never stop.... *

In this excerpt, a Japanese auto worker describes his orientation to work in a huge Toyota plant where workers are considerably more regimented than in Western factories and where rapid production and quality control are emphasized. A neon-lit sign counting auto production, similar to the one described here, was also displayed along a major freeway near Detroit, Michigan.

To protect the U.S. automobile industry from stiff Japanese competition, U.S. automobile manufacturers and the United Auto Workers union pressed the U.S. government to pass legislation requiring Japanese automakers to build automobile plants within the United States and to insist on Japan's self-restriction of exports. Toyota was forced to begin manufacturing in the United States in order to avoid being criticized for flooding the market in the United States and Europe; it was soon followed by a host of other automobile manufacturers from around the world.

*Satoshi Kamata, In the Passing Lane: An Insider's Account of Life in a Japanese Auto Factory, ed. and trans. Tatsuru Akimoto (New York: Pantheon, 1982), pp. 10–11, 195–197.

As part of its Cold War strategy, the United States sought to bolster Japanese economic strength in Asia as a counterweight to Communist power in China and Southeast Asia. To this end, the United States assumed most of the economic burden of Japanese defense by placing Japan under its defense umbrella and by retaining military bases on the islands. Free from burdensome military expenditures, Japan was able to devote almost all its technological and financial resources to economic development.

By the 1980s, the Japanese economy, which was geared toward export-oriented growth, had become the second largest in the world. High-quality Japanese goods flooded world markets, and Japanese technology in fields such as robotics and electronics quickly established itself as the most advanced in the world. This economic preeminence provided for unprecedented domestic prosperity for Japanese workers and the industrialized world's lowest rate of unemployment.

Under authoritarian and highly paternalistic governments, Taiwan, Hong Kong, South Korea, and Singapore also launched impressive programs of industrialization. As in Japan, the Confucian work ethic, respect for education, and a tightly knit family structure provided the basis for economic progress. Productivity in these "little dragons" soared. Economic prosperity provided high employment and rising standards of living as wage levels rose rapidly in the 1980s. On the negative side, the lack of government regulations and labor unions also often resulted in poor working conditions, long hours, and lack of protection for workers, particularly women.

The rising economies of western Europe and the Pacific rim nations deprived the United States of the advantage it had enjoyed in manufacturing goods and technology during the two decades following World War II. This loss of preeminence was a shock to Americans and, coupled with soaring military expenditures, resulted in persistent international indebtedness and trade deficits.

In light of the chronic excess of Japanese exports to imports and Japanese trade laws that protected their domestic markets (especially for agricultural goods), many industrialists and workers in the United States pushed for protectionist and stricter limitations on Japanese imports. This slowed, but did not end, Japan's continued economic growth. During the 1980s and early 1990s, domestic political scandals surrounding key politicians caused considerable uneasiness in Japan. During this era Japanese women emerged for the first time as a key political force demanding internal reforms. Nevertheless, until 1997 the Asian Pacific rim nations appeared likely to maintain their key positions in the global economy (see Chapter 17). They also began to explore the possibilities of forming an economic union similar to that in western Europe.

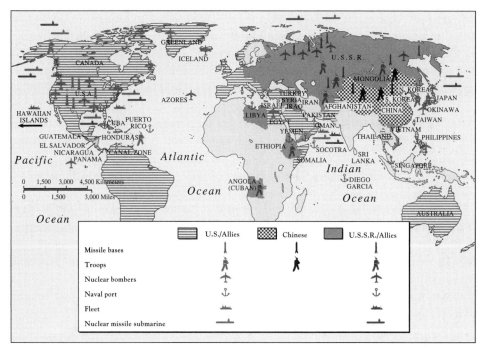

Map 16.6 The Global Cold War, 1950s–1980s. This map only hints at the massive, unprecedented outlay of global military power. Both the United States and the Soviet Union spread their forces and weaponry around the globe, challenging each other on the ground in Europe and East Asia, at sea in every ocean, everywhere in the air, including the poles, and even in outer space. China played a secondary "third-party" role. The enormous cost of this global confrontation put heavy strains on the United States and eventually broke down the Soviet economy, bringing the Cold War to an end by the early 1990s.

Superpower Confrontations and Détentes

Throughout the Cold War, the superpowers alternated between periods of high tension and periods of détente or rapprochement. Also called "peaceful coexistence" or "competitive coexistence," détente centered on the search by the two superpowers for ways of living together in a dangerous world. Détente flourished in the 1960s but ebbed during the Reagan years in the 1980s.

A dramatic easing of Cold War tensions occurred when the United States accepted the legitimacy of the People's Republic of China in the 1970s. Henry Kissinger, President Nixon's secretary of state and global strategist, believed friendly relations between the United States and China would foster a strong balance of power against the Soviet Union. The U.S. rapprochement with China was a pragmatic one for both U.S. President Richard Nixon and Chairman Mao Zedong. The United States had just ended an unsuccessful war in Vietnam, and the People's Republic was recovering from the Cultural Revolution. The Chinese were also motivated by their fear that improved relations between the United States and the Soviet Union would leave it dangerously isolated.

In 1971, as part of its rapprochement with Communist China, the United States accepted the expulsion of the Nationalist government on Taiwan from the United Nations and its replacement by the People's Republic. President Nixon flew to Peking in 1972 for talks with Chinese leaders. The two countries established full diplomatic relations in 1979. Contacts increased after Mao's death. The Chinese especially sought technological and economic assistance from the United States, and the latter in turn wanted to sell manufactured goods in the vast Chinese market. However, the brutal suppression of liberals in China—demonstrating students were ruthlessly gunned down in Beijing's Tiananmen Square in 1989—continued to strain relations between the two and highlighted the Communist party's determination to retain dictatorial powers.

In other Asian nations, détente also suffered setbacks. In 1979 the Soviet Union, in partial response to an Islamic revolution in neighboring Iran, sent troops into Afghanistan in order to bolster its client government, which was crumbling under the armed onslaught of Muslim rebels. (Both superpowers had vital strategic and economic interests in West Asia. Chapter 17 will discuss the key events in this important region, centering on the Arabian Peninsula, the Persian Gulf, and the Arab-Israeli conflict.)

As the United States discovered in Vietnam and France in Algeria, the Soviets soon found themselves bogged down in a protracted and losing guerrilla war in Afghanistan. By the late 1980s, the futility of a continued Soviet military presence in Afghanistan was apparent. Bowing to hostile international pressures and especially to mounting opposition at home, Gorbachev conceded defeat and withdrew the Soviet troops. This failure in Afghanistan was a blow to the already weakened Soviet Union and contributed to its collapse.

During the early 1980s, Cold War tensions increased. Following his election in 1980, President Reagan pursued a vigorous anti-Soviet policy and escalated the arms race by deploying new nuclear weapons to NATO nations in Europe. Reagan characterized the Soviet Union as an "evil empire" to be opposed whenever and wherever possible. The renewal of U.S. commitment to the Cold War in the 1980s was made easier by Soviet weaknesses.

The Arms Race and Disarmament

All of the superpower confrontations during the Cold War carried with them the possibility of nuclear annihilation due to the stockpiles of atomic weapons accumulated by both the United States and the Soviet Union. Popular demands for improved international relations were prompted by fears of nuclear holocaust held by many people around the world, particularly those in eastern and western European nations. The calls for arms control were reinforced by the cost of maintaining military parity, which became increasingly expensive, even prohibitively so.

After the 1962 Cuban Missile Crisis, a contradictory pattern characterized the arms race. On the one hand, with the long-term motive of reducing the terrible danger of atomic war, the superpowers negotiated a series of international agreements for limiting and controlling weapon systems. Under the Nuclear Test Ban Treaty of 1963, more than 100 nations agreed to stop testing nuclear weapons in the atmosphere, under water, or in space. The Nuclear Nonproliferation Treaty, signed by almost 100 nations, committed its signatories to refrain from developing nuclear weapons of their own. However, the number of nations possessing nuclear weapons continued to proliferate as many refused to be bound by the treaty. France, China, India, and Israel all refused to sign and developed their own nuclear weapons and arsenals. The Strategic Arms Limitation Talks (SALT) of 1972 limited the number of ICBMs (intercontinental ballistic missiles), ABMs (antiballistic missiles), and nuclear missile-firing submarines the two superpowers could deploy. Subsequent agreements between the superpowers banned large underground tests and deployment of missiles on the bottom of the sea or in Antarctica.

On the other hand, while the superpowers agreed to some arms limitations, they both continued to manufacture new generations of arms. The two superpowers enhanced some awesome weapons systems not forbidden by treaty. These included multiple, independently targeted reentry vehicles (MIRVs), which were single rockets bearing a number of nuclear bombs programmed to hit different targets; cruise missiles, which could slip in under enemy radar defenses; and neutron bombs, designed to kill humans with minimum damage to property. By the 1980s the superpowers had the nuclear capabilities to destroy the earth at least twelve times over—the "balance of power" had become the "balance of terror."

Space also became an area of superpower competition. In 1961 Soviet cosmonaut Yuri Gagarin became the first human to orbit the earth, followed into space one year later by U.S. astronaut John Glenn. In 1969 Neil Armstrong was the first person to walk on the moon. By the 1970s the Soviet Union was constructing space platforms, and the United States was sending manned shuttles back and forth between earth and space. Both nations sent space probes deep into the solar system to bring back information about other planets. Space research became part of the arms race, as space platforms and "spy" satellites gathered military information that could be used in future wars.

In spite of support for disarmament, the stockpiles of arms grew in the early 1980s. Although many scientists argued the program was unworkable, President Reagan supported a strategic defense initiative (SDI), the building of an elaborate, space-based system of defenses against nuclear attack, popularly known as "Star Wars." Gorbachev and others objected, partly because SDI would be enormously expensive to build and partly because it was viewed as being fundamentally offensive, not defensive. Gorbachev said of the program, "What we need is Star Peace and not Star Wars."

As the debate continued, Reagan and Gorbachev negotiated the Intermediate Nuclear Forces (INF) treaty (ratified in 1988) that provided for the dismantling of some nuclear systems deployed in Europe. This was the first treaty that actually provided for decreasing existing weaponry.

Summary and Comparisons

The collapse of the European overseas empires was a major trend in the decades following World War II. This great liberation movement freed a third of the world's population from foreign rule and marked a major change in the historical development and relationships between the industrialized West and the largely agricultural, poor nations of Africa, Asia, and Latin America.

Many former colonies in West and East Africa achieved independence with relatively little violence, but the Algerians had to fight a long war of liberation. In southern Africa the struggle for independence was even longer.

In the West there was conflict between the two superpowers, the United States and the Soviet Union, and their respective allies in Europe. During the 1950s to 1980s, relations between the superpowers were largely governed by the rise and fall of détente within the larger framework of the Cold War.

Both the Soviet Union and the United States viewed Asia and Latin America through the lens of the Cold War conflict. In largely agricultural Asia, Africa, and Latin America, the masses generally found Marxists more sympathetic to their problems. Mao Zedong, with peasant support, came to power in China, as did Ho Chi Minh in North Vietnam. In Korea, after a bitter war, the superpowers settled for a stalemate and the division of the country. Later, fearing the spread of communism in Southeast Asia, the United States intervened in South Vietnam. Faced with mounting human and economic costs and strong domestic opposition to the war, the United States ultimately withdrew from Vietnam, just as France reluctantly withdrew from Algeria.

As in China and other parts of Asia, social discontent in Latin America also fueled peasant uprisings and revolutions. Personalist dictatorships and revolutionary regimes were two responses to poverty and the wide gap between rich and poor. The most dangerous Cold War incident occurred in Cuba, where Fidel Castro created a peasant-backed Communist state. A U.S. attempt to overthrow him backfired, and when the Soviet Union intervened to protect him and installed nuclear missiles, the United States took measures that threatened war. Although the Cuban Missile Crisis was defused, the potential for atomic holocaust continued to threaten mass destruction on a scale never thought possible in previous conflicts.

Domestically, social reforms in the 1960s made the United States more truly democratic, while cultural changes swept the nation during the 1960s and 1970s. The Soviet Union appeared to achieve political stability, slow economic growth, and military parity with the United States, but the crumbling of the Soviet Empire by 1989 indicated that

C H R O N O L O G Y

1945	Chinese civil war
	Indian independence: Jawaharlal Nehru; Pakistan
	Creation of Israel: Arab-Israeli conflict
	Chinese Communist victory: Mao Zedong
1950	Korean War
	Algerian Revolution
	France withdraws from Indochina
	Bandung: Third World neutralism
	Suez crisis
	Cuban revolution: Fidel Castro
1960	African independence: Jomo Kenyatta, Kwame Nkrumah
	Cuban Missile Crisis
	U.S. civil rights movement: Martin Luther King Jr.
	Cultural Revolution in China
	War in Vietnam
	Man on the moon
1970	OPEC becomes a force in global economics and politics
	Allende's Marxist government overthrown in Chile
	All Vietnam under communism
	Women's liberation movement
	Militant religious movements
	Sandinistas triumph in Nicaragua
1980	Pacific Rim economic boom
	Reagan Cold War pressures on Marxists in Nicaragua and El Salvador
	Mikhail Gorbachev promotes glasnost and perestroika
	Movement toward democratic governments in latin America
1991	

many of its gains had been illusionary. Meanwhile, Europe recovered economically, and democracy flourished in western Europe. In eastern Europe, true autonomy came only in the late 1980s, when Gorbachev ended Soviet domination over the region.

Under U.S. tutelage, Japan became a stable democracy and pro-Western force in the Cold War and enjoyed an unprecedented economic recovery following World War II. The United States gradually lost its preeminent economic position as Japan and the "little dragons" of Taiwan, Hong Kong, Korea, and Singapore became economic powerhouses competing successfully against European- and U.S.-manufactured goods and technology. As a result, the global economic balance shifted in the 1980s toward Asia, just as earlier ages of exploration in the fourteenth and fifteenth centuries had shifted the economic bases of power away from the Mediterranean world to Europe, and the growing power of the United States in the nineteenth and early twentieth centuries had shifted power from Europe to the Western Hemisphere. As in Europe, economic gains in the Communist nations were mostly illusory compared with the rapid strides made in capitalist and democratic countries.

During the Cold War, both superpowers developed arsenals capable of destroying the world. Technological developments meant that nations could not only destroy one another, but also threaten the existence of life on the entire planet. However, just as nations had moved toward some arms control after World War I, during the Cold War the superpowers and others took halting steps toward arms control under treaties designed to limit the arms race.

Selected Sources

Items indicated with an asterisk (*) are available in paperback.

*Anderson, Thomas P. *Politics in Central America.* 1982. Describes developments in El Salvador, Guatemala, Honduras, and Nicaragua.

Antony, A. *Gandhi-Nehru Dynasty.* 1990. On India's most famous family.

Battle of Algiers. An incredible black-and-white film on the Algerian struggle against the French.

Bhutto, Benazir. *Daughter of Destiny: An Autobiography.* 1989. The first female prime minister of a Muslim country writes about herself.

*Chafe, William H. *The Unfinished Journey: America since World War II.* 3d ed. 1995. Expanded assessment of U.S. history during the Cold War and post–Cold War eras.

*Chinodya, Shimmer. *Harvest of Thorns.* 1991. A dramatic and often humorous story of a young African torn between modern and traditional values.

*Cogan, Charles G. *Charles de Gaulle: A Brief Biography with Documents.* 1996. Readable short biography of a key French leader in the twentieth century.

Collins, Larry, and Dominique La Pierre. *Freedom at Midnight.* 1975. Fascinating account of Indian independence in 1947.

*Davidson, Basil. *Modern Africa: A Social and Political History.* 3d ed. 1994. Balanced narrative of independence struggles in Africa.

"The End of Empires." Multicultural Studies. This 48-minute video, hosted by David Frost, includes interviews with soldiers and civilians who fought for independence in African and Asian nations.

Fejto, F. A. *A History of People's Democracies: Eastern Europe since Stalin.* Trans. D. Weissart. 1973. A survey of communism in eastern Europe prior to the collapse of the Soviet system and the emergence of new states.

Fursenko, Aleksandr, and Timothy Naftali. *One Hell of a Gamble: Khrushchev, Castro, and Kennedy, 1958–1964.* 1997. Detailed account of the most dangerous Cold War confrontation, based on latest materials released since the collapse of the Soviet Union.

*García Márquez, Gabriel. *One Hundred Years of Solitude.* 1971. Complex novel on life in Latin America.

Gorbachev, Mikhail. *Perestroika: New Thinking for Our Country and the World.* 1987. The Soviet leader explains his reform plans.

"Half Lives: History of the Nuclear Age." Films for the Humanities and Sciences. A 56-minute video exploring the nuclear age with balanced discussion of key issues surrounding the arms race and nuclear energy.

*Herring, George. *America's Longest War: The U.S. and Vietnam, 1950–75.* 1979. Well-written, concise, and balanced.

*Horne, Alistair. *A Savage War of Peace: Algeria 1954–1962.* 1977. Moving rendition of Algerian struggle for independence.

"India After Independence." Films for the Humanities and Sciences. A short 21-minute video on India from 1947 to the assassination of Indira Gandhi.

"Jomo Kenyatta." A 12-minute film examining Kenyatta's leadership in Kenya. [Films for the Humanities.]

"Kim Phuo." 1984. A 25-minute film account of a young girl's scarring by napalm during the Vietnam war and her struggle to survive.

"The Legacy of Mao Zedong." Insight Media. 1991. A 30-minute video that traces the impact of Mao and communism in China.

Loth, Wilfried. *The Division of the World 1941–1955.* 1988. Scholarly critique of causes for the Cold War.

"Making Sense of the Sixties." PBS. 1991. A six-part video series on the turbulent sixties with interviews with leading figures from the era.

"Martin Luther King, Jr." A 27-minute color video documentary on the Nobel Peace Prize winner and leader of U.S. civil rights movement. [Films for the Humanities.]

*McWilliams, Wayne C., and Harry Piotrowski. *The World Since 1945: Politics, War, and Revolution in the Nuclear Age.* 1987. Comprehensive account of the Cold War and the Third World.

*O'Neill, William. *Coming Apart.* 1971. Spirited account of the United States during the turbulent 1960s.

*Palmer, David Scott, ed. *Shining Path of Peru.* 2d ed. 1994. An updated guide to the organization and program of the revolutionary movement in Peru.

*Patterson, Walter C. *Nuclear Power.* 1976. A lively account of the interconnection of the arms race and the Cold War.

*Powaski, Ronald E. *The Cold War: The United States and the Soviet Union, 1917–1991.* 1998. Cogent narrative of complex interrelationships and conflicts of the two superpowers.

Salisbury, Harrison. *New Emperors: China in the Era of Mao and Deng.* 1992. A masterful analysis of communist China during the last four decades.

**Student Atlas of World Politics.* 1994. Contains accurate current maps and good coverage of independence movements as well as economic and environmental issues.

Szymusiak, Molyda. *The Stones Cry Out: A Cambodian Childhood, 1975–1980.* 1988. Evocative story of terror during Pol Pot regime.

Additional resources, exercises, and Internet links related to this chapter are available at the Book Companion Web site: http://history.wadsworth.com/upshurcompact4/

COMPARATIVE ESSAY 12
Regionalism and Internationalism

Are we ready to abandon the Monroe Doctrine and leave it to other nations to say how American questions shall be settled and what steps we shall be permitted to take in order to guard our own safety? . . . Are we ready to have other nations tell us by a majority vote what attitude we must assume to immigration or in regard to our tariffs?
Senator Henry Cabot Lodge, speech to Senate in pamphlet, Emory University Library, in Elizabeth Stevenson, *Babbitts and Bohemians: The American 1920s* (New York: MacMillan, 1967), p. 64.

The greatest danger for us of the Western nations . . . is that in our affluence we shall become soft and selfish and self-centered . . . and so complacent that we fail to see the dangers of the wider world in time. . . .

    The extent of the dangers is a measure of the need for new effort and for a new sense of urgency, and for new methods. Increasingly we must seek solutions not by old national means but by new international action. The dangers should surely intensify a determination to win freedom from racial discrimination and domination, to settle disputes before violence takes over, to make a new assault on the poverty of more than half the world and . . . to support and strengthen the authority and capacity of the United Nations. Few people will dispute that the dangers exist. The question is whether we understand and care enough to act while there is still time, and time is terribly short.
Hugh Foot, *A Start in Freedom* (London: Hodder and Stoughton, 1964), pp. 231, 246.

These conflicting viewpoints highlight a basic paradox of the post–World War II world. While tribalism, nationalism, and regional loyalties are still strongly felt throughout the world, advanced communications have tied us together in the "Global Village" of interdependence. Senator Lodge's comments are representative of the strong isolationist sentiment held by many in the United States after World War I; Lodge's opposition to U.S. involvement in foreign affairs contributed to the refusal of the U.S. Senate to ratify the Versailles Treaty and of U.S. entry into the League of Nations, the dream project of President Woodrow Wilson. Strong isolationist sentiments are echoed today in the continued opposition among some Americans to the United Nations, except when that organization follows U.S. directives. In contrast, British diplomat Hugh Foot expressed the internationalist viewpoint that stresses the need for cooperation among nations in the latter half of the twentieth century.

Paradoxically, by the year 2000, people in many areas of the world were again espousing narrow ethnic and religious ties. For example, from 1975 to the early 1990s, Maronite Christians and Druze, Sunni, and Shi'i Muslims in Lebanon fought to maintain their separate identities and political power. Similarly, confrontations between ethnic groups in the former Soviet Republic of Azerbaijan threatened to destroy the national unity of that diverse nation. India, too, has been plagued by the sometimes violent separatism of the Sikh minority, while Sri Lanka and Northern Ireland have been torn by ethnic and religious divisions.

On the other hand, stunning advances in transportation and communication technology have tied the world together as never before. Air travel on jet planes has made "globe trotting" commonplace, while satellite transmission, international telephone and telegraph systems, and fax machines enable people around the world to communicate with one another almost instantaneously. These developments have fostered cultural cosmopolitanism and a global economy. Lest the virulent nationalism that led to the world wars resurface, world leaders have turned to strengthening international organizations such as the United Nations and the World Bank to solve national disputes and to encourage international cooperation. Similarly, the Organization of American States (OAS) and the Arab League were created to foster regional cooperation. To promote international trade, most nations joined the General Agreement on Tariffs and Trade (GATT). However, by the 1990s, fear of global economic domination by international corporations and financial institutions had led to a widespread grassroots movement against GATT and similar economic organizations. Similarly, deep-seated national rivalries and emphasis on rights of sovereignty have hampered the efforts of all international organizations.

Since the 1950s, the record of the United Nations has been mixed. On the one hand, it could not prevent wars between Israel and the Arab states or between Iran and Iraq. It also failed to prevent U.S. intervention in Vietnam or the Soviet occupation of Afghanistan. On the other hand, UN peace-keeping forces have helped to prevent full-scale wars in Cyprus and Kashmir. They have also helped in the creation of independent nations; for example, Libya and Namibia. In addition, the UN has helped negotiate settlements to disputes in Latin America.

International organizations such as the Court of Justice at The Hague and the World Health Organization (WHO) have contributed to the lessening of national rivalries and have channeled creative energies toward the solution of national and human problems. The Court, for example, has settled troublesome disputes about fishing rights in coastal waters, and WHO eradicated smallpox, which had ravaged humanity for centuries. Economic organizations such as the World Bank, the Kuwait Fund for Arab Development, and the Asian Development Bank provide finances for development projects at the international and regional levels. On the negative side, the World Bank has funded grandiose development projects in poor Third World nations to the detriment of smaller, local projects such as clean water and sewage systems.

The European Economic Community (EEC) has been the most effective and success-ful movement for regional integration in the post World War II era. Beginning with six nations, the membership of the EEC, later just the European Community (EC), now includes all of western Europe; further, the EC has developed affiliate relationships with eastern Mediterranean nations such as Israel, Turkey, and Cyprus. Following the end of the Cold War and the collapse of the Soviet Union, eastern European nations also sought membership in the EC, which has brought unprecedented prosperity to the citizens of its member nations. The EC has also helped to blunt the rivalries that have for so long divided Europe. The success of the EC has inspired other regions to develop similar cooperative ventures, such as the Association of Southeast Asian Nations (ASEAN).

Private multinational corporations have also become major forces in the global econ-omy. Huge multinational corporations such as Exxon, General Motors, Mitsubishi, and Nestlé operate throughout the world. Some, like General Motors, have annual incomes larger than the combined gross national products (GNP) of many poor Southern Hemi-sphere nations. Their size and wealth place these multinational companies beyond the control of individual governments and international organizations such as the United Nations. For example, nations acting alone have been unable to implement regulations governing the shipment of petroleum by oil tankers. These failures have resulted in major oil spills that caused vast ecological damage from the shores of Alaska to the beaches of France.

Worldwide problems such as pollution, overpopulation, and environmental crises demand global cooperation and financial expenditures far beyond the economic capacity of many poor nations. Whether societies will be able to overcome their national and cultural divisions and cooperate to solve these problems will determine the future of the world.

17

Life in a Multipolar World: The Post–Cold War Era

•

• The Collapse of the Soviet Empire and Changes in Europe •

• Ongoing Conflict and Changes in West Asia and Africa •

• Major Challenges Confronting the Post–Cold War World •

• Summary and Comparisons •

The world in which we live today is radically different from what it was at the beginning or even in the middle of this century. And it continues to change as do all its components.

The advent of nuclear weapons was just another tragic reminder of the fundamental nature of that change. A material symbol and expression of absolute military power, nuclear weapons at the same time revealed the absolute limits of that power.

The problem of mankind's survival and self-preservation came to the fore.

The Soviet Union is prepared to institute a lengthy moratorium of up to 100 years on debt servicing by the least developed countries, and in quite a few cases to write off the debt altogether.

Let us also think about setting up within the framework of the United Nations a center for emergency environmental assistance.

Now let me turn to the main issue—disarmament, without which none of the problems of the coming century can be solved.

The Soviet Union and the United States have built the largest nuclear and missile arsenals. But it is those two countries that, having become specifically aware of their responsibility, were the first to conclude a treaty on the reduction and physical elimination of a portion of their armaments. . . .

I would like to believe that our hopes will be matched by our joint effort to put an end to an era of wars, confrontation and regional conflicts, to aggressions against nature, to the terror of hunger and poverty as well as to political terrorism. This is our common goal and we can only reach it together.*

*Mikhail Gorbachev, quoted in The Manchester Guardian Weekly (December 18, 1988).

In this speech before the United Nations on December 7, 1988, Mikhail Gorbachev, president of the Soviet Union, highlighted the major issues facing the world in the last quarter of the twentieth century; as his remarks make clear, the world today is indeed a global village. While Gorbachev correctly emphasized the need for international cooperation for solving the daunting problems of the twentieth century and for ensuring human progress into the twenty-first, he did not realize that less than two years after delivering this speech he would be forced out of office and the Soviet Union would cease to exist. This chapter will describe the spectacular collapse of the Soviet system and the emergence of numerous new nations in eastern Europe and the old Soviet Union.

It will also describe the ethnic strife jeopardizing both international peace and economic and social development in Europe and much of Asia and Africa. Other "hot spots" will be discussed with particular reference to the ongoing Israeli-Palestinian-Arab conflict and the successful struggle for equality and democracy in South Africa.

Finally, the chapter will survey urgent problems confronting peoples around the world at the turn of the millennium: struggles for democracy; gender and social inequality; technological, economic, and environmental challenges; and cultural tensions.

The Collapse of the Soviet Empire and Changes in Europe

When the idea first came up that I should let my name stand for president of Czechoslovakia, it seemed like an absurd joke. All my life I had opposed the powers that be. I had never held political office. . . .

Slightly less than a month after this shocking proposal was put to me, I was unanimously elected president of my country. It happened quickly and unexpectedly, almost overnight one could say, giving me little time to prepare myself and my thoughts for the job.

It might be said that I was swept into office by the revolution. . . .

The return of freedom to a society that was morally unhinged has produced something we therefore might have expected, but which has turned out to be far more serious than anyone could have predicted: an enormous and dazzling explosion of every imaginable human vice. . . . The authoritarian regime imposed a certain order—if that is the right expression for it—on these vices. . . . This order has now been shattered, but a new order that would limit rather than exploit these vices, an order based on freely accepted responsibility to and for the whole of society, has not yet been built—nor could it have been, for such an order takes years to develop and cultivate.*

*Václav Havel, Summer Meditations (New York: Knopf, 1992), pp. xv, 1–2.

Noted playwright, essayist, and political dissident under the Czechoslovakian Communist regime, Václav Havel (1936–) wrote, in his memoirs, about implications of the fall of the Communist regimes in eastern Europe and his unexpected rise to power in post–Communist Czechoslovakia. In 1989, in an almost bloodless, or "velvet" revolution, the people of Czechoslovakia overthrew the repressive Soviet-dominated regime that had held power almost continuously for forty years. Havel was twice elected president of the new Czechoslovakian federated state but failed to hold the two ethnic groups, the Czechs and Slovaks, together. Two nations emerged as a result, the Czech Republic and Slovakia. In his recollection, cited at the start of this section, Havel describes the euphoria that swept over the peoples of Europe and elsewhere as authoritarian Communist regimes crumbled under the weight of their own internal corruption when faced with popular opposition. As Havel also explains, however, that euphoria quickly disappeared as the difficult tasks of forging democratic and free market institutions began. Following the collapse of the Communist regimes, old ethnic and religious rivalries, long-dormant racism, economic dislocations, and social disruption emerged to threaten the survival of democratic governments and economic development.

This section will describe the collapse of the Communist regimes in eastern Europe and the end of the Soviet Empire and the resulting political, social, and economic dislocations.

The Wall Comes Down. Here enthusiastic crowds of East and West Germans eagerly demolish the Berlin Wall, the hated symbol of the bitter Cold War division of the United States and the Western bloc from the Soviet Union and the Eastern bloc.

Democracy and Capitalism in Post–Cold War Europe

As it became evident that the Soviet Union would no longer use military force to control their internal affairs, the eastern European nations moved away from Soviet domination and, in generally bloodless revolutions, overthrew the Communist regimes that had governed them for over forty years. The process began in the early 1980s with the formation of the Solidarity opposition party in Poland. In 1989 Solidarity candidates won stunning election victories and entered into a coalition government.

By the end of 1989, the old, established Communist leaders had been ousted throughout eastern Europe. In 1989 Václav Havel became the president of Czechoslovakia, and in 1990 Lech Walesa (1943–) of the Solidarity party became the president of Poland. By 1991 the Baltic republics, Estonia, Latvia, and Lithuania, had all obtained complete independence from the Soviet Union. In Bulgaria and Romania, coalition or reformist Communist parties emerged. Even Albania, the poorest nation in Europe with the most hard-line Communist regime, instituted a coalition government in 1991.

In an even more stunning development, East and West Germany were reunified. In November 1989, when a new, reformist East German Communist government responded to popular demonstrations by opening the Berlin Wall—the symbol of the Cold War for almost thirty years—millions of East Germans rushed to visit West Berlin and West Germany. The spring 1990 elections in East Germany resulted in a victory for

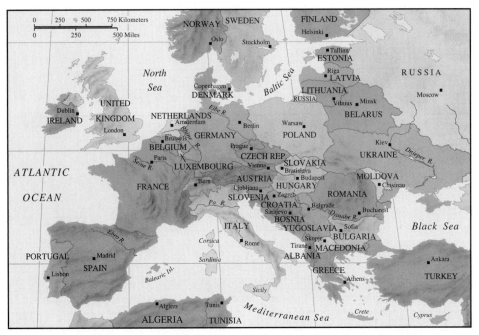

Maps 17.1 Post–Cold War Europe, 2000. With the collapse of the Soviet Empire, former Soviet satellite states in eastern Europe became independent.

a non-Communist coalition, which promptly agreed to the reunification of Germany under the leadership of Helmut Kohl (1930–), leader of the West German Christian Democratic party.

As the new governments across Europe moved to privatize their economies, the era of Soviet domination had clearly ended. In 1991 Soviet forces began to withdraw from eastern Europe, and the Soviet-led military alliance, the Warsaw Pact, was formally dissolved.

The Soviet Empire Crumbles

Mikhail Gorbachev, general secretary of the Soviet Communist party, sought to reform the corrupt and inefficient Soviet economy and government while preserving the socialist system. Having little experience in the Soviet Republics outside the Russian Republic, Gorbachev underestimated the strength of the ethnic loyalties within the multiethnic Soviet Empire. These troubles, bubbling just below the surface, became evident in 1986 when the Kazakhs, under the banner of "Kazakhstan for the Kazakhs," rioted in Alma-Ata, the Kazakh capital. The Armenians followed in 1988 with the slogan "One People, One Republic."

As previously noted (Chapter 16), Gorbachev also faced opposition from hard-liners within the Communist party who both opposed the liberalizing reforms he had initiated and feared that the proposed changes would threaten their privileged positions. Others, particularly his rival Boris Yeltsin (1931–), the elected president of the Russian Republic, demanded more extensive reforms with the creation of a free market economy. After his

Maps 17.2 Former Soviet Union. The Soviet Union ended when former Soviet republics declared their independence. By 2000 most of these weak states, with the exception of the Baltic nations, had joined Russia in the Commonwealth of Independent Nations.

election as chairman of the Russian Republic's Supreme Soviet, Yeltsin publicly challenged Gorbachev to expand both political and economic reforms.

Faced by these demands, Gorbachev reluctantly announced his support for a free market economy in the summer of 1991. Gorbachev's apparent intentions to undercut the authority and power of the Communist party caused the hard-liners within the party to move against him. In August 1991, while he was vacationing in the Crimea, Gorbachev was placed under house arrest. A group of hard-liners, including the KGB (secret police) chief and the defense minister, announced from Moscow that they had taken over the reins of power.

In Moscow, Yeltsin responded by rallying mass demonstrations against the attempted coup. When the military refused to fire on the demonstrators, the coup collapsed and its leaders were imprisoned. A politically weakened Gorbachev returned to power and announced his resignation from the Communist party. In the ensuing backlash against the old Communist party, more and more republics announced their intention to secede from the Soviet Union. The central government, dominated by Russia, was powerless to prevent the breakup. By the end of 1991, Russia, Ukraine, and Belorussia (present-day Belarus) had disbanded the union and formed the Commonwealth of Independent Nations. A number of other republics subsequently joined the loosely organized, decentralized Commonwealth. With no country left to lead, Gorbachev resigned as president in December 1991 and returned to private life. Thus, after more than seventy years, the Soviet Union and its empire had collapsed.

Yeltsin, who had much earlier resigned from the Communist party, continued to head the Russian Federation and emerged as the commonwealth leader until ill health forced him to resign. His hand-chosen successor, Vladimir Putin (1952–), was elected president in 2000. To counter growing opposition and the instability caused by privatization policies, both Yeltsin and Putin increased their executive powers and limited political rights. During his first term in office, Putin worked to restore the economy and public order domestically and to cooperate with the United States in combating international terrorism after the September 11, 2001, terrorist attacks on the United States. He was re-elected to a second term in 2004 with 71 percent of the vote compared with 15 percent for his nearest rival, a Communist party candidate. Although the elections were flawed, Putin's wide margin of victory reflected general satisfaction with his leadership.

New Economic Alliances and Problems

Throughout the 1990s, privatization in both industrial and agricultural sectors and rising prices caused severe economic dislocation throughout the nations of the old Soviet Empire. Although the Soviet economic system had been inefficient, provided few incentives, and produced goods without consideration of consumer demands and cost-effectiveness, it had provided free or low-cost housing, guaranteed employment, transportation, and social services to many citizens. In China, where a similar state-controlled economy had operated, the system of guaranteed jobs was called the iron rice bowl. In addition, under Soviet domination, Communist countries had supplied basic needs for one another through extensive trade. For example, within the Soviet Union, Russia had supplied the Ukraine with petroleum at low prices in exchange for grain.

When these programs abruptly stopped, people on fixed incomes, particularly the elderly (many of them women), found they no longer had enough money to buy food let alone other basic necessities. Inflation skyrocketed, reaching at its peak over 1,000 percent in Poland in the early 1990s. When they could no longer make ends meet, many retired people were forced to sell their guaranteed apartments and to move into cramped quarters with their families or to become homeless. In 1993, Russian women, carrying pictures of Stalin, demonstrated against Yeltsin, demanding a return to family values and government support for the elderly.

As state subsidies and controls disappeared, social problems, crime, declining production, and indebtedness increased. Severe economic hardships led to a broad range of social problems. As health care declined, infectious diseases such as tuberculosis and diphtheria reappeared in Russia and former Soviet republics, alcoholism soared, and life expectancy declined. By 1999 the death rate in Russia exceeded the birth rate, and population continued to decline. Some Russians, desperate to find scapegoats for their economic and social problems, rallied behind openly racist and anti-Semitic extremists who advocated a return to empire.

Meanwhile, other nations formerly under Soviet domination also experienced economic and social dislocations. Western Germany's booming economy was severely strained by its integration with the much poorer and less dynamic former East Germany, wiping out the nation's huge currency reserve. Although citizens of former East Germany generally supported the political and social reforms, many missed such socialist welfare benefits as cheap housing. The integrated economy could not provide jobs for all the new citizens, and unemployment soared, especially in the former East Germany, where Communist-era factories were obsolete. Many in the east also complained that although the stores now carried a wide array of goods, the prices of both consumer goods and basic necessities were much higher. Some, particularly the youth, found outlets for their dissatisfaction by joining neo-Nazi groups or by scapegoating and attacking nonethnic Germans.

Encouraged by the West and international financial institutions such as the International Monetary Fund and the World Bank, the new governments in eastern Europe dismantled their socialist economies, encouraged private enterprise, and established closer ties with the more affluent, capitalist nations of western Europe. At the same time, however, as in Germany, the transition from a Communist to a private enterprise economy was not easy. Former eastern bloc nations lacked efficient communication systems, banks, trained personnel, and computer technology. Rising prices and unemployment caused severe social dislocations and increased crime and corruption. Some former Communist officials and bureaucrats used their connections and experience to manipulate the systems and to further enrich themselves; some formed so-called mafias that often used illegal methods to gain profit. Other enterprising men and women, however, established flourishing businesses and were confident of future prosperity.

Eastern European nations undertook sweeping reforms to qualify for integration into the association of western European economies and governments called the European Union (EU). The EU had been established under the Maastricht agreement of 1991; a common currency, the Euro, had been put into circulation in 2000. In 2000 the EU, with its 338 million generally well-educated and affluent people, was one of the world's three major economic forces, along with the United States and Japan. In 2004 the EU witnessed a dramatic increase to twenty-five members, including even the former Soviet republics of Latvia, Lithuania, and Estonia. Other nations, such as Turkey and Bulgaria, await admission.

Ethnic Diversity and Conflict

Ethnic rivalries also threatened the political and economic well-being of many nations in Europe and elsewhere. As noted in the introduction to this section, in 1993 Czechoslovakia split along ethnic lines into the Czech Republic and Slovakia. Yugoslavia was torn apart by ethnic divisions, as rival Macedonians, Slovenians, Croatians, Serbs, and Muslim Bosnians fought one another over national borders and territory. Conflicts began when Bosnian Serbs launched an "ethnic-cleansing" pogrom, laying siege to the city of Sarajevo and many other Muslim-held Bosnian territories, terrorizing civilian inhabitants with random bombings, raids, rapes, and mass expulsions. The United States, the European nations, and the United Nations attempted to stop the fighting. Finally, in 1995, the United States brought the opposing sides together in Dayton, Ohio. The resultant Dayton Accords called for a Muslim-Croat Federation and a Serb Republic of Bosnia; NATO forces, including U.S. soldiers, were deployed to keep the fragile peace. When

Serbs launched a major offensive in the predominantly ethnic Albanian Kosovar region, NATO forces retaliated by bombing Serb territory. NATO troops have continued to maintain the fragile peace because the future of these weak and poor states remains uncertain.

Partly due to high unemployment, hate crimes against foreign workers (Turks, North Africans, and Asians) increased in Germany, France, and elsewhere in Europe. Reactionary political parties in many European nations campaigned to ban or limit immigration by foreign workers and the granting of political asylum to refugees fleeing war-torn and impoverished countries. Anti-Semitism was on the rise in many countries.

In the United States, racism continued to divide citizens, threatening unity and equal economic development among its diverse ethnic communities. Similarly, racial and sectarian strife racked Sri Lanka, Indonesia, the Philippines, Turkey, Iran, Iraq, and Northern Ireland.

As the quelling of ethnic wars strained the limited budget of the United Nations, Secretary-General Kofi Annan urged nations to increase their financial support. He especially called on the United States to fulfill its financial obligation. Annan has also pushed for the United Nations to respond more rapidly to conflicts before they erupt into full-scale wars and humanitarian disasters. The complexity of the disputes in the Balkans and elsewhere make it likely that the United Nations, NATO, and other multinational forces will have to stop or forestall future wars.

Ongoing Conflict and Changes in West Asia and Africa

The most crucial task which will face the government [the white National Party-led regime] and the ANC will be to reconcile. . . . Such reconciliation will be achieved only if both parties are willing to compromise. The organization will determine precisely how negotiations should be conducted. It may well be that this should be done at least in two stages—the first where the organization and the government will work out together the preconditions for a proper climate for negotiations. Up to now both parties have been broadcasting their conditions for negotiations without putting them directly to each other.

The second stage would be the actual negotiations themselves when the climate is ripe for doing so. Any other approach would entail the danger of an irremovable stalemate. I . . . hope to see the ANC and the government working closely together to lay the foundations for a new era in our country, in which racial discrimination and prejudice, coercion and confrontation, death and destruction, will be forgotten.*

**Nelson Mandela, *Speeches 1990* (New York: Pathfinder, 1990), p. 18.

In this letter written from prison to South African President P. W. Botha in July 1989, Nelson Mandela outlined a plan for negotiations to resolve the long struggle between the white-dominated South African government and the majority black South African population, which was fighting for an end to apartheid and the establishment of a state based on equal rights and self-determination for all its people. Mandela, the leader of the African National Congress, was addressing the protracted conflict in South Africa, but his analysis is equally applicable to the Arab-Israeli conflict, in which two peoples confronted one another to achieve self-determination. This section will trace the ongoing turbulence in West Asia, beginning with Afghanistan in the wake of the Russian withdrawal, and move on to describe the Arab-Israeli conflict and the resolution of strife in southern Africa, with special emphasis on the Republic of South Africa. Despite strides toward conflict resolution in the 1990s, both regions have continued to face major political and economic uncertainties.

The End of Taliban Rule in Afghanistan

Without the active help of its patron, the Soviet Union, the Afghan communist regime was overthrown in 1992, leaving a power vacuum that lasted half a decade. The chief Islamic guerrilla organizations, which had nothing in common except their opposition to communism and foreign rule, turned to fighting each other for political control of the country. Aided by Pakistan and Saudi Arabia, a radical fundamentalist group known as the Taliban slowly gained the upper hand, culminating in their seizure of the Afghan capital of Kabul in 1996. Under the leadership of Muhammad Umar, popularly called Mullah Omar in the West, the Taliban quickly restored order by brutal suppression of any suspected opposition. Their rule, based on a rigorous interpretation of the Qur'an, included the subjugation of women, the destruction of monuments depicting human form, public executions and mutilations for even minor criminal offenses, and the banning of supposed corrupting influences such as music and television.

The Taliban did not attract much attention in the West until they provided training bases and collaborated with a Muslim terrorist faction known as al Qaeda, meaning "the base," led by Osama bin Laden, an Islamic extremist born to extremely wealthy Saudi parents. This network of Arab volunteers had fought under the banner of Islam against the Soviets in Afghanistan in the 1980s. In search of a new jihad (holy war) in the aftermath of the forced Soviet withdrawal from Afghanistan, bin Laden targeted the United States, a country he despised for its secular moral values, its steadfast refusal to endorse lifting UN sanctions imposed on Iraq after the Gulf War, its support for Israel, and its military presence in Saudi Arabia, a supposed affront to Islam in the home of the prophet Muhammad. With a well-financed worldwide network of cells, al Qaeda engineered attacks against the United States that included the bombings of the World Trade Center in New York City (1993), the U.S. military barracks in Saudi Arabia (1996), the U.S. embassies in Kenya and Tanzania (1998), and the USS *Cole* in the port of Aden in Yemen (2000). Though these attacks caused considerable loss of life, the United States failed to initiate any effective response.

On September 11, 2001, commercial airliners hijacked by al Qaeda members slammed into the World Trade Center towers and the Pentagon, killing about 3,000 people. Led by the United States, the United Nations demanded that the Taliban turn over bin Laden. When they defiantly refused to do so, the United States and its allies launched air strikes followed by a ground invasion closely coordinated with the Northern Alliance, an anti-Taliban collection of Afghan militias and war lords. Spearheading the assault, the Northern Alliance rapidly captured one Taliban stronghold after another and in November took Kabul. Thereafter organized resistance melted away, as many of the surviving Taliban surrendered or switched sides. Both Mullah Omar and Osama bin Laden evaded capture, disappearing in the mountains of eastern Afghanistan despite efforts by the American-led coalition to hunt them down.

Following the defeat of the Taliban, the UN assembled the leaders of the chief military factions and brokered an agreement for an interim government headed by Hamid Karzai. The government faced the daunting task of providing basic services, rebuilding the economy, and creating stability in a faction-ridden country torn by two decades of violence and war.

The Israeli-Palestinian-Arab Conflict

A legacy of Western imperialism and the Cold War contributed to the tangle of problems in West Asia (the Middle East). After World War II, Great Britain granted full independence to Transjordan (present-day Jordan) and encouraged Arab nationalism in the neighboring French-held territories of Syria and Lebanon, both of which also received their independence.

Great Britain wanted good relations with the Arab nations because of their strategic locations and their petroleum reserves. The British mandate over Palestine, however, with its majority Palestinian Arab population and growing Jewish minority, who had come mostly from Europe and the United States, posed a problem that defied easy solutions. Jews, pouring into Palestine from the concentration camps of Hitler's Europe, were determined to establish a homeland of their own. To achieve this goal, in the face of frequently hostile British policies, some organized a terrorist underground. The Palestinian Arabs, who accounted for two-thirds of the population and owned 80 percent of the land, were equally determined to defend their rights. Caught in the middle of spiraling violence that their imperial policies had helped to create, the British announced they would leave Palestine in 1948 and turn the entire problem over to the newly formed United Nations. The United Nations recommended the partition of Palestine into a Jewish and an Arab state. Neither side was satisfied with this decision, and fighting between the two conflicting national groups intensified.

Israeli Declaration of Independence

May 14, 1948: A few minutes later, at exactly 4 P.M., the ceremony began. Ben-Gurion, wearing a dark suit and tie, stood up and rapped a gavel. According to the plan, this was to be the signal for the orchestra . . . to play "Hatikvah." But something went wrong, and there was no music. Spontaneously, we rose to our feet and sang our national anthem. Then Ben-Gurion cleared his throat and said quietly, "I shall now read the Scroll of Independence. . . . Accordingly we, the members of the National Council, representing the Jewish people in the Land of Israel and the Zionist movement, have assembled on the day of the termination of the British mandate for Palestine, and, by virtue of our natural and his-

toric right and of the resolution of the General Assembly of the United Nations, do hereby proclaim the establishment of a Jewish state in the Land of Israel—the State of Israel."

The State of Israel! My eyes filled with tears, and my hands shook. We had done it. . . . Whatever happened now, whatever price any of us would have to pay for it, we had recreated the Jewish national home. The long exile was over.*

In this statement, Golda Meir, a future prime minister of Israel, describes the emotions surrounding the declaration of independence for the new Jewish state in 1948.

*Golda Meir, My Life (New York: Dell, 1975), p. 217.

LIVES AND TIMES ACROSS CULTURES

Political Humor

Common people throughout the world have long used humor to express disdain, discontent, and even hatred of politicians and governments. This was, for example, the stock in trade of Aristophanes, whose comedies often satirized the leaders of Athens and their hawkish war policies during the Peloponnesian War. In the ninth century, Arab writers mocked their leaders in satiric essays and poems. The Arabic language lends itself easily to puns and jests; in the Arab world, the Egyptians are particularly famous for making jokes about everything from sex to the bureaucracy to individual politicians. Arab cartoonists caricature their political leaders much as Garry Trudeau in his *Doonesbury* comic strip and Art Buchwald in his columns poke fun at Washington politicos.

During the Cold War, jokes about the repressive Soviet regimes, food shortages, and corruption were popular among eastern Europeans. Similarly, Egyptians who opposed Gamal Abdul Nasser's nationalization policies and growing authoritarianism in the 1960s gleefully shared humorous stories that made fun of the regime. The following witticism was particularly popular.

Nasser was walking around the Great Pyramids and the Sphinx at Giza, when the Sphinx called out, "Nasser, Nasser!" Nasser turned around in amazement, crying, "You have been silent for thousands of years. Caesar, Napoleon, the British all came to you, but you refused to speak. Why now do you speak to me?" And the Sphinx replied, "I want an exit visa."

When the British left Palestine in 1948, the Jews promptly announced the creation of Israel under the leadership of David Ben-Gurion (1886–1973; see the accompanying box). The Palestinians and the Arab nations refused to recognize the new state, and the first Arab-Israeli war began. The Israelis, better equipped, better trained, more unified, and supported by the United States, defeated their Arab adversaries and expanded their territory by one-third. In the course of the struggle, nearly one million Palestinian Arabs fled their villages and sought refuge in squalid camps in the surrounding Arab states. After the war, fearing that the Palestinians threatened the existence of a Jewish state, Israel refused to allow the Palestinian refugees to return. Meanwhile, the Palestinians remained determined to return to their homes and create a Palestinian state. Without resolution of the core of the conflict, namely, implementation of both Israeli and Palestinian rights, the conflict continued.

In many ways Israel, established and governed largely by Jews from Europe and North America, was part of the Western world. Nevertheless, it was surrounded by Arab nations and had many Palestinians living within its borders. The hostility of Israel's Arab neighbors brought conflict punctuated by open warfare. The Israeli refusal to permit the creation of a separate Palestinian state was matched by the Arab denial of the right of Israel to exist.

Arab nationalism peaked in the mid-1950s under the charismatic leadership of Gamal Abdul Nasser (Egyptian leader, 1952–1970). In 1952 Nasser led a military revolt that

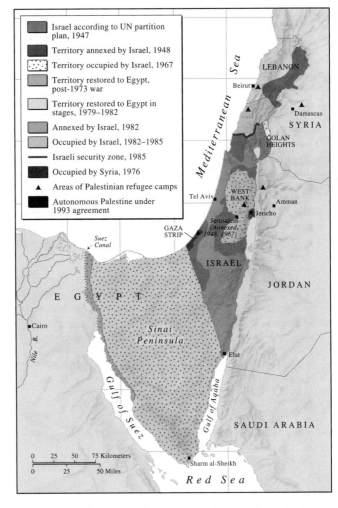

Israel according to UN partition plan, 1947

Territory annexed by Israel, 1948

Territory occupied by Israel, 1967

Territory restored to Egypt, post-1973 war

Territory restored to Egypt in stages, 1979–1982

Annexed by Israel, 1982

Occupied by Israel, 1982–1985

Israeli security zone, 1985

Occupied by Syria, 1976

▲ Areas of Palestinian refugee camps

Autonomous Palestine under 1993 agreement

Map 17.3 The Arab-Israeli Conflict. Two basic facts are set out here: Israel's expansions and annexations from 1948 to 1982, and its occupation of, and subsequent withdrawal from, the Sinai Peninsula and most of southern Lebanon. The autonomous areas of the Gaza Strip and Jericho, agreed upon by Israel and the Palestinian Liberation Organization (PLO) in 1993, are also designated. The future of the rest of the West Bank and East Jerusalem, still under Israeli occupation, remains in doubt.

overthrew the corrupt Egyptian King Faruk. Nasser then instituted a number of reforms, including the redistribution of land to the poor and the building of the huge Aswan High Dam to provide water to irrigate more land and electric power for villages and factories to solve Egypt's economic problems. Nasser was a strong supporter of Palestinian rights, and he suspected continued British and French imperialist designs in the region. To counter Western influence, he sought better relations with the Soviet Union and other eastern bloc nations. In light of the Cold War, the United States viewed Nasser's neutrality with increasing hostility.

When the United States abruptly withdrew its promise to finance the building of the Aswan High Dam, Nasser retaliated by nationalizing the Suez Canal, which was controlled by foreign stockholders. Revenues from the canal fees were diverted to build the Aswan High Dam, which subsequently was also underwritten by Soviet financial and technical aid. Thus challenged, France, Britain, and Israel—all of whom wanted Nasser ousted from power—secretly agreed to take back the canal by force. The subsequent

1956 war resulted in the Israeli occupation of the Sinai Peninsula and the British and French occupation of the canal zone, but the successful tripartite invasion was an unmitigated political disaster for the West. Shocked at this apparent return to nineteenth-century "gunboat diplomacy," the United States entered into a rare agreement with the Soviet Union and compelled its NATO allies (Great Britain and France) to return the canal to Egypt. Nasser, whose charges of continued Western imperialism were justified, emerged as the undisputed leader of the Arab world. Following concerted pressure by the United States to withdraw from Egyptian territory, Israel withdrew from the Sinai after securing U.S. recognition of Israeli shipping rights through the Straits of Tiran to the southern port of Elat. Arab nations opposed this concession, and it became a major cause of the next Arab-Israeli war.

With no peace settlement, both sides continued to prepare for the next confrontation. In May 1967, Nasser, hoping to gain increased popularity among the Arabs, requested the withdrawal of the United Nations forces that guaranteed the safety of Israeli ships passing through the Strait of Tiran and Gulf of Aqaba to Israel's southern port. Acting in accordance with regulations providing that troops could be placed in sovereign territory only with the agreement of the affected nation, the United Nations forces withdrew. Israel viewed any move to close the strait to its ships as an act of war. The United States and the Soviet Union attempted to defuse the crisis, but while negotiations were still in process, Israel attacked the key air installations of the major Arab nations. The 1967 Arab-Israeli war, or the Six Days' War, resulted in a stunning Israeli military victory and Israeli occupation of the entire Sinai Peninsula, the Gaza Strip, the West Bank of Jordan (including eastern Jerusalem, which had been under Jordanian jurisdiction), and the Golan Heights, part of Syrian territory. Israel annexed East Jerusalem, proclaiming the unified city its capital. Following this humiliating defeat, some Palestinians turned to guerrilla raids and terrorist strikes to dislodge Israel from the Occupied Territories and force the creation of a Palestinian state. Under the leadership of Yasir Arafat (1929–), the Palestine Liberation Organization (PLO) became the leading political and military force for Palestinian nationalism.

Nasser died in 1970, and his successor, Anwar Sadat (1918–1981), promised to secure the return of the Sinai to Egypt. In 1973 the Egyptians launched a surprise attack across the Suez Canal against the occupying Israeli forces. Fighting also ensued along the Golan Heights between Israel and Syria. The 1973 war was not a clear-cut victory for either side. The Israelis beat back Syrian attacks on the Golan Heights, but Egyptian forces were able to cross the Suez Canal and establish a foothold on the eastern bank. With this achievement, Sadat later offered peace and recognition of Israel in return for the Sinai. The settlement, brokered by U.S. President Jimmy Carter in 1978, led to a peace treaty between Egypt and Israel in 1979, but it failed to provide for an independent Palestinian state. The peace settlement did, however, mark a break in the solid front of Arab states against Israel and turned Egypt, formerly a Soviet client, into an ally of the United States.

In 1982, Israel invaded its northern neighbor, Lebanon, which had suffered from a destructive civil war since 1975 and had become a major base for the PLO. Exacerbated

Meeting at Camp David. At Camp David in 1978 President Jimmy Carter mediated a formal agreement leading to a full-scale peace treaty between Egypt and Israel in 1979. Here Carter and his wife, Rosalynn, President Sadat of Egypt, and Prime Minister Begin of Israel enjoy a lighthearted moment of relaxation from protracted negotiations that stretched over almost two weeks.

by the Palestinian presence, the civil war in Lebanon stemmed largely from social, economic, and sectarian differences among the various Lebanese religious groups. During the summer of 1982, the Israeli army drove into the Lebanese capital, Beirut, forcing the dispersal of the PLO but not its destruction. Even after the 1982 war, the Lebanese failed to settle their differences, and fighting continued until a fragile peace was established in the late 1980s. Meanwhile, Israel continued to hold a so-called security zone in southern Lebanon, the Gaza Strip, and the West Bank and steadily increased the number of Jewish settlers in this predominantly Palestinian territory. The Israeli occupation in southern Lebanon led to a mounting resistance movement by Hezbollah, a Lebanese Muslim movement supported by Iran and sometimes Syria. After protracted violence, Israel withdrew from Lebanese territory in 2000.

Meanwhile, the Palestinians in the Occupied Territories began a campaign of civil disobedience, attacking Israelis with stones and sticks in 1987. The *intifada*, or uprising, continued unabated in the face of massive repression by the Israelis. In 1988, as the rising spiral of violence continued, the PLO declared Palestinian statehood for the territories of Gaza and the West Bank, the so-called mini-state solution, and recognized Israel's existence (see the accompanying box).

As more and more nations recognized the Palestinian state, the United States reluctantly agreed to mediate between the opposing Israelis and Palestinians and participated in negotiations in 1991. As the negotiations dragged on without results, secret meetings were held between PLO delegates and Israelis that resulted in a stunning Declaration of Principles, whereby the old enemies agreed to recognize one another in September 1993. Further negotiations were to lead to some undefined type of autonomy for the Palestinians in parts of the West Bank and the Gaza Strip, but, once again, the two sides were unable to reach mutually acceptable agreements and the negotiations foundered. Violence between the Palestinians and Israeli settlers in the Occupied Territories escalated, and in 1995 a young Israeli violently opposed to any compromise with the Palestinians assassinated Israeli prime minister Yitzhak Rabin (1922–1995). Although Israel withdrew from some parts of the West Bank and most of the Gaza Strip, major differences over the nature of a Palestinian state, the Israeli settlements, and the status of Jerusalem remained unresolved. Following Ariel Sharon's provocative visit to the holy sites at Haram al-Sharif (the Temple Mount) in Jerusalem in 2000 and his subsequent election as Israeli prime minister, a second Palestinian uprising (the al-Aqsa intifada) broke out. Israel responded by reoccupying a number of West Bank cities and launching military attacks in the Gaza Strip and other West Bank areas. This in turn led to a wave of suicide bombings by Palestinians inside Israel and to the construction of a massive wall in a futile Israeli attempt to gain security while curbing Palestinian opposition. The cycle of violence and reprisal continued as the international community, especially the United States, was largely preoccupied with the ongoing war against terrorism in Afghanistan and Iraq. The failure to resolve the Israeli-Palestinian conflict in an equitable fashion has perpetuated the instability and carnage plaguing the entire Middle East to the present day.

Crises in the Persian Gulf Region

With its vast petroleum reserves and its geopolitical position south of the Soviet Union and astride the intersection between the West and the East, West Asia was of strategic importance to both the superpowers. As a result, during the Cold War both the Soviet Union and the United States sought to reinforce their alliances with key nations in the region. In addition, most western European nations and Japan depended on petroleum from the region for their energy needs and petrochemical industries. Although the Soviet Union was largely self-sufficient in petroleum, whoever controlled the vital petroleum resources of West Asia clearly held an enormous advantage in the global balance of power.

During the 1960s and 1970s, the Shah of Iran had embarked on an ambitious and costly program of industrialization and had built up a huge military machine. Although urban areas experienced rapid economic development, Iran suffered from mounting inflation, declining agricultural output, political repression, and corruption and nepotism at the highest levels of government. As a result, Iranians from all walks of life, particularly the Shi'i clergy, joined forces to overthrow the Shah. The ousting of the Shah in 1979, through a popular revolution championed by the Islamic leader Ayatollah Ruhollah Khomeini (1900–1989), was a severe blow to U.S. interests. Ayatollah Khomeini and the Shi'i mullahs (clergy) established a strict Islamic state that was hostile to secular Western society, which it viewed as immoral. Since Muslims were often disillusioned by the failures of both Western and Soviet models to improve their societies, many in West

Palestinian Declaration of Independence

November 15, 1988: Nourished by many strains of civilization and a multitude of cultures and finding inspiration in the texts of its spiritual heritage, the Palestinian Arab people has, throughout history, continued to develop its identity in an integral unity of land and people and in the footsteps of the prophets throughout this Holy Land, the invocation of praise for the Creator high atop every minaret while hymns of mercy and peace have rung out with the bells of every church and temple. . . .

The Palestine National Council hereby declares, in the Name of God and on behalf of the Palestinian Arab people, the establishment of the State of Palestine in the land of Palestine with its capital at Jerusalem. . . .

The State of Palestine, in declaring that it is a peace-loving State committed to the principles of peaceful coexistence, shall strive, together with all other States and peoples, for the achievement of a lasting peace based on justice and respect for rights. . . .

We give our solemn pledge to continue the struggle for an end to the occupation and the establishment of sovereignty and independence. We call upon our great people to rally to the Palestinian flag, to take pride in it and to defend it so that it shall remain forever a symbol of our freedom and dignity in a homeland that shall be forever free and the abode of a people of free men.*

On November 15, 1988, Chairman Yasir Arafat proclaimed Palestinian independence before the Palestine National Council in Tunis, Tunisia. In many ways his proclamation paralleled Ben-Gurion's declaration of Israeli independence in 1948. Both Israelis and Palestinians seek to exercise their rights to self-determination on the same territory, and therein are the seeds of their ongoing conflict.

*"Palestinian Declaration of Independence," American-Arab Affairs (Fall 1988), pp. 182–185.

Asia and Africa turned to militant Islam. The revolutionary Islamic regime in Iran encouraged and sometimes directly supported militant Islamic movements not only in the Arab world, but elsewhere as well.

Ayatollah Khomeini's attempts to export the Iranian revolution also contributed to the outbreak of a protracted war with neighboring Iraq. The war began in 1980 and dragged on until an uneasy cease-fire was reached in the late 1980s. For both sides the war was a financial and human disaster. Although the war severely strained the Iranian economy, the Islamic state survived both the disasters brought on by the war and the death of Ayatollah Khomeini in 1989.

Iraq emerged from the war with a huge battle-trained army, but with enormous debts. During the war Iraq had been forced to borrow vast amounts of money from oil-rich Arab nations in order to buy arms. The Iraqi regime, under Saddam Hussein (1937–), believed that Iraqis had fought and died in the war in part to protect the Gulf states and Saudi Arabia from possible overthrow by the revolutionary Islamic government of Iran. Consequently, it did not believe it should have to repay the loans. Iraq was also anxious to sell more of its petroleum on world markets to obtain much-needed capital for the rebuilding of its war-damaged infrastructure. When Kuwait began to press for repayment of its loans and massive sales of petroleum by Saudi Arabia and other Gulf states kept the price of petroleum depressed, the Iraqis loudly protested.

After negotiations had failed to resolve these differences, Saddam Hussein took matters into his own hands and launched a massive invasion of Kuwait in August 1990. Most of the international community vigorously condemned the aggression, demanding the immediate withdrawal of Iraq and the return of the Kuwaiti monarchy. With the collapse of the Soviet Union, the United States was the sole superpower, and it was determined to preserve its petroleum and political interests in the region.

Consequently, the United States demanded that economic sanctions be applied against Iraq and that an international coalition under the auspices of the United Nations be organized to force an Iraqi withdrawal by military means. In January 1991, the U.S.-led coalition launched a massive month-long aerial bombardment of Iraq, resulting in numerous Iraqi civilian deaths and widespread destruction. The subsequent ground war into Kuwait by the coalition met with success on all fronts and resulted in the complete withdrawal of Iraqi forces from Kuwait. Although the war ended with a clear-cut military victory for the coalition and the United States and the return of the pro-West Kuwaiti monarchy, U.S. president George H. W. Bush did not remove Saddam Hussein from power when it had the chance.

Despite uprisings among the Kurds in the north of Iraq and the Shi'i in the south, Saddam Hussein's brutal regime survived, contrary to the expectations of the United States and its allies. The United Nations hoped to disarm Hussein by sending inspectors to Iraq to destroy his suspected chemical and biological weapons and the facilities needed to manufacture them. A beaten Hussein was in no position to demur, but he resented the humiliating presence and demands of UN inspectors, who tarnished his

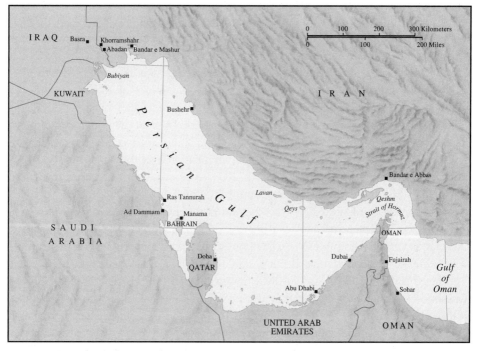

Map 17.4 The Persian Gulf. The gulf, with its vast petroleum reserves and strategic location, became a focus of Cold War rivalry and regional disputes. Iran tried to extend its control of the vital waterway, while Iraq sought to protect and maximize its own interests in the region. As a result, Iran and Iraq fought a long war of attrition in the 1980s. In 1990 Iraq invaded Kuwait but was pushed out by the Allied forces led by the United States in 1991.

image in the Arab world. Weary of Hussein's cat-and-mouse games, the UN inspectors left Iraq in the fall of 1998. As a result, the Clinton administration in the United States indicated it would work to bring about a regime change in Iraq, though nothing was in fact achieved to this end.

In the aftermath of the attack on the United States on September 11, 2001, President George W. Bush redirected American foreign policy to fight the war on terrorism; he declared that the menace posed by a clandestine web of radical terrorists operating in concert with rogue nations required a new policy of preemptive military action. The war in Afghanistan was barely over when the Bush administration accused Iraq of hiding weapons of mass destruction and of having links to al Qaeda. Backed strongly by Britain, the United States proposed a resolution in the United Nations Security Council to authorize the use of military force if Iraq refused to disarm. The measure failed to pass because France threatened to veto it, arguing that the inspectors should be given more time to complete their work. Both Russia and Germany supported the French position.

Unable to obtain UN endorsement for a military strike, American and British forces, aided by a small coalition, went ahead without it, driving into Iraq from neighboring Kuwait in March 2003. The declared purpose of the attack was to remove Saddam Hussein from power, destroy Iraq's chemical and biological weapons, and install a democratic government in Baghdad. Relying on a blitzkrieg of high-tech weapons that struck a variety of targets with pinpoint accuracy, coalition forces routed Iraqi defenders after several weeks of fighting and occupied many of the country's chief cities. As resistance collapsed, the leading members of the Iraqi government fled, but by the end of the year practically all had been captured. Hussein's two sons, Uday and Qusay, who were guilty of unspeakable crimes against the Iraqi people, were killed in Baghdad in July in a firefight with U.S. forces. In December 2003, Hussein himself was taken into custody after he was found hiding in a hole in the ground near his hometown of Tikrit.

Following the overthrow of Hussein's regime, the United States set up a Governing Council representing the Kurds in the north, the Sunni Arabs in the center, and the Shi'i Arabs in the south. Paul Bremer, the top U.S. administrator in Iraq, had to grapple with sectarian tensions exacerbated by fears of Shi'i domination over the Sunni Arab and Kurdish minorities. Bremer managed in March 2004 to persuade all the parties to sign an interim constitution, to remain in effect until a permanent one could be approved by national referendum in late 2005. The adoption of the interim document was a key step in the U.S.-backed plan to hand over power to the Iraqis. U.S. officials and Iraqis still had to agree on a method to create a government that would take power in the summer of 2004 and serve until national elections could take place in January 2005.

Although President Bush had justified the invasion of Iraq by claiming that Saddam Hussein was an immediate threat to the region, no nuclear, biological, or chemical weapons had been found a year after the conclusion of the war. This gave the impression to many, both in the United States and abroad, that Bush had misrepresented or exaggerated the Iraqi threat to suit his own agenda. As a result some Arab and European countries loosened ties with the United States, accusing it of arrogance and seeking hegemony over the oil-rich Middle East.

Iraq remained a dangerous and unstable place. Elements of Hussein's defeated army gradually regrouped and, with the assistance of foreign jihadists, began to mount frequent guerrilla attacks against U.S. troops and conduct acts of terrorism in urban centers. Pacifying and rebuilding Iraq promised to be a lengthy and expensive process.

Struggles for Equality in the Republic of South Africa

By 1991, the Republic of South Africa was the only African state still under white minority rule. South Africa's political and economic system continued to be dominated by Afrikaners, descendants of the Dutch settlers, or Boers, who outnumbered the generally more tolerant English. After World War II, the Afrikaner government perpetuated its system of strict apartheid, or segregation of the races, and tenaciously refused to grant political rights to the majority black population, which numbered approximately 26 million people by the 1980s.

The goals of apartheid were to segregate the races and to perpetuate white control. A complex set of laws required each race—black Africans, Asians, and people of "mixed

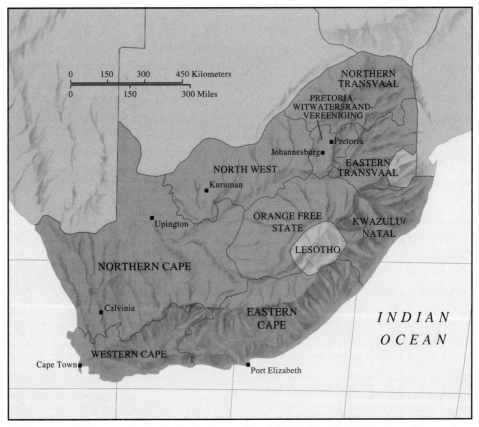

Map 17.5 South Africa. In 1994, in the first elections open to all South Africans, Nelson Mandela won the presidency, ending white minority dominance in the nation. Dire predictions of secession by some tribal groups and whites did not materialize, and the nation remained unified.

races"—to live, go to school, attend church, find recreation, and otherwise spend their lives separate from other races and especially from the whites who ruled them. Interracial marriages were prohibited, and nonwhite South Africans were required to carry special passes. They often had to travel long distances from their segregated living quarters to work at jobs in the white areas.

In the face of mounting international opposition to the denial of political rights to blacks, the Afrikaner South African government created several black African *bantustans*, or "homelands." The government then declared many ethnic Africans citizens of these artificial "states" and compelled them to live in these areas. These homelands were enclaves within the territorial confines of South Africa and were invariably established on the poorest land. In the absence of resources, industry, and jobs, a majority of adult black males and some women had to leave the homelands to find work in white-dominated areas. Populated mainly by the old, women, and children, the homelands remained desperately poor. President P. W. Botha (1916–), leader of the dominant white political organization, the Nationalist party, inaugurated limited parliamentary reforms in the 1980s to satisfy international criticism. Under these reforms some Asians and people of mixed races were granted limited political participation, but the majority black population remained totally outside the political system.

Beginning in the 1950s, black South Africans responded to apartheid with waves of protests. These demonstrations were ruthlessly crushed by police power, and black political organizations such as the African National Congress (ANC), which was formed in 1912 as one of the first African nationalist movements, were outlawed until 1990. Some opponents of the regime adopted guerrilla warfare as a means of fighting the system. The South African government justified its violent suppression of black African nationalist movements by arguing that they were Communist inspired.

Some black South African activists went underground or into exile in neighboring African states to escape death, persecution, or imprisonment at the hands of the government. ANC leader Nelson Mandela (1918–) spent more than twenty-five years in South African jails for his commitment to the cause of justice and equality for his people. Meanwhile, Nobel Peace Prize winners Albert Luthuli (1898–1967) and Bishop Desmond Tutu (1931–), along with Winnie Mandela, wife of the long-imprisoned ANC leader, continued to work for an end to racial discrimination by generating international support for their cause.

The crisis in South Africa continued to mount in the 1980s as the black townships erupted in violence and Western nations intensified pressure on the government through economic sanctions. The threat of withdrawal of Western investment capital, coupled with strains in the South African economy, compelled the government to promise reforms. After considerable political negotiations, the National party led by Frederik de Klerk (1936–) freed Nelson Mandela, who continued to campaign vigorously for an end to apartheid and full voting rights for the majority black population.

After modifying some apartheid regulations, de Klerk opened negotiations with Mandela and the ANC. The two parties subsequently agreed that voting rights would be granted on the basis of one person, one vote, and that new elections would be held in

April 1994. The ANC, which was expected to win a free and open election, campaigned under the simple slogan "Jobs, Peace, Freedom." Since an estimated 47 percent of the labor force was unemployed, it was not surprising that jobs were the ANC's first priority.

Although some extremists attempted to prevent the elections, a record number of voters turned out for the spring 1994 elections, which resulted in a resounding victory for the ANC. Nelson Mandela became the first South African leader chosen in an election open to all South Africans, and South Africa's first black president. A Truth and Reconciliation Commission was established to investigate those accused of crimes against the opponents of the apartheid system, but South African society largely avoided the racial and ethnic violence that had erupted in so many other nations after the Cold War. South Africa also avoided dictatorial rule; Mandela willingly turned over the reins of power to others in the ANC when his term in office expired. He did, however, continue to act as a senior diplomat to negotiate peaceful settlements to disputes and the end to civil wars that plagued other African nations. On the domestic front, South Africa, like many neighboring African nations, continued to face enormous problems of poverty and unemployment.

AP/Wide World Photos

Nelson Mandela. After his election as president of South Africa, Nelson Mandela traveled around the world to gather international support and economic investment for his nation. Here he jokes with schoolchildren after his speech before both houses of the British Parliament.

Political, Social, and Economic Issues in Africa

The struggles in the Republic of South Africa also affected neighboring nations, just as the Arab-Israeli conflict had regional implications in West Asia. During the 1980s, in efforts to destabilize regimes hostile to its apartheid system, the white South African government assisted a number of rebel movements in neighboring countries. It also conducted raids into Mozambique and supported a rebel movement so cruel that the entire international community condemned it. In Angola both the United States and South Africa provided arms and money to Jonas Savimbi, whose UNITA party waged a protracted civil war against the Soviet- and Cuban-backed Popular Movement for the Liberation of Angola (MPLA), led by Jose Eduardo dos Santos. When dos Santos and the MPLA won free and open elections in 1992, Savimbi simply refused to accept the results and resorted to force to achieve political power. In spite of attempted negotiations, fighting continued in much of Angola into 2000. Thus leaders and movements backed by the United States and the West to counter Soviet presence in Africa during the Cold War continued to wage war and threaten democratic, elected governments long after the superpower conflict had ended. Namibia, Angola, Mozambique, and a host of other nations continued to suffer the negative effects of the Cold War.

As in the Balkans, Northern Ireland, and India, ethnic conflicts also erupted in several central African nations. Genocidal warfare between Hutu and Tutsi populations swept through Rwanda and Burundi and spilled over into neighboring Zaire. The aging Zairian dictator, Mobutu Sese Seko, was forced to resign in 1997, having become a multimillionaire through the theft of the wealth of Zaire (now renamed the Congo) for over thirty years. The new Congolese government thus inherited a bankrupt nation and faced the seemingly overwhelming job of rebuilding the economy from the ground up. Eritrea and Somalia in the Horn of Africa confronted similar problems of rebuilding war-torn, impoverished nations. Civil wars have also severely damaged other African nations, including Liberia, Sierra Leone, and Ivory Coast in western Africa. Thus the gap between the prosperous northern nations of Europe, Japan, and the United States and the poor southern states in Africa continued into the twenty-first century.

Major Challenges Confronting the Post–Cold War World

When I got the telegram saying that I was invited by the United Nations [for the International Women's Year Tribunal in Mexico in 1974], I was quite surprised and disconcerted. I called a meeting of the committee and all the compañeras agreed that it would be good for me to travel. . . .

During the trip I thought . . . that I'd never imagined I'd be travelling in a plane, and even less to such a far-off country as Mexico. Never, for we were so poor that sometimes we hardly had anything to eat and we couldn't even travel around our own country. . . .

[At the conference] there'd be two groups: one, on the government level, where those upper class ladies would be; and the other, on the non-government level, where people like me would be, people with similar problems, you know, poor people. It was like a dream for me! Goodness, I said to myself, I'll be meeting peasant women and working women from all over the world.

In the Tribunal I learned a lot. . . . In the first place, I learned to value the wisdom of my people even more. There, everyone who went up to the microphone said: "I'm a professional person, I represent such and such organization. . . ." And bla-bla-bla, they'd begin to give their opinion.

So, I went up and spoke. I made them see that they don't live in our world. I made them see that in Bolivia human rights aren't respected and they apply what we call "the law of the funnel": broad for some, narrow for others. That those ladies who got together to play canasta and applaud the government have full guarantees, full support. But women like us, housewives, who get organized to better our people, well, they beat us up and persecute us. They couldn't see the suffering of my people, they couldn't see how compañeras are vomiting their lungs bit by bit, in pools of blood. They didn't see how underfed our children are. And, of course, they didn't know, as we do, what it's like to get up at four in the morning and go to bed at eleven or twelve at night, just to be able to get all the housework done, because of the lousy conditions we live in.

It was . . . a great experience being with so many women and seeing how many, many people are dedicated to the struggle for the liberation of their oppressed peoples.*

*Dimitila Barrios de Chungara, in Hazel Johnson et al., eds., *Third World Lives of Struggle* (London: Heinemann, 1982), pp. 236–242.

In this excerpt, Dimitila Barrios de Chungara, a miner's wife from Bolivia, vividly describes the vast gulf between the rich and the poor and the problems facing peasants and women throughout most of the contemporary world. She was the leader of a Housewives Committee organized to improve the lot of miners in Bolivia. After a military coup in 1980, her organization was banned and she was forced into exile. De Chungara's description provides a human face to the global problems of poverty, development, and equality described in this section.

Struggles for Democracy

The events of the 1990s indicate that the struggle for democracy is an ongoing one. No one geographic region, people, culture, or religious group seems to have the monopoly either on democracy or dictatorship. The following discussion of the continuing struggle for democratic rights is arranged geographically beginning with Asia and moving to West Asia, Africa, Europe, and the Western Hemisphere.

In Asia the moves toward democracy were mixed. In China, the Communist party stubbornly resisted efforts by the Chinese and international community to democratize. The Chinese government regularly detained dissidents for even planning to protest. After the death of the aged Deng Xiaoping in 1996, the Chinese Communist party has continued to monopolize political power and the policy of economic growth through privatization. China has also joined the World Trade Organization. North Korea remains the most closed and tightly controlled Communist country, with a dynastic style of succession that passed power from Kim Il Sung to his son Kim Jong Il. Despite a collapsing economy, it maintains a huge military and a nuclear arsenal in defiance of the international community.

In Indonesia, the corrupt dictator, General Suharto, was ousted and a fragile, freely elected government was installed in 1998. The new regime quickly moved to end its illegal occupation of East Timor, where since 1975 it had killed over 200,000 people. India, the world's most populous democracy, celebrated fifty years of independence in 1997 and managed to preserve its democratic government. The Indian economy, now largely freed from the shackles of earlier socialist constraints, has forged ahead. The Philippines made some progress in maintaining a democratic government, but the military returned to power in Pakistan. South Korea and Taiwan have become fully democratic and continue to advance economically.

In West Asia long-term rulers died and were succeeded by their sons in Morocco, Jordan, and Syria. Younger rulers also came to power in several Gulf states. This new generation of rulers inherited authoritarian or dictatorial governments but promised both political and economic reforms. Whether they will be able to institute meaningful democratic changes remains to be seen. The Islamic Republic dominated by the clergy remained in power in Iran, but the younger generation and many women voters were particularly outspoken in their demands for reforms and more liberal social policies. Although Israel and Turkey continued their democratic institutions and Lebanon, shattered by years of civil war, reestablished an elected government, many states in the region remained under authoritarian regimes.

In Algeria, when militant Islamic groups seemed certain to win in free elections in the early 1990s, the government cancelled the elections and took firm steps to crush the

Trying to Intimidate the Peasants

The lorry [truck] with the tortured came in.... My mother recognized her son, my little brother, among them. All the tortured had no nails and they had cut off part of the soles of their feet.... They forced them to walk and put them in a line. They fell down at once. They picked them up again.... The officer ... [said] that he had to be satisfied with our lands, ... with eating bread and chile, but we mustn't let ourselves be led astray by communist ideas. Saying that all the people had access to everything, that they were content....

The officer ordered the squad to take away those who'd been "punished." ... They lined up the tortured and poured petrol on them; and then the soldiers set fire to each of them.... When the bodies began to burn they began to plead for mercy....

The officer quickly gave the order for the squad to withdraw.... They roared with laughter and cried, "Long live the Fatherland! Long live Guatemala! Long live [President] Lucas!" ...

[The victims] were Indians, our brothers.... Indians are already being killed off by malnutrition, and when our parents ... make such sacrifices so that we can grow up, then they burn us alive like that.*

The ongoing civil war in Guatemala involved relatively few combatants compared to the struggles in Nicaragua, El Salvador, and elsewhere. Nevertheless, this harrowing scene represents several major trends of the twentieth century: the divisive savagery of guerrilla warfare (many Guatemalan soldiers were Amerindians); the struggle between Marxist revolutionaries and the social and political elite (backed by the United States) in Central America; and the centuries-long suppression and exploitation of indigenous peoples throughout the Western Hemisphere by those of white and mestizo ancestry. Inequalities among peoples of different ethnic heritages persisted after the end of the Cold War. In recognition of the struggle by indigenous peoples for equality, the Nobel Peace Prize committee honored Rigoberta Menchú, an illiterate young Quiche woman who, although her father, mother, and brother had separately met gruesome deaths, had worked for peaceful reforms through publicizing the problems of her people in Guatemala and of Amerindians everywhere. Menchú has been criticized for exaggerating and possibly distorting her own history, but the struggles for equality among indigenous people, particularly in the Western Hemisphere, persist into the twenty-first century.

*Rigoberta Menchú, I, Rigoberta Menchú: An Indian Woman in Guatemala, ed. Elisabeth Bourgos-Debray, trans. Ann Wright (London: Verso, 1984), pp. 176–180.

Islamists, thereby triggering a civil war in which tens of thousands have been killed. The Egyptian government adopted similar martial laws in an increasingly futile effort to stem the tide of Islamic revolution. Meanwhile, the Islamic government in the Sudan failed to resolve the decades-long civil war in that nation and was increasingly isolated by Western nations, which opposed Sudan's militant Islamic program. Much of the mass support for Islamist movements in the Sudan, Algeria, Egypt, and many other Arab nations stemmed from the long-term systematic repression of all other political organizations and the failures of the governments to address the economic problems, job shortages, rising prices, and increasing gaps between the rich elite and the ever-growing number of poor people. The youth, many of whom were unable to find jobs, were particularly hostile to the failed policies of entrenched governments, and many turned to Islamic movements in hopes that they would be able to implement much-needed changes. Thus, if free elections were to be held in many of these nations, Islamist parties would probably win.

In sub-Saharan Africa the picture has been similarly mixed. Although over forty of the continent's fifty-two nations have made commitments to democratic reforms, dictators in many nations have simply refused to step down. For example, when their candidate failed to win in open elections, the military in Nigeria simply jailed the winner and put their own man in office. However, by the mid-1990s it was clear that the "Big Man" method of rule was on the way out as Benin, Niger, and Mali in West Africa moved toward democratic governments. By 2000, even Nigeria, which had had a long history of military coups and dictatorships, returned to elected democratic government under President Olusegun Obasanjo. Unfortunately, as noted in the previous section, ethnic and religious conflicts, sometimes resulting in massive bloodshed, impeded and sometimes destroyed the institution of democratic governments.

European nations, as previously noted, either retained or, in the aftermath of the Soviet collapse, instituted democratic governments. However, the democracies in eastern Europe and the former Soviet republics were new and often rather fragile. As in Africa and Asia, economic problems and ethnic disputes also threatened their survival.

In the Western Hemisphere, the industrialized rich nations, particularly the United States and Canada, continued their democratic traditions. But dictatorship remained in Cuba under Castro, while martial law in Peru curtailed civil liberties. Likewise, the democracies in Argentina, Colombia, and Brazil were undermined by corruption scandals, inflation, indebtedness, inefficiency, and criminal cartels that often attacked or assassinated elected officials. The events of the 1990s have demonstrated that people around the world can attain and ensure democratic governments only through constant work and vigilance.

Struggles for Gender and Social Equality

Throughout the twentieth century, women around the world have continued to struggle for equality. Just as the struggle for democracy has not made steady progress, so too women have gained a voice and political and economic power in many nations but must continue to fight for equality in others. In both rich and poor nations, women are more likely to be poor, and their work remains undervalued and underpaid. The number of women in the workforce in industrialized nations continues to grow, and more women head one-parent households. As a result, the structure of family life has changed, and more financial and social demands are being placed on women.

Similarly, children, especially in poor nations, continue to be used as cheap or free labor, receiving little education and few opportunities. As the United Nations has noted, for many children in poor nations, the "march of progress has become a retreat" as increasing numbers are starving or malnourished, uncared for, or abandoned.

Although in some traditional societies in West Africa and West Asia women enjoy more authority and economic power than outside observers have realized, they continue to face many difficulties. Most traditional cultures have bound women to home and family and have made them subordinate to fathers, brothers, or husbands. Women in poor nations are usually "the poorest of the poor" because they lack education, property rights, or opportunities for employment in the modern sectors of the economy. At the same

AP Photo/John Moore

Refugees from Ethnic Strife. Famine and starvation continue to be major problems through much of Africa. Here starving Somali children wait in line for food provided by a relief agency in the 1990s.

time, as evidence of changing times and customs, women have become presidents and prime ministers in many nations, including India, Israel, Nicaragua, and the Philippines. Benazir Bhutto in Pakistan, Tansu Ciller in Turkey, and Khaleda Zia of Bangladesh all defied stereotypes of the repressed women of Muslim societies to be elected to the highest offices in their countries. Similarly, in Iran, with a conservative Islamic government, large numbers of women are regularly elected to parliament, and many also hold high government positions. However, in most conservative Muslim nations most women remain subordinate and continue to struggle for equal rights. In contrast, with the exceptions of Great Britain and a few others such as Norway, Ireland, and Iceland, most Western nations have not elected women to their top political offices. Although half the voters around the world are women, they hold only 13 percent of the seats in the world's parliaments.

In many nations, women's rights have also been threatened by the growing popularity of militant religious movements that limit women's social and legal rights. The worst case of abuse of women occurred in Afghanistan under the Taliban regime before its ouster in 2002. Although in Algeria and elsewhere thousands of women have demanded that their rights be protected and have led public demonstrations against militant Islamic groups, they have gained little and sometimes lost ground. On the other hand, many Christian religious institutions are according women increasing power, for example, by the ordination of the first women priests in the Church of England in 1994. Most other Protestant denominations also have women ministers. Despite pressures from many Catholic men and women, however, the Pope continued to reject the ordination of women as priests in the Catholic church.

Indigenous peoples around the world, notably in Canada, the United States, Australia, and Latin and South America, have also organized to demand equal rights and economic improvements in their communities. For example, beginning in 1993 Mayan Indians in Chiapas in southern Mexico led a major rebellion demanding land and political reforms, reforms the Mexican government had promised but not delivered for over forty years. By 2000, under new political leadership, the Mexican government promised reforms and resumed negotiations with Chiapas leaders. Hence, the struggles by indigenous peoples promise to be one of the major global issues in the twenty-first century.

Technological and Economic Challenges

The twentieth century saw stunning scientific and technological advances (see Chapter 14). As the twenty-first century begins, humans continue to explore and make new discoveries in medicine, space, genetics, technology, armaments, and many other fields. In 2000 scientists announced that they had successfully mapped the human genome; this accomplishment holds the potential for future cures for a myriad of genetic diseases but also poses complex ethical questions regarding the use of such information about individuals. At the same time, confounding discoveries continue to challenge human knowledge. For example, just as smallpox, a disease that had plagued humans for centuries, was eradicated, a new, more deadly disease, AIDS (acquired immunodeficiency syndrome), appeared. It has ravaged many societies, most notably in sub-Saharan Africa, and so far no cure has been found.

High costs have also often limited scientific development. For example, the World Health Organization in 1993 estimated that it had the scientific knowledge to eliminate leprosy—a disease that has affected humans since the beginning of recorded history—but it lacked the money to institute the necessary drug treatment and caretaking programs. Similarly, just as tests were under way on promising vaccines to treat malaria, which annually kills 3 million people and infects up to 5 million people in over 100 nations, funding for the program was cut. Because leprosy and malaria generally occur among people in the poor nations of the Southern Hemisphere, the rich nations of the Northern Hemisphere have often limited money for research and efforts to prevent these deadly diseases. Likewise, many new drugs that offer some relief and prolong life for a wide variety of diseases—AIDS, for example—are too expensive for people in poor, developing nations to afford.

Although the end of the Cold War promised to provide an economic boost to the economies of the industrialized world, particularly in the United States, which had previously spent a large portion of its budget on arms, the anticipated financial gains were

LIVES AND TIMES ACROSS CULTURES

Monumental Structures

Since ancient times, rulers and governments have built monumental structures as evidence of their power, glory, and wealth. The pyramids of Egypt and Mexico and the Great Wall in China are examples of the achievements of past civilizations. During the twentieth century, first Western nations and then countries around the world have continued the tradition of constructing huge dams, bridges, and skyscrapers. Nations vie for the "bragging rights" of having the world's tallest building or largest dam.

Many nations have built massive dams to provide water for irrigation projects and increased hydroelectric power for industrialization and civilian use. When the Aswan High Dam in Egypt was built during the 1960s, it was the largest project of its type in the world. But by the 1990s, the Ataturk Dam in Turkey, the Tarbela Dam in Pakistan, and the Three Gorges Dam on the Yangtze River in China all surpassed the older Aswan High Dam in size. Although gigantic dams increase nations' economic potential, they also have enormous human and ecological costs. For example, the Three Gorges Dam will displace at least 3 million people.

Bridges and tunnels built to remove barriers to expanding transportation systems are engineering marvels of the twentieth century. Of the world's seven largest suspension bridges, all built since World War II, two are in Europe, two in the United States, one in Hong Kong, and two in Japan, including the Akashi Kaikyo, which, at 6,529 feet, is the longest of all. Seven of the world's sixteen longest railway tunnels are in Europe, two in the United States, and seven in Japan, including the Seikan, which is 33.5 miles in length.

The United States, the birthplace of the skyscraper, continues to build ever-higher buildings. Of the fourteen structures exceeding 1,000 feet (as a reference point, the Eiffel Tower is 984 feet high), eleven are in the United States. Malaysians boast that their twin towers in Kuala Lumpur are part of the world's highest mosque, several dozen stories high. Meanwhile, Morocco claims to have built one of the world's biggest mosques, while the Ivory Coast brags about having the world's largest cathedral.

In reaction to the negative results of mega-projects, proponents of smaller projects applying "appropriate technology" have argued that just because a nation can build the world's largest dam or biggest building doesn't mean that it should. Yet those on the smaller-is-better side of the argument have generally failed to dampen the human fascination with ever-bigger and more monumental construction projects.

slow to materialize. In many rich nations the gaps between the wealthy and the poor continued to widen.

The end of the Cold War did lessen the likelihood of a major nuclear war; however, more nations continued to possess and develop nuclear weapons. Israel, India, and Pakistan developed nuclear capabilities. Iran and North Korea have clandestinely developed nuclear weapons programs that threaten the stability of the region and world. While steps have been taken toward disarmament, the proliferation of nuclear weapons around the world remains a major problem. The maintenance and disposal of aging nuclear weapons pose other problems; the solutions promise to be complex and costly.

One of the most intractable problems of the contemporary era has been the ever-widening gulf between rich industrialized nations (mostly in the Northern Hemisphere) and poor agricultural nations (mostly in the Southern Hemisphere). Economists often refer collectively to these poor nations as the South or Third World and the rich nations as the North. In addition, the gap between the rich and the poor within nations continued to widen. By 1998 the income of more than $1 trillion held by the world's 225 richest people was equal to the income of the poorest 47 percent of the world's population. Three of the richest people—all Americans—had a total equal to the combined gross domestic product (GDP) of the forty-eight poorest nations.

The newly independent nations of the South face an overwhelming array of difficulties. They are almost all poor by affluent Western standards, and their fast-growing populations cause them to fall behind economically every year. While many nations of the North, including Japan, have attained zero population growth and even project future declines, the population of such nations as Kenya doubles every eighteen years. Infertile or overused soil, lack of water, diseases, and low education levels add to the economic problems.

The goal of all poor nations is economic growth, but most of them lack the requirements for industrial development. They are trapped in a cycle of poverty in which lack of capital resulting from low production leads to low savings, which in turn means little or no available capital for future development projects. As producers of raw materials, most poor nations are also limited by a global economy dominated by the nations and multinational corporations of the industrial world, which determine the prices of most raw materials.

Prime Minister Jawaharlal Nehru's comment that in economic spheres "India has to run fast so that it might stand still" continues to apply to most poor, developing nations. These nations also lack skilled technicians and are limited by a minimal infrastructure of roads and communication lines. Some have valuable natural resources, but they have often needed foreign financial and technical help to develop them. In some former colonies, the resources are owned by foreign investors who retain the bulk of the profits and send it out of the country. Some nations have attempted to redress this imbalance by expropriations, but foreign investors and industrialized nations have often retaliated by refusing to buy raw materials that have been expropriated.

Money is a key to economic development. Capital to build schools and roads and dams and factories or to hire foreign technicians is indispensable for economic growth. The major sources of needed funds are trade, foreign aid, and commercial loans; all are difficult to obtain and often come with strings attached. During the Cold War, the superpowers often insisted on alliances or the granting of facilities for military bases in exchange for economic assistance. With the end of the Cold War the remaining superpower, the United States, faced domestic economic pressures and was consequently less inclined to provide foreign aid. By 1997 the United States gave about $7 billion in nonmilitary foreign aid, less than one-tenth of 1 percent of its GDP, making it the lowest donor nation among wealthy donor states. During the 1990s, the International Monetary Fund (IMF), the World Bank, and other Western financial institutions demanded that nations privatize and create capitalist economic systems in order to receive assistance. To comply, many nations were forced to cut back on their social and welfare programs that assisted the very poor.

Other nations, such as Peru, Brazil, Mexico, Nigeria, and others in Africa, remained trapped by debts far in excess of their ability to pay. Massive debts crippled Latin American development plans and have sometimes brought actual declines in living standards. Decades earlier, M. K. Gandhi had warned that the earth "provides enough for every man's need, but not for every man's greed." Many international, nongovernmental organizations (NGOs) that provide relief assistance to the poor and needy around the world urged that far-reaching debt relief plans be adopted, but some wealthier nations and lending institutions opposed these plans.

Rapid urbanization is another global phenomenon that has caused enormous economic and social problems for many nations. Uncontrolled urban growth has reduced arable land, undermined village traditions, and lowered agricultural output. It has also produced massive slums in the cities of poor nations as brutalizing as those found in Europe a century earlier. This growth is caused by the migration of the rural poor to the cities in search of jobs. Many new nations abandoned subsistence farming in favor of cash crops such as coffee, sugar, or cocoa for export. Although this shift brought in badly needed foreign capital to finance development, government planners in these nations often did not divide this capital equitably between the urban and rural sectors. Cities, with their educated and politically influential elites, often retained the bulk of the funds needed for overall development. The shift also caused a decline in essential food production and required the import of grain and other agricultural necessities. When the prices paid for the cash crops declined, villages that had once been self-sufficient could not purchase food needed to survive.

In some nations (for example, Colombia, Peru, Afghanistan, Myanmar, and Thailand) many impoverished peasants stopped growing traditional food crops in favor of vastly more profitable illicit drugs, which were then sold on the international market for consumption in the industrialized world. Recently, newly independent republics in central Asia have also joined in this lucrative trade. The mounting production and consumption of addicting drugs—opium, heroin, and cocaine—thus became a problem for both wealthy, industrialized nations and poor nations.

A decade before the end of the Cold War, one study presciently concluded that the East-West conflict was not the fundamental division that Washington and Moscow believed it to be. The great divide, according to this view, was the conflict between North and South, between the rich nations of the Northern Hemisphere and the poor nations of the tropics and much of the Southern Hemisphere. A number of leaders, joined by theorists concerned with the future of the globe, were instrumental in effecting a new analysis of the basic economic divisions among nations.

Advocates for the poor nations insist that the poverty of the underdeveloped nations was mainly the result of Western imperial exploitation and that therefore the rich nations should make restitution by offering substantial aid for Third World development. They believe a global redistribution of wealth and technology is necessary, pointing out that while citizens of the richest nations of the world spend $9 billion a year on pet food, they refuse to increase the amounts given to the poorest of the world. Many Western liberals have accepted this analysis, but they balk at its conclusions.

The moral appeal of this argument is powerful, especially when the poverty of the Southern Hemisphere is highlighted by disasters such as the great famines that afflicted parts of Africa in the 1970s. The rich nations, however, have refused to accept the argument that Third World poverty is fundamentally rooted in imperialist exploitation. Instead, the United States and other Western nations have pressed the poor nations to follow the Western model of capitalist economic development to secure prosperity. In fact, incentives for private economic initiatives have had some effect in Third World nations since 1975.

Despite these many difficulties, some Third World nations have achieved some significant successes since independence. An example is the building of the Aswan High Dam in Egypt, which fulfilled its economic promise in providing electricity and new arable land, even though it has also had unforeseen environmental ramifications. Scientific breakthroughs in agriculture have allowed many nations to feed their rapidly growing populations. The Green Revolution in agriculture resulted in the development of new highly productive strains of rice, corn, and other grains. These have enabled India, formerly the scene of terrible famines, to become self-sufficient in grain production. By the 1990s, genetically engineered crops promised to increase productivity even further, but their use also raised environmental and health concerns. Many European nations rejected the use or sale of genetically modified crops.

Western assistance and well-conceived development policies have enabled some nations to modernize successfully. The development of export industries along the Asian Pacific rim, for example, has allowed South Korea, Taiwan, Hong Kong, and Singapore to escape the poverty that continues to plague many nations in the Southern Hemisphere. As a result, the peoples in these nations enjoy a high standard of living and a lifestyle approaching that of Western nations. They are the role models for other Asian nations aspiring to achieve the same goals.

Some nations have formed cartels, or international combines, to regulate output and prices of their raw materials. The Organization of Petroleum Exporting Countries (OPEC) successfully forced a reallocation of revenues from this vital energy source. Oil-rich nations like Saudi Arabia, Venezuela, and Nigeria were able to elevate the world price of petroleum several times over during the 1970s and early 1980s. Although oil prices remained depressed for most of the 1990s, when a barrel of oil sold for less than an equal amount of soft drinks, prices rose sharply in 2000. Some producing nations then used their petroleum revenues to finance sweeping development projects. For example, Kuwait acquired sufficient wealth to provide a national welfare system for its citizens that included free education through the university level, low-cost housing and health care, and low-interest or interest-free loans for new businesses.

Some governments, however, committed too many scarce resources to such "prestige projects" as national airlines, new lavish capital cities, or manufacturing plants—projects that offered few immediate benefits to their predominantly peasant populations. Other nations made important shifts in their priorities after the 1970s. One widely heralded new trend was the shift away from big, expensive industrial projects toward "appropriate technologies" that could be cheaply applied at the village level, using local materials and

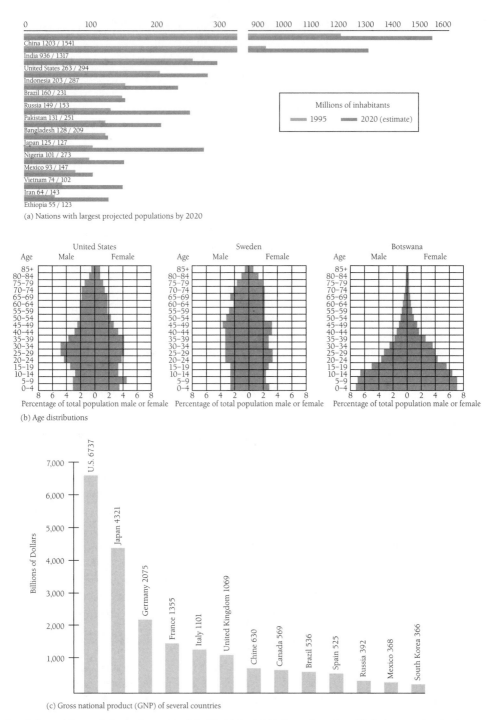

(a) Nations with largest projected populations by 2020

(b) Age distributions

(c) Gross national product (GNP) of several countries

Population and Economic Comparisons around the World. Graph (a) indicates the nations with the largest projected populations by 2020, and graph (b) shows the current age distribution of several nations. Graph (c) shows the huge differences in gross national product (GNP) among a number of countries. These are good indications of the relative economic and social welfare of some nations around the world.

LIVES AND TIMES ACROSS CULTURES

Environmental Cleanups

Growing populations and industrialization have made environmental pollution a mounting problem around the world. Cleaning up the trash of a throwaway, consumer society, in addition to its industrial waste and toxic accidents, is expensive and technologically challenging. As early as the 1950s, Rachel Carson, an early environmentalist, warned about the dangers of chemical pesticides and polluted water systems. But environmental degradation is not unique to the twentieth century.

The Roman Empire, for example, deforested large expanses of Africa and western Asia, and later Westerners have decimated or eliminated countless animal and plant species. Until the mid-nineteenth century, the Thames River, which intersects London, was used as the main sewage dump for one of the largest cities in the world. By the 1850s, the stench from the river was so terrible that members of Parliament could smell the pollution from the open windows of the Parliament building. During one hot summer when the odors were particularly bad, they authorized the construction of a sophisticated sanitation system to solve the problem.

In the mid-twentieth century, the river emptying into Lake Erie from Cleveland, Ohio, was so polluted from industrial waste that it actually caught fire! A massive cleanup effort resulted. In recent years, volunteer groups climbed Mount Everest, not in hopes of reaching the summit, but to pick up the debris discarded by hundreds of mountain climbing expeditions. Huge oil spills in Alaska, off the coast of France, and (in 2000) in Brazil have proven much more difficult to contain. Accidents at atomic energy plants at Three Mile Island in the United States and Chernobyl in the former Soviet Union underscore the dangers and long-term risks to human life and the environment posed by both military and civilian use of nuclear energy.

Driven by poverty and a desperate need for jobs, many poor countries in the global South have welcomed chemical and other industries that have been heavily regulated or outlawed in the rich northern nations. Although these industries provide much-needed jobs, they also destroy both the environment and the health of surrounding populations. For example, the shipyards where huge, outdated oceangoing vessels are dismantled along a six-mile stretch of beach at Alang, India, are one of the most polluted spots on earth. Environmentalists, many from Europe, have called for stricter regulations or the outright banning of such operations. Governments and industrialists in poor nations reply that they provide services that are prohibitively expensive in the West and that poor workers prefer the risks of long-term health problems and pollution to the starvation of their families. Thus the management of human and industrial waste remains a most daunting challenge of the twenty-first century.

requiring little specialized training or expensive repairs. Support for low-impact agriculture or "people-centered" development projects increased. Still other nations continue to ignore the consequences and to indulge in grandiose plans to construct mammoth engineering projects. For example, for China to construct the world's largest dam—the Three Gorges, along the Yangtze River—large areas must be flooded and more than 3 million people must be moved from their homes. Another example is Libya's Grand Mamade River project to construct five hundred miles of pipeline to take water pumped from beneath the Sahara to the Mediterranean coast. In India, work on a huge dam project on the Narmada River was delayed but not canceled despite massive opposition by local peasants and the Japanese government's concern over providing funding for a project that might be damaging to the environment. Critics of these projects argued that they were out of scale with the economic needs of the people they were supposed to benefit and that, furthermore, they posed severe threats to the world's delicate ecological balance. Debates over the relative merits of development projects are legal in democratic India, but they are outlawed in China, where opposition to government programs is forbidden.

From the 1980s, many nations shifted away from government-sponsored economic projects toward entrepreneurial initiatives by private citizens, while central planning gave way to local or grassroots planning. Other new programs earmarked aid for the poorest classes and guaranteed women equal opportunities in education and new jobs. These trends have offered many people some hope for the future.

Environmental Challenges

By 2000 the world's population exceeded 6 billion and was expected to double within the next fifty years. The world now confronts a myriad of complex ecological crises, many of them related to this population growth. The population explosion, particularly evident in nations in the South, has placed sometimes intolerable strains on many of the earth's resources. Whereas Western nations must cope with problems and expenses associated with aging populations, over half the populations in the nations of the South are under the age of twenty-four. Nations with predominantly young populations of a reproductive age are especially afflicted with rapid population growth, high unemployment, and the need for education. As increasing numbers of people in poor nations either flee the countryside in search of better lives in urban areas or emigrate, often illegally, to seek jobs in richer nations, the infrastructures of many cities—for example, Mexico City and Cairo—are strained to the breaking point. In the 1950s Cairo had a population of 1 million; by 2000 its population had soared to over 15 million. In addition to massive social dislocations and a frequent drop in agricultural productivity, urbanization also takes away land from agriculture, diverts water supplies, and contributes to further ecological problems.

In spite of technological advances and increased production levels, the world's 6 billion plus people are consuming increasing percentages of finite resources, such as fossil fuels and foodstuffs, while also contributing to more pollution of the earth's atmosphere, soils, oceans, and fresh water supplies. The quest of people in more countries to better their standard of living places a strain on natural resources. For example, China, where growing industries have improved the living standards of many, has become a huge importer of petroleum and metals, but its factories and dams are causing irreparable environmental degradation. From 1970 to 2000 humans were estimated to have destroyed more than 30 percent of the natural world. The depletion of freshwater resources and global warming are particularly worrisome results. Many of these ecological problems are transnational in nature and can be resolved only through international cooperation on a massive scale. However, nation-states, which emphasize their own self-interest, have often been unwilling or ill-equipped to attack global crises of pollution.

By the 1980s scientists were warning that chemical wastes spewed into the atmosphere might destroy the ozone layer or might also cause a dangerous warming of the earth—the so-called greenhouse effect—that might, for example, turn the American Midwest into a vast dust bowl and cause rising sea levels to flood the eastern and gulf coasts. Toxic pollutants have already caused acid rains, which have damaged large tracts of forests in Canada, Germany, Poland, Russia, and other nations.

Meanwhile, burgeoning populations needing agricultural land, firewood, and money from valuable timber have deforested large areas of jungles and forests, thereby creating new arid, or desert, regions. The cutting down of the tropical Amazonian rain forest at the rate of a football field every five seconds could threaten climatic conditions and the quality of fresh air throughout the Southern and Northern Hemispheres. Massive destruction of rain forests has caused the extinction of many species of plant and animal life and threatens the survival of many others. Even the disposal of garbage for 6 billion people, particularly the heavy consumers of the industrialized world, has become a major problem.

Industrialization and lack of controls over multinational corporations also have contributed to several major ecological disasters in the late twentieth century. Nuclear accidents at Three Mile Island in the United States and Chernobyl in the Soviet Union demonstrated the very real dangers of nuclear energy and have caused many to question the desirability of further proliferation of nuclear reactors. Similarly, the chemical disaster at Bhopal, India, where toxic gas killed and maimed thousands, demonstrated the dangers of such chemicals. Two decades after that accident, survivors continue to suffer, and experts have predicted that people of the affected area will continue to be afflicted with higher rates of cancer for several more decades. Many poor nations are particularly vulnerable to these types of industrial accidents; in their desperate search for outside investment, they have permitted Western corporations to establish plants to produce materials now outlawed in many wealthy nations. Massive oil spills from huge tankers transporting petroleum around the oceans of the world have also resulted in pollution that threatens wildlife and the ecological balance in the Persian Gulf and along the coastlines of Europe, the Gulf of Mexico, and Alaska.

Recognizing these problems, nations have held international conferences and adopted policies to alleviate some of the worst environmental dangers. In 1987, forty-six nations signed a pact to protect the ozone layer by reducing the use of ozone-depleting chlorofluorocarbons. Some critics, however, worried that the measures taken were too little, too late, and they sought additional international legislation to control and limit the use of such materials. In 1992 representatives from around the world met at an "earth summit" in Rio de Janeiro in Brazil to devise solutions to these environmental challenges. Although sharp disagreements arose between the wealthy, industrialized nations, which opposed programs that might threaten their comfortable lifestyles, and the poor nations, mostly in the Southern Hemisphere, they did agree to consider environmental issues in future development plans. Although an international agreement regarding global warming—believed to be largely caused by increased carbon dioxide levels from burning fossil fuels—was reached in 1998, the United States, one of the largest polluters, was reluctant to address the problem. To protect the environment for future generations, northern nations will have to alter their wasteful consumption, and southern nations will have to stem their rapid population growth.

Many individual nations have enacted laws to control pollution and the dumping of toxic materials. Japan and the Netherlands led the way in recycling waste material. In Israel, highly efficient irrigation systems brought substantial savings in water usage, and Kuwait instituted a technologically complex but efficient system to desalinate seawater, which, however, was largely destroyed during the Gulf War. The use of advanced technology and hydroponics (using water for growing foodstuffs) has increased agricultural output in such nations as the Maldive Islands in the Indian Ocean and Japan. Kenya adopted a national system of soil and water conservation, demonstrating that even a relatively poor nation with limited resources can make impressive strides toward controlling environmental damage. All peoples now face the necessity of protecting the global environment, for as former President Jimmy Carter pointed out, "We're all in the same boat." Protecting the fragile environment against the onslaughts of billions of people and growing industrialization is one of the major challenges of the twenty-first century.

Cultural Interactions and Tensions

At the beginning of the twenty-first century, the world is linked together in a vast network of communication systems; the interaction and consequent transformation of societies have resulted not only in profound changes but also in mounting tensions, for example, between those struggling to develop modern secular societies and those adhering to traditional religious values. After World War II, many Western experts predicted that religious values would decline as more societies adopted secular, Western culture. This had been the case in Western Europe. People around the world want Western technology and consumer goods and values, but many also are seeking to avoid the Western problems of drug and alcohol abuse, sexual immorality, divorce, and changing family structures. Many also believe that secularization, with the loss of religious commitment, has been the root of these social problems.

Predictions regarding the decline of religion around the world have proved false. During the 1990s, religious revivals occurred around the globe. Following the lead of the religiously led Iranian revolution, many militant Muslims in other nations are pushing for a return to government under Islamic law. Similarly, some Orthodox Jews advocate rule by Judaic law in Israel. Some fundamentalist Christian groups in the United States have campaigned for a return to religious values and legal restrictions to control personal lives, schools, films, the media, and the press. Religious and sectarian differences have contributed to ongoing violent struggles in nations as diverse as India, Lebanon, Indonesia, Sri Lanka, and Northern Ireland. In the former Soviet republics, decades of antireligious policies failed to stamp out Christianity or Islam, and both experienced a revival of adherents following the collapse of the Soviet Union. Unfortunately, religious differences continue to cause wars among people of differing belief systems. Sectarian struggles in the Balkans, Lebanon, and Northern Ireland have led to thousands of deaths and untold property damage.

Religious zealots in many societies have also sought to control culture and the arts. The authors Salman Rushdie and Naguib Mahfouz were condemned by some Muslim clerics for their allegedly anti-Islamic novels, and some Muslim zealots even put a price on Rushdie's head. Similarly, militant Christians condemn many popular music forms, including rap and heavy metal, and call for strict censorship in the electronic media. Conservative religious activists, even in generally open, secular societies such as Great Britain and the United States, support government censorship or limitations of government funding for works of art they deem blasphemous or pornographic.

The interlocking of global communication systems with broadcasting by satellite, cable television, high-technology telephone and facsimile (fax) systems, e-mail, and computers has made cultural exchanges between people and nations easier than ever. Conversely, authoritarian regimes, for example, in China and Iran, have found it increasingly difficult to control their citizens' access to information. As people of different cultures

© Paul Almasy/Corbis

The Persistence of Religion. Although nations around the world have sought to modernize and adapt to new technologies, religion continues to play a major role in the lives of people. In many traditional societies, religious instruction forms the basis of the educational curriculum. Here a young female student in Nigeria reads the Qur'an aloud as her classmates look on.

intermingle and assimilate other types of music, art, designs, and performing arts, new art forms and modes of expression are constantly emerging. This fusion of cultural traditions is nowhere more apparent than in modern music: around the world, musicians are adapting African, Latin American, and Western music of all types to create constantly changing and evolving music. Similarly, writers such as Naguib Mahfouz (an Egyptian), Derek Walcott (from St. Lucia in the Caribbean), Gabriel Garcia Márquez (a Colombian), and Wole Soyinka (from Nigeria)—all Nobel Prize winners—are indebted to Western literary forms but adapt them to their own cultures.

In popular culture, millions around the world enjoy U.S. movie and television productions such as *Star Wars* or MTV. In Russia, Mexican soap operas are enormously popular, while the Chinese demand more popular music and television shows from Hong Kong and Taiwan. Indian movies made by the hundreds every year in "Bollywood" (Bombay, the center of India's movie industry) are popular throughout South and Southeast Asia. Likewise, Japanese-manufactured Nintendo video games fascinate young people from Tokyo to Kansas City to Riyadh, Saudi Arabia. Some nations, however, have sought to limit cultural diffusion and assimilation. For example, France sought to reduce the number of U.S. films shown and tried to stop the entry of English words into the French vocabulary. Such attempts by governments to limit or reduce cultural interactions are constantly thwarted by technological advances and the demands of citizens. Clearly, the interactions of cultures and religions will continue, and with expanding technology and global communications, new forms will emerge to amaze, delight, or enrage audiences around the world.

Summary and Comparisons

Between 1989 and 1991, Germany was reunified and the nations of eastern Europe broke away from Soviet domination, privatized their economies, and established closer ties with the richer western European nations.

Mikhail Gorbachev tried to preserve the Soviet system through reforms but succeeded only in angering and scaring many Communist party hard-liners, who launched an abortive coup against him in 1991. In the ensuing backlash against the Communist party, Gorbachev lost control of the political system and was forced to resign. As the Soviet Union collapsed, many ethnic groups, including Kazakhs, Armenians, and Ukrainians, demanded and attained national independence. Some then formed the loose, decentralized Commonwealth of Independent States. Economic reforms stressing privatization put the new Commonwealth on the road to capitalism.

There were, however, social and economic costs. Throughout eastern Europe and the former Soviet republics, prices soared and many people lost both their jobs and the safety net of social welfare programs. Crime and social strife, particularly among differing ethnic and religious groups, became more widespread.

Although western Europe continued to move toward greater economic and political unity, many social problems remained unresolved. Ethnic rivalries ignited full-scale war in the former Yugoslavia. Czechoslovakia split along ethnic lines, while Germany, France, and other nations saw an increase in racism, including anti-Semitism, India was threatened with dissolution along ethnic and religious lines. Similar racial and ethnic hatreds also posed problems in the United States.

Political upheaval plagued West Asia and southern Africa. A series of wars led to Israeli victories and expansion of territory but failed to resolve the continuing struggle for Palestinian self-determination. Negotiations between the Israelis and Palestinians in the 1990s led to mutual recognition, but not to an independent Palestinian nation. Consequently, violence in that region continues.

In South Africa, the white minority government and the African National Congress cooperated to dismantle apartheid and to hold open elections based on the principle of one person, one vote. Nelson Mandela won the presidency and moved to lessen old racial tensions and economic disparities between whites and blacks. But in states neighboring South Africa, armed civil strife disrupted and destabilized elected governments.

The progress of democracy around the world met with mixed success. Dictatorships continued in China, much of West Asia, and parts of South America. On the other hand, the fall of the Soviet Empire brought democracies, though sometimes fragile ones, to eastern Europe and the former Soviet republics. Democracy began to grow in much of sub-Saharan Africa and South America as well.

The struggle for gender equality and human rights for minorities and indigenous peoples continues around the world. Women are now a significant political force in many

CHRONOLOGY

1945	
	First Arab-Israeli War
	Second Arab-Israeli War
1965	Arab-Israeli Six Days' War
	Continuing struggle against apartheid in South Africa
1970	Women's liberation movement
	Fourth Arab-Israeli War
	Iranian Revolution: Ayatolla Khomeini
1980	Fifth Arab-Israeli War
	The computer age
	Ecological issues: global warming, acid rain, toxic waste; Green movements
	Crisis in the Persian Gulf
	Reunification of Germany
	Collapse of the Soviet Union
	Boris Yeltsin; Commonwealth of Independent States
	Ongoing civil conflict in northern Ireland
	Israeli-Palestinian accords
	Ethnic warfare in Bosnia
	Nelson Mandela elected president of Union of South Africa
1995	Ongoing ethnic strife: Balkans, India, central Africa
	Islamist movements
	Economic prosperity and recessions
1998	
2001	9/11 terrorist attack on the World Trade Center and Pentagon
2002	U.S.-led overthrow of Taliban regime in Afghanistan
2003	U.S.-led war topples Saddam Hussein in Iraq
2004	

areas of the world and have held the highest offices in numerous nations, but they still suffer economic and social discrimination in much of the world. Likewise, minorities such as the Kurds in Turkey and Iran, Bosnians, Amerindians, and African Americans still seek full equality and civil rights.

In many poor Asian and African nations, economic growth has come slowly, in part because these nations lack everything from adequate health care and education to basic industries; they also usually have poor management and low productivity in both agriculture and manufacturing. Most are also heavily indebted to Western banks. Technological advances like the Green Revolution and genetically altered seeds have rekindled hopes for the future but have also raised fears about negative environmental and long term impacts.

An ever-growing global population has also strained the planet's finite resources. In the early twenty-first century, nations everywhere face ecological crises and problems of pollution. Solutions to these complex problems remain elusive.

Finally, the rapidity of social and cultural transformations has heightened tensions between those advocating liberalization and further change and those championing conservative values and religious traditions. Eagerness to acquire modern technology and consumer goods has not altogether supplanted traditional belief systems and cultural values.

Religion remains a compelling force around the world; clashes between secularists and fervent believers have been frequent and sometimes violent. Sophisticated communication systems and advanced technology allow people to learn about other societies and sometimes to adopt their values by fusing many cultural values and styles into new forms. Rapid communication and interactions among peoples around the globe hold the promise of solutions to the economic, developmental, and environmental challenges of the twenty-first century. It remains to be seen whether we have sufficient determination to meet those challenges.

Selected Sources

Items indicated with an asterisk (*) are available in paperback.

*Aung San Suu Kyi. *Freedom from Fear and Other Writings.* 1991. The Burmese political leader and Nobel laureate pleads for democracy.

Banks, O. *Faces of Feminism.* 1982. A comparison of the U.S. and British feminist movements. Should be read in conjunction with G. W. Lapidus, *Women, Work and Family in the Soviet Union.*

Brzezinski, Zbigniew. *The Choice: Global Domination or Global Leadership.* 2004. President Carter's national security adviser discusses the U.S. role in post-9/11 geopolitics.

*Caplan, Richard, and John Feffer, eds. *Europe's New Nationalism: States and Minorities in Conflict.* 1996. Useful collection of essays on complex issues.

Carrère d'Encausse, Hélène. *The End of the Soviet Empire.* 1993. A scholarly account of various nationalist movements within the former Soviet Union, with an emphasis on the tensions between the Russians and the peoples of their former empire.

Chang, Jung. *Wild Swans: Three Daughters of China.* 1991. On three generations of Chinese women during the twentieth century.

*Critchfield, Richard. *The Golden Bowl Be Broken: Peasant Life in Four Cultures.* Reprinted 1988. Insightful look at daily life in Third World peasant societies.

"A Day With the President." A highly personal 56-minute video of Nelson Mandela as president of South Africa. (Available through First Run/Icarus Films.)

*Filipovic, Zlata. *Zlata's Diary: A Child's Life in Sarajevo.* 1994. A moving account of survival under siege, comparable to Anne Frank's World War II wartime diary. Also on cassette.

*Fisher, Sydney N., and William Ochsenwald. *The Middle East: A History.* 5th ed. Vol. 2. 1997. Readable text with good overview of contemporary West Asia.

*Harrison, Paul. *The Greening of Africa; Breaking Through in the Battle for Land and Food.* 1987. Expert analysis of major development problems and possible solutions.

Havel, Václav. *Open Letters: Selected Writings, 1964–1990*. 1991. Personal observations on the changing political scene by the noted Czech writer and politician.

*Head, Bessie. *A Woman Alone: Autobiographical Writings*. 1990. A personal account of struggles by a powerful South African writer.

"In My Country: An International Perspective on Gender." 1993. This 91-minute video focuses on the problems of gender relations and families and features interviews with experts and everyday people from around the world. (Available through Insight Media.)

*Ishinomori. *Shotaro*. 1988. Amusing and informative study of the Japanese economy in comic book format.

Iwao, Sumiko. *The Japanese Woman: Traditional Image and Changing Reality*. 1993. Good discussion of women and gender roles in Japan since 1945.

Liu, Pin-yen. *A Higher Kind of Loyalty: A Memoir of China's Foremost Journalist*. 1990. The memoir of a loyal Communist turned dissident.

Mama Benz: An African Market Woman. This 49-minute video offers a fascinating look at strong, powerful female merchants in West Africa.

Mazrui, Ali A. *Cultural Forces in World Politics*. 1990. Mazrui argues that Western attitudes toward the Third World have been a "dialogue of the deaf." Discusses Islam, Négritude, traditional societies, and gender issues.

*Rashid, Ahmed. *Jihad: The Rise of Militant Islam in Central Asia*. 2002. Focuses on five of Afghanistan's neighbors: Kazakhstan, Kyrgyzstan, Tajikistan, Turkmenistan, and Uzbekistan.

"A Republic Gone Mad: Rwanda 1894–1994." A 60-minute video that puts crises in Rwanda and central Africa in a historical perspective. (Available through First Run/Icarus Films.)

"Rigoberta Menchú: Broken Silence." This 25-minute film presents the Nobel Prize winner's reflections on the struggles of indigenous peoples for equality. Menchú is also an outspoken advocate for women's rights.

*Smith, Charles. *Palestine and the Arab-Israeli Conflict*. 5th ed. 2004. Highly readable text on the history of this long-lasting conflict.

The South Center: An Interdependent World. 1993. Scholars from around the world discuss North/South relations and the issues of poverty, environmental crises, and political instability.

*Sutcliffe, Bob. *Imperialism after Imperialism*. 1997. Sutcliffe reexamines arguments that imperialism has ended and places the discussion within the context of the internationalization of global economies and the issues of feminism, environmental concerns, and social change.

"Understanding Northern Ireland." This 60-minute film traces the ongoing conflict among Protestants, Catholics, and the British in Northern Ireland. [Films for the Humanities.]

Wei, Jingsheng. *The Courage to Stand Alone*. 1997. China's famous dissident speaks out against the government dictatorship.

Weizsäcker, Ernest U. von. *Earth Politics*. 1993. Assesses the 1992 earth summit in Rio de Janeiro with discussion of problems and strategies for the future.

White, Stephen. *After Gorbachev*. 4th ed. 1994. An overview of the dramatic changes that ushered in the collapse of the Soviet Union.

"Women and Islam." A 30-minute video that describes gender issues in the Muslim world, with sections on marriage and women's rights. (Available through Films for the Humanities and Sciences.)

"Yugoslavia: Origins of a War." Using archival material and firsthand footage, this 58-minute video traces the causes of the breakup of Yugoslavia and the ensuing ethnic warfare. (Available through First Run/Icarus Films.)

 Additional resources, exercises, and Internet links related to this chapter are available at the Book Companion Web site: http://history.wadsworth.com/upshurcompact4/

Romanizing Chinese Words

Two systems are in current use for romanizing Chinese words. The Wade-Giles system has been in use longer than the Pinying system. Scholars of China use both equally. Newspapers tend to use the Pinying system for the People's Republic and the Wade-Giles system for the Republic of China. This book follows the Wade-Giles system for pre-1949 China and the Pinying system for the post-1949 era. The following table equates some of the Wade-Giles and other conventional spellings with the Pinying spelling used in this text. Since not all words differ in the two systems, only those words that do are included.

Wade-Giles	Pinying	Wade-Giles	Pinying
Canton	Guangzhou	Kwangsi	Guangxi
Ch'an	Chan	Kwangtung	Guangdong
Chao	Zhao	Lao Tzu	Laozi
Chekiang	Zhejiang	Li Po	Li Bo
Chengchow	Zhengzhou	Loyang	Luoyang
Ch'ien-lung	Qianlong	Mao Tse-tung	Mao Zedong
Ch'in	Qin	Nanking	Nanjing
Ching-te Cheng	Jingdezhen	Peking	Beijing
Ch'ing	Qing	Shang-ti	Shangdi
Chou	Zhou	Shantung	Shandong
Chu Hsi	Zhu Xi	Shansi	Shaanxi
Chu Yuan-chang	Zhu Yuanzhang	Shensi	Shanxi
Chungking	Chongqing	Sian	Xi'an
Fukien	Fujian	Sinkiang	Xinjiang
Hangchow	Hangzhou	Sung	Song
Honan	Henan	Szechuan	Sichuan
Hopei	Hebei	T'ang	Tang
Hsiung-nu	Xiongnu	T'ang T'ai-tsung	Tang Taizong
Hung-wu	Hongwu	Taoism	Daoism
K'ang-hsi	Kangxi	Tatung	Dadong
Kansu	Gansu	Tien	Tian
Kiangsi	Jiangxi	Tz'u-hsi	Cixi
Kiangsu	Jiangsu	Wu-ti	Wudi
K'ung Fu-tzu	Kong Fuzi	Yang-tze	Yangzi
Kuomintang	Guomindang	Yung-cheng	Yongzheng

Glossary

Abbasid dynasty   The caliphs resident in Baghdad from the 700s C.E. until 1252.

Abbot/abbess   The male/female head of a monastery/nunnery.

Absolutism   A form of government in which the sovereign power or ultimate authority rested in the hands of a monarch who claimed to rule by divine right and was therefore responsible only to God.

Abstractionism   A twentieth-century school of painting that rejected traditional representation of external nature and objects.

Academy   The school founded by Plato; Aristotle is its most famous student.

Actium, Battle of   The decisive 31 B.C.E. battle in the struggle between Octavian Caesar and Marc Antony, in which Octavian's victory paved the way for the Principate.

Agincourt   The great victory of the English over the French in 1415, during the Hundred Years' War.

Agricultural revolution   The substitution of farming for hunting and gathering as the primary source of food by a people.

Ahimsa   The Buddhist doctrine of not harming other living creatures.

A'in Jalut   A decisive thirteenth-century battle in which the Egyptians turned back the Mongols and prevented them from invading North Africa.

Ajanta Caves   Caves in central India that are the site of marvelous early frescoes inspired by Buddhism.

Allah   Arabic title of the one God.

Alliance of 1778   A diplomatic treaty under which France aided the American revolutionaries in their war against Britain.

Anabaptists   Radical Protestant reformers who were condemned by both Lutherans and Catholics.

Analects   The body of writing containing conversations between Confucius and his disciples that preserves his worldly wisdom and pragmatic philosophies.

Anarchism   A political theory that sees all large-scale government as inherently evil and embraces small self-governing communities.

ANC   The African National Congress. Founded in 1912, it was the beginning of political activity by South African blacks. Banned by politically dominant European whites in 1960, it was not officially "unbanned" until 1990. It is now the official majority party of the South African government.

Ancien régime   The "old government"; the pre-Revolutionary style of government and society in eighteenth-century France.

Angkor Wat   A great Buddhist temple in central Cambodia, dating to the twelfth-century C.E. Khmer Empire.

Anglo-French entente   The diplomatic agreement of 1904 that ended British-French enmity and was meant as a warning to Germany.

Anglo-Russian agreement   The equivalent to the Anglo-French entente between Britain and Russia; signed in 1907.

Animism   A religious belief imputing spirits to natural forces and objects.

Anschluss   The German term for the 1938 takeover of Austria by Nazi Germany.

Anthropology   The study of humankind as a particular species.

Antigonid kingdom   One of the Hellenistic successor kingdoms to Alexander the Great's empire.

Anti-Semitism   Hostility toward or discrimination against Jews.

Apartheid   The Afrikaans term for segregation of the races in South Africa.

Appeasement   The policy of trying to avoid war by giving Hitler what he demanded in the 1930s; supported by many in France and Britain.

Archaeology   The study of cultures through the examination of artifacts.

Arianism   A Christian heresy that taught that Jesus was inferior to God. Though condemned by the Council of Nicaea in 325, Arianism was adopted by many of the Germanic peoples who entered the Roman Empire over the next centuries.

Aristocracy   A social governing class based on preeminence of birth.

Arthasastra   An early Indian political treatise that sets forth many fundamental aspects of the relationship of rulers and their subjects. It has been compared to Machiavelli's well-known book The Prince and has provided principles upon which many aspects of social organization have developed in the region.

Aryans   A nomadic pastoral people from Eurasia who invaded the Indus Valley and other regions in about 1500 B.C.E.

Ashikaga clan   A noble Japanese family that controlled political power as shoguns from the 1330s to the late 1500s.

Atatürk, Mustafa Kemal   The "father of the Turks"; a World War I officer who led Turkey into the modern age and replaced the Ottoman Empire in the 1920s.

Audiencia   The colonial council that supervised military and civil government in Latin America.

August 1991 coup   The attempt by hard-line Communists to oust Gorbachev and reinstate the Communist party's monopoly on power in the Soviet Union.

Ausgleich of 1867   The compromise between the Austro-Germans and Magyars that created the "Dual Monarchy" of Austria-Hungary.

Austro-Prussian War   The conflict for mastery of Germany won by the Bismarck-led Prussian kingdom in 1866.

Authoritarian state   A state that has a dictatorial government and some other trappings of a totalitarian state but does not have the same degree of control of the populace and the economy.

Avesta   The holy book of the Zoroastrian religion.

Axis Pact   The treaty establishing a military alliance between the governments of Germany, Italy, and Japan; signed in 1936.

Axum   The center of the ancient Ethiopian kingdom.

Aztec   Last of a series of Amerindian masters of central Mexico prior to the arrival of the Spanish; developers of the great city of Tenochtitlán (Mexico City).

Babylon   Most important of the later Mesopotamian urban centers.

Babylonian Captivity   The transportation of many Jews to exile in Babylon as hostages for the good behavior of the remainder; occurred in the sixth century B.C.E.

Bakufu   The military-style government of the Japanese shogun.

Balance of power   A distribution of power among several states such that no single nation can dominate the others.

Balfour Declaration   The 1917 public statement that Britain was committed to the foundation of a "Jewish homeland" in Palestine after World War I.

Bantu   A language spoken by many peoples of central and eastern Africa; by extension, the name of the speakers.

Barbarian   Greek for " incomprehensible speaker"; uncivilized.

Baruch Plan   An idea put forth early in the Cold War in which all countries would pledge not to make atomic bombs and to allow international inspections; it was rejected by the Soviet Union.

Battle of the Nations   Decisive defeat of the army of Napoleon by combined forces of Prussia, Austria, and Russia in October 1813 at Leipzig in eastern Germany.

Bay of Pigs invasion   A failed U.S.-backed invasion of Cuba by anti-Castro exiles in 1961.

Bedouin   The nomadic inhabitants of interior Arabia; they were the original converts to Islam.

Benedictine Rule   The rules of conduct given to his monastic followers by the sixth-century Christian saint Benedict.

Berbers   Pre-Arab settlers of northern Africa and the Sahara.

Berlin blockade   The 1948–1949 attempt to squeeze the Western allies out of occupied Berlin by the USSR; it failed because of the successful Berlin Airlift of food and supplies.

Berlin Wall   The ten-foot-high concrete wall and "death zone" erected by the communist East Germans in 1961 to prevent further illegal emigration to the West.

Bhagavad-Gita   The best-known part of the *Mahabharata,* it details the proper relations between the castes and the triumph of the spirit over material creation.

Big bang theory   The theory that the cosmos was created by an enormous explosion billions of years ago.

Bill of Rights of 1689   A law enacted by Parliament that established specific rights of English citizens and placed certain limits on royal powers.

Black Death   An epidemic of bubonic plague that ravaged most of Europe in the mid-fourteenth century.

Blitzkrieg ("lightning war")   A war conducted with great speed and force, as in Germany's advance into Poland at the beginning of World War II.

Bodhisattva   In Buddhism, an enlightened being that helps others to reach *nirvana.*

Boer War/Boers   The armed conflict, 1899–1902, between the Boers (the Dutch colonists who had been the earliest European settlers of South Africa) and their British overlords; won by the British after a hard fight.

Bohemia   Traditional name of the Czech Republic, dating from the tenth century C.E.

Bolsheviks   The minority of Russian Marxists led by Lenin who seized dictatorial power in the October Revolution of 1917.

Boule   The 500-member council that served as a legislature in ancient Athens.

Bourgeoisie   The urban middle class; usually commercial or professional.

Boxer Rebellion   A desperate revolt by peasants against the European "foreign devils" who were carving up China in the new imperialism of the 1890s; it was quickly suppressed by Western powers.

Brahman   In Hindu theology, the title of the impersonal spirit responsible for all creation.

Brahmin   The caste of priests, originally found among the Aryans and later spread to the Indians generally.

Bread and circuses   The social policy initiated by Augustus Caesar aimed at gaining the support of the Roman proletariat by supplying them with essential food and entertainment.

Brest-Litovsk Treaty of 1918   The separate peace between the Central Powers and Lenin's government that took Russia out of World War I.

Brezhnev Doctrine   The doctrine, enunciated by Leonid Brezhnev, that the Soviet Union had a right to intervene if socialism was threatened in another socialist state; used to justify the use of Soviet troops in Czechoslovakia in 1968.

Bronze Age   The period when bronze tools and weapons replaced stone among a given people; generally about 3000–1000 B.C.E.

Burning of the books   China's Legalist first emperor attempted to eliminate Confucian ethics by destroying Confucian writings and prohibiting its teaching.

Bushido   The samurai code of honor.

Byzantine empire   The continuation of the Roman imperium in its eastern provinces until its fall to the Muslim Turks in 1453.

Caliph   Arabic for successor (to Muhammad); leader of Islam.

Carthage   Rival in the Mediterranean basin to Rome in the last centuries B.C.E.; it was destroyed by Rome.

Caste   A socioeconomic group that is entered by birth and can only rarely be exited from.

Caudillo   A chieftain (that is, a local or regional strongman) in Latin America.

Central Intelligence Agency   A Cold War creation of the United States, this organization, among other activities, sought to overthrow or destabilize countries deemed too receptive to communism.

Chaeronea   The battle in 338 B.C.E. in which Philip of Macedon decisively defeated the Greeks and brought them under Macedonian rule.

Ch'an Buddhism   Founded by the semilegendary Indian monk Bodhidharma, this Chinese branch of Buddhism (Zen in Japan) focused on meditation and an intuitive understanding of reality.

Chartism   A British working-class movement of the 1840s that attempted to obtain labor and political reform.

Chavin   Early Peruvian Amerindian culture.

Cheka   An abbreviation for the first Soviet secret police.

Chichén Itzá   Site in the Yucatan of Mayan urban development in the tenth to thirteenth centuries.

Ch'ing dynasty   The Manchu dynasty that ruled China from 1644 to 1911.

City of God, The   Written by Augustine in the fifth century C.E., it calls for ultimate allegiance to God, not to earthly rulers.

Civil Code of 1804   Napoleonic law code reforming and centralizing French legal theory and procedures.

Civil constitution of the clergy   1791 law in revolutionary France attempting to force French Catholics to support the new government and bring clergy into conformity with it.

Civil rights   The basic rights of citizens, including equality before the law, freedom of speech and press, and freedom from arbitrary arrest.

Civilization   A complex, developed culture.

Code Napoleon   A system of laws promulgated by Napoleon that upheld many of the ideals of the French Revolution while continuing the subjugation of women and the suppression of unions.

Cold War   The ideological conflict between the Soviet Union and the United States after World War II.

Collective farms   Large farms created in the Soviet Union by Stalin by combining many small holdings into one large farm worked by the peasants under government supervision.

Command economy   The name given to communist economic planning in the Soviet Union after 1929.

Committee of Public Safety   The executive body of the Reign of Terror during the French Revolution.

Commonwealth of Independent States (CIS)   The loose confederation of eleven of the fifteen former Soviet republics formed after the breakup of the Soviet Union in 1991.

Congress of Vienna   A meeting of the major and minor powers of Europe in 1815, called to decide the fate of France and the future of Europe after the defeat of Napoleon. It developed informal structures that kept war in

Europe at low levels throughout much of the nineteenth century.

Conquistadores   Title given to sixteenth-century Spanish explorers/colonizers in the New World.

Conservatism   An ideology based on tradition and social stability that favored the maintenance of established institutions, organized religion, and obedience to authority and resisted change, especially abrupt change.

Consuls   Chief executives of the Roman republic; chosen annually.

Contras   One side of the 1980s civil war in Nicaragua, it was composed in large part of people loyal to the former dictator Somoza; they fought against the Sandinistas.

Coral Sea, Battle of   The naval engagement in the southwest Pacific during World War II that ended the Japanese invasion threat to Australia.

Corpus Juris   "Body of the law"; the final Roman law code, produced under the emperor Justinian in the mid-500s C.E.

Cottage industry   A system of textile manufacturing in which spinners and weavers worked at home in their cottages using raw materials supplied to them by capitalist entrepreneurs.

Creationism   A cosmology based on Christian tradition that holds that the universe was created by an intelligent Supreme Being.

Creole   Term used to refer to whites born in Latin America.

Crimean War   Conflict fought in the Crimea between Russia on one side and Britain, France, and Turkey on the other, from 1853 to 1856; ended by the Peace of Paris with a severe loss in Russian prestige.

Cultural relativism   The belief that no culture is superior to another because culture is a matter of custom, not reason, and derives its meaning from the group holding it.

Culture   The human-created environment of a group.

Cuneiform   Mesopotamian wedge-shaped writing begun by the Sumerians.

Cynicism   A Hellenistic philosophy stressing poverty and simplicity.

Daimyo   Japanese nobles who controlled feudal domains under the shogun.

Dasa   Sanskrit term for "slave" used by Aryans; refers to the dark skin color of Indus Valley peoples.

D Day   June 6, 1944; the invasion of France from the English Channel by combined British and American forces.

Declaration of Independence   The 1776 document approved by the Continental Congress in Britain's American colonies; it asserts the colonies' independence from Britain and provides a logical explanation for doing so.

Declaration of the Rights of Man and Citizen   The epoch-making manifesto issued by the French Third Estate delegates at Versailles in 1789.

Decolonization   The process of becoming free of colonial status and achieving statehood; occurred in most of the world's colonies between 1947 and 1962.

Deductive reasoning   Arriving at truth by applying a general law or proposition to a specific case.

Delian League   An empire of satellite Greek states under Athens in the fifth century B.C.E.

Democracy   A system of government in which the majority of voters decides issues and policy.

Demographic transition   The passage of a large group of people from traditional high birthrates to lower ones, induced by better survival rates among children.

Depression   A severe, protracted economic downturn with high levels of unemployment.

Descent of Man   The 1871 publication by Charles Darwin that applied selective evolution theory to mankind.

Destalinization   The policy of denouncing and undoing the most repressive aspects of Stalin's regime; it was begun by Nikita Khrushchev in 1956.

Détente   Relaxation of tensions; the term used for the toning down of diplomatic tensions between nations, specifically between the United States and the Soviet Union during the Cold War.

Dharma   A code of morals and conduct prescribed for one's caste in Hinduism.

Diaspora   The scattering of the Jews from ancient Palestine.

Diffusion theory   Description of the spread of ideas and technology through human contacts.

Directory   The five-member executive organ that governed France from 1795 to 1799 after the overthrow of the Jacobins and before Napoleon gained control.

Divine right theory   The idea that the legitimate holder of the Crown was designated by divine will to govern; personified by King Louis XIV in the seventeenth century.

Domino theory   The belief that if the communists succeeded in Vietnam, other countries in Southeast and East Asia would also fall (like dominoes) to communism; a justification for the U.S. intervention in Vietnam.

Dorians   Legendary barbaric invaders of Mycenaean Greece in about 1200 B.C.E.

Dream of the Red Chamber   The best-known of the eighteenth-century Chinese novels.

Duce, il   "The Leader"; title of Mussolini, the Italian dictator.

Duma   The Russian legislature created by Tsar Nicolas II.

Dynastic state   A state in which the maintenance and expansion of the interests of the ruling family is the primary consideration.

East India Company   A commercial company founded with government backing to trade with the East and Southeast Asians. The Dutch, English, and French governments sponsored such companies starting in the early seventeenth century.

Economic nationalism   A movement to assert national sovereignty in economic affairs, particularly by establishing freedom from the importation of foreign goods and technology on unfavorable terms.

Edo   Name of Tokyo prior to the eighteenth century.

Eightfold Path   The Buddha's teachings on attaining perfection.

Emir   A provincial official with military duties in Muslim government.

Empirical data   Facts derived from observation of the external world.

Empirical method   Using empirical data to establish scientific truth.

Enclosure movement   An eighteenth-century innovation in British agriculture by which formerly communal lands were enclosed by private landlords.

Encomienda   The right to organize unpaid native labor by the earliest Spanish colonists in Latin America; revoked in 1565.

Encyclopédie, The   The first encyclopedia; produced in mid-eighteenth-century France by the philosopher Diderot.

Enlightened absolutism   An absolute monarchy where the ruler follows the principles of the Enlightenment by introducing reforms for the improvement of society, allowing freedom of speech and the press, permitting religious toleration, expanding education, and ruling in accordance with the laws.

Enlightenment   The intellectual reform movement in eighteenth-century Europe that challenged traditional ideas and policies in many areas of theory and practice.

Epicureanism   A Hellenistic philosophy advocating the pursuit of pleasure (mental) and avoidance of pain as the supreme good.

Equal field system   Agricultural reform favoring the peasants under the T'ang dynasty in China.

Era of Stagnation   The period of Brezhnev's government in the Soviet Union (1964–1982), when the Soviet society and economy faced increasing troubles.

Era of Warring States   The period of Chinese history between about 500 and 220 B.C.E.; characterized by the breakdown of the central government and near-constant feudal war.

Essenes   A Jewish religious group that lived near the Dead Sea at Qumran from around the middle of the second century B.C.E.; some of their ideas were similar to those found in early Christianity.

Estates-General   The parliament of France; it was composed of delegates from three social orders: clergy, nobility, and commoners.

Ethnic, Ethnicity   The racial, cultural, or linguistic affiliation of an individual or group of human beings.

Ethnic cleansing   The policy of killing or forcibly removing people of another ethnic group; used by the Serbs against Bosnian and Kosovar Muslims in the 1990s.

Etruscans   The pre-Roman rulers of most of northern and central Italy and cultural models for early Roman civilization.

European Economic Community   An organization that blossomed after World War II, it fostered economic cooperation among member states, eventually becoming today's European Union.

Excommunication   The act of being barred from the Roman Catholic community by decree of a bishop or the pope.

Existentialism   Twentieth-century philosophy that was popular after World War II in Europe; it insists on the necessity to inject life with meaning by individual decisions.

Exodus   The Hebrews' flight from the wrath of the Egyptian pharaoh in about 1250 B.C.E.

Extended family   Parents and children plus several other kin group members.

Factory Acts   Laws passed by Parliament in 1819 and 1833 that began the regulation of hours and working conditions in Britain.

Fallow land   Land left uncultivated for a period to recover fertility.

Fascism   A political movement in the twentieth century that embraced totalitarian government policies to achieve a unity of people and leader; first experienced in Mussolini's Italy.

Fashoda crisis   In 1898 British forces and French forces, both bent on increasing the imperial holdings of their respective countries, came head-to-head in Fashoda in the Sudan. Diplomacy averted a war between the two countries.

Feminism   The belief in the social, political, and economic equality of the sexes; also, organized activity to advance women's rights.

Fertile Crescent   A belt of civilized settlements reaching from lower Mesopotamia across Syria, Lebanon, and Israel and into Egypt.

Feudal system   A mode of government based originally on mutual military obligations between lord and vassal; later often extended to civil affairs of all types; generally supported by landowning privileges.

Final Solution   Name given by the Nazis to the wartime massacres of European Jews.

First Consul   Title adopted by Napoleon after his coup d'état in 1799.

First Emperor (Shi Huangdi)   The founder of the short-lived Qin dynasty (221–205 B.C.E.) and creator of China as an imperial state.

First Industrial Revolution   The initial introduction of machine-powered production; began in late-eighteenth-century Britain.

Five Pillars of Islam   Popular term for the basic tenets of Muslim faith.

Five-Year Plan   First introduced in 1929 at Stalin's command to collectivize agriculture and industrialize the economy of the Soviet Union.

Floating world   A term for ordinary human affairs popularized by the novels and stories of eighteenth-century Japan.

Forbidden City   The center of Ming and Ching government in Beijing; entry was forbidden to ordinary citizens.

Four Noble Truths   The Buddha's doctrine on human fate.

Fourteen Points   The outline for a just peace proposed by Woodrow Wilson in 1918.

Franco-Prussian War   The 1870–1871 conflict between these two powers, resulting in humiliating defeat for France and German unification.

Frankfurt Assembly   A German parliament held in 1848 that was unsuccessful in working out a liberal constitution for a united German state.

Führer, der   "The Leader" in Nazi Germany—specifically, Hitler.

Fujiwara clan   Daimyo noble clan controlling the shogunate in ninth- to twelfth-century Japan.

Geisha   Women in feudal Japan who entertained men with good conversation, dance, singing, and occasional sexual favors; similar to the *hetairai* of ancient Athens.

Gentiles   All non-Jews.

Gentry   Well-to-do English landowners below the level of the nobility; played an important role in the English Civil War of the seventeenth century.

Geocentric   "Earth centered"; theory of the cosmos that erroneously held the Earth to be its center.

Gestapo   Hitler's secret police, responsible for intimidating the population and helping to rid

Germany of "undesirables" such as Jews and leftists.

Ghana   The earliest of the extensive empires in the western Sudan; also a modern African state.

Ghetto   Italian name for the quarter restricted to Jews.

Gilgamesh   One of the earliest epics in world literature, originating in prehistoric Mesopotamia.

Glasnost   The Russian term for "openness"; along with *perestroika,* it was employed to describe the reforms instituted by Gorbachev in the late 1980s in the Soviet Union.

Glorious Revolution of 1688   The English revolt against the unpopular Catholic king James II and the subsequent introduction of certain civil rights restricting monarchic powers.

Golden Horde   The Russia-based segment of the Mongol world empire.

Gothic style   An artistic style, found mainly in architecture, that came into general European usage during the thirteenth century.

Gracchi brothers   Roman noble brothers who as consuls unsuccessfully attempted reform in the late republican era.

Great Depression   Originating in 1929 in the United States, this global decline in economic output spread throughout the world, causing high unemployment and political unrest; it was a major reason Hitler came to power in Germany.

Great Elector   Frederick William of Prussia (1640–1688); one of the princes who elected the Holy Roman Emperor.

Great Leap Forward   Mao Zedong's misguided attempt in 1958–1960 to provide China with an instantaneous industrial base rivaling that of more advanced nations.

Great Proletarian Cultural Revolution   The period from 1966 to 1969 when Mao inspired Chinese youth to rebel against all authority except his own; caused great damage to the Chinese economy and culture.

Great Purge   The arrest and banishment of millions of Soviet Communist party members and ordinary citizens at Stalin's orders in the mid-1930s for fictitious "crimes against the State and Party."

Great Schism   A division in the Roman Catholic church between 1378 and 1417 when two (and for a brief period, three) popes competed for the allegiance of European

Christians; a consequence of the Babylonian Captivity of the papacy in Avignon, southern France.

Great Trek   The march of the Boers into the interior of South Africa, where they founded the Orange Free State in 1836.

Great Zimbabwe   The leading civilization of early southern Africa.

Greens   A pro-environment, moderately leftist political movement that began in West Germany in the 1970s and has since spread throughout Europe and to other parts of the world.

Grossdeutsch versus *Kleindeutsch*   The controversy over the scope and type of the unified German state in the nineteenth century; *Kleindeutsch* would exclude multinational Austria, and *Grossdeutsch* would include it.

Guild   A medieval urban organization that controlled the production and sale prices of many goods and services.

Habsburg dynasty   The family that controlled the Holy Roman Empire after the thirteenth century; based in Vienna, they ruled Austria until 1918.

Hacienda   A Spanish-owned plantation in Latin America that used native or slave labor to produce export crops.

Hagia Sophia   Greek name ("Holy Wisdom") of the cathedral in Constantinople, later made into a mosque by Ottoman Turkish conquerors.

Hajj   The pilgrimage to the sacred places of Islam.

Han dynasty   The dynasty that ruled China from about 200 B.C.E. to 221 C.E.

Hanoverians   The dynasty of British monarchs after 1714 that came from the German duchy of Hanover.

Harappa   An early Indus Valley civilization.

Hegira   "Flight"; Muhammad's forced flight from Mecca in 622 C.E.; marks the first year of the Muslim calendar.

Heliocentrism   Opposite of geocentrism; recognizes the sun as center of the solar system.

Hellenistic   A blend of Greek and Asiatic cultures, extant in the Mediterranean basin and Middle East between 300 B.C.E. and about 200 C.E.

Helots   Messenian semislaves of Spartan overlords.

Heresy   "Wrong" belief in religious doctrines; often severely persecuted by Christian authorities, including the punishment of execution.

Hetairai   High-class female entertainer-prostitutes in ancient Greece.

Hieroglyphics   Early Egyptian writing consisting of pictographs and symbols for letters and syllables.

Hinayana Buddhism   A strict, monastic form of Buddhism claiming a closer link with the Buddha's teaching than Mahayana Buddhism; often called Theravada.

Historiography   The writing of history so as to interpret it.

History   Human actions in past time, as recorded and remembered.

Hitler-Stalin Pact of 1939   The treaty of nonaggression between Hitler and Stalin in which each agreed to maintain neutrality in any forthcoming war involving the other party.

Hittites   An Indo-European people who were prominent in the Middle East around 1200 B.C.E.

Hohenzollerns   The dynasty that ruled Prussia-Germany until 1918.

Holocaust   The mass executions perpetrated by the Nazi regime of Germany during World War II; its chief victims were 6 million Jews, but hundreds of thousands of gypsies, homosexuals, and others also perished.

Holy Roman Empire   First constituted by Charlemagne, the Holy Roman Empire was a concept that served both political and religious purposes; it was eventually controlled by the Habsburgs centered in Austria, but it essentially had lost all its meaning by the early nineteenth century.

Hominid   A humanlike creature.

Homo sapiens   "Thinking man"; modern human beings.

Hoplites   Heavily armed infantry soldiers in ancient Greece in a phalanx formation.

Huguenots   French Calvinists, many of whom were forced to emigrate in the seventeenth century.

Humanism   The intellectual movement that sees humans as the sole arbiter of their values and purpose.

Hungarian Revolution   The Hungarians' attempt to free themselves from Soviet control in October 1956; crushed by the Soviets.

Hyksos   A people who invaded the Nile delta in Egypt and ruled it during the Second Intermediate Period around 1600 B.C.E.

Ideographs   Written signs conveying entire ideas and not related to the spoken language; used by the Chinese from earliest times.

Iliad   The first of the two epics supposedly written by Homer in eighth-century B.C.E. Greece.

Impressionists   Members of a Paris-centered school of nineteenth-century painting focusing on light and color.

Indian National Congress   Organized in 1885, this secular organization promoted Indian nationalism and lobbied for increased rights of Indians; it became a major force in the struggle for Indian independence.

Individualism   Emphasis on and interest in the unique traits of each person.

Inductive reasoning   Arriving at truth by reasoning from specific cases to a general law or proposition.

Indulgence   The remission of part or all of the temporal punishment in purgatory due to sin; granted for charitable contributions and other good deeds. Indulgences became a regular practice of the Christian church in the High Middle Ages, and their abuse was instrumental in sparking Luther's reform movement in the sixteenth century.

INF (Intermediate Nuclear Forces) Treaty   Negotiated by Mikhail Gorbachev and the Reagan administration in the mid-1980s, it removed all medium-range nuclear missiles from Europe.

Inflation   A sustained rise in the price level.

Inka   Title of the emperor of the Quechuan peoples of Peru prior to arrival of the Spanish.

Inquisition   A systematic attempt by the Roman Catholic church to enforce its religious orthodoxy; the Inquisition tortured and executed hundreds of thousands of people suspected of heresy.

Institutes of the Christian Religion   John Calvin's major work that established the theology and doctrine of the Calvinist churches; first published in 1536.

Intelligentsia   Russian term for a social group that actively influences the beliefs and actions of others, seeking reforms; generally connected with the professions and media.

Iranian Revolution   The fundamentalist and anti-Western movement led by the Ayatollah Khomeini that seized power from the shah of Iran through massive demonstrations in 1979.

Iron curtain   A metaphor employed by Winston Churchill early in the Cold War, it refers to the divide between western and eastern Europe caused by Soviet domination in the latter region.

Isis   A chief Egyptian goddess, represented by the Nile River.

Isolationism   A foreign policy in which a nation refrains from making alliances or engaging actively in international affairs.

Jacobins   Radical revolutionaries during the French Revolution; organized in clubs headquartered in Paris.

Janissaries   An elite troop in the Ottoman army, created originally from Christian boys from the Balkans.

Jesuits   Members of the Society of Jesus, a Catholic religious order founded in 1547 to combat Protestantism.

Jewish War   A rebellion of Jewish Zealots against Rome in 66–70 C.E.

Jihad   Holy war on behalf of the Muslim faith.

Judea   One of the two Jewish kingdoms emerging after the death of Solomon when his kingdom was split in two; the other kingdom was Samaria.

Justification by faith   Doctrine held by Martin Luther whereby Christian faith alone was the path to heavenly bliss.

Ka'bah   The original shrine of pagan Arabic religion in Mecca containing the Black Stone; now one of the holiest places of Islam.

Kali   Wife of the Hindu god Shiva, she was both the cosmic mother and the goddess of destruction.

Kamakura shogunate   The rule by members of a noble Japanese family from the late twelfth to the mid-fourteenth century in the name of the emperor, who was their puppet.

Kami   Shinto spirits in nature.

Kampuchea   Native name of Cambodia, a state of Southeast Asia bordered by Thailand and Vietnam.

Karma   In Hindu belief, the amounts of good and evil done in a given incarnation.

Karnak   The site of a great temple complex along the Nile River in Egypt.

Kashmir   A province in northwestern India that Pakistan also claims.

Kellogg-Briand Pact   A formal disavowal of war by sixty nations in 1928.

KGB   An abbreviation for the Soviet secret police; used after *Cheka* and *NKVD* had been discarded.

Khmers   The inhabitants of Cambodia; founders of a large empire in ancient Southeast Asia.

Kiev, Principality of   The first Russian state; flourished from about 800 to 1240 C.E., when it fell to Mongols.

Kleindeutsch   "Small German"; adjective describing a form of German unification that excluded the multinational Austria; opposite of *Grossdeutsch*.

Knight   Type of feudal noble who held title and landed domain only for his lifetime; generally based originally on military service to his overlord.

Korean War   1950–1953 war between the United Nations, led by the United States, and North Korea; precipitated by the invasion of South Korea by North Korea.

Krishna   An important Hindu god who gives core religious teachings in the *Bhagavad-Gita.*

Kshatriyas   The warrior class of Aryan society.

Kuomintang (KMT)   The political movement headed by Chiang Kai-shek during the 1930s and 1940s in China.

Kurds   A group of people located in an area comprising eastern Turkey, northern Iraq, northern Syria, and northwest Iran; the Kurds have unsuccessfully sought an independent state and have fought with the governments of Turkey and Iraq.

Kush   Kingdom in northeast Africa that had close relations with Egypt for several centuries in the pre-Christian epoch.

Kyoto   Ancient capital of the Japanese Empire and seat of the emperor.

Labour party   Political party founded in 1906 by British labor unions and others for representation of the working classes.

Laissez-faire   "To let alone." An economic doctrine that holds that an economy is best served when the government does not interfere but allows the economy to self-regulate according the forces of supply and demand.

Lascaux   Site of Paleolithic cave paintings in France.

Late Manchu Restoration   An attempt by Chinese reformers in the 1870s to restore the power of the central government after the suppression of the Taiping rebellion.

Lateran Treaty   A 1929 agreement between the pope and Mussolini in which the pope gained substantial sums of money and control over education, while Mussolini gained greater political and economic control of Italy.

League of Nations   An international organization founded after World War I to maintain peace and promote amity among nations; the United States did not join.

Lebensraum   "Living space." The doctrine, adopted by Hitler, that a nation's power depends on the amount of land it occupies; thus, a nation must expand to be strong.

Left   The reforming or revolutionary wing of the political spectrum; associated originally with the ideals of the radical French Revolution.

Legalism   A Chinese philosophy of government emphasizing strong authority.

Legislative Assembly   The second law-making body created during the French Revolution; it was dominated by the Jacobins and gave way to the radical Convention.

Legitimacy   A term adopted by the victors at the Congress of Vienna in 1815 to explain the reimposition of former monarchs and regimes after the Napoleonic wars.

Legitimacy, principle of   The idea that, after the Napoleonic wars, peace could best be reestablished in Europe by restoring legitimate monarchs who would preserve traditional institutions; it guided Metternich at the Congress of Vienna.

Lepanto, Battle of Decisive 1571 naval defeat of the Ottomans at the hands of the Habsburgs and Italian city-states; it marked the beginning of the long decline of the Ottomans.

Liberalism An ideology based on the belief that people should be as free from restraint as possible. Economic liberalism is the idea that the government should not interfere in the workings of the economy. Political liberalism is the idea that there should be restraints on the exercise of power so that people can enjoy basic civil rights in a constitutional state with a representative assembly.

Locarno Pact An agreement between France and Germany in 1925.

Long March, the 6,000-mile fighting retreat of the Chinese Communists under Mao Zedong to Shensi province in 1934–1935.

Lyric poetry Poetry that celebrates the poet's emotions.

Maastricht Treaty Signed in 1991 by members of the European Community; committed them to closer political and economic ties.

Macao Portuguese island colony just off China's coast; founded in 1513.

Maghrib or **Maghreb** Muslim northwest Africa.

Magna Carta A "great charter" issued in 1215 by King John of England that gave the aristocracy substantially increased powers, especially over taxation, and created a more uniform justice system.

Mahabharata A Hindu epic poem; a favorite in India.

Mahavira "Great hero." The term refers to Vardhamana, the founder of Jainism in the sixth century B.C.E.

Mahayana Buddhism A more liberal, looser form of Buddhism; originating soon after the Buddha's death, it de-emphasized the monastic life and abstruse philosophy in favor of prayer to the Buddha and the bodhisattvas who succeeded him.

Mahdi rebellion A serious rebellion against European rule in the Sudan in the 1890s, led by a charismatic holy man ("mahdi") and ended by his death and British attack.

Mali The African Sudanese empire that was the successor to Ghana in the 1300s and 1400s.

Manchu Originally nomadic tribes living in Manchuria who eventually overcame Ming resistance and established the Ching dynasty in seventeenth-century China.

Manchuria Large province of northeastern China, seized in the nineteenth century by Russia and Japan before being retaken by the Maoist government.

Mandarins Chinese scholar-officials who had been trained in Confucian principles and possessed great class solidarity.

Mandate Britain and France governed several Asian and African peoples after World War I, supposedly as agents of the League of Nations.

Mandate of heaven A theory of rule originated by the Chou dynasty in China, emphasizing the connection between an imperial government's rectitude and its right to govern.

Manor An agricultural estate of varying size normally owned by a noble or the clergy and worked by free and unfree peasants/serfs.

Marathon The battle in 490 B.C.E. in which the Greeks defeated the Persians, ending the first Persian War.

March on Rome A fascist demonstration in 1922 orchestrated by Mussolini as a preliminary step to dictatorship in Italy.

Maritime expeditions (China's) Early fifteenth-century explorations of the Indian and South Pacific Oceans ordered by the Chinese emperor.

Marshall Plan A program proposed by the U.S. secretary of state George Marshall and implemented from 1947 to 1951 to aid western Europe's recovery from World War II.

Marxism The political, economic, and social theories of Karl Marx, which included the idea that history is the story of class struggle and that ultimately the proletariat will overthrow the bourgeoisie and establish a dictatorship en route to a classless society.

Mass education A state-run educational system, usually free and compulsory, that aims to ensure that all children in society have at least a basic education.

Matriarchy A society in which females are dominant socially and politically.

Matrilineal descent   Attribution of name and inheritance to children via the maternal line.

Maya   The most advanced of the Amerindian peoples who lived in southern Mexico and Guatemala and created a high urban civilization in the pre-Columbian era.

Medes   An early Indo-European people who, with the Persians, settled in Iran.

Meiji Restoration   The overthrow of the Tokugawa shogunate and restoration of the emperor to nominal power in Japan in 1867.

Mein Kampf   *My Struggle;* Hitler's credo, written while serving a prison term in 1924.

Mercantilism   A theory of national economics popular in the seventeenth and eighteenth centuries, it aimed at establishing a favorable trade balance through government control of exports and imports as well as domestic industry.

Meritocracy   The rule of the meritorious (usually determined by examinations).

Messenian Wars   Conflicts between the neighbors Sparta and Messenia that resulted in Sparta's conquest of Messenia around 600 B.C.E.

Messiah   A savior-king who would someday lead the Jews to glory.

Mestizo   A person of mixed Amerindian and European blood.

Metics   Resident foreigners in ancient Athens; not permitted full rights of citizenship, but did receive the protection of the laws.

Mexican Revolution   The armed struggle that occurred in Mexico between 1910 and 1920 to install a more socially progressive and populist government.

Middle Kingdom   The period in Egyptian history from 2100 to 1600 B.C.E.; followed the First Intermediate Period.

Milan, Edict of   A decree issued by the emperor Constantine in 313 C.E. that legalized Christianity and made it the favored religion in the Roman Empire.

Militarism   A policy of aggressive military preparedness; in particular, the large armies based on mass conscription and complex, inflexible plans for mobilization that most European nations had before World War I.

Ming dynasty   Chinese empire lasting from 1368 to 1644; it overthrew the Mongols and

was replaced by the Ch'ing dynasty of the Manchu.

Minoan civilization   An ancient civilization that was centered on Crete between about 2000 and about 1400 B.C.E.

Missi dominici   Agents of Charlemagne in the provinces of his empire.

Modernism   A philosophy of art of the late nineteenth and early twentieth centuries that rejected classical models and values and sought new expressions and aesthetics.

Mohenjo-Daro   Site of one of the two chief towns of the ancient Indus Valley civilization.

Moksha   In Hinduism, the final liberation from bodily existence and reincarnation.

Monarchy   Rule by a single individual, who often claims divine inspiration and protection.

Mongol yoke   A Russian term for the Mongol occupation of Russia, 1240–1480.

Mongols   Name for collection of savage nomadic warriors of Central Asia who conquered most of Eurasia in the thirteenth century.

Monotheism   A religion having only one god.

Monroe Doctrine   The announcement in 1823 by U.S. president James Monroe that no European interference in Latin America would be tolerated.

Mughal   A corruption of "Mongol"; refers to the period of Muslim rule in India.

Mulatto   A person of mixed African and European blood.

Munich Agreement   The agreement coming from 1938 meetings between Hitler and the British and French prime ministers that allowed Germany to take much of Czechoslovakia; the agreement confirmed Hitler's belief that the democratic governments would not fight German aggression.

Munich beer-hall putsch   The failed attempt by Hitler to seize power by armed force in 1923.

Mutual deterrence   The belief that nuclear war could best be prevented if both the United States and the Soviet Union had sufficient nuclear weapons such that even if one nation launched a preemptive first strike, the other could respond and devastate the attacker.

Mycenaeans   An early and rich Greek culture centered on Mycenae that was destroyed by the

"Sea Peoples" and the influx of Dorians from the north.

Mystery religion   One of various Hellenistic cults promising immortal salvation of the individual.

Nantes, Edict of   A law granting toleration to French Calvinists that was issued in 1598 by King Henry IV to end the religious civil war.

Napoleonic settlement   A collective name for the decrees and actions by Napoleon between 1800 and 1808 that legalized and systematized many elements of the French Revolution.

National Assembly   The first law-making body during the French Revolution; created a moderate constitutional monarchy.

Nationalism   A sense of national con-sciousness based on awareness of being part of a community—a "nation"—that has common institutions, traditions, language, and customs and that becomes the focus of the individual's primary political loyalty.

Nationalities problem   The dilemma faced by the Austro-Hungarian Empire in trying to unite a wide variety of ethnic groups, including, among others, Austrians, Hungarians, Poles, Croats, Czechs, Serbs, Slovaks, and Slovenes in an era when nationalism and calls for self-determination were coming to the fore.

Nationalization   The process of converting a business or industry from private ownership to government control and ownership.

Nation-state   A form of political organization in which a relatively homogeneous people inhabits a sovereign state, as opposed to a state containing people of several nationalities.

Natural rights   Certain inalienable rights to which all people are entitled; include the right to life, liberty, and property, freedom of speech and religion, and equality before the law.

Natural selection   The Darwinian doctrine in biology that changes in species derive from genetic changes that confer an enhanced ability to survive and reproduce.

Navigation Acts   Laws regulating commerce with the British colonies in North America in favor of Britain.

Nazism   The German variant of fascism created by Hitler.

Neanderthal man   A species of *Homo sapiens* flourishing between 100,000 and 30,000 years ago and that mysteriously died out; the name comes from the German valley where the first remains were found.

Négritude   A literary term referring to the self-conscious awareness of African cultural values; popular in areas of Africa formerly under French control.

Neo-Confucianism   An eleventh- and twelfth-century C.E. revival of Confucian thought with special emphasis on love and responsibility toward others.

Neolithic Age   The period from about 7000 B.C.E. to the development of metals by a given people.

Nerchinsk, Treaty of   A 1714 treaty between China and Russia that settled border issues between the two great powers in eastern Asia.

New China movement   An intellectual reform movement in the 1890s that attempted to change and modernize China by modernizing the government.

New Deal   The economic policies of U.S. president Franklin Roosevelt; designed to combat the effects of the Great Depression, they included aspects of Keynesian economics and the first significant social welfare programs in the United States.

New Economic Policy (NEP)   A policy introduced at the conclusion of the civil war that allowed for partial capitalism and private enterprise in the Soviet Union.

New Kingdom or **Empire**   The period from about 1550 to 700 B.C.E. in Egyptian history; followed the Second Intermediate Period. The period from 1550 to about 1200 B.C.E. was the Empire.

Nicaea, Council of   A fourth-century conclave that defined essential doctrines of Christianity under the supervision of the emperor Constantine.

Nicheren sect   A Japanese sect of Buddhism founded by the monk Nicheren; it stressed its supremacy over other religions and glorified Japan.

Niger River   The great river draining most of the African bulge.

Ninety-five Theses   The challenge to church authority put forth by Martin Luther in 1517.

Nineveh   The main city and later capital of the Assyrian Empire.

Nirvana   The Buddhist equivalent of the Hindu *moksha;* the final liberation from suffering and reincarnation.

Nonaligned nations   A large group of countries, most of which became independent after World War II, that desired Cold War alliances with neither the United States nor the Soviet Union.

North American Free Trade Agreement (NAFTA)   An agreement signed by the United States, Canada, and Mexico in 1993 that liberalized trade among these nations.

North Atlantic Treaty Organization (NATO)   An organization founded in 1949 under U.S. aegis as a defense against threatened communist aggression in Europe.

Nuclear family   Composed of parents and children only.

Nuclear test ban   The voluntary cessation of above-ground testing of nuclear weapons by the United States and the Soviet Union; in existence from 1963 to the present.

Nuremberg Trials   Trials conducted in Germany after World War II to determine and punish war guilt among high German officials, resulting in several executions.

October Revolution of 1917   The Bolshevik coup d'etat in St. Petersburg that ousted the Provisional Government and established a communist state in Russia.

Odyssey   The second of the two Homeric epic poems, it details the adventures of the homeward-bound Ulysses coming from the siege of Troy; see also *Iliad.*

Oil boycott of 1973   The temporary withholding of oil exports by OPEC members to Western nations with governments friendly to Israel; led to a massive rise in the price of oil and economic dislocation in many countries.

Old Kingdom   The period of Egyptian history from 3100 to 2200 B.C.E.

Old regime/old order   The political and social system of France in the eighteenth century before the Revolution.

Old Testament   The first portion of the Judeo-Christian Bible; the holy books of the Jews.

Oligarchy   Rule by a few.

Olmec   The earliest Amerindian civilization in Mexico.

Open Door Policy   An early-twentieth-century agreement among the major Western powers that all should have access to trade with weakened China.

Opium Wars   Conflicts that occurred in 1840–1842 on the Chinese coast between the British and the Chinese over the importation of opium into China. The Chinese defeat began eighty years of subordination to foreigners.

Oracle bones   Animal bones used as a primitive writing medium by early Chinese.

Orange Free State   One of the two political entities founded after the Boers' Great Trek in South Africa.

Orders/estates   The traditional tripartite division of European society based on heredity and quality rather than wealth or economic standing, first established in the Middle Ages and continuing into the eighteenth century; traditionally consisted of those who pray (the clergy), those who fight (the nobility), and those who work (all the rest).

Organization for Pan African Unity (OAU)   The present name of the association of African nations founded in 1963 for mutual aid.

Organization of American States (OAS)   An organization founded in 1948 under U.S. auspices to provide mutual defense and aid.

Organization of Petroleum Exporting Countries (OPEC)   Founded in the 1960s by Arab governments and later expanded to include several Latin American and African members.

Origin of Species, On the   Charles Darwin's book that first enunciated the evolutionary theory in biology; published in 1859.

Osiris   A chief Egyptian god, ruler of the underworld.

Ostpolitik   German term for Chancellor Brandt's 1960s policy of pursuing normalized relations with West Germany's neighbors to the east.

Ostracism   In ancient Greece, the expulsion of a citizen for a given period.

Paleolithic Age   The period from the earliest appearance of *Homo sapiens* to about 7000 B.C.E., though exact dates vary by area; the Old Stone Age.

Paleontology   The study of prehistoric things.

Palestine Liberation Organization (PLO)
An organization founded in the 1960s by
Palestinians expelled from Israel; until 1994 it
aimed at destruction of the state of Israel by any
means. Superseded by the autonomous
Palestinian Authority created in 1997.

Pan-Africanism   The concept of African
continental unity and solidarity in which the
common interests of African countries
transcend regional boundaries.

Panama Canal   A canal built across the
isthmus of Panama. Completed in 1914 by the
United States, it linked the Atlantic and Pacific
Oceans, helping international commerce and
extending American naval power.

Pan-Arabism   A movement after World War I
to assert supranational Arab unity, aimed
eventually at securing a unified Arab state.

Pantheism   A belief that God exists in all
things, living and inanimate.

Paris Commune   A leftist revolt against the
national government after France was defeated
by Prussia in 1871; crushed by the
conservatives with much bloodshed.

Parthenon   The classic Greek temple to
Athena on the Acropolis in Athens's center.

Patriarchy   A society in which males have
social and political dominance.

Patricians (*patres*)   The upper class in
ancient Rome.

Patronage   The practice of awarding titles and
making appointments to government and other
positions to gain political support.

Pax Mongolica   The Mongol peace;
between about 1250 and about 1350 in
most of Eurasia.

Pax Romana   The "Roman peace"; the era of
Roman control over the Mediterranean basin
and much of Europe between about 31 B.C.E.
and 180 C.E. or later.

Peace of Augsburg   Pact ending the German
religious wars in 1555, dividing the region
between Lutheran and Catholic hegemony.

Peaceful coexistence   The declared policy of
Soviet leader Khrushchev in dealing with the
capitalist West after 1956.

Pearl Harbor, bombing of   A surprise attack
on December 7, 1941, by Japanese planes on
the American navy at Pearl Harbor, Hawaii; it

brought war between the United States and
Japan.

Peasants' Revolt   An uprising in southern
German states in 1524–1525; it was ruthlessly
suppressed after the peasants were denounced
by Martin Luther.

Peloponnesian War   The great civil war
between Athens and Sparta and their respective
allies in ancient Greece; fought between 429
and 404 B.C.E. and eventually won by Sparta.

Peon   A peasant in semislave status on a
hacienda.

Perestroika   The Russian term for
"restructuring," which, with *glasnost,* was used
to describe the reforms instituted by Gorbachev
in the late 1980s.

Persepolis   With Ecbatana, one of the twin
capitals of the Persian Empire in the 500s B.C.E.

Persian Wars   The conflict between the
Greeks and the Persian Empire in the fifth
century B.C.E., fought in two installments and
ending with Greek victory.

Persians   An early Indo-European tribe that,
along with the Medes, settled in Iran.

Petrine succession   The doctrine of the Roman
Catholic church by which the pope (the bishop of
Rome) is the direct successor of St. Peter.

Pharaoh   The title of the god-king of ancient
Egypt.

Philosophes   A French term referring to the
writers and activist intellectuals during the
Enlightenment.

Phoenicians   An ancient seafaring people
living along the coast north of Palestine; they
dominated trade in the Mediterranean.

Phonetic alphabet   A system of writing that
matches signs with the sounds of the oral
language.

Pictographic script   Uses symbols and
graphs only, with no alphabet; used in Chinese
writing.

Piedmont   "Foot of the mountains"; the Italian
kingdom that led to the unification of Italy in
the mid-nineteenth century.

Platea   The land battle that, along with the
naval battle of Salamis, ended the Second
Persian War with a Greek victory over the
Persians.

Plebeians   The common people of ancient Rome.

Pogrom   Mob violence against local Jews.

Polis The political and social community of citizens in ancient Greece.

Politburo The ruling council of the Soviet Union; it came under the firm control of Joseph Stalin, but reasserted substantial power upon the dictator's death.

Polytheism Belief in many gods.

Popular sovereignty The doctrine that government is created by and subject to the will of the people, who are the source of all political power.

Post-Impressionist A term for late nineteenth-century painting that emphasized color and line in revolutionary fashion.

Praetorian Guard The imperial bodyguard in the Roman Empire and the only armed force in Italy.

Precedent What has previously been accepted in the application of law.

Predestination The belief, associated with Calvinism, that God, as a consequence of his foreknowledge of all events, has predetermined those who will be saved (the elect) and those who will be damned.

Prehistory The long period of human activity prior to the writing of history.

Primogeniture A system of inheritance in which the estate passes to the eldest legitimate son.

Princeps "The First" or "the Leader" in Latin; title taken by Augustus Caesar.

Principate The reign of Augustus Caesar from 27 B.C.E. to 14 C.E.

Proconsuls Provincial governors and military commanders in ancient Rome.

Proletariat Poverty-stricken people without skills; also, a Marxist term for the propertyless working classes.

Provisional Government A self-appointed parliamentary group exercising power in republican Russia from March to October 1917.

Psychoanalysis A psychological technique that employs free associations in the attempt to determine the cause of mental illness.

Ptolemaic Kingdom of Egypt The state created by Ptolemy, one of Alexander the Great's generals, in the Hellenistic era.

Punic Wars The three conflicts between Rome and Carthage that ended with the complete destruction of the Carthaginian Empire and the extension of Roman control throughout the western Mediterranean.

Puranas A collection of mythical stories about Hindu gods and goddesses.

Purdah The segregation of females in Hindu society.

Purgatory In Catholic belief, the place where the soul is purged after death for past sins and thus becomes fit for heaven.

Puritans The English Calvinists who were dissatisfied by the theology of the Church of England and wished to "purify" it.

Pyramid of Khufu (Cheops) The largest pyramid; stands outside Cairo.

Quadruple Alliance The diplomatic pact to maintain the peace established by the Big Four victors of the Napoleonic wars (Austria, Britain, Prussia, and Russia); lasted for a decade.

Quantum theory A theory in physics describing the discontinuous nature of energy. Energy can come only in certain amounts, or quanta.

Quechua The spoken language of the Inca of Peru.

Qur'an The holy scripture of Islam.

Raison d'état The idea that the welfare of the state should be supreme in government policy.

Ramayana A Hindu text that illustrates important aspects of the religion; its heroes, Rama and his wife Sita, are worshiped as the embodiment of the ideal man and woman, especially Sita.

Realpolitik "Politics of reality." Politics based on practical concerns rather than theory or ethics.

Reconquista The recapture of Muslim Spain by Christians; it was completed during the reign of Ferdinand and Isabella.

Red Guard The youthful militants who carried out the Cultural Revolution in China during the 1960s.

Reform Bill of 1832 Brought about a reform of British parliamentary voting and representation that strengthened the middle class and the urbanites.

Reign of Terror The period (1793–1794) of extreme Jacobin radicalism during the French Revolution.

Relativity theory Einstein's theory that holds, among other things, that (1) space and time are not absolute but are relative to the observer and interwoven into a four-dimensional space-time continuum and (2) matter is a form of energy.

Reparations Money and goods that Germany paid to the victorious Allies after World War I under the Versailles Treaty.

Republican government A form of governing that imitates the Roman *res publica* in its rejection of monarchy.

Restoration (English) The period of the 1660s–1680s when Charles II was called by Parliament to take his throne and was thus restored to power.

Revolution A fundamental change in the political and social organization of a state.

Revolutions of 1989 The throwing out of the Communist governments in eastern Europe by popular demand and/or armed uprising.

Rig Veda The oldest of the four Vedas, or epics, brought into India by the Aryans.

Romanov dynasty Ruled Russia from 1613 until 1917.

Rome, Treaty of The pact signed by six western European nations in 1957 that is the founding document of the European Union.

Rubaiyat The verses attributed to the twelfth-century Persian poet Omar Khayyam.

Russo-Japanese War The 1904–1905 conflict that resulted in defeat for Russia, which weakened the position of the Tsar; simultaneously, the international power and prestige of Japan increased substantially.

Safavid The dynasty of Shiite Muslims that ruled Persia from the 1500s to the 1700s.

Sahel The arid belt extending across Africa south of the Sahara; also called the Sudan.

Salamis The naval battle that, with the battle of Platea, ended the Second Persian War with a Greek victory.

SALT (Strategic Arms Limitation Treaty) Two agreements between the United States and the Soviet Union that placed caps on certain types of nuclear weapons.

Samaria One of the two kingdoms into which the Hebrew kingdom was split after Solomon's death; the other was Judea.

Samsara The reincarnation of the soul; a concept shared by Hinduism and Buddhism.

Samurai Japanese warrior-aristocrats of medieval and early modern times.

Sandinistas A left-wing revolutionary group that overthrew the Somoza dictatorship in Nicaragua and found itself the target of the Reagan administration during the 1980s.

Sangha Groupings of Buddhist monks or nuns; one of the "Three Jewels," along with the *dharma* (teachings) and the Buddha.

Sanhedrin The Jewish governing council under the overlordship of Rome.

Sanskrit The sacred language of India; came originally from the Aryans.

Sardinia-Piedmont See Piedmont.

Sati The practice in which a widow committed suicide at the death of her husband in India; also called *suttee*.

Satrapy A province under a governor or *satrap* in the ancient Persian Empire.

Savanna The semiarid grasslands where most African civilizations developed.

Schlieffen Plan The strategic doctrine employed by Germany at the beginning of World War I; it was designed for a two-front war with France and Russia. The bulk of German military forces quickly swept through Belgium into France while fewer forces stayed in the east to hold off the slow-mobilizing Russians.

Schutzstaffel (SS) Hitler's bodyguard; later enlarged to be a subsidiary army and to provide the concentration camp guards.

Scientific method The method of observation and experiment by which the physical sciences proceed.

SDI Strategic Defense Initiative, also known as "star wars." A plan put forth by the Reagan administration to build a space-based missile defense system.

Second Front The reopening of a war front in western Europe against the Axis powers in World War II; eventually accomplished by the invasion of Normandy in June 1944.

Second Industrial Revolution The second phase of industrialization that occurred in the late 1800s after the introduction of electricity and the internal combustion engine.

Second International   Association of socialist parties founded in 1889; after the Russian Revolution in 1917, the Second International split into democratic and communist segments.

Secret speech   Premier Nikita Khrushchev of the USSR gave an account in February 1956 of the crimes of Josef Stalin against his own people that was supposed to remain secret but was soon known internationally.

Secularism   The rejection of supernatural religion as the arbiter of earthly action; emphasis on worldly affairs.

Seleucid kingdom of Persia   The successor state to the empire of Alexander the Great in most of the Middle East.

Self-determination   The doctrine that the people of a given territory or a particular nationality should have the right to determine their own government and political future.

Self-strengthening   The late nineteenth-century attempt by Chinese officials to bring China into the modern world by instituting reforms; it failed to achieve its goal.

Seljuks   Turkish converts to Islam who seized the Baghdad government from the Abbasids in the eleventh century.

Semitic   Adjective describing a person or language belonging to one of the most widespread of the western Asian groups; among many others, it embraces Hebrew and Arabic.

Seppuku   An honorable method of ritual suicide performed by Japanese samurai; it involved disembowelment with a short sword.

Serfdom   Restriction of personal and economic freedoms associated with medieval European agricultural society.

Seven Years' War   Fought between France and England, with their allies, around the world, 1756–1763; won by England with major accessions of territory to the British Empire.

Shang dynasty   The first historical rulers of China; ruled from about 1500 to about 1100 B.C.E.

Shari'a   The sacred law of Islam; based on the Qur'an.

Shiite   A minority sect of Islam; adherents believe that kinship with Muhammad is necessary to qualify for the caliphate.

Shintoism   The earliest religion in Japan, it was polytheistic and stressed the importance of nature; it placed little or no emphasis on theology or ethical conduct.

Shiva   An important member of the Hindu pantheon; he, along with his wife Kali (Durga), is both the creator and the destroyer.

Shogunate   The government of medieval Japan in which the *shogun*, a military and civil regent, served as the actual leader while the emperor was the symbolic head of the state and religion.

Sikhs   Members of a religious group founded in the sixteenth century C.E. by a holy man who sought a middle way between Islam and Hindu belief; centered on the Punjab region in northern India.

Silk Road   A route linking China with the Mediterranean region; it opened during the Han dynasty and was an important conduit for ideas and goods.

Sino-Soviet conflict   Differences in the nature of socialism were accentuated by conflict over proper policy vis-à-vis the United States in the 1950s and 1960s in the twin capitals of Marxist socialism, Moscow and Beijing.

Six Days' War   The 1967 conflict between Israel and its neighbors in which Israel gained much territory.

Social Darwinism   The misadaptation of Darwinian biology to human societies; it stressed competition and struggle between humans and justified the rule of the powerful over the weak.

Social Democrats   Noncommunist socialists who refused to join the Third International and founded independent parties.

Socialism   An ideology that calls for collective or government ownership of the means of production and the distribution of goods.

Socratic method   A form of teaching that uses a question-and-answer format to enable students to reach conclusions by using their own reasoning.

Solidarity   The umbrella organization founded by Lech Walesa and other anticommunist Poles in 1981 to recover Polish freedom; banned for eight years, but continued underground until it was acknowledged as the government in 1989.

Songhai A West African state, centered on the bend of the Niger River, that reached its fullest extent in the sixteenth century before collapsing.

Sophists Wandering scholars and professional teachers in ancient Greece who stressed the importance of rhetoric and tended toward skepticism and relativism.

Soviets Councils of workers' and soldiers' deputies formed throughout Russia in 1917; played an important role in the Bolshevik Revolution.

Spanish Civil War Conflict in Spain lasting from 1936 to 1939 in which authoritarian forces led by Generalissimo Francisco Franco, with the help of Adolf Hitler, triumphed over Republican forces.

Sparta A militaristic Greek city-state that vied with Athens for power in the Peloponnesian War.

Springtime of the Peoples The spring and summer of 1848 when popular revolutions in Europe temporarily succeeded.

Stalingrad, Battle of The 1942 battle that marked the turning point of World War II in Europe.

Stalinist economy Involved the transformation of a retarded agrarian economy to an industrialized one through massive reallocation of human and material resources directed by a central plan; imposed on the Soviet Union and then, in the first years after World War II, on eastern Europe.

Stamp Act A law enacted by the British Parliament in 1765 that imposed a fee on legal documents of all types and on all books and newspapers sold in the American colonies.

State The term for a territorial, sovereign entity of government.

Stoicism A Hellenistic philosophy that emphasized human brotherhood and natural law as guiding principles.

Stonehenge A Neolithic stone arrangement in southern England with a layout based on astronomical principles.

Successor states Usual term for the several eastern European states that emerged from the Paris Treaty of 1919 as successors to the Russian, German, and Austro-Hungarian Empires.

Sudan The arid belt extending across Africa south of the Sahara; also called the Sahel.

Sudras One of the four classes of Aryan society; included serfs and servants.

Suffrage The right to vote.

Suffragists Those who advocate the extension of the right to vote (suffrage), especially to women.

Sufi Arabic name for a branch of Islamic worship that emphasizes emotional union with God.

Sui dynasty Ruled China from about 580 to about 620 C.E.; ended the disintegration of central government that had existed for the previous 130 years.

Sultanate of Delhi The government and state erected by the conquering Afghani Muslims after 1500 in northern India; immediate predecessor to the Mughal Empire.

Sumerians The creators of Mesopotamian urban civilization.

Sung dynasty The dynasty that ruled China from about 1127 until 1219, when the last ruler was overthrown by the Mongol invaders.

Sunni The majority group in Islam; adherents believe that the caliphate should go to the most qualified individual and should not necessarily pass to the kin of Muhammad.

Supremacy, Act of A law enacted in 1534 by the English Parliament that made the monarch the head of the Church of England.

Swahili A hybrid language based on Bantu and Arabic; used extensively in East Africa.

Sykes-Picot Agreement A secret 1916 pact between the British and French to divide up Ottoman holdings in the Middle East after World War I; at the same time the British were promising Arabs independence after the war.

Taipings Anti-Manchu rebels in China in the 1860s.

Taj Mahal The beautiful tomb built by the seventeenth-century Mughal emperor Jahan for his wife.

Tale of Genji First known novel in Asian, if not world, history; authored by a female courtier about life in the Japanese medieval court.

T'ang dynasty Ruled China from about 620 to about 900 C.E. and began the great age of Chinese artistic and technical advances.

Tao Te Ching "The Way and its Power," a text attributed to Lao Tzu; it discusses the

"Tao," the universal source of everything, and also presents ways for attaining the Tao and the best methods of government.

Taoism (Daoism)   A nature-oriented philosophy/religion.

Tariffs   Duties (taxes) imposed on imported goods; usually imposed both to raise revenue and to discourage imports and protect domestic industries.

Tel el Amarna   The site of great temple complexes along the Nile River in Egypt.

Theravada Buddhism   A strict monastic form of Buddhism entrenched in Southeast Asia; same as Hinayana Buddhism.

Thermidorean reaction   The conservative reaction to the Reign of Terror during the French Revolution.

Third Estate   The great majority of Frenchmen: those neither clerical nor noble.

Third International   An association of Marxist parties in many nations; inspired by Russian Communists and headquartered in Moscow until its dissolution in 1943.

Third Reich   The third German empire, self-proclaimed by Hitler. The first was the empire of Charlemagne, the second that of 1871–1918.

Third Republic of France   The government of France after the exile of Emperor Napoleon III; lasted from 1871 until 1940.

Third World   A term in use after World War II to denote countries and peoples in underdeveloped, formerly colonial areas of Asia, Africa, and Latin America; the First World was the West under U.S. leadership, and the Second World was the communist states under Soviet leadership.

Thirty Years' War   A devastating conflict lasting from 1618–1648, it ravaged central Europe. It involved questions of power and religion, and it ended with an agreement that each ruler would determine the religion in his territory.

Tiananmen Square, massacre on   The shooting down of thousands of Chinese who were peacefully demonstrating for relaxation of political censorship by the Communist leaders; occurred in 1989 in Beijing.

Tien   The supreme but impersonal deity of Chou dynasty China.

Time of Troubles   A fifteen-year period at the beginning of the seventeenth century in Russia when the state was nearly destroyed by revolts and wars.

Titoism   The policy of neutrality in foreign policy combined with continued dedication to socialism in domestic policy that was followed by the Yugoslav Marxist leader Tito after his expulsion from the Soviet camp in 1948.

Toltec   An Amerindian civilization centered in the Valley of Mexico; succeeded by the Aztecs.

Torah   The first five books of the Old Testament; the Jews' fundamental law code.

Tordesillas, Treaty of   A 1494 treaty brokered by the pope, it divided the New World between Portugal and Spain, awarding Brazil to Portugal and all the lands west to Spain.

Tories   A nickname for nineteenth-century British conservatives; opposite of Whigs.

Totalitarianism   The attempt by a dictatorial government to achieve total control over a society's life and ideas.

Trench warfare   Warfare in which the opposing forces attack and counterattack from a relatively permanent system of trenches protected by barbed wire; characteristic of World War I.

Trent, Council of   The council of Catholic clergy that directed the Counter-Reformation against Protestantism; met from 1545 until 1563.

Triple Alliance   A pact concluded in 1882 that united Germany, Austria-Hungary, and Italy against possible attackers; the members were called the Central Powers.

Truman Doctrine   The commitment of the U.S. government in 1947 to defend any noncommunist state against attempted communist takeover; proposed by President Harry Truman.

Twelve Tables   The first written Roman law code; established about 450 B.C.E.

Tyrant   In an ancient Greek *polis* (or an Italian city-state during the Renaissance), a ruler who came to power in an unconstitutional way and ruled without being subject to the law.

Ulema   A council of learned men who applied the *shari'a* in Islam; also, a council of religious advisers to the caliph or sultan.

Umayyad dynasty   The caliphs resident in Damascus from 661 to 750 C.E.

Uncertainty principle   The theory in physics that denies absolute causal relationships of matter and, hence, predictability.

Unequal treaties   Chinese name for the diplomatic and territorial arrangements foisted on the weak Ching dynasty by European powers in the nineteenth century; also, the commercial treaties forced on just-opened Japan by the same powers and the United States.

United Nations   Created in 1945, it is the world's most extensive international organization.

Upanishads   The Hindu holy epics dealing with morals and philosophy.

Utopian socialism   The dismissive label given by Marx to previous theories that aimed at establishing a more just and benevolent society.

Vaisyas   The landholder and artisan class of Aryan society.

Vassal   In medieval Europe, a person, usually a noble, who owed feudal duties to a superior, called a suzerain.

Vedas   The four oral epics of the Aryans.

Vernacular   The native oral language of a given people.

Versailles, Treaty of   Negotiated in 1919, it established the League of Nations, created several new states in Europe, set procedures for imperial control of the Middle East, and imposed harsh punishments upon Germany.

Vichy regime   A puppet state in the south of France during World War II, its leaders generally did the bidding of Nazi Germany.

Viet Cong   Pro-independence supporters of Ho Chi Minh active in South Vietnam during the Vietnam War.

Viet Minh   Ho Chi Minh's North Vietnamese troops.

Vishnu   A Hindu god who, through his nine incarnations, saves the world from destruction; in one incarnation he was Krishna, in another Gautama Buddha.

Vizier   An official of Muslim government, especially a high Turkish official equivalent to prime minister.

Wandering of peoples   A term referring to the migrations of various Germanic and Asiatic tribes in the third and fourth centuries C.E. that brought them into conflict with Rome.

War of the Roses   An English civil war between noble factions over the succession to the throne in the fifteenth century.

Wars of the Austrian Succession   Two 1740s wars between Prussia and Austria that gave important advantages to Prussia and its king, Frederick the Great.

Warsaw Pact   An organization of the Soviet satellite states in Europe; founded under Russian aegis in 1954 to serve as a counterweight to NATO.

Watergate   A scandal involving criminal acts by President Nixon; it led to his resignation in 1974.

Waterloo   The final defeat of Napoleon in 1815 after his return from Elban exile.

Wealth of Nations, The   The short title of the path-breaking work on national economy by Adam Smith; published in 1776.

Weimar Republic   The popular name for Germany's democratic government between 1919 and 1933.

Westphalia, Treaty of   The treaty that ended the Thirty Years' War in 1648; the first modern peace treaty in that it established strategic and territorial gains as more important than religious or dynastic ones.

Whigs   A nickname for British nineteenth-century liberals; opposite of Tories.

"White Man's Burden"   A phrase coined by Rudyard Kipling to refer to what he considered the necessity of bringing European civilization to non-Europeans.

World Bank   A monetary institution founded after World War II by Western nations to assist in the recovery effort and to aid the Third World's economic development.

Yalta Conference   Conference in 1945 in which Franklin D. Roosevelt, Josef Stalin, and Winston Churchill (the "Big Three") met to attempt to settle postwar questions, particularly those affecting the future of Europe.

Yamato state   The earliest known government of Japan; divided into feudal subdivisions ruled by clans and headed by the Yamato family.

Yin/yang   Taoist distinction between the male and female characteristics of the universe.

Yom Kippur War   A name for the 1973 conflict between Israel and its Arab neighbors.

Yuan dynasty   Official term for the Mongol rule in China, 1279–1368.

Zama, Battle of   Decisive battle of the Second Punic War; Roman victory in 202 B.C.E. was followed by absorption of most of the Carthaginian Empire in the Mediterranean.

Zen Buddhism   The Japanese form of Ch'an Buddhism.

Zionism   A movement founded by Theodor Herzl in 1896 to establish a Jewish national homeland in Palestine.

Zoroastrianism   A religion founded by the Persian Zoroaster in the seventh century B.C.E.; characterized by worship of a supreme god, Ahuramazda, who represents the good against the evil spirit, identified as Ahriman.

Zulu wars   A series of conflicts between the British and the native Africans in South Africa in the late nineteenth century.

Index

NOTE: **Boldface** numbers indicate illustrations.